The Canterbury and York Society

GENERAL EDITOR: DR P. HOSKIN

ISSN 0262-995X

CANTERBURY AND YORK SOCIETY VOL. CII

Testamentary Records of the English and Welsh Episcopate

1200–1413

WILLS, EXECUTORS' ACCOUNTS AND INVENTORIES, AND THE PROBATE PROCESS

EDITED BY

C. M. WOOLGAR

The Canterbury and York Society

The Boydell Press

2011

First published 2011

A Canterbury and York Society publication
published by The Boydell Press
an imprint of Boydell & Brewer Ltd
PO Box 9, Woodbridge, Suffolk IP12 3DF, UK
and of Boydell & Brewer Inc.
668 Mt Hope Avenue, Rochester, NY 14620, USA
website: www.boydellandbrewer.com

ISBN 978–0–907239–74–1

A CIP catalogue record for this book is available
from the British Library

Details of previous volumes are available from Boydell & Brewer Ltd

Printed in Great Britain by
CPI Antony Rowe, Chippenham and Eastbourne

CONTENTS

ACKNOWLEDGEMENTS

This volume has its origin in an approach made to me by the Canterbury and York Society about editing the records of Bishop Braybrooke of London transcribed by L.H. Butler in his Oxford DPhil thesis of 1951 ('Robert Braybrooke, Bishop of London (1381–1404) and his kinsmen'), a work I have long used in my own research and much admired. My conclusion was that there was a wider interest that an edition might address – as well as covering some of the material for Bishop Braybrooke – by identifying all the surviving probate records for medieval bishops in England and Wales and printing all the unpublished material. The project has been a natural extension of work I have undertaken on the great households of medieval England and their domestic accounts, and it has brought me to a much greater understanding of the spiritual interests and material culture of the episcopate. I am grateful to the Society's General Editor, Dr Philippa Hoskin, for encouraging me to take this broader view of the records.

I have incurred a great many debts in the preparation of this volume, not least to the many archivists who kindly responded to my initial queries about their holdings, even if only to confirm a negative. The burden on others has been greater. Dr Richard Palmer, Mr Giles Mandelbrote and their colleagues at Lambeth Palace Library, Mrs Cressida Williams and her colleagues at Canterbury Cathedral Archives, Dr Sheila Hingley and her colleagues at Durham University Library, Mr Stephen Freeth at the Guildhall Library, London, Mrs Rosalind Caird at Hereford Cathedral Library and Archives, Miss Suzanne Eward at Salisbury Cathedral Library, and Dr Richard Mortimer and his colleagues at Westminster Abbey, have all done much for this volume and I thank them especially. Dr Robert Petre, the Archivist of Oriel College, Oxford, Dr Roger Lovatt, the Archivist of Peterhouse, Cambridge, and the archivists of Clare College, Trinity Hall, and Gonville and Caius College, Cambridge, went out of their way to answer my queries. I have also made extensive use of four doctoral theses: beyond that of Dr Butler, the works of Susan H. Cavanaugh on 'A study of books privately owned in England: 1300–1450' (University of Pennsylvania PhD, 1980); R.G. Davies on 'The episcopate in England and Wales, 1375–1443' (University of Manchester PhD, 1974); R.K. Rose on 'The Bishops and diocese of Carlisle: church and society on the Anglo-Scottish border, 1292–1395' (University of Edinburgh PhD, 1983); and D.A. Williams, 'Aspects of the career of Boniface of Savoy, Archbishop of Canterbury, 1241–70' (University of Wales PhD, 1970), have all given me leads and new perspectives. The identification of the books in the wills and inventories has drawn heavily on the Corpus of British Medieval Library Catalogues and the work of Professor Richard Sharpe, especially his listings at <http://www.history.ox.ac.uk/sharpe/index.htm>; on the work of Professor Kenneth Pennington and his 'Medieval canonists: a bio-bibliographical listing' at <http://faculty.cua.edu/pennington/biobibl.htm>; and I am greatly indebted to James A. Brundage *The medieval origins of the legal profession: canonists, civilians, and courts* (Chicago, 2008).

Beyond this, others have given generously of their advice: Dr Madeleine Gray kindly helped with the identification of Welsh place-names and the wills of the Welsh bishops generally; Professor Paul Harvey, Professor David Hinton and Professor Brian Sparkes assisted with specific queries; Dr Henry Summerson provided information about the Bishops of Carlisle; and Dr Tessa Webber read through **2/1**, **6/2** and **41/4** and helped with the identification of the books they list.

I am grateful to the following for permission to include editions of documents in their care and copyright: the Trustees of Lambeth Palace Library, from whose collections about half the material in this volume is drawn; the British Library (**32**, **43/4**); Canterbury Cathedral Archives (**8**, **9**, **25**, **30**, **35**); the Chapter of Durham Cathedral (**20**); the Dean and Chapter of Hereford Cathedral (**10**, **12**, **15**, **38**, **41**); the Dean and Chapter of St Paul's, London (**2**, **6**, **17**, **18**, **28**); the Dean and Chapter of Salisbury Cathedral (**24**); the National Archives, the Queen's Printer and Controller of Her Majesty's Stationery Office (**1**, **7**, **44**); and the Dean and Chapter of Westminster Abbey (**21**).

My own institution, the University of Southampton, has allowed me a period of leave from my normal duties to carry out the work on this volume, for which I am very grateful and I thank Dr Mark Brown, the University Librarian, for his support. The Centre for Medieval and Renaissance Culture in the Faculty of Humanities has been a stimulating environment for discussion. The Library's Inter-Library Loan section has done more than can be imagined to assist, as have my immediate colleagues in the Special Collections Division of the University Library. For the last eighteen months, much of my time has been focused on other priorities, raising funds to purchase one of our most prominent archive collections, and to return to medieval bishops has been both a challenge and a pleasure.

Much of the preparation of this volume has been undertaken at home and domestic acknowledgements, although last in this list, are first in my mind. I am grateful to Sue, Tom, Matt and Dan for very much more than the space and time to write this book, but without that indulgence I do not think it could have been written.

Christopher M. Woolgar
University of Southampton
30 November 2010

EDITORIAL NOTE AND CONVENTIONS

This edition comprises, firstly, a catalogue of the probate documentation for each bishop, arranged diocese by diocese, summarising the documentation, and giving references to published sources. The see by see arrangement has been chosen in order to present at a single point information relating to the development of testamentary arrangements for each diocese. Bishops are listed in this catalogue by the see they held at the time of death or by the last English or Welsh see they held in the few instances of resignation or translation outside these countries. Manuscripts calendared here and in the texts in the second section of this book use the forms of names given in the originals.

The second section prints a sequence of edited texts, arranged alphabetically by bishop, for those prelates for whom there is hitherto unpublished probate material. These give the full texts of wills, accounts and inventories, and calendar other material. The standard form in grants of probate is omitted. In this the executors undertake to make an inventory of the deceased's goods in the jurisdiction concerned (for example, in that of the archdiocese of Canterbury) and to render an account of their execution of the estate.

The Latin, French and Middle English texts that are published here in full have presented a series of editorial challenges. Although some of the documents are originals, many are copies: this offers special difficulties. There is some doubt whether the clerks of the Archbishop of Canterbury, or the Prior of Christ Church, Canterbury, who were responsible for most of them, always understood exactly what was in front of them (for example, Welsh personal or place-names, or the titles of books).[1] That notwithstanding, the intention has been to set out exactly what each clerk wrote, or what he would have written had he expanded every contraction and abbreviation, so that this volume can serve as a basis for linguistic as well as for historical research. There is in addition sometimes ambiguity over the language in which a word has been written (if the clerk ever considered it). To present this information without overburdening the text with notes, editorial practice has been summarised in the Word List and Glossary. Where documents are not copies, they are preceded by a description setting out how each was compiled and functioned.

In terms of orthography, the exact pattern of the originals has been maintained with the following exceptions. All capitalisation and punctuation are editorial, but the pattern of underlining employed in the manuscripts has been maintained: it is frequently used in the accounts to denominate price per unit, distinguishing it from overall cost. The use of *i*, *j*, *u* and *v* has been standardised: *j* and *v* have been used where the letter has a consonantal value, wherever they occur in the word. Where there has been difficulty establishing, for example, whether a *c* or *t* was intended, or whether a word was written as a single group

[1] Compare the remarks in *Chichele register*, p. v.

of characters or as two or more words, precedents elsewhere in the manuscript in question have been used. Two principles underlie the expansion of contractions and abbreviations. Firstly, all forms that have come from non-Latin words have been expanded using italics, so that editorial additions are clear (where there are examples of ambiguity over the language in which a word was written, it has been treated as if it were in one of the vernaculars and expanded in italics). Secondly, with Latin words, there is much less doubt about expansions: the patterns of classical grammar have been followed, except where there is evidence to the contrary in the manuscript – and here the practice of each clerk has been followed with regard to case, number, gender, tense and grammatical form. The choices in each case are summarised in the Word List and Glossary. There remain cases of uncertainty and ambiguity, however, most frequently over whether a singular or plural form was intended, and in these examples expansions have again been made using italic type. Place-names have not been extended and retain their final suspensions, with the exception of those that are clearly Latin adjectival forms: these last have been expanded. All marginal entries have also been set in italic type. The edition does not mention any notes on documents written after the end of the fifteenth century. The text has only been corrected where there are obvious slips of the pen or where an unusual word formation might mislead, and in all these cases the original form is given in a footnote. There is one set of exceptions to the principle that all words should be written out in full, and that is the frequently occurring words for weights, measures and currency, for which a standardised form has been employed: these are set out below, along with the conventions for insertions, deletions and editorial reconstructions.

In addition to the editorial practices described in the Word List and Glossary, the following abbreviations and conventions have been used.

Abbreviations used for all grammatical forms of these words:

bus.	*bussellus* or bushel (dry measure, capacity)
d.	*denarius*
di.	*dimidia*
fr.	frank[2]
flor.	florin[2]
gross.	gros[2]
lag.	*lagena*, gallon (liquid measure, capacity)
li.	*libra, livre* (sterling)
lib.	*libra* (weight)
liv.	*livre* (weight)
ob.	*obolus*
qua.	*quadrans* (money); also a quarter of an ounce, money used as weight
qr.	quarter (dry measure, capacity)
quart.	quarter (measure of weight, 28 lb, a quarter of a hundredweight)
s.	*solidus, sous*[2]
unc.	*uncia*, ounce (weight)

[2] For these denominations as currency and units of exchange, and the distinction between current and cameral florins, P. Spufford *Handbook of medieval exchange* (Royal Historical Society Guides and Handbooks, 13; 1986) pp. 125–6, 192.

Conventions used:

[ ]	Entry in a second hand
[[ ]]	Entry in a third hand, and so on
\ /	Passage inserted
< >	Passage deleted
’	Unextended suspension
|	End of line

Single quotation marks are used for passages quoted, for example, mottoes or first lines of a folio when describing books.

Wholly editorial reconstructions of missing sections of the text have been placed in square brackets. Missing areas are represented by three points where there is a space that would allow up to three letters and abbreviations to be written. Five points have been employed for more extensively damaged passages, and they have been repeated where the passage continues onto a further line.

References to counties in England and Wales are to those obtaining immediately prior to the changes made in 1974 under the Local Government Act 1972.

ABBREVIATIONS

The place of publication of all works throughout the volume is London unless otherwise stated.

Ancient deeds	*A descriptive catalogue of the ancient deeds in the Public Record Office* ed. H.C. Maxwell Lyte (5 vols., 1890–1906)
AND	*Anglo-Norman dictionary* ed. W. Rothwell *et al.* (2nd edition, in progress, Publications of the Modern Humanities Research Association, 17, 2005–; and on-line at <www.anglo-norman.net/>)
Anglia sacra	H. Wharton *Anglia sacra* (2 vols., 1691)
BL	British Library
Cavanaugh, 'Books'	Susan H. Cavanaugh, 'A study of books privately owned in England: 1300–1450' (unpublished PhD thesis, University of Pennsylvania, 1980; 2 vols., continuously paginated)
CCA	Canterbury Cathedral Archives, Muniments of the Dean and Chapter
CCCM	*Corpus Christianorum. Continuatio medievalis* (in progress, Turnhout, 1954–)
CCH	*Calendar of wills proved and enrolled in the Court of Husting, London, A.D. 1258 – A.D. 1688* ed. R.R. Sharpe (2 vols., 1889–90)
CChR	*Calendar of charter rolls preserved in the Public Record Office* (6 vols., 1903–27)
CClR	*Calendar of close rolls preserved in the Public Record Office* (45 vols., 1892–1954)
CCSL	*Corpus Christianorum. Series Latina* (in progress, Turnhout, 1954–)
CED	*Councils and ecclesiastical documents relating to Great Britain and Ireland* ed. A.W. Haddon and W. Stubbs (3 vols., Oxford, 1869–73)
CFR	*Calendar of fine rolls preserved in the Public Record Office* (in progress, 1911–)
CFR project	Data from the Henry III Fine Rolls Project, in advance of print publication, at <www.frh3.org/home.html>
Chichele register	*The register of Henry Chichele Archbishop of Canterbury 1414–1443* ed. E.F. Jacob and H.C. Johnson (4 vols., CYS, 42, 45–7; 1937–47). References are to volume II (CYS, 42; 1937) unless otherwise stated.
CIPM	*Calendar of inquisitions post mortem* (first series, in progress, 1904–)
Close rolls	*Close rolls of the reign of Henry III* (14 vols., 1902–38)
CPapReg	*Calendar of entries in the papal registers relating to Great Britain and Ireland: papal letters* ed. W.H. Bliss and J.A. Twemlow (14 vols., 1893–1960)

CPapReg: Petitions	*Calendar of entries in the papal registers relating to Great Britain and Ireland: petitions to the pope. Volume 1, 1342–1419* ed. W.H. Bliss (London, 1896)
CPL	E. Dekkers *Clavis Patrum Latinorum* (3rd edition, *CCSL*, 1995)
CPR	*Calendar of patent rolls preserved in the Public Record Office* (in progress, 1891–)
CS	*Councils & synods with other documents relating to the English church. II. A.D. 1205–1313* ed. F.M. Powicke and C.R. Cheney (2 vols., Oxford, 1964)
CUL	Cambridge University Library
CYS	Canterbury and York Society
Davies, 'Episcopate'	R.G. Davies, 'The episcopate in England and Wales, 1375–1443' (3 vols., unpublished PhD thesis, University of Manchester, 1974). All references are to volume III.
DCM	Dean and Chapter muniments
DMLBS	*Dictionary of medieval Latin from British sources* ed. R.E. Latham, D.R. Howlett *et al.* (1975–)
Dom.	Dominus
DUL	Durham University Library, Archives and Special Collections
EEA	*English Episcopal Acta*
Executors	*Account of the executors of Richard, Bishop of London, 1303, and of the executors of Thomas, Bishop of Exeter, 1310* ed. W.H. Hale and H.T. Ellacombe (Camden Society, new series, 10; 1874)
Greenfield register	*The register of William Greenfield Lord Archbishop of York 1306–1315* ed. W. Brown and A.H. Thompson (5 vols., Surtees Society, 145, 149, 151–3; 1931, 1934, 1936–8)
HCA	Hereford Cathedral Archives
Helmholz, *CLEJ*	R.H. Helmholz *The Oxford History of the Laws of England, volume I. The canon law and ecclesiastical jurisdiction from 597 to the 1640s* (Oxford, 2004)
HMC	Historical Manuscripts Commission
HMC, *Report on various collections*	HMC *Report on manuscripts in various collections* (8 vols., 1901–13)
KMED	*Middle English dictionary* ed. H. Kurath, S.M. Kuhn *et al.* (Ann Arbor, Michigan, 1956–)
LPL	Lambeth Palace Library
LS	*A Latin dictionary* ed. C.T. Lewis and C. Short (Oxford, 1879)
Mag.	Magister
Menevia sacra	E. Yardley *Menevia sacra* ed. F. Green (*Archaeologia Cambrensis*, supplemental volume, 1927)
MGH	Monumenta Germaniae Historica
Monnas, *Merchants*	L. Monnas *Merchants, princes and painters: silk fabrics in Italian and northern paintings 1300–1550* (2008)
MRC	*Manorial records of Cuxham, Oxfordshire, circa 1200–1359* ed. P.D.A. Harvey (HMC Joint Publications Series, 23; 1976)

ODNB	*Oxford Dictionary of National Biography* ed. H.C.G. Matthew and B. Harrison (61 vols., Oxford, 2005)
OED	*Oxford English Dictionary*
OPD 1198–1304	J.E. Sayers *Original papal documents in England and Wales from the accession of Pope Innocent III to the death of Pope Benedict XI (1198–1304)* (Oxford, 1999)
Pecham register (CYS)	*The register of John Pecham, Archbishop of Canterbury, 1279–1292* ed. F.N. Davis *et al.* (vol. 1) and D.L. Douie (vol. 2) (2 vols., CYS 64, 65; 1908–69)
Pecham register (RS)	*Registrum epistolarum fratris Johannis Peckham, archiepiscopi Cantuariensis* ed. C.T. Martin (3 vols., RS, 77; 1882–5)
PG	*Patrologiae cursus completus. Series Graeca* ed. J.P. Migne (161 vols. and index, Paris, 1857–66)
PL	*Patrologiae cursus completus. Series Latina* ed. J.P. Migne (217 vols., Paris, 1844–55; index, 4 vols., Paris, 1864)
PRME	*The Parliament rolls of medieval England 1275–1504* ed. P. Brand, S. Phillips, M. Ormrod, G. Martin, C. Given-Wilson, A. Curry and R. Horrox (16 vols., 2005)
RC	*Rotuli chartarum in turri Londinensi asservati* ed. T.D. Hardy (1837)
Registrum … Pontissara	*Registrum Johannis de Pontissara episcopi Wyntoniensis, A.D. MCCLXXXII–MCCCIV* ed. C. Deedes (2 vols., CYS, 19, 30; 1915–24)
Registrum primum	*The first register of Norwich Cathedral Priory* ed. H.W. Saunders (Norfolk Record Society, 11; 1939)
Registrum … Woodlock	*Registrum Henrici Woodlock, diocesis Wintoniensis, A.D. 1305–1316* ed. A.W. Goodman (2 vols., CYS, 42–3; 1940–1)
RLC	*Rotuli litterarum clausarum in turri Londinensi asservati* ed. T.D. Hardy (2 vols., 1833–44)
RLP	*Rotuli litterarum patentium in turri Londinensi asservati* ed. T.D. Hardy (1835)
RMLWL	*Revised medieval Latin word-list from British and Irish sources* ed. R.E. Latham (1965)
RO	Record Office
RPD	*Registrum palatinum Dunelmense: the register of Richard de Kellawe, Lord Palatine and Bishop of Durham, 1311–1316* ed. T.D. Hardy (4 vols., RS, 62; 1873–6)
RS	Rolls Series
Rymer, *Foedera*	*Foedera, conventiones, litterae, et cujuscunque generis acta publica inter reges Angliae et alios …* ed. T. Rymer, new edition ed. A. Clarke, F. Holbrooke and J. Caley (4 vols. in 7, 1816–69)
Sede vacante wills	*Sede vacante wills: a calendar of wills proved before the commissary of the Prior and Chapter of Christ Church, Canterbury, during vacancies in the primacy* ed. C.E. Woodruff (Kent Archaeological Society, Records Branch, 3; 1914)
Sharpe, *Latin writers*	R. Sharpe *A handlist of the Latin writers of Great Britain and Ireland before 1540* (Publications of the *Journal of Medieval Latin*, 1; Turnhout, 1997)

Sheehan, *WME*	M.M. Sheehan *The will in medieval England: from the conversion of the Anglo-Saxons to the end of the thirteenth century* (Toronto, Pontifical Institute of Mediaeval Studies, Studies and Texts, 6; 1963)
STO	*S. Thomae Aquinatis opera omnia jussu impensaque Leonis XIII P. M. edita* (Rome, 1882–)
TDC	*I testamenti dei cardinali del duecento* ed. A. Paravicini Bagliani (Miscellanea della Società Romana di Storia Patria, 25; 1980)
TE I, etc.	*Testamenta Eboracensia or wills registered at York illustrative of the history, manners, language, statistics, etc., of the province of York, from the year MCCC onwards* ed. [J. Raine, J. Raine the younger, and C. Clay] (6 vols., Surtees Society, 4, 1836; 30, 1855; 45, 1865; 53, 1869; 79, 1884; 106, 1902)
Testamenta vetusta	*Testamenta vetusta: being illustrations from wills, of manners, customs, etc.* … ed. N.H. Nicolas (2 vols., 1826)
TNA	The National Archives, Kew
WAM	Westminster Abbey Muniments
Willis, St Asaph	E. Edwards *Willis' Survey of St Asaph, considerably enlarged and brought down to the present time* (2 vols., 1801)
Wills and inventories	*Wills and inventories illustrative of the history, manners, language, statistics, etc., of the northern counties of England, from the eleventh century downwards* ed. J. Raine, W. Greenwell and J.C. Hodgson (3 vols. Surtees Society, 2, 38, 112; 1835–1906)
Winchelsey register	*Registrum Roberti Winchelsey Cantuariensis archiepiscopi* ed. R. Graham (2 vols., CYS, 51–2; 1952–6)

INTRODUCTION

Between 1200 and 1413, 285 individuals held sees in England and Wales. A good deal is known about the pastoral and intellectual activities of these bishops; their buildings, their cathedrals, their tombs, and practices of estate management are equally in evidence in the historical literature. We are, however, less clearly informed about their possessions and the nuances of day-to-day life. The wills of English and Welsh bishops, the activities of their executors and their inventories and accounts, have a very great deal to tell about how these prelates lived their lives, the material culture associated with the episcopate, and the establishment of patterns, ranging from dress, vestments and furnishings, to dining, household structure and other customs of medieval life and death. Many individuals have worked on testamentary documents for the episcopacy;[1] most, however, have looked at individuals, rather than examining the episcopacy as a whole. This volume is founded on the premise that by viewing the probate material as a corpus, we can expect insights that will match studies of the pastoral work of bishops, their expertise as theologians, or their labours as builders of churches and palaces. To this end, this edition surveys all the surviving probate material for English and Welsh bishops between 1200 and 1413. It prints the full texts of the principal elements – the wills, inventories, executors' accounts and receipts – where these have not been published before, calendaring the balance of the unpublished documentation and collating the published references for each bishop.

The start of the thirteenth century marks the first point after the Norman Conquest at which it became common for English bishops to make wills and for there to be documentation about them. Between 1066 and 1200, there are only a handful of references to wills, and in only one instance, that of Theobald, Archbishop of Canterbury, does a will itself survive. Even after 1200, episcopal wills are now scarce, although most bishops made them. It is not until the late thirteenth century, when wills were copied intermittently into the registers of the Archbishops of Canterbury, that larger numbers survive; and only from the archiepiscopate of Simon Islip onwards do they appear there in quantity, in fact, for most bishops who are known to have made a will. The second volume of E.F. Jacob's edition of Archbishop Chichele's register prints many of the episcopal wills from the period 1414–43, which makes the end of 1413 a useful point to conclude this edition.[2] For the 285 bishops (all those who held sees between 1200 and 1413, but excluding those alive at the start of Chichele's archiepiscopate in 1414), 74 wills have survived, of which 22 are unpublished; there are 21

[1] I have used them extensively and it is this interest that has led me to prepare this edition: C.M. Woolgar *The great household in late medieval England* (1999); *The senses in late medieval England* (2006) pp. 190–221.

[2] I have included *sede vacante* material between Arundel's death on 19 February 1414 and the point where Chichele's archiepiscopal administration came into operation.

sets of executors' accounts and inventories, of which eight are unpublished; and there are a further two groups of executors' receipts which provide important evidence for testamentary dispositions in the absence of wills.

The records edited in this volume come from a number of archive repositories. Most of the documents are copies of various kinds, registered in the archiepiscopal archives of Canterbury and York (the former now at Lambeth Palace Library, with Prerogative Court of Canterbury material in the National Archives, and the latter in the Borthwick Institute for Archives at the University of York), in the episcopal registers of individual sees (most commonly in the register of the in-coming bishop), or in *sede vacante* material for Canterbury (in the archives of Christ Church Cathedral Priory) and York (now in the Borthwick Institute). The archives of the cathedrals associated with sees have also been a fruitful source: even if few complete wills have survived in them, they have sometimes yielded material relating to bequests by the bishop to the see. Equally there is documentation among the archives of other beneficiaries, notably among the colleges of Oxford and Cambridge.[3]

At the start of this survey of probate records the proportion of documentary material to have survived appeared disappointing, but contrasts with elsewhere in Europe reveal it to be more impressive. In Normandy between the eleventh and the fifteenth centuries, for example, Marie Casset identified for bishops from the seven Norman sees no more than four wills (all from the early fifteenth century) and three inventories (two from 1388 for the same bishop, and one from 1493).[4] Less surprisingly, the English and Welsh evidence is not as prolific as that for the cardinals of the Roman curia: Professor Paravicini Bagliani identified 45 wills for 30 cardinals, out of a possible 136, in his survey of thirteenth-century cardinals, and documentary traces for 67.[5] The English and Welsh material

[3] The pattern of survival is analogous to that described in *TDC*, p. xxxvii, where, in the majority of cases, the originals of the wills and codicils are in the archives of ecclesiastical institutions that had bequests from cardinals. Other examples include links from the construction of chapels, or tombs, or the presence of an executor associated with an institution. There are further notable groups in Genoese and Roman family archives.

[4] M. Casset *Les Évêques aux champs: châteaux et manoirs des évêques normands au Moyen Âge (XIe–XVe siècles)* (Mont-Saint-Aignan, 2007) p. 19.

[5] *TDC*, pp. xxix–xxxvi. Many more wills survive for English and Welsh bishops than for other senior secular ecclesiastics, but see the inventory and accounts of executors of Andrew Kilkenny, Dean of Exeter, in *Death and memory in medieval Exeter* ed. D. Lepine and N. Orme (Devon and Cornwall Record Society, new series, 47; 2003) pp. 171–202, discussed on pp. 130–8; and D.N. Lepine, ' "Getting and spending": the accumulation and dispersal of a thirteenth-century clerical fortune' *Reports and Transactions of the Devonshire Association for the Advancement of Science* 136 (2004) pp. 37–70; and the account of the executors of Roger de Northampton, chancellor of Lichfield, printed in J.C. Cox, 'Catalogue of the muniments and manuscript books of the Dean and Chapter of Lichfield' *Collections for a history of Staffordshire: Publications of the William Salt Archaeological Society* 6, part 2 (1886) pp. 225–30. Monastic clergy – other than those who became bishops – especially heads of houses, might leave wills, but the tradition had become circumscribed by the end of the thirteenth century. For its evolution, Sheehan, *WME*, pp. 250–2; for references to the practice, *CPR 1272–8*, p. 254; *CPR 1281–92*, p. 389; *CPapReg 1198–1304*, p. 489; *CClR 1296–1302*, p. 585; Richard de Ware, Abbot of Westminster, *CPR 1281–92*, p. 109. Later inventories of the property of a handful of more senior monks at Westminster suggest a process of allocation of their goods on death: WAM 6603, goods of Brother Richard

can be supplemented, however, by the references to the process of making and executing episcopal wills that appear in the records of the English royal Chancery and Exchequer, as well as in papal records; and there is often additional, local information in chronicles of individual churches associated with sees. I have not attempted to survey other documentation, especially to do with the transfer of land and the endowment of chantries, although intended for the benefit of the bishop's soul, and arguably as much a part of the bishop's final intentions as customary practice and formal testamentary disposition,[6] confining myself to material relating to probate and including other material only where there is a close link to the executors and their work.

Some of the documentation is well known: editions of the accounts of the executors of Bishop Richard Gravesend of London and Bishop Thomas Bitton of Exeter, were published by the Camden Society in 1874, and many wills of individual bishops have also been published. Viewing the documentation as a whole, however, allows comparisons to be made across the episcopacy, to demonstrate common patterns, in terms of goods, styles of living and customary practices, that cannot be deduced from single wills, accounts and inventories. It also complements the information that we have about bishops from their household accounts and other sources. What is immediately apparent from looking at the wills as a group is that there was a penumbra of custom surrounding the processes of will-making and administering the goods of the deceased, and we need to see this much more clearly if we are to understand the operation of probate, a bishop's material possessions and what happened to them.[7] Further groups of material – typically receipts transferring to or from a bishop the goods that were customarily associated with the bishop of the see – are included in the documentary survey where I have found them. The documentation also provides references for patterns in the management of goods and property, as mortuary gifts, regalian right, or as custom: some of these practices involved goods of substantial value, often the best goods, and we need to explore this further to understand what were considered a bishop's goods and what might happen to them.

Exeter (Prior, 1377–82; d. 1387); WAM 54446, the account for the distribution of the goods of Abbot Nicholas Litlington, *c.*1387, mentions one or possibly more executors; and WAM 18883, for the goods of Brother John Canterbury, cellarer, *c.*1400. In the fourteenth century, the goods held by the Priors of Christ Church, Canterbury, came to them by indenture, and were returned to the Priory on death: W.H. St John Hope, 'Inventories of the goods of Henry of Eastry (1331), Richard of Oxenden (1334), and Robert Hathbrand (1339), successively Priors of the monastery of Christchurch, Canterbury' *Archaeological Journal* 53 (1896) pp. 258–83.

6 For example, the gifts of William de Longchamp to Ely, 1189 × 1197, *EEA 31: Ely 1109–97* ed. N. Karn (Oxford, 2005) p. 175, number 133; and Walter Mauclerc to Carlisle Cathedral Priory: *EEA 30: Carlisle 1133–1292* ed. D.M. Smith (Oxford, 2005) pp. 54–5, number 71. I have included all references to inquisitions *post mortem*, some of which certainly involved the executors.

7 Helmholz, *CLEJ*, pp. 387–9.

BISHOPS AND WILL-MAKING

We owe the survival of a good deal of the documentation to the claim of the metropolitan to prove all bishops' wills for his province and his special interest in their supervision. The interest of the Church was a broad one, and that meant that bishops' wills had to take account of the wider framework of the canon law, beyond the customary accommodations that were made with ecclesiastical law, in terms of the *ius commune*, relating to probate in England and Wales, the interests of the Crown and the common law.[8] The wills of English and Welsh bishops therefore exhibit a number of features of particular interest. If, by the end of the fourteenth century, English and Welsh bishops made wills, appointed executors who administered their estates, prepared inventories and rendered accounts of their administrations, the development of this pattern was not a foregone conclusion. There was, however, a strong presumption that provision should be made for the disposal of the temporal goods of the episcopacy. Church councils from as early as the fourth century had required the listing of the goods of deceased clergy – and of bishops in particular. There are important examples of wills from the sixth and seventh centuries on the Continent;[9] and they survive for a handful of Anglo-Saxon bishops.[10] Passing references suggest that elements of this practice, including the taking of inventories, survived the Norman Conquest. The *Decretum* and collections of canons focused on property that churchmen owned or administered, and on the protection of gifts for pious uses.[11] In practical terms, however, there was a case to be made with the English Crown for the legal capacity of the clergy in general to leave wills, bequeathing property – beyond their own, personal property – for alms or other purposes. As tenants in chief of the Crown, there were important secular interests in their estates; and they had no right to bequeath property that belonged to the Church (much as the Crown had little right to it during a vacancy, for the Church never died even if incumbents did). The establishment of will-making up to and into the thirteenth century has been described by M.M. Sheehan,[12] but there is scope for examining this process through the thirteenth and fourteenth centuries in more detail, and especially to consider what happened on the death of a bishop. In the case of the episcopacy, usages might be moderated in different ways, in relation to the Crown, the papacy, or ecclesiastical custom generally, as well as by customs local to individual sees.

8 Helmholz, *CLEJ*, pp. 389–96.

9 Will of Remigius, Bishop of Rheims, d. *c.*532: *Testamentum Remigii* ed. B. Krusch (MGH, Scriptores Rerum Merovingicarum, 3; Hanover, 1896) pp. 336–40, and A.H.M. Jones, P. Grierson and J.A. Crook, 'The authenticity of the "Testamentum S. Remigii"' *Revue Belge de Philologie et d'Histoire* 35 (1957) pp. 356–73; will of Bertram, Bishop of Le Mans, made in 616: M. Weidemann *Das Testament des Bischofs Berthramn von Le Mans vom 27. März 616* (Mainz, 1986). T. Reuter, 'You can't take it with you: testaments, hoards and moveable wealth in Europe, 600–1100' in *Treasure in the medieval west* ed. E.M. Tyler (York, 2000) pp. 11–24, summarises the continental evidence for wills at pp. 20–4.

10 *Anglo-Saxon wills* ed. D. Whitelock (Cambridge, 1930) pp. 2–5, 16–17, 52–5, 70–3, 92–3; Sheehan, *WME*, pp. 72, 103, 106.

11 Sheehan, *WME*, pp. 120–62.

12 Sheehan, *WME*, pp. 107–42, 211–19, 241–9.

The earliest post-Conquest episcopal will to survive is that of Theobald, Archbishop of Canterbury. Around 1156, during an illness, Theobald disposed of almost all his property. His will of 1158 × 1161 was intended to be irrevocable; at about the same time he again distributed all his property, save a small portion, which was to be given out in alms by four of his friends; and the document itself largely focused on confirming arrangements with the obedientiaries of Christ Church Cathedral Priory.[13] This focus on almsgiving is important and went to the heart of the question of what a bishop might bequeath. The *ius spolii* – the right to the personal possessions, and potentially to land, of a deceased cleric, exercised by the lay power, either the Crown or the patron of a living, and in time, by the papacy – had made its appearance in England under William Rufus, and was a source of contention between the Crown and the clergy.[14] At first it seemed that bishops in particular should not expect to leave goods in a will, but that distributions of their property should be made as alms while they were alive. We have criticisms of bishops who failed to give alms in this way, like William of Corbeil, Archbishop of Canterbury, who died in 1136.[15] Later in the century, however, the burden of the criticism had shifted to the necessity of making provision to ensure that the Church benefited from the property. Gerald of Wales complained of the intestacy of David FitzGerald, Bishop of St David's. On his death in 1176, his officials divided his gold and silver among themselves before the King's men could arrive; but when they did come, the Bishop's servants were required to pledge themselves to the Crown. They were also powerless to act in the case of a casket, the key for which had been carried round by the Bishop. The casket was found among the relics at St David's, and it contained more than 200 marks. Losses to the Church in cases like this were to be deplored.[16] It appears to have been the case that the King would accept a will only if it were made a reasonable interval before the bishop's death, that is if the bishop's possessions had been distributed in his lifetime.[17] In the case of debts to the Crown, royal interest might overrule any will, as happened in 1196 on the death of Hugh du Puiset, Bishop of Durham, whose goods were seized and his servants required to pay fines at the Exchequer probably because they had started to distribute the Bishop's property.[18] Hugh of Avalon, Bishop of

[13] A. Saltman *Theobald, Archbishop of Canterbury* (1956) pp. 254–7; Sheehan, *WME*, p. 143.

[14] Sheehan, *WME*, pp. 241, n. 41; 242, 249; A.L. Poole *From Domesday Book to Magna Carta, 1087–1216* (2nd edition, Oxford, 1955) pp. 182, 190–1; R. Bartlett *England under the Norman and Angevin Kings, 1075–1225* (Oxford, 2000) pp. 407–8; Helmholz, *CLEJ*, p. 392; *TDC*, p. xlvi.

[15] Sheehan, *WME*, pp. 244–5, citing the criticism of the Archbishop for failure to do so: *Gesta Stephani* ed. and trans. K.R. Potter and R.H.C. Davis (2nd edition, Oxford, 1976) pp. 10–11.

[16] *Giraldi Cambrensis Opera* ed. J.S. Brewer, J.F. Dimock and E.F. Warner (8 vols., RS, 21; 1861–9) iii, pp. 433–4.

[17] The example of Roger, Archbishop of York, who died in 1181, is often cited: he had failed to make a will, despite seizing the goods of other clerics in similar circumstances, and the Crown therefore seized his possessions, including more than £11,000 in silver coin. 'Ymagines historiarum', in *Radulfi de Diceto decani Lundoniensis Opera historica* ed. W. Stubbs (2 vols., RS, 68; 1876) ii, p. 12.

[18] *Chronicles of the reigns of Stephen, Henry II, and Richard I* ed. R. Howlett (4 vols., RS, 82; 1884–9) ii, pp. 439–40; *Historiae Dunelmensis scriptores tres* ed. J. Raine (Surtees Society, 9; 1839) pp. 15–16; Sheehan, *WME*, pp. 244–6; M. Howell *Regalian right in medieval England* (1962) pp. 45–7; *The*

Lincoln, who died in 1200, made a will with reluctance, as he believed all his goods belonged to the Church. He acknowledged that it had become customary for bishops to make wills, and gave as his principal motive in so doing the need to avoid the depredations of the Exchequer.[19] As well as wills, from the late twelfth century there also survive letters, charters and other expressions of a bishop's intentions, made on his deathbed. In 1191, Reginald de Bohun, who died as Archbishop elect of Canterbury, wrote on his deathbed to the Prior and Convent of Canterbury, asking to receive a monastic habit to wear in his last illness.[20] Others confirmed estates to their cathedrals at exactly this point, for example, both Henry of Blois around 1171,[21] and Godfrey de Lucy, in 1204, in favour of St Swithun's, Winchester.[22]

How did bishops make wills? In the first instance they required authority in order to do so from the King and, in some instances, from the Pope. Royal authority covered two aspects, licensing bishops to make wills and establishing what goods might be encompassed within their estates. In a series of charters of 1227, Henry III granted the individuals who at that time were the Bishops of Lincoln, Bath, Winchester, Salisbury and Chichester the right to make a will.[23] This right was confirmed on other occasions, perhaps on each occasion an individual made a will. The example of Chichester shows how this operated. Henry III undertook to Ralph, Bishop of Chichester, in 1227 and 1229 that no sheriff, bailiff, or lay person might interfere with the execution of his will; in 1233, the King ratified any will the Bishop might make, on his deathbed or before.[24] In 1234, the right to make a will was granted to the Bishop, and to his successors.[25] Other bishops, those of Coventry and Lichfield, of Lincoln, and the Archbishop of Canterbury, also acquired in 1234 the extension of the grant of will-making to their successors.[26] These grants need to be seen in the context of the overall relationships between the episcopacy and the Crown.[27]

Episcopal will-making and the powers of the Crown were to continue to be an area of tension through the thirteenth century. Among the complaints against the

chancellor's roll for the eighth year of the reign of King Richard the First, Michaelmas 1196 ed. D.M. Stenton (Pipe Roll Society, new series, 7; 1930) pp. 258–9, 261.

19 Adam of Eynsham *The life of St Hugh of Lincoln* ed. D.L. Douie and H. Farmer (2nd edition, 2 vols., Oxford, 1985) ii, pp. 186–7.

20 *Chronicles and memorials of the reign of Richard I* ed. W. Stubbs (2 vols., RS, 38; 1865) ii, p. 355, number 388; summarised in *EEA 10: Bath and Wells 1061–1205* ed. F.M. Ramsey (Oxford, 1995) p. 137, number 179.

21 *EEA 8: Winchester 1070–1204* ed. M.J. Franklin (Oxford, 1993) pp. 93–7, numbers 131–2; *Chartulary of Winchester Cathedral* ed. A.W. Goodman (Winchester, 1927) p. 12, number 26.

22 *EEA 8: Winchester 1070–1204*, pp. 198–9, numbers 254–5.

23 *CChR 1226–57*, pp. 42–3.

24 *CChR 1226–57*, pp. 43, 178.

25 *The chartulary of the high church of Chichester* ed. W.D. Peckham (Sussex Record Society, 46; 1946) p. 231, number 808.

26 *The great register of Lichfield Cathedral Magnum Registrum Album* ed. H.E. Savage (*Collections for a History of Staffordshire*: William Salt Archaeological Society Collections for 1924 [1926]), number 220; *CChR 1327–41*, p. 148; D. Wilkins *Concilia Magnae Britanniae et Hiberniae* (4 vols., 1737) i, p. 630.

27 N. Vincent, 'Master Alexander of Stainsby, Bishop of Coventry and Lichfield, 1224–1238' *Journal of Ecclesiastical History* 46 (1995) pp. 615–40, at p. 632.

lay power addressed by the bishops and clergy at the legatine council in London in March 1239 (but prepared in 1237) was a plea that the Crown should not impede the execution of the testaments of bishops and others.[28] The complaint was made again at the councils of the Canterbury province at London in January 1253 and in 1257;[29] and the difficulties of executors of bishops' wills also featured in the complaints of the clergy to the Parliaments of 1300–1.[30] The reasons for this conflict are not hard to seek. Bishops were frequently, or had been, career servants of the Crown, and were responsible to the Exchequer for large sums of money. We find an additional category of licence, therefore, indemnifying the Bishop's executors from claims relating to royal office. Richard of Bury, Bishop of Durham, was granted letters patent in 1335 giving his executors free disposal of his goods, considering the service he had given to Edward III and his father, a privilege that was regranted on the same day with more precision, to include any claim from his service as chamberlain of Chester, constable of Bordeaux, a governor of the realm, keeper of the great wardrobe and treasurer of England, also extending to his officials and his accounts at the Exchequer.[31]

Despite the terms of the grants that allowed the Bishop of Chichester to make a will, he felt the need to acquire in 1244 two letters patent which confirmed his ability to include corn sown on the lands of the bishopric, as well as the corn in the barns and all other moveables.[32] The definition of what might be encompassed within the Bishop's goods was an evolutionary process, and it varied from see to see. There was firstly a canonical question about what a bishop's goods might comprise; and secondly there was the relationship with the Crown, the position of regalian right and the extent to which claims of the executors to administer a bishop's goods might be allowed. Under canon law, and by custom, a bishop was at liberty to dispose of the profits of ecclesiastical benefices to which he was wholly entitled in his lifetime and for a certain time afterwards in some cases; but he was not entitled to dispose of property that belonged to the benefices in his charge.[33] There was ambiguity about other areas of ecclesiastical revenue: in 1355, the executors of Bishop Bateman of Norwich petitioned the Pope in order to obtain a decision about sums which the Bishop had disposed of as private property in his will, for pious and other uses, but which derived from the first fruits of vacant benefices.[34] From time to time there might be other restrictions on legacies. The executors of William of Kilkenny, Bishop of Ely, in 1259 were forbidden to pay legacies to Hugh Balsham, Bishop of Ely, and his official, and similar bequests, as the King held that all things not distinctly bequeathed or left in aid of the Holy Land belonged to him by papal indult.[35] A bishop might hold property of his own, both real and moveable, and he might dispose of this in the same way as any other person, once that right had been conceded to him by the Crown. The definition of his moveable goods,

28 *CS*, i, p. 281: 'Item, ne testamentum episcoporum et aliorum impediatur.'
29 *CS*, i, pp. 470, 534, 543.
30 *CS*, ii, p. 1207.
31 *CPR 1334–8*, pp. 117, 120.
32 *CPR 1232–47*, p. 415.
33 Helmholz, *CLEJ*, pp. 389–90; Sheehan, *WME*, p. 241.
34 *CPapReg 1342–62*, p. 565.
35 *CPR 1258–66*, p. 99.

however, might be restricted, especially in regard to items that related directly to the exercise of ecclesiastical and, especially, sacerdotal functions. There was a strong prejudice that these should not be bequeathed, but this was modified in time to a position that permitted them to be devised by will, provided they were not exposed to sale, but given to institutions or to individuals where they could continue to be used for ecclesiastical purposes.[36] Beyond this, ecclesiastical legislation encouraged clerics to make bequests to the Church, as an example to the laity. In 1217 × 1219, those in the diocese of Salisbury were expected to make bequests to the cathedral church.[37]

The position for Welsh bishops was different to English ones, at least until late in the thirteenth century in those sees in areas under the control of the native princes, St Asaph and Bangor. Bishops of St David's made wills in the same way as bishops of English sees, and it may have been possible for Bishops of Llandaff so to do, although this is not entirely clear.[38] Welsh law excluded bishops from the right to bequeath property of any kind, including personal property; and it was only the impact of the Edwardian settlement that changed the position, although Llywelyn may have conceded the position to the Bishop of St Asaph shortly after 1276. Anian, Bishop of Bangor, was permitted by Edward I in 1285 to make a will; and the earliest will for a Welsh bishop now to survive belongs to Anian of St Asaph, from three years later.[39]

Beyond the *ius spolii*, in England and Wales the relationship between the episcopacy and the Crown in terms of regalian right – what the Crown might have the right to take from the bishopric during the vacancy – was important to testamentary practice.[40] There are two areas of interest here: defining what belonged to the estate of the deceased bishop on the one hand, and the establishment of arrangements, see by see, that clarified what one bishop should pass directly to the next, so that the possessions of the bishopric were not completely denuded by the Crown during the vacancy. Regalian right encompassed all the activities that fell within the scope of the temporalities of the see had there been a bishop, for example, in terms of agriculture, especially sales of corn and stock, administration and alms; it might also include a royal tallage of the see, and other payments or goods in kind taken for the King or his treasury.[41] How this came to be

36 *TDC*, pp. lviii–lix; and the admission of the last point in *licencie testandi* of Clement V, p. lix, n. 49.

37 *CS*, i, p. 91.

38 See the catalogue entries for these sees, below.

39 H. Pryce *Native law and the Church in medieval Wales* (Oxford, 1993) pp. 113, 117, 124–7; Howell, *Regalian right*, p. 71; *CED*, i, pp. 512, 520. The English Crown was well aware of the different position and in its response to clerical complaints about spiritualities in the hands of the Crown *sede vacante* made to the Parliament at Westminster in 1280, it noted that Scottish bishops did not make wills, but the Crown had all their goods; that the French Crown had regalian rights in a particular instance in the diocese of Limoges; and that the see of Durham had acquired various rights to spiritualities in the diocese of Carlisle, *sede vacante*, by a fine for a charter from the Crown: *CS*, ii, pp. 281–2. Edward I granted the bishops of Scotland the ability to make wills, just like the bishops of England, 5 October 1296: Rymer, *Foedera*, I, ii, p. 848.

40 For regalian right and how it related to the *ius spolii*, Howell, *Regalian right*, pp. 1, 33–9, 45–9.

41 Howell, *Regalian right*, pp. 50–9.

managed between the Crown and succeeding bishops is an important question,[42] but it is one that only partly relates to the will of a bishop and the administration of his estate by his executors.[43] A keeper (or keepers) of the temporalities of the see was appointed by the Crown as soon as the King learned of the death of a bishop. The keeper was then to account at the Exchequer for his charge until the temporalities were handed to the succeeding bishop. Agriculture, however, was a continuous process and all parties had an interest in seeing that it was not disrupted. The keeper of the archbishopric of Canterbury, for example, was instructed in October 1231 to make sure that the demesne was well cultivated and sown from the issues of the archbishopric, and that the buildings were well kept and not allowed to deteriorate.[44] Agreements were therefore reached with the Crown about what should constitute part of the deceased's estate and what should belong to the Crown. The case of Hugh of Wells, Bishop of Lincoln, is instructive. On 13 July 1231, the Bishop fined with the King in 500 marks in order that he and his successors should have all the moveable goods, including corn sown prior to the Bishop's death and the produce of vineyards for the current year, as far as the Michaelmas (29 September) after the Bishop's death. The executors were to be allowed use of all the buildings, barns, granaries and wine-presses, for storing their goods.[45] Two days later, Hugh received a charter to the same effect, extending these rights to osier beds as well as vineyards;[46] and there was a further charter, based on a similar grant to his brother, Jocelin, Bishop of Bath, on 18 July, which included cider-presses among the list of equipment and buildings to which the executors might have free access until they were required for the crops of the succeeding year.[47] By a general grant of 27 March 1234, Hugh and his successors obtained the right to dispose of their goods, both moveable and immoveable, including the corn sown on their lands.[48] There was a change in position, however, comparatively swiftly. Hugh Foliot, Bishop of Hereford, died on 7 August 1234, that is, during harvest. The Crown's escheators were instructed on 13 August that they were not to impede the executors, as they were free to dispose of the corn of that present harvest, and other goods,

42 For the process, Howell, *Regalian right*, pp. 62–7. To avoid depredation by those who held the see on behalf of the Crown, vacant sees came to be farmed by the chapter of the cathedral church. Fixed levels of payment for the Crown were defined for Lincoln in 1316, for Salisbury and London in 1317, and Llandaff in 1318: *CFR 1307–19*, pp. 272, 348–9, 355–6.

43 Transfers also had to be effected on the translation of bishops: *The register of Walter Giffard, Lord Archbishop of York 1266–1279* ed. W. Brown (Surtees Society, 109; 1904) p. 174, numbers 640–1.

44 *Close rolls 1227–31*, p. 563.

45 *CFR 1224–34*, pp. 386–7 (15/224).

46 *CChR 1327–41*, pp. 147–8.

47 *CChR 1226–57*, p. 137. In 1363, the executors of Ralph of Shrewsbury, Bishop of Bath and Wells, claimed all the corn sown before the Bishop's death, as well as the profits of osiers and vineyards, referring back to the grant to Jocelin and his successors: whatever the general custom, whenever in the year the Bishop of Bath and Wells died, his executors were to have the goods and fruits of the bishopric up to the Michaelmas after the Bishop's death. Further rights, to liberties, had also been granted to Bishop John Droxford, who preceded Ralph of Shrewsbury in the see. *CClR 1360–4*, p. 490.

48 *CChR 1327–41*, p. 148.

provided the Crown had security for any debt owed to it.[49] This notwithstanding, the executors overstepped the mark – or the King realised he had given away more than he had intended. On 11 September, the escheators were told that when the King granted archbishops and bishops the right to dispose in their wills of moveable and immoveable goods, it was not the intention that this would include rents after the time of their deaths (here perhaps mindful of rents that would fall due at Michaelmas) and the profits of vineyards, gardens, mills, tolls, and pannage (that is, in direct contradiction to the grant to Hugh of Wells), but that they should have the corn of their demesnes, cattle and draught beasts, and other moveables. The escheators were to allow the executors of Bishop Hugh Foliot the corn of all the demesnes, along with the cattle and draught beasts, ploughs and carts; they might also have the hay and forage of the previous year, but the hay of the present year was to be kept for the Crown.[50] On 30 September the escheators were instructed to deliver the lands and goods of the bishopric to Ralph Maidstone, the Bishop of Hereford elect; they were not to remove the hay and forage, but were to deliver it to the incoming Bishop.[51] In the case of the estate of William de Blois, Bishop of Worcester, who died on 18 August 1236, letters close to the keepers of the bishopric defined stock as encompassing cattle, sheep, pigs, geese and hens; the executors were to have all other stock and hay from the previous year, as well as hay purchased in the current year, but not the hay made on the demesnes in the current year, nor the produce of the demesne gardens.[52]

Despite the injunction that the estates of bishops might include the corn to the following Michaelmas, further definition was required. The corn had to have been sown already if it was to merit inclusion in the estate. After Archbishop Rich died on 16 November 1240, his executors discovered that the Crown was content for them to have the moveable goods, but not the corn that had been sown by the time letters went to the keepers of the see in February 1241 – this may have been aimed at excluding winter corn which had not been sown at the time of the Archbishop's death, or the corn that was on the point of being sown in the spring, close to the time of the letters.[53] The executors of Ralph Nevill of Chichester were told on 12 February 1244, shortly after this death, that although the licence he had for his will entitled him to dispose of all the corn in the granaries and growing in the fields, it was not the King's intention to include within this seed corn – a remark presumably provoked by the imminence of the spring sowing on the temporalities now in the King's hands – nor corn for the manorial servants and plough animals.[54] William of York, Bishop of Salisbury, died at the end of January 1256; his successor was instructed the following October to let the executors have the corn sown in winter, during the Bishop's lifetime, and which by October would recently have been harvested: this move again excluded all spring-sown corn, limiting the claims of the executors to the corn of

49 *Close rolls 1227–34*, p. 498.
50 *Close rolls 1227–34*, p. 518.
51 *Close rolls 1227–34*, p. 529.
52 *Close rolls 1234–7*, p. 313.
53 *Close rolls 1237–42*, p. 273.
54 *Close rolls 1242–7*, pp. 161–2.

the bishopric.[55] Among the proposals for the protection of ecclesiastical liberties prepared at the provincial council of Canterbury held at London in August 1257 was the desire that the King should not have corn that had been sown.[56] There might be further variation, according to the see. During vacancies, the executors of Bishops of London were bound to sow and cultivate some of the arable of the bishopric by custom.[57] In 1247, the executors of Roger of Salisbury, Bishop of Bath and Wells, were allowed free administration of the Bishop's goods having given surety that any debts to the Crown would be satisfied from the Bishop's best goods (*de primis bonis*).[58]

In terms of the transmission of goods from a bishop to his successor in the see, there developed a range of customary practices. One area, however, was linked closely to the relationship with the Crown and evolved in the same timescale as the establishment of the principle that bishops might make wills. This was a definition of goods that belonged to the see rather than the bishop, and the arrangements necessary for transmitting these goods – such as stock on manors – from one bishop to his successor. These arrangements were sometimes referred to wills, although in some cases they were established separately: they set out a 'complement' (*complementum, implementum*) of stock, and sometimes goods, that were to be transferred, usually by way of the keepers of the see during the vacancy, to the incoming bishop when he received the temporalities. In 1220, Bishop Ranulf of Wareham endowed each of the manors of the bishopric of Chichester with a quota of livestock that was to pass to his successors undiminished.[59] Ranulf's grant was confirmed by Henry III by *inspeximus* on three separate occasions, in 1227, 1228 and 1233.[60] When Bishop Climping added the manor of Drungewick to the bishopric in 1262, he also established the level of stock on that manor to be transmitted to succeeding bishops.[61] Alexander Stavensby made analogous arrangements for Coventry and Lichfield before his death in 1238;[62] the same process was undertaken at Exeter[63] and Winchester.[64] Archbishop Boniface of Savoy set minimum numbers of livestock – 260 horses, 419 oxen and 480 sheep – which were to remain on the Canterbury estates for succeeding archbishops.[65] At Hereford, starting with Bishop Hugh Foliot, bishops bequeathed substantial amounts of cash for seed, as well as for farm stock (**15/2**). Ralph Ireton, Bishop of Carlisle from 1278 to 1292, recognising the poverty to which some prelates

55 *Close rolls 1254–6*, p. 367.

56 *CS*, i, p. 534: 'Item quod dominus rex non impediat testamenta episcoporum, nec extendat manum ad bladum quod seminaverint vel ad alia bona episcoporum defunctorum.'

57 *CClR 1272–9*, p. 65.

58 *Close rolls 1247–51*, p. 19.

59 *EEA 22: Chichester 1215–53* ed. P.M. Hoskin (Oxford, 2001) pp. xxx–xxxi and n. 59, xxxiv.

60 *CChR 1226–57*, pp. 34, 87, 179.

61 *EEA 23: Chichester 1254–1305* ed. P.M. Hoskin (Oxford, 2001) pp. 171–2.

62 *The great register of Lichfield Cathedral Magnum Registrum Album*, p. 309.

63 HMC, *Report on various collections*, iv, p. 71; Exeter Cathedral Archives, Exeter DCM, number 2107.

64 *EEA 9: Winchester 1205–1238* ed. N. Vincent (Oxford, 1994) pp. 34–5.

65 D. Sutcliffe, 'The financial condition of the see of Canterbury, 1279–1292' *Speculum* 10 (1935) pp. 53–67. For the situation at York, *CChR 1257–1300*, pp. 268–9; and with additional funds, *CPR 1396–9*, p. 377.

were exposed on their accession to the see, believed arrangements that guaranteed a successor's estate and equipment should extend beyond his manors, to his chapel, his books, and equipment for household offices, especially the kitchen, bakehouse and brewery. Upon the vacancy in the see, the Bishop's executors were to deliver the stock and goods to the escheators, and to the Chapter of Durham, by indenture, so that the goods could then be delivered to the incoming bishop.[66] Others bequeathed kitchen equipment directly to their successors: in 1310, Bishop Bitton of Exeter included a hand-mill for the ingredients for sauces;[67] the will of John Grandisson of Exeter, 1368, included silver vessels for the household, chargers and plates, along with all wooden utensils;[68] and John Sheppey of Rochester left a long list of ecclesiastical and domestic goods, including the tables in the hall and linen for them, along with equipment for the kitchen, to his successor on condition that he accepted the proposal his will contained about dilapidations (**33/1**).

The estates of bishops contained the profits of a number of different elements beyond the see. Some related to rights of the bishop as a rector, and again there was variation between sees about what might be included. A key date in determining the extent of the bishop's possessions was the Annunciation (25 March). The keepers of the bishopric of Norwich were instructed in May 1326 to let the executors of John Salmon (d. 6 July 1325) have the corn of the 1325 harvest from the churches of Hoxne, Thornham, Terling and Langham, annexed to the see; the custom in that bishopric was to allow the harvest to the estate of rectors who died after the Annunciation.[69] When Robert de Stretton, Bishop of Coventry and Lichfield, died on 28 March 1385, his executors were allowed to take the rents up to the Annunciation, and they were also to have the crop sown by the Bishop in his lifetime as he died after the Annunciation – that is, the harvest of both the winter- and spring-sown corn.[70] Following the death of Silvester Everdon, Bishop of Carlisle, the keeper of the bishopric of Carlisle was instructed in July 1254 that it had been demonstrated by letters patent of the Bishop of Coventry and Lichfield that there was a custom by which all rectors dying after Ash Wednesday might receive for the execution of their wills all profits and offerings of the benefice until the following Michaelmas; and as the Bishop was rector of the church of Melbourne and died after Ash Wednesday, the keeper was to allow the executors to receive all the profits and offerings of the church until the next Michaelmas.[71] After the death of Sewal de Bovill, Archbishop of York, on 10 May 1258, letters close went to the keepers of the archbishopric on 29 May: the executors had claimed the rents and farms of the archbishopric for the term

[66] *CChR 1257–1300*, pp. 408–9; *EEA 30: Carlisle 1133–1292* ed. D.M. Smith (Oxford, 2005) pp. 134–7, number 171. For the process in operation, *CClR 1354–60*, p. 26; and for a supplement and arrangements for dilapidations, the will of Roger Whelpdale, Bishop of Carlisle, 1423, *Chichele register*, pp. 237–8.

[67] *Executors*, p. 43.

[68] *The register of John de Grandisson, Bishop of Exeter (A.D. 1327–1369), with some account of the episcopate of James de Berkeley (A.D. 1327)* ed. F.C. Hingeston-Randolph (3 vols., 1894–9) iii, pp. 1552–3.

[69] *CClR 1323–7*, p. 471.

[70] *CClR 1381–5*, pp. 550–1.

[71] *Close rolls 1253–4*, p. 82.

of Whitsun because the Archbishop's body was not buried before the Wednesday in Whit week (15 May). The keepers were instructed to allow the rents and farms to the executors, pending a discussion before the King whether they should belong to the King or the deceased.[72] At other points, there were specific exemptions that might put goods beyond the reach of both the Crown and the executors. In 1248, Henry III granted Hugh, Bishop of Ely, that during any vacancy of the see the four chaplains appointed by the Bishop to celebrate mass daily for the souls of the King and the Queen, and his ancestors and successors and for the souls of the Bishop, and his predecessors and successors, should receive 20 marks yearly from the issues of the manors of Totteridge and Bramford, which the Bishop had bought for that purpose.[73]

If royal licences protected bishops as testators against the Crown, papal licences had both that effect and also the effect of protecting a bishop's estate from falling into the hands of the papacy. The possession of a papal *licencia testandi* was especially important for cardinals, for bishops and for those who might have aspirations to high office in the church, such as John of Pontoise, who obtained a licence while he was a papal chaplain in 1281, prior to taking up the see of Winchester.[74]

After licences had been obtained, the bishop was free to make his will. The ability to do so, however, also depended on the personal capacity of the bishop, on his spiritual, mental and physical state. In order to ensure the first of these, he needed to make confession. He also had to be of sound mind; his senses had to be fully functioning; and he must not be a criminal who had been condemned to death or a heretic.[75] Individuals addressed these points in their wills, as we shall see below. In addition, it was not expected that former monks and friars would make wills: as they possessed nothing except what had been committed to them by the Church, they had no capacity to make testaments. Thomas Aquinas argued that this applied unless an exception had been made by papal licence.[76] William Bottlesham, making his will (**5/1**) in 1400 as Bishop of Rochester, acknowledged this, but nonetheless sought to make his will in the manner of bishops of the province of Canterbury, so that his soul was not exposed to danger. He was declared intestate, however, on account of his debts (**5/2**) – the ability of the metropolitan to invalidate a bishop's will on these grounds was generally recognised. Debt was a notable problem for those who came to the episcopacy with no goods of their own, especially monks and friars: for example, John Pecham had to borrow substantially from the Crown from the moment he took up the see of Canterbury;[77] and it may have been the underlying cause of the debts of Bishop Tideman of Worcester (**39/1–3**).

English wills might be written, they might be nuncupative, redacted by another party, possibly even written up at a later stage from notes taken by a notary, or they might be a combination of the two. The essential point in the Middle Ages

72 *Close rolls 1256–9*, p. 225.

73 *CChR 1226–57*, p. 329.

74 *TDC*, pp. xlvi–li; Sheehan, *WME*, pp. 241–53; *CPapReg 1198–1304*, p. 463.

75 Helmholz, *CLEJ*, p. 402.

76 *TDC*, p. lix, citing St Thomas Aquinas, *Summa theologica*, II^{a} II^{ae}, qu. 185, art. 8, section 3.

77 Sutcliffe, 'Financial condition of the see of Canterbury', pp. 53–68.

was that the will was made in front of witnesses.[78] Bishops, however, and those who proved their wills were trying to accommodate the demands of Roman and canon law as well as English practice. This had an influence on the way bishops' wills were prepared. Notaries were often present either to assist in the drafting or the process of attestation – and this was far from common in the ordinary practice of will-making in England. Witnesses might be described not only in the forms common in English wills, but also as the 'testes rogati et vocati' expected by the processes of Roman and canon law.[79]

Many episcopal wills were made close to death, a common feature of wills of the medieval period.[80] Of the 28 wills edited in this volume, 22 were made within a year of the testator's death, and two further examples (**18/1** and **40/1**) fall outside this limit by a matter of weeks. Adam Houghton, Bishop of St David's, made his will (**19/1**) on 8 February 1389, and died on 13 February that year; the will of Roger Walden, Bishop of London and sometime Archbishop of Canterbury, was made on 31 December 1405 (**43/1**), and the Bishop died on 6 January 1406; Richard Mitford of Salisbury made his will (**26/1**) on 29 April 1407, and it was proved on 11 May that year (**26/2**). Nuncupative wills were among those that were made closest to death: Robert Stratford's will was recorded briefly in a notarial instrument, presumably effectively dictated to the notary, and was made on the day of his death, 9 April 1362 (**37/1**); the will of Thomas Fastolf of 5 June 1361, who died that month, is recorded in a notarial instrument which contained 'suum nuncupativum testamentum per expressionem verborum' (**14/1**). In March 1350, the executors of Archbishop John Offord were instructed to proceed to execute his will, parts of which were not in writing, by the examination of witnesses and inventorying the deceased's goods.[81]

For other bishops will-making was an activity which they planned and undertook well in advance of death; for some, it occurred regularly, almost as an act of hygiene. The practice may have been more common, but is less well documented as the wills concerned have not survived – and were less likely to if they were superseded by a subsequent will. Hubert Walter, for example, renewed his will every summer over a period of seven years.[82] Something similar may lie behind the multiple form of the documentation which constitutes the will of Llywelyn ap Madoc ab Ellis, 1369 × 1375 (**23/1**). William Spridlington in his will of 1381 included a clause in which he renounced all earlier wills (**34/1**). Others, such as William Lenn, Bishop of Chichester and then Worcester (**22/1**), and John Barnet, successively Bishop of Bath and Wells, and of Ely (**3/1**), did not update wills they had made nearly a decade before death.

Detailed descriptions of the will-making process in action in the thirteenth century survive for three bishops, Hubert Walter, Archbishop of Canterbury, Walter de la Wyle of Salisbury and Oliver Sutton of Lincoln. Hubert Walter

[78] From the sixteenth century, holograph wills might be accepted without witnesses: Helmholz, *CLEJ*, pp. 398–401.

[79] *Chichele register*, pp. xxi–xxii.

[80] *TDC*, pp. lxix, lxxiii; Sheehan, *WME*, p. 165.

[81] *CPapReg 1342–62*, p. 354.

[82] *EEA 3: Canterbury 1193–1205* ed. C.R. Cheney and E. John (1986) pp. 305–7, Appendix II, 'Archbishop Hubert's last will'; *Radulphi de Coggeshall Chronicon Anglicanum* ... ed. J. Stevenson (RS, 66; 1875) p. 157.

made his will after his last visit to Christ Church Cathedral Priory at Canterbury in 1205. Having blessed the convent, he went to Teynham, where he called together the Bishop of Rochester, the Prior of Christ Church, 'and other faithful men, monks, clerks and laymen'. The Archbishop had the will written – it was dictated *satis lucide* and then redacted: he did not write it himself.[83] The cases of Walter and Oliver confirm the importance of the public nature of will-making, with formal declarations by the bishop in the presence of his household that a will had been made. The bishops wanted witnesses to the fact that they had made a will, a new will, or a codicil, and to the sealing of the instruments. In the case of Oliver Sutton, the accounts of the will-making were recorded in his register and, on at least one occasion, by a notary public in addition. Walter de la Wyle, Bishop of Salisbury from 1263 to 1271, made a will at his palace at Sonning on 25 June 1269. A lawsuit between his executors and other parties in 1271–2 gives us a record of the will-making. Master Stephen de Grunville, the precentor of Salisbury, deposed that he heard the Bishop tell him and other clerks and members of his household: 'This is the will that I have made.' The Bishop showed them the will and had it sealed with his greater seal in their presence, in his chamber at Sonning. This happened between mass and *prandium* (the meal that was normally taken around the middle of the day). Stephen also deposed that a little while after, the Bishop had made him read the will to him and instructed that £100 was to be distributed according to its terms among the household, and the sum was distributed during the Bishop's lifetime. Another witness, John de Middleton, the succentor of Salisbury, had written the will: he was the Bishop's chancellor and secretary (*secretarius*) at the time. He was asked by the Bishop to call together his clerks and household: the will was shown to them and John was told to seal it with the Bishop's greater seal, which he did, and he was instructed to tell those present that they were witnesses to it. On the evidence of Stephen de Grunville they included Master William de la Wyle and Laurence de Hakeburn, canons of Salisbury; a knight, Richard de Colsulle; Master Walter de Corffe, Thomas de Beauchamp and many others whose names Stephen could not remember. John stated that the Bishop had not made any will subsequently: as chancellor and *secretarius* he would have known about it. Master William de la Wyle agreed with these depositions, except that he was not present when the will was read. Thomas Wood ('de bosco'), a clerk, reported that he had been instructed by the Bishop to write down the date and names of the clerks and household members who were present.[84]

Oliver Sutton, Bishop of Lincoln from 1280 to 1299, made a will in 1291, another will in 1292, supplemented it with a codicil in May 1294, and made a third will in 1296 – he may, of course, have made many more wills, but these are the ones that we know about.[85] The account from 1291 does not tell us exactly

[83] *The historical works of Gervase of Canterbury* ed. W. Stubbs (2 vols., RS, 73; 1879–80) ii, pp. 412–14. The list of goods and other assets in this source may not have been drawn from the text of the will.

[84] *Select cases from the ecclesiastical courts of the province of Canterbury c.1200–1303* ed. N. Adams and C. Donahue (Selden Society, 95; 1981) pp. 151–3.

[85] The example is partly described by Sheehan, *WME*, pp. 189–90, who was interested in to what exactly the witnesses to the 1291–2 wills were to attest: they had seen the sealing, but had only heard the will in part.

where the Bishop was within his manor of Stow Park when the will was made; but the will was shown and read in part (the Bishop had had it prepared the preceding day), it was then fastened by William de Stockton and sealed closed by Master Jocelin de Kirmington, the keeper of the Bishop's seals, with his great seal and with his small seal on the dorse (probably a counter-seal, rather than one applied to the dorse of the document). The Bishop's official, other canons of Lincoln, a group of chaplains, clerks, and esquires were present, along with a Franciscan friar, Ralph de Tofts, and the Bishop asked them to be witnesses to the act of sealing the will.[86] The will of 28 January 1292 was made by the Bishop seated in his chamber at Fingest, in Buckinghamshire, after vespers, that is early in the evening. It was again sealed by Master Jocelin, in the presence of the archdeacon William de Stockton, who was a canon of Lincoln, and a group of priests and clerks, who could attest to the sealing.[87] It was to this will that Bishop Sutton added a codicil on 28 May 1294, at his manor of Theydon Mount: his register records that the will had been sealed by the Bishop and also by Archbishop Pecham. The Bishop was sitting in the clerks' chamber in the afternoon.[88] He called in the knights of the household (not usually in the clerks' chamber), saying these words (or words to a similar effect): 'We made this our will at Fingest', which he then read out himself; adding, 'This we now approve, with the exception of some changes and additions which are in contained in this codicil', which he displayed sealed with his own seal, asking those present to be witnesses. With the Bishop were the archdeacon of Stow and three others who were canons of Lincoln; a knight, Sir John Burdon; three priests; five clerks, one of whom was a notary public, and six others, members of his household. The notary was instructed to make a public instrument.[89] The Bishop made what was probably his final will on Tuesday 16 October 1296, seated in his chamber at his manor of Stow Park, in the afternoon ('circa medium relevium'). Calling around him many of his household, he declared that he had made his will, and showed a written document. He then instructed the archdeacon of Stow, who was keeper of his seals, to seal it, which he did; and he then asked those present to be witnesses to the time and place. With him on this occasion, besides the archdeacon, were William de Stockton; the knight, Sir John Burdon; two chaplains; three clerks, one a notary public; and nine members of his household, including

[86] *The rolls and register of Bishop Oliver Sutton 1280–1299* ed. R.M.T. Hill (8 vols., Lincoln Record Society, 39, 43, 48, 52, 60, 64, 69, 76; 1948–86) iii, pp. 103–4. The later part of the register was published after Sheehan's volume was printed.

[87] *Rolls and register of Bishop Sutton*, iii, p. 182.

[88] *Rolls and register of Bishop Sutton*, v, p. 3. The timing: Rosalind Hill translates 'circa medium relevium' as 'the middle of recreation'. The *relevium* (or 'getting up again') was the period after the short sleep that followed on from the main meal, *prandium*. As this was a Friday (and the morrow of the Ascension), *prandium* would have been the only meal of the day and it would not have been eaten until all the day's services had been said, including vespers, the hour of which would have been advanced to the middle of the day – so a point in the afternoon is intended here.

[89] *Rolls and register of Bishop Sutton*, v, p. 3.

Gilbert de Sutton – the marshal of the household – and Hamon the doorkeeper, and at least two described as the Bishop's esquires.[90]

These accounts provide us with useful evidence to supplement that of the text of wills themselves. They show us where wills were made: in these examples, in the bishop's household, prepared by the bishop's senior officials, for example, his chancellor. When the document was ready, the bishop summoned as many of his household as he could, and made public the fact that he had made a will, that it was a written document, and he may have read some of it aloud. The document was then sealed by the keeper of the bishop's seal – it was sealed closed in one of these accounts – and the household members were told they must be ready to stand as witnesses to the will-making (which, in the case of Walter de la Wyle, was what they did, in court).[91] The request for a notary to make a public instrument recording the sealing and witnesses underscores the significance of their role in episcopal will-making.

Some bishops wrote their own wills. Richard Gravesend, Bishop of London, wrote his will of 1289 himself (**17/1**), and it was then sealed with his own seal, that of the chapter of St Paul's and the seal of the executors.[92] Llywelyn ap Madoc ab Ellis, Bishop of St Asaph, wrote his will of 1369 himself, along with confirmations of 1372 and 1373; and the additions of 1375 refer to the will as being in 'a parchment roll written in my own hand and sealed with my privy seal'. The copy entered in Archbishop Sudbury's register concludes with a notarial attestation (**23/1**). Walter Suffield, Bishop of Norwich, endorsed his will of 1256 in his own hand.[93]

Writing the will might be a lengthy process: some of the wills are long and complex documents, and some discussion must have gone on as part of the drafting process. The will of William Rede, Bishop of Chichester, was made over three days, 1–3 August 1382; and the registered copy in Archbishop Courtenay's register includes the interjections of the Bishop, faithfully recorded by the notary, concluding the work for the day: 'Et tunc dixit idem venerabilis pater: "Non plus modo, tedet enim me istius laboris, set cras conveniamus in isto loco ubi procedamus in testamento isto."'[94] Archbishop Arundel's will is dated 12 February at the beginning, but has a sealing clause at the end dated 16 February 1414, and one must imagine it took the whole period (Monday to Friday) to draft and complete: that notwithstanding, it must have been written with a sense of urgency, for the Archbishop died shortly after, on 19 February.[95] Notaries and lawyers, however, were not working completely without precedent. While there was a good deal of variety in the text of wills in England, much of the central material was similar – and bishops would have seen a good many wills in the

90 *Rolls and register of Bishop Sutton*, v, p. 188.

91 Sheehan, *WME*, p. 179, on wills sealed closed, and the role of executors sealing the document: the evidence for this from these episcopal households suggests that the executors did not have this role in these cases, although they did in others.

92 *Executors*, pp. 111–16.

93 Printed in full in *EEA 32: Norwich 1244–1266* ed. C. Harper-Bill (Oxford, 2007) pp. 150–6, as number 138.

94 F.M. Powicke *The medieval books of Merton College* (Oxford, 1931) pp. 87–91; comments about the end of the day's work on p. 88, and, quoted here, p. 89.

95 CCA, Register G, ff. 277r–279r; printed in *Sede vacante wills*, pp. 81–5.

course of ecclesiastical business.[96] Although there were comparatively few formularies for wills among those used by clerks in England who commonly wrote routine administrative documents,[97] will-making was covered more extensively in widely copied notarial formularies.[98] Most bishops' wills therefore have elements of a common form.

The structure of episcopal wills

From early in the thirteenth century, wills regularly had a common form. There is little in episcopal wills, other than the character and range of bequests, that distinguishes them from the wills of others.[99] Most episcopal wills start with an invocation of the name of God, sometimes the Trinity, and sometimes separately naming Christ and other saints as well. The will of Michael Northburgh, Bishop of London, of 1361, invoked not only 'sweet Jesus, crucified for me, and his most sweet and most beneficent mother, Mary', but also Mary Magdalen, the apostles Peter, Paul and Andrew, the blessed virgins Katherine, Margaret and Frideswide, and all the saints (**28/1**). Thomas Trillek, Bishop of Rochester, invoked Jesus, Mary and all the citizens of heaven (**42/1**). Many saved their special devotions for the commendations of their soul, in a subsequent clause. Fourteen of the wills edited here chose to make more of the opening of the will, as an *arenga*, or devout preamble. All date from the 1360s onwards with the exception of the wills of Richard Gravesend, Bishop of London (of 1289 and 1302), where the elaboration started a little way into the text. The *arenga* ranged from a few words or a clause, as in the case of John Bottlesham, Bishop of Rochester (**4/1**), in 1404, commenting on fate of the human condition and sensing the danger of death, or Laurence Child, Bishop of St Asaph (**13**), fearing the uncertainty of the end of his life, in 1389; to three difficult but poignant sentences in the will of Roger Walden, as Bishop of London in 1405 (**43/1**), knowing and sensing the complete wreck of life, and acknowledging that there was no end to the sadness, the exile from his country relinquishing the pitiable household of the flesh and seeking for himself his natural place, where he hoped to enjoy his homeland after exile, joy after sorrow, and rest after labour. The longest of the passages in documents edited here comes from the will of John Waltham, Bishop of Salisbury, from 1395 (**44/1**); Waltham's *arenga* was not an original composition, however.[100] It

96 Sheehan, *WME*, p. 193.

97 Sheehan, *WME*, pp. 192–3, especially nn. 110 and 120; J.E. Thorold Rogers, 'Roll of the thirteenth century containing various legal forms' *Archaeological Journal* 22 (1865) pp. 58–62; H.G. Richardson, 'Business training in medieval Oxford', *American Historical Review* 46 (1940–1) pp. 259–80; for the range of work carried out by these clerks, *Household accounts from medieval England* ed. C.M. Woolgar (British Academy Records of Social and Economic History, new series, 17–18; 1992–3) i, pp. 47–8.

98 G. Barraclough *Public notaries and the papal curia: a calendar and a study of a Formularium notariorum curie from the early years of the fourteenth century* (1934) pp. 241–3; *TDC*, p. lxxix.

99 Sheehan, *WME*, pp. 192–5; compare the analysis of the wills of cardinals in *TDC*, pp. xcvii–cli.

100 Although I have not traced the source of the passage, it appears in abbreviated form in an instrument appropriating the church of Bere, in 1334: *Grandisson register*, ii, pp. 731–4,

was at this point, in 1369, that Llywelyn ap Madoc ab Ellis, Bishop of St Asaph, drew attention to the violence of the plague as part of his motives for making his will (**23/1**). Some, like two Bishops of St David's, John Gilbert in 1393 (**16/1**) and Guy Mone in 1407 (**27**), included a formula with the place and date; but for many this was left to the conclusion of the document.

The documents next address the capacity of the testator to make a will. With regard to his spiritual state, there is occasional notice of confession as a preliminary: words to this effect were incorporated in two wills for Bishops of St Asaph, Llywelyn ap Madoc ab Ellis, in 1369 (**23/1**), and Lawrence Child, in 1389 (**13**), which used the same formula verbatim to mention confession to St Asaph.[101] Almost all mentioned the mental state of the testator, frequently contrasting it with his physical state. The important point in defining the last, however, was that the testator should be in possession of all his sensory faculties. In September 1360, John Sheppey, Bishop of Rochester, addressed both areas, stating that he was of sound mind and memory, and had the moistness and use of all his senses, except the ability to walk (**33/1**). Statements about sensory ability, however, are uncommon. Most bishops then declared their intention of making their will, frequently using the first person of the verb: *condo*, *facio*, *ordino*. In 1389 Adam Houghton, Bishop of St David's (**19/1**), used the first person plural, in the expression 'condimus testamentum nostrum in hunc modum' (**19/1**); and a few others, such as Alexander Tottington, Bishop of Norwich (**40/1**), in 1412 also used the plural form.

Most documents are described as testaments, although some use the expression *ultima voluntas*: the distinction between a testament, directly bequeathing chattels, and a last will, encompassing real property, often as a wish expressed to feoffees or executors, rather than a direct instruction, although coming into use in the fourteenth century, is blurred in these examples.[102] Thus the notarial instrument made for Robert Stratford, Bishop of Chichester, set out a 'testament containing his last will' in 1362 (**37/1**), which may have covered both moveable and real property; the testament of Michael Northburgh, Bishop of London, of 1361, included real property (**28/1**); William Lenn, Bishop of Chichester, in 1363 (**22/1**), and Thomas Trillek, in 1372 (**42/1**), both left a 'testamentum sive ultimam voluntatem'; and John Gilbert's dispositions of 1393 (**16/1**) were contained in a document described as both – 'testamentum meum et meam ultimam voluntatem'. Alexander Tottington, Bishop of Norwich and formerly Prior of the Cathedral Priory there, left two instruments executed on the same day in 1412 (**40/1**), the first, a testament, concerned with chattels and cash bequests, but including an annual sum from the manor of Brundall, covered in more detail in a codicil; and the codicil itself, described as *ultima voluntas*, which gave the use of Brundall to the Priory in perpetuity, and covered other things,

at pp. 731–2; in the will of Master John de Branketre, 1375: P. Chaplais, 'Master John de Branketre and the office of notary in Chancery, 1355–1375' *Journal of the Society of Archivists* 4 (1970–3) pp. 169–99, at p. 190; and in full in the will of Ralph, Lord Cromwell, of 1451: *TE II*, pp. 196–200, at p. 196. The *arenga* to the will of Cardinal Giacomo Savelli, of 1279, may also be related to this text: *TDC*, p. 197.

[101] Cardinals were expected to confess to the Pope before making a will; in some areas, a priest was expected to be present at will-making by the laity. *TDC*, p. li, and n. 30.

[102] Compare Helmholz, *CLEJ*, pp. 398–9.

including chattels. The will starts by saying that the intention was not to revoke 'aliam nostram voluntatem in quodam testamento nostro', but rather to declare and make plainer the Bishop's intentions to his executors. The term 'codicil' is applied to all instruments modifying a testament or will without further distinction.[103]

The bishop's first bequest was of his soul, to God and to a selection of saints, those of especial importance to him. Thus the two Bottleshams, Bishops of Rochester, commended their souls to St Andrew, their patron (**4/1**, **5/1**); John Burghill, Bishop of Coventry and Lichfield, left his soul to God, to blessed Mary and to his saints (**9/1**); Richard Mitford of Salisbury (who had formerly been Bishop of Chichester) recalled St Richard, his patron (**26/1**); and Thomas Trillek and Roger Walden both commended their souls to Christ (**42/1**, **43/1**). John Sheppey's rather particular document was more expansive: hoping that his soul might be placed with those of the elect, he asked for any impediment to be pointed out to him that he might purge himself of it in his lifetime (**33/1**). The second dispositive element in the will almost always specified the burial of the bishop's body and the arrangements for the funeral, including the provision of memorial stones or tombs. In 1361 Michael Northburgh asked that his funeral take place while his face could be shown without any sign of decay, and with the tokens that befitted a bishop (*presulatus*) (**28/1**). Llywelyn ap Madoc ab Ellis, of St Asaph, left all the utensils of house to be divided between his nephews, with the exception of one lead vat, in which he was to be buried (**23/1**). William Lenn, who made his will while Bishop of Chichester in 1363, envisaged burial in the cathedral there in front of the altar of St Mary Magdalen, before the door which led into the chapel of the Virgin (**22/1**). There was considerable variation here, from those who left everything to the discretion of their executors, such as Bishop Trefnant of Hereford (**41/1**), to Stephen Gravesend of London, who in 1337 left 100 marks for his funeral expenses and not more because, according to St Augustine, funerary pomp and crowds are solace for the living, not a help to the dead (**18/1**). He also asked for £100 to be distributed among his poor tenants, rather than the poor at the funeral. Others envisaged distributions to large numbers – Alexander Tottington leaving £20 to be distributed *denariatim* to the poor on the day of his burial (**40/1**).[104] Public ceremony, the attendance and clothing of the poor carrying candles around the corpse, were set out in the will of Michael Northburgh, Bishop of London, in 1361 (**28/1**); and, in the case of Lewis Charlton, Bishop of Hereford, in 1369, there was an injunction 'quod fiat convivium die sepulture mee' (**12/2**). The members of the cathedral were often singled out for reward if they attended the funeral and took part in the commemorations and spiritual devotions connected to it. Bishop Mitford of Salisbury made provision for every canon of Salisbury, every vicar in the church, chantry chaplain, chorister and other ministers of the church who were present at the funeral, and on the vigil at the *placebo* and *dirige* (**26/1**). In some instances, the executors were enjoined to start on major campaigns of spiritual commemo-

[103] Sheehan, *WME*, p. 192; *Chichele register*, pp. xix–xxi. Codicils in English wills did not usually name an executor: Helmholz, *CLEJ*, p. 401.

[104] But dwarfed by the number who came to Bishop Richard Gravesend's funeral in 1303: *Executors*, p. 100.

ration: Guy Mone envisaged 10,000 masses, which were to be commenced with the greatest expedition after his death (**27**).

Twelve of the wills edited then contain explicit provision for the payment of debts. John Sheppey required his executors 'statim spiritu exalato' to make proclamations in London, Dartford, Rochester, Newington and Sittingbourne, advertising a place and time for claimants to demonstrate their debts, bringing documentation, charging the executors to pay all before providing for the legacies in the will (**33/1**); others, such as William Spridlington in 1381, required property to be sold in order to pay debts (**34/1**). In addition to the texts edited here in full, both wills of Richard Gravesend listed his debts in detail (**17/1–2**).

The wills then proceed through bequests, briefly in some instances, in other cases at great length; sometimes setting out first those to the cathedral church of the see or other establishment with which there was to be a special connection (for example, through burial), pious legacies alongside gifts to individuals, to relations, servants and tenants.[105] Some of these legacies form part of broader patterns – and the role of customary practice upon the death of a bishop is examined in more detail below.

Pious bequests, especially to the cathedral church, to churches in the diocese, to friaries and other religious houses, were a principal feature of episcopal wills. Support for cathedral churches ranged from, for example, Lawrence Child, Bishop of St Asaph, who left 100 marks for buying vestments, as well as bequeathing vestments, a psalter and a long, wooden chair, perhaps a settle, for the rectors in the choir (**13**); to Adam Houghton, Bishop of St David's, who in 1389 left silver plate and vestments, along with £10 for remaking the walls of the cathedral close (**19/1**). Some wills have long lists of bequests to religious institutions, as, for example, the will of John Burghill (**9/1**); sometimes the focus is on specific institutions, such as the investment made by Guy Mone in the church of Maidstone, where three chaplains were to celebrate for seven years after his death (**27**); or the arrangements for a chantry in Christ Church, Canterbury, that were made under the will of John Buckingham, Bishop of Lincoln, and revised by agreement between the Prior and chapter of Christ Church and the priests concerned in the early fifteenth century (**8**). Sometimes the arrangements for chantries were made well in advance of death, such as the preparations made by Cardinal Langham for his chantry at Westminster Abbey (**21**), or Bishop Hatfield of Durham at Stratford, and Bishop Skirlaw at Durham.[106] Occasionally the bequests were given to individual religious. Dame Margery Fokerham, a nun of Romsey, and Dame Margery Artur, a nun of Amesbury, each received 40*s.* in the will of Thomas de Ringstead, Bishop of Bangor, in 1365 (**31/1**). Others directed bequests to the support of university education, ranging from Walter of Merton, Bishop of Rochester, who established Merton College, Oxford, under his will of 1276 and codicil of the following year;[107] to Michael Northburgh, who made a bequest for supporting 12 scholars in civil and canon law at Oxford in 1361 (**28/1**), and Thomas de Ringstead, Bishop of

105 For charitable bequests, *piae causae*, Helmholz, *CLEJ*, pp. 417–19.

106 DUL, Durham DCM, Miscellaneous Charters 6000 and 7169.

107 *The early rolls of Merton College Oxford* ed. J.R.L. Highfield (Oxford Historical Society, new series, 18; 1964) pp. 79–89.

Bangor, who bequeathed £100 in 1365 for sending five scholars from his diocese to Oxford or Cambridge (**31/1**).

General charity could extend much further. The residual estate of Stephen Gravesend, Bishop of London, in his will of 1337, was to be sold and the proceeds put to three uses: supporting the poor, repairing roads, and providing marriage portions for women of good repute (**18/1**). A later Bishop of London, Michael Northburgh, in 1361, also provided marriage portions. In addition he established a loan chest, with 1,000 marks for Londoners in need who had the means to obtain pledges for repayment, and left £10 towards the improvement of muddy roads in Essex (**28/1**). In 1365 Thomas de Ringstead left 20 marks to two sisters, probably religious, whom his suffragan knew well, to be distributed by them among the poor: they were to have 40*s.* themselves from this sum (**31/1**). The scale of the charity depended on the wealth of the individual bishop, and some prelates had very substantial resources to bequeath.

Besides customary gifts to the archbishops, they received specific legacies. In 1389, Adam Houghton left William Courtenay a silver cup, with a gilt cover of exquisite work, with a flying dragon on the top, along with 20 marks in the cup (**19/1**). There were bequests to both Archbishops in the will of John Waltham, Bishop of Salisbury, of 1395 (**44/1**). Guy Mone, Bishop of St David's, left Archbishop Arundel a gold cup worth £40 and £40 in cash (**27**); and the Archbishop also received Bishop Mitford's best pontifical, with the injunction to exercise good lordship to his executors (**26/1**). Equally, there were often bequests to other bishops, or evidence that these had been made; and some of these may have attracted special reverence. Stephen Gravesend of London in 1337 left the Archbishop of Canterbury a great ring with a sapphire, which had belonged to the recently canonised Thomas Cantilupe. Listed among his jewels John de Sandale had a belt that had belonged to Robert Winchelsey which was considered to be a special relic of the Archbishop (**32**: p. 212).

Some bishops made extensive lists of bequests to individuals, especially their own relations, and delineating the arrangements for real property that formed a part of their personal estate – as opposed to the lands of the bishopric – was a clear purpose in some of these documents. Roger Walden, for example, asked his executors to enfeoff his brother John and his wife, and John's heirs in tail male, with the manor of Tottenham (**43/1**), with further provisions for the sale of the manor and the expenditure of the proceeds in works of charity. But it was one thing to make a bequest in a will; another for that intention to be completed, and Richard Scot, one of Walden's executors, reported his frustration and concern that the manor had been sold and some of the proceeds had been loaned rather than being disbursed (**43/4**). Among bequests to individuals, the choice of leaving textiles to close female relatives, especially to a bishop's sister, was a common one, and it was a practice that was probably already of some antiquity by the period of the wills edited in this volume. Stephen Gravesend asked that the contents of his wardrobe and bedding be sold and the proceeds given to the executors of his sisters, to be disbursed for the benefit of their souls (**18/1**). John Sheppey left his sister Alice 20 marks and all his furs not yet in use (**33/1**). John Waltham left his sister Joan a silver gilt cup, and all the beds, utensils and moveables at Waltham, and his sister Cecily another complete suit of clothes, with fur (**44/1**). His successor in the see of Salisbury, Richard Mitford, left his best suit of clothes of scarlet to his sister Alice; her three daughters also received clothing; and further bequests of clothing were made to other female relatives (**26/1**). Three of the bishops covered in this volume had extensive libraries – Ralph Baldock (**2/1**), Cardinal Langham (**21/8**) and John Trefnant (**41/4**) – and many others had smaller collections of books.[108]

The series of bequests to servants is especially noteworthy, rewarding them on the basis of rank, and paying attention to common and perhaps customary practice in terms of their goods. Michael Northburgh, in 1361, left payments to all the esquires, valets, pages and grooms in his household according to the judgement of his executors, except one of the valets, Simon, to whom he left 100*s.* if he wished to marry, and 40*s.* and a robe if he did not (**28/1**). In 1393, John Gilbert, Bishop of St David's, required his executors to remunerate all his household and servants, both greater and lesser, for their services 'debito modo'; the executors, we are told, knew and know well the household and servants and their labours for and on account of the Bishop (**16/1**). Many named their household servants, and specified individual bequests. William Lenn left at least £40 to Robert Wyk' who had served him from boyhood, besides a further £5 and 100 sheep (**22/1**). Richard Mitford of Salisbury left 5 marks to his chamberlain and 5 marks to one Roger Cook (probably a cook), as well as making general bequests to all his lay and clerical servants not individually named (**26/1**).

Charity to poor tenants was also a feature. William Bottlesham had proposed in 1400 that a distribution should be made among his poor tenants at Halling, Snodland and Trottiscliffe (**5/1**); in 1412, John Burghill, Bishop of Coventry and Lichfield, had asked that his executors reward his poor tenants who were not otherwise in receipt of bequests, according to their discretion (**9/1**); and also in 1412, Alexander Tottington of Norwich provided legacies for his poor tenants, estate by estate (**40/1**).

Most wills concluded with clauses that covered the residue of the estate, the appointment of executors – along with supervisors and bequests to those, especially archbishops, who might influence the execution of the document – and, if they had not already done so, encompassed the dating, witnessing and sealing of the document. The residuary estate was most often committed to the executors to dispose of either as they saw best for the testator's soul, or to address particular objects. In 1381, William Spridlington, Bishop of St Asaph, proposed the division of the residue into two equal parts, one to be paid to chaplains celebrating for the Bishop's soul, those of his parents, friends and benefactors, for as long as possible; and the other to be given to his servants, poor and disabled widows, and other poor tenants, and in other alms, but firstly and principally to his poor tenants in five named places, as well as elsewhere at the discretion of the executors (**34/1**). Roger Walden, who died in January 1406 as Bishop of London, but who had held the see of Canterbury from 1397 until he was deprived in October 1399, asked for the residue to be devoted to the salvation and cure of his soul, and those of Richard II, his wife Anne, and John Waltham, Bishop of Salisbury; the souls of his parents and benefactors, and of all the faithful departed; and in works of charity (**43/1**). The disposition of the residue was normally

108 For comparative material, *TDC*, pp. cxxxiii–cxliii; D.S. Chambers *A renaissance cardinal and his worldly goods: the will and inventory of Francesco Gonzaga (1444–1483)* (Warburg Institute Surveys and Texts, 20; 1992); *Chichele register*, p. xxxv and ff.

more briefly accomplished: Robert Stratford, in 1362, simply enjoined that the other parts of his will having been performed, the residue might be disposed of as seemed best for the benefit and salvation of his soul (**37/1**). Alexander Tottington of Norwich, envisaging the possibility that there might be no residue, added here the instruction to his executors that if his goods did not suffice to pay the legacies, they should reduce them all proportionately (**40/1**).

From the middle of the thirteenth century, most wills then went on to name the executors. One element, however, might go hand-in-hand with this, perhaps as an oral act. Adam of Eynsham's account of Hugh of Avalon making his will concludes with him pronouncing a formal anathema against all those who sought to disrupt it.[109] The will of Richard Wich of Chichester of *c.*1253 is unusual in putting this in written form: preceding the names of his executors is a clause anathematising and excommunicating those who impeded his will.[110] The bishops in the wills edited in this volume named between one (**19/1**) and eleven executors (**44/1**), but more commonly between three and five. When wills were proved, however, the pattern was to commit the execution usually to three or four individuals, reserving the power of admitting other executors named in the will (**34/2**). The choice of executors was important: executors did not have to accept their charge, and if they all refused it, the bishop would be deemed intestate, as was the case with Robert Wyvil, Bishop of Salisbury, who died in 1375.[111] The executors commonly included ecclesiastics, especially members of the chapter of the bishop's cathedral: for example, Stephen Gravesend, in 1337, named the chancellor of St Paul's along with a canon of the same church (**18/1**); in 1362, Robert Stratford named the chancellor, treasurer and a canon of Chichester (**37/1**); and in 1393, Edmund Bromfield named two canons of Llandaff (**7**). Other bishops were sometimes named: John Trefnant named John Trevor II, Bishop of St Asaph (**41/1**); Thomas de Ringstead, Bishop of Bangor, named his suffragan, Thomas, Bishop of Lviv (**31**); Bishop Swinfield of Hereford was to act as executor of his predecessor in the see, Thomas Cantilupe (**10/2**); and Robert Baldock, dean of St Paul's and subsequently Bishop of London, was named as executor of Richard Gravesend, even though he did not then proceed to act in that capacity.[112] Others selected their officials (**33/1**) or chaplains (**1/1**, **13**). As well as a prominent clerical contingent among the executors, there were also family members (**12/2**, **17/1**, **19/1**), and household officials (**12/2**, **27**, **37/1**, **44/1**). It was not unusual to find at least one layman named, and some were locally prominent individuals. The sole executor named by Adam Houghton was a knight, John Joce (**19/1**); Alexander Tottington of Norwich included Edmund Oldehalle, esquire, and William Paston (**40/1**).

As well as naming executors, there were additional clauses about the actions of the executors. Thomas de Ringstead required there to be at least two executors to give an acquittance (**31/1**); and Michael Northburgh was concerned that should an executor die, the executors of the deceased executor should have no power with regard to his will, permitting his own executors to appoint a further person in the stead of the deceased (**28/1**). Another clause introduced

109 Adam of Eynsham, *Life of St Hugh of Lincoln*, ii, pp. 186–7.

110 *EEA 22: Chichester 1215–1253*, p. 160.

111 LPL, Register of Simon Sudbury, f. 79v.

112 *Executors*, p. 114.

at this point allowed the executors themselves to purchase goods that were part of the estate, usually at an agreed valuation (**28/1**, **33/1**, **43/1**). Some of the bishops appointed individuals to supervise their executors. John Sheppey made a bequest of a ring with a diamond to William of Wykeham out of friendship to ensure his supervision and protection of his executors (**33/1**); John Waltham, Bishop of Salisbury, selected both archbishops for this role in 1395 (**44/1**); and in 1407 his successor in the see, Richard Mitford, shrewdly nominated Henry Chichele, then chancellor of Salisbury, for this task, along with John Gaweyn, an esquire (**26/1**). These appointments recognised the uncertainties of the probate process and the power and influence that was necessary in some instances for the successful completion of the execution of the will.

In establishing that the will was genuine, three further elements were crucial: a sealing clause; a dating clause, frequently with a note of both place and time; and a statement of witnesses. They are sometimes found in combination, sometimes separately. These elements are also important in understanding what type of instrument the document was and how it worked. Sealing by the testator was essential to giving legal force to wills in England from the thirteenth century onwards,[113] but the purpose of applying seals to episcopal wills is a little more complex and, at times, opaque. Its aim was not only to give force to the document, but also to guarantee its authenticity – and to that end, other seals beyond those of the testator might be employed. Many of the originals of the copies of the documents edited in this volume were sealed and we must suppose that in most cases the bishop's formal, episcopal seal was employed. Few of the copies specify whether this was used, or whether a private seal was preferred. The will of Stephen Gravesend, of which we have the original (and which has no sealing clause), employed two vesica-shaped seals (formal, ecclesiastical seals), one of which was probably his own (**18/1**). John Waltham used his great seal in 1395 (**44/1**); but Llywelyn ap Madoc ab Ellis used his private seal (**23/1**), John Bottlesham his private signet (**4/1**), and John Trefnant his round (*rotundum*) seal, that is, his personal seal as opposed to the vesica-shaped episcopal seal (**41/1**). John Sheppey marked his will with the seal of his most blessed patron (St Andrew, the patronal saint of the cathedral of Rochester), 'cum manu mea tremula' (**33/1**). In 1289, Richard Gravesend of London employed not only his own seal, but also procured that of the Chapter of St Paul's, along with the seal of the executors (**17/1**). The will of Walter Suffield, Bishop of Norwich, of 1256 was sealed by the Bishop with his episcopal seal, and it also has seven smaller seals attached.[114] The number was probably significant. Roman law required a solemn testament 'in scriptis' to have seven witnesses, and for them to subscribe and/or seal the document; canon law was more flexible, and from the time of Pope Alexander III only two witnesses were required.[115] The will of Nicholas Longespee of Salisbury had seven seals, one of which was that of the Dean and Chapter; it is stated to have been sealed by the executors as well as the Bishop, procured 'ad memoriam futurorum';[116] the will of Richard Kellaw, Bishop of Durham, of 1316, was also

[113] Sheehan, *WME*, p. 189.

[114] *EEA 32: Norwich 1244–1266*, p. 150.

[115] *TDC*, pp. lxxxi–lxxxiii.

[116] A.R. Malden, 'The will of Nicholas Longespee, Bishop of Salisbury' *English Historical Review* 15 (1900) pp. 523–8, at pp. 526–7.

sealed by his executors.[117] As well as a seal, a will might be subscribed by the testator. John de Grandisson of Exeter added a personal subscription to his will in his own hand.[118] Witnesses might also add their own subscriptions, as in the example of the will of Thomas Brantingham of Exeter, of 1393.[119]

Sealed episcopal wills as we now have them look to all intents and purposes like charters. The will of Simon of Wells, who died in 1207, is described as having his seal hanging from it ('a quo sigillum suum dependet').[120] There was an important difference, however: charters were patent, that is, they were not sealed closed – and while the examples of wills that we have now may look like charters today, many of them also employed seals to keep them closed. This was the case with the will of Alexander Tottington, in 1412 (**40/1**), and the formal process of opening the will, described below, implies that this is likely to have been true more generally of thirteenth-century episcopal wills. Sheehan's wider survey of thirteenth-century original wills noted that many had been folded, employing a thong to keep them closed, and that some had been sealed closed across the thong.[121] The will of Hugh, Bishop of Ely, was sealed closed by the Bishop's seal; it also had a pendant seal of the Bishop's, as well as many other pendant seals attached – when Archbishop Pecham came to add his own great seal to it in 1279, it was already sealed closed and his register transcribed the endorsement confirming that it was Hugh's will and that the witnesses had added their own seals at the Bishop's request, in the presence of the greater part of his household.[122]

The will might have schedules attached to it, or additional documents. Notable among these were inventories of goods: that of William of Wykeham was transcribed at probate into Archbishop Arundel's register,[123] but others are mentioned only in passing, for example, the sealed inventory joined or tied to the will of John Waltham (**44/1**). A list of books, vestments, clothing, cups and other jewels and utensils was sealed with the will of Bishop Skirlaw of Durham: it also listed to whom the goods should be distributed and for what purposes.[124]

A will recorded in a notarial act superseded the need, in canon law, for the instrument to be sealed, as it was a public instrument in its own right – and its contents would have been publicly declared, in contrast to the wills that were sealed closed. Six of the wills edited here are formal notarial instruments (**14**, **23/1**, **26/1**, **34/1**, **37/1** and **41/1**). A further four (**12/2**, **13**, **22/1** and **31/1**)

117 *TE I*, pp. 1–2.

118 *Grandisson register*, iii, p. 1557: 'Subscripcio domini Exoniensis episcopi de manu sua propria: Johannes de Grandissone predictus predicto testamento subscribo in hac precelsa festivitate beatissime semper virginis Marie, que gaudium annunciavit universo mundo, ex qua ortus est sol justicie, Christus Dominus noster, qui solvens malediccionem dedit benediccionem, et confundens mortem donavit nobis vitam sempiternam. Amen.'

119 *The register of Thomas de Brantyngham, Bishop of Exeter (A.D. 1370–1394)* ed. F.C. Hingeston-Randolph (2 vols., London and Exeter, 1901–6) ii, pp. 742–9, at p. 748.

120 *RLC*, i, p. 92.

121 Sheehan, *WME*, p. 192.

122 *Pecham register (CYS)*, ii, p. 79.

123 A 'codicellus sive rotulus de quo supra fit mentio', printed in R. Lowth *Life of William of Wykeham* (2nd edition, London, 1759) pp. xlvii–li, from the probate copy in Arundel's register.

124 *TE I*, pp. 310–11.

may also have been recorded in this way – the first two mention the writing of the document, but have no reference to it being sealed. The will of William Lenn (**22/1**) was formally recited before him and acknowledged by him in the presence of a notary and other witnesses. Notaries also appear among the witnesses in the will of John Gilbert (**16/1**) and Alexander Tottington (**40/1**), and the use of the phrase 'testibus ad premissis vocatis specialiter et rogatis' in this last instance suggests that a notarial instrument was made or intended. The wills of Llywelyn ap Madoc ab Ellis (**23/1**), Richard Mitford (**26/1**) and William Spridlington (**34/1**) were sealed by the bishops as well as being recorded as public acts by notaries.[125]

The public character of a notarial act could be obtained for a will as a special part of the probate process, the formal opening, or *apertio*, of the will.[126] The *apertio* of the will of John Pecham on 22 December 1292, by the Prior of Christ Church, Canterbury, in his greater chapel, in the presence of the official of Canterbury, many monks and secular clerks, was recorded in both the Prior's *sede vacante* register and by notarial instrument. The Prior also administered the oath to the executors, that they would faithfully make an inventory and administer the goods of the deceased, rendering an account for the same.[127] The grant of probate endorsed on the will of Nicholas Longespee of Salisbury noted the formal opening of the will in front of the Archbishop of Canterbury.[128] The will of Anthony Bek, Bishop of Durham, was proved first before the Archbishop of Canterbury and was subsequently brought for probate before Archbishop Greenfield of York in May 1311 in a small box (*pixide*), which was sealed with the privy seal of the Archbishop of Canterbury; the box was opened and the Archbishop of York added his own seal to mark probate in his archdiocese.[129] It is probable that wills were read publicly at the point of opening. The note of the probate of the will of Richard Gravesend of London in 1304 recorded that it was read in the presence of the Archbishop of Canterbury.[130] Although the probate process and registration of the will guaranteed the document's authenticity, the creation of a notarial record added a further dimension of value in the administration of episcopal estates, validating it in a way that was recognised on the Continent and in ecclesiastical processes more generally.

With both sealed wills and notarial instruments, witnesses were important for guaranteeing the authenticity of the document. Two were formally required under canon law, as we have seen. In many wills the list of witnesses is introduced in much the same way as in charters, 'Hiis testibus ...', as in the will of Gervase de Castro (**11/1**), or 'Presentibus ...', as in the will of John Gilbert (**16/1**).[131] The lists of witnesses usually followed a place/time dating formula, unless the

125 For the will of Edmund Stafford, Bishop of Exeter, similarly sealed and notarised, *Chichele register*, pp. xxii, 158.

126 *TDC*, pp. lxxxii, lxxxvi–lxviii.

127 CCA, Register Q, f. 12r; Chartae Antiquae A13A.

128 Malden, 'Will of Nicholas Longespee', pp. 527–8.

129 *Greenfield register*, v, p. 94, number 2544.

130 'Probatur fuit istud testatmentum apertum lectum coram venerabili patre domino R. dei gratia Cantuariensi archiepiscopi ...': *Executors*, pp. 115–16.

131 For witness clauses in charters and land grants, J.M. Kaye *Medieval English conveyances* (Cambridge, 2009) p. 15.

document had already been dated at the beginning, in which case a formula like 'Data die loco mense et anno domini supradictis' might be employed (**4/1**). The information in these clauses is useful for what it tells us of episcopal life, placing bishops at their manors – for example, Adam Houghton, Bishop of St David's, at his manor of Lamphey (**19/1**); or even in certain rooms – Thomas Percy, Bishop of Norwich, made his will in his oratory at South Elmham (**29/1**).

A number of other practices should be noticed briefly. Some bishops turned to ways of managing business and their sees from beyond the grave. One area especially, dilapidations, concerned the testator, his executors and the incoming bishop. The principle here was that the outgoing bishop should leave his lands and the goods of the see in the same state that he found them. In practice, however, this was difficult to establish, especially if the episcopate had been a long one. The extent to which the Crown had drawn upon the property during the vacancy might also have an impact on negotiations. To take the example of Chichester: Robert Stratford, succeeded to the see in 1337; his predecessor, John Langton, had held it for more than 30 years. Stratford came to a formal agreement with his predecessor's executors, enrolled in Chancery, whereby he was granted the corn of the bishopric in the barns of the see in order that he might make repairs to buildings and episcopal ornaments; there were two further recognisances for debts totalling approximately £600 between the parties, to even out the balance.[132] Stratford then held the see for some 25 years and his successor, William Lenn, was to complain in his will of 1363 that he received only a modest amount from Stratford's executors – Lenn demanding that his successor settle for no more than 300 marks, as he had held the bishopric such a short time (his will was made about 18 months after his provision to the see). Lenn was equally unimpressed in this short time with the way the Dean and Chapter of Chichester administered their finances, and counselled his executors carefully about the restitution of episcopal goods to them (**22/1**). We do not know what composition was made with Lenn's successor, William Rede, on Lenn's translation to Worcester in 1368; but Rede left his successor 500 marks in his will of 1385, on the condition that this sum was accepted effectively as a composition for all dilapidations.[133] Similar clauses appear in other wills, for example, that of John Sheppey, Bishop of Rochester, who left the mitre that had been made by John of Cologne for the use of his successor, as well as a whole succession of goods, on conditions relating to claims for dilapidations (**33/1**). Conditional gifts of moveables, as much as real property, allowed bishops to make these adjustments.

The probate process and its documentation

The form of the medieval English will was ambulatory, that is, it did not come into effect until the death of the testator. Death therefore provoked activity on the part of those interested or concerned, both formally and informally. Bishops were wealthy individuals and there were temptations for those interested in their property and power. The events on the death of Richard Blund, Bishop of

132 *CClR 1337–9*, pp. 285, 385.

133 Powicke, *Medieval books of Merton College*, p. 87.

Exeter, in December 1257 are instructive: as the Bishop lay dying, and immediately after his death, a group of clerics and household members without the Bishop's knowledge continued to write and seal documents, granting benefices and disposing of his goods. Blund's successor, Bishop Bronescombe excommunicated those involved in February 1259, and in the following months received confessions from those who had taken part.[134] The keepers of the see of Winchester on the death of John de Sandale in November 1319 recorded how the Bishop's treasurer and another had taken a pack-horse load of cash from Farnham to London in order to facilitate the arrangements for the Bishop's burial. Thomas de Folquardby had a large sum of cash that had belonged the Bishop, but it was not known where he had taken it. The treasurer had also taken to an unknown destination from the palace at Wolvesey two cart-horses laden with silver and jewels.[135] Opportunities for depredation like this meant that it was essential for wills to be proved swiftly and for executors to secure the deceased's goods.[136]

Obtaining probate required the formal production of the will and its recognition as authentic in the appropriate church court.[137] The metropolitans claimed jurisdiction over the testaments of their suffragans, as well as over what were known as *bona notabilia* – larger estates, often taken as those worth more than £10 (including debts, but excluding land), but in practice the limit varied and was disputed.[138] On the death of the metropolitan, wills were proved under *sede vacante* arrangements; those for Canterbury were undertaken by the Prior of Christ Church, Canterbury, as noted above in the case of Pecham, and those for York, by the Dean and Chapter of York.[139] The probate of the will required it to be formally opened in court (*apertio*), to be read, that is, published (*insinuatio*) and confirmed as authentic by the presence of witnesses or the executors named in the will. The archbishop, or whoever had his delegated authority, then committed the estate to the executors named in the will, or to a subset of them, in order to execute the testator's wishes. Executors were not obliged to take up their position, and numbers refused: for example, in 1348, Mag. Richard Vaughan, archdeacon of Surrey, and Ralph, Bishop of London, refused to take on the execution of the will of Archbishop Stratford (**35/2**, **4–5**); and in 1361, Mag. David Ley, the precentor of St David's, refused the execution of the will of Bishop Thomas Fastolf, on the grounds that he was still fully engaged as an executor of the preceding Bishop, Henry Gower, who had died 14 years earlier (**14/2**). If all the executors refused the charge, or if the bishop had no will, he was declared to have died intestate, and the archbishop, or his delegate, then committed the administration of the goods to others. The grant of probate required the executors to take an oath to perform certain tasks: firstly, faithfully to complete an inventory of the goods, usually delivering it into the court before proceeding to execute the will. In tandem with this, however, it might

[134] *EEA 11: Exeter 1046–1184* ed. F. Barlow (Oxford, 1996) pp. liii, lxxix–lxxx.

[135] **32**, below, pp. 185, 188.

[136] *Chichele register*, p. xxv.

[137] Helmholz, *CLEJ*, pp. 414–16, summarises the process generally.

[138] Helmholz, *CLEJ*, p. 428.

[139] D.M. Smith *Guide to bishops' registers of England and Wales: a survey from the Middle Ages to the abolition of the episcopacy in 1646* (1981) pp. 232–3.

be necessary to make and carry out the arrangements for the funeral, and there might be other measures that were necessary, for example, in relation to perishable goods.[140] The executors also swore that they would submit to the court an account of their execution of the estate. The court would then gave them a formal acquittance, either conditional or absolute, in regard to their charge.[141]

All these stages had documentary consequences. Although it is hard now to establish exactly what was involved at each point, the documentation edited and summarised in this volume and the fragments of the *sede vacante* administration which survive at Canterbury confirm the process and demonstrate the character of the records. The wills were formally endorsed in the court with a note of probate. The probate act, or a notarial instrument recording it, sometimes survives as a separate document.[142] The Prior of Christ Church, Canterbury, seems to have retained some wills, for example, that of Anian II, Bishop of St Asaph, of 1289, endorsed with a the grant of probate of 1293.[143] Inventories are mentioned in the twelfth and first part of the thirteenth century, and there are occasional examples of them surviving attached to wills.[144] The presence in the Canterbury archives of a mid-thirteenth-century executor's account for the estate of John de Hamtum' suggests that inventories and accounts were delivered into the court from this point.[145] Further examples of the operation of *sede vacante* jurisdiction survive from vacancies from the late thirteenth century onwards: inventory and account were sometimes combined in one document.[146]

By the late thirteenth century, episcopal wills and the associated inventories and accounts that went with the probate process were typically submitted to the metropolitans or their officials – and it is important to note that the metropolitans were often personally involved in the proving of the wills of their suffragans.[147] That the process may have caused some apprehension among testators is apparent from the will of John Sheppey. He made a series of bequests to ensure the safe passage of his will through probate, along with the submission of the inventory and the executors' accounts – 50 marks to the Archbishop of Canter-

140 Sheehan, *WME*, p. 214.

141 Sheehan, *WME*, pp. 195–219; 241–8.

142 As in the case of Pecham, n. 127 above.

143 CCA, *Sede Vacante* Scrap Book II/187/1.

144 Sheehan, *WME*, pp. 211–14.

145 CCA, RE/122A.

146 For example, CCA, *Sede Vacante* Scrap Book II/185/2, inventory of Adam del Seche, 1270 × 1279; DE/205, late thirteenth-century inventory of Hamo de Polletun'; RE/122B, late thirteenth-century will, inventory and account of executors of Emma Gobilond; Inventories/23, inventory of Thomas Romayn of London, 1313.

147 For the presence of the Archbishop of Canterbury, *Chichele register*, p. xxvii. The processes were similar for the northern province, although there might be additional requirements for probate within the palatinate of Durham: the will of Richard Kellaw, Bishop of Durham, who died in 1316, was proved *sede vacante* at York after it was proved at Durham: *TE I*, pp 1–2; *Greenfield register*, v, p. 296, number 2912; the official of Durham received a commission from the Archbishop of York to grant probate of the will of Lewis de Beaumont, d. 1333, *The register of William Melton, Archbishop of York, 1317–1340* ed. R.M.T. Hill *et al.* (in progress, CYS 70–1, 76, 85, 93; 1977–) i, pp. 96–7, numbers 323–5; and the will of Thomas Hatfield was proved before the Archbishop of York on 6 June 1381, *TE I*, pp. 121–2, after it had been proved by the Archbishop of Canterbury, 11 May 1381, LPL, Register of Simon Sudbury, ff. 107v–108r.

bury, 5 marks to his chancellor, 40*s.* to the auditor of causes, 2 marks to his registrar and 1 mark to the apparitor of the court, all on condition that there was no impediment for the executors (**33/1**). Documents were scrutinised closely. The grant of probate endorsed on Richard Gravesend's will of 1302 noted that there was nothing interlined or cancelled on the document when it was formally opened, except in the fifteenth and eleventh lines from the end, setting out the words in question.[148] Elements of the will or the process of proving it might be varied at this point, as in the case of John Barnet, Bishop of Ely (**3/2**), where probate was granted in 1373 as set out in the will with the exception of the place of burial, to take account of the Bishop's translation from Bath and Wells to Ely. In September 1404, the executors of Bishop Braybrooke of London received a commission allowing them to sell goods without sight of the inventory 'on account of distance', but required them to prove the will in the Archbishop of Canterbury's presence the following Saturday (**6/1**).

Episcopal registers have commissions to hear executors' accounts, but the more important of them, and the records of the execution of many episcopal wills, appear to have been rendered before the Archbishop in person.[149] The presumption was that both the compilation of the inventory, and the execution of the will, would be completed as soon as possible. For example, on 26 November 1299, the archdeacon of Bedford was sent a commission to receive the oath from the executors of Oliver Sutton, Bishop of Lincoln, that they would take an inventory of the estate and administer it faithfully, instructing them to present their inventory and account before Ash Wednesday (24 February 1300).[150] The Archbishop might also summon creditors,[151] issue commissions to assist executors,[152] and grant letters of administration.[153] Account rolls of executors were sometimes physically delivered to the Archbishop. The discharge of the executors of Roger, Bishop of Norwich, in October 1279, noted that they were bound to particular creditors, as was set out in the account roll in the Archbishop's possession ('prout in rotulo compoti sui penes nos residente particulariter apparet').[154] In other instances, the Archbishop may have had only a summary. When the executors of Walter of Merton, Bishop of Rochester, were examined, it was noted that the original accounts of the executors were in the treasury of St Paul's. One of Walter's executors, William de Ewell, was a canon of St Paul's, and one of those commissioned to examine the accounts was the chancellor of that church.[155] The registers of Archbishops Pecham and Winchelsey contain summaries of some of the accounts of executors. For example, in 1308 Winchelsey recorded a formal notification that the executors of Walter Haselshaw, Bishop of Bath and Wells, had rendered their accounts and administered the will, summarising the

148 *Executors*, pp. 115–16.

149 *Winchelsey register*, ii, pp. 1146–53; separate commissions to hear accounts, for example, those of the executors of Ralph Walpole, Bishop of Ely: *Winchelsey register*, i, p. 505.

150 *Winchelsey register*, i, pp. 368–9.

151 *Winchelsey register*, i, pp. 36–7.

152 *Winchelsey register*, i, pp. 384, 781.

153 *Winchelsey register*, i, pp. 440–1.

154 *Pecham register (CYS)* ii, p. 93.

155 *Pecham register (CYS)* i, pp. 182–4.

principal elements from a financial point of view.[156] It is possible that there was a standard abbreviated form in which accounts were submitted, like that prepared later for the estate of Archbishop John Stratford in 1349, which survives as a single, separate membrane (**35/6**). Another possibility is that executors submitted a summary account which was essentially just the foot of the account (*pes compoti*), noting the total receipt, total expense and summarising the balance and on-going arrangements for the funds, as in the case of Ralph Stratford, Bishop of London, a document copied into the register of Simon Islip (**36**). Either way, we know from the separate examples that survive that the full inventories and accounts of the executors were much more substantial documents, such as those for Bishop Richard Gravesend of London, Bishop Thomas Bitton of Exeter, and Bishop Walter Stapledon of Exeter.[157] The executors of Walter Stapledon submitted an inventory that they had sealed, stating that they would include in the account of the execution any things that came into their possession beyond this.[158]

There were further requirements for probate in other jurisdictions. Wills relating to real property and moveables within the city of London had to be proved and enrolled in the city's Court of Husting.[159] In practice these enrolments covered only those elements of the will relating to London, as in the case of the wills of the Bishops of Ely relating to property in Holborn.[160] The will of Michael Northburgh, Bishop of London, is endorsed with a note of the probate in the Court of Husting, in this case more than three months after the grant of probate by the official of Canterbury.[161]

The probate documentation, especially the inventories and accounts, are powerful evidence that the resources in the hands of some bishops were very considerable indeed. The goods of Bishop Sandale of Winchester recorded for the Exchequer in 1319 amounted to £5,498 (**32**, p. 217). Matthew Parker accused Archbishop Pecham of avarice, arguing that most of the £5,305 that his executors accounted for was spent on his tomb; but this seems highly unlikely. A substantial proportion of this must have been the valuation of the goods of the see, on its manors, which had to be passed on to his successors under the arrangements we have already seen; and there was probably little in cash or treasure – although one notes that his tomb effigy, albeit of wood, had, until the Reformation, a mitre of silver and possibly other precious decoration.[162] Behind these figures lies an uncertainty that can only be unravelled through careful assessment of the sources. Bishop Barnet in his will of 1364 × 1366, made while he held the see of Bath and Wells, claimed not to know the scale of his patrimony and goods (**3/1**). The information from wills is opaque, as valuations were not commonly included, although there were some important bequests of cash. For

156 *Winchelsey register*, ii, pp. 1077–8.

157 *Executors*; *The register of Walter de Stapeldon Bishop of Exeter (A.D. 1307–1326)* ed. F.C. Hingeston-Randoph (London and Exeter, 1892) pp. 562–79.

158 *Stapeldon register*, p. 575.

159 *CCH*, i, pp. xxiv–xxvi.

160 *CCH*, i, pp. 90–1, 138.

161 **28/1–3**; the probate entry on the Husting court roll is summarised in *CCH*, ii, pp. 61–2.

162 Sutcliffe, 'Financial condition of the see of Canterbury', pp. 53–68, discusses Pecham's chronic indebtedness, citing M. Parker, *De antiquitate Britannicae ecclesiae* (1572) p. 206; J. Keates and A. Hornak *Canterbury Cathedral* (revised edition, 2005) p. 55.

example, in December 1365, Thomas de Ringstead, Bishop of Bangor, in a display of exceptional prejudice, left £100 to the fabric of the cathedral church on the condition that his successor was an Englishman (**31/1**). Some bishops had substantial resources in cash. The executors of Richard Gravesend, Bishop of London, found £148 in cash in his treasury when he died in 1303; those of Bishop Thomas Bitton of Exeter accounted for £1,026 in his treasury – that this was cash is suggested by the following passage in the account which covers small change (62*s.* 10*d.* in farthings) and assorted foreign coins.[163] A calculation of overall worth is also difficult to derive from the accounts of executors, as they were working towards a balance of zero, or as close to that as possible, having made their distributions. Their initial inventories, however, can give us something of a guide. The executors of Ralph Stratford, the Bishop of London who died in 1354, had goods in his inventory worth £1,826. By the time his executors had paid for his funeral, debts and legacies, they had a little over £270 in hand, which was then allocated out in further payments (**36**). Cardinal Langham's executors accounted for 7,904 florins' worth of goods (at about 3*s.* to the florin, some £1,185), including eight bales of books worth 1,122 florins (**21/8**). The executors of Roger Skerning, Bishop of Norwich, in 1279 accounted for a charge of £1,533,[164] and in 1283, at their final account the executors of Walter Bronescombe, Bishop of Exeter, covered assets worth £2,803.[165] Against this background it is easy to understand the wonderment of Bishop Dalderby of Lincoln, in relation to the estate of a proctor of the Templars. The man had apparently latterly lived a secluded life, without recourse to his neighbours, and was known for his parsimony. Dining at Banbury Castle, with the Abbot of Eynsham, Dalderby recounted how the executor had come to him and accounted for £300 as set out in the will. At the end of the will, however, had been a note 'Ad hec autem omnia remanent octo sub cathedra', which no one had understood. A chair was found in a remote room: digging under it, a chest containing £8,000 was found – and the principal executor had sought the Bishop's advice. As Dalderby commented at table: '£8,000, Lord Abbot, he had £8,000 in his treasury and never ate a good meal!'[166]

Executing the will

The bishop made his will, he died, the will was proved, the goods were inventoried and the executors were then set on the course of administering the estate.[167] Despite

[163] *Executors*, pp. 1, 47.

[164] *Pecham register (CYS)*, ii, p. 93.

[165] *Pecham register (CYS)*, ii, p. 205.

[166] 'Huyt mille liverez! Huyt mille liverez, sire abbé, en tresorie avoyt, e unqes un bon repast manger ne poeit!': *Les Contes moralisés de Nicole Bozon frère mineur publiés pour la première fois d'après les manuscrits de Londres et de Cheltenham* ed. L. Toulmin Smith and P. Meyer (Société des anciens textes français, Paris, 1889) pp. 179–82.

[167] In a few, rare instances, the executors took on their role in advance of the testator's death. Walter Mauclerc, Bishop of Carlisle, resigned in 1246 and died in 1248. The Bishop became a Dominican friar in 1246 and the executors started work then: 'civil death' came with religious

demands that executors do their work promptly – Roman law and some diocesan statutes set a limit of one year[168] – it is apparent from the records summarised in this volume that the estates of some of the episcopate were complex and their administration long drawn out. The executors of Robert Burnell, Bishop of Bath and Wells, and Chancellor of England, who died in 1292, had a good deal of financial work, possibly even lending money themselves;[169] and in turn, the executors of one of the Bishop's executors, William de Hamelton', had to petition Parliament partly about the debts of the Bishop, in May 1319.[170] Even when executors had been formally discharged from their responsibility, they might need to take action and make further distributions, sometimes decades after the administration of the estate was ostensibly complete. A comparatively straightforward, but lengthy, will was that of Bishop Mitford of Salisbury. The Bishop made his will (**26/1**) at his manor of Potterne on 29 April 1407. It was witnessed by Dom. John Wyther, the subdean of Salisbury, Andrew Swynford, rector of nearby Marston, Thomas Thirlewall, clerk, and others, as well as John Holand, a notary public. The Bishop's household account for this day simply records the presence of eight outsiders to the establishment; the preceding day it noted three visiting rectors and four visiting chaplains. On 30 April the account records the presence of Mag. Roger Harwell, who was one of the Bishop's executors, and the day after he was joined by John Wilmington, another executor. Mag. Thomas Thirlewall, one of the witnesses, visited on Tuesday 3 May; and Harwell again on 4 May. On 5 May, three of the executors were present: Mag. Walter Mitford (the Bishop's brother), Mag. Roger Harwell and John Wilmington; the first two were to have special oversight of the will, with the counsel of John, and the same day John Gaweyn was present, who had been designated to oversee the executors. Harwell stayed in the Bishop's household until 15 May. On 11 May, another of the executors, Laurence Drew, appeared – the day probate was granted to Walter Mitford (there was a commission issued for admitting the other executors to the administration of the will the preceding day). He stayed for two days. Walter Mitford returned on 16 May, Wilmington on 24–25 May and Roger Harwell on 26 May. We do not know the exact date of the Bishop's death, but it must have occurred on or shortly after 29 April. One of the Bishop's sisters was present in the household from 2 May until 24 May. The household moved to Salisbury during 27 May to make preparations for the funeral. At this point, the domestic expenses of a group from the household, including Walter Mitford, George Louthorp (another executor) and John Gaweyn, who had been at Salisbury for 12 days for arranging the funeral, were paid. The Bishop was buried at Salisbury on 7 June – the Bishop of Norwich headed the list of guests in the household that day, and the funeral meal included portions for some 1,450 individuals. The Bishop's household seems to have been broken up about 11 June.[171]

profession and wills were used to effect the distribution of property at that point. *EEA 30: Carlisle 1133–1292*, p. xl; *Close rolls 1242–7*, p. 456; Sheehan, *WME*, p. 250.

168 Helmholz, *CLEJ*, p. 416.

169 See the catalogue entry, below, especially the enrolments of bonds and obligations on the close roll.

170 *PRME*, iii, pp. 359–60.

171 *Household accounts from medieval England*, i, pp. 378–405.

The executors worked swiftly, and were acquitted by the Archbishop on 27 June (**26/4**). Even though elements of their business continued – on 31 July 1407 the Dean and Chapter of Salisbury gave them a receipt for goods, ornaments and jewels bequeathed to them (**26/5**) – the work appears to have been completed in around three months.

Bishop Swinfield of Hereford died on 15 March 1317. His executors, Dom. John de Kemeseye, treasurer of Hereford (**38/1**), Dom. John de la Felde and Mag. Robert de Icclesham, canons of Hereford, and Dom. Roger de Breynton' (**38/21**), were in a position to start paying legacies and distributing goods by the end of April, but even they may not have anticipated that elements of business relating to the estate would endure for almost 30 years, although the bulk of the work would be completed in a decade. The first receipt for a legacy is dated 26 April, at Hereford (**38/1**), and the executors continued to work at Hereford, obtaining further receipts on 28 and 30 April (**38/2–7**), and on 2 May (**38/9**); they visited nearby Aconbury on 30 April to give to the Prioress there the cup which her late father, Geoffrey de Geneville, had sent Swinfield from Ireland (**38/8**). On 3 May, they were at the episcopal manor of Bosbury (**38/10**) and at Ledbury (**38/11**), on 5 May at Bosbury (**38/12**) and Hereford (**38/13**), where they were also at work on 9, 10, 12, 14 and 16 May (**38/14–22**). They were at Ludlow on 16 May (**38/23**) and back at Hereford on 17, 18, 19, 21 and 22 May (**38/24–34**). There was then a caesura in their distributions until 12 July, when they handed over in London a gold ring with a sapphire to Adam de Herwynton (**38/35**). Their next receipt, the following day, is dated at London and Wingham, to the east of Canterbury, where Adam de Cranebrok and his wife Gunnora de Boynton' made use of the seal of the provost of the church there to give their acquittance, as their own seals were unknown to many (**38/36**). The executors then proceeded to make other disbursements in Kent (Swinfield came from a Kentish family), at Canterbury on 13 and 14 July (**38/37–45**), at Wingham again on 15 July (**38/46**), and back at Canterbury on 16 and 17 July (**38/47–8**). They were in London on 2 August to hand over a ring with an emerald (**38/49**), and back in Hereford making a further distribution on 9 September (**38/50**). In the main, these receipts were for single items or small legacies; the executors clearly thought that many of the legatees were sufficiently obscure for them to need to use one of the Hereford decanal seals, the seal *ad causas*, to give authority to their receipts (e.g. **38/1–2**). A mandate for hearing the executors' account was given by the Archbishop of Canterbury to Adam Orleton, Bishop of Hereford, in July 1320 (**38/52**), but the work of the executors continued. It was seven years later, however, before the Dean and Chapter of Hereford gave their acquittance for their legacies under the will, particularly those relating to the construction of their new chapter house (**38/53**); and in 1328 Adam Orleton was able formally to complete the task with which he had been charged in 1320, giving the executors their acquittance after rendering their accounts (**38/54**). This was not, however, to be the end of the matter. Between 1340 and 1347, Dom. Roger de Breynton, probably the only surviving executor, had to settle with a range of parties to clear any further claims on the residuary estate resulting from a clause in the will for distributing funds to Swinfield's poor, blood relations (**38/55–60**).

Custom

Beyond the written will, but sometimes apparent in it and in the inventories and accounts documenting the work of the executors, were customary practices that mitigated what might constitute a bishop's estate and how he might dispose of it. These fall into three groups: customary patterns relating to the episcopacy in general; customs relating to individual sees – although these might be effectively local variations on general customs; and customs to do with death generally and goods of the deceased in a great household.

There is occasional evidence for the network of customary transactions that punctuated episcopal daily life and especially the more important ceremonial occasions. Termed 'fees', courtesies, or customs, these were typically due to the Crown and to the metropolitan.[172] Executors rendered to the Crown a bishop's best palfrey and his episcopal ring. These renders might also feature as bequests: thus in 1233, Hugh of Wells bequeathed directly to the King the more beautiful ('pulcriorem') of his palfreys and his best cup.[173] In March 1271, 110 marks were allowed to the executors of Archbishop Boniface of Savoy, offsetting some of the debts the Crown owed them. Of these, 10 marks were for the sum the Crown customarily received in lieu of a palfrey on the death of an Archbishop of Canterbury.[174] The executors of Robert Winchesley gave the King his best palfrey, ring, his cup and a pack of hounds.[175] A glance at royal wardrobe accounts reveals the extent of this practice. In 1299–1300, the jewels in the wardrobe included a ring with four great rubies that had belonged to Archbishop Pecham, as well as rings that had belonged to the Archbishops of Dublin and York, and the Bishops of St Asaph, Bath, Coventry and Lichfield, Exeter, and Salisbury.[176]

On the death of any bishop of the archdiocese of Canterbury, it was established by the end of the thirteenth century that *sede plena*, the Archbishop, and *sede vacante*, the Prior of Christ Church, Canterbury, were to receive all seals and the bishop's second-best ring (the best having passed to the Crown). In addition, on the death of the Bishop of St Asaph or of Bangor, the render was to include their palfreys, with harness and saddle, along with the Bishop's rain-cloak and hood (extended to his leggings or boots (*ocrias*) and spurs on the death of Alexander Bache of St Asaph in 1394, **1/3**). The case of the Bishop of Rochester was slightly different, partly because the operation of regalian right in this see

172 For customs or renders due on consecration, see, for example, the fee claimed by the Archbishop of Canterbury on the enthronement of the Bishop of Norwich: from William Ayermine this amounted to 10 marks, a palfrey, a cope, a cup, a chapel and a pair of boots. LPL, Register of Archbishop Walter Reynolds, f. 148r. Further customs related to the Crown, some on consecration, some on death: *EEA 1: Lincoln 1067–1185* ed. D.M. Smith (Oxford, 1980) p. xxxiii, for a valuable mantle due from each Bishop of Lincoln to the Crown.

173 *The acta of Hugh of Wells Bishop of Lincoln 1209–1235* ed. D.M. Smith (Lincoln Record Society, 88; 2000) pp. 191–5, at p. 194.

174 *CPR 1266–72*, pp. 524–5.

175 *Winchesley register*, i, p. xxxiii; ii, pp. 1345–7.

176 *Liber quotidianus contrarotulatoris garderobe anno regni regis Edwardi primi vicesimo octavo A.D. MCCXCIX & MCCC* ed. Anon (1787) pp. 343–6; see also J. Cherry, 'The medieval episcopal ring', in *The medieval English cathedral: papers in honour of Pamela Tudor-Craig. Proceedings of the 1998 Harlaxton Symposium* ed. J. Backhouse (Harlaxton Medieval Studies, 10; Donington, 2003) pp. 208–17, at pp. 210–11.

had been remitted to the Archbishop of Canterbury. The Archbishop was due the Bishop's palfrey, his silver cup, his entire pack of hunting dogs; he was also due all the seals and the Bishop's best ring. If the archbishopric were vacant, however, the King would receive the palfrey, the hunting dogs, the cup and the best ring, as well as custody of all the temporalities of the see of Rochester. In this case, too, the Prior of Christ Church was to have all the seals and the Bishop's second-best ring, as in the case of other deaths while the archbishopric was vacant.[177] The ring is sometimes described as a pontifical ring as, for example, in the case of Lewis Charlton, of Hereford, delivered in 1370 (**12/4**).

The relationship between the bishop and his cathedral church was marked by a number of general customs. Among these was the practice of passing the contents of the episcopal chapel, that is, the textiles and furnishings associated with liturgical practice, to the cathedral church on the bishop's death. In the fifteenth century, Durham Cathedral Priory under Prior Wessington could list goods of the bishop's chapel, which had been received as *funeralia* or mortuary payments from individual bishops going back to William of St Carilef (d. 1096).[178] For Nicholas de Farnham – who had resigned the see in 1249, but did not die until 1257 – Durham received the horses that had brought Nicholas' body to Durham, as well as the horse bringing two chests with the chapel, that is, a chasuble of red samite, decorated with many jewels, in which the Bishop celebrated mass on Palm Sunday; two tunics of the same cloth; a cope, stole and maniple, and an embroidered red alb; a chalice with precious stones in the foot, and a silver thurible, along with many other ornaments.[179] Bishop Richard Kellaw sought the chapel goods from the executors of his predecessor, Anthony Bek, and Richard of Bury's letter book recorded it was the custom of Bishops of Durham to leave their whole and complete chapel ('capellam integram et honestam') either by will or to be assigned by custom by their executors[180] – and the seals of the Bishops of Durham were left to the shrine of St Cuthbert, within their cathedral church.[181] Hubert Walter, on his death in 1205, left his chapel to Canterbury, as its Archbishop – on condition that the monks spent 300 marks for his soul, perhaps a negotiation of custom. The chapel's richness, however, attracted the attention of King John, who asked for it and gave it to Peter des Roches, the new Bishop of Winchester.[182] Hugh of Wells, Bishop of Lincoln, in what was perhaps a variation of this custom, in 1233 left his chapel

177 These customs are recorded in two records from Canterbury Cathedral Priory, a *sede vacante* register, CCA, Register G, ff. 23r–v, and in the register and memorandum book of Henry de Eastry, BL MS Cotton Galba E IV, f. 25v.

178 *Wills and inventories*, i, prints what are described on p. 1 as mortuary payments on the death of the bishop, listing typically the goods of the chapel or ornaments left to Durham Cathedral Priory, from DUL, Durham DCM, Miscellaneous Charter 2622.

179 *Wills and inventories*, i, p. 5.

180 *RPD*, iv, pp. 429–30.

181 B.M. Bedos-Rezak, 'L'Au-delà du soi. Métamorphoses sigillaires en Europe médiévale' *Cahiers de Civilisation Médiévale* 49 (2006) pp. 337–58. The article also notes the formal breaking of the episcopal seals on the death of the Bishop of Durham, a practice which also happened in the case of other prominent individuals: e.g. William de Valence, in 1296, before the Archbishop of Canterbury, Woolgar, *Great household*, p. 107

182 *Historical works of Gervase of Canterbury*, ii, pp. 98, 413–14.

to his altar;[183] and in 1368 Thomas Percy of Norwich left his cathedral his principal vestments, along with a cross and pontifical which he had received from the executors of his predecessor in the see; the chapel goods that were for daily use, however, he bequeathed for the use of the chapel in the bishop's palace, to remain there in perpetuity (**29/1**).

It is not always easy to see how or when these transactions happen. For a bishop to give ecclesiastical goods to his cathedral was not an unusual act; but whether the transaction was made in his lifetime, or at his death, is not always clear. For example, at Ely, the continuation of the *Historia Eliensis* records a whole succession of goods that came to the cathedral priory from the bishops, but exactly when these transfers were made is more opaque. On the death of John Ketton, in 1316, the chronicle records that the ornaments of the Bishop's chapel were brought to Ely: one suspects that his happened on the deaths of at least some of the other bishops, and that it was part of a broader pattern, but it is not so easily demonstrated.[184] The suspicion that this was the expected pattern is underpinned by the events on the death of Bishop John Fordham, in 1425. Here the chronicler records that two basins were given for the high altar, along with £50 for the bishop's chapel. This looks as if it was a gift of money in lieu of a customary bequest of his chapel: it is not mentioned separately as a bequest in Fordham's will, although his executors had discretion to make further bequests as they considered best for the salvation of Fordham's soul and unburdening of their consciences.[185] There is evidence for transfers of this nature at other sees, for example, Chichester;[186] and numbers of bishops made bequests of mitres, croziers or rings to their successors in the see, usually bequeathing them as well to the cathedral church.[187] Godfrey Giffard of Worcester left his cathedral his best mitre, which he had as gift from his brother, the Archbishop of York, along with other vestments. At the same time, all the vestments that he received from the sacrist of Worcester on taking up the see were to be returned.[188] Thomas Cobham, also of Worcester, left the cathedral the beautiful mitre he had received from the Archbishop of Canterbury, to remain at Worcester in perpetuity, although there was a complication in terms of pledges relating to it. A further great mitre, which had belonged to Walter Maidstone and which he had in turn bought from John Droxford of Bath and Wells, had been seized in London by the king's justices, and assigned to Cobham in part payment of damages: Cobham left it to his successor and Adam Orleton, who succeeded him, gave a receipt for it.[189] In 1365, Thomas de Ringstead, Bishop of Bangor, left the church there his

183 *Acta of Hugh of Wells*, p. 193.

184 *Anglia sacra*, i, p. 642.

185 Will printed in *Chichele register*, pp. 327–9; *Anglia sacra*, i, p. 666.

186 *Chartulary of the high church of Chichester*, pp. 275–82, gifts recorded in the catalogue of bishops, number 903; and a direct bequest by William Rede to his successor of his chapel, with his mitre, crozier and 'other ornaments': Powicke, *Medieval books of Merton College*, p. 87.

187 For example, Walter of Merton, Bishop of Rochester, 1276: *Early rolls of Merton College Oxford*, p. 80.

188 *The register of William de Geynesburgh, Bishop of Worcester, 1302–1307* ed. J.W. Willis Bund with an introduction by R.A. Wilson (Worcestershire Historical Society, 22; 1907–29) p. 50.

189 *The register of Thomas de Cobham, Bishop of Worcester, 1317–1327* ed. E.H. Pearce (Worcestershire Historical Society, 40; 1930) pp. 49–50.

pastoral staff, which he had had made from new, but made bequests of many chapel goods elsewhere, leaving some to the Dominicans in London, so that when the convent was visited by bishops there would be liturgical equipment ready for their use (**31/1**). While there is variation here, the point is that although some wills list large quantities of ecclesiastical goods as bequests to their cathedral church (e.g. **40/1**, **43/1** (to both Canterbury and London) and **44/1**), the act of bequeathing these goods may have been little different from what would have happened by custom had these legacies not been mentioned. One of the reasons for this is that many of these goods, commonly relating to the bishop's chapel, may have been in the possession of the cathedral church in the first instance, and had been delivered to the bishop on his consecration, with the expectation that they were to be returned on resignation from the see or by the bishop's executors on his death.[190] At Worcester, the Prior and Convent passed a mitre that had belonged to Bishop Giffard, as well as vestments, chalices, and other goods for his chapel, to his successor, Walter Reynolds, and then had considerable difficulty recovering the mitre from Reynolds once he had been translated to Canterbury.[191] These goods were often augmented by bequests (**28/1**). Simon Mepham, on entering the see of Canterbury in 1328, received goods including Pecham's mitre and great pontifical, Winchelsey's gloves, candelabra and bible, and the crismatorium of Walter Reynolds (**25/1**).[192] In 1361, on taking up the see of Hereford, Lewis Charlton received goods held by the chapter for the use of the Bishops of Hereford (**12/1**). In the case of Bishop Mitford of Salisbury, the old pastoral staff which he had received was remade and was then bequeathed to his cathedral church, but not without noting that the value of the silver in the old staff (the stock of which had been made of wood) was 5 marks, presumably to forestall a claim against his executors (**26/1**). Custom and practice also mutated into ecclesiastical law. A case of 1347, involving the executors of Bishop Ross of Carlisle, was taken by the early seventeenth century as demonstrating that the ornaments of the bishop's chapel belonged to the succeeding bishop, but other chattels belonged to the executors. Historical practice, however, suggests a more complex picture.[193]

Not all the transfers from bishop to bishop took place on a customary basis. Many had the opportunity of purchasing episcopal ornaments and goods from the executors or administrators of their predecessors. Thomas Charlton of Hereford, for example, had an antiphoner of the use of Hereford, which he acquired from the administrators of John Trillek (**12/2**).

Other customs related to grave goods and to funerals. Although they are not mentioned in wills, it was common practice for bishops to buried with episcopal

[190] For example, HMC *Calendar of the manuscripts of the Dean and Chapter of Wells* (2 vols., 1907–14) i, p. 224; **22/1**.

[191] *The 'Liber albus' of the priory of Worcester* ed. J.M. Wilson (Worcestershire Historical Society, 35; 1919) pp. 40, 68, 73.

[192] For the transfers of some of these goods to and from Reynolds, **30/1–2**.

[193] Referred to in 12 Coke's Reports, pp. 105–6, Corven *v.* Pym: *The twelfth part of the reports of Sir Edward Coke, kt. …* (1656) pp. 105–6; and in E. Gibson *Codex juris ecclesiastici Anglicani* (2 vols., 1713) i, p. 195. Both give the reference 21 E. III, 48, Gibson repeating Coke: I have not traced this further. Later authorities, e.g. R.J. Phillimore *The ecclesiastical law of the Church of England* (2 vols., 2nd edition, 1895) i, p. 65, refer back to Gibson.

insignia and vestments, as well as chalice and paten.[194] Rings with sapphires, perhaps of lesser quality, have been found in a least a dozen burials.[195] Nicholas Longespee of Salisbury, who died in 1297, asked that his heart be buried at Lacock Abbey, along with his silver crucifix.[196] Bishop Grandisson of Exeter was unusual in specifying an inscription on a lead plaque that was to placed with his body.[197]

Provision for funeral feasts is sometimes mentioned. The executors of John Salmon, Bishop of Norwich, who died in 1325, were permitted to hunt and take deer in the Bishop's parks, woods and chases, and fish the ponds and fisheries in order to make suitable provision for the funeral.[198] Similar provision for venison and fish for the feasting accompanying the funeral was made on the death of William Zouche, Archbishop of York, in 1352.[199] John Grandisson of Exeter in his will of 1368 tells of a custom for which there is little other evidence, prohibiting drinking with spices at night around the body in the choir of the church (presumably part of the wake), but conceding that it might happen in the chapter house or other fit place. He also did not wish his household members to dress in black at the commemorative services that would follow the funeral, asking them to wear their livery for that year, and for the priests and clerks of his chapel their surplices and hoods as they would normally have done.[200]

Although they are not mentioned in the probate documents edited here, the commemoration of the dead was sometimes marked by a further custom, the creation of obituary rolls, which were taken round religious fraternities seeking intercessory prayers on behalf of the deceased, and which were duly subscribed. At Durham, rolls survive for Bishops Robert of Holy Island, Thomas Hatfield and Walter Skirlawe.[201]

Wills are also immensely useful for what they tell us about household customs generally and the bishop's goods – just as the transfer of the bishop's chapel to his cathedral had a customary dimension, so too did other practices relating to domestic goods that might, or not, appear in wills. John Sheppey, Bishop of Roch-

194 N. Stratford, P. Tudor-Craig and A. Muthesius, 'Archbishop Hubert Walter's tomb and its furnishings' *Medieval art and architecture at Canterbury before 1220: British Archaeological Association Conference Transactions* 5 (1982) pp. 71–93; and the account of the attempted robbery of grave goods from the corpse of Richard Grant, Archbishop of Canterbury: *Matthaei Parisiensis monachi sancti Albani Chronica majora* ed. H.R. Luard (7 vols., RS, 57; 1872–83) iii, p. 206.

195 R. Gilchrist, 'Magic for the dead? The archaeology of magic in later medieval burials' *Medieval Archaeology* 52 (2008) pp. 119–69, at p. 138; Cherry, 'Medieval episcopal ring', pp. 209–10.

196 Malden, 'Will of Nicholas Longespee', p. 524.

197 *Grandisson register*, iii, p. 1557: 'Hic jacet Johannes de Grandissone | Miserabilis episcopus Exoniensis | Matris misericordie miserrimus servus | Cujus misericors filius ejus precibus est miseratus | Ut de misero fieret beatus | Et ceteris miseris spes detur flendi reatus.'

198 *CClR 1323–7*, p. 388.

199 *CPR 1350–4*, p. 311. For the scale of feasting at the funeral of Bishop Mitford of Salisbury in 1407, n. 171 above.

200 *Grandisson register*, iii, pp. 1549–50.

201 DUL, Durham DCM, Locellus I 1, Robert of Holy Island; 2–3, Hatfield; 4, Skirlawe; *The obituary roll of William Ebchester and John Burnby, Priors of Durham, with notices of similar records preserved at Durham from the year 1233 downwards* … ed. J. Raine (Surtees Society, 31; 1856) pp. xvii–xx, also mentioning a roll for a Bishop of Ely, p. xvii; the texts of the rolls are printed on pp. 51–63.

ester from 1352 until his death in 1360, mentions in his will of 21 September 1360 a good deal of especial interest with regard to servants and their perquisites. He left John Barbour, his chamberlain, 10 marks and a silver-plated cup, and John Moys, the valet of the chamber, 60*s*. But, he noted, because chamberlains generally claimed as a courtesy after the death of their lords their belt, with whatever might be attached to it, that is, knives, purses and whatever might be contained in the purse (with the exception of the seal and secret writings of the lord), as well as all the fittings (*apparatus*) of the chamber, and that as a consequence there was often fraud, Sheppey specified exactly what goods the chamberlain was to have – a canvas (i.e. a cover), two mattresses, two linen sheets, two pillows, a good quilt, a coverlet with a tester, two tapets and three curtains and nothing more. The two Johns were also to receive all the equipment used with spices (**33/1**). This association between servants, the goods they worked with in their professions, and perquisites on death can be seen in other wills. Thomas Percy of Norwich left his chamberlain his best bed and all the textiles belonging to it, along with a robe of scarlet and 60*s*. He also left his falconer all his falcons, his tercilet and lanners; and another servant, John Waryn, was left all the Bishop's saddles (**29/1**). William Bottlesham's marshal and another servant, Henry Walpool, were to have their customary fees; and the Bishop's chamberlain was to have the cover of the bed, and bedding in which the Bishop slept (**5/1**). John Braytoft, the cook of William Spridlington of St Asaph, was to have at least 40*s*. worth of cloth or household utensils; his chamberlain at the time of his death was to have a green bed and its accoutrements (**34/1**).[202] The presence of these transactions shows us that we need to look beyond the text of wills to comprehend the full range of proceedings on a bishop's death. The testamentary records catalogued and edited in this volume document only a part of these arrangements.

[202] For the case of the cook and butler of Richard Gravesend, Bishop of London, Woolgar, *Great Household*, p. 33, citing *Executors*, pp. 58, 109.

CATALOGUE OF PROBATE DOCUMENTATION

BANGOR

As Edward I noted in his grant to Bishop Anian in May 1285, 'from ancient custom' Welsh bishops were not permitted to make wills: the princes of Wales and Welsh law had not expected or allowed them to do so.[1] Anian was the first Bishop of Bangor permitted to make a will – by the English – but there is nonetheless some suggestion that earlier Bishops, even under Welsh law, may have had property that they considered their own and at their disposal. When Bishop Cadwgan resigned the see in 1235 × 1236, he became a monk at the Cistercian abbey of Dore, making his profession 'in ultima et libera voluntate mea' at his 'civil death'. In the instrument of profession he gave the abbey for the safety of his soul all that he possessed, 'whether in books or in horses, or in any other thing'.[2] The licence granted in 1285 did not apply to Anian's successors, and Anian Sais therefore obtained his own licence to make a will in 1311,[3] as did Bishop Matthew de Englefield in 1329 shortly after taking up the see.[4] The poverty of the see was a major problem and in 1320 Anian Sais asked that on his death his executors might have the vacancy – by which he meant that the King should forego his right to the temporalities – so that the church might be repaired and his debts paid. The King's council regarded the request as unconventional and did not grant it.[5]

On the death of a Bishop of Bangor, the Archbishop of Canterbury, *sede plena*, or the Prior of Christ Church, Canterbury, *sede vacante*, was entitled to the Bishop's palfrey and harness, his rain-cloak and hood, all his seals and his second best ring.[6]

Notes

1 *CED*, i, p. 584.

2 *CED*, i, p. 464, from T. Madox *Formulare Anglicanum or a collection of ancient charters and instruments …* (1702) pp. 302–3; Sheehan, *WME*, p. 250.

3 *CPR 1307–13*, p. 391.

4 *CPR 1327–30*, p. 387.

5 *PRME*, iii, p. 398.

6 CCA, Register G, f. 23v; BL MS Cotton Galba E IV, f. 25v.

Robert of Shrewsbury (1197 – d. 1212 × 1213)

No documentation traced.

Cadwgan [or Martin] (1215 – res. 1235 × 1236)

Wills: None surviving.
Other grants and gifts: CED, i, p. 464.

Richard (1237 – d. 1267)

No documentation traced.

Anian (1267 – d. 1305 × 1306)
Licences: CED, i, p. 584, reprinting Rymer, *Foedera*, I, i, p. 654; brief summary in *CPR 1281–92*, p. 161.

Gruffydd ab Iorwerth (1307 – d. 1309)
No documentation traced.

Anian Sais (1309 – d. 1328)
Licences: CPR 1307–13, p. 391.
Wills: None surviving.
Other grants and gifts: PRME, iii, p. 398.

Matthew de Englefield [Madoc ab Iorwerth] (1328 – d. 1357)
Licences: CPR 1327–30, p. 387.
Wills: None surviving.

Thomas de Ringstead (1357 – d. 1366)
Wills: Will, 3 December 1365, **31/1**, LPL, Register of Simon Islip, ff. 245v–246r.
Executors: Dom. Thomas [de Illeye], Bishop of Lviv (*Lambergensis*), Mag. Ralph de Ryngestede, Brother Nicholas de Mo*n*yngton' and Dom. Thomas de Thorp, rector of the church of Tydd, with power to include Brother John de Beauchamp (**31/1–2**).
Probate process and execution: **31/2–3**.

Gervase de Castro (1366 – d. 1370)
Wills: Will, 24 September 1370, **11/1**, LPL, Register of William Whittlesey, ff. 117r–117v.
Executors: Howel ap Tud*ur* Gruffuth', Treffegoet Ll*oyt* ap Howel, Brother Howel de sancto Hillario, Ieuan ap David Vych*aun*, Eign*ion* ap Ll*oyt*, Howel ap Ior*werth* Vych*aun*, Gruffuth' ap Mad*og* Clodayth' and Edmund ap Eygn*ion* Lloyt named in will (**11/1**). Probate granted to Gruffuth' ap Mad*og* Clodayth (**11/2**).
Probate process and execution: **11/2–3**.

Hywel ap Gronow (1371 – d. 1372)
Wills: None surviving; died intestate.
Executors: Administrator: Gronow ap Tudir.
Probate process and execution: Commission to Gronow ap Tudir to administer the goods of Howel, last Bishop of Bangor, who has died intestate 'ac ipsa bona in pios usus pro salute anime ipsius defuncti prout secundum deum tibi melius videbitur expedire distribuenda et eciam eroganda'. Croydon, 13 February 1372. LPL, Register of William Whittlesey, f. 137r.

John Swaffham (1376 – d. 1398)
No documentation traced.

BATH AND WELLS

On his deathbed, around Christmas Day 1191, Reginald de Bohun (FitzJocelin), Bishop of Bath and Archbishop elect of Canterbury, sent a letter to Prior

Geoffrey and the convent of Canterbury, asking to be brought a monastic habit in his last illness.[1] There is no evidence, however, that he left a will. The first Bishop for whom there is evidence of will-making is Jocelin of Wells. In July 1231, Henry III granted Jocelin – just as he had done for his brother, Hugh of Wells, Bishop of Lincoln – the right for him and his successors in the see to make wills, confirming at the same time that notwithstanding any custom to the contrary, their estates were to include all the moveable goods and all the produce of the bishopric, explicitly noting corn and the produce of vineyards, until the Michaelmas after the bishop's death. The executors were also to be allowed to use the buildings – including the barns, granaries and wine-presses – of the bishopric until they were needed for the produce of the following year.[2] Edward III confirmed the rights to Ralph of Shrewsbury, extending them to the liberties and quittances due to the bishopric.[3]

In addition to wills listed here, John Barnet, who died in 1373 as Bishop of Ely, made his will (**3/1**) while Bishop of Bath and Wells.

Notes

1 Printed in *Chronicles and memorials of the reign of Richard I* ed. W. Stubbs (2 vols., RS, 38; 1865) ii, p. 355, number 388; summarised in *EEA 10: Bath and Wells 1061–1205* ed. F.M. Ramsey (Oxford, 1995) p. 137, number 179.

2 *CFR 1224–34*, pp. 386–7 (15/224); *CChR 1226–57*, p. 137. The Michaelmas date was further confirmed in 1237: *CPR 1232–47*, p. 184.

3 *CClR 1360–4*, p. 490.

Savaric FitzGeldewin, Bishop of Bath (and Glastonbury from 1197) (1191 – d. 1205)

No documentation traced.

Jocelin of Wells (Jocelin Trotman), Bishop of Bath and Glastonbury (1206 – d. 1242)

Licences: CChR 1226–57, p. 42; *CFR 1224–34*, p. 387 (15/224); *CChR 1226–57*, p. 137; *CPR 1232–47*, p. 184.

Wills: None surviving.

Probate process and execution: Close rolls 1242–7, p. 78.

Roger of Salisbury, Bishop of Bath and Wells (1244 – d. 1247)

Wills: None surviving.

Probate process and execution: Close rolls 1247–51, p. 19.

William of Bitton I (1248 – d. 1264)

Licences: CPR 1247–58, p. 192.

Wills: None surviving.

Probate process and execution: Close rolls 1261–4, pp. 352–3.

William of Bitton II (1267 – d. 1274)

Wills: None surviving.

Executors: Thomas de Bitton, archdeacon of Wells, and Roger de Cruk, provost of Wells (HMC *Calendar of the manuscripts of the Dean and Chapter of Wells* (2 vols., 1907–14) i, p. 379, from Liber Albus II, f. 132).

Robert Burnell (1275 – d. 1292)
Wills: None surviving.
Executors: Mag. William Burnel, Dean of Wells (*CClR 1272–9*, p. 568; *CClR 1288–96*, p. 264, etc.), William de Hamelton, archdeacon of York (*CClR, 1288–96*, p. 264, etc.), and Dionysius Well (*CClR 1279–88*, p. 554).
Probate process and execution: CIPM, iii, pp. 44–51 (number 65); *CFR 1272–1307*, p. 316; *PRME*, ii, p. 113; *CPR 1292–1301*, p. 264; *CPR 1292–1301*, p. 560; *PRME*, iii, pp. 359–60.
Recognisances for debt to the executors or payments acknowledged by the executors: CClR 1272–9, p. 568; *CClR 1279–88*, pp. 44, 246, 484, 494, 554; *CClR 1288–96*, pp. 38, 46, 120, 264, 315, 316, 318, 319, 322, 323, 384, 386, 387, 389, 405 (two), 446, 454, 500 (two); *CClR 1296–1302*, pp. 133, 187, 193–4, 320, 343, 350, 429, 451; *CClR 1307–13*, p. 64.

William of March (1293 – d. 1302)
Wills: None surviving.
Executors: Thomas de Berkeley, knight, Mag. Peter de Avebur', archdeacon of Taunton, Mag. Antony de Braden', canon of Wells, and John de Marchia and Richard de Rodeneye, laymen (*Winchelsey register*, i, pp. 440–1).
Probate process and execution: *CIPM*, iv, p. 61 (number 94); *Winchelsey register*, i, pp. 440–1; *CClR 1302–7*, p. 5; HMC, *Calendar of the manuscripts of the Dean and Chapter of Wells*, i, pp. 240, 245–8 (from Liber Albus I, ff. 202, 206–8).

Walter Haselshaw (1302 – d. 1308)
Wills: None surviving.
Executors: Mag. Henry de Schavynton, archdeacon of Taunton, Mag. Robert de Heselschawe, provost, Hugh de Pencriz, canon of Wells, Richard de Rodeneye and William de Hesselschawe (*Winchelsey register*, ii, p. 1077).
Probate process and execution: Winchelsey register, ii, pp. 1077–8.

John Droxford (1309 – d. 1329)
Wills: None surviving.
Probate process and execution: CIPM, vii, pp. 160–1 (number 218); account of John de Clyveden for the sale of corn of the late Bishop, seized for his debts to the King, 3 Edward III, TNA E 101/507/12.

Ralph of Shrewsbury (1329 – d. 1363)
Licences: CPR 1361–4, p. 346.
Wills: Will, dated 12 May 1363, LPL Register of Simon Islip, f. 244r, calendared in *Somerset medieval wills (second series) 1501–30, with some Somerset wills preserved at Lambeth* ed. F.W. Weaver (Somerset Record Society, 19; 1903) pp. 286–7. Bequests of books noted in Cavanaugh, 'Books', p. 788.
Executors: William Camel, precentor and canon of Wells, Mag. Robert de Nettelton, canon of Wells, William Derby, canon of Wells, Robert de Samborn, canon of Wells, and John Lombard, canon of Wells, named in the will (*Somerset medieval wills (second series) 1501–30*, p. 287).
Probate process and execution: CClR 1360–4, p. 490; *CClR 1369–74*, p. 425; HMC, *Calendar of the manuscripts of the Dean and Chapter of Wells*, i, pp. 292–3.

Acquittance of the executors of Bishop Ralph, 30 May 1364. LPL, Register of Simon Islip, f. 202v.

John Harewell (1366 – d. 1386)
Wills: Will, dated 29 June 1386, LPL Register of William Courtenay, ff. 218v–219, calendared in *Somerset medieval wills (second series) 1501–30*, pp. 289–90.
Executors: Henry Segrave, knight, John, Prior of Bath, Mag. Thomas Spert, the Bishop's official, John Waryn, canon of Wells, John de Harewell, the Bishop's nephew, John Bryngton, John Grene, canon of Wells, and John de Tuttebury (*Somerset medieval wills (second series) 1501–30*, p. 290).

Ralph Erghum (1388 – d. 1400)
Wills: Will, 31 January 1398, LPL Register of Thomas Arundel, vol. I, ff. 168r–169v, calendared in *Somerset medieval wills (second series) 1501–30*, pp. 294–7.
Executors: Agnes Rabbas, the Bishop's sister, Thomas Terry, canon of Wells, John Podmore, and John Carethorp the younger (*Somerset medieval wills (second series) 1501–30*, p. 297).
Probate process and execution: CPR 1405–8, p. 136; *CPapReg 1404–15*, p. 133.

Commission to the Abbot of Glastonbury to act in a dispute relating to bequests under the will, of £100 to John Carethorp the younger, *nepos* of Ralph of Shrewsbury, and of £20 to Eustachia, his sister. John Carethorp the younger has died and his father, John Carethorp, his executor, is moving the case. The executors of the Bishop's will, Thomas Terry, canon of Wells, and John Podmore, esquire, have been released from their charge. Given at Lambeth, 16 February 1402. LPL, Register of Thomas Arundel, vol. I, f. 117v.

CANTERBURY

The will of Archbishop Theobald is the earliest post-Conquest episcopal will to survive. The munificence and wealth of earlier Archbishops is detailed in other records: for example, Bartholomew Cotton notes Lanfranc (Archbishop 1070–89) rebuilding the church and its courts at Canterbury, and endowing it with books and ornaments; but no mention is made of these gifts being made at his death.[1] In 1136 William of Corbeil was known at his death to be very wealthy, a subject of unfavorable comment, but he did not leave a will.[2] From the time of Archbishop Baldwin of Forde onwards, most Archbishops made wills: Hubert Walter, for example, made them regularly. A formal royal licence to make a will was granted in 1234 to Edmund Rich, extending the right to his successors as well.[3] Boniface of Savoy set minimum levels of livestock on the manors of the estate which were to pass from one Archbishop to his successor,[4] but this may reflect earlier arrangements: in 1228, the executors of Stephen Langton fined with the King for having the livestock of the estate which had previously been left there by Hubert Walter (that is, the same quantity), as well as corn, wines and cider.[5] In terms of customary expectation, the Archbishop's chapel often passed to Canterbury Cathedral Priory and incoming Archbishops received ecclesiastical ornaments and goods from its sacrist, augmented from time to time by gifts or bequests of further goods (**25/1**, **30/1–2**).[6] Well before the late thirteenth century, it was the custom that on the death of the Archbishop his best palfrey, ring, cup and his pack of hounds passed to the Crown – a practice so long accepted that 10 marks in lieu of the palfrey were allowed to the executors of Boniface of Savoy in settling the debts the Crown owed to the former Archbishop;[7] the Prior of the Cathedral Priory received the second best ring and the Archbishop's seals.[8]

Notes

1 Bartholomew Cotton, 'Liber de archiepiscopis et episcopis Angliae', in *Bartholomaei de Cotton monachi Norwicensis Historia Anglicana (A.D. 449–1298) necnon ejusdem Liber de archiepiscopis et episcopis Angliae* ed. H.R. Luard (RS, 16; 1859) p. 364.
2 Sheehan, *WME*, pp. 244–5, at n. 56.
3 D. Wilkins *Concilia Magnae Britanniae et Hiberniae* (4 vols., 1737) i, p. 630.
4 *Winchelsey register*, i, p. xxxiii; for levels of stock after the end of the archiepiscopate of Robert Kilwardy, BL MS Cotton Galba E IV, ff. 2v–3v.
5 *CFR 1224–34*, p. 227 (13/20).
6 Winchelsey's bible, which appears in Mepham's list, may have been the one bequeathed to Winchelsey's nephew, Mag. John de Wynchelsey: *Winchelsey register*, ii, p. 1341.
7 *CPR 1266–72*, pp. 524–5.
8 BL MS Cotton Galba E IV, f. 25v.

Theobald (1138 – d. 1161)
Wills: Disposed of his property during an illness, *c.*1156: *The letters of John of Salisbury* ed. W.J. Millor, H.E. Bulter, revised by C.N.L. Brooke (revised edition, 2 vols., 1979–86) i, p. 14, number 8; i, p. 261 for the date; discussed in Sheehan, *WME*, pp. 142–3.

Will, 1158 × 1161: CCA, Chartae Antiquae A3, printed in *Sede vacante wills*, pp. 61–2; *Letters of John of Salisbury*, i, pp. 245–8; and A. Saltman, *Theobald, Archbishop of Canterbury* (1956) pp. 254–7. Discussed in Sheehan, *WME*, p. 143.

Thomas Becket (1162 – d. 1170)
Wills: The 'magna carta sancti Thome', transcribed in LPL, MS 1212, ff. 133r–133v, where it is described as 'testamentum beati Thome martiris gloriosi conditum per paucos dies ante mortem suam', is a thirteenth-century forgery from Christ Church Cathedral Priory, Canterbury, copied in the early fourteenth century: *Sede vacante wills*, p. vi; *EEA 2: Canterbury 1162–1190* ed. C.R. Cheney and B.E.A. Jones (1986) pp. xli, 4–5; *EEA 3: Canterbury 1193–1205* ed. C.R. Cheney and E. John (1986) p. 305; C.R. Cheney, 'Magna carta beati Thome: another Canterbury forgery' *Bulletin of the Institute of Historical Research* 36 (1963) pp. 1–26, reprinted in C.R. Cheney, *Medieval texts and studies* (Oxford, 1973) pp. 78–110.

Richard of Dover (1173 – d. 1184)
No documentation traced.

Baldwin of Forde (1184 – d. 1190)
Wills: None surviving.
Executors: Hubert Walter (*Radulfi de Diceto decani Lundoniensis Opera historica* ed. W. Stubbs (2 vols., RS, 68; 1876) ii, p. 88; *Rogeri de Wendover Liber qui dicitur flores historiarum* … ed. H.G. Hewlett (3 vols., RS, 84; 1886–9) i, pp. 189–90).
Probate process and execution: Radulfi de Diceto decani Lundoniensis Opera historica, ii, p. 88; *Rogeri de Wendover Liber qui dicitur flores historiarum* …, i, pp. 189–90.

Hubert Walter (1193 – d. 1205)
Licences: Charters of John of 1199 and 1203 confirm wills made by Hubert Walter: *RC*, pp. 23a, 110a. The charter of 1199 in Rymer, *Foedera*, i, p. 78, is a copy of that in *RC* drawn from a Canterbury register.
Wills: Hubert Walter made wills annually during the last seven years of his life: *Radulphi de Coggeshall Chronicon Anglicanum* ... ed. J. Stevenson (RS, 66; 1875) p. 157. The making of his last will is described in *The historical works of Gervase of Canterbury* ed. W. Stubbs (2 vols., RS, 73; 1879–80) ii, pp. 412–13. For further descriptions and other references to Hubert Walter's estate: C.R. Cheney *Hubert Walter* (1967) pp. 175–6, and especially *EEA 3: Canterbury 1193–1205*, pp. 305–7, Appendix II, 'Archbishop Hubert's last will'.
Other grants and gifts: His chapel, which was to go to Christ Church, Canterbury, on condition that the convent spent 300 marks for the benefit of the Archbishop's soul, was taken by King John for the new Bishop of Winchester: *Historical works of Gervase of Canterbury*, ii, p. 98. Its contents are listed in a receipt given by the King's clerks to the Templars in London, who had temporary custody of it: *RLP*, p. 58b, also printed in *EEA 3: Canterbury 1139–1205*, p. 306. See also *RLP*, p. 60b, for instructions to deliver the chapel to the Bishop of Winchester, presumably for his consecration.

Stephen Langton (1206 – d. 1228)
Wills: None surviving.
Probate process and execution: Close Rolls 1227–31, p. 67; *CFR 1224–34*, pp. 227 (13/20), 252 (13/189).

Richard Grant (Wethershed) (1229 – d. 1231)
Wills: None surviving.
Probate process and execution: Letters close about the corn and stock of the estates: *Close rolls 1227–31*, p. 561; *Close rolls 1227–34*, pp. 112, 189.
Other grants and gifts: For the events around his death and burial, *Matthaei Parisiensis monachi sancti Albani Chronica majora* ed. H.R. Luard (7 vols., RS, 57; 1872–83) iii, p. 206.

Edmund Rich (1233 – d. 1240)
Licences: D. Wilkins *Concilia Magnae Britanniae et Hiberniae* (4 vols., 1737) i, p. 630.
Wills: None surviving.
Probate process and execution: References to bequests in *Le Vie seint Richard evesque de Cycestre by Pierre d'Abernon of Fetcham* ed. D.W. Russell (Anglo-Norman Text Society, 51; 1995) pp. 56–7; pallium taken to Catesby Priory after his death: 'Liber miraculorum beati Edmundi archiepiscopi' in *Thesaurus novus anecdotorum* ed. E. Martène and U. Durand (5 vols., Paris, 1717) iii, cols. 1888–9; letters close to the keepers of the archbishopric, about the moveable goods of the Archbishop: *Close rolls 1237–42*, pp. 273 (two), 387–8, 418–19.

Boniface of Savoy (1241 – d. 1270)
Licences: CPR 1232–47, p. 446 (securing repayment of a loan from Richard, Earl of Cornwall).
Wills: Boniface made at least two wills (*CPapReg 1198–1304*, p. 444). The will made at Tournon, 11 October 1264, is printed and discussed in D.A. Williams,

'Aspects of the career of Boniface of Savoy, Archbishop of Canterbury, 1241–70' (unpublished PhD thesis, University of Wales, 1970) pp. 487–9, from the edition by J.L. Wurstemberger *Peter der Zweiter Graf von Savoyen, Margraf in Italien, sein Haus und seine Lande. Ein Charakterbild des dreizehnten Jahrhunderts diplomatisch bearbeitet, ...* (4 vols., Bern, Zürich, 1856–8) iv, number 665. The Tournon will set aside all former wills.
Executors: Mag. Stephen, archdeacon of Canterbury, Mag. H. de Mortuo Mari, Mag. P. de Ausona, official of Canterbury, Mag. P. de Sableria, Mag. P. de Mota, Mag. P. de Camberiaco, and Dom. P. de Creysiaco (Williams, 'Aspects of the career of Boniface of Savoy', p. 489).
Probate process and execution: Close rolls 1268–72, pp. 218, 236–7; *CPR 1266–72*, pp. 524–5; *CFR* project, 55/401: TNA C 60/68, mem. 12r; *CPR 1266–72*, p. 568; *CPapReg 1198–1304*, p. 444; *CPR 1272–81*, p. 64.

Robert Kilwardby (1273–8; d. 1279)
Licences: Papal *licencia testandi*, *TDC*, p. 33.
Wills: No will traced and he probably died intestate: *TDC*, p. 33, n. 2.
Probate process and execution: Memorandum of stock left on the manors of the archbishopric of Canterbury after the archiepiscopate of Robert Kilwardby, with a note of all the vessels and utensils, along with ploughs, carts and other equipment found on the manors at the time of the archbishop's death; 1278. BL MS Cotton Galba E IV, ff. 2v–3v.

John Pecham (1279 – d. 1292)
Wills: Bequests of a mitre and pastoral staff noted in **30/1–2**.
Executors: Mag. Luke, treasurer of Hereford and rector of the church of Reculver (Raculure), Nicholas de [?]*Cernomule* (*Knonile* in M. Parker, *De antiquitate Britannicae ecclesiae* (1572) p. 206), rector of the church of Maidstone, and Simon de Grely, rector of Godmersham, executors named in the will (CCA, Register Q, f. 12r).
Probate process and execution: Winchelsey register, i, pp. 191, 239–40. Parker, *De antiquitate Britannicae ecclesiae*, p. 206, prints figures that were probably derived from a summary of the probate account, which no longer survives, submitted *sede vacante* to the Prior of Christ Church, Canterbury, between the archiepiscopates of Reynolds and Mepham. For a further view of the finances at probate, D. Sutcliffe, 'The financial condition of the see of Canterbury, 1279–1292' *Speculum* 10 (1935) pp. 53–68, at p. 67 n. 2, citing TNA E 372/140, mem. 28r, for payments by the executors; and 'Annales de Dunstaplia', in *Annales monastici* ed. H.R. Luard (5 vols., RS, 36; 1864–9) iii, p. 373.

Probate of the will, before Henry de Eastry, Prior of Christ Church, Canterbury, by Mag. Luke, treasurer of Hereford and rector of the church of Reculver (Raculure), Nicholas de [?]*Cernomule*, rector of the church of Maidstone, and Simon de Grely, rector of Godmersham, executors named in the will, in his greater chapel at Canterbury, in the presence of Mag. J., official of Canterbury, and many monks of the church, as well as secular clerks, namely R. de Adesham, then subprior, W. de Chil*in*derne, Thomas Beloysel, R. de Scharstede, J. Hardnes, J. Achard and Thomas de Wynchelese, monks; Mag. W. de Sarden', Martin, rector of the church of Hykham, Thomas, rector of the church of Adesham, P. de Geldeford, Mag. J. de Redingate, Mag. Roger de Canterbury and Edmund de Verdon, notary public, and others. The will was opened by the Prior and the oath administered to the executors, that they will faithfully make an inventory and administer the goods of the deceased, rendering an account for the same. 22 December 1292. CCA, Register Q, f. 12r.

Notarial instrument (damaged by damp) recording the proving of Pecham's will, 2[2] December 1292. As above, but noting that William de Sardene was a canon of St Paul's and P. de Geldeford a canon of Bosham. CCA, Chartae Antiquae A13A.

Commission from Henry de Eastry, Prior of Christ Church, Canterbury, to the official of the Bishop of Chichester and Gilbert Henday, rector of the church of Stedehame. As the account of the executors of Archbishop Pecham has not yet been heard, they are to summon the executors and other, interested parties in order to speed the conclusion of this business, reserving to the Prior the power of acquitting the executors. In chapter at Canterbury, 8 April 1294. CUL MS Ee. V. 31, f. 60v.

Robert Winchelsey (1293 – d. 1313)
Wills: Will, 1313, printed in *Sede vacante wills*, pp. 63–7, and in *Winchesley register*, ii, pp. 1340–5 (from a fresh transcript by W.P. Blore), from CCA, Chartae Antiquae W218. There is a description of the will and the process of its execution in *Winchelsey register*, i, pp. xxxii–xxxiv. The documentation is (a) a notarial copy of the will and a codicil and (b) a second codicil, recorded in a further notarial instrument. **30/1** contains further detail on the vestments bequeathed to Canterbury Cathedral Priory. Winchelsey's books were bequeathed to Canterbury Cathedral Priory: M.R. James *The ancient libraries of Canterbury and Dover: the catalogues of the libraries of Christ Church Priory and St Augustine's Abbey at Canterbury and of St Martin's Priory at Dover* (Cambridge, 1903) pp. 135–7; Cavanaugh, 'Books', pp. 936–8. The gift of vestments and books is noted in the 'Dies obituales archiepiscoporum Cantuariensium', *Anglia sacra*, i, pp. 52–64, at p. 59.
Executors: Henry, Prior of Christ Church, Canterbury; Richard de Rokesle, knight, steward of the Archbishop's lands, Mag. Michael de Bereham, chancellor, Mag. William de Swanitone, steward of the Archbishop's household, Robert Crul, clerk, and Geoffrey de Brampton, clerk, named in the will; probate committed to Michael de Bereham, William de Swanitone and Dom. Robert Crul, with the other executors at that point (*Winchesley register*, ii, pp. 1342–3).
Probate process and execution: Summary executors' accounts, including a summary inventory, printed in *Winchesley register*, ii, pp. 1345–7, from CCA, Chartae Antiquae A34. *PRME*, iii, pp. 117–18; *CClR 1323–7*, p. 379.

Walter Reynolds (1313 – d. 1327)
Wills: Will, 11 November 1327, **30/3**, CCA, Chartae Antiquae A14; printed in J.R. Wright, 'The testament or last will of Archbishop Walter Reynolds of Canterbury 1327' *Mediaeval Studies* 47 (1985) pp. 445–73. Bequests of books in the will noted in Cavanaugh, 'Books', p. 721.
Executors: Twelve executors are named in the will: Walter de Norwich, knight, Mag. John de Bruytone, Mag. John de Reddeswell, steward of the Archbishop's lands, Mag. Robert de Reddeswelle, chancellor, Mag. Ralph de Wyndesore, Dom.

John de Ringwode, treasurer of Canterbury, Mag. Adam de Penytone, Dom. John de camera, the Archbishop's clerk, Dom. Thomas de Stowe, Dom. Richard de Kyngtone, the Archbishop's almoner, John de Breydistone, the Archbishop's steward of the liberties of Christ Church, and William Moraunt. Archbishop Mepham claimed that they refused to administer the will (*CClR 1330–3*, p. 104; Wright, 'The testament or last will of Archbishop Walter Reynolds', p. 458); **30/5** shows their work in progress immediately after the proving of the will. **30/4** absolves Thomas de Stowe from the execution.
Probate process and execution: **30/4–5**. Receipts of the Crown's keepers of temporalities, which show the receipt of jewels, etc., in three almost identical indentures: TNA SC 6/1128/7–8, and E 372/173/44; printed in Wright, 'The testament or last will of Archbishop Walter Reynolds', pp. 460–5. *CPR 1313–17*, p. 112; *PRME*, iv, p. 89; *CClR 1330–3*, pp. 104, 451–2.

Simon Mepham (1327 – d. 1333)
Wills: None surviving.
Executors: Mag. Laurence Fastolf and Dom. Thomas de Woghope, the other executors declining the task at probate (**25/2**).
Probate process and execution: **25/2–3**. *CClR 1333–7*, pp. 231, 593; *CClR 1337–9*, p. 505; 'Dies obituales archiepiscoporum Cantuariensium', *Anglia sacra*, i, pp. 52–64, at p. 59.
Other grants and gifts: Cavanaugh, 'Books', p. 583.

John Stratford (1333 – d. 1348)
Licences: CPR 1334–8, p. 193 (a pardon allowing the Archbishop and his executors free administration of his goods).
Wills: Will, 1347, **35/1**, CCA, Chartae Antiquae W219; printed in *Sede vacante wills*, pp. 72–6; and in abstract, along with the executors' account, **35/6**, in R.M. Haines *Archbishop John Stratford: political revolutionary and champion of the liberties of the English church ca. 1275/80–1348* (Toronto, Pontifical Institute of Medieval Studies, Studies and Texts, 76; 1986) pp. 507–13; Cavanaugh, 'Books', pp. 329–30.
Executors: Dom. Robert, Bishop of Chichester, Ralph, Bishop of London, Mag. John de Lecch', Mag. Richard Vaughan, archdeacon of Surrey, John de Pulteneye, knight, Dom. John de Egleshale, and Richard de Twynerton, clerk (**35/5**). Ralph, Bishop of London (**35/4–5**), and Richard Vaughan (**35/2**) refused the executorship.
Probate process and execution: **35/2–7**. **35/6** is the executors' account. *CClR 1349–54*, p. 4; *CPR 1348–50*, p. 258; *CClR 1349–54*, p. 124.
Recognisances for debt to the executors or payments acknowledged by the executors: CClR 1343–6, p. 564; *CClR, 1346–9*, pp. 36, 138, 239.
Other grants and gifts: Gifts to Canterbury Cathedral Priory are noted in the 'Dies obituales archiepiscoporum Cantuariensium', *Anglia sacra*, i, pp. 52–64, at p. 59; Cavanaugh, 'Books', p. 330.

John Offord (1348 – d. 1349)
Wills: None surviving; his will was in part nuncupative (*CPapReg 1342–62*, p. 354).
Executors: Richard de Plessys, archdeacon of Colchester, Stephen de Brokesbourn,

rector of Holingbourn, and Robert de Morton, rector of Neuchurch, diocese of Canterbury (*CPapReg 1349–50*, p. 337).
Probate process and execution: CPapReg 1342–62, pp. 337, 354–5.

Mandate on behalf of the administrators of the goods of John Offord, threatening excommunication against those concealing goods and impeding the execution of Offord's will, listing those principally concerned, 18 April 1350. LPL, Register of Simon Islip, ff. 43v–44r.

Thomas Bradwardine (d. 1349)
No documentation traced.

Simon Islip (1349 – d. 1366)
Wills: Extracts from his will appear in the 'Dies obituales archiepiscoporum Cantuariensium', *Anglia sacra*, i, pp. 52–64, at pp. 60–1. CCA, Chartae Antiquae A15, 7 January 1362, is a gift of vestments, plate and a flock of 1,000 ewes, to Christ Church Cathedral Priory, Canterbury, to endow a chantry; transcribed in *Sede vacante wills*, pp. 77–9. Calendared in HMC, *Appendix to 5th Report*, p. 436.
Executors: Walter Dautre and Thomas Woltone (R.N. Swanson, 'Simon Islep', *ODNB*, xxix, pp. 433–5).
Probate process and execution: Books bought from his executors by William Rede, Bishop of Chichester: Cavanaugh, 'Books', pp. 461–2.

Simon Langham (1366 – res. 1368; d. 1376, at Avignon)
Wills: Notarial exemplification, 14 August 1377, of his will of 28 June 1375, WAM 9225, **21/5**; printed in R. Widmore *An history of the church of St Peter, Westminster, commonly called Westminster Abbey, chiefly from manuscript sources* (1751) pp. 184–91; discussed in M. Harvey, 'The household of Cardinal Langham' *Journal of Ecclesiastical History* 47 (1996) pp. 18–44.
Executors: Cardinal Pierre de Monteruc, Bishop of Pamplona, Cardinal Guillaume d'Aigrefeuille, Dean of Clermont, Dom. Nicholas, Abbot of Westminster, Adam de Eston, monk of Norwich, Laurence, monk of Battle, first of the English nation at the papal curia, Thomas de Southam, archdeacon of Oxford, Langham's auditor, William Palmer, canon of Derby, and John Boukenhull, monk of Westminster (Widmore, *History of … Westminster Abbey*, pp. 188–9).
Probate process and execution: **21/1–4, 6–16**.
Other gifts and grants: Gifts to Ely Cathedral Priory of vestments, possibly at his consecration as Bishop of Ely, and on his promotion to the cardinalate, listed in *Anglia sacra*, i, pp. 663–4.

William Whittlesey (1368 – d. 1374)
Wills: Will, 5 June 1374, CCA, Register G, ff. 170v–171r, and f. 208r, printed in *Sede vacante wills*, p. 80.
Executors: Dom. John Wodehull, Dom Walter Dautri, Dom. John Sulthorn, William Topclif, John Marcheforde, William Islep, John Tolthorp, John Knyvet, Mag. Nicholas de Chaddesden, and John Holt (*Sede vacante wills*, p. 80).
Probate process and execution: Cavanaugh, 'Books', pp. 942–3.

Grant of probate to Dom. John de Wodhull', Dom. John de Tolthorp', priests;

William Topclife, Mag. John Marcheford, and Ralph Marcheford, executors named in the will, 13 June 1374. CCA, Register G, f. 171r and f. 208r.

Simon Sudbury (1375 – d. 1381)
Wills: Certificate of probate and grant of administration, 12 October 1381, reciting the Archbishop's nuncupative testament dated 12 June 1381, CCA, Chartae Antiquae W220A; transcribed in *Sede vacante wills*, p. 81, from CCA, Register G, f. 228r.
Executors: Dom. William Rysing', prior of Holy Trinity, London, John Charceseye [Chertsey], Dom. John Ovyng', and Dom. Thomas Crocyer [Grocier] (CCA, Register G, f. 228r; *CClR 1381–5*, p. 394).
Probate process and execution: CClR 1381–5, p. 394; *CClR 1392–6*, p. 106.

Acquittance of the executors, by John, Prior of Christ Church, Canterbury, at Canterbury, 15 October 1381. Bodleian Library, MS Ashmole 794, f. 251v.

Other grants and gifts: Cavanaugh, 'Books', pp. 834–5.

William Courtenay (1381 – d. 1396)
Wills: Will, probably from the summer of 1395 (R.N. Swanson, 'William Courtenay' *ODNB*, xiii, pp. 687–92, at p. 691), with codicil dated 28 July 1396, CCA, Register G, ff. 258r–261v, printed in L.L. Duncan, 'The will of William Courtenay, Archbishop of Canterbury, 1396' *Archaeologia Cantiana* 23 (1898) pp. 55–67; part printed in translation in W.F. Hook *Lives of the Archbishops of Canterbury* (12 vols., London, 1860–76) v, pp. 394–6, and translated in full in J.H. Dahmus *William Courtenay, Archbishop of Canterbury, 1381–1396* (University Park, Penn., 1966) pp. 265–76. Bequests to Canterbury Cathedral Priory are noted in the 'Dies obituales archiepiscoporum Cantuariensium', *Anglia sacra*, i, pp. 52–64, at pp. 61–2.
Executors: Thomas Chillinden, Prior of Christ Church, Canterbury, Mag. Adam de Mottrum, archdeacon, Dom. Guy Mone, rector of the church of Maidstone, John Frenyngham, esquire, Dom. William Baunton, rector of Harrow, John Dodyngton, rector of Crewkerne, Mag. Robert Hallum, rector of Northfleet, Dom. John Wotton, rector of Staplehurst (Duncan, 'The will of William Courtenay', p. 66).
Probate process and execution: CClR 1396–9, p. 76; *PRME*, vii, pp. 321–2 (CCA, Chartae Antiquae T33); *CPapReg 1398–1404*, p. 96; *CClR 1396–9*, p. 408; *CClR 1399–1402*, pp. 121–2.

Probate, with deathbed codicil, granted by the commissary of Canterbury Cathedral Priory, to Thomas Chillynden, Dom. John Dodyngton, Mag. Robert Hallum and Dom. John Wotton, executors named in the will, Lambeth, 15 September 1396. CCA, Register G, ff. 261v–262r.

Other grants and gifts: Cavanaugh, 'Books', p. 214.

Thomas Arundel (1396–7 [trans. St Andrews]; restored 1399 – d. 1414)
Wills: Will, 12–16 February 1414, CCA, Register G, ff. 277r–9r; printed in *Sede vacante wills*, pp. 81–5.

Executors: Dom. Gilbert Humfrevyle, Prior of Christ Church, Canterbury, Mag. Philip Morgan, Mag. William Milton, Dom. John Wotton, master of the college of Maidstone, Bartholomew Brokesby, and William Maydeston (*Sede vacante wills*, p. 85).
Probate process and execution: CIPM, xx, pp. 90–1 (numbers 276–7), with an inventory of Leeds Castle. An abbreviated inventory of his goods, in the form usually submitted for probate, is printed in Hook, *Lives of the Archbishops of Canterbury*, v, pp. 527–8. *The fabric rolls of York Minster* ed. J. Raine the younger (Surtees Society, 35; 1859) p. 39. Gifts to Canterbury Cathedral Priory by his executors are noted in the 'Dies obituales archiepiscoporum Cantuariensium', *Anglia sacra*, i, pp. 52–64, at pp. 62–3.

Grant of probate, 24 March 1414, CCA, Register G, f. 279v.

Other grants and gifts: Fabric rolls of York Minster, p. 309; Cavanaugh, 'Books', pp. 52–5.

Roger Walden (1397–9 [deprived]; Bishop of London 1404 – d. 1406)
Licences: Letters patent with general pardon and discharge to the Archbishop, for all debts to the Crown, and all suits and actions, to include his heirs, successors and executors, 21 November 1398, *CPR 1396–9*, p. 448.
Wills: Will, 31 December 1405, **43/1**, LPL, Register of Thomas Arundel, vol. I, ff. 227r–228r.
Executors: John Walden', the Bishop's brother, Richard Clyderow, esquire, John Shordiche the younger, esquire, Mag. William Bulcote, Mag. Henry Hamerton, John Bernard, clerk, Thomas Wysebech', clerk, and Richard Scot, clerk (**43/1**); probate granted to the executors, except Thomas Wysebech', for whom a power of admission to the administration was reserved (**43/2**).
Probate process and execution: **43/2–4**. *CPapReg 1404–15*, p. 227.

CARLISLE

Hugh of Beaulieu is the first Bishop of Carlisle known to have made a will. His successor, Walter Mauclerc, was granted licences in 1230 and 1245 enabling him to bequeath property, both moveable and immoveable, along with wardships.[1] In 1291 Ralph Ireton obtained royal confirmation of the stock and equipment of the bishopric estates, along with domestic moveable goods, which were to pass unabated from bishop to bishop.[2] Letters close of 1354 show the system in operation, with the delivery of stock at the episcopal manor of Horncastle in Lincolnshire by the escheator to Bishop Gilbert Welton.[3] A law suit in 1347, about the ornaments of the episcopal chapel and involving the executors of Bishop Ross, established the general principle that these goods should belong to succeeding bishops rather than to the executors as part of the deceased's personal estate.[4]

Notes
1 *CChR 1226–57*, pp. 121–2; *CPR 1232–47*, p. 456.
2 *CChR 1257–1300*, pp. 408–9.
3 *CClR 1354–60*, p. 26.
4 *The twelfth part of the reports of Sir Edward Coke, kt. …* (1656) pp. 105–6; E. Gibson *Codex juris ecclesiastici Anglicani* (2 vols., 1713) i, p. 195.

Bernard (1203 – d. 1214)
No documentation traced.

Hugh of Beaulieu (1218 – d. 1223)
Wills: None surviving.
Probate process and execution: EEA 30: Carlisle 1133–1292 ed. D.M. Smith (Oxford, 2005) p. 51, number *67; *RLC*, i, p. 578.

Walter Mauclerc (1223 – res. 1246, d. 1248)
Licences: CChR 1226–57, pp. 121–2; *CPR 1232–47*, p. 456.
Wills: None surviving. *EEA 30: Carlisle 1133–1292*, p. 80, number *100, summarises references to his will.
Executors: Richard the chaplain, parson of Rothbury, and Robert, parson of Horncastle (*EEA 30: Carlisle 1133–1292*, p. 80, number *100, citing TNA E 159/31, mem. 10d; E 159/47, mem. 20d; E 159/48, mem. 27; E 159/49, mem. 31; E 159/51, mem. 1, 11).
Probate process and execution: Close rolls 1242–7, p. 456 (three letters). The Bishop's executors started their work when Mauclerc resigned the see to become a Dominican friar in August 1246, on his profession and 'civil death'. He made substantial gifts to the Dominican friary in Oxford: *EEA 30: Carlisle 1133–1292*, p. xl; W.A. Hinnebusch *The early English Friars Preachers* (Rome, 1951) pp. 11–12, 15, 17.

Silvester Everdon (1246 – d. 1254)
Wills: None surviving. *EEA 30: Carlisle 1133–1292*, p. 95, number *120, brings together references to his will.
Executors: Simon de Trop', William de Suyneford' of Northumberland and others (*Close rolls 1253–4*, p. 41).
Probate process and execution: Close rolls 1253–4, pp. 41, 57, 82.

Thomas Vipont (1254 – d. 1256)
No documentation traced.

Robert de Chaury or Chause (1257 – d. 1278)
Wills: None surviving. *EEA 30: Carlisle 1133–1292*, p. 131, number *166, brings together references to a will and executors.
Probate process and execution: CPR 1272–81, pp. 419–20; *CClR 1288–96*, p. 208.

Ralph Ireton (1278 – d. 1292)
Licences: CPapReg 1198–1304, pp. 534–5.
Wills: Charter, 20 November 1291, setting out an endowment for the see, in goods (including domestic goods) and stock, exemplified 1 December 1291, in *CChR 1257–1300*, pp. 408–9 (where the original is dated 14 November 1291); edited in *EEA 30: Carlisle 1133–1292*, pp. 134–7, number 171. There was a further document, a will, beyond this charter: references summarised in *EEA 30: Carlisle 1133–1292*, pp. 167–8, number *208.
Probate process and execution: CFR 1272–1307, p. 307.

John of Halton (1292 – d. 1324)
Wills: None surviving. Bequest of a silver or gold cup ('argenteam sive auream')

to the Archbishop of York recorded in *The register of William Melton, Archbishop of York, 1317–1340* ed. R.M.T. Hill *et al.* (in progress, CYS, 70–1, 76, 85, 93; 1977–) i, p. 85, number 263.
Probate process and execution: CClR 1330–3, p. 95.

John Ross (1325 – d. 1332)
Wills: None surviving.
Executors: Mag. Robert de Askeby, Mag. Nicholas de Rosse, Mag. John de Rosse and John de la Calow (*The register of John Kirkby, Bishop of Carlisle, 1332–1352, and the register of John Ross, Bishop of Carlisle, 1325–32* ed. R.L. Storey (2 vols., CYS, 79, 81; 1993–5) i, p. 27, number 139).
Probate process and execution: The twelfth part of the reports of Sir Edward Coke, kt., pp. 105–6; Gibson, *Codex juris ecclesiastici Anglicani*, i, p. 195.

John Kirkby (1332 – d. 1352)
No documentation traced.

Gilbert Welton (1353 – d. 1362)
Other grants and gifts: An obit for the Bishop is noted in *Valor ecclesiasticus temp. Henr. VIII auctoritate regia institutus* ed. J. Caley and J. Hunter (6 vols., 1810–34) v, p. 276.

Thomas Appleby (1363 – d. 1395)
Wills: None surviving.
Executors: William Strickland, Bishop of Carlisle (*CPR 1408–13*, p. 258).
Probate process and execution: CPR 1408–13, p. 258.

Thomas Merk (1397 – 1399 [trans. Salmas, d. 1409])
No documentation traced.

CHICHESTER

The first Bishop of Chichester for whom there is evidence for a will is Simon FitzRobert (d. 1207), whose executors had a licence from King John to execute it 'according to the tenor of its authentic writing, from which his seal hangs', as far as moveables were concerned, excluding stock, chattels and other things which belonged to the bishopric when he received the temporalities, and a bequest of 100 marks for the soul of Hubert Walter.[1] Ralph Nevill received grants from Henry III in 1227, 1229 and 1233 that the execution of his will would be unimpeded by any royal official or secular person.[2] In 1234, he was one of the bishops who received grants that both he and his successors in the see might make wills with this same protection.[3] Nevill was Henry III's chancellor 1226–44 (although he was not the keeper of the great seal 1238–42); on 8 January 1244, about three weeks before his death, he found it prudent to obtain royal letters patent to make it clear that the property of which he might dispose by will was to include the corn sown on the lands of the see. It seems probable that these letters were incorrectly drafted, for he was granted further letters patent the following day confirming that his will might encompass in addition corn already harvested and all moveables.[4]

Arrangements for the stock of the see to transfer from each bishop to his successor were set out by Ranulf of Wareham in 1220,[5] and were confirmed by royal *inspeximus* in 1227, 1228 and 1233, coinciding with the grants to Nevill that he might make his will unimpeded.[6] When Bishop Climping added the manor of Drungewick to the lands of the bishopric in 1262, he also confirmed for that manor the level of stock that would pass to his successors.[7]

It appears to have been the practice for Bishops of Chichester to give their chapels to the cathedral church: the records of their gifts are recorded in a medieval catalogue of the Bishops.[8]

In addition to the documentation noted below, the will of William Lenn (**22/1**) was made in 1363 while he was Bishop of Chichester and was not revised after his translation to Worcester in 1368.

Notes

1 *RLC*, i, p. 92a: 'iuxta tenorem autentici scripti sui a quo sigillum suum dependet ... de rebus suis mobilibus salvis instauris et aliis catallis et rebus quas invenit in eadem episcopatu'.

2 *CChR 1226–57*, pp. 43, 178.

3 *The chartulary of the high church of Chichester* ed. W.D. Peckham (Sussex Record Society, 46; 1946) p. 231, number 808.

4 *CPR 1232–47*, p. 415.

5 *EEA 22: Chichester 1215–53* ed. P.M. Hoskin (Oxford, 2001) p. xxx and n. 59, citing Liber Y (West Sussex RO, Chichester DCM, Ep/VI/1/6), f. 108v, a list of stock on episcopal manors.

6 *CChR 1226–57*, pp. 34, 87, 179.

7 *EEA 23: Chichester 1254–1305* ed. P.M. Hoskin (Oxford, 2001) p. 171, number 200; *CChR 1327–41*, p. 441.

8 *Chartulary of the high church of Chichester*, pp. 275–82, number 903, from Liber E (West Sussex RO, Chichester DCM, Ep/VI/1/4, ff. 169–73).

Seffrid II (1180 – d. 1204)

No documentation traced.

Simon FitzRobert (Simon of Wells) (1204 – d. 1207)

Wills: None surviving.
Probate process and execution: RLC, i, p. 92a.

Ranulf of Wareham (1217 – d. 1222)

Wills: None surviving.
Other grants and gifts: In 1220, he established the arrangements for the stocking of the manors of the bishopric: West Sussex RO, Chichester DCM, Liber Y, Ep/VI/1/6, f. 108v.

Ralph Nevill (1222 – d. 1244)

Licences and protections: CChR 1226–57, pp. 43 (two), 178; *Chartulary of the high church of Chichester*, p. 231, number 808; *CPR 1232–47*, p. 415 (two).
Wills: Extracts from his will, relating to the Dean and Chapter of Chichester, and to Chichester: Liber Y (West Sussex RO, Chichester DCM, Ep/VI/1/6), ff. 102r–v, 179v; Liber B (West Sussex RO, Chichester DCM, Ep/VI/1/2), ff. 47v, 83r; Liber K (West Sussex RO, Chichester DCM, Cap I/12/2) pp. 127–8; printed in *EEA 22: Chichester 1215–53*, pp. 85–6 (number 106); HMC, *Report on various collections*, i, pp. 191–2; calendared in *Chartulary of the high church of Chichester*, pp. 52–3, number 212.
Executors: G. the dean, E. the precentor, John the chancellor, also archdeacon of

Chichester, Raynder, Prior of Tortint', and Walkelin of Chichester (HMC, *Report on various collections*, i, p. 191).
Probate process and execution: CIPM, i, p. 8 (number 27); *Close rolls 1242–7*, pp. 160 (two), 161–2, 179.

Memorandum dated December 1247 that at the distribution of the goods left for pious uses by Bishop Ralph, by his executors at Guildford, January 1245, the executors granted £140 for the fabric of the cathedral at Chichester. Liber Y (West Sussex RO, Chichester DCM, Ep/VI/1/6), f. 69r; partly transcribed in HMC, *Report on various collections*, i, pp. 191–2, calendared in *Chartulary of the high church of Chichester*, p. 9, number 37.

Other grants and gifts: The catalogue of bishops, Liber E (West Sussex RO, Chichester DCM, Ep/VI/1/4), f. 171r, records his gifts of land at Greylingeswell and Seman Wood, along with 130 marks for the church fabric, his chapel furniture and ornaments: *Chartulary of the high church of Chichester*, p. 278.

Richard Wich (or of Wyche) (1245 – d. 1253)
Licences and protections: CPR 1247–58, p. 75.
Wills: A fourteenth-century copy of a will, *c.*April 1253, is in Liber E (West Sussex RO, Chichester DCM, Ep/VI/1/4), ff. 165r–165v; printed in W.H. Blaauw, 'The will of Richard of la Wych, Bishop of Chichester, commonly called Saint Richard, who died A.D. 1253' *Sussex Archaeological Collections* 1 (1848) pp. 164–92, and in *EEA 22: Chichester 1215–53*, pp. 158–60 (number 188); translated in *English Historical Documents 1189–1327* ed. H. Rothwell (London, 1975) pp. 776–9, and *Saint Richard of Chichester: the sources for his life* ed. D. Jones (Sussex Record Society, 79; 1995) pp. 66–70. A short extract from the will, taken from BL MS Lansdowne 1000, is printed in *Testamenta vetusta*, i, pp. 47–8, with a translation of a longer extract at ii, pp. 761–2.
Executors: The Archbishop of Canterbury, Dom. John Mansell, provost of Beverley, the Dean of Chichester, the precentor of Chichester, Mag. Hugh de sancto Edmundo, canon of St Paul's, London, Dom. Simon de Teryngg', Walter de Campeden and William de Seleseya (*EEA 22: Chichester 1215–53*, p. 160); Robert de Purle, canon of Chichester, and Ivo de Whistring (*CPR 1272–81*, p. 148).
Probate process and execution: Close rolls 1251–3, p. 340; *CPR 1247–58*, p. 190; *CPR 1272–81*, pp. 63, 148.

John Climping (1253 – d. 1262)
Wills: None surviving.
Executors: William [de Bracklesham], chancellor, S[imon de Clymping], archdeacon of Lewes, and Robert de Purle (*Chartulary of the high church of Chichester*, p. 169, number 656).
Probate process and execution: Chartulary of the high church of Chichester, p. 169, number 656.
Other grants and gifts: EEA 23: Chichester 1254–1305, pp. 167–8, number 196.

Stephen Bersted (1262 – d. 1287)
Wills: None surviving.

Probate process and execution: CClR 1288–96, p. 340 (two); *CClR 1296–1302*, p. 336 (two).

Gilbert of St Leofard (1288 – d. 1305)
Wills: None surviving. See *Other grants and gifts* below.
Probate process and execution: PRME, ii, pp. 76, 216–17 and 286–7; *CClR 1302–7*, p. 254; *CClR, 1330–3*, p. 103.
Other grants and gifts: The catalogue of bishops, Liber E, f. 171v, records gifts, some of which took place during the Bishop's lifetime, of land of Racham and Norton; the manor of Torring, stocked with 8 oxen, 2 steers, 100 wethers and 100 ewes; the commencement of the chapel of St Mary in the cathedral at Chichester; 1,250 marks towards the cathedral fabric; 100*s.* rent for two boys censing the host at high mass; land in Oving purchased for £200 for his anniversary; for 56*s.* 8*d.* [annual rent] for the communar for distribution at this time; and of his chapel furniture and ornaments: *Chartulary of the high church of Chichester*, p. 278; *EEA 23: Chichester 1254–1305*, pp. 270–1, number 308, for the 100*s.* rent, dated 11 October 1304; p. 271, number *310, for a note of the gift of the 56*s.* 8*d.* for the obit. The chapel and ornaments were probably in part a customary transaction.

John Langton (1305 – d. 1337)
Wills: None surviving.
Executors: John de sancto Paulo, Mag. John de Belegrave, Mag. John de Mitford, Mag. William de Fissheburn, William de Langeton, clerks, and William de Preston, executors (*CClR 1337–9*, p. 285).
Probate process and execution: CClR 1337–9, p. 285; *CPR 1338–40*, p. 296.
Recognisances for debt to the executors or payments acknowledged by the executors: CClR 1337–9, pp. 285, 378 (two), 385.
Other grants and gifts: The catalogue of bishops, Liber E, records gifts of £100 to the fabric of the cathedral, along with his chapel, with other relics, jewels and ornaments, which may have been received on his death on a customary basis: *Chartulary of the high church of Chichester*, p. 279, number 38.

Robert Stratford (1337 – d. 1362)
Wills: Will, 9 April 1362, **37/1**, LPL, Register of Simon Islip, f. 185r.
Executors: Mag. Henry Cockham, chancellor, John de Wendlingburgh', treasurer, Robert de Wendlingburgh', canon of Chichester, Dom. William Horewyk, rector of the church of Bury and steward of the Bishop's household, Richard Clere, marshal of the household, and Richard Cha*u*nz of Appledram (**37/1**); probate granted to Mag. Henry Cookham, chancellor of Chichester Cathedral, Robert de Wendlynghburgh', canon of Chichester Cathedral, and William Horewyk', rector of Bury (**37/2**).
Probate process and execution: **37/2–3**.

William Rede (1369 – d. 1385)
Wills: Will, 1 August 1382, LPL, Register of William Courtenay, ff. 212v–213v, printed in F.M. Powicke *The medieval books of Merton College* (Oxford, 1931) pp. 87–90; bequests and gifts of books noted and discussed in Cavanaugh, 'Books', pp. 689–721.
Executors: Mag. John Bloxham, warden of Merton College, Oxford; Richard

Pestour, rector of Selseye; Geoffrey Spede, rector of Middleton; Dom. John Bampton, rector of Denton; Mag. Walter Roberti, rector of Nuthurst, listed in the will (Powicke, *Medieval books of Merton College*, p. 90); probate granted to them with the exception of John Bloxham, who declined to administer the will, and with the addition of Mag. William Scaldewell (Powicke, *Medieval books of Merton College*, pp. 90–1).
Probate process and execution: Probate of will, 4 November 1385, printed in Powicke, *Medieval books of Merton College*, pp. 90–1.
Other grants and gifts: Powicke, *Medieval books of Merton College*, lists the books he gave to New College, Oxford, on pp. 91–2; and prints a catalogue of Rede's library at Merton on pp. 162–83; Cavanaugh, 'Books', pp. 461–2.

Thomas Rushook (1385–8, translated to Kilmore, d. 1393)
No documentation traced.

COVENTRY AND LICHFIELD

In 1234, Henry III granted Alexander Stavensby and his successors in the see the right to make a will.[1] The arrangements for the stock on manors of the bishopric to transfer to subsequent bishops were also established by Alexander Stavensby, who left in his will probably of *c.*1238 13 plough-teams for the use of his successors.[2] The number was, however, not firmly established at that point, as Roger Longespee, in his will close to the end of the thirteenth century, bequeathed 12 plough-teams of eight oxen to his successor.[3]

Notes
1 *The great register of Lichfield Cathedral Magnum Registrum Album* ed. H.E. Savage (*Collections for a History of Staffordshire*: William Salt Archaeological Society Collections for 1924 [1926]) pp. 102–3, number 220.
2 *The great register of Lichfield Cathedral Magnum Registrum Album*, p. 309, number 651.
3 *The great register of Lichfield Cathedral Magnum Registrum Album*, p. 309, number 652.

Geoffrey Muschamp (Bishop of Coventry 1198 – d. 1208)
No documentation traced.

William Cornhill (Bishop of Coventry 1214 – res. 1223, d. 1223)
No documentation traced.

Alexander Stavensby (Bishop of Coventry 1224–8, then Coventry and Lichfield 1228–38)
Licences: The great register of Lichfield Cathedral Magnum Registrum Album, pp. 102–3, number 220.
Wills: Memorandum about the arrangements for stocking the bishopric during vacancies, under the Bishop's will, calendared in *The great register of Lichfield Cathedral Magnum Registrum Album*, p. 309, number 651, and noted in J.C. Cox 'Catalogue of the muniments and manuscript books of the Dean and Chapter of Lichfield' *Collections for a history of Staffordshire: Publications of the William Salt Archaeological Society* 6, part 2 (1886) p. 149.
Other grants and gifts: Evidence for a deathbed grant endowing a hospital at

Denhall, Wirral: *The registers or act books of the Bishops of Coventry and Lichfield. Book 5, being the second register of Bishop Robert de Stretton, A.D. 1360–1385* ed. R.A. Wilson (*Collections for a History of Staffordshire*: William Salt Archaeological Society Collections for 1905) p. 132; and endowment of chantry in Lichfield Cathedral, *The great register of Lichfield Cathedral Magnum Registrum Album*, p. 309, number 651; p. 352, number 740.

Hugh Pattishall (1239 – d. 1241)
Wills: None surviving.
Executors: Thomas [de Wymundham], precentor, and Peter [de Radenoure], archdeacon of Salop and canon of Lichfield (*The great register of Lichfield Cathedral Magnum Registrum Album*, p. 106, number 231); Brother Andrew, Prior of Darley, acting on behalf of the executors (*Close rolls 1237–42*, p. 510).
Probate process and execution: Close rolls 1237–42, p. 379; *CPR 1232–47*, p. 275; *Close rolls 1237–42*, p. 510; *CFR* project, 27/50: TNA C 60/40, mem. 8r.
Other grants and gifts: Establishment of a chantry, post mortem, in Lichfield Cathedral: *The great register of Lichfield Cathedral Magnum Registrum Album*, pp. 106–10, numbers 231–7.

Roger Weseham (1245 – res. 1256, d. 1257)
No documentation traced.

Roger Longespee (Meuland) (1257 – d. 1295)
Wills: Memorandum of plough oxen bequeathed to his successor in the see, drawn from the will, 6 May 1292: *The great register of Lichfield Cathedral Magnum Registrum Album*, p. 309, number 652.
Probate process and execution: CPR 1292–1301, p. 215; *The great register of Lichfield Cathedral Magnum Registrum Album*, p. 309, number 652; *Winchelsey register*, i, pp. 67–8, 97, 197–8.

Walter Langton (1296 – d. 1321)
Wills: None surviving. The construction of the Lady Chapel, in Lichfield Cathedral, was funded in part by a bequest in his will: Thomas Chesterfeld, 'Historia de successione episcoporum Conventrensium et Lichfeldensium', *Anglia sacra*, i, p. 442.
Executors: Mag. Gilbert de la Dorner', John de Langeton' and John de Peateshull' (BL Harley Charter 46 G. 7).
Probate process and execution: CIPM, vi, pp. 194–8 (number 330); *CClR 1296–1302*, p. 478; *CPR 1321–4*, pp. 119, 180; *CClR 1330–3*, p. 182.

Receipt by Richard de Perar', sheriff of Hertfordshire, by William Hemelhamsted, under-sheriff, by the hands of Thomas de Harpesfield, for 20*s*. from the goods and chattels of Ralph de Brok' and Laurence de Brok', by virtue of a writ from the King at the suit of Mag. Gilbert de la Dorner', John de Langeton' and John de Peateshull', executors of the will of Walter Langton, owed from lands and tenements in Chesham leased to Ralph by the Bishop; given at Westminster, 5 January 1327. BL Harley Charter 46 G. 7.

Other grants and gifts: Gifts to Lichfield Cathedral, most during his lifetime, listed in Thomas Chesterfeld, 'Historia de successione episcoporum Conventrensium et Lichfeldensium', *Anglia sacra*, i, p. 442.

Roger Northburgh (1321 – d. 1358)
Wills: None surviving.
Executors: Reference to them, unnamed, in LPL, Register of Simon Islip, f. 172r.
Probate process and execution: CClR 1354–60, p. 583.

Commission to Mag. William de Witlesey and Mag. Richard de Plessys to hear the accounts of the executors of Roger, Bishop of Coventry and Lichfield, Mayfield, 12 April [1360 ?]. LPL, Register of Simon Islip, f. 172r.

Robert Stretton (1358 – d. 1385)
Wills: Will, 19 March 1385, LPL Register of William Courtenay, f. 211r, printed in translation in W.G.D. Fletcher, 'Robert de Stretton, Bishop of Coventry and Lichfield, 1360 to 1385' *Associated Architectural Societies' Reports and Papers* 19 (1887–8) pp. 198–208, at pp. 204–5.
Executors: Mag. Richard de Bermynchin and Mag. William de Neuhash, canons of Lichfield, Mag. Richard de Torpeclyfe, archdeacon of Stafford, Dom. John de Stretton and John de Utoxhatr', canons of the collegiate church of St Chad, Salop, and Roger de Outheby, chaplain; probate granted to William Newhash and John Uttoxhatre, with Richard Topclyf and Roger Oudeby subsequently admitted (Fletcher, 'Robert de Stretton', p. 205); Mag. Thomas Stretton (Osbern, 'Continuatio historiae Lichfeldensis', *Anglia sacra*, i, p. 449).
Probate process and execution: CClR 1381–5, pp. 550–1; Fletcher, 'Robert de Stretton', p. 205.

Mandate to the executors of the Bishop of Coventry and Lichfield, 1385. LPL, Register of William Courtenay, f. 346v.

Other grants and gifts: 200 marks given to Lichfield Cathedral on his deathbed, of which the greater part was appropriated for the use of the vicars choral by the will of his executor, Mag. Thomas Stretton: *Anglia sacra*, i, p. 449.

John Burghill (1398 – d. 1414)
Wills: Will, 21 June 1412, **9/1**, CCA, Register G, ff. 289v–290v.
Executors: Mag. William Newport and Mag. John Pulford (**9/2**), but unable to administer the will, and power to do so granted to Richard, Prior of Coventry, Mag. Robert Walden and John Bakford (**9/4**).
Probate process and execution: **9/2–4**.
Other grants and gifts: Anglia sacra, i, p. 452, summarises his benefactions.

DURHAM

The first Bishop of Durham that we know left a will was Hugh du Puiset, but his goods were seized by the keepers of the see for debts to the Crown and his servants also had to pay fines at the Exchequer, perhaps because they had started to distribute the Bishop's possessions.[1] The executors of his successor, Philip of Poitiers, were also required to hand over to the Exchequer all that Bishop's jewels.[2] Richard Poore, while Bishop of Salisbury, a year before his translation to Durham in 1228, acquired a licence to make a will;[3] and his successor at Durham, Nicholas Farnham, also had a licence to make a will, in 1244.[4] The arrangements for transfer of stock and goods from one bishop to the next are not wholly clear, but it seems probable that they followed a pattern familiar from other sees. In 1283, the keepers of the bishopric in the vacancy after the death of Robert of Holy Island delivered to Anthony Bek, the Bishop elect, all the corn, cattle and stock which they had bought from Robert's executors for the price which they had paid for them, deducting Crown expenses for wainage and the collection of first fruits – and this may indicate the mechanism by which these transfers took place, but here subject to some royal charges.[5] There may also have been other goods that transferred between bishops: in 1237, John de Romsey, steward and executor of Bishop Richard Poore, was instructed to deliver to the keeper of the bishopric all the arms which Poore had received after the death of his predecessor, Richard Marsh; the keeper was to have the arms appraised and give the value to John de Romsey and his fellow executors.[6]

The relationship between the Bishops of Durham and their cathedral priory was a critical one for their executors and the transmission of their goods – and there is evidence of extended disputes between these parties. Bishops of Durham, by custom, gave all the goods of their chapel to the cathedral priory.[7] Prior Wessington was able in the early fifteenth century to list the goods received in this way from each Bishop as *funeralia*, from William of St Carilef (d. 1096), to Walter Skirlaw (d. 1406) – and Thomas Langley's goods were entered after his death in 1437 – noting that according to ancient custom the goods of each Bishop were displayed at the mass for his obit.[8] The sections of Wessington's roll listing goods for Bishops William of St Carilef, Ranulf Flambard (d. 1128) and Geoffrey Rufus (d. 1141) are printed in *Wills and inventories*, i, pp. 1–3. Sections for other bishops are noted below.

Durham is noteworthy for the survival of obituary rolls for some of its Bishops, a custom which was probably widespread, although we have now have little evidence for it.[9]

Notes

1 *Chronicles of the reigns of Stephen, Henry II, and Richard I* ed. R. Howlett (4 vols., RS, 82; 1884–9) ii, pp. 439–40; *Historiae Dunelmensis scriptores tres* ed. J. Raine (Surtees Society, 9; 1839) pp. 15–16; Sheehan, *WME*, pp. 244–6; M. Howell *Regalian right in medieval England* (London, 1962) p. 45; *The chancellor's roll for the eighth year of the reign of King Richard the First, Michaelmas 1196* ed. D.M. Stenton (Pipe Roll Society, new series, 7; 1930) pp. 258–9, 261.

2 *The great roll of the pipe for the tenth year of the reign of King John Michaelmas 1208* ed. D.M. Stenton (Pipe Roll Society, new series, 23; 1945) p. 59.

3 *CChR 1226–57*, p. 43.

4 *CPR 1232–47*, p. 435.

5 *CFR 1272–1307*, p. 189.

6 *Close Rolls 1234–7*, p. 437.

7 *RPD*, iv, pp. 429–30.

8 DUL, Durham DCM, Miscellaneous Charter 2622 (originally in Locellus II).

9 *The obituary roll of William Ebchester and John Burnby, Priors of Durham, with notices of similar records preserved at Durham from the year 1233 downwards* ... ed. J. Raine (Surtees Society, 31; 1856), prints the rolls for Robert of Holy Island, Thomas Hatfield and Walter Skirlawe: DUL, Durham DCM, Locellus I, 1–4.

Hugh du Puiset (1153 – d. 1195)
Wills: None surviving, but according to William of Newburgh he did make one: *Historia rerum Anglicarum* in *Chronicles of the reigns of Stephen, Henry II, and Richard I*, ii, pp. 439–40.
Probate process and execution: William of Newburgh, as above; Geoffrey of Coldingham in *Historiae Dunelmensis scriptores tres* ed. J. Raine (Surtees Society, 9; 1839) pp. 15–16; *The chancellor's roll for the eighth year of the reign of King Richard the First, … 1196*, pp. 258–9, 261.
Other grants and gifts: Goods left to Durham Cathedral Priory as a mortuary, as well as books: *Wills and inventories*, i, pp. 3–4; the listing of these books is also given in *Catalogi veteres librorum ecclesiae cathedralis Dunelm* … ed. B. Botfield (Surtees Society, 7; 1838) pp. 118–19.

Philip of Poitiers (1195 – d. 1208)
Wills: None surviving.
Executors: Aimericus, archdeacon of Durham (*The great roll of the pipe for the tenth year of the reign of King John … 1208*, p. 59).
Probate process and execution: The great roll of the pipe for the tenth year of the reign of King John … 1208, p. 59; *OPD 1198–1304*, pp. 24–5, number 44 (DUL, Durham DCM, 3. 1 Pap. 5).
Other grants and gifts: Goods left to Durham Cathedral Priory as a mortuary: *Wills and inventories*, i, p. 4.

Richard Marsh (1217 – d. 1226)
Wills: None surviving.
Probate process and execution: CFR 1234–42, p. 214 (21/104); *Close rolls 1234–7*, p. 437.
Other grants and gifts: Goods left to Durham Cathedral Priory as a mortuary: *Wills and inventories*, i, p. 5.

Richard Poore (1228 – d. 1237)
Licences: CChR 1226–57, p. 43.
Executors: Mag. Elias de Derham, John de Rumeseye, Stephen de Burthon and others (*CPR 1232–47*, p. 180).
Probate process and execution: CFR 1234–42, p. 214 (21/104); *CPR 1232–47*, p. 180; *Close rolls 1234–7*, pp. 437, 449, 455–6 (three); *Close rolls 1237–42*, pp. 9–11 (two).
Other grants and gifts: Goods left to Durham Cathedral Priory as a mortuary: *Wills and inventories*, i, p. 5.

Nicholas Farnham (1241 – res. 1249; d. 1257)
Licences, protections and pardons: CPR 1232–47, p. 435; *CFR* project, 33/141: TNA C 60/46, mem. 9r; *CFR* project, 36/128: TNA C 60/49, mem. 21r; *CFR* project, 40/1297: TNA C 60/53, mem. 1r; grants relating to the provision from the manors of Howden, Stockton and Easington assigned to him on his resignation from the see: *CChR 1226–57*, p. 338; *CPapReg 1198–1304*, p. 348.
Wills: None surviving.
Probate process and execution: Close rolls 1256–9, p. 216.
Other grants and gifts: Goods left to Durham Cathedral Priory as a mortuary: *Wills and inventories*, i, p. 5.

Walter Kirkham (1249 – d. 1260)
Wills: None surviving.
Probate process and execution: Close rolls 1259–61, pp. 102–6 (four); *CPR 1258–66*, p. 91; *Close rolls 1259–61*, pp. 110–11; **20**; *Close rolls 1259–61*, p. 356 (two); *Close rolls 1268–72*, pp. 463–4.
Other grants and gifts: Goods left to Durham Cathedral Priory as a mortuary: *Wills and inventories*, i, p. 11.

Robert Stichill (1260 – d. 1274)
Wills: None surviving.
Executors: Mag. Roger of Seaton and others (*CFR 1272–1307*, p. 26), Mag. Thomas of Levesham (*RPD*, i, p. 318), Hugh of Darlington (TNA CP 40/9, mem. 11d).
Probate process and execution: CFR 1272–1307, p. 26.
Other grants and gifts: Goods left to Durham Cathedral Priory as a mortuary: *Wills and inventories*, i, p. 12.

Robert of Holy Island (1274 – d. 1283)
Wills: None surviving.
Executors: Robert Avenel, clerk, Gwischard de Charron, knight, and others (*OPD 1198–1304*, p. 389, number 861); Henry of Holy Island, Thomas de Levesham (*OPD 1198–1304*, p. 410, number 908).
Probate process and execution: CFR 1272–1307, pp. 186, 189; *OPD 1198–1304*, p. 389, number 861 (Durham DCM 4. 2 Pap. 4), and p. 410, number 908 (Durham DCM, 4. 1 Pap. 29); *RPD*, iv, pp. 51–3.

A roll of documents from Durham Cathedral Priory about the claim of the Prior against the executors of the Bishop to goods, including silver vessels, along with tithes of various mills, with an account of legal expenses, late thirteenth century. DUL, Durham DCM, Miscellaneous Charter 7160.

Statement of Henry of Holy Island, executor, about a sentence of greater excommunication falsely alleged by various parties against the Bishop, 1283: contemporary copy. DUL, Durham DCM, Locellus XIV 1k.

Process, before judges delegate, for the claim of the Prior and convent of Durham against the executors, for the recovery of expenses incurred at the election of the Bishop, 1288. DUL, Durham DCM, Locellus VI 15.

Other grants and gifts: Goods left to Durham Cathedral Priory as a mortuary: *Wills and inventories*, i, p. 12.

Obituary roll: 1283. DUL, Durham DCM, Locellus I 1, printed in *The obituary roll of William Ebchester and John Burnby*, pp. 51–3.

Anthony Bek (1283 – d. 1311)
Licences and prospective arrangements: CPR 1301–7, p. 334.
Wills: None surviving.
Executors: Robert Winchelsey, Archbishop of Canterbury, Robert de Wylughby, knight, Thomas de Goldesburgh', archdeacon of Durham, and others (*Winchelsey*

register, ii, pp. 1245–6; *Greenfield register*, v, pp. 94, 97–8, numbers 244, 247); John de Foxle (from *c.*1315, *RPD*, ii, pp. 1102–8).
Probate process and execution: CIPM, v, pp. 150–1 (number 274); *CFR 1307–19*, pp. 84–5 (three); probate and grant of administration, 16 March 1311 (*Winchelsey register*, ii, pp. 1245–6); grant of probate for the archdiocese of York, 4 May 1311, 3 June 1311 (*Greenfield register*, v, pp. 94, 97–8, numbers 2544, 2547); *Greenfield register*, v, p. 82, number 2526; *CPR 1307–13*, p. 354; *RPD*, iv, p. 98; *RPD*, i, pp. 112–13; *CPR 1307–13*, pp. 356, 360, 385; *CPR 1313–17*, p. 209; *CFR 1307–19*, p. 249; *CPR 1313–17*, pp. 290–1; *RPD*, ii, pp. 1102–8 (three); *CPR 1313–17*, p. 437; *CClR 1313–18*, pp. 474 (two), 572–3; *CClR 1318–23*, pp. 37, 63–4, 81; *CPapReg 1305–42*, p. 451.
Other grants and gifts: Goods left to Durham Cathedral Priory as a mortuary: *Wills and inventories*, i, pp. 12–13. For the dispute over his chapel, *RPD*, iv, pp. 429–30.

Richard Kellaw (1311 – d. 1316)
Wills: Will, 26 September 1316, printed in *TE I*, pp 1–2, from Borthwick Institute for Archives, York, *Sede vacante* register A, f. 184v; a short extract from the will, from BL Lansdowne MS 1000, is printed in *Testamenta vetusta*, i, p. 53; noted in *Greenfield register*, v, pp. 295–6, number 2912.
Executors: Patrick de Kellowe, the Bishop's brother, Sir Thomas de Hessewell, rector of Seggefeld, Sir Robert de Brumpton, prebendary of Auckland, and Sir Robert de Saxton, rector of Aberford, named in the will (*TE I*, p. 1); William de Denum added at probate, Patrick de Kellawe refusing to undertake the administration (*Greenfield register*, v, p. 296, number 2912).
Probate process and execution: Probate at Durham, 24 December 1316, and at York, 24 January 1317, *Greenfield register*, v, p. 296, number 2912; *CClR 1313–18*, p. 474.
Other grants and gifts: Goods left to Durham Cathedral Priory as a mortuary: *Wills and inventories*, i, p. 21.

Lewis de Beaumont (1317 – d. 1333)
Wills: None surviving.
Executors: Possibly Lady de Vescy (*The register of William Melton, Archbishop of York, 1317–1340* ed. R.M.T. Hill *et al.* (in progress, CYS 70–1, 76, 85, 93; 1977–) i, p. 97, numbers 325 and 328).
Probate process and execution: Register of William Melton, i, pp. 96–7, numbers 323–5; *CClR 1333–7*, p. 138.
Other grants and gifts: Goods left to Durham Cathedral Priory as a mortuary: *Wills and inventories*, i, p. 23.

Richard of Bury (1333 – d. 1345)
Licences: CPR 1334–8, pp. 117, 120.
Wills: None surviving.
Probate process and execution: CPR 1343–5, p. 455; *CClR 1343–6*, pp. 538, 561; *RPD*, iv, p. 263.
Other grants and gifts: Goods left to Durham Cathedral Priory as a mortuary: *Wills and inventories*, i, pp. 25–6. The reference in W.J. Courtenay, 'Richard Bury' *ODNB*, ix, pp. 67–9, at p. 69, to his executors selling his books, filling more than five large carts, is based on *Adae Murimuth Continuatio chronicarum* ... ed. E.M. Thompson (RS, 93; 1889) p. 171, which does not mention the executors or the sale; one of

the books Bishop Richard acquired from St Alban's was bought from the executors by the Abbot (BL MS Royal 13 D IV), and others may have returned in similar circumstances: Cavanaugh, 'Books', pp. 152–3.

Thomas Hatfield (1345 – d. 1381)
Wills: Will, made 28 March 1381 and proved in the presence of the Archbishop of York on 6 June 1381, printed in *TE I*, pp. 121–2, from Borthwick Institute for Archives, York, Register of A. Neville, f. 114; a further copy of the will is in LPL, Register of Simon Sudbury, ff. 107v–108r, with minor textual differences, the addition of a notarial attestation by William Mundy, clerk of Winchester diocese, and a grant of probate by the Archbishop of Canterbury, 11 May 1381, committing the administration to two executors named in the will, Mag. John Ma*u*ndour and John de Popeham, *domicellus*. A very short extract from the will appears in *Testamenta vetusta*, i, p. 113.
Executors: John, Bishop of Hereford, Brother Thomas de Stubbes, STP, William de Walleworth, mayor of London, Dom. John de Hanlee, treasurer of the Bishop's household, John de Popham, the Bishop's nephew, Mag. John Maundour, chancellor of the Bishop's household, John Rous, citizen of London, Dom. John Attelee, the Bishop's almoner, and Dom. William de Brantyngham, Dean of Lanchester (*TE I*, p. 122).
Probate process and execution: Probate noted above. *CClR 1381–5*, p. 554; *CClR 1385–9*, pp. 336–7, 512.
Other grants and gifts: Goods left to Durham Cathedral Priory as a mortuary: *Wills and inventories*, i, pp. 36–7, with a note of building works and other gifts on pp. 37–8.

Ante mortem agreement between the Cistercian convent of Stratford and the executors, about the establishment of a chantry, 2 September 1380: an indenture, with a notarial attestation. DUL, Durham DCM, Miscellaneous Charter 6000.

Obituary roll: DUL, Durham DCM, Locellus I 2 and 3, printed in *The obituary roll of William Ebchester and John Burnby*, pp. 54–6.

Walter Skirlaw (1388 – d. 1406)
Wills: Will, with inventory and notes of where goods were given by the executors, printed in *TE I*, pp. 306–25 (where it is dated 7 March 1403), from a book *sede vacante*, 1285–1554, in the Prerogative Court of York (*The York sede vacante register 1405–1408* ed. J. Kirby (Borthwick Texts and Calendars, 28; 2002) p. 62: number 507, ff. 327–8, will of Walter Skirlaw, 17 March 1403; 508, ff. 328r–328v, notarial attestation of the same by Robert Blundell, chaplain, 17 March 1403; 509, codicil to the above, 25 July 1404; 510, notarial attestation of the same, 25 July 1404; 511, ff. 328v–329v, further codicils, 30 July, 1 August, 18 September, 8 December 1404; 512, notarial attestation of the codicils; 513, f. 329v, grant of probate of the will and codicils by the custodian of the spirituality of the archdiocese, 21 April 1406; 514, ff. 330–2, inventory of the valuables and plate, chapel books, chapel vestments and cloths (*vestes et panni*) in the wardrobe of Walter Skirlaw recorded in the will and codicils, together with the named recipients, and 515, memorandum of the audit of the account and acquittance of the executors of the will, 1 February 1408.

Executors: Robert, Bishop of London, Mag. Thomas de Weston, archdeacon of Durham, Mag. Richard de Holme, rector of the parish church of Wearmouth, Mag. Robert Wiclyf, rector of the parish church of Rudby, Mag. Alan de Newerk, canon of the church of Lanchester, Peter de la Hay, *domicellus*, John de Hildyard and John Burgh, canons of the collegiate churches of Auckland and Chester le Street (*TE I*, pp. 311–12).
Probate process and execution: Probate summarised above.
Other grants and gifts: Goods left to Durham Cathedral Priory as a mortuary: *Wills and inventories*, i, pp. 43–4. Gifts to Lichfield by his executors and in his lifetime noted in *Anglia sacra*, i, p. 450. The books in his will and inventory, along with other gifts of his books, are noted in Cavanaugh, 'Books', pp. 790–4.

Indenture of account of Thomas de Lyth', monk of Durham, for monies belonging to the chantry of Bishop Skirlaw, 1 November 1403 to 20 March 1406, paid to Mag. Thomas Weston' and Peter del Hay, the executors: DUL, Durham DCM, Miscellaneous Charter 7169.

Obituary roll: DUL, Durham DCM, Locellus I 4, printed in *The obituary roll of William Ebchester and John Burnby*, pp. 56–63.

ELY

Bishop Eustace (d. 1215) is the first Bishop of Ely for whom there is firm evidence that he made a will, King John instructing the sheriff of Norfolk and Suffolk to distrain all the Bishop's debtors that they might pay the executors.[1] In 1248 Henry III granted special protection during vacancies to revenues from two manors purchased by Hugh of Northwold, in a guarantee that the four chaplains the Bishops of Ely appointed to celebrate daily for the souls of the King and Queen, their ancestors and successors, and Bishops of Ely, past, present and future, would continue to receive 20 marks from the keepers of the manors of Totteridge and Bramford.[2] But there was no more general relaxation of the Crown's interest. When Hugh died in early August 1254, at harvest time, his estate was entitled to the corn sown on the lands, but not the means of gathering it in: the King, however, allowed the executors to have the harvest works of the bishopric as far as Michaelmas, provided they answered to the Crown for the value of those works and allowed the livestock of the bishopric to be kept in pasture.[3]

Records of gifts by individual bishops to the cathedral church at Ely, especially of chapel goods, are recorded in the continuation of the Ely chronicle.[4] In the case of Bishop John Ketton (d. 1316), it describes 'haec autem ornamenta capellae suae delata sunt ad ecclesiam suam Elyensem post obitum suum.'[5] By the time of John Fordham (d. 1425) there is a suggestion that the gift of the chapel was a custom that had been commuted for a cash payment. £50 was given 'pro capella sua': this payment is not mentioned separately as a bequest in his will, although his executors had discretion to make further bequests as they considered best for the salvation of his soul and unburdening of their consciences.[6]

Notes
1 *RLC*, p. 188a–b.

2 *CChR 1226–57*, p. 329.
3 *CFR* project, 38/776: TNA C 60/51, mem. 3r.
4 'Monachi Eliensis Continuatio historiae Eliensis ab anno MCLXIX ad annum MCCC LXXXVIII', *Anglia sacra*, i, pp. 631–74.
5 *Anglia sacra*, i, p. 642.
6 Fordham's will is printed in *Chichele register*, pp. 327–9; his gifts to Ely are listed in *Anglia sacra*, i, p. 666.

William de Longchamp (1189 – d. 1197)
Wills: None surviving.
Other grants and gifts: Notification, generally addressed, in favour of Ely Cathedral Priory, of the grant in free alms of 100 acres of land from the Bishop's assarts at Somersham, for feeding 100 paupers on the anniversary of the Bishop's death, 31 December 1189 × 31 January 1197, prob July × October 1191, *EEA 31: Ely 1109–97* ed. N. Karn (Oxford, 2005) p. 175, number 133.

Eustace (1197 – d. 1215)
Licences: Sheehan, *WME*, p. 246.
Wills: None surviving.
Probate process and execution: RLC, p. 188a–b.
Other grants and gifts: Gifts to Ely, including those for his anniversary and chapel goods, noted in *Anglia sacra*, i, p. 634.

John of Fountains (1220 – d. 1225)
Wills: None surviving.
Other grants and gifts: Gifts to Ely, including an endowment for his anniversary and chapel goods, listed in *Anglia sacra*, i, p. 635.

Geoffrey de Burgo (1225 – d. 1228)
Wills: None surviving.
Probate process and execution: Close rolls 1259–61, p. 464.
Other grants and gifts: Gifts to Ely, including the endowment of his anniversary and chapel goods, listed in *Anglia sacra*, i, p. 635.

Hugh of Northwold (1229 – d. 1254)
Licences: CChR 1226–57, p. 329.
Wills: None surviving.
Probate process and execution: CFR project, 38/776: TNA C 60/51, mem. 3r; *Close rolls 1253–4*, p. 95; *Close rolls 1259–61*, p. 464.
Other grants and gifts: Gifts to Ely of chapel goods, listed in *Anglia sacra*, i, p. 636.

William of Kilkenny (1254 – d. 1256)
Wills: None surviving.
Executors: Henry de Kylkenny (*Pecham register (CYS)*, ii, p. 94); Simon de la More, knight (*Pecham register (CYS)*, ii, p. 108); Mag. Guy de Castro Bernardi and others (*CPR 1258–66*, p. 99); and J. de Lascy, called to the execution in 1280 (*Pecham register (RS)*, i, p. 110).
Probate process and execution: Close rolls 1256–9, p. 1; *CFR* project, 41/924: TNA C 60/54, mem. 2r; *CFR* project, 41/925: TNA C 60/54, mem. 2r; *Close rolls 1256–9*, p. 94; *CPR 1247–58*, pp. 580, 605, 622; *CPR 1258–66*, p. 99; *Close rolls*

1259–61, p. 464; *Pecham register (CYS)*, ii, pp. 94, 108–9; *Pecham register (RS)*, i, p. 110.
Other grants and gifts: Gifts to Ely, including chapel goods and 200 marks for two chaplains to pray for his soul, noted in *Anglia sacra*, i, p. 636.

Hugh Balsham (1256 – d. 1286)
Wills: Record of the sealing of his will by John Pecham, 28 July 1279, *Pecham register (CYS)*, ii, p. 79. Bequest of 300 marks for building at Peterhouse possibly bequeathed in a further will or codicil: 'Ipse insuper in extremis laborans dictis scolaribus ad edeficii de novo contruenda trescentas marcas legavit …', Bodleian Library, Oxford, MS Laud misc. 647, f. 176r, with notes of legacies on f. 174v.
Executors: Ralph de Walepol, archdeacon of Ely, and Ralph de Fotheringheye, clerk (*Ancient deeds*, ii, p. 30).
Probate process and execution: Ancient deeds, ii, p. 30; *PRME*, i, p. 334.
Other grants and gifts: Gifts to Ely noted in *Anglia sacra*, i, p. 637.

John of Kirkby (1286 – d. 1290)
Wills: Will, relating to property (Ely Place and related lands) in Holborn, London, bequeathed to the bishopric of Ely, enrolled in the Hustings Court for 28 May 1290, following a challenge from William de Kirkebi, knight, the Bishop's heir, relating to vineyards outside the city: *CCH*, i, pp. 90–1.
Executors: William de Kyrkeby, Mag. Gwydo de Tyllebrok', Philip de Everdon' and John Cotoun (*PRME*, i, pp. 239–40).
Probate process and execution: CClR 1288–96, pp. 95, 156; *PRME*, i, pp. 239–40, 242, 269, 287; *CClR 1288–96*, p. 190; *CPR 1301–7*, p. 125.
Other grants and gifts: Gifts to Ely for his anniversary noted in *Anglia sacra*, i, p. 638.

William of Louth (1290 – d. 1298)
Wills: Will, relating to property in Holborn, enrolled in the Court of Husting, 18 October 1298, *CCH*, i, p. 138.
Executors: R[ichard Gravesend], Bishop of London, W[alter Langton], Bishop of Coventry and Lichfield, and others (*CPR 1292–1301*, p. 439).
Probate process and execution: CPR 1292–1301, pp. 439, 474–5; *CClR 1296–1302*, p. 343; *Executors*, p. 112.

Commission of Walter Reynolds, Archbishop of Canterbury, to Mag. G. de Middelton', his official, asking him to hear, examine and determine the disputes relating to the will of William, late Bishop of Ely; given at Canterbury, 2 November 1316. LPL, Register of Walter Reynolds, f. 91r.

Ralph Walpole (1299 – d. 1302)
Wills: None surviving.
Executors: Hervey de Staunton, a justice in eyre in Kent, and others (*CClR 1313–18*, p. 20).
Probate process and execution: Winchelsey register, i, p. 505; *CClR 1313–18*, p. 20.
Other grants and gifts: Gifts to Ely, including chapel goods and books, noted in *Anglia sacra*, i, p. 640; Cavanaugh, 'Books', p. 906.

Robert Orford (1302 – d. 1310)
Wills: None surviving.

Probate process and execution: Commission, possibly part of a formulary, *sede vacante*, for the Prior of Christ Church, Canterbury, to A. and B., to hear the accounts of the Bishop's executors. CCA, Register Q, f. 104r. No date: the next item is dated 14 August 1313 (f. 104v).
Other grants and gifts: Gifts to Ely, including chapel goods, noted in *Anglia sacra*, i, p. 641.

John Ketton (1310 – d. 1316)
Wills: None surviving.
Executors: Richard de Ikene, Mag. John Caleys and Godfrey, parson of the church of Snailwell, executors (*CClR 1318–23*, p. 70).
Probate process and execution: CPR 1313–17, p. 468; *CClR 1313–18*, p. 292; *CClR 1318–23*, pp. 70, 197.
Other grants and gifts: Gifts to Ely, principally his chapel, listed in *Anglia sacra*, i, p. 642.

John Hotham (1316 – d. 1337)
Licences and grants: CPR 1334–8, p. 94.
Wills: None surviving.
Executors: Simon de Drayton, knight, and Nicholas de Stokton, clerk (*CClR 1337–9*, pp. 171–2).
Probate process and execution: CClR 1337–9, pp. 98–9, 171–2.
Other grants and gifts: Gifts to Ely, including funds from the executors, and goods given on his death, listed in *Anglia sacra*, i, pp. 644, 646–9.

Simon Montacute (1337 – d. 1345)
Wills: None surviving.
Probate process and execution: CIPM, viii, p. 459 (number 617).
Other grants and gifts: Gifts to Ely, including his chapel and funds for the building of the Lady Chapel, noted in *Anglia sacra*, i, p. 652.

Thomas de Lisle (1345 – d. 1361)
Wills: None surviving.
Other grants and gifts: Goods – vestments and vessels – left in the custody of Ely Cathedral Priory shortly before he left England (he died at Avignon), listed in *Anglia sacra*, i, p. 662. Books given to Peterhouse, Cambridge: Cavanaugh, 'Books', pp. 523–4, citing M.R. James *A descriptive catalogue of the manuscripts in the library of Peterhouse* (Cambridge, 1899) pp. 55, 67–9, 77, 135–6.

Simon Langham
Listed under Canterbury.

John Barnet (1366 – d. 1373)
Wills: Will, made while Bishop of Bath and Wells, 1364 × 1366, **3/1**, LPL, Register of William Whittlesey, f. 127v.
Executors: Mag. Stephen Pympell', Dean of Wells, John Barnet, archdeacon of Essex, Dom. Roger de Bello Campo (Beauchamp), rector of Hampton Monialium [Minchinhampton], Stephen Ro*t*he, rector Bisley, Glos., and William de

Petteworth', rector of the parish church of St Anthony, London (**3/2**); probate granted to Mag. John Barnet, Dom. Roger de Bello Campo (**3/3**).
Probate process and execution: **3/2–3**.
Other grants and gifts: Gifts to Ely of chapel goods, listed in *Anglia sacra*, i, p. 664.

EXETER

The probate material for the Bishops of Exeter is among the most complete to have survived for English and Welsh sees. Henry Marshal (d. 1206) is the first bishop known to have made a will, even though the text no longer survives.[1] It is possible that by the time of the death of Simon of Apulia, the arrangements for stock of the see to pass between bishops had been established: his executors made a fine for 50 marks with the King in 1223 for all the Bishop's chattels that were in the custody of the keeper of the bishopric, along with all the horses, oxen, cows, pigs and sheep that the Bishop had received on first coming to the see.[2] The pattern of transfer had certainly been established by 1280 when, on the death of Walter Bronescombe, 10 plough-teams, each of 10 oxen, were to pass to succeeding bishops.[3] The operation of these arrangements can be traced through the fourteenth century: they were augmented by Bishop Stapledon;[4] Bishop Grandisson passed to his successor 1,000 sheep, if he had that many, as well as the 100 oxen.[5] It is possible that other goods passed from bishop to bishop and there were, for example, bequests of domestic utensils to their successors by both Bishops Bitton and Grandisson.[6] An inventory of vestments and other ecclesiastical ornaments in the cathedral, updated to the late fourteenth century, includes gifts from Bishops Leofric (d. 1072), Bartholomew (d. 1184), Henry Marshal, Simon of Apulia, William Briwere, Richard Blund, Walter Bronescombe, James Berkeley and John Grandisson, some of which may derive from their chapels.[7]

Notes

1 *RLC*, p. 76a.
2 *CFR 1216–24*, p. 333 (7/316).
3 HMC, *Report on various collections*, iv, p. 71; Exeter Cathedral Archives, Exeter DCM, number 2107.
4 G. Oliver *Lives of the Bishops of Exeter, and a history of the cathedral* (Exeter, 1861) p. 63; Exeter Cathedral Archives, Exeter DCM, number 2197, printed in *The register of Walter de Stapeldon Bishop of Exeter (A.D. 1307–1326)* ed. F.C. Hingeston-Randoph (London and Exeter, 1892) pp. 579–80, and in *The register of John de Grandisson, Bishop of Exeter (A.D. 1327–1369), with some account of the episcopate of James de Berkeley (A.D. 1327)* ed. F.C. Hingeston-Randolph (3 vols., London and Exeter, 1894–9) iii, pp. 1557–8.
5 *Grandisson register*, iii, p. 1553.
6 Introduction, above, p. xxviii; *Executors*, p. 43; *Grandisson register*, iii, pp. 1552–3.
7 *Ordinale Exoniense* ed. J.N. Dalton and G.H. Doble (4 vols., Henry Bradshaw Society, 27–8, 63, 79; 1909–40) ii, pp. 546–7, 549.

Henry Marshal (1194 – d. 1206)

Wills: None surviving.
Probate process and execution: RLC, p. 76a.

Simon of Apulia (1214 – d. 1223)

Wills: None surviving.
Executors: S., archdeacon of Exeter, S., archdeacon of Cornwall and others (*CFR 1216–24*, p. 333 (7/316)).

Probate process and execution: CFR 1216–24, p. 333 (7/316).

William Briwere (1223 – d. 1244)
Wills: None surviving.
Probate process and execution: CFR project, 29/71: TNA C 60/42, mem. 15r; *CFR* project, 29/505: TNA C 60/42, mem. 4r.

Richard Blund (1245 – d. 1257)
Wills: None surviving.
Probate process and execution: Close rolls 1256–9, p. 183.
Other grants and gifts: Events on his death are described in *EEA 11: Exeter 1046–1184* ed. F. Barlow (Oxford, 1996) pp. lxxix–lxxx.

Walter Bronescombe (1258 – d. 1280)
Wills: None surviving.
Executors: Dom. Roger de Derteford and Dom. Reginald le Arcevek, canons of Exeter, Dom. Peter de Guldeford, chaplain, and Mag. Gervase de Credintonia (*Pecham register (CYS)*, ii, p. 202); Hugh de Plumptone and Richard de Grangiis (*Pecham register (CYS)*, ii, p. 206).
Probate process and execution: HMC, *Report on various collections*, iv, p. 71 (Exeter Cathedral Archives, Exeter DCM, number 2107); *CClR 1279–88*, p. 101; *Pecham register (CYS)*, ii, pp. 150–1, 197–8, 202, 205 (discharge of the executors, with summary of their account, listing goods remaining in their hands, 26 November 1283).

Peter Quinel or Quivel (1280 – d. 1291)
Wills: None surviving.
Executors: Mag. Andrew de Kilkenny, Mag. Peter de Insula and Mag. Robert de Veteri Terra (*CPR 1281–92*, p. 513).
Probate process and execution: CIPM, iii, pp. 34–5 (number 41); *CClR 1288–96*, p. 212; *CPR 1281–92*, p. 513; *Registrum … Pontissara*, ii, p. 731.

Thomas Bitton (1292 – d. 1307)
Wills: None surviving.
Executors: Walter Stapledon, Thomas de Cherlton, John de Button, John de Bureton, Thomas de Henton, Richard de Hacche and Geoffrey de Lucy (*Executors*, p. 34).
Probate process and execution: CIPM, v, pp. 9–10 (number 35).

Executors' accounts, Devon RO, Exeter, Archives of the City of Exeter, Miscellaneous Roll 1, printed in *Executors*, pp. 1–45; discussed in Cavanaugh, 'Books', pp. 101–2.

Receipt by Walter Stapledon, Bishop of Exeter, Thomas de Cherleton', archdeacon of Wells, and Thomas de Henton, treasurer of Exeter, executors of Bishop Bitton, for letters of obligation under the statute merchant, received from John de Button', son and heir of Sir John de Button, knight, one of the co-executors of Bishop Bitton, by the hands of John de Pederton', by which Richard de Rodeney of Somerset was bound to the Bishop in £30, to be paid the octave of Hilary next after the making of the letters; Bristol, 16 December

1305. Receipt given in the priory of Polsdon next Exeter, 30 September 1319. BL Add. Charter 6517.

Walter Stapledon (1308 – d. 1326)
Wills: None surviving, but part recited in a receipt, noted below.
Executors: Mag. Richard Coletone, Dom. Thomas de Stapeltone, Dom. Richard Brayle, Dean and canons of Exeter, and Robert de Tautone (*Stapeldon register*, p. 561).
Probate process and execution: CFR 1319–27, p. 423; *CClR 1327–30*, p. 184 (printed in *Stapeldon register*, p. 561); *CClR 1323–7*, p. 144; *PRME*, iv, p. 150 (two).

Receipt from Bishop John Grandisson for 100 oxen received as a legacy from Bishop Stapledon, reciting part of his will, 28 June 1328. Exeter Cathedral Archives, Exeter DCM, number 2197; copy in a cartulary, Exeter Cathedral Archives, Exeter DCM, number 3672, p. 374. Printed in *Stapeldon register*, pp. 579–80; and in *Grandisson register*, iii, pp. 1557–8.

Inventory, June 1328, Exeter Cathedral Archives, Exeter DCM, number 2847, printed in *Stapeldon register*, pp. 562–75; Cavanaugh, 'Books', pp. 811–14.

Sentence of excommunication by John Stratford, Bishop of Winchester, at the request of the executors (named), against those detaining the goods of Bishop Stapledon in the diocese of Winchester, 9 February 1329. Hampshire RO, A1/5, Bishop Stratford's Register, f. 44. Printed in *Stapeldon register*, pp. 561–2.

Accounts of the executors (the first membrane only, with sewing holes for a further membrane or membranes at the foot), 6 August 1331, Exeter Cathedral Archives, Exeter DCM, number 2848, printed in *Stapeldon register*, pp. 575–9.

James Berkeley (1326 – d. 1327)
Wills: None surviving.
Probate process and execution: Commission to Mag. Adam Murimuth, canon of the cathedral church of Hereford, to prove the will of James Berkeley, Bishop of Exeter, and to admit the executors named in the will or other suitable people to its administration, the will and the account of the administration to be exhibited before the Archbishop. South Malling, 4 July 1327. LPL, Register of Walter Reynolds, f. 155r.

Letters of the Archbishop to Mag. John de Bruyton, canon of Wells, and Mag. Adam Murimuth, canon of Hereford, asking them, at the request of the executors of James Berkeley, Bishop of Exeter, to establish what livestock, goods and profits of sale and purchase on the manors of the bishopric belonged to Berkeley and what to his successor. Given at Mayfield, 27 July 1327. LPL, Register of Walter Reynolds, f. 158r.

John Grandisson (1327 – d. 1369)
Wills: Will, 8 September 1368, LPL, Register of William Whittlesey, ff. 103v–105, printed in *Grandisson register*, iii, pp. 1549–57, with translation on pp. 1511–23; Cavanaugh, 'Books', pp. 371–81.

Executors: Dom. John de Monte Acuto, his nephew, Mag. Philip de Bellocampo (d. 23 May 1369, before the Bishop), *pronepotem meum*, papal nuncio, Mag. Stephen de Pempel, Dean of Wells, Mag. John de Shareshulle, precentor, John Wyliethe, chancellor, Robert de Wykforde, John de Holande, and Nicholas de Braybroke, canons of Exeter, Dom. Andrew de Moore, warden of the collegiate church of St Mary Ottery, William de Braybroke, Dom. John de Mounceaux, Dom. Thomas Sage and Dom. Thomas Tugge, named in the will (*Grandisson register*, iii, p. 1556).
Probate process and execution: CIPM, xii, pp. 340–1 (number 354).

Thomas Brantingham (1370 – d. 1394)
Wills: Will, 13 December 1393, registered copy in TNA PROB 11/1 (4 Rous), ff. 24v–25v, printed in *The register of Thomas de Brantyngham, Bishop of Exeter (A.D. 1370–1394)* ed. F.C. Hingeston-Randolph (2 vols., London and Exeter, 1901–6) ii, pp. 742–9; with an abstract in *Wills and inventories*, i, p. 248; discussed in Cavanaugh, 'Books', pp. 126–7.
Executors: Dom. Hugh Hykelyng', Dom. Robert Rygge, Dom. Thomas Barton, Dom. John Lugans, Dom. John Copleston (grant of probate, below).
Probate process and execution: CClR 1396–9, p. 53. The work of Thomas Barton, one of Brantingham's executors, is discussed in M.C. Burson, '"... for the sake of my soul": the activities of a medieval executor' *Archives* 13 (1977–8) pp. 131–6.

Probate granted 30 December 1394 to Dom. Hugh Hykelyng', Dom. Robert Rygge, Dom. Thomas Barton, Dom. John Lugans, Dom. John Copleston, executors named in the will, by Robert de Hallum, canon of St Asaph, commissary of the Archbishop of Canterbury. TNA PROB 11/1 (4 Rous), f. 25v.

HEREFORD

Hugh Foliot is the first Bishop of Hereford known to have made a will, although its text has not survived.[1] The King acted in September 1234 to clarify the goods that might be treated as part of the Bishop's estate, defining a general principle for the estates of bishops and archbishops and restricting Hugh's executors to the corn of the demesnes, along with cattle and draught oxen, the ploughs and carts. They were to be allowed the previous year's hay and forage, but the hay that had been recently mown, a valuable commodity, was reserved to the Crown.[2] Ralph Maidstone, in 1237, acknowledged that he had received from his predecessor's estate £26 towards the sowing of the demenses of the bishopric in both winter and spring, along with ploughs and stock. He allowed an equivalent sum of money to his successor, if the lands of the bishopric had not been sown at the time of his death. If he died after harvest, and the lands had been sown, he promised the fruits of the harvest, along with the ploughs and stock to his successor – nothwithstanding any will he might subsequently make or the privilege of the King to the contrary. He also attempted to bind his successors in the see to the provision of the same benefit (**15/2**). Bishop Peter d'Aigueblanche enjoined his successors each to leave 30 plough-teams of oxen to the following Bishop.[3] Thomas Cantilupe received 500 marks from the executors of John Breton for the stock of the see and promised that his successor should have as much from his estate.[4]

Ecclesiastical goods were held by the chapter of Hereford for the use of the Bishops of the see. The receipt given by Bishop Lewis Charlton in 1361 (**12/1**) reveals, inter alia, vestments given by John Breton nearly a century earlier, along with others from Thomas Charlton and the mitre of Bishop Swinfield.

Notes

1 *Close Rolls 1227–34*, p. 498.
2 *Close Rolls 1227–34*, p. 518.
3 *CChR 1226–57*, p. 346.
4 *Registrum Thome de Cantilupo, episcopi Herefordensis, A.D. MCCLXXV–MCCLXXXII* ed. R.G. Griffiths and W.W. Capes (CYS, 2; 1907) p. 139.

Giles de Braose (1200 – d. 1215)
No documentation traced.

Hugh de Mapenore (1216 – d. 1219)
No documentation traced.

Hugh Foliot (1219 – d. 1234)
Wills: None surviving.
Executors: Mag. Thomas Foliot, treasurer of Hereford (**15/2**).
Probate process and execution: **15/1–2**; *Close rolls 1227–34*, pp. 498, 518.
Other grants and gifts: Grant by Hugh Foliot for the endowment of two chaplains in St Catherine's Chapel, Hereford, under the supervision of the Dean and Chapter, with payments to the cathedral canons and clerks of the choir on the anniversary of Hugh's death, 14 March 1232 or 13 March 1233. HCA 2098, printed in *EEA 7: Hereford 1079–1234* ed. J. Barrow (Oxford, 1993) pp. 272–4.

Ralph Maidstone (1234 – res. 1239; d. 1245)
Wills: None surviving.
Other grants and gifts: **15/2**.

Peter d'Aigueblanche (1240 – d. 1268)
Licences: CPR 1232–47, p. 276; *CPR 1247–58*, p. 52.
Wills: Inspeximus by Nicholas of Ely, Bishop of Winchester, and Mag. Hugh de Mortuo Mari, official of Canterbury, reciting the Bishop's will, dated November 1268, CCA, Chartae Antiquae W238A. Codicil: CCA, Add. MS 128/68. Printed by C.E. Woodruff, 'The will of Peter de Aqua Blanca Bishop of Hereford (1268)' in *Camden Miscellany XIV* (Camden, 3rd series, 37; 1926) pp. i–xi, 1–13.
Executors: John, Dean of Hereford (*Close rolls 1268–72*, pp. 18–19; Woodruff, 'Will', pp. 6–7); Eymeric, chancellor, and Aymo, precentor, of Hereford (Woodruff, 'Will', p. 7).
Probate process and execution: Close rolls 1268–72, pp. 18–19; *CPR 1266–72*, p. 345.

Grant of administration, CCA, Chartae Antiquae W238B, of 1268; printed in Woodruff, 'Will', pp. 8–9.

Other grants and gifts: Arrangements for stock of the see to pass to succeeding Bishops, *CCR 1226–57*, p. 346.

John Breton (1268 – d. 1275)
Wills: None surviving.
Executors: Probably Thomas Cantilupe, Bishop of Hereford, and Walter de Rudmarelee, [canon of Hereford] (*CFR 1272–1307*, p. 49); possibly also Thomas Breton, canon of Hereford, and Brother John, called Ros, canon of Wormsley (*Pecham register (CYS)*, ii, p. 62).
Probate process and execution: CPR 1272–81, p. 88; *CFR 1272–1307*, pp. 46, 49; *Registrum Thome de Cantilupo* ..., p. 139.

Thomas Cantilupe (1275 – d. 1282)
Wills: Record of the sealing of his will by Archbishop Pecham, 28 July 1279, *Pecham register (CYS)*, ii, p. 79.
Executors: Richard Swinfield, Bishop of Hereford, Mag. William de Monteforti, precentor of Hereford (*Pecham register (CYS)*, i, p. 197).
Probate process and execution: **10/1–4**; *CFR 1272–1307*, p. 170; *CClR 1288–96*, p. 345; *CClR 1302–7*, pp. 7–8. The initial stages of the process following the Bishop's death in Italy are described in R.C. Finucane, 'The Cantilupe-Pecham controversy' in *St Thomas Cantilupe, Bishop of Hereford: essays in his honour* ed. M. Jancey (Hereford, 1982) pp. 103–23, at pp. 118–19.

Richard Swinfield (1282 – d. 1317)
Wills: None surviving.
Executors: Dom. John de Kemeseye, treasurer of Hereford (**38/1**), Dom. John de la Felde and Mag. Robert de Icclesham, canons of Hereford, and Dom. Roger de Breynton' (**38/21**); Mag. Richard Hamenherse (**38/43**).
Probate process and execution: **38/1–60**.

Thomas Charlton (1327 – d. 1344)
Wills: None surviving. Bequests to Lewis Charlton, later Bishop of Hereford, and his brother, Mag. Humphrey Charlton, are noted in **12/2**.
Executors: John de Cherleton the younger (*CClR 1343–6*, p. 284).
Probate process and execution: CClR 1343–6, p. 284.

John Trillek (1344 – d. 1360)
No documentation traced.

Lewis Charlton (1361 – d. 1369)
Wills: Will, 23 May 1369, **12/2**, LPL, Register of William Whittlesey, ff. 102r–103r.
Executors: Dom. William Charleton', 'germanum meum', Dom. Adam Exseg*er*, Roger de Otery and Thomas Bisshbury, canons of Hereford, and William Bar*id*-hurst, 'domicellum meum' (**12/2**); probate granted to Mag. Roger de Otery and Dom. Thomas Bisshebury (**12/4**).
Probate process and execution: **12/3–5**.

John Trefnant (1389 – d. 1404)
Wills: Will, 1 March 1404, notarial copy, 21 March 1404, **41/1**, LPL, Register of Thomas Arundel, vol. I, f. 207r.
Executors: John, Bishop of St Asaph, Dom. Richard Kyngeston', Dean of Windsor;

Mag. Reginald Wolston', Dom. John Proute [Prat], Dom. Hugh Harper and Dom. Thomas Bussh*e*bury, canons of Hereford; Richard de la Bere, Thomas Wallewayn' and William Wallewayn, his brother, and John Crosset, rector of the church of Hartlebury, named in the will (**41/1**); probate granted to Wolston and Crosset (**41/2**).
Probate process and execution: **41/2–3**; inventory, **41/4**; *CIPM*, xviii, p. 412 (number 1194).

LINCOLN

Hugh of Avalon is the first Bishop of Lincoln for whom there is firm evidence that he made a will – although he did not approve of the custom – primarily to avoid the depredations of the Exchequer.[1] There are two wills surviving for Hugh of Wells, of 1212 and 1233, and there may have been others. Henry III granted Hugh a licence in 1227, possibly in 1229, to make a will.[2] This was followed in 1231 by a royal grant to Hugh – in terms similar to his brother, Jocelin of Wells – that both he and his successors might make wills, and that those wills could include all their moveable goods and all the corn sown on the lands of the bishopric and fruits of vineyards up to the Michaelmas after their death, notwithstanding any custom to the contrary.[3] The right of Bishops of Lincoln to make wills was confirmed by a further charter of 1234.[4]

John de Schalby's 'Lives of the Bishops of Lincoln' records gifts by twelfth-century Bishops to the cathedral, for example, chapel goods from Robert Bloet (1093–1123), and later Bishops may also have given their chapels in this way.[5]

Notes

1 Adam of Eynsham *The life of St Hugh of Lincoln* ed. D.L. Douie and H. Farmer (2nd edition, 2 vols., Oxford, 1985) ii, pp. 186–7.
2 *CChR 1226–57*, p. 42.
3 *CFR 1224–34*, pp. 386–7 (15/224); *CChR 1327–41*, pp. 147–8; *CChR 1226–57*, p. 137.
4 *CChR 1327–41*, p. 148.
5 *Giraldi Cambrensis Opera* ed. J.S. Brewer, J.F. Dimock and G.F. Warner (8 vols., RS, 21; 1861–91) vii, pp. 193–216, at p. 195.

Hugh of Avalon (1186 – d. 1200)

Wills: Adam of Eynsham, *Life of St Hugh*, ii, pp. 186–7, records Hugh making a will. Roger de Houeden and Matthew Paris both record that King John visited Hugh and confirmed the will: *Chronica Magistri Rogeri de Houedene* ed. W. Stubbs (4 vols., RS, 51; 1868–71) iv, pp. 140–1; *Matthaei Parisiensis, monachi sancti Albani, Chronica majora* ed. H.R. Luard (7 vols., RS, 57; 1872–83) ii, p. 471.

William of Blois (1203 – d. 1206)

No documentation traced.

Hugh of Wells (1209 – d. 1235)

Licences: CChR 1226–57, p. 42 (there is a small group of charters at this point on the roll with this type of grant from 1227, but the year may possibly be 1229, if the marginal note is followed); *CFR 1224–34*, pp. 386–7 (15/224); *CChR 1327–41*, pp. 147–8 (two, 1231 and 1234); *CChR 1226–57*, p. 137.
Wills: Will, made on St Brice's Day, 13 or 14 November 1212, surviving in an

early sixteenth-century copy in Wells Cathedral Library, Wells DCM, Liber Albus II, ff. 248v–249v, relating to goods to be restored to him in England: printed in HMC *Calendar of the manuscripts of the Dean and Chapter of Wells* (2 vols., 1907–14) i, pp. 431–2; and full text in *The acta of Hugh of Wells Bishop of Lincoln 1209–1235* ed. D.M. Smith (Lincoln Record Society, 88; 2000) pp. 3–5, number 2, which also notes that it is printed (with translation) in *Lincolnshire Notes and Queries* 2 (1890–1) pp. 172–6, and that there is a brief abstract in C.M. Church, 'Jocelin, Bishop of Bath, 1206–1242' in *Archaeologia* 51 (1888) pp. 281–346, at pp. 312–13.

The will of 1 June 1233 survives in Lincolnshire Archives Office, Lincoln DCM, doct. Dj/20/1/7; and A/1/8, number 379. The first of these, possibly the original or a contemporary copy, is the basis for the text printed in *Giraldi Cambrensis Opera*, vii, pp. 223–30, with commentary on pp. xc–xcv, and for the text in *The Registrum Antiquissimum of the cathedral church of Lincoln* ed. C.W. Foster and K. Major (10 vols. and 2 vols. of facsimiles, Lincoln Record Society, 27–9, 32, 34, 41–2, 46, 51, 62, 67–8; 1931–73) ii, pp. 70–5, number 372. The will is edited from both texts in *Acta of Hugh of Wells*, pp. 191–5.

Executors: Will of 1212: names the Bishop of Bath and Mag. Elias de Derham (*Acta of Hugh of Wells*, p. 4); will of 1233: names the Bishop of Bath, his brother; Robert, archdeacon of Lincoln; Walter the treasurer, J., archdeacon of Northampton, and W., archdeacon of Leicester, Warin and Robert, his chaplains, Gilbert de Treilly, Radulph de Waravill', Thomas de Askeb', John de Crakall and John de Burgo, his clerks (*Acta of Hugh of Wells*, p. 194).

Probate process and execution: CPR 1232–47, pp. 94–5, 174.

Robert Grosseteste (1235 – d. 1253)

Wills: None surviving. His will included a bequest of all his books to the Franciscans at Oxford: *F. Nicholai Triveti de ordine fratrum praedicatorum Annales sex regum Angliae … (A.D. MCXXXVI – MCCCVII)* ed. T. Hog (English Historical Society, 1845) p. 243.

Probate process and execution: Close rolls 1251–3, p. 420; *CPR 1247–58*, p. 459.

Henry Lexinton (1253 – d. 1258)

Wills: None surviving.

Probate process and execution: CIPM, i, p. 109 (number 402); *Close rolls 1256–9*, p. 260 (three); *CFR* project, 42/1028: TNA C 60/55, mem. 2r; *CFR* project, 42/1029: TNA C 60/55, mem. 2r.

Richard Gravesend (1258 – d. 1279)

Wills: None surviving.

Executors: Mag. Richard de Graveshend (*CFR 1272–1307*, p. 122).

Probate process and execution: CFR 1272–1307, p. 122.

Other grants and gifts: Goods given to Lincoln described in John de Schalby, 'Lives of the Bishops of Lincoln', in *Giraldi Cambrensis Opera*, vii, p. 207; R.M. Haines, 'Richard of Gravesend (d. 1279)' *ODNB*, xxiii, pp. 402–3, mentions a book, possibly two, BL MS Royal 3 B XIII and 2 F XII, left to Rochester Cathedral Priory.

Oliver Sutton (1280 – d. 1299)

Wills: Sutton made at least three wills, one with a codicil. The will-making is

described in *The rolls and register of Bishop Oliver Sutton 1280–1299* ed. R.M.T. Hill (8 vols., Lincoln Record Society, 39, 43, 48, 52, 60, 64, 69, 76; 1948–86) iii, pp. lxxxv, 103–4, 182; v, pp. 3, 188.
Executors: Mag. Thomas de Sutton, Mag. Goscelin de Kirmington', archdeacon of Northampton and Stow, Dom. William de Stoketon', Dom. John Maunsel and Dom. Hugh de Normanton', canons of Lincoln; Mag. Walter de Wotton', archdeacon of Huntingdon, and Mag. Robert de Kelingeworthe, canon of Lincoln (*Winchelsey register*, i, pp. 368–9, 378–9).
Probate process and execution: Winchelsey register, i, pp. 368–9, 378–9; *CPR 1292–1301*, p. 501.
Other grants and gifts: Building work at Lincoln noted in John de Schalby, 'Lives of the Bishops of Lincoln', in *Giraldi Cambrensis Opera*, vii, pp. 210–11.

John Dalderby (1300 – d. 1320)
Wills: None surviving.
Executors: Mag. Thomas de Langetoft and others (*CClR 1318–23*, p. 339); Mag. John de Stretford, archdeacon of Lincoln, who nominated as his attorneys Mag. Thomas de Langetoft and Nicholas de Welton (*CPR 1321–4*, p. 41).
Probate process and execution: CClR 1318–23, p. 339; *CPR 1321–4*, p. 41.

Henry Burghersh (1320 – d. 1340)
Wills: None surviving.
Executors: Nicholas de Falle (*CClR 1343–6*, p. 111); John de Hale (*CClR 1343–6*, p. 395).
Probate process and execution: CIPM, viii, pp. 210–12 (numbers 288–9); *CClR 1341–3*, pp. 260, 311, 348–9; *CClR 1343–6*, pp. 111, 395; *CClR 1346–9*, p. 48.

Letters of Simon Islip, Archbishop of Canterbury, instructing the executors of Henry Burghersh to appear before him or his commissary on the first law day after the feast of St Luke [18 October] in the collegiate church at Wingham to give an account of their administration of the estate, Mayfield, 5 September 1350. LPL, Register of Simon Islip, f. 31v.

Thomas Bek (1341 – d. 1347)
Wills: Will, 18 November 1346, with codicil, 11 February 1347, printed in *TE I*, pp. 24–8, from Borthwick Institute for Archives, York, Register of Archbishop Zouche, Prerogative Court of York, Register 10, ff. 310v–312r. Cavanaugh, 'Books', p. 85.
Executors: Named in the will: Mag. Walter de Stauren', treasurer of Lincoln, Mag. William de Haryngton, rector of Herpiswell, Dom. William de sancto Quintino, Mag. Richard de Retford, Mag. John de Carleton, Mag. Walter de Grewick, Dom. John de Pappeworth, Dom. William de Grantham, and Mag. William de Burton (*TE I*, p. 27); acting: William de St Quintin and John de Pappeworth, knights, and Mag. William de Burton (CCA, Register G, f. 36v).
Probate process and execution: CClR 1343–6, pp. 114–15.

Mandate by Robert, Prior of Christ Church, Canterbury, addressed to John Gynwell, Bishop of Lincoln: William de St Quintin and John de Pappeworth, knights, and Mag. William de Burton, clerk, executors of the will of Thomas

Beek, were recently in negotiation with Archbishop Stratford about legal matters, but the matter was not concluded. Robert instructs the Bishop of Lincoln to cite the executors to appear before the Prior or his commissary on the first law day after St Denis [9 October] to give a final account of their administration of the estate, Canterbury, 10 September 1348. CCA, Register G, f. 93v.

Acquittance by Robert, Prior of Christ Church, Canterbury, and the chapter, to William de St Quintin and John de Pappeworth, knights, and Mag. William de Burton, executors of Bishop Thomas de Beek, late Bishop of Lincoln, 14 October 1348. CCA, Register G, f. 36v.

Commission by Robert, Prior of Christ Church, Canterbury, to the Priors of the Priory of St Mary, Huntingdon, and St Ives, to conclude actions relating to the executors of Thomas Beek, who had been executor of Thomas Beek, in regard to 300 marks and two rings, 14 October 1348. CCA, Register G, ff. 98v–99v.

Acquittance of the executors of Thomas Beek, by Robert, Prior of Christ Church, Canterbury, 14 October 1348. CCA, Register G, f. 99v.

A second copy of all these documents is in CCA, Register Q, ff. 214r–214v.

Instruction to Mag. John de Lech, the Archbishop's official, and Mag. Richard de Plessys, Dean of Arches, about the case between the former Archbishop of Canterbury, John Stratford, and his commissary on the one part, the Dean and Chapter of Salisbury, on the second part, and William Seyntquintyn, John Pappeworth, knights, and William de Burton, executors of Bishop Thomas of Lincoln, Lambeth, 7 April 1350. LPL, Register of Simon Islip, f. 48v.

Letters of Simon Islip, Archbishop of Canterbury, instructing John de Pappeworth, knight, and Mag. William de Burton, executors of Thomas Bek, to appear before him on the second law day after the feast of the translation of St Edward the King [13 October] at Canterbury, with the will, inventory and account of their administration of the estate, Mayfield, 5 September 1350. LPL, Register of Simon Islip, f. 31v.

John Gynwell (1347 – d. 1362)
Wills: None surviving.
Probate process and execution: Commission to hear the account of the executors of John Gynwell, 27 May 1364. LPL, Register of Simon Islip, f. 202r.

John Buckingham (1362 – res. 1398; d. 1399)
Wills: Will, 9 February 1399, and codicil, CCA, Chartae Antiquae W220, copy of the testament of John Buckingham, Bishop of Lincoln; related charters, Chartae Antiquae C146–50. Will printed in *Sede vacante wills*, pp. 100–5; noted in Cavanaugh, 'Books', p. 147.
Executors: Dom. Thomas Chelenden, Prior of Canterbury Cathedral Priory, Mag. Peter Dalton, treasurer of Lincoln, Mag. John Botlysham and Dom. John Forest, canons of Lincoln, Dom. John de Lydyngton, rector of Irnham, and John Park, the Bishop's esquire (*Sede vacante wills*, p. 103).

Other grants and gifts: CPR 1396–9, p. 568, mortmain licence for the chantry at Canterbury, the revision of the operation of which is the subject of **8**.

LLANDAFF

The first Bishop of Llandaff known to have made a will was William de Radnor (d. 1266); as his executors were not discharged until 1284, however, it is not clear how easy it was to establish the principle that Bishops of Llandaff should make wills.[1] Between 1148 and 1229, the see was held by monks, who would not normally have been expected to hold property of their own.[2] Henry III exercised regalian right in the bishopric during vacancies, and it is noteworthy that in 1219, following the death of Henry de Abergavenny, as well as the temporalities of the bishopric, he committed to custody all the chattels and goods of the late bishop.[3] The Crown made grants of chapel goods to bishops in many sees at their election, and Henry III did so for William de Burgh in 1244, giving rich textiles for his chapel, along with a mitre worth 10 marks.[4] In 1318, Bishop John de Monmouth and the chapter of Llandaff were granted the right to hold the temporalities of the see during vacancies instead of the property being committed to the royal escheators and bailiffs, to avoid the depredations that occurred during vacancies, for an annual sum (or pro-rata for a part year) during vacancies of £93 9*s*. 8*d*.[5]

In addition to the individuals listed here, John Burghill, who held the see 1396–8, made a will as Bishop of Lichfield (**9**).

Notes

1 *Pecham register (CYS)*, i, p. 214. The date is incorrectly given in the document as A.D. 1288, but correctly as the sixth year of Pecham's archiepiscopate.

2 *Llandaff episcopal acta 1140–1287* ed. D. Crouch (South Wales Record Society, 5; 1988) p. xv; *Episcopal acts and cognate documents relating to the Welsh dioceses, 1066–1272* ed. J. Conway Davies (2 vols., Historical Society for the Church in Wales, Cardiff, 1946–8) ii, p. 542.

3 *CPR 1216–25*, p. 195.

4 *Close rolls 1242–7*, p. 214.

5 *CFR 1307–19*, pp. 355–6.

Henry de Abergavenny (1193 – d. 1218)
No documentation traced.

William de Goldcliff (1219 – d. 1229)
No documentation traced.

Elias de Radnor 1230 – d. 1240
No documentation traced.

William de Christchurch (1240 – res. before 1244)
No documentation traced.

William de Burgh (1245 – d. 1253)
No documentation traced.

John la Warre (1254 – d. 1256)
No documentation traced.

William de Radnor (1257 – d. 1266)
Wills: None surviving.
Executors: Mag. William de Radenor, Mag. Simon de Radenor (*Pecham register (CYS)*, i, p. 214).
Probate process and execution: Pecham register (CYS), i, p. 214.

William de Breuse (1266 – d. 1287)
No documentation traced.

John de Monmouth (1297 – d. 1323)
Wills: None surviving.
Executors: Mag. Alexander de Munemuta, archdeacon of Llandaff, Dom. John de Middelton, canon of Llandaff, Dom. Vincent de Bergeveny, chaplain, and Mag. Richard de Halton (LPL, Register of Walter Reynolds, f. 164v).
Probate process and execution: Letters of Archbishop Reynolds acquitting Mag. Alexander de Munemuta, archdeacon of Llandaff, Dom. John de Middelton, canon of Llandaff, Dom. Vincent de Bergeveny, chaplain, and Mag. Richard de Halton, executors of John, late Bishop of Llandaff, of their administration of the will: they have exhibited the will, inventory and account rolls relating to the case. £97 17*s.* 8¾*d.* remains in their hands, however, for the marriage portions of female relations of the deceased ('pro maritagiis consanguinearum dicti defuncti') and other women of the diocese of Llandaff as set out in the will, and they are to provide a further account of this money. Given at Lambeth, 27 October, 1324. LPL, Register of Walter Reynolds, f. 164v.
Other grants and gifts: Cavanaugh, 'Books', pp. 590–1.

John de Eclescliff [Eaglescliffe] (1323 – d. 1346)
No documentation traced.

John Paschal (1344 – d. 1361)
No documentation traced.

Roger Gradock, or Craddock (1361 – d. 1382)
No documentation traced.

Edmund Bromfield (1389 – d. 1393)
Wills: Will, 10 June 1393, **7**, TNA PROB 11/1 (3 Rous), f. 10v.
Executors: Mag. Roger Croke and Thomas Orwell', canons of Llandaff, Dom. Henry Cha*u*nce and Arnold Whitchurche (**7**).

Andrew Barret (1395 – d. 1396)
No documentation traced.

LONDON

William of Ste-Mère-Église had a licence from King John to make a will, but Eustace of Fauconberg is the first post-Conquest Bishop of London known to have made one.[1] While in 1228 Alexander de Dorset was instructed to take the keepership of all the lands and tenements that belonged to the Bishop, at the King's pleasure,[2] the instructions to the keeper of the bishopric in 1274, following the death of Henry of Sandwich, excepted lands which the executors were required, by custom, to sow and cultivate when the see was vacant.[3] Other concessions were made by the Crown from time to time. In April 1242, more than six months after the death of Roger Niger in 1241, the executors were given remission for an amercement of 10 marks owed to the Crown, the sum to be used to provide a light or wax candle, to burn next to the body of the Bishop in St Paul's.[4] Roger's executors had continued to cultivate the lands of the see after his death, and also in April 1242 they were allowed to have all the manorial works up to 1 August.[5] In 1317, Bishop Richard Newport and the Dean and Chapter of St Paul's gave 400 marks for a fine to have the custody of the see during vacancies, agreeing to pay the Exchequer £1,000 a year, and pro-rata for a longer or shorter period, to avoid the depredation of the see at these times.[6]

There is good evidence for ecclesiastical goods given by Bishops of London to their cathedral, perhaps the customary practice of handing over their chapels, and for some of these goods subsequently being held by later incumbents of the see. A visitation of the cathedral treasury in April 1295 recorded goods that had come from as far back as Bishop Gilbert (although it is unclear whether this was Gilbert the Universal (d. 1134), or Gilbert Foliot (d. 1187)), and from almost every Bishop from Richard FitzNeal (d. 1198) onwards. Some goods were in the custody of the current Bishop of London, Richard Gravesend.[7] Gravesend's executors returned some items to St Paul's, especially books, as well as handing over further bequests; but they did not pass to St Paul's all the goods of the Bishop's chapel: a portion of these may have belonged to William of Louth, whose executor Gravesend was, but it is also likely that the extent of the chapel was limited by custom.[8]

Notes

1 Sheehan, *WME*, p. 246; *Close rolls 1227–31*, p. 122.
2 *Close rolls 1227–31*, pp. 119–20.
3 *CClR 1272–9*, p. 65.
4 *Close rolls 1237–42*, p. 416.
5 *Close rolls 1237–42*, p. 416.
6 *CFR 1307–19*, p. 349. This arrangement was in contemplation under Bishop Baldock: **2/1**, roll 1, 'peccunia numerata', p. 77.
7 W. Dugdale *The history of Saint Paul's Cathedral in London* … revised by H. Ellis (1818) pp. 310–35.
8 *Executors*, pp. 47–50, 112.

William of Ste-Mère-Église (1198 – res. 1221; d. 1224)
Licences: Sheehan, *WME*, p. 246.
Wills: None surviving.

Eustace of Fauconberg (1221 – d. 1228)
Wills: None surviving.
Executors: archdeacons of Huntingdon, London and Middlesex (*Close rolls 1227–31*, p. 122).
Probate process and execution: Close Rolls 1227–31, p. 122; *CFR 1224–34*, p. 227 (13/21); *Close Rolls 1227–31*, pp. 125, 132.

Roger Niger (1228 – d. 1241)
Wills: None surviving.
Probate process and execution: CFR 1234–42, p. 469 (25/754); *Close rolls 1237–42*, p. 416 (two).

Fulk Basset (1241 – d. 1259)
Executors: Walter [de Cantilupe], Bishop of Worcester, Philip Basset, Robert, Dean of St Paul's, and Richard, treasurer of the same. Mentioned in a grant by Matthew del Paundfreit of land for 3 chaplains to pray for Basset's soul (HMC, *Appendix to the Ninth Report*, p. 10).

Henry of Wingham (1259 – d. 1262)
Licences: CPR 1247–58, p. 188 (1253).
Wills: None surviving.
Executors: H., Prior of St Radegund's, Mag. J. de Chishull and H. de Wengham, archdeacon of London and Middlesex, J. de Wengham, precentor of St Paul's, London, H. de Stokes and others (*CPR 1258–66*, p. 239).
Probate process and execution: Close rolls 1261–4, pp. 154–5, 197, 202; *CPR 1258–66*, pp. 239–40; *Close rolls 1268–72*, pp. 133–4.
Other grants and gifts: A.J. Musson, 'Henry of Wingham', *ODNB*, lix, pp. 739–40: 'a memorandum arising from council business noted that the executors of the Bishop of London had given security to the King for all the bishop's debts.' In 1298 a document of the Abbot of Beeleigh records the Bishop's grant of 360 marks to Beeleigh Abbey, in return for 2 priests to say mass for his soul for 6 marks a year, 4 marks a year to be distributed on his obit and half a mark a year to St Martin-le-Grand (Guildhall Library, London, MS 25501, f. 70r).

Henry of Sandwich (1262 – d. 1273)
Wills: None surviving.
Executors: Archbishop Kilwardby, Nicholas of Lenham and Roger of Tilmanstone (C.H. Knowles, 'Henry of Sandwich', *ODNB*, xlviii, pp. 107–8, from *CFR 1272–1307*, p. 11).
Probate process and execution: CClR 1272–9, p. 65; *CPR 1272–81*, p. 60.

John Chishull (1273 – d. 1280)
Wills: None surviving.
Executors: Robert de Drayton, Mag. Ralph de Baldok and Mag. Ralph de Ivyngho (*CClR 1279–88*, p. 550).
Probate process and execution: CClR 1279–88, p. 550; *CClR 1288–96*, pp. 30, 342. The executors are mentioned in **17/1** and **17/3**.

Richard Gravesend (1280 – d. 1303)
Wills: Will, 20 May 1289, **17/1**, Guildhall Library, London, MS 25271/14A; will, 1302, **17/2**, Guildhall Library, MS 25271/14.
Executors: Will of 1289: Mag. John de Selviston', rector of Stepney, Mag. J. de sancto Claro, rector of Fulham, Mag. Thomas, rector of Hadham, and Stephen, the Bishop's brother (**17/1**); will of 1302: Mag. Radulph de Baudak', Dean of St Paul's, John de Bedford, archdeacon of London, Richard de Neuport,

archdeacon of Middlesex, and Stephen de Gravesende, rector of Stepney, the Bishop's nephew (**17/2**); Ralph Baldock did not appear at probate.
Probate process and execution: **17/3–5**; inventory, **17/6**; *CIPM*, iv, p. 130 (number 207); *CFR 1272–1307*, p. 486; *CPR 1301–7*, p. 299; *CPR 1307–13*, p. 11.

Ralph Baldock (1304 – d. 1313)
Wills: None surviving.
Executors: Mag. Robert de Baldok, archdeacon of Middlesex, and William de Meleford, archdeacon of Colchester (*CPR 1317–21*, p. 532).
Probate process and execution: Inventories, 1313–14 (**2/1–2**); *CPR 1317–21*, p. 532 (mortmain licence, 1320).

Commission from Henry de Eastry, Prior of Christ Church, Canterbury, to the Prior of Holy Trinity, London, noted in a document in part designed as a formulary, instructing him to receive from A., B., C., D., etc., executors named in the will of R[alph], Bishop of London, the oath that they will make a faithful inventory of the deceased's goods, and faithfully administer them. The oath has not before been taken because of the election to the see of London and other pressing matters from the period of the vacancy of the see. The inventory is to be exhibited to the Prior of Holy Trinity and Mag. W. de M', archdeacon of Colchester. An account of the administration, *sede vacante*, is to be exhibited before the Prior of Christ Church, or before others, *sede plena*. The oath to be received by the counsel of Mag. William Russel and Philip de Pateneye, 'juratorum nostrorum', or others if they are present in London who are not of the collegiate church of London (St Paul's). CCA, Register Q, f. 103v. No date: the entries immediately preceding are not dated, and the closest entries that are dated (on f. 101v) come from 29 July 1313 and 1 August 1313.

Grant of probate to the executors of R[alph], Bishop of London; possibly intended as an example in a formulary. CCA, Register Q, f. 104r. No date: the entries immediately preceding are not dated, and the closest entries that are dated (on f. 101v) come from 29 July 1313 and 1 August 1313.

Gilbert Segrave (1313 – d. 1316)
Wills: None surviving.
Other grants and gifts: Exemplification under the seal of the Exchequer of certain accounts of the guardians of the see of London after the death of Gilbert Segrave, Bishop of London, in the tenth year of King Edward II (1316–17), 27 April 1406. Guildhall Library, London, MS 25241/35.

Richard Newport (1317 – d. 1318)
Wills: Passages in the will, 22 August 1315, relating to property in the city of London, enrolled in the Court of Husting, 11 November 1318: *CCH*, i, p. 281.
Probate process and execution: Commission to Mag. William de Bray and Mag. Robert de Do*n*ebregg', canons of St Paul's, London, to hear the accounts of the executors of Richard de Neuport, late Bishop of London, and to give them their acquittance, given at Lambeth, 27 March 1324. LPL, Register of Walter Reynolds, f. 132r.
Other grants and gifts: Cavanaugh, 'Books', p. 607.

Stephen Gravesend (1318 – d. 1338)
Wills: Will, 19 February 1337, **18/1**, Guildhall Library, London, MS 25271/27.
Executors: Thomas Durant, chancellor of St Paul's, Henry de Iddesworth', canon of St Paul's, Robert de Teye, Dom. John de Teversham, Dom. Richard de Bursted and Dom. William Vygerous (**18/1**).
Probate process and execution: Executors' accounts, **18/2**; *CIPM*, viii, pp. 108–9 (number 176); *CPR 1345–8*, pp. 349, 356 (mortmain licences, 1347).

Richard Bintworth (1338 – d. 1339)
Wills: None surviving.
Probate process and execution: CClR 1339–41, pp. 372–3, 398, 547.

Ralph Stratford (1340 – d. 1354)
Wills: None surviving.
Probate process and execution: Foot of the executors' account, *c.*1356, **36**.

Michael Northburgh (1354 – d. 1361)
Wills: Will, 23 May 1361, **28/1**, Guildhall Library, London, MS 25271/47; *inspeximus* and confirmation of that part of the Bishop's will relating to the bequest of a loan chest containing 1,000 marks to the treasurer of St Paul's, 5 February 1375, *CPR 1374–7*, p. 75.
Executors: Mag. Michael Fre, John de Cantebrugg' and Mag. John, his son, and Thomas Frowyk' (**28/1**); probate granted to Mag. Michael Fre, Mag. John de Cantebreg' and Thomas Frowyk (**28/2**).
Probate process and execution: **28/2–3**; *Ancient deeds*, ii, p. 268.

Robert Braybrooke (1381 – d. 1404)
Wills: None surviving.
Executors: Gerard Braybrok, knight, Edward Hamden, esquire, Mag. William Stukley, Dom. John Wyke, Roger Albryghton and Thomas Lyes (**6/4**).
Probate process and execution: **6/1–4** (**6/2** is an indenture with an inventory of the goods of the Bishop); *CIPM*, xviii, p. 351 (number 1011); *CPapReg 1404–15*, p. 154.
Other grants and gifts: Grant by Gerard Braybrok the younger, knight, Edmund Hampden, John Boys and Roger Albryghton, the executors, during the lifetime of the Bishop, for the establishment of a chantry at the altar of the BVM within the palace of the Bishop of London, 1 May 1404. BL Harley Charter 47 B. 14, printed in Dugdale, *History of Saint Paul's*, p. 357.

Roger Walden (1404 – d. 1406)
Listed under Archbishops of Canterbury.

NORWICH

Rather than a grant of a general licence to a Bishop of Norwich and his successors in the see to make wills, Bishops appear to have sought licences individually. These now survive for Walter Suffield, Roger Skerning (two, one from Edward I confirming that of Henry III), John Salmon and William Ayermine (in recognition of his service to Edward I, Edward II and Edward III).[1] The Crown confirmed in 1326 that the custom of the bishopric was that rectors who died after the Annunciation should have the profits of the next harvest, and that the Bishops were therefore entitled to it as part of their estates.[2]

The obituary notices in the *Liber de archiepiscopis et episcopis Angliae* of Batholomew Cotton and his continuator, and in the *Registrum primum* of Norwich Cathedral Priory, record gifts to the cathedral church of Norwich from Herbert Losinga onwards, although it is not clear when these gifts were made.[3]

Notes

1 Listed under these individuals below.

2 *CClR 1323–7*, p. 471.

3 For example, for Bishop Losinga, Bartholomew Cotton, 'Liber de archiepiscopis et episcopis Angliae' in *Bartholomaei de Cotton monachi Norwicensis Historia Anglicana (A.D. 449–1298) necnon ejusdem Liber de archiepiscopis et episcopis Angliae* ed. H.R. Luard (RS, 16; 1859) p. 391; *Registrum primum*, p. 56.

John of Oxford (1175 – d. 1200)
Wills: None surviving.
Other grants and gifts: Obituary notice in the *Registrum primum*, p. 82.

John de Gray (1200 – d. 1214)
Wills: None surviving.
Other grants and gifts: Obituary notice in the *Registrum primum*, p. 88.

Pandulf Verraccio (1215 – d. 1226)
Wills: Will, with gifts to the crusade, his successor at Norwich and to Norwich Cathedral Priory, noted in *Regesta Honorii Papae III* ed. P. Pressutti (2 vols., Vatican City, 1888–95) ii, p. 441, number 6032; *EEA 21: Norwich 1215–1243* ed. C. Harper-Bill (Oxford, 2000) p. xxiii.
Other grants and gifts: Gift to Norwich of an *archa* with relics noted in *Bartholomaei de Cotton … Liber de archiepiscopis et episcopis Angliae*, p. 394.

Thomas Blundeville (1226 – d. 1236)
Wills: None surviving.
Probate process and execution: Close Rolls 1234–7, pp. 384, 389.

Walter Suffield (1244 – d. 1257)
Licences: CPR 1247–58, p. 92.
Wills: Will, 19 June 1256, Norfolk Record Office, NCR Case 24b/2, summarised in F. Blomefield *Topographical history of Norfolk* (5 vols., Fersfield, etc., 1739–75) ii, pp. 345–6; F. Blomefield and C. Parkin *An essay towards a topographical history of the county of Norfolk* (2nd edition, 11 vols., 1805–10) iii, pp. 486–92; printed in full in *EEA 32: Norwich 1244–1266* ed. C. Harper-Bill (Oxford, 2007) pp. 150–6, number 138.
Executors: Walter de Calethorp, 'nepotem meum', Geoffrey de Lodn', William de Whitewell', William de Pakeham, Dom. Hamo, master of the Hospital of St Giles, Mag. Hugh de Corbrig' and William de Wichingham (*EEA 32: Norwich 1244–1266*, p. 155).
Probate process and execution: Close rolls 1256–9, p. 59.

Simon Walton (1257 – d. 1266)
Wills: None surviving.
Probate process and execution: Close rolls 1264–8, p. 166.

Roger Skerning (1266 – d. 1278)
Licences: CPR 1266–72, p. 619; *CPR 1272–81*, p. 252.
Wills: None surviving.
Executors: William de Pakeham, Geoffrey de Thorp, chaplain, and Thomas de Pulham (*Pecham register (CYS)*, ii, p. 92).
Probate process and execution: CFR 1272–1307, p. 93; discharge of the executors, including a summary of their accounts, 30 October 1279, *Pecham register (CYS)*, ii, pp. 92–4.

William Middleton (1278 – d. 1288)
Wills: None surviving.
Probate process and execution: CClR 1279–88, p. 515.

John Salmon (1299 – d. 1325)
Licences: CPR 1324–7, p. 51.
Wills: None surviving.
Executors: Walter de Norwyco, Richard Lieu, Simon de Claxby, William de Culpho, John le Croter and John de Sutton (*CClR 1323–7*, p. 518).
Probate process and execution: CClR 1323–7, pp. 388, 471, 518; *CClR 1327–30*, p. 252.
Other grants and gifts: Gifts to Norwich Cathedral Priory recorded in 'Continuatio historiae Bartholomaei Cotton', *Anglia sacra*, i, p. 413.

William Ayermine (1325 – d. 1336)
Licences: CPR 1334–8, p. 239.
Wills: None surviving.
Executors: Richard de Ayremynn, Mag. Thomas Sampson, Robert de Usseflete, Mag. Gilbert de Yareswell, Ivo de Clynton and William de Salteby (*CClR 1337–9*, p. 137).
Probate process and execution: CPR 1334–8, p. 239; *CClR 1337–9*, p. 137; *CPR 1338–40*, p. 313.
Other grants and gifts: Gifts to Norwich Cathedral Priory noted in 'Continuatio historiae Bartholomaei Cotton', *Anglia sacra*, i, p. 414.

Anthony Bek (1337 – d. 1343)
Wills: None surviving.
Other grants and gifts: Cavanaugh, 'Books', pp. 84–5, citing C.L. Shadwell, 'The catalogue of the library of Oriel College in the fourteenth century', in *Collectanea I* ed. C.R.L. Fletcher (Oxford Historical Society, 5; 1885) p. 69.

William Bateman (1344 – d. 1355)
Licences: CPapReg: Petitions, i, p. 265.
Wills: None surviving.
Executors: Simon de Babbingle, Ralph Urry, Robert de Waltone and John de Wynestone (*CPapReg 1342–62*, p. 565).

Probate process and execution: CPapReg 1342–62, p. 565; R.M. Haines, 'William Bateman' *ODNB*, iv, pp. 309–11. A gift by the executors to Thomas Percy, the succeeding Bishop of Norwich, is noted in **29/1**.

Acquittance of Dom. Simon de …, Dom. Ralph Urry, Dom. Robert de Walton' and Mag. John de Wyneston, executors of Bishop Bateman, Lambeth, December 1355. LPL, Register of Simon Islip, f. 104v.

Other grants and gifts: Gifts to Norwich Cathedral Priory noted in 'Continuatio historiae Bartholomaei Cotton', *Anglia sacra*, i, p. 414; R.M. Haines, 'William Bateman' *ODNB*, iv, pp. 309–11.

Thomas Percy (1355 – d. 1369)
Wills: Will, 25 May 1368, **29/1**, LPL, Register of William Whittlesey, ff. 105v–106r; a short extract, taken from BL MS Harley 6148, is printed in *Testamenta vetusta*, i, p. 84.
Executors: Dom. Henry de Percy, lord of Alnwick, Mag. William de Blyth', archdeacon of Norfolk, Dom. William de Swynflet, archdeacon of Norwich, Dom. Richard de A*n*la*n*dby, vicar of Mildenhall, and Dom. William Malbus, rector of Wheatacre (**29/1–3**).
Probate process and execution: **29/2–4**; *CIPM*, xii, p. 426 (number 450).
Other grants and gifts: Gifts to Norwich Cathedral Priory and work of executors noted in 'Continuatio historiae Bartholomaei Cotton', *Anglia sacra*, i, p. 415.

Henry Dispenser (1370 – d. 1406)
Wills: None surviving. Died intestate (Davies, 'Episcopate', p. cx).
Other grants and gifts: Cavanaugh, 'Books', p. 801.

Alexander Tottington (1406 – d. 1413)
Wills: Will and codicil, 20 April 1412, **40/1**, LPL, Register of Thomas Arundel, vol. II, ff. 165r–166v.
Executors: Mag. Thomas Dallyng, Mag. William Bernham and Mag. John Thornham, clerks, Edmund Oldehalle, esquire, and William Paston named in will (**40/1**); probate granted to Mag. William Berham and William Paston (**40/2**).
Probate process and execution: **40/2–3**.

ROCHESTER

The temporalities of the see of Rochester were held from the Archbishop of Canterbury, to whom regalian right had been remitted. On the death of the Bishop of Rochester, therefore, it was the Archbishop who received the Bishop's palfrey, his silver cup, his pack of hounds, all his seals and his best ring. Canterbury *sede vacante*, control of the temporalities passed to the Crown, and the Prior of Christ Church, Canterbury, had all the Bishop's seals and his second best ring.[1] Gilbert Glanvill was the first Bishop of Rochester to have a licence for making a will, from King John, in June 1213.[2]

The will of John Sheppey (**33/1**) mentions an agreed level of stock and goods on the bishopric – 'implementum ab antiquo consuetum' – which a bishop's executors were expected to pass to his successor.

Notes

1 CCA, Register G, f. 23v; also recorded in Henry de Eastry's memorandum book, BL MS Cotton Galba E IV, f. 25v.

2 Sheehan, *WME*, p. 246.

Gilbert Glanvill (1185 – d. 1214)
Licences: Sheehan, *WME*, p. 246.
Wills: None surviving.

Benedict de Sausetun (1215 – d. 1226)
No documentation traced.

Henry Sandford (1226 – d. 1235)
No documentation traced.

Richard Wendene (1235 – d. 1250)
No documentation traced.

Lawrence of St Martin (1250 – d. 1274)
Wills: None surviving.
Executors: John de sancto Dionsio, archdeacon of Rochester (*CClR 1272–9*, p. 491).
Probate process and execution: CClR 1272–9, pp. 154, 464, 491. The claims of the executors against Bishop Walter of Merton were noted in the codicil to the will of that Bishop, 1277: *The early rolls of Merton College Oxford* ed. J.R.L. Highfield (Oxford Historical Society, new series, 18; 1964) p. 85.

Walter of Merton (1274 – d. 1277)
Wills: Will, 29 March 1276, with codicil, 26 October 1277, Merton College, Oxford, Records 4234a, printed in *Early rolls of Merton College*, pp. 79–89.
Executors: Mag. William de Ewelle, canon of St Paul's, London, John de Merstune, John de Catheleyne, Ranulph, perpetual vicar of Greenwich, Ralph de Ripplingeham, clerk, and William Dudekin, lay person (*Pecham register (CYS)*, i, p. 183); the will names Mag. William de Ewell', John de Merston, chaplain, Brother Thomas de Woldeham, John de Catteloin, Radulph de Riplingham, and William Dodekin (*Early rolls of Merton College*, p. 83).
Probate process and execution: Early rolls of Merton College discusses the execution of the will on pp. 54–8 and prints the accounts of the executors on pp. 90–169. Mandate for hearing the accounts of the executors, as there is dispute among the executors, 22 April 1282 (*Pecham register (CYS)*, i, p. 182); record of the audit, the approval of the funeral expenses and note of sums not yet in the hands of the executors, 1–13 May 1282 (*Pecham register (CYS)*, i, pp. 183–4). *CIPM*, ii, p. 145 (number 247); *CClR 1272–9*, pp. 446–7 (five), 491; *CPR 1272–81*, p. 259; *CClR 1272–9*, p. 559; *CPR 1272–81*, p. 317.

John Bradfield (1277 – d. 1283)
Wills: None surviving.

Executors: Mag. Henry le Affeyte and Dom. Robert, rector of Southfleet, administrators (*Pecham register (CYS)*, ii, p. 207).
Probate process and execution: Pecham register (CYS), ii, p. 207.

Thomas Ingoldsthorpe (1282 – d. 1291)
Wills: Extract from his will relating to lands in the city of London, enrolled 3 May 1292 in the Court of Husting: *CCH*, i, p. 105.

Thomas Wouldham (1291 – d. 1317)
No documentation traced.

Hamo Hethe (1317 – res. 1352; alive in 1357)
No documentation traced.

John Sheppey (1352 – d. 1360)
Wills: Will, 21 September 1360, **33/1**, LPL, Register of Simon Islip, ff. 169v–170r.
Executors: Mag. Thomas de Bradwell, rector of Shoreham and the chapel of Otford, the Bishop's official, Dom. Robert de Pleseley, rector of Southfleet, and Dom. Stephen Randulph, rector of Cowden (**33/1**).
Probate process and execution: **33/2**; *CClR 1354–60*, p. 434. Books sold by his executors, along with one given to Rochester Cathedral Priory: Cavanaugh, 'Books', pp. 783–4.

Thomas Trillek (1364 – d. 1372)
Wills: Will, 11 December 1372, **42/1**, LPL, Register of William Whittlesey, ff. 126v–127r.
Executors: Mag. Robert de Bourne, rector of Southfleet, and Dom. William Durrant, rector of St Michael Queenhithe ('ad ripam regine'), London (**42/1**).
Probate process and execution: **42/2**. He had a substantial library and those volumes purchased probably after his death by William Rede, Bishop of Chichester, passed mainly to Merton College, Oxford, and New College, Oxford: Cavanaugh, 'Books', pp. 883–7.

Thomas Brinton (1373 – d. 1389)
Wills: Will, 29 April 1389, printed in *The sermons of Thomas Brinton, Bishop of Rochester, 1373–1389* ed. M.A. Devlin (2 vols., Camden 3rd series, 85–6; 1954) ii, pp. 503–4, from LPL, Register of William Courtenay, f. 231v; noted in Cavanaugh, 'Books', p. 140.
Executors: Mag. Robert de Bradgare, the Bishop's official, William Makenade, Mag. John Charyington, clerk, and John Blyklyng, under the supervision of Dom. John de Cobham (*Sermons of Thomas Brinton*, ii, p. 504).
Probate process and execution: CClR 1392–6, pp. 273–4.

Indenture noting that John Bliklyng, executor of Bishop Brinton, has accounted with John de Cobham, lord of Cobham, for all the goods that the latter has received from the estate of Bishop Brinton, and that he holds 63*s.* 3*d.*, from which he has paid 40*s.* to Thomas Clier' of Fleet Street, London, in part payment (*parpayement*) for the glazing of the windows of Dertford, 1 February 1392. BL Harley Charter 46 E. 24.

William Bottlesham (1389 – d. 1400)
Wills: Will, 16 February 1400, **5/1**, LPL, Register of Thomas Arundel, vol. I, ff. 166v– 167r; deemed to have died intestate because of the scale of his debts, **5/2**.
Executors: Brother Roger Dymmok', STP, Mag. John La*u*nce, rector of Southfleet, Brother William Bozun and Brother John Sayl (**5/1**); goods administered by Mag. John La*u*nce and William Bamburgh' (**5/2**).
Probate process and execution: **5/2–3**.

John Bottlesham (1400 – d. 1404)
Wills: Will, 15 April 1404, **4/1**, LPL, Register of Thomas Arundel, vol. I, ff. 206r–206v.
Executors: Mag. Robert Hallum, Dom. Roger Cherch', rector of Bromley, Mag. Robert Ely, Mag. John Bosham and Mag. John Hoke, clerks, and Robert Rycroft (**4/1**).
Probate process and execution: **4/2**.

ST ASAPH

Following the practices of Welsh law, Bishops of St Asaph did not make wills, until Anian II, who had letters patent from Edward I permitting him to make one.[1] The next two Bishops, Llywelyn de Bromfield and Dafydd ap Bleddyn, obtained letters patent at the start of their episcopates permitting them also to make wills[2] – and Dafydd had those he had received from Edward II confirmed by Edward III shortly after that King obtained full power.[3] When John Trevor I left the greater part of his goods to St Asaph, however, they were seized by officials of Black Prince on the grounds that, by custom, no Welsh bishop might make a will without leave of the Prince of Wales. Trevor's successor, Llywelyn, petitioned the Pope for the return of the goods, and the Pope duly wrote to the Prince to this end.[4]

On the death of a Bishop of St Asaph, fees were due to the Archbishop of Canterbury *sede plena* and to the Prior of Christ Church, Canterbury, *sede vacante*. These typically included the Bishop's palfrey and harness, rain-cloak and hood, along with all seals and his second best ring.[5]

Notes
1 *CFR 1272–1307*, p. 319.
2 *CPR 1292–1301*, p. 97; *CPR 1313–17*, p. 371.
3 *CPR 1327–30*, p. 174.
4 *CPapReg: Petitions*, p. 328.
5 CCA, Register G, f. 23r; BL MS Cotton Galba E IV, f. 25v; **1/3**.

Reiner (1186 – d. 1224)
No documentation traced.

Abraham (1225 – d. 1233)
No documentation traced.

Hugh (1235 – d. 1240)
No documentation traced.

Hywel ab Ednyfed (1240 – d. 1247)
No documentation traced.

Anian I [Einion] (1249 – d. 1266)
No documentation traced.

John II (1267 – d. 1267 × 1268)
No documentation traced.

Anian II (1268 – d. 1293)
Wills: Will, declared 21 February 1289 and confirmed with seal of John Pecham, 19 March 1289, endorsed with probate in the name of Henry de Eastry, Prior of Christ Church, Canterbury, St Mary of Arches, 1 May 1293: CCA, *Sede Vacante* Scrap Book II/187/1, calendared in *Sede vacante wills*, p. 116; also calendared, with some additions, in J. Fisher, 'Three Welsh wills' *Archaeologia Cambrensis* 6th series, 19 (1919) pp. 181–92, at pp. 181–7.
Executors: Griffith, archdeacon of St Asaph, Keneuerth Lloyd, canon of St Asaph, and Brother Adam de Nannew (Fisher, 'Three Welsh wills', p. 187).
Probate process and execution: CFR 1272–1307, p. 319.

Probate granted by Henry de Eastry, Prior of Christ Church, Canterbury, and Mag. J., official of Canterbury, to Dom. Griffin, archdeacon of St Asaph, Keneuerth Lloyd, canon of St Asaph, and Brother Adam de Nanneu. The executors delivered to the Prior two seals of the Bishop and his second best ring, swearing to make a faithful inventory and render account when required. The form of probate was endorsed on the will. St Mary of Arches, London, 1 May 1293. CCA, Register Q, f. 14r.

Llywelyn de Bromfield (1293 – d. 1314)
Licences: CPR 1292–1301, p. 97.
Wills: None surviving.

Dafydd ap Bleddyn (1315 – d. 1346)
Licences: CPR 1313–17, p. 371; *CPR 1327–30*, p. 174.
Wills: None surviving.

John Trevor I (1346 – d. 1357)
Wills: None surviving.
Probate process and execution: CPapReg: Petitions, p. 328. BL Add. MS 25459, ff. 191–2, is a post-medieval copy of a list of his books in the possession of John de Brunham the younger, receiver and administrator of his goods, 31 Edward III (1357–8); transcribed in Cavanaugh, 'Books', pp. 879–81.

Llywelyn ap Madoc ab Ellis (1357 – d. 1375)
Wills: Will, 10 November 1369, with confirmations 4 October 1372, 17 January 1374, and confirmation with additions, 12 October 1375, **23/1**, LPL, Register of Simon Sudbury, ff. 88v–89r; translation in *The Cheshire Sheaf* 28 (1933) pp. 13–14.

Executors: Dom. Gruffuth ap Ieuan [Grath], canon of St Asaph, and Madoc ap Gronw Loyt, executors named in the testament, Dom. Madoc Moel declining to act in this capacity (**23/2**).
Probate process and execution: **23/2–4**.

William Spridlington (1377 – d. 1382)
Wills: Will, 30 June 1381, with notarial confirmation, 6 September 1381, **34/1**, LPL, Register of William Courtenay, ff. 196v–197v. *Willis, St Asaph*, ii, pp. 96–8.
Executors: Dom. Richard de Stokes, Dom. Richard de Spridelyngton', Dom. Roger de Wymondham, Dom. Hugh de Wolaton' and Dom. John Brigg' named (**34/1**); Dom. Richard de Spridlyngton', Dom. Roger de Wymondham and Dom. Hugh de Wolaton act (**34/3**).
Probate process and execution: **34/2–3**.

Lawrence Child (1382 – d. 1389)
Wills: Will, 10 November 1389, **13**, LPL, Register of William Courtenay, f. 232v. *Willis, St Asaph*, ii, pp. 100–1.
Executors: Dom. Thomas Pece and Dom. Richard de Sta*u*ndon', clerks and the Bishop's chaplains (**13**).

Alexander Bache (1390 – d. 1394)
Wills: Will, 13 August 1394, **1/1**, TNA PROB 11/1 (3 Rous), f. 22v. *Willis, St Asaph*, ii, pp. 103–4.
Executors: Mag. John Prophet, 'consanguineum meum', Brother William Syward' and John Graunger, the Bishop's chaplain (**1/1**); probate granted to Graunger (**1/2**).
Probate process and execution: **1/2–3**. *Willis, St Asaph*, ii, pp. 105–6.

John Trevor II (1394 – d. 1410 or later)
No documentation traced. Died abroad (Davies, 'Episcopate', p. ccxc).

ST DAVID'S

Unlike bishops of the sees in North Wales, Bishops of St David's made wills in the early thirteenth century and may have had the capacity to do so earlier. Gerald of Wales remarked on the death of Bishop David FitzGerald in 1176 that he had died intestate – that is, it was expected that he could have made a will – and that the cathedral could not therefore counter the seizure of more than 200 marks by the Crown which the Bishop had kept in a chest among the relics at St David's.[1] Bishop Iorwerth (d. 1229) is the first Bishop who is known to have left a will.[2] Statutes dating from 1259 for the cathedral chapter, issued by Bishop Richard de Carew, confirmed the custom that executors of Bishops of the see and canons of the cathedral might receive from the date of death, for a whole year, the profits of the prebends of the deceased, and that these benefits might be disposed of according to the will of the deceased.[3]

Notes
1 *Giraldi Cambrensis Opera* ed. J.S. Brewer, J.F. Dimock and E.F. Warner (8 vols., RS, 21; 1861–9) iii, pp. 433–4.

2 *Close rolls 1227–31*, p. 146.
3 *St David's episcopal acta 1085–1280* ed. J. Barrow (South Wales Record Society, 13; 1998) pp. 146, 152.

Geoffrey de Henlaw (1203 – d. 1214)
No documentation traced.

Iorwerth [Gervase] (1215 – d. 1229)
Wills: None surviving.
Probate process and execution: Close rolls 1227–31, p. 146.

Anselm le Gras (1230 × 1231 – d. 1247 × 1248)
Wills: None surviving.
Probate process and execution: CFR project, 31/251: TNA C 60/44, mem. 7r; *CFR* project, 31/359: TNA C 60/44, mem. 5r.

Thomas le Waleys (1248 – d. 1255)
No documentation traced.

Richard de Carew (1256 – d. 1280)
Wills: None surviving.
Executors: Mag. Adam, archdeacon of Brecon, and William de Bureht (*CFR 1272–1307*, pp. 133–4).
Probate process and execution: CFR 1272–1307, pp. 133–4; *Pecham register (RS)*, ii, p. 404.

Thomas Bek (1280 – d. 1293)
Wills: None surviving.
Executors: As below.
Probate process and execution: CClR 1288–96, p. 340.

Probate of the will, before Henry de Eastry, Prior of Christ Church, Canterbury, and the official of Canterbury, in St Mary of Arches, London, by Dom. Anthony Bek, Bishop of Durham (the deceased's brother), William, Bishop of Ely, Henry de Lacy, Earl of Lincoln, R. Tybetot, knight, William le Moyne, archdeacon of Carmarthen, and William de Bruere, canon of St David's. The form of probate was endorsed on the will. The executors were granted administration of the will, with the exception of Henry de Lacy, who declined to act, and administration was placed in the hands of the Prior of Llanthony (on behalf of the Bishop of Durham), William le Moyne and William de Bruere. As the Bishop of St David's had many goods in diverse dioceses, the Prior of Christ Church granted the executors his letters patent (copied in the register) confirming the probate. 14 May 1293. CCA, Register Q, ff. 14r–v.

David Martin (1296 – d. 1328)
Wills: None surviving.
Executors: Henry Gower, Bishop of St David's, Mag. David Fraunceys and Walter del Hull (*CClR 1330–3*, p. 168).
Probate process and execution: CIPM, vii, p. 99 (number 113); *CClR 1330–3*, p. 168.

Henry Gower (1328 – d. 1347)
Wills: None surviving.
Executors: Mag. David Ley (LPL, Register of Simon Islip, f. 175r).
Probate process and execution: CIPM, ix, p. 79 (number 77); administration of his will still in progress, 20 June 1361: given as a reason by Mag. David Ley, executor, for refusing to be an executor of the will of his successor, Thomas Fastolf (**14/2**).

Thomas Fastolf (1352 – d. 1361)
Wills: Will, 5 June 1361, **14/1**, LPL, Register of Simon Islip, f. 175r; part printed in *Menevia sacra*, p. 370.
Executors: Mag. David Ley, precentor of St David's, Robert de Grymeston', co–parcener of the church of Dysserth', Philip Dyer', rector of Llanychlwydog (**14/1**); Ley and Dyer refused to act (**14/2**).
Probate process and execution: **14/2–5**.

Adam Houghton (1362 – d. 1389)
Wills: Will, 8 February 1389, **19/1**, LPL, Register of William Courtenay, ff. 231v–232r; printed in *Menevia sacra*, pp. 370–1.
Executors: John Joce, knight (**19/1**), supervised by Dom. John Hyot, canon of St David's, with Dom. Gilbert Nichol, canon of the collegiate church of Abergwili, appointed to assist in the administration (**19/2**).
Probate process and execution: **19/2**.

John Gilbert (1389 – d. 1397)
Wills: Will, 24 November 1393, **16/1**, LPL, Register of Thomas Arundel, vol. I, ff. 160r–v; printed in *Menevia sacra*, pp. 377–8.
Executors: Dom. John Godmaston', canon of St David's, and John Ewias, esquire (**16/1**).
Probate process and execution: **16/2**. *CPR 1396–9*, p. 327; *CClR 1399–1402*, p. 121; *CPapReg 1404–15*, p. 134.

Guy Mone (1397 – d. 1407)
Wills: Will, 17 August 1407, **27**, LPL, Register of Thomas Arundel, vol. I, ff. 246v–247r; printed in *Menevia sacra*, pp. 378–9.
Executors: Drew Barentyne, William Walderne, Henry Pomfreyt, citizen of London, Thomas Rede, 'domicellus' from Wales, Mag. Robert Raulyn, canon of St David's, and William Maydenston', the Bishop's chamberlain (**27**).
Probate process and execution: CPapReg 1404–15, p. 134.

SALISBURY

While arrangements were made for celebrating the anniversary of the death of Bishop Jocelin de Bohun (d. 1184) at some point between 1155 and 1165, providing two daily 'commons' for this purpose,[1] there is no evidence for a Bishop of Salisbury making provision for a will before Richard Poore, who obtained a licence to make one in 1227, before his translation to Durham in 1228.[2] Bishop William of York died at the end of January 1256: after harvest, in September, there was a dispute with the Crown whether the executors might have the winter corn already sown at the Bishop's death, valued at nearly 400 marks, a case that was resolved in the executors' favour.[3] In 1317, Bishop Roger Martival and the Dean and Chapter made a fine with Edward II also for 400 marks to have control of the lands of the bishopric during vacancies, a right extended to their successors, paying the King £1,021 7*s.* 11*d.* a year (and pro rata for lesser or greater periods).[4]

Notes

1 *EEA 18: Salisbury 1078–1217* ed. B.R. Kemp (Oxford, 1999) pp. 94–5, number 125.
2 *CChR 1226–57*, p. 43.
3 *CFR* project, 40/1122: TNA C 60/53, mem. 3r; *Close rolls 1254–6*, p. 367.
4 *CFR 1307–19*, pp. 348–9.

Herbert Poore (1194 – d. 1217)
No documentation traced.

Robert Bingham (1228 – d. 1246)
Wills: None surviving.
Probate process and execution: Close rolls 1242–7, p. 483.

William of York (1246 – d. 1256)
Wills: None surviving.
Executors: William [of Bitton I], Bishop of Bath and Wells, and Fulk Basset, Bishop of London (TNA SC 1/2/145).
Probate process and execution: Close rolls 1254–6, p. 272; *CFR* project, 40/1122: TNA C 60/53, mem. 3r; *Close rolls 1254–6*, p. 367; *CPR 1247–58*, p. 504.

Giles of Bridport (1256 – d. 1262)
Wills: None surviving.
Probate process and execution: CFR project, 47/120: TNA C 60/60, mem. 12r.

Walter de la Wyle (1263 – d. 1271)
Wills: None surviving. He made a will at Sonning on 25 June 1269: *Select cases from the ecclesiastical courts of the province of Canterbury c.1200–1303* ed. N. Adams and C. Donahue (Selden Society, 95; 1981) pp. 151–3.
Executors: Mag. John de Burton, archdeacon of Dorset, and Dom. John de Middleton, succentor of Salisbury (*Select cases from the ecclesiastical courts of the province of Canterbury c.1200–1303*, p. 77).
Probate process and execution: References to his will and the work of executors in law suits in *Select cases from the ecclesiastical courts of the province of Canterbury*, pp. 77–86, 145–53.

Robert Wickhampton (1271 – d. 1284)
Wills: None surviving. Bequest to Nicholas Longespee, later Bishop of Salisbury, noted in Longespee's will: A.R. Malden, 'The will of Nicholas Longespee, Bishop of Salisbury' *English Historical Review* 15 (1900) pp. 523–8, at p. 524.
Probate process and execution: CFR 1272–1307, p. 202; *CPR 1281–92*, p. 237; *CClR 1288–96*, pp. 12, 280; *CClR 1296–1302*, p. 157; *CClR 1302–7*, pp. 149–50 (two).

Walter Scammel (1284 – d. 1286)
No documentation surviving.

Henry Brandeston (1287 – d. 1288)
Wills: None surviving.
Executors: Mag. Ralph le Waleys, precentor of Salisbury, Mag. William de Berges, archdeacon of Berkshire, and others (*CClR 1279–88*, p. 533).
Probate process and execution: CClR 1288–96, pp. 62–3.
Recognisances for debt to the executors or payments acknowledged by them: CClR 1279–88, p. 533 (four).

William de la Corner (1288 – d. 1291)
Wills: None surviving.
Probate process and execution: CClR 1302–7, pp. 265–6, 277; *PRME*, ii, pp. 95, 114, 236, 286–8, 307.

Nicholas Longespee (1291 – d. 1297)
Wills: Will, 14 February 1296, Salisbury Cathedral Library and Archives, Salisbury DCM, printed in Malden, 'Will of Nicholas Longespee', pp. 523–8, and *EEA 37: Salisbury 1263–1297* ed. B.R. Kemp (Oxford, 2010) number 450.
Executors: Mag. Richard de Sottewell, canon of Salisbury, Dom. Stephen de Remmesburia, succentor of Salisbury, Dom. William de Braybrok, rector of Wittenham, John de Herteriggh and William de Barnevile (Malden, 'Will of Nicholas Longespee', p. 526).
Probate process and execution: The will is endorsed with the grant of probate, 29 May 1297 (Malden, 'Will of Nicholas Longespee', pp. 527–8); *Winchelsey register*, i, p. 169; ii, pp. 1069–70.

Simon of Ghent (1297 – d. 1315)
Wills: None surviving.
Probate process and execution: CClR 1313–18, p. 250.

Roger Martival (1315 – d. 1330)
Wills: None surviving. Bequests of books and ornaments to the cathedral are recited in an indenture between Bishop Robert Wyvil and the chapter, 2 July 1330: HMC, *Report on various collections*, i, p. 355, Salisbury Cathedral Library and Archives, DCM Salisbury, Press 3; further bequests noted in Cavanaugh, 'Books', pp. 573–4.
Executors: Mag. Richard de Stretton, Mag. Thomas de Bocton, Mag. William de Lubbenham, Mag. Robert de Worth, Hugh de Knossyngton and John de Wynterburn (*CClR 1330–3*, p. 165).
Probate process and execution: HMC, *Report on various collections*, i, p. 355; *CClR 1330–3*, p. 165; **24**.

Robert Wyvil (1330 – d. 1375)
Wills: None surviving. Although he made a will and named executors, they declined to administer the will and he was pronounced intestate.
Executors: Administrators, as noted below.
Probate process and execution: Commission for the administration of his goods to Dom. John Stone and Dom. Nicholas Loswyk', chaplains, John Paier and Richard Swetyngg', 26 September 1375. LPL, Register of Simon Sudbury, f. 79v.

Acquittance to the administrators of the goods, Philip FitzWaryn, knight, and Dom. William David, clerk, and other administrators, given at Lambeth, 29 June 1376. LPL, Register of Simon Sudbury, f. 91v.

Other grants and gifts: Cavanaugh, 'Books', pp. 943–4.

John Waltham (1388 – d. 1395)
Wills: Will, 2 September 1395, **44/1**, TNA PROB 11/1 (5 Rous), ff. 32r–33r.
Executors: Dom. William Lescrop, knight; Dom. Roger Walden', Mag. Radulph Selby, Mag. William Waltham, Mag. Richard Holm, Dom. George Louthorp', Dom. Thomas Haxey, Mag. Richard Pittes, canons of Salisbury; William Holym and William Dyones, chaplains; and John Gowayn, 'domicellus' (**44/1**).
Probate process and execution: F.L. Harrison *Music in medieval Britain* (London, 1958) pp. 83–4 refers to an item in Salisbury DCM, a decree of Archbishop William Courtenay, relating to the will of John Waltham, about paying choristers to sing a Marian antiphon each day; discussed in N. Morgan, 'Marian liturgy in Salisbury cathedral' in *The medieval English cathedral: papers in honour of Pamela Tudor-Craig. Proceedings of the 1998 Harlaxton symposium* (Donington, 2003) pp. 89–111, at p. 104.
Other grants and gifts: agreement, 15 July 1412, between the Abbot and convent of Westminster, and the executors, for the celebration of the Bishop's obit annually on the day of his death, 18 September, or within seven days before, the Bishop's body having been buried in the Abbey; enrolled on the close roll, 17 February 1413, *CClR 1409–13*, pp. 418–19.

Richard Mitford (1395 – d. 1407)
Wills: Will, 29 April 1407, **26/1**, LPL, Register of Thomas Arundel, vol. I, ff. 237v–238v; translated in D. Martin, 'Hospitality and household: Bishop Metford's household accounts October 1406 – June 1407' (unpublished MA thesis, Macquarie University, 2002) pp. 129–32.
Executors: Mag. Walter Medeford', his brother, Dom. George Louthorp, Mag. Roger Harewell', and Dom. Thomas Wysbech', canons of Salisbury, Laurence Drewe and John Wylmyndon' (**26/1**).
Probate process and execution: **26/2–5**.

WINCHESTER

Although we do not have separate wills for them, Bishops William Giffard (d. 1129), Henry of Blois (d. 1171) and Godfrey de Lucy (d. 1204) appear to have made grants either in the last year of life or very close to death in favour of St Swithun's Cathedral Priory.[1] The first Bishop for whom there is unambiguous evidence for a will – in fact, for a succession of them – is Peter des Roches, who had licences to make a will in 1221 and 1227,[2] and whose will of 1236, made at Rochester in the presence of the executors, was confirmed by the Crown.[3] Des Roches bequeathed stock to the bishopric, and this was regarded as constituting an endowment to be passed to the incoming bishop.[4] The executors delivered this stock to the keepers of the see by chirograph, and were instructed by the King to deliver it to the incoming bishop, William Raleigh, on 10 September 1244, some six years after Des Roches' death.[5] In 1250, Raleigh's executors in turn handed on the stock. They obtained from the Crown freedom to dispose of the Bishop's goods, excluding the stock destined for the incoming bishop by ordinance of Peter des Roches, but including all salt and utensils not bound to the land, and in addition by the King's special grace all hay from that year's harvest as well as that from previous years which was in hand on the eve of the Bishop's death on 1 September.[6] In 1331, Bishop John Stratford, consecrated as Bishop of Winchester in 1323, was still struggling to resolve the position with regard to the stock following the death of his predecessor but one, John de Sandale, in 1319. Stratford petitioned the Crown in 1331, stating that the King had taken in hand cattle to the value of more than £550, and that there was a custom at Winchester that every Bishop, on his death, passed to his successor 127 plough beasts, 1,556 oxen, 4,495 wethers, 4,358 ewes and 2,697 hoggets, which were known as the *implementum* of the church.[7]

Notes

1 Giffard: *EEA 8: Winchester 1070–1204* ed. M.J. Franklin (Oxford, 1993) pp. 12–14, numbers 20–1 (number 20 possibly in part a forgery); Henry of Blois: *EEA 8: Winchester 1070–1204*, pp. 93–7, numbers 131–2; *Chartulary of Winchester Cathedral* ed. A.W. Goodman (Winchester, 1927) p. 12, number 26; Godfrey de Lucy, below.

2 *CPR 1215–25*, p. 286; *CChR 1226–57*, p. 42.

3 *CPR 1232–47*, p. 166.

4 *Close rolls 1237–42*, pp. 62–3; *CFR 1234–42*, pp. 241 (22/36), 242 (22/40–1).

5 *CFR* project, 28/441: TNA C 60/41, mem. 2r.

6 *CFR* project, 35/162: TNA C 60/48, mem. 20r.

7 *CPR 1330–4*, pp. 230–1.

Godfrey de Lucy (1189 – d. 1204)

Wills: None surviving.

Other grants and gifts: Two acta in favour of St Swithun's, Winchester, both dated 25 August 1204, shortly before his death: *EEA 8: Winchester 1070–1204*, pp. 198–9, numbers 254–5; and a confirmation to Geoffrey de Lucy, on the date of the Bishop's death, 11 September 1204, of a manor held by the Bishop: *RC*, p. 137.

Peter des Roches (1205 – d. 1238)

Licences and confirmations: CPR 1215–25, p. 286; *CChR 1226–57*, p. 42; *CPR 1232–47*, p. 166.

Wills: EEA 9: Winchester 1205–1238 ed. N. Vincent (Oxford, 1994) prints on pp. 34–5, as numbers *42, *42A and *43, evidence for three wills, of April 1221, June 1227 and 1236, although in none of these instances does the will itself survive.

Executors: Luke, called 'Diuti', canon of Salisbury (*CPapReg 1198–1304*, p. 260).

Probate process and execution: CFR 1234–42, pp. 241 (22/36), 242 (22/40–1); *Close rolls 1237–42*, pp. 62–3 (five), 79; *CPR 1232–47*, p. 231; *Close rolls 1237–42*, p. 105; *CPR 1232–47*, p. 423; *CFR* project, 28/441–2: TNA C 60/41, mem. 2r; *CPapReg 1198–1304*, p. 260.

William Raleigh (1242 – d. 1250)

Wills: None surviving. Bequest of 100 marks to Shaftesbury Abbey noted in *CFR* project, 35/162: TNA C 60/48, mem. 20r.

Probate process and execution: Close rolls 1247–51, pp. 327, 329–30 (two); *CFR* project, 35/162: TNA C 60/48, mem. 20r; *Close rolls 1251–3*, p. 146.

Aymer de Valence (1250 – d. 1260)
Wills: None surviving.
Executors: Mag. Peter de sancto Mario and others (*Close rolls 1261–4*, pp. 154–5).
Probate process and execution: CPR 1258–66, p. 215; *CPR 1266–72*, p. 732; *Close rolls 1261–4*, pp. 154–5; *CPapReg 1198–1304*, pp. 380, 392; *CPR 1272–81*, p. 88.

John Gervais (1262 – d. 1268)
Wills: None surviving.
Executors: William Gervays, Guido de Mulbrok, Adam de Ilegh, William de Wyntreshull', Walter de la Croce, Thomas de Wynton (*Registrum … Pontissara*, ii, pp. 727–34).
Probate process and execution: CIPM, i, p. 222 (number 702); *Registrum … Pontissara*, ii, pp. 727–34.
Other grants and gifts: On his deathbed, surrendered to the monks of Winchester his right to nominate their Prior: *Chartulary of Winchester Cathedral*, pp. 10–11, number 23.

Nicholas of Ely (1268 – d. 1280)
Wills: None surviving. Bequests to Worcester Cathedral Priory of 30 marks for a pittance and of a bible, as well as 50 marks which the Bishop had already given; 60 marks were received by the sacrist of Worcester for rebuilding the tower of the Cathedral Priory: *Annales monastici* ed. H.R. Luard (5 vols., RS, 36; 1864–9) iv, p. 480. Durham Cathedral Priory received a bible: *Catalogi veteres librorum ecclesiae cathedralis Dunelm* … ed. B. Botfield (Surtees Society, 7; 1838) p. 127.
Executors: Ralph de Staunford and others (*CClR 1279–88*, p. 152); Mag. Hugh Tripacy (*CClR 1296–1302*, p. 274); Willelmus de Combe and Radulfus de Stamford (*Registrum … Pontissara*, ii, pp. 733).
Probate process and execution: Pecham register (RS), i, pp. 118–19; *Registrum … Pontissara*, ii, pp. 718–19; *CClR 1279–88*, p. 152 (two); *Registrum … Pontissara*, i, pp. 263–4; *CClR 1279–88*, p. 263; *Registrum … Pontissara*, ii, pp. 727–34; *CClR 1296–1302*, pp. 54, 274.
Other grants and gifts: Charter establishing a chantry for the Bishop at Waverley Abbey, *Registrum … Woodlock*, i, pp. 470–1.

John of Pontoise (1282 – d. 1304)
Licences: Licencia testandi to John of Pontoise as a papal chaplain, *CPapReg 1198–1304*, p. 463.
Wills: None surviving.
Executors: Hugh le Despenser, Robert de Harewedon, Simon de Farham, William de Staunford, Walter de Preston and Henry de Lyscret (*CClR 1307–13*, p. 374); Mag. James de Florencia, archdeacon of Winchester, Mag. Philip de Barton, archdeacon of Surrey, Michael de Huleston, rector of Meonstoke, William de Staunford, rector of West Meon, and Henry de Lyskeret, rector of Wydehaye (*CPR 1317–21*, p. 269).
Probate process and execution: J.H. Denton, 'Complaints to the apostolic see in an early fourteenth-century memorandum' *Archivum Historiae Pontificiae* 20 (1982) pp. 389–402; *Registrum … Woodlock*, i, pp. 12–13, 387; ii, 902, 906, 908–9, 912–14, 917, 920, 924–5; *PRME*, ii, pp. 77, 95, 225–6, 295–6; *The register of William de Geynesburgh, Bishop of Worcester, 1302–1307* ed. J.W. Willis Bund, with an introduc-

tion by R.A. Wilson (Worcestershire Historical Society, 22; 1907–29) pp. 15–16; *CClR 1307–13*, p. 374 (four); *CPR 1317–21*, p. 269; *CPapReg 1305–42*, pp. 190, 425, 446.

Memorandum of a royal writ addressed to the Abbot of St Augustine's, Canterbury, instructing him to deliver four chests, containing jewels and other items, and sealed by the executors of John of Pontoise, to the treasurer and barons of the Exchequer on 30 September, in order that the executors might satisfy their debts to the Crown, given at Waverley, 22 July 1306; with a memorandum that John de Intebergh, clerk, delivered the chests on 30 September 1306 in the presence of John de Drokenesford, lieutenant of the treasurer and the barons, and that they were found to contain silver vessels and diverse jewels ('vasa argentea et diversa jocalia') but no cash; the goods were then replaced in the chests and delivered to Robert de Harewedon' and Michael de Hellestone, executors of the Bishop, in order to satisfy their debts to the Crown, and the Abbot of St Augustine's was held quit of them. BL MS Cotton Julius D II, f. 206v.

Memorandum of a bond ('littera obligatoria') for £100 from Mag. James de Florence, executor of the will of John of Pontoise, and his co-executors, on the instructions of the [Archbishop of Canterbury], brought by Mag. R. de Norton', to be repaid at Easter following. Lambeth, 6 November 1317. LPL, Register of Walter Reynolds, f. 284r.

Letters of Walter Reynolds, Archbishop of Canterbury, binding him to the executors of John of Pontoise, late Bishop of Winchester, in the sum of £1,200 loaned from the goods of the estate, with letters to the executors of Henry Woodlock, and a memorandum about the bonds. 23 July 1326. LPL, Register of Walter Reynolds, f. 278r.

Other grants and gifts: Cavanaugh, 'Books', pp. 660–1.

Henry Woodlock (1305 – d. 1316)
Wills: None surviving.
Executors: Mag. Richard de Wodelok (*CPR 1317–21*, p. 527).
Probate process and execution: CPR 1317–21, p. 527.

Letters of Walter Reynolds, Archbishop of Canterbury, noting that he has received from the executors of Henry, late Bishop of Winchester, the sum of £1,200 in cash and other goods. Bishop Henry had been bound in this sum to John of Pontoise, his immediate predecessor, by way of a loan. Given at St Ives, 23 July 1326. LPL, Register of Walter Reynolds, f. 278r.

Letters of Walter Reynolds, Archbishop of Canterbury, noting that he has received from the executors of Henry, late Bishop of Winchester, the sum of £300 in cash and other goods. Bishop Henry had been bound in this sum to the serjeant cook of the Pope. [23 July 1326] LPL, Register of Walter Reynolds, f. 278r.

John de Sandale (1316 – d. 1319)
Licences and indemnities: CPR 1313–17, p. 112.

Wills: None surviving.
Executors: John de Cokermuth and John de Heyden (*CClR 1318–23*, p. 294).
Probate process and execution: CIPM, vi, p. 130 (number 125); *CClR 1318–23*, p. 107; *CFR 1319–27*, pp. 9, 12–13; *CPR 1317–21*, p. 412; *CClR 1318–23*, p. 294; *CClR 1323–7*, p. 52; *CClR 1330–3*, pp. 475–6; *CClR 1333–7*, pp. 49–50; *CPR 1334–8*, p. 412.

The registers of John de Sandale and Rigaud de Asserio, Bishops of Winchester (A.D. 1316–1323) ed. F.J. Baigent (Hampshire Record Society, 8; 1897) prints from Exchequer records extracts from the account for his household after his death (TNA E 101/506/24) on pp. 620–4; and on pp. 624–6, payments to household members. Baigent also printed two documents now bound into the register of Henry Woodlock (Hampshire RO 21M65/A1/2), the first (ff. 8*–13*, printed on pp. 234–53) listing the stock on the episcopal manors in Hampshire and Surrey at John de Sandale's death, crops sown, wood sales, defects of buildings, noting sales and transactions by the executors, as far as the delivery of the temporalities to Rigaud of Assier, with notes of crops sown on the manors of Harwell, Brightwell and Witney; and the second (ff. 14*–15*, printed on pp. 254–64), from June to July 1320, memoranda of the delivery of the livestock on each of the manors to the reeves by the agent of Rigaud of Assier.

Inventory and valuation of the goods of John de Sandale, Bishop of Winchester, made before Adam de Lymbergh' and Richard de Pottesgrave, 2 November 1319, delivered to the Exchequer 24 April 1322: **32**, BL Add. MS 57334.

Royal writ against John de Cockermouth, executor of the will of John de Sandale, requiring him to answer Mag. Thomas de St Alban's in a plea that he return £200 that he, along with John de Sandale, canon of the church of the BVM of Southwell, and John de Heydon unjustly withhold. The sheriff of Hampshire has returned that John de Cockermouth has no lay fee. Given at Westminster, 30 June 1321. Note of the Archbishop's return: that John de Cockermouth has no ecclesiastical benefice in his diocese by which he could compel him to appear. LPL, Register of Walter Reynolds, f. 299v.

Royal writ, noting that as John de Cockermouth and John de Heydon, executors of the will of John de Sandale, have found sufficient surety at the Exchequer for paying all debts of the deceased to the Crown, the King has permitted them to have the administration of all the goods and chattels of the deceased; and the Archbishop is not to allow any prosecution by R[igaud, Bishop of Winchester], before him to impede any settlement between the executors and the Crown. Given at Westminster, 28 July 1322. LPL, Register of Walter Reynolds, f. 299v.

Royal writ requiring the Archbishop of Canterbury not to hear cases against John de Cockermouth and John de Heydon, executors of the will of John de Sandale, brought at the instance of R[igaud, Bishop of Winchester], while the executors remain to account at the Exchequer for debts of the deceased from the time he was chamberlain of Scotland and from other points when he was in royal service. Given at Westminster, 20 October 1322. LPL, Register of Walter Reynolds, f. 300v.

Rigaud of Assier (1319 – d. 1323)
No documentation traced.

Adam Orleton (1333 – d. 1345)
Wills: None surviving.
Executors: Mag. Thomas de Trillek, Sire Rogier de Breyntone, Sire Walter Carles, canons of Hereford; Mag. Johan de Usk and Mag. Nichol de Kaerwent, parsons of Burghclere and Colesbourne (*Registrum Johannis de Trillek, episcopi Herefordensis, A.D. MCCCXLIV – MCCCLXI* ed. J.H. Parry (CYS, 8; 1912) p. 133).
Probate process and execution: Registrum … Trillek, p. 55; *CPR 1343–5*, p. 538; *Registrum … Trillek*, p. 77; *CClR, 1346–9*, p. 122; *CPR 1345–8*, p. 291; *Registrum … Trillek*, pp. 23–4, 73–5, 130, 133–5.

Memorandum relating to a claim brought by Roger de Breynton, canon of Hereford, against Thomas Trillek and Walter Calres, executors of the will of Adam, late Bishop of Winchester, about a claim for £500 unjustly withheld causing a loss of £1,000; the executors cannot contradict the bonds for the £500 which are adjudicated to Roger, who settles for the value of the bonds, *c.*1345. HCA 1378.

Other grants and gifts: Bishop Edendon's chantry at Edington also commemorates Adam Orleton, *CPapReg 1342–62*, p. 539. Cavanaugh, 'Books', pp. 628–9.

William Edendon (1345 – d. 1366)
Wills: Will, 11 September 1366, LPL, Register of Simon Langham, ff. 110–11, printed in *Registrum Simonis Langham, Cantuariensis archiepiscopi* ed. A.C. Wood (CYS, 53; 1956) pp. 318–25; probate copy of the will: CCA, *Sede Vacante* Scrap Book c. 24, 1366, listed in HMC, *Appendix to the Fifth Report*, p. 460.
Executors: Dom. Nicholas Kaerwent, rector of Crondall, Dom. John de Bleoberi, rector of Witney, Thomas Hungreford, the Bishop's steward, Mag. Walter de Sevenhampton, rector of Alresford, and Mag. John Corf, rector of Collingbourne Abbots (*Registrum Simonis Langham*, p. 323)
Probate process and execution: Registrum Simonis Langham, pp. 324–5; *CClR 1349–54*, pp. 362, 517; *CClR 1364–9*, p. 270; *CPR 1370–4*, p. 439; 'Dies obituales archiepiscoporum Cantuariensium', *Anglia sacra*, i, pp. 52–64, at p. 61.

Probate of the will by the Prior of Christ Church, Canterbury, granted to Dom. Nicholas ….., Mag. John de Corfe, Thomas de Hungerford and Mag. John Beautr'; with notarial attestation of the will, fifth year of Pope Urban V, in the presence of Dom. Richard … …cler', John de Fairford, rector of Dupeden', Winchester diocese, John de …, 1366. CCA, Register G, f. 138r.

Agreement between the executors of William Edendon and Bishop William of Wykeham, Burghclere, 6 February 1372; printed in *Wykeham's register* ed. T.F. Kirby (2 vols., Hampshire Record Society, 11, 13; 1896–9) ii, pp. 151–6; formal recognition of the indenture before the Archbishop of Canterbury, 29 April 1372, LPL, Register of William Whittlesey, ff. 52v–53r.

William of Wykeham (1366 – d. 1404)
Wills: Will, 24 July 1403, with list of names, with plate and cash allocated to each

(said to be on an annexed roll), a codicil of 10 January 1404, printed in R. Lowth *Life of William of Wykeham* (2nd edition, London, 1759) pp. xxxiv–liv, from LPL, Register of Thomas Arundel, vol. I, ff. 215–18, collated with Winchester College Muniments (WCM) 22992, Liber albus or Vetus registrum, ff. 151–4v. The *Life* is reprinted in *Robert Lowth (1710–1787): the major works* ed. D.A. Reibel (8 vols., London, 1995) ii. A translation is printed in *Testamenta vetusta*, ii, pp. 763–76. Other copies of the will are: BL MS Cotton Titus A XXIV, ff. 5r–10v, possibly late fifteenth or early sixteenth century, but not including the annexed roll, and followed by a metrical life of Wykeham in Latin, ff. 11r–14r; WCM 1472, a sixteenth-century copy of the Winchester College statutes with the will; WCM 21482, an eighteenth-century[?] copy of the will 'copied from that which is at the end of the old statute book in the outward chapel' (now Winchester College, Fellows' Library MS 55); abstract of the will: BL Add. MS 5538, p. 19.
Executors: Robert, Bishop of London, Mag. Nicholas Wykeham, Mag. John Elemere, Mag. John Campeden, Thomas Chelrey, steward of the lands of the bishopric, Thomas Wykeham, 'consanguineus' and heir, and Dom. Thomas Ayleward, rector of Havant (Lowth, *Life of William of Wykeham*, p. xlv).
Probate process and execution: CIPM, xviii, pp. 411–12 (numbers 1192–3); grant of probate and commission to commit the administration of the will, 9 October 1404, LPL, Register of Thomas Arundel, vol. I, f. 218, printed in Lowth, *Life of William of Wykeham*, pp. liii–liv.

Acquittance by Archbishop Thomas Arundel of Mag. Nicholas Wykeham, Mag. John Elmere, Mag. John Campeden, Thomas Chelrey, Thomas Wykeham and Dom. Thomas Ayleward, rector of Havant, as executors of Wykeham's will, Lambeth 23 October 1405. LPL, Register of Thomas Arundel, vol. I, f. 225v.

Other grants and gifts: An undated, but fifteenth-century, inventory of jewels given by William of Wykeham and other, unnamed, benefactors to Winchester College. WCM 21856.

WORCESTER

Aside from a bequest ('legavit') of a cope by Bishop Wulfstan (d. 1095) to Robert the Lotharingian, Bishop of Hereford, recorded by Bartholomew Cotton,[1] the earliest evidence for testamentary dispositions by post-Conquest Bishops of Worcester is for William de Blois.[2] On 20 August 1236, two days after the Bishop's death, Henry III granted the executors free administration of his goods,[3] but about a fortnight later he became suspicious that the Bishop had in fact died intestate. The Bishop of Coventry and Lichfield, along with his fellow executors, was summoned to meet the King in Yorkshire to discuss the case with him, his council, the Archbishop of York and the Bishop of Durham.[4] Agreement must have been reached by 20 September, at which point the keepers of the bishopric were ordered to let the executors have all the corn and stock on the manors, including stock and hay from the previous year, along with hay bought by the Bishop in the present year, but excluding the hay of the demesnes and the produce of demesne gardens of the present year.[5]

In the late thirteenth and early fourteenth century, Bishops of the see received ecclesiastical goods from the Cathedral Priory, to be returned at the close of their episcopate.[6]

Notes

1 Bartholomew Cotton, 'Liber de archiepiscopis et episcopis Angliae' in *Bartholomaei de Cotton monachi Norwicensis Historia Anglicana (A.D. 449–1298) necnon ejusdem Liber de archiepiscopis et episcopis Angliae* ed. H.R. Luard (RS, 16; 1859) p. 407.

2 There are three acta of Bishop Simon, purportedly made on his deathbed in 1150, in favour of Worcester Cathedral Priory, about the church of St Mary-le-Strand, London, which survive in mid-thirteenth-century copies – and which may well be forgeries: *EEA 33: Worcester 1062–1185* ed. M. Cheney, D. Smith, C. Brooke and P.M. Hoskin (Oxford, 2007) pp. xlii–xliv, 78–80, numbers 111–13.

3 *CFR 1234–42*, p. 174 (20/460).

4 *CFR 1234–42*, p. 181 (20/500).

5 *Close rolls 1234–7*, p. 313.

6 *The 'Liber albus' of the priory of Worcester* ed. J.M. Wilson (Worcestershire Historical Society, 35; 1919) p. 40, number 604; p. 68, numbers 860–1; p. 73, numbers 952–3.

Mauger (1199 – d. 1212)
No documentation traced.

Sylvester (1216 – d. 1218)
No documentation traced.

William de Blois (1218 – d. 1236)
Wills: None surviving.
Executors: Alexander Stavensby, Bishop of Coventry and Lichfield, and others (*CFR 1234–42*, p. 174 (20/460)).
Probate process and execution: CFR 1234–42, p. 174 (20/460); *CFR 1234–42*, p. 181 (20/500); *Close rolls 1234–7*, p. 313.
Other grants and gifts: EEA 13: Worcester, 1218–1268 ed. P.M. Hoskin (Oxford, 1997) pp. 25–6, number 35, is a grant probably of 1235 in favour of Worcester Cathedral Priory providing for a payment of 1 mark annually for a pittance on the Bishop's anniversary.

Walter Cantilupe (1236 – d. 1266)
Licences: CPR 1247–58, p. 398.
Wills: None surviving.
Executors: Mag. Thomas de Cantilupo and others (*CPR 1258–66*, p. 596); Walter Giffard, Archbishop of York, declined to act (*The register of Walter Giffard, Lord Archbishop of York 1266–1279* ed. W. Brown (Surtees Society, 109; 1904) pp. 178–9, number 164).
Probate process and execution: CPR 1258–66, p. 596; *Close rolls 1264–8*, p. 238; *CPR 1258–66*, p. 570; *Register of Walter Giffard*, pp. 178–9, number 164; *CClR 1279–88*, pp. 43–4.
Other grants and gifts: Thomas Cantilupe (later Bishop of Hereford), possessed a hair garment that had belonged to his uncle, who was reputed for his sanctity: C.M. Woolgar *The senses in late medieval England* (2006) p. 197, n. 66, citing Biblioteca Apostolica Vaticana MS Vat. Lat. 4015, f. 107v.

Godfrey Giffard (1268 – d. 1302)
Wills: Will, 13 September 1301, Worcestershire RO, Register of Bishop William

Gainsborough, ff. 17–18, printed in *The register of William de Geynesburgh, Bishop of Worcester, 1302–1307* ed. J.W. Willis Bund with an introduction by R.A. Wilson (Worcestershire Historical Society, 22; 1907–29) pp. 48–54, with translation on pp. 54–60; Cavanaugh, 'Books', pp. 360–1.
Executors: Dom. Walter de Berton, rector of Bredon, Mag. John de Rodgeberge, rector of Hartilbury, Dom. Bartholomew de Devyses, John de Staneway, rector of Ripple, and Geoffrey de Hembury (*Register of William de Geynesburgh*, p. 54); they may, initially, have refused to act: *The 'Liber albus'*, p. 7, number 84.
Probate process and execution: CIPM, iv, pp. 66–7 (number 101); *The 'Liber albus'*, p. 7, number 84; *CClR 1296–1302*, pp. 523, 608; *Register of William de Geynesburgh*, p. 44; *CClR 1302–7*, p. 321; *CPR 1301–7*, p. 343; *CClR 1302–7*, pp. 267–8; *The 'Liber albus'*, p. 23, numbers 369–72, p. 27, number 421.

William Gainsborough (1302 – d. 1307)
Wills: None surviving.
Executors: Mag. Benedict de Fereby and John de Geynesbergh' (*Winchelsey register*, ii, p. 1239).
Probate process and execution: Winchelsey register, ii, pp. 1239–40.

Walter Maidstone (1313 – d. 1317)
No documentation traced.

Thomas Cobham (1317 – d. 1327)
Wills: The register of Thomas de Cobham, Bishop of Worcester, 1317–1327 ed. E.H. Pearce (Worcestershire Historical Society, 40; 1930) pp. vi, 49–50, prints extracts from his testament relating to Worcester Cathedral and the Bishop's successors. They are on a larger piece of parchment that is now bound up with the register, which contains on the other side documents of 1324–5 relating to Robert de Somery's chantry at Bishampton.
Executors: Thomas de Hevere (*CClR 1327–30*, p. 191).
Probate process and execution: CClR 1327–30, p. 191; *CClR 1330–3*, p. 193; *CPR 1338–40*, p. 509.

Letters of the Archbishop of Canterbury to Mag. Robert de Valoignes and Mag. Nicholas de Gore, rectors of the churches of Northfleet and Stistede, instructing them to commit the administration of the will of Thomas, Bishop of Worcester, which has been proved before the Archbishop, to the executors, admitting them on oath, and requiring them to bring an inventory of the deceased's goods to the Archbishop in Canterbury before Easter next. Robert and Nicholas are to certify to the Archbishop by letters patent that the executors have been admitted to their administration. Given at Oftord, 23 September 1327. LPL, Register of Walter Reynolds, f. 206v.

Other grants and gifts: Oriel College records ed. C.L. Shadwell and H.E. Salter (Oxford Historical Society, 85; 1926) pp. 24–7, prints a memorandum about the construction by Cobham of a building for the congregations and councils of the University of Oxford, the execution of his will and bequests; Cavanaugh, 'Books', pp. 201–2.

Thomas Hempnall (1337 – d. 1338)
No documentation traced.

Wulstan Bransford (1339 – d. 1349)
Wills: None surviving.
Executors: As below.
Probate process and execution: CFR 1368–77, pp. 161–2.

Probate, granted by Robert, Prior of Christ Church, Canterbury, and the chapter, committing the administration to Thomas atte Mulne, Richard de Bromwych' and John de Wych', executors named in the will, reserving the power of committing the administration to the Prior of Worcester, Hugh de Cokesey, Walter de Shakemherst, Peter de Cruce[?], John de Selverley, archdeacon of Worcester, Dom. William de Sallewarp', Mag. Hugh de Penebregg' and Mag. Henry de Niwebolt', other executors in the will, 7 September 1349. CCA, Register G, f. 72v.

Reginald Brian (1352 – d. 1361)
No documentation traced.

William Lenn (1368 – d. 1373)
Wills: Will, 29 December 1363, **22/1**, LPL, Register of William Whittlesey, ff. 128v–129r, made while Bishop of Chichester.
Executors: Thomas de Lexham, rector of St Mary, Feltwell, diocese of Norwich, Dom. William de Thufford', Thomas le Hunte, Roger Schire, and Robert Wyk' (**22/1**); Mag. Thomas Lexham, Mag. William Thirford, archdeacon of Gloucester, Mag. Robert Wyk' and Adam Feurother (**22/4**).
Probate process and execution: **22/2–5**; *CIPM*, xiii, p. 272 (number 308).

Henry Wakefield (1375 – d. 1395)
Wills: Will, 10 March 1395, TNA PROB 11/1 (4 Rous), f. 26r, printed in *A calendar of the register of Henry Wakefield, Bishop of Worcester, 1375–95* ed. W.P. Marett (Worcestershire Historical Society, new series, 7; 1972) pp. xliv–xlvi; abstract in *Wills and inventories*, i, pp. 248–9.
Executors: Mag. Robert de la More, the Bishop's official, Dom. John Besford, Richard Thurgrym, Thomas Hodynton, Thomas Throgmarton, and John Newman (*Register of Henry Wakefield*, p. xlv).
Probate process and execution: Commission for probate, 14 March 1395, probate, 27 March 1395, and acquittance of the executors, 25 June 1396: TNA PROB 11/1 (4 Rous), ff. 25v, 26r, 36v; probate, *Register of Henry Wakefield*, pp. xlv–xlvi.

Letter from the Abbot of Gloucester to the Archbishop of Canterbury: he has received the Archbishop's letter of 14 March 1395 authorising him to prove the will of Henry, Bishop of Worcester. He has proved the will and committed its execution to Mag. Robert de la More, John Besford, Richard Thyngrynne, Thomas Hadynton and John Newman. A true copy of the will is sent. 27 March 1395. TNA PROB 11/1 (4 Rous), f. 25v.

Tideman of Winchcombe (1395 – d. 1401)
Wills: None surviving: died intestate and heavily in debt.
Probate process and execution: **39/1–3**.

YORK

Archbishop Roger de Pont l'Évêque obtained a ruling from Pope Alexander III which appropriated to his use those goods which clerics, who had made a will *in extremis*, failed to distribute by their own hands before death. Ralph de Diceto noted with some satisfaction that the Archbishop himself died in exactly this position, and that on his death in 1181 £11,000 in old, silver coin, and £300 in gold, as well as silver vessels, were confiscated by the Crown.[1] The first Archbishop for whom there is evidence that he made a will is Walter de Gray, who had a royal licence in 1245 to this end and whose executors were granted free administration of his goods in 1255.[2] While in some sees the estate of a bishop encompassed rents as well as the profits of the lands up to the Michaelmas after the death of the bishop, this may not have been the case at York. Archbishop Sewal de Bovill died on Friday 10 May 1258, two days before Whitsun. His executors then claimed the rents due at Whitsun as he was not buried before the following Wednesday. The keepers of the see were instructed on 29 May to allow these rents to the executors, pending a discussion with the King whether they should belong to the estate or to the Crown. The outcome is not known, but the fact that the assumption was challenged is of interest.[3] Arrangements for the stock of the see to be passed to each succeeding Archbishop were set out by William Wickwane in 1283, and were confirmed by Edward I. Wickwane set the complement at about 600 oxen and 54 horses, for agriculture, that is, for ploughs, carts, and so on; and 1,000 sheep (possibly 1,200), made up equally of wethers and ewes. The King was to have the use of the stock and implements during vacancies and the keepers of the see were to undertake on oath to pass them to the new Archbishop when he received the temporalities.[4] Richard II confirmed to Archbishop Richard le Scrope in 1398 as part of the complement sums of money owed to Archbishops Thomas Arundel and Alexander Neville, which were granted to Robert Waldby as part of the complement.[5]

An inventory of the jewels, plate, vestments and other goods of York Minster, *c.*1510, includes items, principally liturgical goods, that had belonged to Walter de Gray, Walter Giffard, John Thoresby, Alexander Neville, Thomas Arundel, and Richard le Scrope.[6]

Notes

1 'Ymagines historiarum', in *Radulfi de Diceto decani Lundoniensis Opera historica* ed. W. Stubbs (2 vols., RS, 68; 1876) ii, p. 12.

2 *CPR 1232–47*, p. 454; *Close rolls 1254–6*, p. 74.

3 *Close rolls 1256–9*, p. 225.

4 *CChR 1257–1300*, pp. 268–9. The executors of Archbishop Newark were bound for sums relating to the 'complementum' in 1311, just as the Archbishop had been: *Greenfield register*, i, p. 135, number 302. In 1316, Archbishop Greenfield's executors were granted free administration of his goods, excepting corn bought by the King from them and the oxen, plough animals and livestock, which passed by custom to the Archbishop's successor: *CPR 1313–17*, p. 382.

5 *CPR 1396–9*, p. 377.

6 *The fabric rolls of York Minster, with an appendix of illustrative documents* ed. J. Raine the younger (Surtees Society, 35; 1859) pp. 212–35.

Geoffrey (1189 – d. 1212)

No documentation traced.

Walter de Gray (1216 – d. 1255)
Licences: CPR 1232–47, p. 454.
Wills: None surviving; 350 marks bequeathed to the King, *CPR 1247–58*, p. 409.
Probate process and execution: Close rolls 1254–6, p. 74 (two); *CPR 1247–58*, p. 409.

Sewal de Bovill (1255 – d. 1258)
Wills: None surviving.
Probate process and execution: Close rolls 1256–9, p. 225 (two), 250.

Godfrey Ludham (1258 – d. 1265)
Wills: None surviving.
Probate process and execution: The register of Walter Giffard, Lord Archbishop of York 1266–1279 ed. W. Brown (Surtees Society, 109; 1904) pp. 172–3, number 637; *The register of John le Romeyn, Lord Archbishop of York 1286–1296* [ed. W. Brown] (2 vols., Surtees Society; 123, 128; 1913–16) ii, pp. 162–3, number 1488.

Walter Giffard (1266 – d. 1279)
Wills: None surviving.
Probate process and execution: CFR 1272–1307, pp. 110–11, 113; *The register of William Wickwane, Lord Archbishop of York 1279–1285* ed. W. Brown (Surtees Society, 114; 1907) pp. 8–9, number 27; pp. 243–4, number 600; p. 257, number 632; p. 260, number 643; pp. 280–1, number 701; p. 325, number 844; *Register of John le Romeyn*, ii, pp. 162–3, number 1488.

William Wickwane (1279 – d. 1285)
Wills: None surviving. *Inspeximus* of arrangements, 23 September 1283, for stocking the see, 6 October 1283: *CChR 1257–1300*, pp. 268–9.
Executors: Mag. Walter de Gloucestre, archdeacon of York, and Mag. Thomas de Wakefield, subdean of York (*Register of John le Romeyn*, ii, p. 163, number 1488).
Probate process and execution: Register of John le Romeyn, i, p. 37, number 91; pp. 354–5, number 1016; ii, pp. 162–3, number 1488.

John le Romeyn (1285 – d. 1296)
Wills: None surviving.
Probate process and execution: CClR 1288–96, p. 477.

Henry Newark (1296 – d. 1299)
Wills: None surviving.
Probate process and execution: The register of Thomas of Corbridge, Lord Archbishop of York, 1300–1304 ed. W. Brown (2 vols., Surtees Society, 138, 141; 1925–8) i, p. 9, number 18; pp. 11–12, number 27; *PRME*, ii, p. 396; *CClR 1296–1302*, p. 546; *Greenfield register*, i, p. 135, number 302.

Thomas Corbridge (1299 – d. 1304)
Wills: None surviving.
Executors: Dom. Lambert de Trikyngham, Mag. John de Nassington the elder and Dom. William de Jafford (*Greenfield register*, i, p. 111, number 241A; pp. 114–15, number 247).

Probate process and execution: CFR 1272–1307, pp. 503–4; *Greenfield register*, i, p. 111, number 241A; i, pp. 114–15, number 247; i, pp. 126–7, number 286.

William Greenfield (1304 – d. 1315)
Wills: None surviving. Bequest of books to St Alban's noted in Cavanaugh, 'Books', p. 387.
Executors: Thomas of St Alban's, Richard de Henneye, Nicholas de Molyns and William de Grenefeld (*CPR 1313–17*, p. 382); Thomas of St Alban's, canon of Southwell, and William, son of Robert de Grenefeld (*CClR, 1327–30*, pp. 131–2).
Probate process and execution: CFR 1307–19, p. 266; *Greenfield register*, v, pp. 243–4, number 2782 (*sede vacante* register); *CPR 1313–17*, p. 382; *CClR 1318–23*, p. 88; *CClR 1327–30*, pp. 131–2.

William Melton (1316 – d. 1340)
Wills: None surviving.
Executors: Mag. William de la Mare, canon of St Peter's, York, William de Wirkesworth and William de Feriby (*CClR 1349–54*, p. 593).
Probate process and execution: CIPM, viii, pp. 198–9 (number 274); *CClR 1333–7*, p. 109; *CClR 1337–9*, p. 145; *CClR 1339–41*, pp. 386, 633; *CClR 1349–54*, p. 593.

William Zouche (1340 – d. 1352)
Wills: Will, 28 June 1349, proved 27 July 1352, printed in *TE I*, pp. 55–6, from a volume of Acta capitularia, in the registry of the Dean and Chapter of York (Register E, f. 7), now in the Borthwick Institute for Archives, York.
Executors: Dom. Radulph Nevyll, lord of Raby, Dom. Roger la Zouche, the Archbishop's brother, Marmaduke Constable, knight, William de Playce, knight, Christopher Malore, knight, Mag. Gilbert de Welton, Dom. William de Ferriby, Dom. Roger de Stiendby, clerks, and Anketil Malore, esquire, *literatus* (*TE I*, p. 56).
Probate process and execution: CPR 1350–4, p. 311.

John Thoresby (1352 – d. 1373)
Wills: Will, 12 September 1373, printed in *TE I*, pp. 88–91, from a book marked B. y. in the registry of the Dean and Chapter of York, now in the Borthwick Institute for Archives, York.
Executors: Dom. Richard le Scrop, knight; Mag. John de Waltham, Mag. John de Thoresby, Dom. Henry de Barton, canons of York; and Mag. Henry de Greymesby (*TE I*, p. 90).

Alexander Neville (1373 – trans. St Andrews, 1388; d. 1392)
Wills: No will surviving.
Other documentation: TNA E 36/66, ff. 17–19, 27, a list of goods forfeited to the Crown in February 1388 when the Archbishop was found guilty of treason, printed in Anon., 'Inventory of the goods of Alexander Neville, Archbishop of York, 1388' *Yorkshire Archaeological Journal* 15 (1900) pp. 476–88; see also R.G. Davies, 'Alexander Neville, Archbishop of York, 1374–1388' *Yorkshire Archaeological Journal* 47 (1975) pp. 87–101, at p. 99.

Robert Waldby (1396 – d. 1398)
Wills: None surviving.

Probate process and execution: His will, if he had made one, was to be admitted to probate by Bishop Skirlaw of Durham, when directed by the chapter of York, 6 January 1398. Borthwick Institute for Archives, York, Reg/5a, *Sede vacante* register 1398, f. 211v.

Richard le Scrope (1398 – d. 1405)
Wills: None surviving. Davies, 'Episcopate', p. ccxlv: died intestate; as he was executed for treason, his will, if there had been one, would have been set aside.
Other grants and gifts: Gift to Lichfield Cathedral for his anniversary, made before his translation to York: *Anglia sacra*, i, p. 451. Books he may have owned are noted in Cavanaugh, 'Books', p. 772.

TEXTS

1 Alexander Bache, Bishop of St Asaph

1/1 Will, 13 August 1394 *TNA PROB 11/1 (3 Rous), f. 22v*

In nomine summe et individue Trinitatis amen. Casus mortiferus primi parentis de statu innocencie immortalitatem mortalitate infelici conversio commutavit et adeo dire infeccionis rivolos diriuavit in posteros ut genus humanum ab infectis radicibus propagatum racione ipsius originalis contagii exinde resolucionis pateretur discrimina et divina voluntate justificante decetero matris semitas incedere cogeretur quod ego Alexander episcopus Assavensis et confessor domini regis revolvens in *anima* dum recenti gaudeo memoria ad testamentum condendum procedere censui in hunc modum. In primis lego animam meam deo et beate Marie et beato Assapho confessori glorioso et omnibus sanctis corpus meum ad sepeliendum in conventu fratrum predicatorum He*re*fordensi ubicumque fratres eiusdem loci voluerint. Item lego domino Johanni Graunge[1] xx marcas sterlingorum unum equum nigrum super quo solebat equitare. Item lego Waltero Feelde consanguineo meo x marcas sterlingorum et unum equum super quo solebat equitare. Item lego Gruffino Percyvale camerario meo x marcas sterlingorum et unum equum[2] optimum quem voluerit eligere de chariettis. Item lego Johanni Cutwele barbitonsori meo v marcas sterlingorum et unum equum secundum disposcionem executorum meorum. Item lego Johanni Halgrave v marcas sterlingorum et unum equum secundum disposicionem executorum meorum. Item lego Willelmo Ravenyng' xl s. sterlingorum et unum equum quem solet equitare. Item lego garcioni meo Wallico xl s. et unum equum secundum disposicionem executorum meorum. Item lego Willelmo Newe xl s. Item lego tribus pueris de stabulo cuilibet eorum xiii s. iiii d. Item lego Ieuan nuncio meo xl s. et unum equum quem solet equitare. Item lego unum par vestimentorum blodio et rubio bipartitorum de aurotexato in camera mea London' existentem conventui fratrum predicatorum He*re*fordie. Item lego conventui fratrum predicatorum London' xx li. Item lego conventui fratrum predicatorum Herefordie xl s. sterlingorum. Item volo quod hospicium meum apud Lymhost juxta London' in Forbourlane vendatur et distribuatur pro anima mea secundum disposicionem executorum meorum. Item lego fratri Thome Castell x marcas. Item lego ad distribuendum pauperibus in die sepulture mee xx li. sterlingorum. Residuum autem omnium bonorum meorum volo executores meos ordinare et disponere prout eis melius videatur expedire. Ad hanc autem ultimam voluntatem meam fideliter exequend*um* constituo executores meos magistrum Johannem Prophet consanguineum meum fratrem Willelmum Syward' et predictum Johannem Graunger capellanum meum. In quorum omnium testimonium sigillum meum presentibus est appensum. Datum apud Clatford xiii^{mo} die mensis Augusti anno domini millesimo CCC^{mo} nonogesimo quarto. Et nostre consecracionis anno quinto.

Notes
1 Possibly intended to be read as 'Graung*ere*'.
2 MS: 'equm'.

1/2 Probate granted to Dom. John Graunger, chaplain, executor named in the will, 15 September 1394, at Tonbridge Castle. *TNA PROB 11/1 (3 Rous), ff. 22v–23r.*

1/3 Memorandum of fees due to the Archbishop of Canterbury on the death of the Bishop of St Asaph and received on the death of Bishop Alexander. *TNA PROB 11/1 (3 Rous), f. 23r.*

Feoda debita domino Et memorandum quod de consuetudine a tempore et per tempus cuius contrarii memoria hominum non existit pacifice et inconcusse observata legitimeque prescripta et obtenta dominus archiepiscopus Cantuariensis qui pro tempore fuerit percipiet et habebit a quolibet episcopo Assavensi decedente anulum suum pontificalem et signetum suum sigillum suum oblongum optimum palafridum optimum ciphum capam pluvialem cellam et frenum capillum ac ocrias et calcaria quibus idem episcopus dum vixit utebatur. Et hec omnia et singula percepit et habuit de executoribus predicti domini Alexandri episcopi defuncti reverendissimus in Cristo pater dominus meus archiepiscopus qui nunc est.

2 Ralph Baldock, Bishop of London

2/1 Inventory, 1313–14 *Guildhall Library, London, MS 25271/17*

Five parchment rolls, as follows: 1. A roll of one membrane, indented down the right-hand side, with a slit at the top, which could have been used for a seal on a tag, and/or for linking this roll to the other rolls in this group. Dated 1313 at the head; acknowledged at the foot by the chapter of St Paul's to have been delivered to them, with a sealing clause dated August 1314. There are two notes on the dorse: (a) In an early fourteenth-century hand: 'Memorandum de diversis bonis datis ecclesie sancti Pauli per R' de Baldok' episcopum London'' (b) In a late fourteenth- or early fifteenth-century hand: 'Sub altari iiii^{to} de diversis bonis Radulphi Baldok datis ecclesie sancti Pauli'.

2. A roll of one membrane, containing a copy of part of roll 1. There is one small slit at the foot and there are no contemporary endorsements. The roll has a circle, about 2 cm in diameter, bottom left, perhaps the traces of an applied seal.

3. A roll of one membrane, containing a copy of part of roll 1. There is a late fourteenth-century endorsement: 'Jocalia Radulphi episcopi Lon' que dedit ecclesie sancti Pauli sub altari iiii^{to}'. Rolls 2 and 3 are in the same hand, and have nearly the same content.

4. A roll of one membrane, with a small slit at the foot and no contemporary endorsements.

5. A roll of one membrane, with a small slit at the foot and with an early fourteenth-century endorsement: 'Libri in camera domini'.

The books in the inventories were noted in part in HMC, *Appendix to Ninth Report,*

p. 46 (box A66, no. 17); more fully (but without identification) in A.B. Emden *A biographical register of the University of Oxford to A.D. 1500* (3 vols., Oxford, 1957–9) iii, pp. 2147–19; and in Cavanaugh, 'Books', pp. 64–9.

Roll 1

Memorandum de diversis bonis recolende memorie Radulphi nuper Londoniensis episcopi per eum causa mortis donatis et legatis ecclesie sue sancti Pauli London et eius ministris in capella libris jocalibus peccuniis et rebus aliis partim in vita partim post mortem eius per executores suos ipsi ecclesie et ministris eiusdem liberatis anno domini M^{o}CCC^{mo}xiii^{o}

Hec sunt que Radulphus episcopus Londoniensis de novo providit in capella sua que dedit ecclesie sue sancti Pauli London' videlicet i missale novum i evvangelistarium novum i librum pontificale i collectarium et capitularium novum i manuale novum i psalterium bonum. Item i libellus qui vocatur Bretoun.[1] Item unum vestimentum integrum de diaspre cum capitibus alis et pedibus aquilarum intextis continens quatuor pecias. Item unum vestimentum integrum purpurei coloris cum duplici casula continens septem pecias. Item i vestimentum integrum nigri coloris continens sex pecias. Item i vestimentum integrum indei coloris continens sex pecias. Item quatuor albe cum paruris et aliis actinentibus brudatis. Item vii capse corporalium brudate. Item ii calices pulcri et bene operati. Item i turribulum novum cum tinnatorio novo. Item i mitra nova cum baculo pastorali de argento. Item ii paria cirotecarum cum anulo magno de opere Romano. Item i anulus cum anatisto triangulo. Item i anulus cum saphiro magno. Item i anulus cum rubio precioso. Item i superaltare de lapide jaspidis cum preciosis reliquiis in eodem inclusis quod fuit bone memorie Thome de Cantilupo. Item ii vascula argentea ad conservandum crisma et oleum benedictum et tercium ad oleum infirmorum. Item ii phiale rotunde argentee. Item ii phiale argentee sexangulares. Item ii pelves argentee. Item i tabula plicata bene depicta. Item i crux metallica deaurata. Item alia crux nigra cum ymaginibus eburneis. Item ii pelvinaria brudata cum flosculis. Item ii panni de baudekyno ad ornandum altare. Item i martilogium. Item i morsus cum capite sancti Pauli deauratus cum lapidibus insertis. Item alius morsus aureus cum quinque lapidibus. Item ii pelvinaria cooperta de veluto et tercium pelvinarium operatum de viridi sandoco. Item nova cathedra episcopalis. Item tunica dalmatica et capa chori de albo diaspre. Item i pecten eburneus cum capsa de corio quod fuit sancti Edmundi archiepiscopi Cantuariensis. Item ii tunice ii dalmatice de rubeo sandaco tulee. Item i casula de rubeo sameto intexto cum flosculis. Item capa tunica et dalmatica de panno Tarsensi cum flosculis indici coloris quas dominus fieri fecit de novo. Item ii panni subtiles offertorii ad tenendum patenam in missa. Item pixis cum balsamo. Item i antiphonarium notatum quod dominus fieri fecit de novo.

Libri scolastici Una bibilia nova. Alia bibilia in duobus voluminibus. Tercia bibilia parva. Duo volumina ewangeliorum cum glossis Thome de Aquino.[2] Concordancie bibilie in duobus voluminibus.[3] Glose Cassiodori super psalterium.[4] Esdras Paralipomenon Machabeorum glosati. Isayes Jeremias glosati. Ezechiel Daniel glosati. Regum glosatus. Job Cantica canonic*orum*[5] et Apocalipsis glosati. Historie scolastice[6] cum aliis scriptis. Liber senteanciarum.[7] Rowelle super summas.[8] Tercia pars Alexandri super summas.[9] Prima secunde secunda secunde.[10] Item quarta pars \ et ultima.[11] / Postille super Matheum et Lucam. Postille super Ecclesiasticum et librum Sapientie. Postille super epistolas Pauli. Postille super Cantica et flores Bernardi.[12] Postille super Job. Postille super xii prophetas. Postille super Genesim Exodum et Leviticum. Postille super epistolas Pauli. Postille antique super epistolas Pauli. Postille super Ysaiam et Jeremiam. Postille super Cantic*um* et Apocalipsim et Egidius de regimine principum[13] et de corpore Cristi.[14] Postille super canonic*a* et Johannem et coment*ari*um super angelicam jerarchiam.[15] Item auora.[16] Tractatus super septem donis cum aliis magistralibus.[17] Prima pars originalium Augustini. Seconda pars. Tercia pars. Encheridion[18] et dialogi.[19] Speculum super moralia.[20] Remediarium conversorum super moralia.[21] Hugo de sacrament*is*.[22] Gregorius super Ezechielem[23] et alia magistralia. Omelie Gregorii.[24] Verbum abreviatum[25] et pastoralem Gregorii.[26] Breviloquium et alii tractatus.[27] Legenda sanctorum. Liber de officiis ecclesie.[28] Apochalipsis depictus.[29] Brutus[30] et testamenta prophetarum.[31] Epistole Petri Blesensis.[32] Questiones Bonaventure super quartum summarum.[33] Summa Prepositini cum collacionibus.[34] Questiones magistrales super summas. Questiones magistrales super summas cum tabula Kylewardby.[35] Pastoral*e* Gregorii.[36] Cinomina vel soliloquia Ysodori[37] et compassio Augustini de beata virgine.[38] Item decretales glosate. Decretales antique glossate. Decretales glosate.[39] Glosse Innocencii cum variis lecturis et distincionibus.[40] Summe Roffredi Goffredi et Reymundi.[41] Commentarium Hostiensis super decretales in duobus voluminibus.[42] Repertorium aur*eum*[43] cum aliis tractatibus. Apparatus decretalium.[44] Casus Bartholomei super decreta et decretales.[45] Summa de viciis et virtutibus. Sextus liber decretalium cum apparatu et cum statutis et consuetudinibus de Arcubus et forma litterarum.[46] Casus decretorum cum historiis et cas*us* Bernardi super decretales[47] et questiones Bartholomei.[48] Summa Hugucionis.[49] Item abbicianus minor.[50] Varie collaciones in corio velluto. Collaciones Kylewardeby.[51] Collecta collacionum. Themata diversa cum aliis tractatibus. Gubertus ad omnem statum in uno volumine et super evvangelia in alio volumine.[52] Omelie antique super evvangelia et epistole in rubio corio. Omelie antique cum aliis tractatibus in corio albo. Omelie Odonis.[53] Omelie super psalterium. Omelie ad Cistercienses.[54] Divisiones thematum et alii tractatus cum littera A. Themata sanctorum. Duo volumina magna omeliarum Bede in Anglico.[55] Oraciones Anselmi et Augustini et meditaciones varie.[56] Ysodorus de summo bono[57] et summa Reymundi.[58] Vita sancti Anselmi cum meditacionibus de gaudiis beate Marie et aliis tractatibus.[59] Distinciones Biard' et alii tractatus.[60] Distincciones Nicholai cum alii tractatibus. Distincciones Mauricii.[61] Distincciones magistrales cum collacionibus et epistolis Jeromini et Augustini.[62] Libellus de laudibus salvatoris.[63] Tractatus de justic*ia*. Tractatus de lingua. Tractatus de oculo. Exposcio Anglici[64] cum aliis tractatibus. Liber parvulus in nigro coreo de collacionibus. Item alius liber in panno viridi omeliarum. Parvum volumen.[65] Digestum novum.[66] Codex.[67] Inforciatum.[68] Summa Azonis.[69] Casus inforciati. Statuta Otonis et Octoboni et aliorum.[70] Liber naturalium.[71] Summe Thome de Aquino circa metaphisicam et animam.[72] Parvi libri naturales et de animalibus[73] et Albimazar.[74] Tabula super librum naturalem.[75] Conclusiones heticorum[76] et tractatus varii de p*redica*m*enta*.[77] Congregacio multorum super jure civili. Notule super logicalia.[78] Kylewardeby super Priscianum.[79] Varie practice medicinales. Macer[80] cum aliis tractatibus. Practica Bede in Anglico.[81] Duo parvi libri practicales. Brito super bibiliam[82] liberatur inter libros de capella. Liber Papie.[83] Liber Hugucionis de dirivacione.[84] Donatus vetere in Anglico.[85] Liber Alfragani[86] et Petri Arfronsi[87] et alii tractatus. Spera.[88] Compotus Algorismi.[89] Tractatus Willelmi de Conchis de motibus astrorum[90] et Thimeo super Platonem.[91] Papirus non scriptus. Cronica plenar*ia* ab origine mundi.[92] Cronica Henrici archidiaconi Huntyngd' ab anno domini M°Cxlv usque ad tempus Henrici primi.[93] Item sciendum est quod cum dictus testator in suo memorando librorum in vita sua describi fecisset certos libros sub quibusdam intitillacionibus qui quidem libri descriptis per eum titulis concordes non poterant inveniri cum alii libri superessent qui in dicto memorando suo non fuerunt expressi loco descriptorum huiusmodi librorum deficiencium fiebat subrogacio aliorum librorum equivalencium juxta conjecturaciam defuncti voluntatem per executores suos prout sequitur. Pro questionibus Thome de veritate liberatur liber contra gentiles.[94] Pro libro eticorum liberatur liber de predestinacione et de formatione corporis humani et flores eticorum et concordancie juris civilis.[95] Pro questionibus Thome de potencia et malo admittitur Cassiodorus super psalterium.[96] < Pro Fysacre liberatur manipulus florum >[97] Pro parvunculis questionibus theologie[98] liberatur quidam libellus de quiditate dei et de causis et aliis tractatibus. Pro prima parte Thome de Aquino liberatur liber histor*iarum* super bibliam et libellus Nicholi Byard de sermonibus super dominical*es*.[99] Pro ympnar*io* glosato liberatur libellus de coronacione regis et regine.[100] Pro questionibus super sentencias liberatur quidem libellus de sermonibus discontinuatis qui incipit 'dedicacio ecclesie'.

Jocalia Anuli in uno baculo ix communes. Item in alio baculo xvii majoris precii. Item in quodam alio minori baculo sex anuli solempnes. Item in quodam alio minori baculo unus anulus cum loupa. Item in quodam alio minori baculo vii boni anuli magni precii. Item in quodam chinchio v casse anulorum aureorum sine lapidibus. Firmacula v magna firmacula et i parvum in quodam cinchio.

Floreni Item octies viginti floreni parvi de Florencia et i magnus florenus cum cathedra. Item i berillus in circulo argento.

Peccunia numerata In primis quadragente libre ut inde procuretur erga regem ut in qualibet vacacione \ ecclesie / sancti Pauli London' custodia omnium temporalium episcopatus sit in manu capituli prout in testamento dicti defuncti plenius invenietur. Item triginta libre sterlingorum assignate per dictum Radulphum episcopum ecclesie sue predicte in recompensacionem cere quam solebat ecclesia sancti Pauli habere in sepultura predecessorum suorum. Item pro xii parvis canonicis ecclesie xii li. sterlingorum videlicet pro quolibet xx s. Item pro xxi vicariis xiiii li. videlicet pro quolibet xiii s. iiii d. Item pro xxiiii capellanis celebrantibus in ecclesia sancti Pauli xi li. vi s. viii d. pro quolibet vi s. viii d. Item pro vii secondariis capellanis in dicta ecclesia xiiii s. videlicet pro quolibet ii s. Item pro v servientibus ecclesie xxxiii s. iiii d. pro quolibet vi s. viii d. Item pro octo pueris elemosinarie xxxii s. pro quolibet iiii s. Item pro ii garcionibus ecclesie iiii s. videlicet pro quolibet eorum ii s.

Summa totalis peccunie CCCClxxi li. et x s.

Nos vero capitulum ecclesie sancti Pauli London' vacante ipsius ecclesie decanatu fatemur omnia et singula premissa prout supra scribuntur fuisse et esse nobis et ecclesie predicte ac ministris eiusdem partim in vita bone memorie Radulphi de Baldok' condam Londoniensis episcopi et partim per executores suos post mortem eiusdem liberata tradita et soluta de quibus omnibus et singulis ipsos executores liberatos esse reputamus et quietos. In premissorum vero testimonium sigillum nostrum commune presentibus est appensum. Data in capitulo nostro London'[101] die Augusti anno domini millesimo trecentesimo quartodecimo.

Roll 2
Hec sunt que Radulphus episcopus Londoniensis de novo providit in capella sua et que dedit ecclesie sue sancti Pauli London' videlicet i missale novum i ewangelistarium novum i librum pontificalem novum i collectarium et capitularium novum i manuale novum i psalterium bonum. Item libellum que vocatur Bretoun.[102] Item i vestimentum integrum de albo diaspro cum capidibus alis et pedibus aquilarum intextis \ iiii peciarum. / Item i vestimentum integrum purpurei coloris cum duplici casula \ vii peciarum. / Item i vestimentum integrum yndici coloris \ vi peciarum. / Item i vestimentum \ integrum / nigri coloris \ vi peciarum. / Item iiii albas cum paruris et aliis attinentibus broydatis. Item vii capsas broidas ad corporalia. Item ii calices pulcres et bene operatos novos. Item i turribulum novum cum thimiaterio novo. Item i mitram novam cum baculo pastorali de argento. Item ii paria cirothecarum cum anulo magno de opere Romano. Item i anulum cum ametisto triangulo. Item i anulum cum saphiro magno. Item i anulum cum rubeo precioso. Item i superaltare de lapide jaspidis cum preciosis reliquiis in eadem inclusis quod fuit bone memorie Thome de Cantilupo. Item ii vascula argentea ad conservandum crisma et oleum benedictum et tercium ad oleum infirmorum. Item ii phiolas rotondas argenteas. Item ii phiolas argenteas sexangulares. Item ii pelves argenteas. Item i tabulam plicatam bene depictam. Item i crucem metallicam deauratam. Item aliam crucem nigram cum ymaginibus eburneis. Item ii pulvinaria broydata cum flosculis. Item ii pannos de baudkino ad ornandum altare. Item i marthilogium. Item i morsum cum capite sancti Pauli deauratum cum lapidibus incertis.[103] Item alium morsum aureum cum v^{que} lapidibus. Item ii pulvinaria cooperta de veluto et tercium pulvinarium operatum de viridi sandato. Item novam cathedram episcopalem. Item tunicam dalmaticam et capam cori de albo diaspre. Item i pecten eburneum cum capsa de coreo quod fuit sancti Edmundi archiepiscopi Cantuariensis. Item ii tunicas ii dalmaticas de rubeo sandato tulee et i casulam de rubeo sameto intexto cum flosculis. Item ii pannos subtiles offert*orios* ad tenendum patenam in missa. Item pixidem cum balsamo.

Roll 3
Entries in a second hand are in square brackets.

Hec sunt que Radulphus episcopus Londoniensis de novo providit in capella sua et que dedit ecclesie sue sancti Pauli London' videlicet unum missale novum unum ewangelistarium novum unum librum pontificalem novum unum collectarium et capitularium novum unum manuale novum unum psalterium bonum. Item libellum qui vocatur Breton.[104] Item unum vestimentum integrum de albo diaspre cum capitibus alis et pedibus aquilarum intextis. Item unum vestimentum integrum purpurei coloris cum dupplici casula. Item unum vestimentum integrum yndici coloris. Item unum vestimentum integrum nigri coloris. Item quatuor albas cum paruris et aliis attinentibus broidatis. Item < quatuor > \ [septem] /

capsas broidatas ad corporalia. Item duos calices pulcros et bene operatos novos. Item unum thurribulum novum cum thimiaterio novo. Item mitram novam cum baculo pastorali de argento. Item duo paria cyrothecarum cum anulo magno de opere Romano. Item unum anulum cum ametisto triangulo. Item unum anulum cum saphiro magno. Item unum anulum cum rubeo precioso. Item unum superaltare de lapide jaspidis cum preciosis reliquiis in eodem inclusis quod fuit bone memorie Thome de Cantilupo. Item duo vascula argentea ad conservandum crisma et oleum benedictum \ [et tercium ad oleum informorum.] / Item duas phiales argenteas rotundas. Item duas phialas argenteas sexangulares. Item duas pelves argenteas. Item \ [unam] / tabulam plicatam bene depictam. Item unam crucem metallicam deauratam. Item aliam crucem nigram cum ymaginibus eburneis. Item duo pulvinaria broidata cum flosculis. Item duos pannos de baudekyno ad ornandum altare. < Item unum portiforium > \ [rubeum][105] / et unum martilogium. Item unum morsum cum capite sancti Pauli deauratum cum lapidibus insertis. Item alium morsum aureum cum quinque lapidibus. Item duo pulvinaria cooperta de veluto et tercium pulvinarium operatum de viridi cendato. Item novam cathedram episcopalem. Item tunicam dalmaticam et capam chori de albo diaspre. Item unum pecten eburneum cum capsa de corio quod fuit sancti Edmundi archiepiscopi Cantuariensis. Item duas tunicas duas dalmaticas de rubeo sandato tulee et unam casulam de rubeo sameto intexto cum flosculis. Item duos pannos subtiles offertor*ios* ad tenendum patenam in missa. Item pixidem cum balsamo.

Roll 4
Inventa in capella domini Radulphi episcopi Londoniensis in vigilia sancti Jacobi

In primis i vestimentum integrum album videlicet tunica dalmatica pro diacono et subdiacono casula et capa
Item tunica dalmatica et pro diacono et subdiacono yndei coloris et capa
Item i alba amicta stola phanula et zona pro domino
Item alia alba amicta stola phanula cum scutis et zona et casula rubea
Item tercia alba amicta stola phanula et casula duplex
Item quarta alba amicta stola et phanula debili et i casula < deb > virid*is* cum iii amictis
Item alba amicta stola phanula casula tuallia cum parura et frontale alb*a* modici valoris

Item vii corporalium capse brudate sollempnes
Item ii capse corporalium virides brudate cum ymaginibus aureis
Item i crux deaurata
Item duo baudekini pro altari
Item i pannus pro altari de samite stragulat*o*
Item i pannus ad lectrinum
Item i frontale altaris cum bestiis
Item ii tuallie altaris cum paruris brudat*is* cum scutis
Item ii alie tuallie altaris
Item iii manutergia
Item i tuallia ad cooperiendum altare de opere Romano
Item ii pulvinaria brudata cum flosculis

Item duo tapeta de pilis camelorum pro altari
Item duo tapeta pro domino yndei coloris
Item x superplicia et i rochet
Item amictum et ii superplicia pro domino

Item i calix argenteus deauratus. Item i pixis brudata sollempnis
Item ii phiali argentei
Item iii phiali argentei pro oleo sancto crisma et oleo infirmorum
Item i crismatorium cum stola et rotulo et ceteris appendicibus
Item iiii candelaria de opere Limonitensi. Item iii sconse
Item i thurribulum vetus argenteum deauratum
Item i navis ad idem pro incenso cum cocleario argenteo

Item i portiforium album plenarium
Item aliud portiforium nigrum
Item tercium portiforium in duobus voluminibus
Item unum psalterium cum ympnario album
Item i graduale nigrum et i troperium pro domino
Item i graduale album et troperium album
Item i graduale nigrum et troperium nigrum
Item i liber qui vocatur Briton[106]
Item i liber albus qui vocatur Remediarium conversorum[107]
Item i diurnale
Item i missale rubeum
Item i epistolarium rubeum
Item i tabula depicta sollempnis
Item ii pecie remanencium de vestiment*is*
Item i martilogium
Item i magna campanula pro capella
Item i parva campanula
Item ii cathedre pro domino
Item i frontale quadragesimale
Item i pixis vitrea ligata cum virgis
Item alia pixis debilis

Roll 5
Libri inventi in studio episcopi Londoniensis apud Stebb' xiiii kal. Julii anno gracie M^{o}CCC^{mo}xiii^{o}

Una parva biblia bene correcta
Decretales glossate
Inventarium juris canonici per Berengarium[108]
Salines super decreta[109]
Sextus liber decretalium cum glosis Guidonis et aliis tractatibus[110]

Statuta Oxon' Lamheye Ottonis et Ottoboni cum aliis tractatibus[111]
Practica medicine
Legenda sanctorum duplex
Themata diversa de sanctis et de temporali

Sermones Guiberti de dominicis et festis
Sermones Guiberti ad omnem statum[112]
Anglicum expositum per ordinem alphabeti[113] cum aliis tractatibus
Tractatus qui intitulatur Dominus < Jhesus noster > judex noster[114]
Sermones fratris Nicholai Byart[115]
Collecti sermones diversorum doctorum in libello rubeo
Exposiciones cymbolorum cum aliis tractatibus in parvo libello rubeo[116]
Sermones Kylewardeby[117]
Themata de epistolis artificiosa prosecuta
Breves collaciones de epistolis et evangeliis per annum in coreo nigro
Collaciones magistrales in corio albo
Collaciones breves in panno virido
Flores philosophie
Cronice
Registrum ecclesie London' cum multis tractatibus
Aliud registrum ecclesie antiquum cum taxacione beneficiorum diocesis Lond'[118]
Visitacio maneriorum sancti Pauli cum visitacione cantariarum sacristie et thesaurarie
Processus contra templarios[119]

Notes

1 The description of this book later in the document (see notes 82, 102, 104, 106) as 'Brito super bibiliam' delivered among the books of the chapel, makes most likely the identification of the text as William Brito *Expositiones vocabulorum Bibliae* ed. L.W. and D.A. Daly (Padua, 1975).

2 Thomas Aquinas *Catena aurea in quatuor ewangelia* ed. A. Guarienti (Rome/Turin, 1953).

3 Perhaps the *Concordantia maior*, prepared by the Dominicans of Saint-Jacques, Paris.

4 Cassiodorus *Expositio Psalmorum* ed. M. Adriaen (*CCSL*, 97–8; 1958).

5 For 'Cantica canticorum'.

6 Petrus Comestor *Historia scholastica*, edited in *PL* 198, cols. 1053–1722.

7 Various possibilities, the most likely of which is Petrus Lombardus *Libri sententiarum*, published as *PL* 192, cols. 521–962.

8 William Rothwell, abbreviated commentary on Petrus Lombardus *Libri sententiarum*; unpublished; see K. Emery, 'The sentences abbreviation of William de Rothwell OP' *Recherches de Théologie Ancienne et Médiévale* 51 (1984) pp. 69–135; Sharpe, *Latin writers*, p. 805.

9 Alexander of Hales *Glossa in quatuor libris sententiarum Petri Lombardi*, probably on the third book, printed in *Bibliotheca Franscicana Scholastica medii aevi*, 12–15 (Quaracchi, 1951–7).

10 Thomas Aquinas *Summa theologica*, printed in *STO*, iv–xii: I^{a} IIe and II^{a} IIe.

11 Thomas Aquinas *Summa theologica*: perhaps the second section, on the fourth part of the *summa*, and III.

12 William of Tournai *Flores Bernardi* (Bernard of Clairvaux); unpublished.

13 Aegidius Romanus (Giles of Rome, Archbishop of Bourges) *De regimine principum*, printed 1473.

14 Aegidius Romanus *Theoremata de corpore Christi*, printed Rome, 1554.

15 One of the commentaries on Pseudo-Dionysius *Hierarchia caelestis*.

16 Identified by Emden as probably Petrus Riga *Aurora*; published as *Aurora. Biblia versificata* ed. P.E. Beichner (Notre Dame, Indiana, 1965).

17 A treatise on the seven gifts of the Holy Spirit.

18 The works of Augustine of Hippo, in three parts, followed by his *Enchiridion*, the last ed. E. Evans (*CCSL*, 46; 1969) pp. 21–114.

19 Gregory the Great *Dialogi* ed. A. de Vogüé (3 vols., Sources chrétiennes, 251, 260, 265; Paris, 1978–80).

20 Adalbert of Metz *Speculum Gregorii*, preface printed in *PL* 136, cols. 1309–12 (a collection of excerpts from Gregory the Great *Moralia in Job*).

21 Peter of Waltham, archdeacon of London *Remediarium conversorum* ed. J. Gildea (Villanova, Pennsylvania, 1984), a synthesis of Gregory the Great's *Moralia in Job*.

22 Probably Hugh of St Victor *De sacramentis Christianae fidei*, *PL* 176, cols. 173–618.

[23] Gregory the Great *Homiliae in Ezechielem* ed. M. Adriaen (*CCSL*, 142; 1971).

[24] Probably Gregory the Great *Homiliae XL in evangelia*, *CPL* 1711.

[25] Petrus Cantor *Verbum abbreviatum*, *PL* 205, cols. 23–554.

[26] Further works of Gregory the Great, including either the *Regula pastoralis*, *CPL* 1712, or an abbreviated form.

[27] Bonaventure *Breviloquium pauperis seu compendium sacrae scripturae*, printed in *S. Bonaventurae Opera omnia* (10 vols., Quaracchi, 1882–1902) v, pp. 201–91; and other works.

[28] There are several possible identifications: Isidorus Hispalensis (Isidore of Seville) *De ecclesiasticis officiis* ed. C.M. Lawson (*CCSL*, 113; 1989), *CPL* 1207; perhaps Guido of Orchelles *De officiis ecclesiae*, ed. E. Kennedy, 'The Summa de officiis ecclesiae of Guy d'Orchelles' *Mediaeval Studies* 1 (1939) pp. 33–62; less likely is William of Auxerre *Summa de officiis ecclesiasticis* ed. F. Fischer, <www.thomasinst.uni-koeln.de/sdoc/start.html>.

[29] An illuminated Apocalypse.

[30] Perhaps a copy of Geoffrey of Monmouth *Historia regum Britanniae*.

[31] Perhaps the *Testamentum xii patriarcharum*, translated by Robert Grosseteste, *PG* 2, cols. 1038–1150. Note a copy also paired with a Brutus, *English Benedictine libraries: the shorter catalogues* ed. R. Sharpe, J.P. Carley, R.M. Thomson and A.G. Watson (Corpus of British medieval library catalogues, 4; 1996) p. 191, B39.197a.

[32] Peter of Blois *Epistolae*, *PL* 207, cols. 1–560.

[33] Bonaventura, Commentary on Peter Lombard's *Sentences*, printed in *S. Bonaventurae Opera omnia*, i–iv.

[34] Praepositinus (Gilbert Prévostin) of Paris *Summa theologica*, parts 1 and 4 published: part 1, ed. G. Angelini, *Analecta Gregoriana* 183 (Rome, 1972) pp. 191–303; part 4, *Praepositini cancellarii de sacramentis et de novissimis* ed. D.E. Pilarczyk (Rome, 1964).

[35] Robert Kilwardby, Archbishop of Canterbury *Tabulae super originalia patrum*, unprinted; Sharpe, *Latin writers*, p. 564.

[36] Gregory the Great *Regula pastoralis*, *CPL* 1712.

[37] Isidorus Hispalensis *Synonyma* ed. J. Elfassi (*CCSL*, 111B; 2009); *CPL* 1203.

[38] Not traced now as a work by Augustine, but perhaps a work by Oglerius of Tridino, extracts of which circulated widely as the *Planctus Mariae*, under the authorship of Bernard of Clairvaux (printed Cologne, 1470), *PL* 182, cols. 1133–42, and ed. C.W. Marx, *Journal of Medieval Latin* 4 (1994) pp. 118–29.

[39] Gregory IX, *Decretales*, printed in *Corpus iuris canonici* ed. E. Friedberg (2nd edition, 2 vols., Leipzig, 1922) ii, cols. 1–928; with gloss.

[40] Perhaps including Innocent IV *Apparatus in quinque libros decretalium*, printed Strassburg, 1477.

[41] Works on civil law by Roffredus Beneventanus (perhaps his *Libelli de iure canonico*, printed Avignon, 1500), Goffredus de Trano (*Summa super titulis decretalium*: see M. Bertram, 'Der Dekretalenapparat des Goffredus Tranensis' *Bulletin of Medieval Canon Law*, new series, 1 (1971) pp. 79–83), and Raymund of Peñafort *Summa iuris canonici*, published as *Summa de iure canonico* ed. X. Ochoa and A. Diez (Rome, 1975).

[42] Probably Henricus de Segusio, Cardinal Bishop of Ostia *Lectura super decretales*, printed Strassburg, 1512.

[43] Willelmus Durandus *Breviarium sive repertorium aureum iuris canonici*, printed Rome, 1474.

[44] Perhaps Innocent IV *Apparatus in quinque libros decretalium*, printed Strassburg, 1477.

[45] Bartholomaeus Brixiensis (Bartholomew of Brescia) *Casus decretorum*, printed Basel, 1489.

[46] The *Liber sextus*, with decretals from Gregory IX to Boniface VIII, printed in *Corpus iuris canonici*, ii, cols. 933–1124, with gloss; and with the customs and statutes of the Court of Arches and a formulary.

[47] Possibly Bernardus de Botone Parmensis (Bernard of Parma) *Casus longi super decretales*, printed Venice, 1477; Bernard of Compostella *Notabilia et casus super decretales*, unprinted, or Bernardus Papiensis (Balbus) (Bernard of Pavia) *Casus decretalium*, printed in *Bernardus Papiensis Faventini episcopi Summa decretalium* ed. E.T. Laspeyres (Regensburg, 1860) pp. 327–52.

[48] MS: possibly 'questionum'. Bartholomaeus Brixiensis (Bartholomew of Brescia) *Quaestiones dominicales et veneriales*, unprinted.

[49] Hugutio of Pisa *Summa decretorum*, unprinted: see L. Prosdocimi, 'La "Summa decretorum" di Uguccione da Pisa: studi preliminari per una edizione critica' *Studia Gratiana* 3 (1955) pp. 349–74, and *idem*, 'I manoscritti della "Summa decretorum" di Uguccione da Pisa' *Studia Gratiana* 7 (1959) pp. 251–72.

[50] MS obscure. Perhaps a text for language teaching, but not identified from T. Hunt *Teaching and*

learning Latin in thirteenth-century England (3 vols., Cambridge, 1991); the same text may be recorded below, note 113.

51 Treatises, etc., by Robert Kilwardby; Sharpe, *Latin writers*, pp. 560–4.

52 From the works of Guibertus Tornacensis (Gilbert of Tournai), perhaps from his sermons. See note 112 below, which probably describes the same works.

53 Perhaps Odo de Cheriton *Sermones dominicales*, unprinted.

54 Perhaps from Bernardus Claraevallensis *Sermones*.

55 Bede *Homeliae evangelii* (and perhaps other works in addition) ed. D. Hurst (*CCSL*, 122; 1955) pp. 1–378; *CPL* 1367. It was unusual for the text to circulate in Old or Middle English, as noted here.

56 Anselm of Canterbury *Orationes* and *Meditationes*, published in *Sancti Anselmi Opera* ed. F.S. Schmitt (6 vols., Seckau, Rome, Edinburgh, 1938–61) iii, pp. 3–91; and probably devotional texts attributed to Augustine of Hippo (such as Pseudo-Augustine *Liber soliloquiorum animae ad deum* and *Meditationes de spiritu sancto*), like those found combined with Anselm's prayers and meditations in books from Leicester Abbey (*The libraries of the Augustinian canons* ed. M.T.J. Webber and A.G. Watson (Corpus of British medieval library catalogues, 6; 1998) pp. 179–80, A20.306; p. 201, A.20.435-6). I am grateful to Tessa Webber for this suggestion.

57 Isidorus Hispalensis *Sententiae* (also known as *De summo bono*), *CPL* 1199.

58 Raymund of Peñafort *Summa de casibus poenitentiae* ed. U.X. Ochoa and A. Diez (Rome, 1976).

59 Eadmer of Canterbury *Vita S. Anselmi* ed. R.W. Southern (2nd edition, Oxford, 1972); and Anselm of Canterbury *Orationes* and *Meditationes*, as note 56.

60 Nicholas de Byard *Distinctiones theologicae veteris et novis testamenti*; the following item may be a duplicate of this entry. L.J. Bataillon, 'The tradition of Nicholas of Biard's distinctiones' *Viator* 25 (1994) pp. 245–88.

61 Mauricius Hibernicus *Distinctiones*, part printed Venice, 1603.

62 Jerome *Epistulae*, *CPL* 620–1, 633 (many MSS collections are incomplete); Augustine of Hippo *Epistulae*, *CPL* 262.

63 Libellus de laudibus salvatoris: unidentified.

64 Perhaps one of the commentaries of Nicholas Trevet.

65 The *Parvum volumen* was a standard collection of Roman law: Justinian *Codex*, X–XII; the *Codex* is printed in *Corpus iuris civilis* ed. T. Mommsen, P. Krüger, R. Schöll and W. Kroll (3 vols., Berlin, 1872–7) ii.

66 The second part of Justinian's *Digest* to become known in the West, containing the last books, XXXIX–L; printed as part of the *Digestum* in *Corpus iuris civilis*, i, part 2.

67 Justinian, *Codex*, printed as above, note 65.

68 The last part of the *Digest* to become known in the West, containing books XXIV, 3, to XXXVIII; printed as part of the *Digestum* in *Corpus iuris civilis*, i, part 2.

69 Azo of Bologna *Summa codicis* and *Summa institutionum*, printed Venice, 1610.

70 Cardinal Otto de Monteferrato *Constitutiones* (1237), printed in *CS*, i, pp. 245–59; and Ottobuono Fieschi *Constiutiones* (1268), printed in *CS*, ii, pp. 747–92; see note 111 below.

71 Aristotle *Libri naturales*, collected works, described in *English Benedictine libraries: the shorter catalogues*, at e.g. pp. 218, 356.

72 Thomas Aquinas, Commentary on Aristotle's *Metaphysica*, ed. M.R. Cathala and R.M. Spiazzi (Turin, 1964); and his Commentary on Aristotle's *De anima*, *STO*, xlv, part i, pp. 3–260.

73 Aristotle *Parvi libri naturales*, a collection containing *De sensu et sensato*, *De memoria et reminiscentia*, *De somno et vigilia*, and *De longitudine et brevitate vitae*; the books of *De animalibus*, in the translation of William of Moerbeke, appearing in *Aristoteles Latinus* (31 vols., Bruges, Paris, Leiden, 1961–) xvii.

74 Several works of Albumasar (Abu Ma'shar, d. 885) were in circulation in Latin translations: F.J. Carmody *Arabic astronomical and astrological sciences in Latin translation: a critical bibliography* (Berkeley, CA, 1956) pp. 88–102.

75 An index or guide to the *Libri naturales*.

76 One of the translations of Aristotle's *Ethica* ed. R.A. Gauthier, *Aristoteles Latinus* (31 vols., Bruges, Paris, Leiden, 1961–) xxvi, parts 1 to 3.

77 Possibly works of the *Logica vetus* of Aristotle and others, including the *Categoriae* (known as the *Praedicamenta*); the contracted form of the word, 'pma', is concise.

78 Notes on works of logic, possibly the *Logica nova* and *Logica vetus* of Aristotle and others, described in *English Benedictine libraries: the shorter catalogues*, p. 356.

79 One of the commentaries of Robert Kilwardby on the works of Priscian or pseudo-Priscian, listed in Sharpe, *Latin writers*, p. 561.

80 Odo Magdunensis (Odo of Meung, 'Macer Floridus') *De viribus herbarum*, printed Naples, 1477, and ed. L. Choulant (Leipzig, 1832) pp. 28–132, reprinted in *Höhepunkte der Klostermedizin: Der Macer Floridus und das Herbarium des Vitus Auslasser* ed. and trans. by J.G. Mayer and K. Goehl (Holzminden, 2001).

81 Some of the scientific works attributed to Bede: see C.W. Jones *Bede's Pseudepigrapha: scientific writings falsely attributed to Bede* (Ithaca, NY, 1939); Sharpe, *Latin writers*, pp. 74–6. That they are in English is unusual: see note 55 above.

82 William Brito *Expositiones vocabulorum Bibliae*, as note 1.

83 Papias *Elementarium doctrinae rudimentum*, printed Milan, 1476; new edition in progress, ed. V. de Angelis (Milan, 1977–80).

84 Hugutio Pisanus *Liber derivationum*, unprinted; A. Marigo, *I codici manoscritti delle Derivationes di Uguccione Pisano* (Rome, 1936) lists manuscripts.

85 One of the works of Donatus, perhaps an adaptation or abbreviation: works of Donatus edited by L. Holtz, *Donat et la tradition de l'enseignement grammatical* (Paris, 1981); Middle English text not traced, but for Middle English grammars and knowledge of *The Accedence*, based on Donatus' *Ars minor*, in the fourteenth century, D. Thomson *A descriptive catalogue of Middle English grammatical texts* (London, 1979) p. 11.

86 A translation of one of the works of Alfraganus (Al Farghani, d. post 863).

87 One of the works of Petrus Alfonsi, perhaps his *Dialogus contra Judaeos* or *De disciplina clericali*: for these works, *PL* 157, cols. 535–706.

88 Perhaps Johannes de Sacrobosco *De sphaera mundi*, printed in L. Thorndike *The Sphere of Sacrobosco and its commentators* (Corpus of medieval scientific texts, 2; Chicago, 1949).

89 Possibly two works by Alexander de Villa Dei: *Algorismus*, ed. J.O. Halliwell, *Rara mathematica* (1841) pp. 73–83, and *Massa compoti*, ed. R. Steele *Opera hactenus inedita Rogeri Baconi* (16 vols., Oxford, 1905–40) vi, pp. 268–89. It is possible the *Compotus* and *Spera* listed in note 88 are works of Robert Grosseteste, the *Compotus correctorius* printed in *Opera hactenus inedita Rogeri Baconi*, vi, pp. 212–67; *De Sphaera*, ed. L. Baur *Die philosophischen Werke des Robert Grosseteste, Bischofs von Lincoln* (Beiträge zur Geschichte der Philosophie des Mittelalters, 9; Münster, 1912) pp. 10–32.

90 From the works of William of Conches, perhaps *De philosophia mundi libri quatuor*, *PL* 90, cols. 1127–78 (where it is attributed to Honorius of Autun), and *Elementorum philosophiae libri quatuor*, *PL* 172, cols. 41–102 (where it is attributed to Bede), printed as Wilhelm von Conches *Philosophia* ed. G. Maurach (Pretoria, 1980).

91 William of Conches, Commentary on Plato's *Timaeus*, published in *Guillelmi de Conchis Glosae super Platonem* ed. E. Jeauneau (*CCCM*, 203; 2006).

92 A chronicle sometimes attributed to Ralph Baldock: N.R. Ker, 'Books at St Paul's Cathedral before 1313', in *idem*, *Books, collectors and libraries: studies in medieval heritage* ed. A.G. Watson (London, 1985) pp. 209–42, at p. 236, entry 124a; A. Gransden *Historical writing in England c.550 to c.1307* (London, 1974) pp. 522–3.

93 Henry of Huntingdon *Historia Anglorum* ed. T. Arnold (RS, 74; 1879). The four versions are described at pp. xi–xiv: the first two ran to 1129 and 1135; the fullest to 1145, and this may account for some of the confusion about the date here.

94 In place of Thomas Aquinas *De veritate*, printed as *STO*, xxii; another work by Aquinas, *Summa contra gentiles*, *STO*, xiii–xv.

95 In place of Thomas Aquinas, Commentary on Aristotle's *Ethica* (*Scriptum super libros Ethicorum*: *STO*, xlvii): Augustine's *De praedestinatione sanctorum*, *CPL* 354; a work of Giles of Rome, printed as *Aegidii Romani Opera omnia II.13 De formatione humani corporis in utero* ed. R. Martorelli Vico (Testi e studi per il 'Corpus philosophorum medii aevi', 22; Florence, 2008); a compilation directly from or based around Aristotle's *Ethica*; and a concordance to the *Corpus iuris civilis*.

96 In place of Thomas Aquinas *De potentia dei*, printed as Thomas Aquinas, *Quaestiones disputatae II* ed. P.M. Pession (Turin/Rome, 1949); and *De malo*, printed as *STO*, xxiii: Cassiodorus Senator *Expositio Psalmorum* ed. M. Adriaen (*CCSL*, 97–8; 1958); *CPL* 900.

97 In place of a work probably by Richard Fishacre (Sharpe, *Latin writers*, pp. 476–7): Thomas Hibernicus *Manipulus florum*, printed Piacenza, 1483 (see also R.H. and M.A. Rouse *Preachers, florilegia, and sermons: studies on the Manipulus florum of Thomas of Ireland* (Toronto, 1979)).

98 First four words written over an erasure: various, unidentified sets of *questiones*.

99 In place of Thomas Aquinas *Summa theologica*, I: a volume of tales based on the bible, and some of the many sermons of Nicholas de Byard (for a listing, J.B. Schneyer *Repertorium der lateinischen Sermones des Mittelalters für die Zeit von 1150–1350* (11 vols., Münster, 1969–90) iv, pp. 228–50). See also note 115, below.

100 An unidentified coronation order.
101 Followed by a blank space.
102 See note 1.
103 For 'insertis'.
104 See note 1.
105 It is not clear what 'rubeum' relates to, unless it is the deleted entry for the portiforium.
106 See note 1.
107 Peter of Waltham *Remediarium conversorum*; see note 21.
108 Berengarius Fredoli *Inventarium sive repertorium super Speculum Durantis*, printed Rome, 1474.
109 An unidentified work of Petrus de Salinis on Gratian's *Decretum*.
110 The *Liber sextus*, see note 46 above; the gloss: perhaps the work of Guido de Collemedio (d. 1306), his *Repertorium* to Innocent IV's *apparatus decretalium*. A. Bernal Palacios, 'Repertorios del commentario de Innocencio IV a las Decretales de Gregorio IX' *Escritos del Vedat* 17 (1987) pp. 149–52.
111 Probably the 1222 Council of Oxford and the May 1261 Council of Lambeth (although this could possibly refer to the Councils of Lambeth of 1281 and 1309), statutes printed in *CS*, i, pp. 100–125, 660–92. For Cardinal Otto de Monteferrato, *Constitutiones* (1237), and Ottobuono Fieschi, *Constiutiones* (1268), see note 70 above.
112 Guibertus Tornacensis (Gilbert of Tournai) *Sermones*, probably the same as the works in note 52 above. Guibertus' sermons are listed in Schneyer, *Repertorium der lateinischen Sermones*, ii, pp. 282–318.
113 Possibly a text for teaching English, perhaps that in note 50.
114 Possibly a work based on Isaiah 33: 22.
115 Probably the works recorded in note 99 above: Nicholas de Byard *Sermones*.
116 Perhaps catechistical works.
117 Possibly as note 51: Robert Kilwardby *Sermones*, listed in Sharpe, *Latin writers*, p. 563; and in Schneyer, *Repertorium der lateinischen Sermones*, v, p. 195.
118 Presumably the *matricula* of Fulk Basset, Bishop of London: D.M. Smith, *Guide to bishop's registers of England and Wales: a survey from the Middle Ages to the abolition of the episcopacy in 1646* (1981) p. 136 and n. 3.
119 I am grateful to Helen Nicholson for the suggestion that this manuscript is now either Bodleian Library, Oxford, MS Bodley 454, or the Templar trial material bound into BL MS Cotton Julius B XII. See *The trial of the Templars in the British Isles: an edition and translation of the trial proceedings* ed. H.J. Nicholson (Aldershot, 2010).

2/2 Inventory of silver vessels at Stepney, 12 June 1313 *Guildhall Library, London, MS 25121/1712*

A roll of one membrane, pointed at the head, now folded in squares. Passages in square brackets were written in a second hand, except in the concluding entry, which was written by the first hand on a second occasion. Endorsed (a) At the foot, inverted, in the main hand of the front: 'Ultimum inventarium vasorum argenteorum' (b) In a late fourteenth- or early fifteenth-century hand: 'Sub altari iiii°. Inventarium de bonis Radulphi Baldok episcopi Lond'. Item de jocalibus suis datis ecclesie sancti Pauli.'

[*Recto*]

Inventarium vasorum argenteorum factum apud Stebbenheth' ii idus Junii anno gracie 1313°

In primis quatuor charjor*s* ponderis x li.
Item sex salsaria magna ponderis lx s.
Item due pelves magne ponderis vi li. xiii s. iiii d.
Item due pelves magne ponderis Ciiii s. ii d.
Item due pelves minores ponderis iiii li. iiii s.
Item due pelves minores ponderis iiii li.

[iii quia inter legata ecclesie sancti Pauli] Item due pelves pro capella ponderis iiii marce ii s. iiii d.
Item i olla cum catulo ponderis lxii s. vi d.
Item alia olla magna ponderis lviii s. ix d.
Item tercia olla magna ponderis xlv s. vi d.
Item quarta olla magna ponderis iiii marce
Item i olla sexangula ad aquarium ponderis xxvii s. ii d.
Item alia olla cum ii tuelliis ad aquarium ponderis xv s. x d.
Item tercia olla cum iii tuelliis ad aquarium ponderis xxii s. vi d.
Item i salarium cum ymagine ponderis xxi s.
Item i salarium sine cooperculo ponderis xiiii s. vi d.
Item i cuppa pro domino ponderis xl s.
Item alia cuppa cum pede sexangulo ponderis xxiiii s.
Item tercia cuppa quo solebat uti dominus ponderis xxxvii s. vi d.
Item quarta cuppa quo solebat uti dominus ponderis xlvi s.
Item v cuppa plana cum pede sexangulo ponderis xxii s.
Item vi cuppa cum pede sexangulo ponderis xxii s.
Item unus ciphus deauratus duplex interius sine cooperculo ponderis xix s. vi d.
Item una cuppa gravata cum magno pomello deaurata ponderis iii marce
Item alia cuppa deaurata cum opere levato ponderis lix s. ii d.
Item alia cuppa deaurata cum scutis ponderis lii s. vi d.
[*Vacat quia*] Item alia cuppa deaurata ponderis xxxiiii s. ii d. data \ [per dominum] / fratri Johanni de Eggesclive [in vita sua]
Item alia cuppa deaurata ponderis xxvii s. x d. Sciendum quod omnes alie cuppe que fuerunt scripte in anterioribus inventariis date sunt diversis amicis [in vita domini].
Item xxiiii coclearia ponderis xxxv s. vid.
Item xxvi coclearia ponderis xxxviii s. iiii d.
Item xii coclearia ponderis xiiii s. iiii d.
Item xii coclearia ponderis xii s.
Item una plata ad species cum scuto ponderis xiiii s. vi d.
Item i vas ad species cum pede ponderis xxxv s.
Item i nux cum pede argenteo deaurato precii xxiiii s.
Item xii disci argentei minoris forme ponderis xv li. xvi s. viii d.
Item xii disci argentei majoris forme ponderis xvi li.
Item xii disci argentei parvi ponderis x li viii s.
Item vi disci profundi ponderis iiii li. ii s.
Item xxiiii salsaria argentea ponderis viii li.
Item xii salsaria argentea ponderis lix s.
Item due pecie argentee in fundo aumellate cum cooperculis ponderis lvii s. x d.
Item iiii pecie argentee plane majoris forme ponderis iiii marce
Item vii pecie argentee plane minoris forme ponderis vi marce vi s. ii d.
[Item ii coclearia argentea ad species quorum i deauratum ponderis ii s. x d.]
Summa huius < Cxlix li. ii s. xi d. > secundum pondus vasorum \ [Cxlvii li. xi s. vii d.] /

Item unus calix magnus deauratus ponderis xliiii s. ii d. Legatus domino Hugoni de Veer una cum pat*er*nost*er* de ambra et appendiciis que fuerunt matris sue
Item alius calix deauratus ponderis xxii s. vi d.

Item tercius calix deauratus ponderis xxvii s.
Item quartus calix deauratus ponderis xx s.
Item due phiale argentee ponderis xviii s. iiii d.
Item due phiale sexangule ponderis xi s. viii d.
Item i thurribulum novum argenteum deauratum ponderis xxxvii s. vi d.
Item alium thurribulum argenteum vetus deauratum ponderis xxiiii s.
Item thimiaterius argenteus cum cocleario ponderis xxi s.
Item i phiala nova ad oleum infirmorum ponderis viii s. viii d.
Item due alie majores cum crismate et oleo sancto
Item i morsus argenteus deauratus cum capite Pauli et lapidibus[1] insertis ponderis xiiii s. vi d.
[Item alius morsus aureus aumallatus cum quinque lapidibus insertis ponderis vi s. viii d.]
Summa huius < xi li. xiiii s. x d. > secundum pondus

Notes
1 MS: 'lapill''.

3 John Barnet, Bishop of Ely

3/1 Will of John Barnet, Bishop of Ely, made while he was Bishop of Bath and Wells, 1364 × 1366 *LPL, Register of William Whittlesey, f. 127v*
In dei nomine amen ego Johannes permissione divina Bathoniensis episcopus et Wellensis infirmus corpore sit laus altissimo sanus mente meum in hunc modum facio testamentum. In primis lego animam meam deo et beate Marie ac omnibus sanctis eius corpusque meum ad sepeliendum in ecclesia cathedrali Wellensi si illuc commode valeat deportari alioquin in ecclesia sancti Pauli London' si in civitate London' aut eius suburbio me contigerit expirare. Et volo quod expense funerariorum fiant considerato meorum onere debitorum que quidam debita volo quod pre omnibus aliis exceptis expensis funerariorum moderatis ut premittitur exsolvantur. Item volo quod de residuo bonorum meorum per executores meos fiat distribucio inter servientes et familiares meos bene meritos unicuique juxta gradum et suorum exigenciam meritorum. Et quia ignoro quantitatem et substanciam meorum patrimonii et bonorum discrecioni executorum meorum totaliter hec committo ipsorum in hiis onerans consciencias apud deum. Ad execucionem autem presentis mee ultime voluntatis meos ordino facio et constituo executores magistros Stephanum Pymp*e*ll' decanum ecclesie Wellensis Johannem Barnet archidiaconum Essex' in ecclesia sancti Pauli London' dominos Rogerum de Bello Campo et Stephanum Ro*t*he rectores ecclesiarum de Hampton' Monialium et de Bisle Wygorniensis diocesis necnon Willelmum de Petteworth' rectorem ecclesie parochialis sancti Antonii London'.

3/2 Grant of probate to Mag. John Barnet, lately archdeacon of Essex in the church of London, Dom. Roger de Bello Campo [Beauchamp], rector of the parish church of Hampton Monialium [Minchinhampton], and Dom. William de Petteworth, lately rector of the church of St Anthony, London, as set out in the will with the exception of the place of burial: 'et pro eodem testamento et ipsius domini Johannis ultima voluntate corporis sui sepultura quam post translacionem suam ab ecclesiis Bathoniensi et Wellensi ad ecclesiam Eliensem in ipsa Eliensi ecclesia elegit dumtaxat excepta', 13 June 1373. *LPL, Register of William Whittlesey, f. 127v.*

3/3 Commission to Mag. Thomas Wormenhale, bachelor of both laws, and Mag. John Ware, *juris perito*, to grant the administration of goods to other executors, to Mag. Stephen Pympell', Dean of the church of Wells, and Dom. Stephen Rothe, lately rector of Bisley, diocese of Worcester, named in the will. Otford, 15 June 1373. *LPL, Register of William Whittlesey, f. 127v.*

4 John Bottlesham, Bishop of Rochester

4/1 Will, 15 April 1404 *LPL, Register of Thomas Arundel, vol. I, ff. 206r–206v*
In dei nomine amen die martis in crastino sancti Tiburcii et Valeriani martirorum videlicet xv die mensis Aprilis anno domini millesimo CCCC^{mo} quarto in manerio meo de Trottesclyve ego Johannes Bottesham permissione divina Roffensis episcopus licet indignus sortem condicionis humane in fragilitate assidua persistere attendens michique mortis periculum senciens iminere condo testamentum meum in hunc modum. In primis lego animam meam deo omnipotenti beatissimeque virgini Marie matri sue ac beato Andree patrono meo necnon omnibus sanctis dei et corpus meum sepeliendum in ecclesia mea cathedrali Roffensi. Item lego eidem ecclesie cathedrali centum marcas argenti ut summa huiusmodi ponatur in cista quadam ad comparandum staurum ad ecclesiam meam huiusmodi in principio anni intra*ntis*[1] videlicet liberaturas familiarium et aliorum ac alia necessaria pro stauro suo. Ita quod tanta summa reponatur in ipsa cista citra festum [*f. 206v*] nativitatis sancti Johannis Baptiste proximum sequens ibidem remansura usque ad festum sancti Michaelis tunc proximum futurum ad causam stauri comparandi ut supra. Item lego eidem ecclesie mee cathedrali mitram meam et baculum meum pastoralem ad finem et effectum quod quicumque seculares vel regulares saltem possessionati successores mei habeant usumfructum eorundem ad terminum vite eorundem et statim post decessum cuiuslibet eorundem restituantur ecclesie cathedrali predicte. Et si contingat ibidem aliquem esse successorem de ordine mendicancium volo quod habeat usumfructum eorundem in ecclesia cathedrali et civitate Roffensi dumtaxat. Item lego domino meo specialissimo domino Thome dei gracia Cantuariensi archiepiscopo tocius Anglie primato et apostolice sedis legato prout alias coram magistro Roberto Hallum et aliis executoribus meis plenius declaravi ut idem dominus meus in cuius dominacione fiduciam gero specialem sit michi et executoribus meis infrascriptis in executione testamenti huiusmodi sullevator pater et protector. Item lego ecclesie Cristi Cantuarensi unum memoriale capam videlicet precii xx^{ti} li. ea intencione ut nulla alia que illa ab executoribus meis exigatur. Item lego ad reparacionem murorum civitatis Cant' pro tutamine tuciori martiris ibidem gloriosi centum marchas argenti. Item lego collegio sancti Petri Cantubrig' omnes libros meos tam juris civilis quam canonici[2] exceptis libris Johannis in novella[3] in duobus voluminibus qui debentur monasterio de Croulond. Volo tamen et concedo quod si Nicholaus Swafham nepos meus scolas ibidem intendat

excercere habeat dictos libros et usu*m*fructum eorundem ad terminum vite sue prestita primitus caucione sufficienti collegio memorato pro libris predictis et si non posset caucionem pro omnibus ponere ponat saltem pro illis quos in hac parte recipiet. Item lego quatuor ordinibus mendicancium Cantubrig' cuilibet videlicet x marcas. Item lego quatuor ordinibus mendicancium London' cuilibet x marcas. Item cuilibet provinciali ordinum eorundem seu eorum vicariis xx s. Item lego monasterio de Croulond Lincolniensis diocesis centum marcas sub eisdem modo et forma quibus ecclesie Roffensi superius legavi. Item lego ecclesie parochiali de Yngoldesby unum vestimentum precium x li. Item lego ecclesie parochiali de Kemsale unum vestimentum precium x li. Item lego ecclesie prebendali de Brampton' unum vestimentum precium x li. Item lego domino Willelmo Barnefader capellano cantarie in ecclesia Cristi Cantuariensi pro anima domini Johannis Bukyngham quondam episcopi Lincolniensis fundate perite et dotate missale meum optimum quod quondam fuit suum. Item lego eidem cantarie missale meum novum. Item ecclesie parochiali de Yngoldesby missale meum parvum. Item lego capelle episcopi Roffensis qui pro tempore fuerit unum missale et volo quod ita intituletur inter alios libros de capella predicta. Item volo quod grangia rectorie de Fryndesby per me de novo iam incepta complete reperetur. Residuum vero omnium bonorum meorum non legatorum do et lego executoribus meis infrascriptis ut ipsi disponant pro anima mea et animabus illorum quibus sum vel fui aliqualiter obligatus ac animabus omnium fidelium defunctorum in causas pias prout voluerint alibi respondere cum celeritate possibili quos constituo per presentes magistrum Robertum Hallum dominum Rogerum Cherch' rectorem ecclesie parochialis de Bromlegh' magistros Robertum Ely Johannem Bosham et Johannem Hoke clericos ac Robertum Rycroft executores meos. In quorum omnium testimonium sigillum meum una cum privato signeto presentibus est appensum. Data die loco mense et anno domini supradictis. Et[4] mee consecracionis anno quarto.

Notes

1 MS: 'intra' followed by 6 minims.

2 Listed in M.R. James *A descriptive catalogue of the manuscripts in the library of Pembroke College, Cambridge* (Cambridge, 1905) p. xiii, with one addition noted in Cavanaugh, 'Books', p. 115.

3 Johannes Andreae *Novellae in decretales*, printed Venice, 1489.

4 MS: 'Est'.

4/2 Grant of probate, before the Archbishop of Canterbury, to Dom. Robert Cherch, rector of Bromley, Mag. Robert Ely, Mag. John Bosham, Mag. John Hoke, clerks, and Robert Rycroft, reserving the power of committing the administration to Mag. R. Hallum, archdeacon, the Archbishop's chancellor, named in the will. Lambeth, 24 April 1404. *LPL, Register of Thomas Arundel, vol. I, f. 206v.*

5 William Bottlesham, Bishop of Rochester

5/1 Will, 16 February 1399/1400 *LPL, Register of Thomas Arundel, vol. I, ff. 166v–167r*

In dei nomine amen nos frater Willelmus permissione divina Roffensis episcopus ex una parte recolens determinacionem sancti doctoris sancti scilicet Thome de Aquino per quam licitum non videtur assumpto de statu religioso ad presulatum condere testamentum nisi papa ad hoc suam amplictacionem dispensacionem[1] ex alio latere sperans ratihabicionem domini pape quo ad illam ratihabicionem amplictacionem que dispensacionis habende et ex alio latere volentes uti jure episcoporum Cantuariensis provincie in hac parte si quod habeant nullo modo exponens animam meam periculo ego frater Willelmus predictus sane mentis et integre memorie condo testamentum meum in hunc modum. In primis lego animam meam deo et beate Marie beato Andree apostolo beato Dominico et omnibus sanctis corpusque meum sepeliendum in conventu fratrum ordinis predicatorum London' que sepultura infra triduum meum post obitum fiat sine dilacione ulteriori in qua ardeant quinque cerei proprii[2] et xii torticii conducticii quos teneant xii pauperes quorum quilibet habeat xii d. Item volo quod conventus ille habeat unam pitanciam cum illis qui veniunt ad sepulturam faciendam. Item volo quod distribuantur inter pauperes tenentes meos de Hallyng' Snodelonde et Trottysclyve xl s. ad que perficienda volo et assigno de bonis meis xx li. Ita quod quicquid de illis xx^{ti} li. remanere poterit habeat idem conventus racione sepulture mee predicte. Item lego conventui Cantebrig' ordinis predicatorum xx li. Item conventui Lynme ordinis predicti x li. si tanta summa salvis debitis meis et expensis de bonis meis levari poterit et plus usque ad centum li. conventui Cantabrig' et quinquaginta li. conventui Lynme predictis si tanta summa de bonis meis predictis debitis prius persolutis remanere contigerit quia tantum et plus debeo conventibus supradictis. Item lego fratri Willelmo Bozun capam habitum et mantellum cooperculum lecti cum tapeto ii langella pulvinarium et i canvas meliora que habeo excepto cooperculo cum tapeto super magnum lectum meum. Item lego fratri Rogero Dymmok magistro capam et habitum. Item lego fratri Johanni Sayll' capam et habitum sed habeat Rogerus predictus de istis duobus meliores. Item volo quod Johannes Fynchyngfeld' marescallus et Henricus Walpool habeant feoda sua consueta. Item lego Johanni Barbour camerario meo cooperculum lecti cum tapeto curtinis selatura langell*um* et matteris in quibus jaceo. Item Thome Broman et Johanni Cuppere ii qr. frumenti per equales porciones. Item lego Johanni Sewale Thome Boteller Willelmo Totyngton et Johanni Wrenne viii s. per equales porciones ad orandum pro anima mea. Item volo quod omnes servitores mei habeant stipendia sua plen*e* [*f. 167r*] pro presenti termino. Residuum vero omnium bonorum meorum do et lego executoribus meis infrascriptis ut ipsi disponant pro anima mea sicut coram summo judice voluerint respondere. Et supplico reverendissime paternitati domini archiepiscopi Cantuariensis quatinus cordi capiat disposicionem meam supradictam sic quod pro viribus facultatum mearum deductis precipue debitis meis voluntas mea supramemorata suum habeat effectum ut est expressum et quod idem reverendissimus pater superintendat ad administracionem paucorum bonorum meorum et committat administracionem eorundem bonorum personis et executoribus per me nominatis sub auctoritate et defensione suis quia alias ut dicunt nolunt intromittere de eisdem. Executores huius testamenti ordino facio et constituo fratrem Rogerum Dymmok' theologie professorem magistrum Johannem Launce rectorem ecclesie parochialis de Suthflette fratres Willelmum Bozun et Johannem Sayl eiusdem ordinis. In cuius rei testimonium sigillum meum presentibus est appensum. Data in manerio meo de Trottesclyv' xvi^{to} die mensis Februarii anno domini millesimo CCC^{mo} nonagesimo nono. Et mee translacionis anno undecimo.

Notes

1 Thomas Aquinas *Summa theologiae*, II^{a} IIe, qu. 185, art 8.

2 MS obscure: 'proprii', 'own', as opposed to the 'torticii', which are 'hired'.

5/2 Power given to Mag. John La*u*nce, rector of the parish church of Southfleet, and William Bamburgh', administrators, for selling the goods of William, Bishop of Rochester, deceased, listed in the annexed inventory, as he has died intestate owing large sums of money and goods to his church of Rochester and to divers other creditors, rendering an account of the sale when required. Sealed. Date not recorded. *LPL, Register of Thomas Arundel, vol. I, f. 167r*

5/3 Letters releasing Mag. John La*u*nce, rector of the parish church of Southfleet, and William Bamburgh', esquire, from any further account for the estate of William, late Bishop of Rochester, their accounts having been heard, with the exception of £54 17*s.* 8¾*d.* worth of goods not yet sold. Canterbury, 24 May 1402. *LPL, Register of Thomas Arundel, vol. I, f. 167r*

6 Robert Braybrooke, Bishop of London

6/1 Commission from Thomas Arundel, Archbishop of Canterbury, to Sir Gerard Braybrok, knight, and Edmund Hampdene, *domicello*, executors of Bishop Braybroke's will, on account of the distance allowing them to sell goods of the Bishop to perform his will without the Archbishop's sight of [the inventory], but requiring them to prove the will in the Archbishop's presence the following Saturday [22 September 1404]; Slindon, 17 September 1404. *LPL, Register of Thomas Arundel, vol. I, f. 214v.*

6/2 Indenture with an inventory of the possessions of Robert Braybrooke, Bishop of London, at the date of his death, 27 August 1404

Guildhall Library, London, MS 25271/58

An indenture of two membranes, sewn Chancery fashion, as a deed, with a third membrane, the certificate (**6/3**), fixed to the foot of the lower membrane and sealed on a tongue through it. Fragmentary traces of a seal in red wax remain. The inventory is the indented copy, prepared as part of the probate process, and acknowledged by the indenture between the executors on the one hand, and the Archbishop of Canterbury's register on the other, to be a true listing and valuation of the goods of the estate. Endorsed in a sixteenth- or early seventeenth-century hand: 'Inventarium bonorum domini Roberti Braybroke episcopi London' cum administrationis litteris annexis anno domini 1404'. The inventory is transcribed in L.H. Butler, 'Robert Braybrooke, Bishop of London

(1381–1404) and his kinsmen' (unpublished DPhil thesis, University of Oxford, 1951) pp. 539–59.

In dei nomine amen. Inventarium omnium bonorum que fuerunt bone memorie Roberti Braybrok' nuper episcopi Londoniensis die quo obiit videlicet vicesimo septimo die mensis Augusti anno domini millesimo quadringentesimo quarto per ipsum dimissorum et in locis infrascriptis per Gerardum Braybrok' militem Edmundum Hamden armigerum Johannem Wyke et Rogerum Albryghton' clericos executores testamenti eiusdem domini episcopi inventorum ac ad manus ipsorum executorum qualitercumque perveniencium per viros fidedignos noticiam rei pleniorem obtinentes[1] appreciatorum de mandato reverendissimi in Cristo patris ac domini domini Thome dei gracia Cantuariensis archiepiscopi tocius Anglie primatis et apostolice sedis legati qui testamentum predictum approbavit per eosdem executores antequam administracionem in bonis predictis attingerent confectum et reverendissimo patri predicto realiter traditum et liberatum ac penes registrum eiusdem reverendissimi patris per modum indenture dimissum sequitur in hunc modum.

In primis in studio episcopi predicti tam apud Hadham quam in palacio London' una biblioteca precium x li. Item una legenda sanctorum precium xlvi s. viii d. Item i catholicon precium lxvi s. viii d.[2] Item una policronica precium lx s.[3] Item i racionale divinorum precium xl s.[4] Item i par decretorum precium xiii s. iiii d.[5] Item i par decretalium debilis precium vi s. viii d. Item i aliud par decretalium precium xvi s. viii d.[6] Item i liber sextus cum tribus glosis precium xl s.[7] Item i par Clementinarum precium xl s.[8] Item i Innocencius albo corio coopertus precium xiii s. iiii d.[9] Item i Innocencius rubeo corio coopertus precium xvi s. Item i archidiaconus in rosario precium lx s.[10] Item Johannes in novellis super sextum precium xxiii s. iiii d.[11] Item i Hostiensis in lectura in duobus voluminibus precium iiii li. vi s. viii d.[12] Item i speculum judiciale precium l s.[13] Item i Hostiensis in summa precium xl s.[14] Item Gesselinus super sextum precium xiii s. iiii d.[15] Item Willelmus super sextum precium vi s. viii d.[16] Item Bernardus Maynard' super Clementinas v s.[17] Item historie decretorum et unum provinciale precium iiii s.[18] Item Isidorus ethemologiarum precium xx s.[19] Item i parvus liber de sermonibus antiquis precium ii s. Item Isidorus de summo bono[20] cum vita beati Thome martiri[21] et Gregorio in pastoralibus[22] precium vi s. viii d. Item Titus Livius in iii voluminibus precium xiii s. iiii d.[23] Item questiones sancti Thome de veritate precium x s.[24] Item bellum Trojanum precium xiii s. iiii d.[25] Item i parvus liber continens in prosa historias biblie precium iii s. Item unus liber rubeus de xii capitulis Ricardi heremite precium iii s. iiii d.[26] Item i quarternus albus de xii capitulis proximis predictis et de incendio amoris precium ii s.[27] Item ii parvi quaterni precium xii d. Item liber Salustii Crispi historiographi precium ii s.[28] Item tractatus qui dicitur pars oculi precium v s. iiii d.[29] Item quidam liber qui sic incipit 'de quolibet festo' rubrica precium vi s. viii d. Item quidam liber qui sic incipit in rubrica 'liber colleccionum' precium x s. Item liber Julii Solini precium xii d.[30] Item unum corpus juris civilis precium lxvi s. viii d.[31] Item unus liber de taxis omnium beneficiorum Angl*ie* precium xxvi s. viii d.[32]

Secuntur libri in capella predicti domini episcopi inventi videlicet unum missale magnum precium xiii li. vi s. viii d. i missale parvum precium iiii li. Item i missale novum albo corio coopertum precium xii li. i missale rubeum precium x li. i antiphonare precium xiii li. vi s. viii d. i portiforium non notatum precium xii li. i liber novus continens prefaciones et benedicciones pontificales per totum annum precium xl s. i antiphonare magnum precium xii li. tria antiphonaria magna precium xxvi li. i antiqum antiphonare precium xlvi s. viii d. i portiforium notatum precium lx s. i portiforium portativum precium x li. ii gradalia scripta in motelyn' precium C s. ii gradalia scripta in velym precium vi li. xiii s. iiii d. i graduarium precium liii s. iiii d. i legenda in ii voluminibus precium xiii li. vi s. viii d. i evangelizarium et i epistolarium precium lxvi s. viii d. i collectarium precium lx s. i manuale precium xxx s. iiii^{or} processionalia precium Cvi s. viii d. i processionarium antiqum precium x s. i liber organicus precium x s. i psalterium precium xxvi s. viii d. i liber continens unum provinciale et modum serviendi pape in missa precium vi s. viii d. i liber pontificalis precium lxvi s. viii d. Item i alius liber pontificalis precium lxvi s. viii d. i liber pontificalis in papiro precium vi s. viii d. ii quarterni de historia sancte Anne precium ii s.[33] iiii^{or} quarterni unius secte pro dedicacionibus ecclesiarum precium viii s. i liber solus pro eodem officio precium iii s. iiii d. i missale abbreviatum precium xx s. i hympnarium non ligatum precium ii s. i portiforium continens partem sanctor*alis* dumtaxat precium xx s. i ordinale antiqum de usu Sarum precium vi s. viii d.

Item in capella predicta unus anulus pontificalis cum petra viridi precium xlvi s. viii d. Item unum vestimentum \ cum tribus capis / de panno aurei de Cipre precium xxvi li. \ xiii s. iiii d. / Item unum vestimentum absque capis de panno aurei rubeo cum orfrayes de velwet blodi*o* precium vi li. Item i vestimentum cum quinque capis de ragmas blodi*o* precium x li. Item i vestimentum cum quinque capis de ragmas rube*o* precium x li. Item i vestimentum cum iii capis de baudekyn blodi*o* precium x li. Item i vestimentum absque capis de baudekyn rube*o* precium xl s. Item i vestimentum absque capis de baudekyn rube*o* et nigr*o* xl s. Item i vestimentum absque capis de samyt steignat*o* cum toto apparatu eidem pertinenti precium lx s. Item vestimentum de velwet crymsye rube*o* cum i pari sandalium eiusdem secte absque capis precium x li. Item i vestimentum de baudekyn coloris crocei absque capis precium xxxiii s. iiii d. Item vestimentum de baudekyn blodi*o* absque capis precium xx s. Item i vestimentum antiqum de tartaryn viridi precium xx s. Item i vestimentum antiqum de samyt rube*o* precium vi s. viii d. Item i vestimentum de bokacyne alb*o* pro quadragesima tam pro capella quam pro oratorio precium lxvi s. viii d. Item i calix argenti deauratus ponderis de Troy i lib. iii qr. precium lib. xxviii s. xxix s. ix d. Item i deosculatorium habens in utroque latere columpnam ponderis de Troy i lib. i unc. precium i lib. xxviii s. xxx s. iiii d. Item ii phiole argenti albi ponderis de Troy v unc. i qr. precium unc. xxvi d. xi s. iiii d. Item i frount' et i reredos embraudat*i* cum magnis ymaginibus precium xx li. Item i fro*u*ntell' de velwet nigr*o* embraudat*o* cum sole et cignis precium xxvi s. viii d. Item i fro*u*ntell' de damask alb*o* embraudat*o* cum apostolis precium lxvi s. viii d. Item i fro*u*ntell' de velvet rube*o* embraudat*o* cum rosis precium xl s. Item i fro*u*ntell' embraudat*us* cum griphonibus et rosis precium xvi s. viii d. Item i ymago Trinitatis embraudata super velwet rube*o* precium xiii s. iiii d. Item i capsa embraudata cum salutacione et nativitate beate Marie precium xiii s. iiii d. Item i capsa pro corporali embraudata cum armis Braybrok' precium vi s. viii d. Item i capsa de velwet rube*o* et i capsa embraudata cum leonibus precium v s. Item i pilwe de velwet rube*o* precium vi s. viii d. Item i capsa embraudata cum Cristo sedente in judicio precium iiii s. Item i moce pro capa embraudat*us* cum salutacione beate Marie precium iii s. iiii d. Item vi moces pro capis in una pecia de armis Braybrok' precium xiii s. iiii d. Item ii parvi crucifixi cum Maria et Johanne embraudati precium x s. Item i remanens panni aurei \ rubei / et i remanens de velwet rube*o* et i remanens panni aurei imperialis precium xii s. Item xii pecie de velwet rube*o* et nigr*o* precium xxvi s. viii d. Item i celur' et ii curtini de tartaryn viridi radiat*o* ii curtini de tartaryn viridi et alb*o* paleat*o* et ii curtini de tartaryn blodi*o* radiat*o* precium xxvi s. viii d. Item v sudaria precium xii s. Item i par dalmaticularum panni aurei imperialis precium vi li. xiii s. iiii d. Item i par dalmaticularum de satyn rube*o* vi li. xiii s. iiii d. Item i par dalmaticularum de satyn alb*o* precium xx s. Item i par dalmaticularum de tartaryn viridi ex una parte samyt purple ex alia parte precium xx s. Item i alba et i amicta cum stola et manipulis embraudat*e* et cum ii cingulis inscriptis cum evangeliis 'In principio' et 'Missus est' precium x s. Item i amicta precium x s. Item unum par sandalinorum et sabatinorum de velwet blodi*o* cum i pari de galoches precium xx s. Item i par sandalinorum et sabatinorum de damask' precium vi s. viii d. Item duo paria sandalinorum precium vi s. viii d. Item unum par cirothecarum precium xl s. Item v^{que} alia paria cirotecharum precium v s. iiii d. Item viii panni aurei diversarum sectarum precium ix li. Item vi panni de bokacyne alb*o* radiat*o* precium iiii li. Item viii antique albe et vi amicte precium xii s. Item i superpellicium de lawne precium viii s. Item unum superpellicium de Champeyne Reynes precium vi s. viii d. Item xl superpellicia precium vi li. Item i capa de panno nigro linato cum satyn precium xxx s. Item \ ix / superpellicia puerorum precium xiiii s. viii d. Item xvi palle altaris precium ix s. vi d. Item v^{que} manutergia precium x d. Item viii carpete precium vi li. xv s. Item decem costere de worsted ii tapeti de opere tapeserie et vi pecie de tapeserie viridi precium xx s. viii d. Item i tabula de Trinitate depicta que legatur ecclesie de Horsingdon' precium xiii s. iiii d. Item i alia tabula de passione depicta que legatur domino Reginaldo Braybrok militi precium xl s. Item tres tabule depicte precium xxix s. Item una campana cum bolstero pro somero episcopi in sua visitacione precium ii s. Item iii ciste vocate standardes precium liii s. iiii d. Item i par de trussyngcofres precium xlvi s. viii d. Item ii alia paria de trussyngcofres precium xv s. Item i stoppe cum aspersorio i par candelabrorum i pila et i skonce de laton' precium v s. Item xiii skonces ligne*i* precium ii s. viii d. Item vi spereshaftes precium iii s. Item ii pelves vitree duplicate precium viii d. Item unum par organ*or*um precium liii s. iiii d. Item i aliud par organorum portativorum precium xxxiii s. iiii d. Item i clothesak' pro capella precium v s. Item i cathedra ferrea precium xxvi s. viii d.

Secuntur inventa in garderoba predicti episcopi tam in palacio suo London' quam in manerio suo de Hadham predicto. In primis unus lectus de syndone rube*o* de Tripe embraudatus cum i traille cum vi costeris ii tapetis et vi cussinis de worsted' ac iii banqueris de tapeserie precium vi li. Item unus alius lectus de worsted' viridi plan*o* cum curtinis de tartaryn xii costeris quinque tapetis et vi cussinis de worsted' precium xlvi s. viii d. Item i lectus albus de worsted' embraudatus cum rosis et armis domini episcopi predicti precium xxvi s. viii d. Item vi costere plane de worsted' rube*o* precium x s. Item ii lecti de worsted' blodi*o* cum curtinis set absque costeris precium xxviii s. Item i lectus de worsted' rube*o* precium xiiii s. Item unus lectus de worsted' viridi et alb*o* cum curtinis de carde precium xiii s. iiii d. Item i lectus de worsted' rube*o* cum curtinis de tartaryn ac vi costeris ii tapetis i banquero et vii cussinis de worsted' precium iiii li. Item ii antiqua coopertoria absque testuris precium viii s. iiii d. Item ii ridell*i* de sindone rube*o* et v^{que} tapeta antiqua de tapeserie cum armis regis Anglie precium xiii s. iiii d. Item i lectus de worsted' viridi embraudatus cum una cerva jacente in una rosa cum xi costeris iii curtinis ii tapetis et i banquero precium liii s. iiii d. Item i lectus operatus ad modum assheler de worsted' rube*o* cum iii curtinis viii costeris viii cussinis iii banqueris precium iiii li. Item i lectus de serico operatus ad modum assheler qui legatus est Edmundo Hamdene cum i canevass' i matrass' i pari fustianorum i pari linthiaminum de Reynes et una pana furrata cum menyver*e* ac omnibus costeris banqueris et cussinis eidem lecto pertinentibus precium x li. Item unus lectus de serico pulverizatus cum boterflyes qui legatus est domino Gerardo Braybrok' militi cum i canvas' i matras' i pari fustianorum i pari linthiaminum de Reynes una pana furrata cum menyver ac omnibus costeris banqueris et cussinis eidem lecto pertinentibus precium x li. Item ii cussini de serico coloris blodii et viridis precium x s. viii d. Item i lectus simplex de worsted' cum curtinis de tartaryn precium xxx s. Item vii canevas' et iii presseclothes precium xiii s. iiii d. Item ii pailett*es* xii d. Item quinque bolstere et xviii pulvinaria de downe precium xl s. iiii d. Item ii fetherbeddes precium xxvi s. viii d. Item decem paria blanketorum precium xlii s. Item ii paria fustianorum antiqorum precium xv s. Item i par staminorum precium vi s. viii d. Item viii matras' precium liii s. iiii d. Item i quylt debil*is* precium ii s. Item xxiiii paria linthiaminum i foteshete et iiii hedeshetes precium Cix s. Item vi mantell' precium xxiii s. iiii d. Item furrure de menyver precium xiiii li. Item i furrura de grey precium xvi s. viii d. Item una amic*t*a de grey precium xxxiii s. iiii d. Item vestes usuales pro corpore domini episcopi predicti precium vii li. xv s. Item una capella de velwet nigr*o* precium vi s. viii d. Item ii rochet*i* antiq*i* de Reynes precium xiii s. iiii d. Item iiii rocheti de panno lineo precium viii s. Item xii arcus et viii duodene catapultarum precium xxxi s. viii d. Item i olla zinziberis in sirupo precium iiii s. vi d. Item due ciste computatorie precium x s. Item i canapium de filo lineo precium xiii s. iiii d. Item i corium Hispanie precium iiii li. Item i remanens blanketi precium viii s. Item i remanens panni linei precium xvi s. viii d. Item i tabellaria de prucia precium x s.

Secuntur bona in aula predicti domini episcopi inventa. In primis una aula steignata de panno lineo precium C s. Item i aula operata ad modum assheler precium xliii s. iiii d. Item i aula de worsted' viridi cum racione 'Come dieu le veult' precium xxxiii s. iiii d. Item i doserium et i banquerum steignata cum hawthornes precium x s. Item i tentorium cum toto apparatu precium vi li. xiii s. iiii d. Item iii olle enee vocate chaufours precium v s. viii d.

Item bona in panetria et boteria dicti domini episcopi inventa. In primis unus ciphus argenti deauratus qui legatus est domine comitisse Hereford' precium viii li. Item duo paria de panyers vocatis gardeviandes precium x s. Item bordeclothes towailles safnapes et browers tam nova quam antiqua precium vii li. ii s. Item octo olle de corio precium ii s. vi d.

Coquina. In primis quinque cigni apud Fulham inventi precium x s. Item i par de barelferers precium vi s. Item i par de fisshebarels precium iii s. iiii d. Item xix lag. mellis precium xix s. Item ii bus. di. de semine sinap*ii* precium iii s. iiii d. Item ii fryyngpannes precium vi s. viii d. Item ii wortknyves precium xii d. Item iii paria de aundirnes precium xiii s. Item i pestell' et i morter' precium iii s. Item vasa de peutre ponderis iiii^{xx}xiiii lb. precium xv s. x d. Item olle enee vii^{tem} precium xliii s. viii d. Item viii patelle cupr*ee* precium lxv s. i d.[34] Item iiii broches ferri precium x s. x d. Item i firfork' i grydirne vii broches et i magn*um* rak' ferri precium lxviii s. iiii d. Item alia necessaria et utensilia coquine modici valoris per se precium xxiiii s. iiii d.

Eweria et candelaria. In primis duo paria pelvium argenti cum armis domini episcopi predicti ponderis de Troy xv lib. x unc. di. precium lib. xxvi s. viii d. xxi li. iii s. iiii d. Item cera ponderis xl lib. precium lib. v d. xvi s. viii d. Item weke pro torticiis ponderis viii stone precium iii s. iiii d.

Item secuntur bona in stabulo predicti domini episcopi et aliis officiis et locis diversis ad eundem episcopum spectancia. In primis unus equs niger ambulans precium xxvi s. viii d. Item i equs sorell' ambulans precium xxvi s. viii d. Item i equs bay hakenay nuncupatus precium x s. Item i equs pro somero coquine precium xx s. Item iii pulli equini precium x li. Item iii eque stodemares precium xl s. Item i charietta cum vii equis et toto apparatu precium xvi li. Item ii somersadeles ii clothesakkes ii barhides i male i malesadell' precium xliiii s. iiii d. Item i incus precium x s. viii d. Item diversa necessaria hospicii apud Hadham inventa ut de exitibus coquine pistrine et lardar*ii* et consimilium precium xxxiiii li. xiiii s. v d. Item i aper et xii porci apud Hadham inventi precium liiii s. iiii d. Item xxix qr. brasei apud Hadham inventa precium viii li. xiiii s. iii d. Item xlii qr. brasei apud Roiston' inventa precium ix li. ii s.

Sequitur staurum tam vivum quam mortuum in diversis maneriis ad episcopatum Londoniensem spectantibus.[35] Et primo in manerio de Claketon' unus taurus precium x s. Vacce l precium capitis x s. Hurtardi xiii precium capitis xv d. Multones CCC precium capitis xvi d. Oves matrices CCCxxvii precium capitis xv d. lxvi li. xv s.

Item in manerio de Wykeham de ordeo iiii qr. vii bus. precium qr. iii s. iiii d. De drageto iiii bus. precium bus. iiii d. De vestura frumenti xxxvii acrarum precium acre v s. De vestura myxtilionis xiiii acrarum precium acre iii s. iiii d. De vestura avenarum xliii acrarum precium acre iii s. De equis pro caruca vii precium capitis x s. De bobus iiii precium capitis xiii s. iiii d. De vaccis lii precium capitis ix s. De hurtardis et ovibus matricibus Clxxv precium capitis xii d. lvii li. iiii s. vii d.

Chelmesford'. De frumento xvi qr. precium qr. xl d. De ordeo viii qr. precium qr. xl d. De avenis xx qr. precium qr. ii s. De stottis iiii precium capitis xviii s. De tauris i precium x s. De vaccis xxiiii precium capitis x s. De ovibus matricibus iiii^{xx} precium capitis xvi d. De feno ibidem ix carectate precium carectate ii s. De terra warecta xl acre precium acre viii d. De terra rebinata xxx acre precium acre xii d. De terra compostata viii acre precium acre ii s. Item i carecta cum toto apparatu precium xxvi s. viii d. xxxiii li. vi s.

Suthmynstr'. De acris seminatis cum frumento xxxviii precium acre v s. De acris seminatis cum siligine xv acre precium iii s. iiii d. De equis carectatis viii precium capitis xx s. De tauris et vaccis Cxii precium capitis x s. De hurtardis et ovibus matricibus CClxxiiii precium capitis xx d. De agnis CCCxiiii precium viii li. De stramine et palea precium lxv s. viii d. Cx li. ii s. iiii d.

Neylond'. De acris seminatis cum frumento lv acre precium acre v s. De jumentis x precium capitis x s. De pullanis masculis ii precium capitis x s. De vaccis xii precium capitis x s. De stramine et palea precium xxxi s. ii d. Summa xxvii li. vi s. ii d.

Althorne. De acris seminatis cum frumento xl acre precium acre v s. De jumentis x precium capitis x s. De pullanis annal*ibus* vi precium capitis ii s. De tauris et vaccis vii precium capitis x s. De hurtardis et ovibus matricibus iiii^{xx}viii precium capitis xviii d. Summa xxv li. xiiii s.

Storteford'. De cignis aier*iis* ii precium xiii s. iiii d. De cigniculis ii precium iiii s. De feno ibidem precium xx s. Summa xxxvii s. iiii d.

Leyndon'. De ovibus matricibus Cxl precium capitis xviii d. Summa x li. x s.

Hadham. De vestura frumenti lvi acre precium acre v s. De vestura pisarum xiii acre precium acre iii s. De vestura avenarum lxxviii acre precium acre iii s. De equis carectatis v precium capitis x s. De stottis vi precium capitis x s. De bobus iiii precium capitis xiii s. iiii d. De tauris et vaccis xxxii precium capitis viii s. De multonibus CCiiii^{xx} precium capitis xviii d. De feno ibidem xxiiii carectate precium carectate ii s. De feno eciam ibidem precium C s. Item carbones ibidem existentes precium l s. Summa lxxix li. x s. iiii d.

Stebbenhith. De feno ibidem remanenti precium C s. Item i batella precium vi s. viii d. Summa Cvi s. viii d.

Fulham. De frumento ibidem in manibus firmarii xxiii qr. ii bus. precium qr. v s. De siligine xxx qr. vii bus. precium qr. iiii s. De pisis i qr. precium iii s. iiii d. De ordeo lvii qr. precium qr. iiii s. De avenis viii qr. ii bus. precium qr. ii s. De equis carectatis iii precium capitis x s. De stottis iiii precium capitis x s. De bobus xii precium capitis xiii s. iiii d. De tauris et vaccis xli precium capitis x s. De vitulis i precium iii s. De multonibus Ciiii^{xx}vi precium capitis xviii d. De ovibus matricibus et aliis lxv precium capitis xiiii d. De agnis liiii precium capitis xii d. Summa lxxvi li. xvi s. xi d.

Wormeholt. De bobus viii precium capitis xiii s. iiii d. De tauris et vaccis xxix precium capitis x s. De terra warecta xxvi acre precium acre xii d. Summa xxi li. ii s. viii d.

ȝillyng. De equis carectatis ii precium xv s. De stottis iiii precium capitis vi s. viii d. De bobus iiii precium capitis xiii s. iiii d. De tauris et vaccis xx precium capitis x s. [*Mem. 2r*] Summa xiiii li. xv s.

Secuntur debita et arreragia ballivorum et receptorum denariorum domini episcopi supradicti. In primis Thomas de Lyes debet xlix s. vii d. Item dominus Johannes Wyke de denariis per eum receptis debet Ciiii^{xx} li. ii s. vii d. Item Rogerus Pynchepole de denariis per eum receptis debet Clxxiii li. iii s. xi d.

Item apud Ȝyllyng Thomas Burton debet x s. ii d. ob. Robertus Burton debet xxv li. Willelmus Cony debet xiiii li. x s. Item apud Wormeholt Johannes Danyell debet xii li. x s. Johannes Norman debet xl s. Item apud Fulham Johannes Clerk' firmarius ibidem debet xxxiiii li. xviii s. Johannes Nottele collector ibidem debet C s. Johannes Adam nuper bedellus debet xl s. Item apud Fynchesley Johannes Saneye collector ibidem debet xxxv s. Item apud Harengeye Thomas Hougwe debet xl s. Johannes atte Fryth' debet xxx s. Hugo Buxton' debet li s. xi d. Thomas Pope debet lxxvi s. viii d. Apud palacium London' Willelmus Fraunceys debet vi li. iiii s. Apud Stebbenhith Thomas Whytyng debet xx li. Thomas Potter debet ix li. xiii s. iiii d. Item apud Hakeney Willelmus Salm*a*n debet xxx li. Item apud Hadham Ricardus Pernell debet iiii li. vi s. Item apud Branketre Johannes Redeman debet lxiiii s. Robertus Ro*u*ton' debet xx s. Willelmus Coupehood debet xxv s. Item apud Claketon' Thomas Joman debet ix li. Item apud Wykeham Johannes Sharp' debet vii li. Johannes Godwynsey debet xl s. Johanna Grafton debet ix s. Johannes Boget debet xl s. Thomas Saward' debet iiii li. Item apud Chelmesford' Nicholaus Waleys debet x li. Thomas Wyllynghale debet xl s. Johannes Harry debet iiii li.[36] Item apud Orsete Johannes Dudley debet viii li. Preterea Nicholaus Tannere debet xvii s. Item Philippus Englefeld debet xvi s. viii d. Item Reginaldus Braybrok' miles debet Cl li. Item Bartholomeus Bourchier miles debet vi li. xiii s. iiii d. Item magister Adam atte Welle debet xxxii li.

Secuntur debita desperata. In primis prior de Colne debet l li. Item Thomas Bradewardyne medicus debet vi li. xiii s. iiii d. Item Thomas dominus de Morle debet x li. Item Alexander Burton' de Fulham debet x li. Item executores testamenti Johannis Radenor debent xxii s. x d. Item magister Willelmus Bron' debet xli s. iii d. ob. Item Robertus Brounyng de Stebbenhith debet xxx li. Item Thomas Potter' de eadem debet xxxiii li. xii s. Item Johannes Gray de Coppeford debet xxvii s.

Summa omnium bonorum predictorum preter debita et arreragiorum MCCviii li. vii s. viii d.
Summa debitorum et arreragiorum speratorum viiClxxviii li. vi s. iiii d. ob.
Summa bonorum et debitorum speratorum MixCiiii^{xx}vi li. xiiii s. ob.
Summa debitorum et arreragiorum desperatorum Cxliiii li xvi s. v d. ob.
Summa totalis omnium bonorum et debitorum et arreragiorum predictorum MMCxxxi li. x s. vi d.

Notes

1 Followed by a space, with line filler.

2 John of Genoa (Johannes Januensis) (compiler) *Catholicon*, printed Mainz, ?1460.

3 Probably Ranulf Higden *Polychronicon* ed. C. Babington and J.R. Lumby (9 vols., RS, 41; 1865–6).

4 Willelmus Durandus the elder *Rationale divinorum officiorum*, printed Mainz, 1459.

5 Gratian *Decretum*, printed in *Corpus iuris canonici* ed. E. Friedberg (2nd edition, 2 vols., Leipzig, 1922) i.

6 Gregory IX *Decretales*, printed in *Corpus iuris canonici*, ii, cols. 1–928.

7 *Liber sextus decretalium*, with the Decretals from Gregory IX (1234) to Boniface VIII (1298), printed Strassburg, 1465; *Corpus iuris canonici*, ii, cols. 933–1124. The three glossators: Guido de Baysio, Johannes Andreae and Johannes Monachus.

8 *Liber septimus decretalium*, with the Decretals from Boniface VIII (1298) to Clement V (1314), *Corpus iuris canonici*, ii, cols. 1129–1200.

9 This and the following volume: presumably Innocent IV *Apparatus in quinque libros decretalium*, printed Strassburg, 1477.

[10] Guido de Baysio *Rosarium seu apparatus ad decretum*, printed Strassburg, 1472.
[11] Johannes Andreae *Novellae in decretales*, printed Venice, 1489.
[12] Henricus de Segusio, Cardinal Bishop of Ostia *Lectura super decretales*, printed Strassburg, 1512.
[13] Willelmus Durandus the elder, *Speculum judiciale*, printed Strassburg, 1473.
[14] Henricus de Segusio, Cardinal Bishop of Ostia *Summa super titulis decretalium*, printed Rome, 1473.
[15] Jesselin de Cassagnes *Apparatus ad librum sextum*, unprinted; J. Tarrant, 'The life and works of Jesselin de Cassagnes' *Bulletin of Medieval Canon Law*, new series, 9 (1979) pp. 37–64.
[16] Willelmus de Monte Lauduno *Lectura super sextum*, printed Toulouse, 1524.
[17] Bernardus Maynard, unpublished commentary on *Liber septimus decretalium*, known as the *Constitutiones Clementinae*: J. Kejr, 'Der Apparat zu den Klementinen von Bernardus Maynardi' *Bulletin of Medieval Canon Law*, new series, 13 (1983) pp. 49–56.
[18] A collection of decretals and a *provinciale*, a book of provincial constitutions: for sources of these, see C.R. Cheney, 'William Lyndwood's *Provinciale*', reprinted in his *Medieval texts and studies* (Oxford, 1973) pp. 158–84, at 162–77.
[19] Isidorus Hispalensis (Isidore of Seville) *Etymologiae*; printed as *Isidori Hispalensis episcopi etymologiarum sive originum libri XX* ed. W.M. Lindsay (2 vols., Oxford, 1911).
[20] Isidorus Hispalensis *Sententiae*, *CPL* 1199.
[21] A life of Thomas Becket.
[22] Gregory the Great *De cura pastorali*, *CPL* 1712.
[23] Presumably Titus Livius *Historiarum ab urbe condita libri*, printed Rome, 1469.
[24] Hugo Ripelinus *Compendium veritatis theologicae* ed. A. Borgnet *Alberti Magni Opera omnia* (38 vols., Paris, 1890–9) xxxiv, pp. 1–270 (often attributed in the Middle Ages to Thomas Aquinas).
[25] Probably Dares Phrygius *De excidio Troiae historia* ed. F.O. Meister (Leipzig, 1873).
[26] Richard Rolle of Hampole *Emendatio vitae*, printed Paris, 1510; ed. N.J. Watson (Toronto medieval Latin texts, 21; Toronto, 1995).
[27] As note 26, along with Richard Rolle of Hampole *Incendium amoris* ed. M. Deanesly (Manchester, 1915).
[28] Works of C. Sallustius Crispus, probably the *Bellum Catalinae* and *Bellum Jugurthinum*.
[29] Willelmus de Pagula *Oculus sacerdotis*, unprinted: L.E. Boyle, 'The *Oculus sacerdotis* and some other works of William de Pagula' *Transactions of the Royal Historical Society*, 5th series, 5 (1955) pp. 81–110.
[30] C. Julius Solinus *Rerum memorabilium collectanee*, printed Rome, 1474; *C. Iulii Solini Collectanea rerum memorabilium*, ed. T. Mommsen (Berlin, 1895).
[31] Justinian, *Corpus iuris civilis*, ed. T. Mommsen, P. Krüger, R. Schöll and W. Kroll (3 vols., Berlin, 1872–7).
[32] Perhaps the taxation of Pope Nicholas of 1291 (*Taxatio ecclesiastica Angliae et Walliae auctoritate P. Nicholai IV, circa A.D. 1291* [ed. T. Astle, S. Ayscough and J. Caley], 1802). Bishop Baldock had a volume which recorded the taxation of benefices in the diocese of London: **2/1**, p. 81.
[33] An unidentified life of St Anne.
[34] MS: 'lxv s.' over erasure.
[35] MS: this sentence in larger letters.
[36] MS: 'iiii li.' over erasure.

6/3 Certification of the inventory, annexed to it: letters from Thomas Arundel, Archbishop of Canterbury, noting that, wheareas the executors of the will of Bishop Braybrooke, namely Gerard Braybrok, knight, Edmund Hamdene, esquire, John Wyke and Roger Albryghton' clerks, appeared before the Archbishop and exhibited the will, 21 September 1404, and he granted probate, they were required to produce an inventory of Braybrooke's goods appraised by those that knew them; the executors have now produced the inventory, annexed to the present letters, and have made an indenture of it with the Archbishop's register. Lambeth, 22 February 1405. *Guildhall Library, London, MS 25271/58*

6/4 Acquittance of Sir Gerard Braybrok, knight, Edmund Hamden, esquire, Mag. William Stukley, Dom. John Wyke, Roger Albryghton and Thomas Lyes, executors of Robert Braybroke, Bishop of London, Lambeth, 7 August 1406. *LPL, Register of Thomas Arundel, vol. I, f. 232v*

7 Edmund Bromfield, Bishop of Llandaff

Will, 10 June 1393 *TNA PROB 11/1 (3 Rous), f. 10v*
In dei nomine amen die martis decimo die Junii anno domini millesimo CCC^{mo} nonogesimo tercio ego Edmundus permissione divina Landavensis episcopus languins in extremis condo testamentum meum quatenus de jure permittitur in hunc modum. In primis lego animam meam deo eiusque gloriose virgini Marie et omnibus sanctis corpusque meum ad sepeliendum in ecclesia cathedrali Landavensi. Item volo quod omnia debita mea plene de bonis meis persolventur. Item lego Simoni Abraham servienti meo xl s. Item lego Ricardo Taillour camerario meo xx s. Item lego residuum omnium bonorum meorum non legatorum executoribus meis ad distribuendum pro anima mea prout eis melius videbitur expedire. Et ad istud testamentum bene et fideliter exequendum ordino facio et constituo executores meos videlicet magistrum Rogerum Croke Thomam Orwell' canonicos ecclesie nostre cathedralis Landavensis dominum Henricum Cha*un*ce et Arnoldum Whitchurche. Datum apud Lank'[1] die et anno domini supradictis.

Notes
1 The Bishops of Llandaff had estates at Llangadwaladr (Bishton), Monmouthshire; their residence there was sometimes referred to as Lankes Castle.

8 John Buckingham, Bishop of Lincoln

Draft for an agreement between the Prior and Chapter of Christ Church, Canterbury, and the priests serving the chantry established under the will of John Buckingham, Bishop of Lincoln, n.d. early fifteenth century *CCA, DE/177*
One paper, a fragment torn at the foot; the dorse is blank.

..... incumbencia priori et capitulo ecclesie Cristi Cantuar' < secundum > et de quibus annuatim oneratis secundum tenorem et formam ordinacionis cantarie domini Johannis Bokyngham nuper episcopi Lincolniensis < secundum vim et effectum > facte per venerabiles viros dominos Thomam Chylyndem' ad tunc priorem dicte ecclesie Cristi Johannem Bodysham Johannem Forest canonic*os* ecclesie Lincolniensis Johannem Lydyngcote rectorem ecclesie parochialis de Irnham eiusdem diocesis et Johannem Park' domicellum < prefati domini episcopi > executores < ipsius > \ dicti / domini episcopi Lincolniensis et eorum sigill*is* confirmate[1]

In primis \ iidem prior et capitulum / onerantur per ipsam ordinacionem solvere duobus capellanis eiusdem cantarie < annuatim > \ annis singulis inperpetuum / xx marcas secundum formam ..... in eodem
Item sacerdoti celebranti \ i / missam \ de requiem / in die anniverarii < sui > \ ipsius domini episcopi / vi s. viii d.
Item diacono et subdiacono legentibus ewang*elium* et epistolam in eadem missa vi s. viii d.

Item cuilibet monacho eiusdem ecclesie eadem die<s> scilicet iiii^{xx}xii vii li. xiii s. iiii d.
Item pro elemosina eodem \ die / inter pauperes distribuenda scilicet C pauperibus viii s. iiii d.
Summa < istius oneris > \ < istorum > istius oneris / in denariis xxii li. xx d.

Item prefati prior et capitulum \ ultra premissas soluciones faciendas in denarios annuatim ut prefertur / habent supportare juxta tenorem prefate ordinacionis omnia onera reparacionum domorum capellanorum predictorum quocienscumque indignerint reparare ac providere pro eisdem cantaria et capellanis eiusdem \ cantarie / honesta sacerdotalia vestimenta pannos pro altari i missale portiforium de usu Sarum calicem fiolas manutergium panem ceram vinum et cistam comunem pro rebus suis et minuta opera facienda que casualiter possunt extendere ..... ad onera infinita.

Habita igitur consideracione onerum premissorum < videat eisdem > \ volumus quod si / dicti capellani velint se contentare cum summa eis < assignata > superius per ordinacionem ut premittatur assignata unde quidem < ab > sin autem evacuentur \ et deleantur / omnia in eadem ordinacione < deposita[2] > \ assignata / et ordinata et fiat nova ordinacio et dabimus eis xx li. juxta peticiones eorundem.

Notes
1 MS: 'confirmatam'.
2 MS obscure.

9 John Burghill, Bishop of Coventry and Lichfield

9/1 Will, 21 June 1412 *CCA, Register G, ff. 289v–290v*

The will was copied on the last folios of this volume, which are now damaged by damp and mould, with some loss of text. Approximately 10 lines have been lost at the beginning of f. 290v: what is legible is transcribed preceded by a line number. Line breaks are indicated by | at the close of the text. In other places, conjectural readings of missing passages have been supplied in square brackets.

In dei nomine amen ego Johannes Bourghull' permissione divina Coventriensis et Lichfeldensis episcopus vicesimo primo die mensis Junii anno domini millesimo CCCC^{mo}xii^{mo} sanus mente condo testamentum meum in hunc modum. In primis lego animam meam deo beate Marie et sanctis eius corpusque m[eum] ad sepeliendum in ecclesia mea cathedrali Lichfeldensi in loco pro sepultura mea ordinato et preparato. Item lego xxiiii pauperibus tenentibus torticos circa corpus meum pro vestura eorundem viii li. Item lego apparat*ui* ferrei mei x li. et majus si necesse fuerit. Item lego ad distribuendum pauperibus pro anima mea die sepulture mee xvi li. Item lego pro expensis meis funeralibus xl li. vel majus vel minus juxta discrecionem et disposicionem executorum meorum juxta numerum amicorum me[orum] in exequiis meis et in die sepulture mee existencium. Item lego in panno nigro pro vestura in die sepulture mee xl marcas vel majus vel minus secundum discrecionem executorum meorum. Item lego cuilibet canonico dicte ecclesie venienti et existenti in exequiis et in missa die sepulture rew..... vi s. viii d. Item lego cuilibet vicario dicte ecclesie Lichfeldensis existenti in dictis exequiis et ..... iii s. iiii d. Item lego cuilibet capellano cantariam perpetuam in dicta ecclesia obt.....[1] et in dictis exequiis et missa existenti vicariis in dicta ecclesia cantariam obtentibus exceptis x... Item cuilibet alteri capellano tam fratribus quam aliis in dictis exequiis et missa exist..... [*f. 290r*] Item lego ad celebrandum pro anima mea duo milia missarum infra duos menses post mortem meam ..... li. vi s. viii d. vel majus si necesse fuerit secundum disposicionem executorum meorum. Item lego Thome [Bo]urgh*u*ll' fratri meo uxori sue [et] liberis suis xx li. Item lego Willelmo Bourgh*u*ll' fratri meo x li. ..... Johanni Dene nepoti meo ..... Item lego Rogero Solers nepoti meo x li. Item lego Roberto Solers xl s. Item fratribus predicatoribus Oxon' C s. Item fratribus predicatoribus Cant*u*brigge C s. Item lego fratribus predicatoribus London' xl s. Item lego fratribus predicatoribus ..... xl s. Item fratribus predicatoribus H*er*ford' ad celebrandum pro anima mea et parentum meorum x li. Item lego fratribus predicatoribus de Novo Castro xx s. Item lego fratribus predicatoribus Derb' xx s. Item lego fratribus predicatoribus Salop' xx s. Item lego fratribus predicatoribus Cestr' xxvi s. viii d. Item lego fratri Ricardo[2] Runcorne xiii s. iiii d. Item lego monialibus monasterii de Pollesworth' vi s. viii d. Item lego monialibus prioratus de Farewall' vi s. viii d. Item lego monialibus prioratus Cestr' vi s. viii d. Item lego monialibus de Hynwode vi s. viii d. Item lego monialibus albis de Brewode vi s. viii d. Item lego monialibus nigris de Brewode vi s. viii d. Item lego monialibus prioratus Derb' vi s. viii d. Item fratribus minoribus Coventr' vi s. viii d. Item fratribus Carmelitis Coventr' vi s. viii d. Item fratribus Augustinis de Admiston' vi s. viii d. Item fratribus minoribus Lich' vi s. viii d. Item fratribus minoribus Staff' vi s. viii d. Item fratribus Augustinis Staff' vi s. viii d. Item fratribus minoribus de Brugnorth' vi s. viii d. Item fratribus minoribus Salop' vi s. viii d. Item fratribus Augustinis Salop' vi s. viii d. Item fratribus minoribus Cestr' vi s. viii d. Item fratribus Carmelitis Cestr' vi s. viii d. Item fratribus Augustinis de Werynton' vi s. viii d. Item lego Margaret*e* Podemour priorisse de Fardwall' vi s. viii d. Item lego fratribus predicatoribus de Langley ad celebrandum pro anima mea et anima Ricardi regis Anglie etc. et animabus parentum mearum x li. et unum par integrum vestimentorum videlicet unam casulam cum ii tuniculis de panno rubeo de velwet cum leonis de auro cum iii aub*is* et toto apparatu eorundem et unum missale de usu fratrum predicatorum. Item lego fratribus predicatoribus Hareford' in Vallia xx s. Item lego fratribus predicatoribus de Breconia xx s. Item lego fratribus ..... de Gloucestr' xl s. Item lego magistro Willelmo Newport illum ciphum quem michi dona..... cum pede argenti deaurato cum cooperturio et unam ollam eneam secundum meliorem et unum ..... blodium quem michi idem Willelmus donavit. Item lego fratri Thome Lyngesbone capellano ..... C s. Item lego Willelmo Rogers capellano meo C s. Item lego Waltero capellano meo ..... Item lego Henst' capellano meo xl s. Item lego Thome Fyssher lxvi s. viii d. Item ..... magistro Willelmo [Adm]uston' sequestratori meo C s. Item lego Thome Admuston' receptori meo C s. Item lego Ricardo [Ger]fray armigero meo C s. Item lego Henrico Barbour Alicie uxori ..... et liberis suis iiii li. ..... Item lego Johanni Chikenes armigero meo x ls. Item lego Thome S..... armigero meo xl s. Item lego Willelmo de camera valetto meo xl s. Item lego Willelmo B..... et Agneti uxori sue xl s. Item lego Ricardo Botler valetto meo C s. Item lego cuilibet alteri valetto in domo mea deservienti tempore mortis mee xiii s. iiii d. Item lego cuilibet gercioni meo in domo mea michi deservienti tempore mortis mee vi s. viii d. Item lego domino Johanni Batford' xx s. Item lego domine Elizabeth*e* Ypstons i peciam argenti deauratam flat' cum cooperturio. Item lego domino Ade Pershall' militi illum ciphum argenti deauratum quem episcopus Eliensis donavit michi. Item lego Alicie Ferour vi s. viii d. Item lego priori et conventui sancti Thome Staff' xl s. Item lego ecclesie mee de Wibbenbury unam casulam cum i aube et apparatum blodii coloris cum una capa eiusdem coloris et pann*um* de serico cum bestiis de auro. Item lego Roberto Waller clerico meo xl s. Item lego Johanni Luggor' rectori de .....cumpton' x li. Item lego domino Thome Aston' militi C s. Item lego ecclesie mee Lichfeldensi ad celebrandum pro anima mea et anima Ricardi nuper regis Anglie meam capam rubeam meliorem de auro. Item lego Johanne uxori Willelmi Smerley unam peciam argenti cum cooperturio quam [d]onavit michi dominus Johannes Kyngeston'. Item lego fratribus minoribus de H*er*ford' vi s. viii d. Item lego fratribus minoribus de Glouc' vi s. viii d. Item lego fratribus Carmelitis de Glouc' vi s. viii d. Item lego Willelmo Kent ballivo meo de Brewode xiii s. iiii d. Item lego domino [Hugoni] Malpas illum ewor quem michi donavit et unam peciam argenti deauratam ad [*f. 290v*] [1] ..... sufraganeo meo ..... [2] ..... [3] ..... [4] ..... Johanni diac..... [5] ..... al..... .....p..... .....b..... [6] ..... choro et le..... [7] ..... Item lego priori et conventui ..... bona que ..... [8] ..... die mortis ..... Item lego ..... Item lego [9] anulum ..... Item lego Thome Polynton' ..... s. iiii d. Item [10] lego cuilibet monacho predicti conventus Coventr' dicto priore ..... et ..... vi s. viii d. Item lego Jo..... .....sford capellano meo i goblet deaurat*o* cum cooperturio de [eo]dem. Item lego Willelmo Bridley valetto meo in coquina xl s. Item lego fratri Nich..... ..... s. Item lego Johann*i* fili*o* Ricardi Botler xl s. Item lego Johanne uxori Ricardi .... s. Item lego ..... Henrico Ad..... i murram cum cooperturio Mag. W..... Bullok cum pede argenti deaurat*o*. Item lego ..... Bromwich' et uxori sue xx s. Item lego Johanni Pulford capellano meo i olla... ..... existentem apud Eccleshall' et mantellum meum optimum. Item lego Johanni Dene ..... meum chimerum meliorem. Item lego cuilibet executorum meorum onus ....nent' pro labore suo vi li. xiii s. iiii d. priore Coventr' excepto ...... Willelmo Pa*r*me xx s. Et si contingat aliquam personam cui pro me superius ...... lega..... mortem meam decedere volo tunc quod illud legatum illi ..... vel leg'..... penitus sit momenti vel valoris. Item volo quod remunere f...... meis et pauperibus meis tenentibus quibus per me non extitit remuneratis secundum disposicionem executorum ...... ordino facio et constituo per presentes videlicet Ricardum C[rosby]..... ecclesie mee cathedralis Li..... priorem magistros Robertum .....en[3] Willelmum Newport Johannem Pulford ecclesie ..... Lichfeldensis canonicum et magistrum Johannem B*o*lford' ecclesie prebend..... de Eccleshall' vicar..... bona mea legata et non legata pro salute anime mee cum res..... ...... animarum et omnium fidelium def..... ordinant et disponant et .... execut' et disp..... ..... deberent ..... Item ..... | .... Item volo quod non obst..... quocumque jure sive ..... | ...... de bonis meis emant et pro justo precio ..... | ..... alii extranei sol..... vellent. In cuius ..... | ...... presentibus tunc ibidem domino Hugone Mal.....| ..... P..... ...vell' fratre Thome ...... | ...... Tho..... .....fford' et Ricardo M.....| ...... supradictis.

Notes

1 MS obscure.

2 MS repeats 'Ricardo'.
3 *Chichele register*, iv, p. 15, gives the name as Robert Walden: **9/4**.

9/2 Probate, granted *sede vacante* by the Prior of Christ Church, Canterbury, to ...., Mag. William Newport and Mag. John Pulford, executors named in the will, 27 [.....] 1414. *CCA, Register G, f. 290v*

9/3 Commision to Mag. William Newhagh and Walter Bullok, canons of Lichfield, to admit to the execution of the will other executors, as those originally appointed, William Newport and John Pulford, are in remote parts, 25 June 1414. *Chichele register*, iv, p. 6.

9/4 Commission to Walter Bullok and William Newhagh to hear the account of the executors appointed to administer the will, who have drawn up and exhibited the inventory, but are now in remote parts; transferring the administration to Richard, Prior of Coventry, Mag. Robert Walden and John Bakford, executors named in the will, 5 October 1414. *Chichele register*, iv, pp. 14–15.

10 Thomas Cantilupe, Bishop of Hereford

10/1 Notarial instrument recording the distribution of legacies, 31 August 1282 *HCA 1414*

One membrane, written in an Italian hand. There is a late thirteenth- or early fourteenth-century endorsement in an English hand: 'Instr..... ..... de diversis legatis diversis personis solutis'.

In nomine domini amen anno nativitatis eiusdem millesimo CC° octuagesimo secundo pontificatus domini Martini pape quarti anno secundo indiccione decima mense Augusti die ultima in presencia mei infrascripti notarii et testium subscriptorum ad hoc specialiter vocatorum et rogatorum magister Adam de Fileby archidiaconus Solopsir' in ecclesia Herefordensi[1] confessus est et recognovit se habuisse et recepisse unam pixidem argenteam ad oblata tria bankaria cum floribus liliorum. Item magister Robertus de Redeswelle confessus est et recognovit se habuisse et recepisse decem marcas sterlingorum tresdecim solid*os* et quatuor denari*os* sterlingorum pro marca qualibet computans unam bibliam et unum anulum. Item dominus Johannes de Clara confessus est et recognovit se recepisse et habuisse quadraginta marcas sterlingorum unum anulum et unam peciam integram de profundo persio. Item dominus Johannes de Kemeseye confessus est et recognovit se recepisse et habuisse viginti marcas et unam robam yemalem cum mantello furrato de griseo et unam nigram clokam cum duobus capuciis. Item magister Galfridus de Bradeham confessus est et recognovit se habuisse et recepisse triginta marcas sterlingorum. Item dominus Robertus de Wichio presbiter confessus est et recognovit se recepisse et habuisse viginti marcas sterlingorum et unam peciam de albo persio quinque ulnarum et dimidie et unum equm qui vocatur Assh et unam clokam furratam cum capucio. Item dominus Nicolaus de Oxon' presbiter confessus est et recognovit se habuisse et recepisse quindecim marcas sterlingorum et unam robam estivalem de albo persio integram cum capucio et unam clokam de bluetto cum capucio. Item idem magister Adam de Fileby confessus est et recognovit se recepisse et habuisse vice et nomine Nicolai de Hodenet viginti quinque marcas et unum pullanum griseum. Item idem dominus Johannes de Clara confessus est et recognovit se recepisse et habuisse vice et nomine Riccardi dicti pape tres marcas. Item idem dominus Johannes confessus est et recognovit se recepisse et habuisse vice et nomine Willelmi de Cantilupo studentis Parisivis[2] triginta marcas. Item idem dominus Johannes confessus est et recognovit se recepisse et habuisse pro expensis funeris et ad distribuendum pauperibus et aliis piis locis quadraginta marcas. Item idem dominus Johannes confessus est et recognovit se recepisse et habuisse quinquaginta marcas pro faciendis expensis familie antedicti[3] episcopi usque ad partes Anglicanas. Item idem dominus Johannes confessus est et recognovit se recepisse et habuisse pro ecclesia Flore*ncia*[4] centum soldos paparinorum. Item Johannes de Parisivis[5] cocus confessus est et recognovit se recepisse et habuisse quindecim marcas. Item Johannes marescallus confessus et recognovit se recepisse et habuisse viginti marcas et unum equm album. Item idem Johannes marescallus confessus est et recognovit se recepisse et habuisse vice et nomine Picca*ud*i tres marcas. Item Johannes de Basevylla confessus est et recognovit se recepisse et habuisse viginti quinque marcas et unum equm qui vocatur Butleye. Item Rubinettus pincerna confessus est et recognovit se recepisse et habuisse viginti sex marcas et unam robam furratam ad opus uxoris sue. Item Riccardus scissor confessus est et recognovit se recepisse et habuisse quinque marcas et unum equm qui fuit dicti Rubinetti. Item Robertus ferrator confessus est et recognovit se habuisse et recepisse septem marcas et dimidiam. Item Petrus Nu*nn*us confessus est et recognovit se recepisse et habuisse septem marcas et dimidiam. Item Robertus Deynte confessus est et recognovit se recepisse et habuisse viginti marcas et lectum dicti domini episcopi integre cum lintheaminibus culcitra coopertorio et alio coopertorio corino ac canavacio. Item Guillelmus janitor confessus est et recognovit se recepisse et habuisse quinque marcas. Item Thomas frater dicti Guillelmi confessus est et recognovit \ se recepisse et habuisse /[6] quinque marcas. Item Robertus Harlond confessus est et recognovit se recepisse et habuisse decem marcas. Item Thomas pistor confessus est et recognovit se recepisse et habuisse tres marcas. Item Gille de coquina confessus est et recognovit se recepisse et habuisse tres marcas. Item Walterius pagius confessus est et recognovit se recepisse et habuisse unam marcam. Que omnia legata fuerunt omnibus et singulis supradictis in testamento venerabilis patris bone memorie domini Thome dei gracia quondam Herefordensis episcopi sicut apparet per instrumentum confectum per manum mei notarii infrascripti ipsius domini episcopi sigillo munitum. De quibus omnibus et singulis supradictis prefati omnes et singuli se quietos et bene pacatos vocaverunt. Renunciantes omnes et singuli exception*e* non solute et non numerate eis predicte quantitatis pecunie et non datarum et assignatarum predictarum jurum et omnium alii juris et legum auxilio canonici et civilis feceruntque michi notario infrascripto recipienti nomine et vice illorum quorum interest vel intererit de omnibus et singulis finem quietacionem refutacionem et pactum de ulteriori non petendo. Promittentes insuper predicti omnes et singuli predictas solucionem dationem et assignacionem omnium predictorum et omnia et singula suprascripta firma et rata semper habere et tenere et per se vel per alium seu alios nullo tempore contra facere vel venire aliqua racione vel causa de jure vel de facto sub pena dupli dicte

quantitatis pecunie et rerum predictarum et pena soluta vel non contractus iste et singula que continentur in eo in suo nichilominus robore perseverent. Actum in palacio monasterii sancte crucis de Urbe Veteri presentibus hiis testibus Thoma de Redeswelle Hugone de < Kyggeho >[7] Kameseya Guillelmo de Kyggeho et Waltero de Bromhart'. Et ego Petrus Bartholomei de Guartino sancte Romane ecclesie publicus notarius omnibus predictis interfui rogatus scripsi et publicavi meoque signo consueto signavi.
[*Notarial sign*]

Notes
1 MS: 'Herefodensi'.
2 MS: 'Parisiiis' (three minims).
3 MS unclear: water damage.
4 MS unclear.
5 MS 'Parisiiis' (three minims).
6 Insertion in MS, written immediately before the notarial attestation at the end of the document.
7 Deleted by subscript points.

10/2 Grant of formal administration of the will to Richard, Bishop of Hereford, and Mag. William de Monteforti, precentor of Hereford, 11 May 1283. *Peckham register (CYS)*, i, p. 197.

10/3 Receipt from the Archbishop of Canterbury for a legacy, 21 October 1283 *HCA 1050*
A narrow strip of parchment, with a seal on a tongue, and a wrapping tie, both cut from the bottom left side. Seal: in green wax, a fragment of the centre section of a vesica-shaped seal of the Archbishop in pontificals, now 65 mm × 27 mm. Contemporary endorsement: 'Aquietancia domini archiepiscopi pro legato recepto'.

Universis presentes litteras inspecturis vel audituris frater J. permissione divina Cantuariensis ecclesie minister humilis salutem in domino. Noveritis nos recepisse ab executoribus bone memorie Thome quondam Herefordensis episcopi viginti libras sterlingorum pro palefrido et anulo in testamento suo nobis relictis per manum magistri Rogeri de Sevenak' dictam summam pecunie Rogero Burde thesaurario nostro numerantis ex parte executorum predictorum. In cuius rei testimonium sigillum nostrum fecimus hiis apponi. Valete. Data apud Lambache xii kal. Novembris anno domini M°CC° octogesimo tercio ordinacionis nostre quinto.

10/4 Letters of the Archbishop of Canterbury appointing the Abbot of Oseney, the warden of the Friars Minor in Oxford, and Mag. Harvey de Saham, professor of canon law, to hear the account of the executors of the will of Bishop Cantilupe, which he witnessed (*testatus est*) in the Roman curia, and to absolve them from the administration, making the necessary allowances for its execution, allowing two of them to act if they cannot all do so, and reporting to the Archbishop by 1 August next by letters patent; Mortlake, 30 April 1285. *HCA 1416.* There is also a notarial instrument exemplifying these letters, Hereford, 26 October 1305. *HCA 1417.*

11 Gervase de Castro, Bishop of Bangor

11/1 Will, 24 September 1370 *LPL, Register of William Whittlesey, ff. 117r–v*
In dei nomine amen ego Gervasius dei gracia episcopus Bangorensis compos mentis condo testamentum meum in hunc modum. In primis lego et commendo animam meam deo omnipotenti et beate Marie virgini et omnibus sanctis corpus vero meum ad sepeliendum in choro fratrum predicatorum Bangorensium. Item lego fratribus predicatoribus Bangorensibus i casulam cum ii tuniculis et iii albis de eadem secta. Item eisdem fratribus ii vasa pro corporalibus custodiendis. Item eisdem i capam de panno deaurato. Item eisdem fratribus lego omnes lectos meos et linthiamina mea et omnes pannos meos excepto lecto meo stellato cum avibus quem lego Galfrido nepoti meo cum i opere linthiamini. Item eisdem fratribus ii corporalia. Item eisdem fratribus lego xii ciphos meos argenteos de eadem secta. Item lego Ll*oyt* ap Howel i ciphum argenteum cum cooperculo suo meliorem de duobus ciphis cum cooperculis de eadem secta. Item Howello ap Tud*ur* i ciphum cum cooperculo de eadem secta. Item lego Gruff*uth* Treffgoet[1] i ciphum argenteum quem prior London' michi dedit. Item omnibus notifico quod crismatorium meum argenteum cum ii fialiis de argento i campanam de argento i turribulum de argento deaurato i navem argenteam i cocliarium argenteum [*f. 117v*] pro thure iii pelves de argento cum iii lavatoriis argenteis de eadem secta donavi a diu ecclesie cathedrali Bangorensi et volo quod illa donacio imperpetuum valeat. Item lego fratri Howelo de sancto Hillario[2] dorserium aule mee cum ii costeris suis et iii bankeris de eadem secta. Item lego fratribus predicatoribus predictis xiiii coclearia mea argentea. Item fratribus minoribus Lanvasie[3] xl s. Item fratribus predicatoribus de Ruthlan' lx s. Item lego Edmundo ap Eign*ion* Lloyt[4] xl s. Item lego Galfrido nepoti meo lx s. Item fratri Howelo i capam et habitum meum. Item lego David O*n*yth xx s. Item lego Ior*werth* Vych*au*m de Novo Burgo[5] xx s. Item lego cuilibet sorori mee xl s. Item lego Mad*og* Bach nepoti meo xx s. Item lego Galfrido nepoti meo viii boves qui sunt apud Treff*os*.[6] Item lego Deikwes ap Rys xx s. Item fratri Lewelino Deff*v*aii xx s. Item lego Ior*werth* ap David D*u*y vii vaccas cum vitulis suis que sunt in custodia sua apud Treffos. Item lego Galfrido nepoti meo averia unius anni que sunt apud Treffos. Item lego Ior*werth* ap Tud*ur* Llyot xx s. Item Mad*og* fratri eius xx s. Item lego Ll*oyt* ap Mered*uth* ii vaccas. Item lego Ieuan ap Yge*nn*at xx s. Item Edmundo coco x s. Item lego Llamogwas vi s. viii d. Item Ieuan Lloyt vi s. viii d. Item Ieuan D*u*y ap David D*u*y x s. Item Ririt Saer xiii s. iiii d. Item lego Rys ap Tud*ur* xl s. Item lego Atha ap Ieuan de Gog*er*th[7] x s. Item lego Ieuan ap David Vych*au*n xxvi s. viii d. Et ad omnia fideliter facienda et exequenda et funeralia mea facienda ordino facio et constituto executores meos videlicet Howel ap Tud*ur* Gruffuth' Treffegoet Ll*oyt* ap Howel fratrem Howelum de sancto Hillario Ieuan ap David Vych*au*n et Eign*ion* ap Ll*oyt* et Howel ap Ior*werth* Vych*au*n. Item lego Ieuan Lloyt rectori ecclesie de Eglwyseil[8] xx s. Item si sit aliquod residuum deductis legatis meis et solutis debitis meis lego medietatem residui omnium bonorum meorum Galfrido nepoti meo et aliam medietatem ad disposicionem et ordinacionem executorum meorum ad dividendum pro salute anime mee. In cuius rei testimonium huic presenti testamento meo sigillum meum apposui. Hiis testibus Rys ap Tud*ur* Edmundo ap Eign*ion* Lloyt David Roffair' notario publico Ior*werth* Vach*au*n de Novo Burgo Daikwes ap Ris Ieuan ap Yge*nn*at et Gruffuth' ap Eygn*ion* cum multis aliis. Data in hospicio fratrum predicatorum Bangorensium vicesima quarta die

mensis Septembris anno domini millesimo CCC^{mo}lxx^{o}. Item volo quod Gruffuth' ap Mad*og* Clodayth'[9] et Edmundus ap Eygn*ion* Lloyt sint executores mei cum predictis executoribus meis et lego Gruffuth' ap Mad*og* predicto xl s. Item lego Howel ap Ior*werth* Vach*au*n xl s. cum predictis testibus et Galfrido filio Gronw. Data die loco et anno supradictis.

Notes

1 Possibly a place-name that might now be Tref-y-coed: not traced in Gwynedd, probably a farm name. I am grateful to Dr Madeleine Gray for advice on the place-names in this will.
2 Perhaps linked to a church dedication: possibly Llanrhos, near Conwy, Caerns., and in the diocese of St Asaph.
3 MS: three minims for 'nv'; Llanfaes, Anglesey.
4 MS: 'Eignlloyt'.
5 Newborough, Anglesey.
6 Treffos, Anglesey.
7 Perhaps Gogarth, Caerns., near Llandudno, where the Bishop of Bangor had a palace.
8 Eglwys Ail/Llangadwaladr, Anglesey.
9 Possibly Gloddaeth, Caerns., near Llandudno.

11/2 Probate granted to Gruffuth' ap Mad*og* Clodayth', one of the executors named in the will, 30 October 1370, at Lambeth. *LPL, Register of William Whittlesey, f. 117v.*

11/3 Commission to Dom. John Dibyll, vicar and keeper of the spiritualities of the city and diocese of Bangor, to admit further executors to the administration of the will, 31 October 1370, at Lambeth. *LPL, Register of William Whittlesey, f. 117v.*

12 Lewis Charlton, Bishop of Hereford

12/1 Receipt for goods held for the use of Bishops of Hereford by the Chapter of Hereford, 22 December 1361 *HCA 1448*

Two membranes, both indentures, fastened together with a parchment thong at the bottom left.
1. With the letters 'ABCDEFG' inverted at the head, transcribed below; with a fragment of the vesica-shaped episcopal seal in green wax on a tag. 2. A small piece of parchment, now almost entirely illegible, mid to late fourteenth century, probably with a memorandum of goods remaining to the Chapter of Hereford, held for the use of the Bishops of Hereford. Occasional words are legible: e.g. 'volumine'; 'fial''.

Hec indentura testatur quod die mercurii proximo post festum sancti Thome apostoli videlicet vicesimo secundo die mensis Decembris anno domini millesimo CCC^{mo} sexagenta primo venerabilis in Cristo pater dominus Ludowicus dei gracia Herefordensis episcopus a capitulo ecclesie cathedralis Herefordensis per manus venerabilis viri magistri Griffini de Ch*er*leton' canonici Herefordensis res recepit subscriptas videlicet unum librum pontificale cum rubio corio coopertum unum gradale cum tropero cum corio piloso coopertum. Item unam albam cum stola manipul*o* et amict*a* de dono Johannis de Brecon'. Item unam albam cum stol*a* manipul*o* et amict*a* de dono domine Elianore regine. Item unam albam cum stola manipulo et amicta de dono Thome Ch*er*leton' quondam episcopi. Item unam casulam cum duobus tuniculis eiusdem secte de dono Henrici Schorne. Item unam capam albam de dono episcopi Exoniensis. Item unam albam capam de dono Rogeri de Breynton'. Item duos pannos de plonkett pulverizatos cum leopardis aureis. Item unam mitram preciosam que fuit domini Ricardi quondam episcopi Herefordensis. Item unum par sandalium unum par sotularium. Item unum par cerotecarum. Item unum anulum pontificalem in quo deficiunt novem lapides. Item unam dalmaticam cum tunica de panno < a > deaurato. Item unam mitram albam de dono Grauntson'. Item unam aliam mitram debilem albam pro consecracione. Item unum baculum pastoralem de ligno cum capite argenti et deaurato. Item duo tuallia pro baculo pastorali. Item unum turibulum cum cathenis argenti. Eodem ecclesie cathedrali restituendas. In quorum omnium testimonium tam predictus dominus Lodewicus episcopus .... capitulum predictum huic indenture sigilla sua alternatim apposuerunt. Data Hereford' die et anno domini supradictis.

12/2 Will, 23 May 1369 *LPL, Register of William Whittlesey, ff. 102r–103r*
In dei nomine amen ego Lodowicus de Cherleton' permissione divina Herfordensis episcopus sanus et in bona memoria existens condo testamentum in hunc modum. In primis lego animam meam deo et beate Marie virgini et omnibus sanctis et corpus meum sepulture in ecclesia cathedrali Herfordensi. Item lego mitram meam rubeam cum cirothecis meis de serico et anulum meum pontificalem et sandalia mea eidem ecclesie. Item lego coopertorium lecti mei cum celura eiusdem secte et operis de serico viridi et cortinis de taffata viridi et dorsoria mea de passione domini nostri Jhesu Cristi cum sex quissyns de velvett' viridi et duas parvas pelves argenteas de capella habentes arma mea de *cun*al'[1] in fundo magno altari ecclesie Herfordensis ut diebus festivis ornent idem altare donec usu consummantur. Item lego ecclesie Herfordensi catholicon[2] meum et bibliam meam glosatam et librum vocatum pars oculi[3] et librum concordancie[4] et magistrum historiarum[5] qui incipit in tercio folio 'velut ex' et doctorem de Lira super quinque libros Moysy[6] quos volo quod executores mei faciant in aliquo tuto loco infra dictam ecclesiam ubi volentes intueri libros poterunt libere accedere sumptibus meis cathenari. Item lego fabrice ecclesie Herfordensi quadraginta li. Item lego feretro sancti Thome Herfordensi omnes anulos meos preter duos unum videlicet cum magno saphiro perforato in quo fui consecratus Avinon' quem cum saphiro lego feretro sancti Edwardi regis apud Westm'. Item lego ecclesie de Pontesbury Herfordensis diocesis missale meum de usu Herfordensi habens in principio tercii folii hoc verbum 'cum potestate' et unum gradale de usu Herfordensi sine tropario. Item unum portiforium quod incipit in tercio folio 'videt vultus' et unum antiphonarium de usu Herfordensi quod incipit in tercio 'susceperunt me' quos libros emi de administratoribus bone memorie domini Johannis Tryllek' predecessoris mei. Item rubea vestimenta que emi de eisdem administratoribus videlicet unam casulam duas tunicas unam capam unum pannum pro altari consimilis secte que habent aves et bestias cum capitibus deaurat*as* et duas albas cum stol*is* et manipulis de armis de Corbet de Caus. Item lego ecclesia de Pola Assavensis diocesis vestimenta mea alba que emi de dictis administratoribus videlicet unam casulam duas tunicas unam capam unum pannum pro altari consimilis secte que habent aves et bestias aureas. Item lego ecclesie de

Guldesfeld' eiusdem diocesis unum pannum album de serico pro altari de secta vestimentorum legatorum ecclesie de Pola et majus gradale meum de usu Sarum coopertum rubeo quod incipit in tercio folio 'libri bil*ium*'. Item lego ecclesie de Meyvot eiusdem diocesis aliud magnum gradale meum de usu Sarum coopertum nigro corio et unum pannum de rubeo serico pro altari de secta vestimentorum legatorum ecclesie de Pontesbury supradicte. Item lego ecclesie prebendali de Welyngton' sub D*une*mor' Herfordensis diocesis duas capas de serico videlicet unam albam capam de secta vestimentorum legatorum ecclesie de Pola et aliam rubeam capam de secta vestimentorum legatorum ecclesie de Pontesbury. Item lego ecclesie de Codeshale Lychfeldensis diocesis missale meum notatum de usu Sarum et albam casulam cum stol*a* et manipulo usitat*is* communibus diebus in capella mea et unam albam cum amictu habentem paruris de rubeo cum avibus deauratis in capite. Item lego antiquum gradale meum de usu Sarum quod fuit exemplarium omnium aliorum quod incipit in tercio folio 'adventu' ecclesie de Tottenhale eiusdem diocesis ut deserviat stallo prebende de Codeshale. Item lego ecclesie beate Marie de Otery Exoniensis diocesis viridia vestimenta mea michi per dominum Johannem de Grandissono dei gracia episcopum Exoniensem missa vel decem li. ut orent pro anima dicti domini Exoniensis. Item lego fabrice campanilis ecclesie beate Marie Oxon' xl s. quos promisi. Item lego fabrice ecclesie abbatie de Strata Marcella Assavensis diocesis xx marcas. Item lego fratribus minoribus Salop' x marcas et fratribus predicatoribus ibidem v marcas. Item fratribus minoribus Herfordensibus x marcas et fratribus predicatoribus ibidem v marcas. Item monialibus de Lyngbrok' x marcas. Item monialibus de Acornebury x marcas. Item fratribus predicatoribus Oxon' v marcas et fratribus minoribus ibidem v marcas et fratribus Augustinis ibidem v marcas et fratribus Carmelitis ibidem v marcas. Item fratribus Augustinis de Lodelowe v marcas. Item fratribus Carmelitis ibidem v marcas. Item lego magistro Umfredo germano meo partem meam omnium legatorum sibi et michi in communi per bone memorie Thomam nuper Herfordensem episcopum avunculum nostrum videlicet de albis vestimentis scilicet de una casula ii tunicis una capa debili[7] magna quam idem Umfredus habet in custodia sua de uno calice deaurato quem idem Umfredus eciam habet de i turribulo argenteo que omnia reliquit[8] nobis dictus Thomas in testamento suo. Item lego dicto Umfredo sex discos cum sex salsariis argenteis de armis meis et cuppam argenteam cum coopertorio de qua solitus sum potare cum uno parvo aquario [*f. 102v*] argenteo habenti unum babwyn de animal*ibus* in summitate coopertorii. Item lego Willelmo de Cherleton' germano meo librum meum vocatum summa summarum[9] et ii ollas argenteas pro vino de armis meis et vi ciphos argenteos de armis meis et xii discos cum xii salsariis argenteos de armis meis. Item lego Griffino germano meo sex discos cum salsariis argenteos de armis meis et iii ciphos argenteos de armis meis et meum sextum librum decretalium[10] et usum libri decretalium[11] meorum ad terminum vite sue et volo quod post vitam suam eundem librum decretalium faciat tradi et liberari abbathie de Hamond' Lychfeldensis diocesis ex dono magistri Johannis de Cherleton' quondam rectoris de Wrocwardyn avunculi domini patris mei. Item lego Rogero germano meo sex discos cum sex salsariis argenteos de armis meis. Item lego domino Ade Eseg*er* duas pelves argenteas in fundo ainnelatas. Item lego magistro Rogero Otery bibliam meam parvam et unum aquarium argenteum in summitate ainnelatum et vi godettos in eodem aquario inclusos. Item lego domino Johanni rectori ecclesie de Brompton' xl s. cum i cipho argenteo. Item lego domino Thome Webbe capellano xl s. Item lego Nicholao clerico capelle C s. et peciem meam argenteam cum coopertorio habentem clowes depictos in fundo. Item lego domino Philipo Wayte ad celebrandum pro anima mea per biennium x marcas et consimiliter lego domino Johanni Frome x marcas. Item lego Ricardo Thurban' clerico xl s. Item lego domino Hervico vicario de Ledeby xl s. Item lego domino Thome Bisshbury rectori de Aysshbury Sarum diocesis illam preciosam casulam de rubeo cum avibus et bestiis habentibus capita et pedes de auro et albam cum amictu stol*a* et manipulo de armis Genevil' et i corporale cum meliori bursa corporalium et ii meliora linthiamina pro altari et tercium linthiaminum cum frontali meliori et amiciam meam meliorem et melius superpellicium meum et parvum missale meum de usu Sarum quod feci scribi Oxon' et est in maximis dupplicibus festis notatum et gradale meum parvum coopertum rubeo quod habet arma mea depicta in litteris in festis majoribus. Item lego sibi parvum jornale meum de usu Herefordensi in quo solebamus similiter dicere horas canonicas et i anulum aureum habentem rosam cum perles et diamantem in medio et meliorem calicem deauratam cum ii melioribus fialis argenteis et omnia bankara camere mee et omnes quissinos preter supra legata et iiii coffr*as* depictas quas voluerit eligere ex omnibus et omnes mappas et manutergia mea cum omnibus ciphis meis de maser' et xii discos cum xii salsariis argenteos non signatos armis meis quos discos et salsaria habui de magistro Thoma Trillek' episcopo Roffensi. Item lego eidem Thome Bisshbury bollam meam argenti cum coopertorio que fuit domine matris mee et habet in fundo arma de Pola et eciam in coopertorio arma episcopi Thome de Cherleton'. Item i sallarium argenti et xii coclearia argenti que sunt de una secta et ii pelves argenti de armis meis que sunt magni ponderis fere x lib. vel circiter et ii ollas argenti pro vino et omnes tankardos meos de nigro corio et ii melios saccos camere cum ii melioribus barhud*is* et ii meliores cellas cum frenis pro somere et ii meliores equos et vi parvas ollas coquine et iii broch*is* de ferro pro coquina ut oret et orare faciat pro me. Item lego Willelmo Brandhurst domino de Whytyngton' xx marcas. Item Johanni de Brandhurst germano suo xx marcas. Item lego Ricardo Bysshebury xx marcas cum ii lectis et ii melioribus robis meis. Item lego Johanni[12] filio Thome xx li. Item lego Ricardo Brugge famulo camere mee lx s. et i de robis meis. Item lego Alano Pa*mter* lx s. Item Janyn Pa*mter* xl s. Item Simoni Porter xl s. Item Johanni coco de Lodelowe xl s. Item Willelmo pagetto coquine xx s. Item Nicholao Baker xl s. Item Willelmo Baker xl s. Item Thome Baker famulo Nicholai xx s. Item Ade Buk' famulo Willelmi Bar*und*h' xl s. Item famulo meo Johanni Frenche xl s. Item Johanni Falwode famulo meo xl s. Item lego Johanni Jones famulo meo lx s. et i de robis meis. Item lego Ricardo Taunton' famulo meo xl s. Item lego Ricardo Pola nuper famulo meo xl s. Item Johanni Bot*er*ley de Pola uxorato apud Malpas nuper famulo me*o*[13] xl s. Item Johanni Walyngford' nuper famulo meo xx s. Item antiquo Willelmo coco meo nuper Oxon' xl s. Item magistro Philippo de la More Herford' C s. Item lego Waltero de Eton' nepoti magistri Walteri Moryn xx marcas. Item magistro Johanni Turk' executori magistri Walteri Moryn xx marcas ad perficiendum quantum poterit testamentum magistri Walteri Moryn qui in comitiva mea obiit Avinon'. Et quicquid residuum fuerit [*f. 103r*] de bonis meis non legatis lego executoribus meis ad disponendum et ordinandum obitum meum perpetuum in ecclesia cathedrali si fieri poterit et ad faciendum libere pro anima mea et animabus omnium fidelium defunctorum prout melius viderint et deliberaverint expedire juxta discrecionem eis a deo datam. Et post sumptus sepulture mee quos nolo esse excessivos set moderatos videlicet ut quilibet pauper veniens die sepulture mee ad orandum pro anima mea habeat denarium et quilibet canonicus ecclesie cathedralis dicens psalterium more consueto et presens in exequiis et in missa di. marcam et quilibet vicarius ecclesie similiter presens xl d. et quilibet sacerdos alius quam vicarius chori presens in exequiis et in missa xii d. Et volo quod fiat convivium die sepulture mee. Executores meos ordino facio et constituto dominos Willelmum Charleton' germanum meum Adam Exseg*er* Rogerum de Otery Thomam Bisshbury canonicos ecclesie Herfordensis et domicellum meum Willelmum Bar*i*dhurst. Scripta apud Whytbourne feria iiii[a] quatuor temporum in ebdomada Pentecost*es* videlicet xxiii die mensis Maii anno domini millesimo CCC[mo] lxix[o]. Et consecracionis me*i*[14] anno octavo.

Notes

1 MS obscure: possibly intended for 'cunabulo', the arms which he had from birth.

2 Johannes Januensis (John of Genoa) *Catholicon* (printed, Mainz, ?1460). For these bequests and other books owned by Charlton, Cavanaugh, 'Books', p. 178.

3 Willelmus de Pagula *Oculus sacerdotis* (unpublished). *Pars oculi* could be both a summary of the work, which circulated independently, and a reference to the whole work: L.E. Boyle, 'The *Oculus sacerdotis* and some other works of William of Pagula' *Transactions of the Royal Historical Society*, 5th series, 5 (1955) pp. 81–110.

4 Possibly the *Concordancia major*, the work of the Dominicans of Saint-Jacques, Paris.

5 Petrus Comestor *Historia scholastica*: *PL* 198, cols. 1053–1722.

6 Nicholas de Lyra *Postillae super Pentateuchum*; printed as part of his *Postilla litteralis in Vetus et Novum Testamentum*, Rome, 1471–2.

7 MS: 'debilia'.

8 MS: possibly 'reliquid'.

9 Willelmus de Pagula *Summa summarum* (unpublished): L.E. Boyle, 'A study of the works attributed to William of Pagula, with special reference to the *Oculus sacerdotis* and the *Summa summarum*' (unpublished University of Oxford DPhil thesis, 1956).

10 *Liber sextus decretalium*, containing the Decretals from Gregory IX to Boniface VIII, printed in *Corpus iuris canonici* ed. E. Friedberg (2nd edition, 2 vols., Leipzig, 1922) ii, cols. 933–1124.

11 Gregory IX *Decretales*, printed in *Corpus iuris canonici*, ii, cols. 1–928.

12 MS repeats 'lego Johanni'.

13 MS: 'me'.

14 MS: 'me'.

12/3 Memorandum of a commission to Mag. Nicholas de Chaddesden, Dean of Arches, then in London, to receive and admit the probate of the will of Lewis, Bishop of Hereford, to publish the will and to commit the administration of the testator's goods to the executors named in the will, London, 27 June 1369. *LPL, Register of William Whittlesey, f. 101v.*

12/4 Probate granted by Nicholas de Chaddesden, Dean of Arches, in his dwelling house in the parish of St James Garlickhithe, London, to Mag. Roger de Otery and Dom. Thomas Bisshebury, canons of the church of Hereford, named as executors in the will, 29 June 1369. The executors are assigned the first law day after the feast of St Luke [18 October] to appear before the Archbishop of Canterbury with the inventory of the deceased's goods. On 21 January [1370] Mag. Richard de Wormyngton', the Archbishop's chancellor, assigned Dom. Thomas Bisshebury the second law day after the second Sunday in Lent for exhibiting the inventory. On 8 March 1370, Mag. Roger and Dom. Thomas appeared personally in the chapel at Otford and exhibited the inventory, with its valuation of the items listed. The document was admitted and the [chancellor] required the executors to restore to him the fruits of the last harvest due to the church of Bosbury belonging to the Archbishop in right of the spiritualities of the see of Hereford, which the executors had received, along with the pontifical ring of the deceased. He set the second law day after the feast of St Nereus and St Achilleus [12 May] for them to appear with a fuller inventory of the deceased's goods and an account of their administration of them. On 14 May 1370 the executors appeared before the [chancellor] at Otford and delivered the pontifical ring and paid £20 for the fruits of the church of Bosbury. *LPL, Register of William Whittlesey, f. 103r.*

12/5 Acquittance of the executors by the chancellor, Otford, 14 May 1370. *LPL, Register of William Whittlesey, f. 103r.*

13 Lawrence Child, Bishop of St Asaph

Will, 10 November 1389 *LPL, Register of William Courtenay, f. 232v*
In dei nomine amen ego Laurencius episcopus Assavensis sanus mente et corpore prout percipere possum aut sentire timens tamen incertitudinem finis vite mee testamentum meum condo ordino et facio in hunc modum. In primis confisus meritis et precibus sanctissimi Assaphi episcopi et confessoris patroni mei lego animam deo omnipotenti et beatissime Marie virgini matri eiusdem et omnibus sanctis corpusque meum ad sepelliendum in choro ecclesie cathedralis Assavensis ante summum altare sub pedibus capellani ubi celebrare solet. Item lego eidem ecclesie centum marcas argenti pro vestimentis emendis ad serviendum in eadem ecclesia dum durare poterunt. Item lego eidem ecclesie mee unam casulam meam de panno serico rubeo cum una auba et amict*a* stola et fanon*a* ac parures de eadem secta ad serviendum in eadem ecclesia. Item lego eidem ecclesie unum psalterium meum ad serviendum in eadem. Item lego eidem ecclesie unam cathedram ligneam et longam ad serviendum in eadem pro rectoribus chori. Item lego Johanni Andrewe omnes libros meos juris canonici et civilis. Item lego eidem Johanni Andrewe unum lectum integrum rubeum videlicet cum curtenis eiusdem coloris una cum i canavas i mattras i quilte blanketys et linthiaminibus pro eodem lecto. Item lego xl s. distribuendos per executores meos prout eis melius visum fuerit pro anima magistri Meyvot nuper rectoris ecclesie de Llanarmon'.[1] Deinde volo et precipio per executores meos de residuo omnium bonorum meorum creditoribus < vel > \ ac / servitoribus meis fideliter computantibus pro eorum labore et servicio satisfieri. Et ad hoc testamentum meum bene et fideliter exequendum facio et ordino executores meos dominos Thomam Pece et Ricardum de Sta*u*ndon' clericos et capellanos meos. Scripta apud castrum de Pola[2] decimo die mensis Novembris anno domini millesimo CCC^{mo} octagesimo nono.

Notes
1 Llanarmon: it is unclear which of the several locations with this name in Denbighshire and Flintshire is intended here.
2 Powis Castle.

14 Thomas Fastolf, Bishop of St David's

14/1 Will of Thomas Fastolf, Bishop of St David's, 5 June 1361 *LPL, Register of Simon Islip, f. 175r*

In nomine domini amen anno ab incarnacione eiusdem secundum cursum et computacionem ecclesie Angl*icane* M°CCC^{mo}lxi° indiccione xiiii pontificatus sanctissimi in Cristo patris et domini nostri domini Innocencii divina providencia papa vi anno ix° mense Junii die quinta in mei notarii publici et testimonio subscriptorum presencia constitutus reverendus in Cristo pater et dominus dominus Thomas dei gracia episcopus Menevensis compos mentis corpore tamen eger existens suum nuncupativum testamentum per expressionem verborum condidit in hunc modum videlicet: in nomine patris et filii et spiritus sancti amen. Ego Thomas episcopus Menevensis lego deo ac sancte et individue Trinitati et beatissime semper virgini Marie animam meam et corpus meum ecclesiastice sepulture tradendum a dextris ymaginis eiusdem beatissime Marie in capella ipsius in ecclesia Menevensi. Item committo ordinacioni et disposicioni magistrorum David Ley precentoris nostre ecclesie Menevensis Roberti de Grymeston' comparcionarii ecclesie de Dysserth'[1] Philippi Dyer' rectori ecclesie de La*n*nerth' Loydok'[2] mee diocesis omnia bona mea ut ipsi aut duo eorum de eisdem bonis disponant et ordinent prout eis pro meo[3] comode et honore videbitur melius expedire et prout inde coram deo pro me et seipsis voluerint respondere. Quos quidem magistrum David principalem et autenticum, Robertum vero et Philippum aut duos eorum huius testamenti mei executores constituo ac eciam ordino. Super quibus omnibus et singulis prefatus reverendus pater requisivit me infrascriptum notarium conficere publicum instrumentum. Data sunt hec apud Lantefey[4] in interiori camera prefati domini episcopi manerii sui ibidem prefate diocesis Menevenis presentibus domino Johanne Ace rectore ecclesie de Lanmadok'[5] eiusdem Menevensis et Willelmo Lonyet presbitero Herefordensis diocesis vocatis testificandis ad premissa.

Notes

1 Diserth and Tre-goed (also known as Diserth in Elfael), Radnorshire, in the diocese of St David's.
2 For Lannerch, i.e. Llanychlwydog, Pembs.
3 MS: possibly 'meis'.
4 Lamphey, Pembs., a palace of the Bishop of St David's: the Welsh spelling is Llandyfai.
5 Perhaps Llanmadoc, on the Gower Peninsula.

14/2 Notarial instrument recording the renunciation of the executorship by those named in the will, 21 June 1361 *LPL, Register of Simon Islip, f. 175r*

Die etc. vicesima prima predicti mensis Junii annis ab incarnacione domini et pontificatus ac indiccionis prefatis constitutis in[1] presencia mei notarii et testimonio subscriptorum venerabilibus et discretis viris magistris Davido Ley et Philippo Dyer' superius nominatis. Idem magister David asseruit atque dixit quod ipse multociens ante illud tempus jura intrat ut nunquam velle esse executorem testamenti alicuius nec administracionem bonorum cuiuscumque defuncti recipere admittere nec subire donec complev*i*t execucionem unius testamenti videlicet domini Henrici quondam episcopi Menevensis nondum completi ut dixit. Et ideo idem magister David execucionem testamenti domini Thome Menevenis episcopi supradicti et administracionem bonorum suorum renunciavit palam publice et expresse. Et inmediate postea subsequenter prefatus magister Philippus Dyere dixit et protestatus fuit publice et expresse se nolle intromittere quovismodo de execucione huius testamenti sepedicti domini Thome episcopi et execucionem ipsius renunciavit ac onus eiusdem penitus recusavit. Acta sunt infra clausum Menevense ante portam pallacii episcopalis ibidem presentibus discretis viris magistris Philippo Fysgard' clerico notario publico Bryano Ley clerico prefate diocesis Menevensis testibus in premissis. Et ego Thomas de Bockyng' clericus Londoniensis diocesis publicus apostolica auctoritate notarius legacioni commissioni constitucioni assercioni renunciacioni et recusacioni omnibusque aliis et singulis dum sit ut supra scribuntur de annis domini pontificatus mensibus diebus et lectis predictis agerentur et fierent. Una cum prenominatis testibus presens personaliter interfui eaque sic omnia < fi > vidi fieri et audivi et ideo hoc presens publicum instrumentum inde confeci quod manu mea scripsi et publicavi signoque meo solito consignavi rogatus in fidem et testimonium eorundem.

Notes

1 MS repeats 'in'.

14/3 Commission to Mag. Griffin ap Res, archdeacon of Brecon, for the probate of the will, 22 June 1361. *LPL, Register of Simon Islip, f. 174r.*

14/4 Probate committed to Mag. Robert de Grymeston', executor named in the will, Mayfield, 1 July 1361. *LPL, Register of Simon Islip, f. 175r.*

14/5 Commission to Mag. Philip Dyer, rector of the church of Lann*er*thloydokt [Llanychlwydog], diocese of St David's, to hear the petition of the executors of the Bishop of St David's against some of his debtors, Mayfield, 1 July 1361. *LPL, Register of Simon Islip, f. 175r.*

15 Hugh Foliot, Bishop of Hereford

15/1 Agreement relating to the estate of the Bishop, post 7 August 1234 *HCA 2118*

One membrane, with the remains of three tongues at the bottom left. No contemporary endorsement.

Universis Cristi fidelibus presens scriptum visuris Henricus Craft Willelmus filius Thome Theob' Willelmus filius Stephani Theob' Johannes Theob' cives Herefordenses salutem in domino. Noveritis nos recepisse viginti solidos argenti ad opus Alicie uxoris Restold' a magistro Thoma Foliot thesaurario Herefordensi executore H. Foliot bone memorie quondam episcopi Herefordensis de bonis eiusdem defuncti in testamento hospitali de Ledebir' relictis quos viginti solidos permisimus solvere dicto executori vel dicto hospitali cum pena quadraginta solidorum si dicta Alicia domum juxta domum Willelmi Wyber quam dotem suam dixit esse unquam petat vel dictum hospitale vel aliquem qui dictam domum inhabitaverit racione dotis vel alterius juris ad ipsam pertinentis inquietaverit et hoc permisimus stipulatione sollempni interveniente fide eciam nostra vallata obligando unumquemque nostrum insolidum et heredes nostros et omnia bona nostra renunciando in omnibus et singulis supradictis articulis omni juris civilis et canonici auxilio et beneficio legitime prohibicionis omnibus inpetratis et inpetrandis. In cuius rei testimonium presentibus literis sigilla nostra apposuimus. Hiis testibus magistro H. Buistard' archidiacono Herefordensi magistro Roberto de Cotinton' magistro Hugone de furcis Willelmo Romano et aliis.

15/2 Agreement relating to the estate of the Bishop and the bequest of stock and seed on episcopal manors in future, May 1237 *HCA 1401*
One membrane, with fragments of a vesica-shaped seal, now 64 mm × 37 mm, in white wax on a tag. A bishop in pontificals. Legend .....V' | RADV..... Contemporary endorsement: 'Radul*ph*us episcopus Herefordensis de terris seminandis in maneriis episcopatus'.

Omnibus Cristi fidelibus ad quos presens scriptum pervenerit Radul*ph*us dei gracia Herefordensis episcopus eternam in domino salutem.[1] Noverit universitas vestra nos recepisse a magistro Thoma Foliot thesaurario Herefordensi executore bone memorie domini H. predecessoris nostri quondam Herefordensis episcopi sex viginti libras sterlingorum ad terras episcopatus seminandas in utroque tempore seminandi et carucas cum stauro quales in episcopatu fuerunt relicte. Et quia volumus ut tantum beneficium nobis collatum futuris temporibus prosit ecclesie nostre Herefordensi permittimus nos tantundem pecunie successori nostro relicturos nisi fuerint terre tempore nostri decessus seminate. Quod si forte disponente domino contingat nos in fata decedere citra autumpnum terris seminatis volumus quod fructus autumpni sequentis cedant in usus successoris nostri cum carucis stauro suppellectalibus ad culturam terre convenientibus privilegio domini regis episcopi Anglie concesso non obstante nullo eciam testamento a nobis aliquando faciendo huic nostre ordinacione voluntati et permissioni prejudicante. Volumus eciam et ordinamus quantum in nobis est ut omnes successores nostri futuri episcopi in ecclesia Herefordensi ad simile beneficium quale a nobis relictum fuerit in perpetuum obligentur. Et in huius rei testimonium decano et capitulo nostro Herefordensi ....tes direximus volentes et petentes ut ab eodem capitulo hac nostra ordinacio confirmetur. Data anno domini M°CC° tricesimo septimo mense Maio.

Notes

1 An *inspeximus* of this document by the Dean of Hereford, from June 1237, is printed in *Registrum Thome de Cantilupo episcopi Herefordensis A.D. MCCLXXV–MCCLXXXIII* ed. R.G. Griffiths and W.W. Capes (CYS, 2; 1907) pp. 38–9. The text is also summarised in *Charters and records of Hereford Cathedral* ed. W.W. Capes (Hereford, 1908) p. 75.

16 John Gilbert, Bishop of St David's

16/1 Will, 24 November 1393 *LPL, Register of Thomas Arundel, vol. I, ff. 160r–v*

In dei nomine amen anno domini millesimo CCC^mo nonogesimo tercio mensis Novembris die vicesimo quarto in castro de Lawhaden' Menevensis diocesis ego Johannes Menevensis episcopus indignus sanus mente eger tamen corpore senioque confractus et considerans terminum vite mee iminere ordino et facio testamentum meum et meam ultimam voluntatem declaro et dispono sub hac que sequitur forma. In primis do lego et commendo animam meam peccatricem deo salvatori meo et sue misericordie ac matri sue virgini Marie et omnibus sanctis celestis curie et corpus meum ad sepeliendum in ecclesia conventuali fratrum predicatorum Haverford' dicte Menevensis diocesis. Item volo ordino et executoribus meis infrascriptis precipio quod ipsi solvant seu solvi faciant omnia debita mea personis singulis quibus teneor sicut ipsi velint et debeant. Si hoc non fecerint coram deo propter hoc respondere. Item do et lego ecclesie conventuali[1] predicte quandam albam sectam vestimentorum presbiteri diaconi et subdiaconi cum quatuor capis eiusdem secte. Item do et lego eidem centum li. argenti secundum disposicionem et ordinacionem executorum meorum. Item do et lego residuum omnium bonorum meorum et rerum presencium et futurorum superius non legatorum ubicumque existencium executoribus meis subscriptis ut ipsi executores mei nomine meo solvant satisfaciant et remunerent debito modo omnes familiares et servientes meos majores et minores pro suis serviciis et laboribus michi et causa mei factis. Et quia executores mei subscripti omnes et singulos familiares et servientes meos et eorum labores ac merita plenius noverunt ac noscunt eciam in presenti dictis executoribus meis firmiter precipio quod dictis familiaribus meis et servientibus sic remuneratis subscripti executores mei [*f. 160v*] distribuant de residuo predicto inter pauperes et egenos et conferant ad alia pietatis opera pro salute anime mee sicut eis secundum bonam conscienciam melius et salubrius videbitur expedire. Et ad faciendum exequendum ac fideliter et plenarie adimplendum testamentum et ultimam voluntatem huiusmodi omniaque alia et singula suprascripta per me data facta et declarata dilectos michi in Cristo et confidentissimos servientes meos dominum Johannem Godmaston' canonicum ecclesie cathedralis Menevensis et Johannem Ewias armigerum ordino facio et constituo executores meos quibus do et concedo plenam potestatem testamentum et ultimam voluntatem huiusmodi ac omnia et singula suprascripta per me declarata et dicta faciendi exequendi ac finaliter et plenarie adimplendi. Et insuper injungo et precipio executoribus meis et eos per viscera Jhesu Cristi firmiter requiro quod ipsi predicta omnia et singula celeriter et fideliter perficiant adimpleant et exequantur sicut ipsi velint et debeant super premissis omnibus ante tribunale eterni judicis respondere. Presentibus dominis Willelmo Thornbury et Willelmo Ly*v*y capellanis Roberto Hethe et Ricardo Wheolar' notariis publicis Henrico Schavot et Philipo Craboll' armigeris.

Notes

1 MS originally 'conventul', then rewritten as 'conventuali'.

16/2 Insinuation and grant of probate to Dom. John Godmaston, canon of

St David's, and John Ewias, esquire, executors named in the will, 11 August 1397. Place not clear. *LPL, Register of Thomas Arundel, vol. I, f. 160v.*

17 Richard Gravesend, Bishop of London

17/1 Will, 20 May 1289 *Guildhall Library, London, MS 25271/14A.* Printed in *EEA 39: London 1280–1303* ed. P.M. Hoskin (forthcoming, 2011) pp. 264–5, number 380.

17/2 Will, 1302 *Guildhall Library, London, MS 25271/14* (formerly Archives of the Dean and Chapter of St Paul's, A., Box 66, no. 14). Printed in *Executors*, pp. 111–16, and in *EEA 39: London 1280–1303*, pp. 266–9, number 381. Endorsed with grant of probate, 20 December 1303.

17/3 Agreement between Ralph Baldock, Dean of St Paul's and Bishop Elect of London, and the executors of Bishop Richard Gravesend, August 1304 *Guildhall Library, London, MS 25121/1961*
One membrane, an indenture, to which a seal, of which nothing remains except small traces of green colour, was affixed on a tongue. There is an early fourteenth-century note on the dorse: 'Summa solucionum domini el*ec*ti ... ix^{xx} v li. ix d ...', written over an erasure, probably 'xix s. ...'

Cyrographum

Memorandum quod \ anno gracie millesimo CCC° quarto mense Augusti / habita racione diligenti inter magistrum Radulphum de Baudak' decanum ecclesie Londoniensis et eiusdem electum confirmatum ex parte una et magistros Johannem de Bedeford archidiaconum London' Ricardum de Neuport archidiaconum Middelsex' et Stephanum de Graveshende executores testamenti bone memorie Ricardi de Graveshende nuper Londoniensis episcopi ex altera super quibusdam pecuniarum summis dicto decano et electo debitis ab executoribus memoratis iidem executores satisfecerunt prefato magistro Radulpho de centum marcis in quibus dictus defunctus eidem decano tenebatur per quoddam instrumentum obligatorium sigillo ipsius defuncti signatum quod prefatus decanus suprascripto magistro Stephano liberavit. Item satisfecerunt prefato decano de sexaginta marcis quas dictus testator fatebatur in testamento suo se debere executoribus testamenti bone memorie Johannis de Chishulle quondam episcopi Londoniensis. Item satisfecerunt predicto magistro Radulpho de viginti septem li. et duobus solidis per eundem solutis Johanni de Burford civi London' pro cera empta ad exequias dicti R. de Graveshende cuius debiti talliam prefatus decanus dicto magistro Stephano liberavit. Item satisfecerunt predicto magistro Radulpho de centum solidis quos solvit per manum domini Simonis rectoris ecclesie de Orsete pro minutis expensis factis die sepulture dicti testatoris. Et vult dictus decanus quod obligacio quam dictus rector sibi fecit de dictis centum solidis eximit pro nulla et irrita penitus habeatur. Item satisfecerunt de sex solidis et quinque denariis quos dictus decanus pro obligacionibus debui[1] fecit die mensis post sepulturam dicti testatoris. Et de quinque marcis quas solvit marmorario facienti lapidem superponendum tumulo dicti testatoris. Et de undecim solidis et quatuor denariis quos solvit clericis domini archiepiscopi die administracionis concesse in bonis dicti testatoris. Item satisfecerunt dicto magistro Radulpho de quadraginta duabus li. in quibus dicebat manifeste liquere dictum testatorem executoribus predecessoris sui obligatum fuisse qua satisfaccione prefato magistro Radulpho facta restituit suprascriptis magistris Johanni Ricardo et Stephano omnia vasa argentea et libros que de bonis dicti testatoris nomine pignoris habebat in custodia sua. Et dicti magistri Johannes Ricardus et Stephanus restituerunt dicto magistro duas obligaciones quas prius eis fecerat de centum li. sibi solutis per eosdem unam videlicet obligacionem de sexaginta li. receptis per manum dicti archidiaconi London' et aliam obligacionem de quadraginta li. receptis per manum Henrici Balb*in* de Suthmymstr'. In premissorum vero testimonium sigillum prefati magistri Radulphi electi uni parti huius memorande cyrographate est appensum. Et sigilla predictorum magistrorum Johannis Ricardi et Stephani alteri parti [sunt a]ppensa.[2]

Notes

1 MS: perhaps intended for 'deberi', or 'debitis'.

2 Text concealed under tongue.

17/4 Letters of Ralph Baldock, Bishop of London, asking the executors to render their accounts, Stepney, 10 May 1308. Printed in *Registrum Radulphi Baldock, Gilberti Segrave, Ricardi Newport, et Stephani Gravesend* ed. R.C. Fowler (CYS, 7; 1911) p. 56.

17/5 Letters of Archbishop Walter Reynolds citing Mag. Stephen de Gravesende, executor of the last will of Richard, late Bishop of London, to appear before the Archbishop on the fourth law day after Trinity, with the will, inventory and all legal documents touching the possessions of the deceased, to give an account of his administration. No date given: the last dated entry in the register (f. 63r) preceding these letters was given at Lambeth, 25 April 1315. *LPL, Register of Walter Reynolds, f. 63v.*

17/6 Executors' accounts, Guildhall Library, London, MS 25176 (formerly Archives of the Dean and Chapter of St Paul's, A., Box 53, 18), a Chancery fashion roll of 11 membranes. Printed in *Executors*, pp. 47–110. The accounts must date from after **17/5**, and include on mem. 11r a reference to Archbishop Reynolds seeking, on behalf of the executors, to recover a debt from the executors of Archbishop Winchelsey. Cavanaugh, 'Books', pp. 382–5.

18 Stephen Gravesend, Bishop of London

18/1 Will, 19 February 1337 *Guildhall Library, London, MS 25271/27*
Two separate membranes: 1. A sealed copy of the will, with two seal tags, (a) with a vesica-shaped episcopal seal, a bishop in pontificals, in green wax on the right-hand tag, badly damaged, and (b) on the left-hand seal tag, a fragment of a seal, with a bishop in pontificals, in green wax. There are also traces of an applied circular seal in red wax on the dorse. An erasure and addition were made in the text before it was sealed, confirmed by the final clause of the will. The edited text is based on this document. The membrane is endorsed with: (a) A contemporary note of the grant of probate to Mag. Thomas Durant, Mag. Henry de Iddesworth, Mag. Robert de Teye, Dom. John de Teversham and Dom. William Vygerous, named in the will as executors; Richard de Burstede to be admitted as a co-executor at his request; the inventory to be exhibited before Michaelmas next; and the will has been sealed with the Archbishop's seal, 16 April 1338. (b) Around the right-hand seal tag in a contemporary hand: 'Hoc est testamentum venerabilis patris domini Stephani dei gracia Londoniensis episcopi factum et asignatum apud Stebbenheth' in camera eiusdem patris ibidem die jovis videlicet decimo nono die mensis Februarii anno domini millesimo CCC^{mo} tricesimo ..... Presentibus in assignacio huius domino Nicholao Hosebo*u*nde Willelmo Prat' et Willelmo de Langedich' et Ada atte Watere. Mayden' [*notarial sign*] N. Housebonde de int' fact'.' (c) Near the left-hand seal tag: 'Stephani Graveshend' testamentum anno domino M^{o} CCC xxxvi^{o}'. (d) 'Cij^{o}'.
2. A contemporary copy of the will, possibly written in the hand which wrote the executors' accounts (**18/2**). It does not have the passage about the erasure. There is a late fourteenth-century endorsement: 'Testamentum Stephani Gravesend' ..... sigillatum. Cii^{o}'.

In dei nomine amen ego Stephanus permissione divina Londoniensis ecclesie minister licet indignus die lune decimo nono die mensis Februarii anno domini millesimo CCC^{mo} tricesimo sexto sanus corpore et compos mente condo testamentum meum in hunc modum. In primis lego animam meam deo et corpus meum ad sepeliendum in ecclesia sancti Pauli London' juxta tumulum bone memorie domini Ricardi avunculi mei quondam Londoniensis episcopi. Item lego centum marcas pro funeraris die sepulture mee nec volo quod plus expendatur quia secundum beatum Augustinum pompa funeris agmina exequiarum sunt vivorum qualiacumque solacia non adjutoria mortuorum.[1] Et volo quod sunt viginti quatuor cerei circa corpus meum et non plures. Item lego centum li. pauperibus tenentibus maneriorum nec volo quod aliqua pecunia distribuatur pauperibus die sepulture mee sed postea in locis episcopatus ubi videbitur executoribus meis magis expediens. Item lego Ricardo de Bursted' unam cuppam. Item lego domino Willelmo de Cantuar' unam peciam argent*i* de majoribus. Item lego domino Willelmo de Munden' unam cuppam. Item lego domino Stephano de Scaldeford' unam cuppam. Item lego Johanni de Teversham meliorem cuppam secundam. Item lego domino archiepiscopo Cantuariensi unum anulum magnum cum saphiro qui fuit bone memorie quondam domini Thome Herefordensis episcopi. Item lego omnes libros meos de arte dialetica pauperibus scolaribus de Merton'.[2] Item lego pauperibus scolaribus de aula universitatis Oxon' librum de veritate in uno volumine[3] et librum de potencia mala in alio volumine.[4] Item lego pauperibus scolaribus de Bailolph decem marcas. Item scolaribus de novo fundatis quibus est ecclesia beate Marie apropriata terciam partem summe fratris Thome de Alquino[5] et quodlibet magistri Henrici de Landavo in duobus voluminibus.[6] Item lego magistro Thome Durant cancellario ecclesie sancti Pauli London' librum concordanciarum.[7] Item lego domino Willelmo Vygerous parvam bibliam meam et unam cuppam qua utor cotidie. Item volo quod tota garderoba mea et lectualia exponantur vendicioni et pecunia illa liberetur executoribus sororum mearum ad distribuendum pro animabus earum. Item lego domino Willelmo de Bohoun meliorem equm quem ego habeo et duas pelves argenteas. Item lego Hugoni de Nevill' cursorem meum qui vocatur Lumbard.[8] Item lego Johanni filz Walter duodecim discos argenteos cum totidem salsariis et duas pelves planas. Item lego domino Ricardo de Ha*ul*e cursorem meum nigrum quem emi de Johanne de Pulteneye. Item lego Henrico Chamberleyn decem li. Item lego Thome filio suo decem marcas et cursorem meum album qui vocatur Hungrie. Item lego Johanni de Claketon' decem marcas. Item lego Reginaldo Filet' centum solidos et unam peciam de majoribus. Item lego magistro Willelmo coco centum solidos. Item lego Egidio falconario centum solidos. Item lego cuilibet armigero domestico deservienti in domo mea de residuis quinque marcas. Item lego Gautro*u*n quinque marcas. Item lego Proude quatuor marcas. Item lego magistro Johanni coco centum solidos. Item lego cuilibet officiario de residuis quatuor marcas. Item lego Willelmo Prat centum solidos. Item lego Osberto centum solidos. Item lego Longedich' decem marcas. Item lego Johanni Lyne centum solidos. Item lego cuilibet de garcionibus meis propriis de residuis quadraginta solidos. Item lego Johanni de Cornewaille quatuor marcas. Item lego unam cuppam deauratam quam habui ex legato bone memorie domini Rogeri de Mortevaux quondam episcopi Sarum successori meo. Et volo quod aliquis executorum meorum notificet sibi quot virorum valencium fuit illa cuppa. Item lego ecclesie sancti Pauli London' decreta mea in quo volumine continentur multa memoranda tangencia statum ecclesie.[9] Et volo quod successor meus habeat usum libri illius et statim post decessum illius restituatur ecclesie. Item lego Willelmo de Stocton' unam cuppam argenteam. Item lego majoribus canonicis presentibus in sepulture mee decem li. Item lego cuilibet minori canonico presenti unam marcam argenti. Item lego cuilibet capellano ecclesie presenti duos solidos. Item lego cuilibet vicario ecclesie presenti dimidiam marcam. Item lego pueris elemosinarie viginti solidos. Item lego quinque servientibus ecclesie et garcionibus eorum viginti solidos. Item lego magistro Henrico de Iddesworth' unam cuppam et unam ollam argenteam pro vino. Item lego domine de Clare discum meum pro elemosina. Item lego Thome nepoti meo omnia animalia et blada existencia in maneriis hereditatis mee excepto marisco de Plumberwe. Et lego eidem quadraginta libras pro patronatu alicuius ecclesie emendo loco ecclesie de Thurrok'. Et si contingat dictum Thomam reddere se difficilem in dimittendo ecclesiam de Thurrok' executoribus meis nolo quod habeat aliquid de sibi legatis. Item lego fratri Willelmo de la More priori fratrum predicatorum London' quinque marcas et conventui suo quinque marcas. Item lego fratribus minoribus quinque marcas. Item lego fratribus Carmelitis quinque marcas. Item lego fratribus sancti Augustini quinque marcas. Item lego fratribus sancte crucis quadraginta solidos. Item lego minorissis London' quadraginta solidos. Item lego aliis monialibus London' quinque marcas. Item lego Roberto de Teye decem li. et meliorem summarium quem habeo. Item lego cuilibet ordini mendicancium

Essex' quadraginta solidos. Item lego Willelmo de Teye unam cuppam. Item lego Johanne atte Grave unam cuppam et duas pecias de majoribus. Item lego Johanni de Kyngesdon' et Johanni de Huntyngdon' cuilibet quinque marcas. Item lego Johanni de Brightlyngeseye Willelmo de Apoldre et Thome de Branketr' clericis de capella mea non promotis cuilibet eorum viginti solidos. Item lego domino Ade ate Water x li.[10] Huius autem testamenti mei constituto et ordino executores meos Thomam Durant cancellarium ecclesie sancti Pauli Lond*onie* et Henricum de Iddesworth' ipsius ecclesie canonicum Robertum de Teye et dominos Johannem de Teversham Ricardum de Bursted et Willelmum Vygerous. Et volo quod omnia bona mea residua executores mei convertant in tres usus pios videlicet in pauperibus sustentandis viis reparandis et in mulieribus bone fame maritandis. Rasura superius inter illa verba 'Lumbard' et 'Item lego Johanni filz Walt*er*' facta fuit ante consignacionem huius testamenti.

Notes

1 Augustine *De civitate dei* ed. B. Dombart and A. Kalb (*CCSL*, 47–8; Turnhout, 1955) i, p. 14 (Book 1, chapter 12).

2 For the books bequeathed to Merton, F.M. Powicke *The medieval books of Merton College* (Oxford, 1931) p. 51; for these volumes and others owned and bequeathed by Gravesend, Cavanaugh, 'Books', pp. 325–7.

3 Thomas Aquinas *De veritate*, printed in *STO*, xxii.

4 Thomas Aquinas *De malo*, printed in *STO*, xxiii.

5 Thomas Aquinas *Summa theologica*, part III, printed in *STO*, iv–xii.

6 'Landavo' for 'Gandavo': Henricus de Gandavo (Henry of Ghent) *Quodlibeta*, printed Paris, 1518.

7 Perhaps the *Concordantia maior*, compiled by the Dominicans of Saint-Jacques, Paris; printed Strassburg, before 1474.

8 MS: followed by a line filler over an erasure.

9 Gratian *Decretum*, printed in *Corpus iuris canonici* ed. E. Friedberg (2nd edition, 2 vols., Leipzig, 1922) i: a copy in current administrative use.

10 This sentence written over an erasure, in a second hand.

18/2 Account of the executors, *c*.1340–1 *Guildhall Library, London, MS 25177*

A roll of two membranes, sewn Chancery fashion with brown thread. The roll is damaged at the head, and the top only remains at the extreme right- and left-hand sides. There are no contemporary endorsements beyond 'Compotus executorum Cii^{o}' in a fourteenth-century hand on mem. 1d. The paragraph totals appear at the right-hand side. Stephen Gravesend died on 8 April 1338. The account was written throughout largely in a single hand, with a second hand making some additions, including entries in the final paragraph which take the work of the executors past the third anniversary of Gravesend's death. There are no separate signs of auditing.

[*Mem. 1r*] ..... episcopi de

Expense ante sepulturam In primis ..... sabati xxv diem carnium mensis ..... ord' xvi qr. precii lxiiii s. De aven*is* lii qr. In iiii bus. p*isarum* precii ..... precii xxxiiii s. De multonibus iii precii v s. De p*or*cellis i precii iiii d. De caponibus ii precii v d. De agnis xvi precii iiii s. ..... precii xx s. Summa huius stauri xvi li. v s. iii d. ob. qua. Item computat in diversis empcionibus per dictum tempus et aliis expensis forinc*ecis* xix li. ii s. vi d. qua.

Summa xxxv li. vii s. x d.

......*ue*nt' Item ..... factis et die dominica xxvi die Aprilis quo die fumus aportabatur London' usque diem veneris proximam tunc sequentem ..... videlicet xx qr. ii bus. frumenti precii iiii li. xii d. De braseo ordei xvi qr. precii lxiiii s. De avenis xx qr. iiii bus. precii xli s. ..... De i pipa vini precii xx s. De porcis l precii lxx s. De multonibus lx precii lx s. De vitulis iii .....xx s. De agnis Cv precii xxxv s. De porcellis li precii xvii s. De pavonibus lxviii precii xx ..... ix d. ob. De cignis ii precii xx s. De aucis iiii precii x d. Summa huius stauri xxxi li. ix s. vii d. ob. Item computat in diversis empcionibus die sepulture xliiii li. ii s. ix d. qua.

Summa lxxv li. xii s. iiii d. ob. qua.

Expensis forincecis dicto die In primis soluti Johanni le Barber pro cimentariis carpentariis et garcionibus eorundem ac eciam aliis expensis neccessariis circa repparacionem aule coquine et aliarum domorum in palacio lxix s. vi d. ob. Item soluti Gilberto le Wodemongere pro bordis cleyes et aliis rebus ab eodem emptis a[1] diem sepulture xl s. Item soluti pro uno plumbo empto et aliis plumbe[2] emendandis vi s. Item soluti pro seruris a diversa ostia in palacio ii s. Item in canabo empto lx s. vi d. Item in xii ulnis pro streynours emptis ii s. vi d. In ix paner*es* ii s. In cariagio aque ad coquinam iii s. v d. In ixC vasis ligneis emptis xxxiii s. iiii d. In ..... verjus empt*is* xi s. viii d. In pestello empto xviii d. In trowes et bolles emptis iii s. iii d. In lxvii qr. et di. carbonum ..... ob. In C et di. fagettorum emptis v s. In xiiii tonellis et iii pipis vacuis emptis xvii s. vii d. In viii cuvellis emptis ..... convens' fact' pro cignis capiendis ... et hero*u*ncellis gerendis et pascendis iii s. ix d. In expensis quatuor hominum per viam ..... in doleis ..... circul' emend' pro eisdem ii s. iiii d. In diversis portagiis viii d. In speciebus emptis dicto die et pro choro ..... existent' apud palacium per tempus pro providencia facienda iiii s. vi d. ob. Item soluti pro allocacione panni de Cand..... ..... aula vi s. ..... In cuppis emptis pro aula xviii d. Item soluti pro factura unius olle enee vi d. Item dati Ricardo Hura*u*nt xxvi s. viii d. Item dati ....as... ... vi s. Item datis Alano le Fruturer iii s. Item dati hominibus coquentibus carnes grossas vi s. viii d. Item dati torn...roche iiii s. ii d. Item dati hominibus rumpentibus carnes grossas vi d. Item dati tribus hominibus laborantibus circa mortarium xv d. Item dati coco domine Ide de Nevill' iii s. iiii d. Item dati magistro Willelmo Chapeler ii s. Item dati coco Henrici Chamb*er*leyn xii d. Item dati coco domini Nicholai Hosebonde ii s. Item dati servientibus vicecomitum London' x s. Item dati garcionibus eorundem v s. Item pauperibus istronibus v s.

Summa xxi li. xix s. x d. ob.

Expense circa exequias Item computat pro Cxiiii ulnis nigri panni emptis pro cotis hominum deferencium torticos circa fumus per viam Cxiiii s. iii d. Item liberati cissor*ibus* pro eisdem cotis faciendis ix s. iii d. Item soluti pro quadringenta lib. cere emptis pro torticis cereis et candelis faciendis ix li. xii s. ii d. Item soluti candelario pro factura cerorum torticorum et candelarum et pro cista reperpanda ad fumus liiii s. ii d. Item soluti pro feretro ligneo de novo facto ad fumus portandam vi s. x d. Item liberati ad pitanciam ministris ecclesie sancti Pauli die sepulture xxxiii li. xvii s. iiii d. In oblacionibus eodem die ix s. vi d.

Summa liii s. li iii s. vi d.

Alie expense forincece In primis soluti pro oblacione testamenti xx s. Dati clerico registri iii s. iiii d. Item soluti pro batellagio executorum euntium per diversas vices apud Westm' et Lamheth' iiii s. vi d. Item in expensis tricesima die mensis xlvii s. xi d. Item liberati eodem die ministris ecclesie pro pitancis ix li. iiii s. rectoribus civitatis London' pro processione et classica in eadem xl s. Item soluti pro ymagine episcopi sculpanda super lapidem defuncti cum aliis ymaginibus vi li. xv s. i d. Item in expensis et vadiis solutis a die sepulture usque diem mensis et extunc per xiiii dies quousque equi venditi xlvi s. ii d. In ferris equorum per idem iii s. vi d. Item in prebenda eorundem equorum per diem tempus vi qr. vi bus. avenarum precii xiii s. vi d. In expensis dominorum Johannis Brid et Willelmi Vigorus euntium in Essex' pro juvento faciendo x s. iiii d. In expensis euntium per diversa maneria episcopatus pro implemento liberato xxxvi s. vi d. In expensis Roberti de Treye et Willelmi Vigerus euntium in banco pro colloquio habendo cum domino Thoma de Aldon' pro negocio defuncti vi s. viii d. Item in expensis auditorum compotorum servientium et prepositorum episcopatus xxvi s. x d. Item dati Johanni de Leyre clerico compoti pro labore suo xl s. Item dati cuidam alii clerico pro labore iii s. iiii d. Item soluti Ricardo de Hakeneye pro canabo empto ab eodem pro lana anni preteriti et presentis lxxiiii s. Item dati Thome de Hamme pro reperpacione lane xiii s. iiii d. In lana ponderanda vi d. Item liberati Roberto de Teye venienti London' per vices pro negoc*io* defuncti xx s. Item liberati domino Johanni Brid pro labore xl s. Item soluti xvii officiariis pro calcituara eorum debito tempore vite domini lx s. Item xx garcionibus pro eadem xxx s. Item vii pagiis pro eadem vii s. In xxiiii ulnis panni de Candelwykstret' emptis pro dictis pagiis quia non habuerunt robas tempore vite domini xx s. vi d. In percamenum emptum per vices iii s. iiii d. Item dati cuidam clerico scribenti inventarium et ad tangencium negocia defuncti iii s. iiii d. Item soluti diversis hominibus de famulia[3] a retro de serviciis suis xiii li. vi s. iiii d. Item dati pro anima defuncti Marie nepte eiusdem monali apud Berkyngg' xl s. Item dati Willelmo de Longedych' pro longo servicio suo lx s. Item dati cuidam puero elemosinarie pro anima defuncti ad introitum suum apud sanctam Ositham pro neccessariis suis et habitu suo emendo lx s. Item soluti cuidam scanonario pro vendicione librorum xvi s. Item liberati ministres[4] ecclesie sancti Pauli die anniversarii dicti defuncti ad pitanciam cum oblacionibus vii li. xvii s. Item soluti pro quadam via reparanda inter Acton' et London' xv li. xiii s. iiii d. Item pro quadam via reparanda apud Oresete C s. Item soluti duobus capellanis celebrandis pro anima defuncti vi li. xiii s. iiii d.

Summa Ci li. \xv/iii s. \ viii d. /[5]

Debita et alia soluta In primis solute Willelmo de Joneston' de debitis domini x li. Item soluti Johanni Perles attornato domini de debitis eiusdem xi s. viii d. Item soluti camerario ecclesie sancti Pauli pro arreragiis pitancie quinque annorum de ecclesia de Brokesbourn' pro anima Ricardi episcopi tercii[6] xvi li. xiii s. iiii d. Item solute eidem camerario pro arreragiis pitancie trium annorum de redd*itibus* in Maldon' pro anima regis Henrici tercii x li. Item solute pro secunda medietate anni decime triennalis pro episcopatu Londoniensi post mortem dicti defuncti l li. Item liberati cuidam nuncio domini regis ex promissa domini in vita sua vi s. viii d. Item soluti pro uno equo empto cum sella et misso domino cardinali Mountfavensi per executores Ciiii s. Item solute domino Willelmo de Cossale pro arrerragiis annue pensionis sex annorum xii li. Item soluti ministris ecclesie sancti Pauli in anniversario quondam Ricardi de Graveshende episcopi

Londoniensis xl s. Item soluti executoribus testamenti magistri Petri de Askern' de debitis defuncti C s. Item magistro Thome de Plumstok' de debitis defuncti lx s. Item abbati de Stratford' de debitis defuncti xxi s. Item solute magistro Bernardo Cistr' clerico pape pro denariis beati Petri existentibus aretro per biennium de archidiaconatu Essex' xi li. Item liberati decano et capitulo xii panni de serico et i carpita precii xvi li.

Summa Cxlii li. xvi s. viii d.

Implementum et defectus domorum In primis liberat*i* successori pro implemento vii equos carectarios precii vi li. xiii s. iiii d. Item CCiiii^{or} stottos precii Cii li. Item CC boves precii Cxxxviii li. Item duo tauros xxi vaccas precii vi li. xviii s. Item vi^{xx} et xv capita porcorum precii x li. ii s. vi d. Item MMCCCxxviii capita bidencium precii Cxvi li. viii s. Item liberate eidem successori pro defectibus domorum in maneriis episcopatus DClxvi li. xiii s. iiii d.

Summa Mxlvi li. xv s. ii d.

Item soluti eidem successori pro diversis debitis et accionibus ac calumpniis et pro emendo defectuum domorum CCClvii li. xii s. ii d. qua. precii

Summa iiiClvii \ li. /[7] xii s. ii d. qua.

Libri legatti In primis liberate successori et ecclesie sancti Pauli libre decretorum[8] precii C s. Item magistro Thome Duraunt librum concordancie[9] precii liii s. iiii d. Item domino Willelmo Vigerus parvam bibliam precii xl s. Item scolaribus Oxon' de novo fundatis quibus est ecclesia beate Marie apropriata tercia pars fratris Thome de Aquino[10] et quodlibet magistri Henrici de Landavo precii xxvi s.[11] Item pauperibus scolaribus de Merton' omnes libri de arte dealetica precii iiii li. vii s. v d. Item pauperibus scolaribus de aula universitatis Oxon' ii libri de veritate potencia et malo precii xl s.[12]

Summa xvii li. vi s. ix d.

Vasa argentea legatta et data In primis data domino regi i cuppa ponderis x li. Item eidem i annulum precii xx li. Item date successori ii pelves cum castell*is* precii Ci s. ii d. Item liberate magistro Henrico de Iddesworth' ex legatto i cuppa et i olla pro vino ponderis C s. x d. Item liberata domino Ricardo de Burgsted' ex legato una cuppa ponderis xxxviii s. iiii d. Item liberata[13] domino Willelmo Vigerus una[14] cuppa ponderis lxvi s. viii d. Item Johanni de Teveresham i cuppa ponderis Cxi s. viii d. Item domino Stephano de Scaldeford i cuppa ponderis xxvi s. viii d. Item domino Willelmo de Mundene i cuppa ponderis xxx s. Item Willelmo de Stokton' i cuppa ponderis xlvi s. viii d. Item Willelmo de Teye i cuppa ponderis xxxiii s. iiii d. Item Johanni de la Gravei i cuppa ii pecie ponderis lxi s. viii d. Item successor*i* ex legato i cuppa ponderis lx s. Item domino Willelmo de Cant' i pecia precii xiii s. iiii d. Item Reginaldo Filett' i pecia ponderis xiii s. iiii d. Item domine de Clare i discus pro elemosina ponderis iiii li. x s. Item domino Willelmo de Bohun ii pelves ponderis vi li. Item Johanni fitz Waut' xii disci[15] xii salsaria et ii pelves plana ponderis xix li. vi s. viii d.

Summa iiii^{xx}xv li. iiii d.

Item liberata magistro Ricardo de Bynteworth clerico Lond' per manus J. de Teversham in presencia archidiaconi Middelsex' et magistri Henrici de Idesworth' executorum vasa argentea ad valorem lxii li. ii s. x d. pro quibus nichil soluta[16]

Denarii legatti et soluti In primis liberate domino Ade atte Watere ex legato x li. Item Johanni de Kyngeston' clerico lxvi s. viii d. Item Johanni de Huntyngdon' clerico lxvi s. viii d. Item Johanni de Britȝlyngeseye clerico xx s. Item Willelmo de Apuldre clerico xx s. Item Thome de Branketre clerico xx s. Item Henrico Chamb*er*leyn x li. Item Thome filio eiusdem vi li. xiii s. iiii d. Item Johanni de Claketon' vi li. xiii s. iiii d. Item Reginaldo Filett' C s. Item Willelmo coco C s. Item Egidio falconario C s. Item Waltero le Groos lxvi s. viii d. Item Ricardo de Frowesby lxvi s. viii d. Item Johanni de Otle lxvi s. viii d. Item Johanni Gobion lxvi s. viii d. Item Roberto de Teye x li. Item Johanni de Ferrar' lxvi s. viii d. Item Ricardo Ga*u*tro*u*n lxvi s. viii d. Item Roberto Proude liii s. iiii d. Item Johanni coco C s. Item Johanni Ly*n*e C s. Item Willelmo Prat C s. Item Willelmo Longedych vi li. xiii s. iiii d. Item Willelmo pistori liii s. iiii d. Item Johanni de Bokherst liii s. iiii d. Item Eustacio de garderobe liii s. iiii d. Item Johanni le Barber liii s. iiii d. Item Stephano piscatori liii s. iiii d. Item Thome falconario liii s. iiii d. Item Ricardo carectario liii s. iiii d. Item Johanni janitori liii s. iiii d. Item Humfr*id*o clerico capelle xl s. Item Johanni Osebern' C s. Item Johanni de Cornwell' liii s. iiii d. Item Roberto pistor*i* xl s. Item Johanni Squiller xl s. [*Mem. 2r*] Item Eustacio de coquina xl s. Item Willelmo vigili xl s. Item Roberto palefridario xl s. Item Johanni Meleward xl s. Item Ricardo Ferrar' xl s. Item Willelmo de paner*ia* xl s. Item Scot' xl s. Item Johanni venatori xl s. Item Willelmo Dawe xl s. Item Willelmo Makke xl s. Item Willelmo cursori xl s. Item Johanni Dagenet' xl s. Item Johanni Fleg' xl s. Item Roberto Frebern' xl s. Item Nicholao falconario xl s. Item fratribus predicatoribus London' lxvi s. viii d. Item fratribus sancti Augustini de eadem lxvi s. viii d. < viii d. >[17] Item fratribus Carmelitis de eadem lxvi s. viii d. Item fratribus sancte crucis de eadem xl s. Item dati ii pauperibus scolaribus Oxon' de parentibus dicti defuncti xl s. Item liberati minorisse extra Allegate London' lxvi s. viii d. Item monialibus sancte Elene Clerkenewell' et Haliwell' lxvi s. viii d. Item scolaribus Balliolhalle Oxon' vi li. xiii s. iiii d. Item liberati fratribus predicatoribus Chelm*e*sford' xl s. Item fratribus Carmelitis de Maldon' xl s. Item fratribus minoribus Colec' xl s. Item pauperibus tenentibus per diversa maneria episcopatus C li. Item liberati Thome de Graveshende de stauro in maneriis hereditatis ad valorem Clxiiii li. xii s. ii d. ob. Item fratri Willelmo de Mora de ordine predicatorum lxvi s. viii d. Item fratribus minoribus London' lxvi s. viii d.

[*Mem. 1r*] Summa CCCCiiii^{xx}i li. [*Mem. 2r*] xviii s. x d. ob.

Equi legatti et dati Primo datum domino regi i palefrey nigrum precii xx li. Item liberatum domino comiti Norhampton' unum palefrey grey ex legatto precii xx li. Item Hugoni de Neuville ex legato i palefrey vocatum Lumbard precii xiii li. vi s. viii d. Item Roberto de Teye ex legato i sommarium precii lxvi s. viii d. Item datum pro anima defuncti cuidam pauperi reperpanti viam regiam inter London' et Braynfford' i sommarium vetus et debile precii xiii s. iiii d.

Summa lvii li. vi s. viii d.

Allocaciones In primis petunt executores allocacionem de xx qr. vii bus. frumenti captis per homines domini regis precii iiii li. iii s. vi d. Item de xxii qr. ii bus. avenarum captis per eosdem precii xliiii s. vi d. Item de vi qr. iii bus. pisarum captis per eosdem precii xv s. vii d. ob. Item petunt allocacionem de xvi qr. frumenti datis pauperibus pro anima defuncti precii lxiiii s. Item petunt allocacionem de diversis morinis in episcopatu post confeccionem inventarii antequam staure vendebantur successori Cx s. Item petunt allocacionem de xxviii ovibus matricibus[18] et xxxii agnis liberatis uxori Johannis Stork' de debitis defuncti precii xxvi s. viii d.

Summa xvii li. iiii s. iii d. ob.

Alie expense Item computat liberati[19] Johanni Grene et Symoni Bargeman pro arreragiis serviciorum[20] suorum xl s. Item cuidam Ricardo le Wollepakker' pro eodem x s. Item Johanni lotrario pro eodem v s. Item Johanni de Leyere clerico compoti maneriorum pro eodem xxx s. Item cuidam magistro capelle de Graveshende de debitis patris dicti defuncti xx s. Item de Roberto le Port*er* pro arreragiis servicii sui xx s. Item soluti pro expensis executorum apud Croydon' et batellagio versus Lamheth' iii s. xi d.

Summa vi li. ix s. xi d.

Alie expense facte post compotum Item liberate clerico archiepiscopi auditoribus compoti[21] iiii li. Item liberati Johanni de Stelb' carectario pro arreragiis servicii sui vi s. viii d. Item liberate archiepiscopo Cantuariensi pro acquietancia habenda de ministracione bonorum domini Stephani de Graveshende quondam episcopi Londoniensis lx li. Item liberati ministris ecclesie sancti Pauli die anniversarii quondam Ricardi de Graveshend' episcopi xl s. Item liberati magistro Ricardo de Wermington' executori*bus* pro copia libelli et scripcione diversarum excepcionum et ii procurationum iii s. i d. Item Johanni atte Pole executori domine Alicie pro tercia \ parte /[22] gardrobe domini ix li. xii d. Item liberati Egido falconario pro arreragiis pensionis sue de Graveshende lx s. Item liberati ministris ecclesie sancti Pauli die anniversarii Stephani de Graveshende pro secundo anno lx s. Item liberati pro expensis executorum die anniversarii dicti Stephani vi s. v d. ob. Item liberate magistro Michaeli de Nortburn' advocato executorum pro uno anno[23] iiii li. Item liberati magistro Ricardo de Warmington' procuratori dictorum executorum pro uno anno[24] xl s. Item liberate Willelmo de Fulham piscenario London' de antiquo debito prout ostendit per talli*am* x li. Item liberati pro certis locatis et expensis cere die anniversarii pro secundo anno dicti defuncti ii s. viiii d.[25] Item liberati pauperibus apud Stebb' ultra viii li. v s. vi d. Item liberate executoribus Johanne de Hastynges sororis[26] episcopi Londoniensis de garderoba sua ix li. Item[27] liberati pro scripcione copie compoti viii d. Item liberati Ricardo le Avener pro arreragiis servicii sui xiii s. iiii d. Item liberati ministris ecclesie sancti Pauli ad pitanciam die anniversarii dicti defuncti pro tercio anno lx s. Item liberati pro cereis locatis eodem die iii s.

Notes

1 In this paragraph, 'a' followed by the accusative is used to mean 'ad'; it is possible the clerk was thinking in French.

2 Possibly a French form.

3 MS has 6 minims for 'mu'.

4 Possibly a French form.

5 Insertions in a second hand.

6 Richard FitzNeal, Bishop of London (d. 1198).

7 Insertion in a second hand.

8 Gratian *Decretum*, as **18/1**, note 9.
9 Perhaps the *Concordantia maior*, as **18/1**, note 7.
10 Thomas Aquinas *Summa theologica*, part III, as **18/1**, note 5.
11 Henricus de Gandavo (Henry of Ghent) *Quodlibeta*, as **18/1**, note 6.
12 Thomas Aquinas *De veritate*, as **18/1**, note 3; and Thomas Aquinas *De malo*, as **18/1**, note 4.
13 MS: 'liberate'.
14 MS puts this in the accusative, 'unam', whereas all other examples are in the nominative or without indication of case.
15 MS: 'discus'.
16 This sentence in a second hand.
17 Erased, rather than deleted.
18 MS: 'matrices'.
19 MS: 'liberate'.
20 MS: 'servicorum'.
21 MS: 'Item ..... compoti' in a second hand, over an erasure.
22 Insertion in a second hand.
23 MS: 'pro uno anno' in a second hand, over an erasure.
24 MS: 'pro uno anno' in a second hand, over an erasure.
25 For 'ix d.'
26 Final 's' of 'sororis' in a second hand.
27 The four concluding sentences are written in a second hand.

19 Adam Houghton, Bishop of St David's

19/1 Will, 8 February 1389 *LPL, Register of William Courtenay, ff. 231v–232r*
In nomine sancte et individue Trinitatis patris et filii et spiritus sancti amen. Nos Adam Houton' divina miseracione Menevensis episcopus sane mentis et bone memorie in manerio nostro de Launtefay[1] octavo die mensis Februarii anno domini millesimo CCC^{mo} octogesimo nono condimus testamentum nostrum in hunc modum. Primitus commendamus animam nostram deo omnipotenti beatissime virgini Marie matri sue et omnibus sanctis et corpus nostrum sacre sepulture tradendum in parte boriali capelle cantarie quam deo favente fundamus juxta ecclesiam nostram cathedralem Menevensem in honore dicte beatissime virginis Marie. Item legamus ii pelves nostras meliores argenteas cum scutis armorum nostrorum ii phialas argenteas xii discos argenteos cum totidem[2] salsariis argenteis ecclesie nostre cathedrali Menevensi. Item legamus dicte ecclesie nostre cathedrali i casulam i tunicam i dalmaticam i capam i pannum pendentem ante altare i pannum pro fronte altaris i frontellum consutum cum linthiamine ii redillos et i casam corporal*ium* de albo et puro satyn embroudatam cum mitris aureis et crucibus sancti Andree aureis ac duabus litteris principalibus nominis nostri videlicet 'AH' auro communito necnon tres albas et iii amictas de panno lineo cum paruris stolis et phanulis de eadem secta. Item legamus x li. que sunt in manibus domini Willelmi Nicol archidiaconi de Kerverdyn[3] ad fabricam et refectionem murorum et clausur*e* ecclesie Menevensis predicte. Item legamus reverendissimo in Cristo patri et domino nostro carissimo domino Willelmo Courtenay archiepiscopo Cantuariensi unum ciphum argenteum cum uno cooperculo argenteo deauratum exquisiti operis continentem unum draconem volantem in summitate unacum xx marcarum in dicto cipho. Item legamus cuilibet canonico Menevensi interessenti in exequiis et sepultura nostra xx s. Item legamus cuilibet vicario presbitero ecclesie nostre Menevensis predicte x s. Item cuilibet vicario diacono et subdiacono in eadem ecclesia cathedrali vi s. viii d. Item cuilibet presbitero

cantariarum infra dictam ecclesiam nostram cathedralem iii s. iiii d. Item cuilibet presbitero interessenti in exequiis et sepultura nostris preter vicarios et presbiteros predictos ad celebrandum pro anima nostra iii s. iiii d. Item legamus quatuor choristis in ecclesia nostra Menevensi viii s. inter eos equaliter dividendos. Item volumus quod restituantur[4] ecclesie collegiate de Abbergwyly[5] i casula i tunica i dalmatica et iii cape de albo serico ac unum missale que quondam[6] fuerunt in custodia domini Reginaldi de Briane nuper episcopi Menevensis. Item legamus eidem ecclesie nostre collegiate de Abb*er*gwly C s. pro i pari vestimentorum emendorum ad eandem. Item legamus cuilibet vicario presbitero in eadem ecclesia collegiate vi s. viii d. Item cuilibet vicario diacono et subdiacono in eadem v s. Item legamus x li. ad emendum ea que magis < nuc > neccessaria sunt ad ecclesiam nostram collegialem de Landebre*v*y[7] ad ordinacionem executorum nostrorum. Item legamus cuilibet vicario presbitero in dicta ecclesia collegiali de Landebrevy vi s. viii d. Item cuilibet vicario diacono et subdiacono in eadem v s. Item legamus conventui fratrum predicatorum Haverfordie xl s. Item conventui fratrum minorum de Kermerdyn xl s. Item conventui fratrum predicatorum Brecon' xl s. Item conventui fratrum Augustinorum de Lodelowe xx s. Item conventui Carmelitorum[8] fratrum ibidem xx s. Item legamus in exequiis et sepultura nostris faciendis ad disposicionem executorum nostrorum. Item legamus organa nostra cantarie nostre beate Marie Menevensi ubi corpus nostrum requiescet. Item legamus magistro Johanni Sampson xl s. Item domino Johanni Port*er* xl s. Item domino Johanni Hyot C s. Item fratri Henrico Morice monacho de Pulla[9] xl s. Item fratri Johanni Giffard' monacho < lvi > lxvi s. viii d. Item domino Philippo Bemond' xl s. Item domino Roberto Bro*u*n xl s. Item domino Johanni Kedwelly xl s. Item Thome Pope xl s. Item Johanni Laurence xl s. Item Nicholao Baker xl s. Item Waltero Hugyn xl s. Item [*f. 232r*] Ricardo Wader xl s. Item domino Henrico Lloyd xl s. Item domino Johanni Mabo*u*ce xl s. Item domino Johanni Huchyn xl s. Item Ade Blakeman nepoti nostro xl s. Item Johanni Castel xl s. Item Henrico Ma*u*ncel xl s. Item Johanni Daskervyle xl s. Item Johanni Jamys xl s. Item Johanni Fauley xl s. Item omnibus aliis de familia nostra remunerandis juxta ordinacionem executoris nostri. Residuum vero omnium bonorum nostrorum hic non legatorum legamus et assignamus ad ordinacionem et disposicionem executoris nostri ut ipse dispon*a*t et ordinet de eisdem ad salutem anime nostre prout sibi secundum deum melius videbitur expedire. Et ad istud testamentum nostrum fideliter exequendum dilectum consanguineum nostrum dominum Johannem Joce militem huiusmodi ultime voluntatis nostre constituimus et preficimus executorem.

Notes

1 Lamphey, Pembs.
2 MS: 'todicem'.
3 Carmarthen: in Welsh, Caerfyrddin.
4 MS: 'restitituantur'.
5 Abergwili, Carmarthenshire.
6 MS: 'quodam'.
7 Llanddewi Brefi, Cardiganshire.
8 MS: 'Carmelitorum' preceded by a superscript letter 'b'.
9 The Cistercian abbey of Strata Marcella, near Welshpool.

19/2 Probate granted to John Joce, knight, as executor named in the will, with Dom. John Hyot, canon of St David's, appointed as supervisor, in the chapel at

Croydon, 23 May 1389. Dom. Gilbert Nichol, canon of the collegiate church of Abergwili, is appointed to assist in the administration of the will, 24 May 1389. *LPL, Register of William Courtenay, f. 232r.*

20 Walter Kirkham, Bishop of Durham

Account of debts and stock on manors, late September 1260 *DUL, DCM Durham, Locellus V 14*

A roll of one membrane. A document possibly prepared for the executors of the Bishop, in its present state probably from late September 1260. Bishop Kirkham died on 9 August 1260; the royal writ at the start of the roll is dated 5 September 1260, and the listing of livestock is dated 24 September 1260. The valuation of the livestock was left incomplete in many places. Endorsed at the foot in a mid to late thirteenth-century hand: 'Infrascripta tangentia testamentum Walteri quondam Dunelmensis episcopi'.

[*Recto*]
Rex vicecomiti Northumbr' salutem. Quia reddidimus et concessimus W. quondam Dunelmensi episcopo et ecclesie sue Dunelmensi sequestrum ecclesiarum quas episcopus Karlionensis et ecclesia sua in episcopatu Dunelmensi usibus suis propriis habent assignatas per finem videlicet mille marcarum quem dominus episcopus Dunelmensis nobiscum fecit et quo fine nobis solvendo executores dicti episcopi plenam nobis securitatem fecerunt tibi precipimus quod quicquid de sequestro predicto de duabus ultimis vacacionibus episcopatus Karlionensis ad manus tuas vel ballivorum tuorum devenit executoribus predictis sine dilacione restitui facias et omnes illos qui in arreragiis aliquibus tenentur ex empcione sequestri predicti distringas ad arreragia illa prefatis executoribus sine dilacione reddenda et taliter te habeas in hac parte ut diligenciam tuam exinde debeamus habere commendatam. Teste me ipso apud Clarendon' v die Septembris anno regni nostri xliiii^{o}.

Hec sunt debita que dominus W. Dunelmensis ..... die quo obiit anno gracie scilicet M^{o}CClx^{mo}
In \ archi/episcopatu Cantuariensi x li.
xx marce prout in rotulo magistri R. de Seyton'[1]
In episcopatu Elyensi xx li. pro Eustachio
In episcopatu eodem viii li. vi s. et viii d.
Item executoribus magistri R. de Kyrkh' CCCxliii li. xviii s. ii d. et ob.
Roberto de Wytheby xxxiii li. vi s. et viii d.
Petro Sarazeno xxvi li. xiii s. iiii d.
Domino priori Dunelmensi CC marce
Ricardo Belle x li.
Domino Thome de Huk' C marce
Domino J. de ballivo de mutuo aberrenti C li.
Wyberto de Cancia C marce
Alano Sampson' de Ebor' iiii^{xx} li. unde R. le burs' respond*et*
Arnaldo Pychard xlv li. viii s.

Executoribus Gace de Chaumund xxxiiii li.
Serloni de Staingat' xiii li. vi s. et viii d.
Roberto de Brompholm' xi li. ix s. iiii d.
Thome Benet xxxviii li. vii s. et i d.
Stephano aurifabro xiiii li. xiiii s.
Domino regi DCC marce
Mercatoribus Sen*ensibus* D marce
Mercatoribus Florentinis CCC li.
Domino J. de Eggesclive iiii^{xx} li.
Item eidem C marce
Domino J. Walran' C s.
Domino Alano de Kyrkh' xxv li. vi s. viii d.
Summa hucusque MMCCCiiii^{xx}viii li. iii s. iii d. ob.

Item domino priori de Dunelm' per P. de Brandon' iiii^{xx} li.
Petro de Novo Castro xxxii li. v s.
Domino archidiacono Dunelmensi xx li.
Pro diversis prisis captis in Dunelm' per B. de Ely xxx li.
Dominus dixit.[2]
Pro vino empto apud Novum Castrum iiii^{xx} li.
Pro expensis coquine Cxxxvii li. iiii s. et iii d.
Item pro aliis expensis domus de quibus G. de Elm' se onerat CCxiii li. ix s. et ix d.

Instaurum episcopi W. quondam Dunelmensis episcopi die veneris proxima post festum sancti Mathei apostoli anno gracie M^{o}CC^{o}lx^{mo}
Vaccaria de Escardford' In custodia Johannis Faxrem sunt l vacce unde xxx sunt lactrices cum xxii vitulis lactantibus precium cuiuslibet vacce cum vitulo di. marca cuiuslibet vacce prengnantis di. marca et cuiuslibet kebbe vi s. que sunt sine vitulo et tunc lactrices.
In custodia eiusdem est unus taurus precium vi s.
In custodia eiusdem sunt xxiii stirki in secundo anno quorum xiii sunt masculi precium cuiuslibet ii s. et x femelli precium cuiuslibet xx d.

Vaccaria de Swynehop' In custodia Radul*ph*i \ de M*er*ley / sunt lviii vacce unde xxxii sunt lactrices cum xxiii vitulis lactantibus precium cuiuslibet cum vitulo vi s. et vi d. cuiuslibet prengnantis vi s. et cuiuslibet kebbe v s.
In custodia eiusdem est unus taurus precium vi s.
In custodia eiusdem sunt xvii stirci in secundo anno quorum xi famelli precium cuiuslibet xviii d. Et vi masculi precium cuiuslibet ii s.

Vaccaria de Hundesschelford' In custodia Ade de Rokehop' sunt xlix vacce unde xxiiii sunt lactrices cum xxi vitulis precium cuiuslibet cum vitulo vii s. cuiuslibet prengnantis vii s. Et cuiuslibet kebbe vi s.
In custodia eiusdem est unus taurus precium v s.
In custodia eiusdem sunt xxiiii stirci in secundo anno quorum xi sunt masculi precium cuiuslibet ii s. vi d. et xiii famelli precium cuiuslibet ii s.

Vaccaria de Blakedenn' In custodia Alani Todde sunt l vacce unde xxiiii sunt

lactrices cum xxxiii vitulis precium cuiuslibet cum vitulo vii s. cuiuslibet prengnantis vii s. et cuiuslibet kebbe vi s.
In custodia eiusdem sunt xxv stirki in secundo anno quorum x sunt masculi precium cuiuslibet ii s. et vi d. et xv femelli precium cuiuslibet ii s.

Vaccaria apud Hyreshop' In custodia Willelmi Todd sunt xlviii vacce unde xxxiii sunt lactrices cum xxviii vitulis precium cuiuslibet cum vitulo di. marca cuiuslibet prengnantis di. marca et cuiuslibet kebbe v s. vi d.
In custodia eiusdem est unus taurus precium di. marca.
In custodia eiusdem sunt xviii stirki in secundo anno quorum x sunt masculi precium cuiuslibet ii s. iiii d. et viii famelli precium xx d.

Vaccaria de Brunhop' In custodia Willelmi Paulin sunt xlix vacce unde xxx sunt lactrices cum xxv vitulis precium cuiuslibet cum vitulo vi s. cuiuslibet prengantis di. marca et cuiuslibet kebbe v s.
In custodia eiusdem est unus taurus precium vi s.

Item vaccaria apud Brunhopp' In custodia Willelmi Colier sunt lv vacce unde xxix sunt lactrices cum xxv vitulis precium cuiuslibet cum vitulo di. \ marca / cuiuslibet prengnantis di. marca et cuiuslibet kebbe vi s.
In custodia eiusdem[3]

Prima vaccaria in Woskerhop' In custodia Thome Hulyn sunt liiii vacce unde xxx sunt lactrices cum xxvii vitulis precium cuiuslibet cum vitulo[4]
Item in custodia eiusdem[5]
In custodia eiusdem sunt xvii stirchi quorum x sunt masculi precium cuiuslibet[6] et vii femelli precium cuiuslibet[7]

Secunda vaccaria ibidem In custodia Willelmi de Alwendall' sunt lviii vacce unde xxxiii sunt lactrices cum xxx vitulis precium cuiuslibet cum vitulo[8]
In custodia eiusdem[9]
In custodia eiusdem sunt xvii stirci quorum xi sunt masculi precium cuiuslibet[10] et vi famelli precium cuiuslibet[11]

Tercia vaccaria ibidem In custodia Johannis Todde sunt xliii vacce unde xxii sunt lactrices cum xxii vitulis precium cuiuslibet cum vitulo[12]
In custodia eiusdem[13]
In custodia eiusdem sunt xix stirci quorum ix sunt masculi precium cuiuslibet[14] et x famelli precium cuiuslibet[15]

Item Brunhop' Sunt eciam in altera foresta scilicet Brunhop' in custodia Ricardi Boves' et Roberti Bu*n*kemann' xl boviculi in quarto anno precium cuiuslibet v s.
Item in custodia eorundem ibidem sunt v^{xx}xiii boviculi in tercio anno precium cuiuslibet iiii s.
Item in[16] custodia eorundem sunt ibidem lxxviii boves ad larderium precium cuiuslibet vi s. vi d.

Esydehop' Item in custodia Andree Hyne in Midelhop v^{xx}viii juvence in tercio anno precium cuiuslibet v s.

Item[17] pro uno equo empto et amigdan*is* et cera et canabaco emptis de Jordino cissore de Houeden' lviii s. et v d. Item Robert*o* de Novo Monasterio xv < marc*e* > li.

[*Dorse*]
......ibend' staurum et .... ali..... et ea apprecianda[18]
Nomina juratorum ad appreciandum instauri episcopi W. quondam Dunelmensis
Walter de Alanseles
Rogerus marescallus
Robertus filius Godiffr'
Robertus filius Martini
Willelmus filius Rad*ulphi*
Adam de Paris
Robertus Poer
Robertus filius Alicie
Ricardus Smelter'
Ro... ...m*er*ley
Walterus .....crof'
David' filius Willelmi

Summa boum de maneriis infra Tynam et Teysam et extra preter Werdall' DCCCiiii^{xx} et xvi precium cuiuslibet vi s. viii d. unde summa CCiiii^{xx}xviii li. xiii s. iiii d.
Summa affrorum lxxiiii et i pullus precium cuiuslibet vi s. et viii d. unde summa xxv li.
Summa vaccarum DCCCii et xiiii taurorum precium cuiuslibet v s. et sex den. unde summa CCxxiiii li. et viii s.
Summa vitulorum CCv precium cuiuslibet xviii d. unde summa xv li. vii s. et sex den.
Summa stircorum in secundo anno Cxli precium cuiuslibet iii s. unde summa xxxvi li. et iii s.
Summa porcorum CCClviii precium cuiuslibet xii d. unde summa xvii li. et xviii s.
Summa ovium matricium MMMCliii precium cuiuslibet xii d.
Summa angnorum utriusque sexus MDCxxxv eiusdem precii
Summa multonum MMCCxviii eiusdem precii
Summa CCC li. et vi s. Summa capitum viiMvi[19]
Summa equarum Cxlvii et iii stalones precium cuiuslibet x s. unde summa lxxv li.
Summa pullorum in primo anno iiii^{xx} et i precium cuiuslibet iii s. unde summa xii li. iii s.
Summa pullorum et pultrarum in secundo anno lxix precium cuiuslibet vi s. unde summa xx li. xiiii s.
Summa pullorum in tercio anno xxxiiii precium cuiuslibet xiii s. et quatuor den. unde summa xxii li. xiii s. et iiii d.
Summa summarum tocius precii MCxliii li. et xiiii d.

Gwanagium episcopi supradicti infra Tynam et Teysam et extra ut supra
Idem episcopus habet apud Norham' Horneclive et Fennewik' ganagium xiii carucarum precium cuiuslibet caruce x li. unde summa Cxxx li.

Idem habet apud Alv*er*ton Creyk' et Houeden' ganagium xi carucarum precium cuiuslibet caruce x li. unde summa Cx li.

Summa CCxl li.

Maneria inter Tynam et Teysam
Apud Haulthon' et Hetton' habet vii carucas precium caruce ut supra.
Apud Rikenhall' habet sex carucas precium cuiuslibet ut supra.
Apud Hethkington' tres carucas precium caruce ut supra.
Apud Miderig' sex carucas precium cuiuslibet ut supra.
Apud Gundon' quinque carucas precium ut supra.
Apud Aukeland duas carucas precium ut supra.
Apud Wlsingh' et F*ro*sterley sex carucas eiusdem precii
Apud Midelham' quinque eiusdem precii
Apud Querendon' quatuor carucas eiusdem precii
Apud Houthton' quatuor carucas eiusdem precii
Apud Newbotel quatuor carucas eiusdem precii
Apud Weremue tres carucas precii eiusdem
Apud Refhopp'quatuor carucas eiusdem precii
Apud Hesington' due caruce precii eiusdem
Apud Stoketon' et Herdwik' x carucas eiusdem precii

Summa carucarum infra Tynam et Teysam lxxi caruce
Summa carucarum infra et extra iiii^{xx}xv caruce
Summa precii carucarum infra Tynam et Teysam DCCx li.
Summa precii summarum infra et extra DCCCCl li.

Memorandum quod magister R. de Kyrkham' debet domino episcopo C li. per compotum R. le burs'. Item debet eidem per compotum eiusdem iiii^{xx}xiiii li. ix d. ob.

Summa omnium summarum precedencium excepto debito magistri R. de Kyrkham iiMiiiiCxiii li. xiiii d.

Notes

1 Entry in another hand. 'prout in rotulo': MS obscure.
2 Entry in another hand. 'dominus': MS obscure.
3 Followed by a blank space.
4 Followed by a blank space.
5 Followed by a blank space.
6 Followed by a blank space.
7 Followed by a blank space.
8 Followed by a blank space.
9 Followed by a blank space.
10 Followed by a blank space.
11 Followed by a blank space.
12 Followed by a blank space.
13 Followed by a blank space.
14 Followed by a blank space.
15 Followed by a blank space.
16 MS omits 'in'.
17 These two sentences in another hand.
18 This entry in another hand.
19 Bracketed against the preceding three entries for sheep.

21 Simon Langham, Cardinal, formerly Archbishop of Canterbury

Simon Langham was Abbot of Westminster (1349–62), Bishop of Ely (1362–6), Archbishop of Canterbury (1366–8), Cardinal-Priest of St Sixtus (1368–73), and Cardinal Bishop of Palestrina, 1373–6 – known as the 'Cardinal of Canterbury'. Between 1368 and 1376 he established a chantry at Westminster Abbey, worth 1,000 marks. He died at Avignon on 22 July 1376, leaving a major part of his estate to the Abbey for the upkeep of its fabric, along with a substantial library. The documentary consequences of this bequest remain in one principal group in the Abbey's archives, with further scattered elements. Monks of Westminster remained in close contact with their former Abbot at Avignon and were present there during the period when his will was made in 1375.[1]

Notes

1 J.A. Robinson, 'Simon Langham, Abbot of Westminster' *Church Quarterly Review* 66 (1908) pp. 339–66, summarises some of the correspondence, notably a letter from John Bokenhull, Avignon, to Nicholas Litlington, Abbot of Westminster, 9 May 1375, from two fragments, WAM 9236 and 9239, on pp. 358–60. For Langham's endowment of the Abbey, B.F. Harvey *Westminster Abbey and its estates in the Middle Ages* (Oxford, 1977) pp. 40, 395–6, 418.

21/1 Fragment of a letter from John Bokenhull, [Avignon], to Nicholas Litlington, Abbot of Westminster, conveying news of the death of Cardinal Langham. '..... vasa argentea transmitt...r' hiis diebus quid ..... bonis vero ac plenius eiusdem domini mei sunt in manibus domini Willelmi Palmer .....' Post 22 July 1376 (death of Cardinal Langham). *WAM 9236**.

21/2 Fragment of a letter from the subprior of Westminster, [Avignon], to Nicholas Litlington, Abbot of Westminster, mentioning the body of Cardinal Langham. '.... prosequitur alius medio tempore pro negociis nostris in partibus Avunon' pro corpore domini nostri cardinalis una cum aliis rebus monasterii nostri ....nalem legatis ad partes nostras deferendas suam in hac parte opportet diligenciam et sic sperans quod utrumque negocium .....' n.d. post 22 July 1376. *WAM 9235**.

21/3 Fragment of a letter from Adam Eston, monk of Norwich, Avignon, to Nicholas Litlington, Abbot of Westminster, about the bequests of Cardinal Langham to Westminster. He asks for a copy of the dicts of John Wyclyf, who, it is said, has preached in Oxford against the [Benedictine] order, 18 November [1376]. Printed in *Documents illustrating the activities of the general and provincial chapters of the English Black Monks, 1215–1540* ed. W.A. Pantin (3 vols., Camden, 3rd series, 45, 47, 54; 1931–7) iii, pp. 76–7. *WAM 9229**

21/4 Fragment of a letter from W. Colchester, monk of Westminster, Avignon, to Nicholas Litlington, Abbot of Westminster, referring to conflict of opinion between counsel at Westminster and at Avignon over the execution of Langham's estate, asking for instructions. '... pro testamento bone memorie domini Symonis cardinalis auctoritate quorum ..... pecuniam dicti cardinalis in manibus domini Willelmi Palmere et Lombar.... dictus W. Palmere ut asseritur a solucione omnium benefic.... summa juxta dictum magistrum Thomam de ..... pro duobus annis integris respondeant Lombardi suis obligacionibus quorum nomina invenientur in .....' Between 24 July and 19 August 1377. *WAM 9229***.

21/5 Notarial exemplification, 14 August 1377, of Langham's will of 28 June 1375, printed by R. Widmore *An history of the church of St Peter, Westminster, commonly called Westminster Abbey, chiefly from manuscript sources* (1751) pp. 184–91. *WAM 9225.*

21/6 Notarial instrument about the benefices of Cardinal Langham in England, 14 August 1377 *WAM 9223**

One membrane, folded into 16. Late fourteenth- or early fifteenth-century endorsement: 'Instrumentum transsumptum de arendacione sive firma beneficiorum cardinalis in Anglia'.

Universis sancte matris ecclesie filiis ad quos presentes littere pervenerint Robertus de Suardeby bacallarius in decretis publicus auctoritate apostolica notarius clericus Eboracensis diocesis salutem in domino et presentibus fidem credulam adhibere. Noverit universitas vestra quod presens publicum instrumentum per magistrum Thomam de Southam executorem testamenti bone memorie domini Symonis quondam cardinalis Anglie deputatum coram me exhibitum vidi et inspexi in hec verba. In dei nomine amen. Per hoc presens publicum instrumentum cunctus appareat evidenter quod anno a nativitate domini millesimo trecentesimo septuagesimo tercio secundum cursum Romane curie indiccione undecima mensis Januarii die secundi pontificatus sanctissimi in Cristo patris et domini nostri domini Gregorii divina providencia papa undecimi anno secundo in mei notarii publici infrascripti testimoniumque subscriptorum presencia personaliter constitutus reverendissimus in Cristo pater et dominus dominus Symon miseracione divina tituli[1] sancti Sixti sancte Romane ecclesie presbiter cardinalis et ex sua certa sciencia tradidit et ad firmam dimisit domino Willelmo Palmere canonico Derbeye ibidem presenti et onus suscipienti omnia beneficia sua in Anglia exiscencia cum omnibus juribus et pertinenciis eorundem usque ad beneplacitum dicti reverendissimi patris domini Symonis cardinalis ita videlicet quod idem Willelmus solvat seu solvi faciat eidem reverendissimo patri vel quibuscumque seu cuicumque assignaverit annuatim pro tempore quo dicta beneficia ad firmam habere et tenere contigerit hic in Anglia vel in Romana curia mille trecentas et sexaginta marcas sterlingorum seu valorem summe antedicte videlicet ad festa purificacionis beate Marie et sancti Johannis Baptiste per equales porciones. Item voluit dictus reverendissimus pater et eciam ordinavit quod triginta marce de summa suprascripta pro reparacione beneficiorum huiusmodi et alia triginta marce pauperibus in dictis beneficiis suis existentibus distribuende comiterentur annuatim. Ad que omnia et singula tenenda et observanda tam dictus reverendissimus pater dominus Symon cardinalis quam Willelmus Palmere antedictus sigilla sua alternatim presentibus apposuerunt et apposuit quilibet eorundem. Acta fuerunt hec in prioratu Roffensi sub anno indiccione pontificatu mense et die quibus supra. Presentibus discretis viris domino Thoma Garlekhethe canonico Wellensi et Petro de Nascia clerico Cameracensis diocesis notario publicco testibus ad premissa vocatis specialiter et rogatis. Et ego Ricardus de Croxton' clericus Eliensis diocesis publicus apostolica et imperiali auctoritate notarius ac reverendissimi in Cristo patris et domini Symonis cardinalis scriba premissis omnibus et singulis prout suprascribuntur sub anno indiccione pontificatu mense die et loco predictis una cum prenominatis testibus presens interfui ac ea omnia et singula sic fieri vidi et audivi et in hanc publicam formam redegi per alium scribi feci signo eciam meo una cum appensione sigillorum dictorum domini Symonis cardinalis et Willelmi Palmere signavi rogatus et requisitus in testimonium omnium premissorum. Acta sunt hec Avunion' in domo habitacionis ipsius magistri Thome de Sutham prope dominam nostram de miraculis situata anno a nativitate domini millesimo trecentesimo septuagesimo septimo indiccione xv pontificatus sanctissimi in Cristo patris et domini nostri domini Gregorii divina providencia pape xi^{mi} anno septimo mense Augusti die xiiii. Presentibus discretis viris dominis Willelmo de Colcestr' et Johanne Farvyngho monachis monasterii Westmonasterii ordinis sancti Benedicti prope London' et Johanne Kentyf' clerico Sarum ac Gehado Euschede clerico Monasteriensis diocesis testibus ad premissa vocatis specialiter et rogatis.

Et[2] ego Robertus de Suardeby clericus Eboracensis diocesis publicus apostolica et imperiali auctoritate notarius supradictus diversis negociis occupatus presens transsumptum per alium scribi feci et de ipso transsumpto cum suo originali personaliter una cum testibus suprascriptis anno indiccione pontificatu mense die et loco quibus supra collacionem feci diligentem et quia inveni idem transsumptum cum huiusmodi suo originali in omnibus concordare hic me subscripsi et signum meum solitum et consuetum apposui per prefatum magistrum Thomam de Southam rogatus in fidem et testimonium omnium premissorum.

Notes

1 MS obscure.

2 Preceded by a notarial sign; the attestation is written in a second hand.

21/7 Letter from R. Merston, Prior of Westminster, to Nicholas Litlington, Abbot of Westminster, about the estate of Cardinal Langham, 14 October [1377] *WAM 9232*

One paper, folded in the past as a letter, with nine groups of four slits cut through the paper for a wrapping tie, and traces of red wax on the dorse around one of these groups of four. Endorsed in a contemporary hand, with the address: 'Reverendo in Cristo ac domino domino N. abbati Westmonasterii'.

[*Recto*] Reverende pater et domine debita recomendacione premissa noverit vestra paternitas predilecta quod die sabbati xi^{o} die Octobris ante horam vesperarum ad Avunon' perveni cum omnibus ad me pertinentibus benedicto altissimo totus sanus et in quatuordecim diebus de Brugis applicui dictum locum. Et in crastino de consilio magistri Adam de Eston' monachi Norwic' magistri Thome Southam \ fratris Johannis Bukenhull' / magistri Ricardi de Croxton' et aliorum famuliarum quos inveni accessi ad dominum cardinalem Pampilonencem principalem executorem domini nostri cardinalis Cantuariensis et sibi presentavi in eorum presencia eidem domino cardinali Pampilonenci litteras domini nostri regis quas statim cum reverencia accepit et perlegit responsionem subjungendo ad singulas partes eius et statim petivit procurr*atorium* et perlegit in aliqua parte calumpnia faciens de concencis sed finaliter \ ad / < a > bonum propositum condessendit. Concedens quod sub periculo nostro omnia bona domini nostri mortui ecclesie nostre legata michi liberarentur et ubi desideraveram pro comodo ecclesie ducerentur. Quia vero idem dominus cardinalis reputatus omni discrecione et sapientia precipuus de cariagio bonorum versus Angliam propter pericula itineris difficultatem maximam pretendebat de consilio predictorum domini nostri mortui famuliarum et executorum cum mercatoribus de Luca finaliter sic conveni quod omnia bona finaliter estimarentur et ipsi ad Brug*is* ducerent omnia sic legata sub periculo eorundem quod ad omne periculum sub equali valore ad nostram ecclesiam respondebunt sub obligacione debita inde facta. Actam pro tali manucapcione oportet magnas pecunias solvere videlicet pro quolibet centenario florenorum quinque florenos. Et istud non solum de consilio meo set de consilio omnium amicorum ecclesiam diligencium fuerat ordinatum presertim propter insidiatores que circa bona huiusmodi spolianda vigilar*e*nt. Et sic domino concedente omnia legata in vasis argenteis in vestimentis in libris et aliis sicud in testamento continetur ad villam de Brug*is* securissime conducentur nisi pro meliore de vasis argenteis planis contingat vendere aliqua sicud reputatur ecclesie magis bonum. De pecunia vero nichil inveni sed omnia quid per legatum quid per debita omnia fuerant ante adventum \ meum / persoluta. Et adhuc de diebus in dies pro reparacionibus in beneficiis plurimi multum clamant. Inventi fuerant solum decem milia et iiiC vel circa florenorum pecunia numerata. Ceterorumque confrater noster dominus Bokenille habet ex provisione domini nostri pape prioratum de Derhurst et solum timetur in curia de impedimento per dominum nostrum regem amore dei et zelo monasterii nostri a contemplacione mei servi vestri si placet placeat vestre paternitati apud dominum nostrum regem manus apponere adjutrices qua gracia habita dicti domini regis magister Ricardus Croxton' cum vestro adjutorio et consilio contra priorem pretensum residuum prosequetur. Et cum idem ad parternitatem vestram pervenerit singula magis plane declarabit et cum plura occurrerint vestre paternitati specialiter intimabo. Et quia superius scripsi quod de pecunia nichil fuerat inventa ultra legata et expensas interim factas prout per compotum executorum inde factum bene apparet scire dignemini quod sunt in manus diversorum creditorum circa sex milia florenorum de camera ut patet per certas obligaciones[1] inde factas qui ad fabricam monasterii in eventu ut speramus bene poterunt levari. Paternitatem vestram asservet altissimus per tempora longiora. Scipt*e* Avicnon' xiiii^{mo} die mensis Octobris

Vester devotus orator R. Merston' prior Westmonasterii

Notes

1 MS: 'obligacones'.

21/8 Inventory and accounts for the goods of Cardinal Langham, late 1377 – early 1378 *WAM 9225* and 9226*

The inventory survives in two versions, WAM 9225*, and WAM 9226, both paper booklets of 8 folios. WAM 9226 is in a rougher hand and does not contain the final section of notes on the administration of Langham's estate; it has also been damaged by damp and, although conserved, substantial sections are no longer easily legible. WAM 9225* is a fair copy, which was subsequently audited and cash sums amended. Both documents were used to check the contents of Langham's goods shipped to Bruges by a merchant of Lucca in late 1377 or early 1378: the agreement described in **21/9** required goods to be delivered there within three months of 17 October 1377. Both copies have been marked up accordingly. WAM 9225* in its concluding section notes the goods and Langham's remains sent by Mag. Thomas Southam on 11 March 1378 (for which there is a separate listing of items received by Brother Richard Exeter, **21/10**); so this copy of the document must have been in use for a period of some months over the close of 1377 and first months of 1378. WAM 9225* also contains a short section eulogising Langham's achievements for the benefit of Westminster. The edition is based on WAM 9225*, with variants from WAM 9226 noted. The listing of books was printed by J.A. Robinson and M.R. James *The manuscripts of Westminster Abbey* (Cambridge, 1909) pp. 4–7, is given in Cavanaugh, 'Books', pp. 495–9, and in *English Benedictine libraries: the shorter catalogues* ed. R. Sharpe, J.P. Carley, R.M. Thomson and A.G. Watson (Corpus of British medieval library catalogues, 4; 1996) pp. 613–25, from which the identification of the books has been taken. The sections in square brackets have been written by two hands (just possibly one) other than that of the main text, one adding the marginal notes 'Comperta' against each section, the other various parts of the totalling process.

[*f. 1r*] Estimacio librorum bone memorie domini cardinalis Cantuariensis

Prima cista [*Comperta*][1] In primis dictionarius in tribus voluminibus iiC fr.
Item iiii ewangelia glosata in uno volumine xx fr.
Item summa Valencii ii fr.
Item constituciones Benedictini cum aliis viii s.
Summa iiCxvii fr. viii s.[2]

Secunda [*Comperta*]
Item Gregorius super Ezechielem iii fr.
Item Ricardus de Media Villa viii fr.
Item quodlibet Hervei iii fr.
Item quedam facta circa ordinem monachorum per beatum Bernardum in parvo volumine i fr.
Item actus et exilium sancti Thome in quarternis. Creditur esse Cant' ii fr.
Item repertorium de paupere de materia indugenciarum di. fr.
Item ultima pars summe sancti Thome sine asseribus iii fr.
Item Crisostimus super Mathium cum aliis parvis scriptis vi fr.
Item Lira super iiii ewangelia et epistolas Pauli xxxvii fr. et di.
Item milleloquium Augustini iiii^{xx} fr.
Item quedam tabula de diversis doctoribus ii fr.
Item temata divisa per alphabetum cum una tabula in fine iii fr.
Item diversa originalia Agustini quindecim in uno volumine xii fr.
Item tabula Berengarii super speculum xiii fr.
Item Augustinus super psalterium abbreviatus cum septem quarternis non ligatis i fr.
Item tercia pars Lire continens Ysaiam Jeremiam Trenorum Daniel Makebeorum xii prophete minores Baruk Ezechiel xxxvii fr. et di.
Summa iiCxii fr. et di.[3]

Tercia [*Comperta*][4]
Item Lewes super iiii^{or} sentenciarum xii fr.

Item sermones Borage vi fr.
Item originale Agustine de Trinitate cum aliis xii fr.
[*f. 1v*] Item prima pars et secunda pars Thome super ewangelia in ii^{bus} voluminibus xx fr.
Item Gregorius in pastoralibus et exameron Ambrosii sine asseribus ii fr.
Item passio sancti Thome cum epistolis suis et privatus sancti Gregorii i fr.
Item secundum volumen Lire continens Esdras Nemias Ester Job Tobias Judit Psalterium Proverbia Ecclesiastes Cantica Sapiencia Ecclesiasticus xxxvii fr. et di.
Item Armakanus de questionibus Armenorum cum sermonibus suis xxx fr.
Item par decretalium xxii fr.
Item biblia in parvo volumine xii fr.
Item de claustro anime iiii fr.
Item libri beati Bernardi xii fr.
Item distincciones Malicii ii fr.

Summa Clxxii fr. et di.[5]

Quarta [*Comperta*]
Item Innocencius super decretales xii fr.
Item Egidius de regimine principum iiii fr.
Item parve concordancie i fr.
Item de exemplis scripturarum sacrarum ii fr.
Item speculum historiale prima pars l fr.
Item Augustinus de civitate dei xii fr.
Item de proprietatibus rerum vi fr.
Item decreta xx fr.
Item dealogus Gregorii iiii fr.
Item Johannes Calderini et unus tractatus < cont’ > de paupere contra prophesias de Rapitifa i fr.
Item Thomas de veritate vi fr.
Item epistole Pauli glosate xvi fr.
Item Josue Judit Esdras Makabeorum cum aliis xii fr.

[Summa Cxlvi fr.][6]

[*f. 2r*] *Quinta* [*Comperta*]
Item tabula sermonum sancti Augustini cum Armakanis de pauperie salvatoris iiii fr.
Item Thomas de Equino super de anima ii fr.
Item primum volumen de Lira xxxvii fr. et di.
Item Thomas super primum sentenciarum iii fr.
Item Lira moralizans totam bibliam xxx fr.
Item Marcus et Matheus glosati vi fr.
Item Ezechiel et Daniel glosati viii fr.
Item Genesis et Exodus glosati viii fr.
Item Regum et Parolipominon glosati viii fr.[7]
Item Leviticus Numerum Deuteronomii glosati viii fr.
Item concordancie biblie xv fr.
Item tercium et quartum scriptum Durandi vi s.
Item vita sancti Thome monachi et martiris Deverre vi s.
Item quarterni de propheciis vi s.

Summa < Clv fr. vi s.> [Cxxxv fr. et di.][8]

Sexta [*Comperta*]
Item prima pars summe sancti Thome iii fr.
Item Hugo super Johannem et super aliis monasterii de Flandria iiii fr.
Item sentencie Petri Lumbardi vi fr.
Item Thomas super quart*um* sentenciarum vi fr.
Item epistole sancti Augustini viii fr.
Item Boicius de consolacione philosophie cum aliis x fr.
Item Thomas super libros phisicorum iii fr.
Item Thomas super librum metaphisicie iii fr.
Item secunda pars summe sancti Thome vi fr.
Item summa contra gentiles vi fr.
Item tabula originalium xx fr.
Item libri Ancelmi viii fr.
Item Ysaias Jeremias Trenorum glosati vi fr.
Item xl quarterni Bartholomei Jacobi Berengarii involuti in duobus manutergiis que sunt Thome de Southam xvi fr.

Summa Cv fr.[9]

[f. 2v] *Septima* [*Comperta*]
Item summa Hostiensis xx fr.
Item liber sextus cum Clementinis et cum glosis xvi fr.
Item Thomas super secundum sentenciarum vi fr.
Item liber Salamonis glosatus vi fr.
Item Thomas super tercium sentenciarum vi fr.
Item unum Mariale iiii fr.
Item psalterium glosatum xii fr.
Item xii prophete parvi glosati iiii fr.
Item registrum Gregorii ii fr.
Item liber de consideracione sancti Bernardi cum aliis iii fr.
Item historia ecclesiastica. Creditur Cristi Cant' viii fr.
Item cronica Martiniana Beda de gestis Anglorum et vita sancti Thome in uno volumine x fr.
Item Thomas de malo vi fr.
Item de potencia dei iiii fr.
Item excepciones librorum beati Gregorii ii fr.
Item Ancelmus de similitudinibus ii fr.
Item exposicio super Ester et Judit ii fr.

Summa Cxiii fr.[10]

Estimacio vestimentorum

Octava
Item tres cape de panno aureo cum literris Sarazenorum date per regem Cxx fr.
Item una casula eiusdem secte xxv fr.
Item due tunicelle eiusdem secte xxx fr.
Item frontale magnum inferius eiusdem xii fr.
Item frontale superius eiusdem cum crucifixo xx fr.
Item unus planus lettori*s* eiusdem iiii fr.

Item unum frontale strictum eiusdem iii fr.
[*f. 3r*] [*Comperta*]
Item due ridelle de auro verberato viii fr.
Item albe cum paruris et amictis ii^{bus} stolis et iii^{bus} manipulis xii fr.
Item una casula cum capa et duobus tunicellis de satino nigro operato de floribus cum tribus albis et amict*is* stola et tribus manipulis lxx fr.
Item ii^{e} tunicelle de satino nigro plane xvi fr.
Item ii^{e} tunicelle virides de taffata plana viii fr.
Item ii^{e} parure deaspino et parura unius amicte et i frontale de samita plana alba i fr.
Item ii^{e} stole cum ii manipulis i fr. et di.
Item ii panni de blaneo cum armis regis Anglie xxxii fr.
Summa iiiClxii fr. et di.

Nona [*Comperta*][11]
Item ii casule de panno aureo violato cum avibus in arboribus iiii^{xx} fr.
Item una capa eiusdem secte xxx fr.
Item due tunicelle eiusdem xii fr.
Item una casula de panno aureo rubeo cum aurifirario imaginato de auro xl fr.
Item ii^{e} tunicelle eiusdem cum stola et duobus manipulis xx fr.
Item una capa eiusdem secte xxxv fr.
Item due albe cum paruris cum duabus paruris amictorum iiii fr.
Item unum frontale strictum cum capitibus apostolorum x fr.
Item due cape de panno aureo deaspino viridis coloris lv fr.
Item una casula eiusdem xxxv fr.
Item ii^{e} tunicelle eiusdem xl fr.
Item ii^{e} stole cum iii^{bus} manipulis eiusdem i fr.
Item ii^{e} tunicelle de samito simplices indici coloris viii fr.
Item ii^{e} tunicelle de panno aureo viridi deaspino xlii fr.
Item una capa de panno aureo cum cauda pavonis xl fr.
Item ii^{e} tunicelle de panno aureo albo cum paruris et casula xlv fr.
Item una stola cum duobus manipulis de panno aureo albo i fr.
Item due tunicelle de camaca alba cum paruris de panno aureo rubeo cum stola et manipulo xx fr.
Item ii^{o} frontalia de panno aureo albo lata xx fr.
Item ii ridelli de serico albo i fr. et di.
[*f. 3v*] Item una alba et amictus cum paruris de panno albo aureo i fr. et di.
Item unum calballium album de panno aureo v*ir*gato pro patena i fr.
Item paramentum pro altari de serico albo cum radiis de auro in finibus viii fr.
Item ii panni de blaneo cum scutis regis Anglie xxxii fr.
Summa vCiiii^{xx}ii fr.

Decima [*Comperta*]
Item una capa de satin blanido multis ymaginibus de auro C fr.
Item una capa rubea de camaca cum imaginibus de auro et angelis lx fr.
Item una capa rubea de satin cum coronis de auro xl fr.
Item una casula de panno aureo violac*io* cum ursis de auro et nodis xxx fr.
Item una capa rubea de aspino xx fr.
Item unum colerium cum ymaginibus de auro et perlis xii fr.

Item alia duo coleria de auro simplici viii fr.
Item unum corporale cum ymaginibus cum sancto agno et iiii^{or} angelis ii fr.
Item unum corporale i fr.
Item duo paria sidaliorum cum sotularibus i fr.
Item i par sirotecarum xxx fr.
Item cathedrale de viridi deaspino ii fr.
Item cathedrale de panno aureo deaspino columbini coloris ii fr.
Item unum cathedrale de panno aureo albo ii fr.
Item unus pannus de auro viridi cum apris de azuro et duo gremialia eiusdem coloris iiii fr.
Item ii ridelli blani simplices de taffata i fr. cum di.
Item duo ridelli virides virgati de taffata i fr.
Item ii aurifricus de velveto rubeo cum rosis de auro vi fr.
Item una alba cum amitta stola et manipulo cum paruris de auro et de ymaginibus xviii fr.
Item iiii^{or} panni de auro viridi cum armis regis Anglie rotundis lxiiii fr.
Item littere domini Johannis Moris conparatoris familiarum et ewangelia iiii fr.[12]
Item fardellus parvus pro magistro Ricardo de Croxton'

Summa iiiiCviii fr. cum di.

[*f.* 4*r*] *Undecima* [*Comperta*]
Item una mitra cum perlis et lapidibus precosis viiiC fr.
Item una casula deaspino panno aureo viridi cum aurifirario de angelis et stell*is* cum duobus tunicellis alba et amicte cum stola et manipulo xvi fr.
Item una casula de panno albo aureo operata cum arboribus et avibus et duobus tunicellis eiusdem secte et duabus capis legatis ecclesie Cristi Cant' Cxx fr.
Item una casula de panno viridi aureo deaspino et duabus capis eiusdem secte cum duobus tunicellis legatis ecclesie Eli*e*ensi C fr.
Item una capa de velveto indicii coloris cum delphinis aureis legata ecclesie Lincolniensi xl fr.
Item una casula de camaca blaneo cum duabus tunicellis cum tribus albis et amicte cum duobus stolis iii^{bus} manipulis et ii^{bus} frontalibus[13] < albis > latis superioris et inferioris cum frontale stricto pro altari et pro homer'[14] legatis ecclesie de Langham xxv fr.
Item unum mantellum dupplicatum domini regis et Side[15] cum tribus capuciis xvi fr.

Summa M^{l}Cxvii fr.

Duodecima [*Comperta*]
In primis una navis argentea pro elemosina ponderis xxi marcharum marcha valet vi fr.
Item una plata pro speciebus ponderis xi marcharum i unc. marcha valet vi fr. et quart.
Item una crux cum ymaginibus ponderis xxiiii marcarum unum unc. marcha valet viii fr. et di.
Item una navis cum cocliare deaurata ponderis viii marcarum i unc. marcha valet v fr. et di.
Item due pelves argentee deaurate ponderis xxiiii marcarum iii unc. et qua. marcha valet vi fr. et di.

Item due fiole deaurate ponderis iii marcarum xv d. marcha valet vi fr.
Item unum deosculatorium ponderis i marce vi unc. et i qua. marcha valet vii fr.
Item quatuor candelabra ponderis xxvii marcarum v unc. marcha valet vi fr. xii s.
Item unum turribulum ponderis xxv marcarum marcha valet vi fr.
Item unum aquarium amelatum ponderis iii marcarum vi unc. xiiii d. marcha valet vii fr.
Item due fiole deaurate ponderis i marce vi unc. iii qua. marcha valet vii fr. et di.
Item unus liber Willelmi de Laduno[16] et tres alii quarterni que sunt Thome Southam valet i fr.

Summa valor ixCxvii fr. xii s. x d.

[*f. 4v*] Ista sunt vasa vendita mercatoribus

In primis xii picheria ponderis lxxi marcarum i unc. Marcha valet v flor. ix gross. quod valet in toto iiiiCviii flor. xxiiii s.
Item ix aquaria ponderis xxi marcharum. Et marcha valet v flor. ix gross.
Cxx flor. xviii s.
Item ii aquaria deaurata ponderis iii marcarum vi unc. Marcha valet vi flor.
xxii flor. xii s.
Item una navis pro elemosina ponderis xiiii marcarum vii unc. Marcha valet vi flor.
iiii^{xx}ix flor. vi s.
Item una calix deaurata ponderis iii marcarum xiiii d. Marcha valet viii flor.
xxiiii flor. xiiii s.
Item una ydria ponderis xx marcarum et di. unc. Marcha valet vi flor. iiii gross.
Cxxvii flor. vi d.
Item duo candelabra ponderis v marcarum i unc. et iii qua. Marcha valet v flor. et di.
xxviii flor. xvi s. x d.
Item una plata pro speciebus ponderis viii marcarum ii unc. et ii qua. Marcha valet vi flor.
xlix flor. xxi s.
Item una navis pro elemosina ponderis xvii marcarum iiii unc. Marcha valet vi flor. iiii gross.
Cx flor. xx s.
Item viii basini ponderis xlv marcarum iii unc. et di. Marcha valet v flor. viii gross.
iiClvii flor. xi s. vi d.
Item una coupa deaurata ponderis ii marcarum viii unc. et di. Marcha valet vii flor.
xvii flor. xvii s. iii d.
Item una coupa deaurata cum litteris Sarazenorum ponderis iii marcarum ii unc. iii d. Marcha valet vii flor.
xxii flor. xxi s.
Item una coupa in cuius summitate cooperculi est draco ponderis vi marcarum i unc. Marcha valet viii flor.
xlix flor. xii s.
Item una coupa plana deaurata ponderis vii marcarum ii unc. xviii d. Marcha valet vi flor. cum di.
xlviii flor. xiii s.

Item xv tasse ponderis xv marcarum vii unc. xix d. Marcha valet v flor. ix gross.

iiii^{xx}xi flor. xx s. iiii d.

Item vi tasse deaurate interius ponderis xii marcarum i unc. iiii d. Marcha valet vi flor.

lxxii flor. xxi s.

Item unum aquarium et sex gobollette interius ponderis vi marcarum iiii unc. xxi d. Marcha ad v flor. et ix gross.

xxxviii flor.

Item ii pelves pro capella ponderis xii marcarum vii unc. et di. Marcha ad v flor. et ix gross.

lxxiiii flor. ix s. iiii d.

Item ii alii pelves pro capella ponderis xii marcarum ii unc. Marcha ad vi flor.

xxxi flor. et di.

[*f. 5r*] Item unum salsarium ponderis iii marcarum et i unc. Marcha ad vii flor. cum di.

xxiii flor. x s. vi d.

Item una coupa plana deaurata coronata ponderis iii marcarum ii unc. xii d. Marcha ad vi flor. vi gross.

xxi flor. vi s.

Item iii salsaria x coclearia i campana et duo aspersoria ponderis x marcarum ii unc. xxi d. Marcha ad v flor. et vi gross.

lv flor. vi s.

Item vi cocliaria deaurata ponderis i marce iiii unc. xviii d. Marcha ad vii flor.

xi flor. vi s. iiii d.

Item xii plate magne ponderis liii marcarum iii unc.
Item liiii scutelle ponderis Cxvi marcarum vii unc.
Item xii platelle ponderis xx marcarum vi unc.
Item xxiiii platelle ponderis liii marcarum vi unc.
Item xxiii salsaria ponderis xviii marcarum xv d.
Item i vas pro aqua benedicta ponderis iii marcarum vi unc.

Summa marcarum CClx marce vi unc. xxi d. Marcha ad v flor. et ix gross.

M^{l}vCxxviii flor. xvi s. vi d.

Item vii tasse x cocliaria et i aquarium ponderis x marcarum v unc. viii d. Marca ad v flor. ix gross.

lxi flor. viii s.

Item una calix deaurata ponderis ii marcarum v unc. et di. Marcha ad viii flor.

xxi flor. viii s.

Summa vasorum venditorum mercatoribus de Luk' iiiM^{l}iiiiC flor. xii s. x d. qui valent de moneta nostra in Anglia vCxi li. xiiii s. vi d. Et sic obolo dempto de quolibet flor. pro excambio faciendo in Angliam quod se extendit ad vii li. ii s. i d. et ob. Restat ad solvendum vCiiii li. xii s. v d. unde solvent infra quindenam Natalis Domini proximo futuram C li. et totum residuum ad nativitatem sancti Johannis Baptiste tunc proximo sequentem pro qua solucione mercatores predicti obligantur abbati priori et conventui Westm' et camere domini pape per instrumentum publicum vobis transmissum.

[*f. 5v*] Item venduntur diversis hominibus diversa vasa argentea et quedam deaurata appreciata ad iiiClvii flor. camere qui valent liii li. xi s.
Item una crux appreciata ad iiC fr.

Inde solutum est mercatoribus de Luk' de summa predicta pro cariagio librorum vestimentorum et aliorum jocalium usque Brugges missorum CCiiii^xx. Item solutum pro diversis expensis ut patebit in futurum in villa Avunon' lx flor.

Nomina debitorum bone memorie domini cardinalis Cantuariensis
In primis dominus Gregorius papa undecimus tenetur in \3/M^l flor. camere solvendis in Anglia mense Januarii proximo venturo de quibus solvendis habemus bullam in qua dictus dominus papa obligat sedem appostolicam et fructus redditus et proventus dicte camere et eius habemus bullam directam collectori Anglie ad solvendos dictos flor. dicto termino.
Item dominus cardinalis de Vernhi*no* tenetur in mille flor. camere pro quibus habemus obligacionem scriptam manu sua eidem solvendam quandocumque fuerit requisitus qui habet beneficia in Anglia videlicet archidiaconatum Exoniensem et canonicatum et prebendum de Alesbury in ecclesia Lincolniensi. Ideo de eo eritis securi.
Item dominus Jacobus de Urcinis cardinalis tenetur in mille flor. camere de quibus habemus obligacionem sigillo suo signatam ad solvendum dicto domino meo vel eius procuratori quandocumque fuerit requisitus qui eciam habet beneficia in Anglia videlicet decanatum ecclesie Sarum et archidiaconatum Dunolmensem.
Item dominus cardinalis de Arogonia tenetur eidem in quingenta flor. camere de quibus habemus eciam obligacionem ad solvendum quandocumque fuerit requisitus qui habet canonicatum et prebendum in ecclesia Wallensi et archidiaconatum Batoniensem de quibus omnibus debit premissis estis securi.
Item dominus Willelmus de Hoo tenetur dicto domino in centum flor. camere. Dies solucionis transiit.
Item dominus episcopus Xancomensis de Vasconia tenetur eidem in centum flor. camere.
Item dominus episcopus Dagorenciensis tenetur eidem in octogenta flor. camere solvendis in Anglia de mense Januarii proximo venturo et recipiatis pro flor. iii s. i d. de ipso juxta cambium quod fecerunt domino meo camsores.

Summa flor. debitorum viM^lvC qui valent de moneta Anglie ixClxxv li. computando flor. ad tres solidos.

Item xi^o die Marcii transmisit magister Thomas Southam ista infrascripta[17]
In primis unam modicam techam coopertam nigro panno in qua continentur ossa etc.
Item ii nouchis ad modum viii fibularum context*a* cum peryll*is*
Item sigillum eiusdem cardinalis
Item capellum cum suis appendiciis
Item pallium eiusdem cardinalis

Item[18] dominus Willelmus Palm*er* arendatarius omnium beneficiorum domini cardinalis in Anglia debet M^l marcas.
Item Johannes Credi socius mercatorum Scrociis[19] debet iiiiM^l flor.

Item Franciscus de Kyte factor de comitiva[20] de Bruges debet octo milia flor.
Item dominus cardinalis misit ad monasterium de Avinona unum jocale et unum missale appreciata ad mille marcas sterlingorum
Item dominus cardinalis per duos annos contulit fabrice Westm' CCCC li. quolibet anno ducentas
[*f. 6v*] Item idem dominus cardinalis contulit Westm' premanibus M^{l} marcas ad perquirendum terras et possessiones ad valorem xl^{a} marcarum pro sustentacionem iiii^{or} monachorum per quos deberet augeri numerus monachorum Westm'. De cuius summe parte perquiruntur Westm' manerium de Bekleswelle et molendina apud Mulsham.
Item iste dominus in minoribus constitutus quando scilicet erat abbas Westm' exoneravit ecclesiam Westm' de debito predecessor*is* ad summa iiM^{l}iiC marcarum.
Item contulit unum preciosum vestimentum de blodio felwete ad valorem C marcarum.
Item perquisivit de quodam Nicholo Gangere sergersiam infra celarium Westm' dicto Nicholo jure hereditario pertinentem ad utilitatem conventus iiii^{xx} li.
Item perquisivit sumptibus suis propriis ad utilitatem conventus in Fynchesle quoddam manerium vocatum Wydyke et aliud manerium vocatum le Fryte < uniqu... > \ juxta Hendone / < habendo > pro vestura conventus amplianda.
Item iste dominus nunquam oneravit porcionem conventus sed semper ipsam fovit nichil a conventu in exenniis extorsit[21] sed ea relaxavit nichil in participacionibus regimine seu alio modo ab eis abstulit sed semper fatebatur porcionem conventus nimis fuisse exilem.
Item iste dominus pro utilitate et honesta conversacione conventus ordinavit domum misericordie que prius erat inusitata ubi tam senes quam juvenes alterius diebus carnium honorifice recreantur.
Item iste dominus prout seniores retulerunt quasi antiquum statum monasterii sencierunt ita monasterium in tam debita regula et sub tam bono gubernaculo stabilivit quod et si nichil aliud boni fecisset monasterio nisi dumtaxat monasterium sub tam gubernaculo statuendo potuit fundatori aut renovaturi in meritis sociari.
Item iste dominus totali et tanto patrono dilexit conventum quod porcio conventus sibi proximior quam sua omni tempore videbatur et in eius recessu sui monachi ut de Martino discipuli condolebant ipsius viciosum affectum ad conventum in vita sua approbant eius facta cui mors eciam attestatur nam post mortem se dedit conventui atque sua.[22]

Notes

1 MS: the marginal notes 'Comperta' are set against the entries for each chest or bale, although sometimes not on the same folio as the start of the entry for it.

2 Books in the first bale: *Dictionarius*, perhaps the *Catholicon*; *Summa Valencii*: probably a commentary on Peter Lombard's *Sentences*; the *Constitutiones ad monachos nigros* of Benedict XII.

3 Books in the second bale: Gregory the Great *Homiliae in Ezechielm*; Richard of Middleton, commentary on Peter Lombard's *Sententiae*; Hervé Nédellec *Quodlibet*; perhaps St Bernard *Apologia ad Guillelmum S. Theodorici abbatem*; an unidentified collection on the life of St Thomas Becket; a collection, written on paper, of material on indulgences; Part III of Thomas Aquinas *Summa theologica*; probably pseudo-John Chrysostom *Opus imperfectum in Mattheum*; Nicholas of Lyre *Postilla litteralis* on the Gospels and Pauline Epistles; Augustinus Triumphus of Ancona and Bartholomew of Urbino (attrib.) *Milleloquium veritatis*; an index of the work of various doctors; perhaps Peter of Capua *Alphabetum in artem sermocinandi*; various works of Augustine; Berengarius Fredolis *Inventarium*

sive repertorium super speculum Durantis; an abbreviation of Augustine *Enarrationes in Psalmos*; Nicholas of Lyre *Postilla litteralis* on the Major and Minor Prophets, and Maccabees.

4 MS: 'Comperta' on f. 1v.

5 MS: the second 'x' in 'Clxxii' is an insertion. Books in the third bale: Lewes and Borage not identified; Augustine *De Trinitate*; Thomas Aquinas *Catena aurea in Evangelia*; Gregory *Regula pastoralis*; Ambrose *Hexaëmeron*; Thomas Becket *Epistulae* and other collected materials; Nicholas of Lyre *Postilla litteralis* on the Wisdom Books and Psalter; Richard FitzRalph *Summa de quaestionibus Armenorum*, and *Sermones*; the *Decretales* of Gregory IX; a bible; Hugh of Fouilloy *De claustro animae*; works of St Bernard; Mauritius *Distinctiones*.

6 Books in the fourth bale: Innocent IV *Apparatus super decretales*; Aegidius Romanus (Giles of Rome) *De regimine principum*; a volume with small, or short, concordances; Nicholaus de Hanapis *Liber de exemplis sacrae scripturae*; Vincent of Beauvais *Speculum historiale*; Augustine *De civitate dei*; Bartholomaeus Anglicus *De proprietatibus rerum*; Gratian *Decretum*; Gregory *Dialogi*; Giovanni Calderini, works, and a treatise against the prophecies of Jean de Roquetaillade (Rupescissa); Thomas Aquinas *De veritate*; the Epistles of Paul, glossed; the books of Joshua, Judith, Esther and Maccabees.

7 MS: the figures of the cash sum are written in a second hand over an erasure.

8 Books in the fifth bale: a list or index of the sermons of Augustine; Richard FitzRalph *De pauperie salvatoris*; Thomas Aquinas, Commentary on Aristotle's *De anima*; Nicholas of Lyre *Postilla litteralis* on Genesis to 2 Chronicles; Thomas Aquinas, Commentary on Petrus Lombardus *Sententiae*, Book I; Nicholas of Lyre *Biblia moralisata*; glosses to books of the bible and a concordance to the bible; Durandus de S. Porciano (attrib.), Commentary on Petrus Lombardus *Sententiae*, Books III–IV; life of St Thomas de la Hale; quires of prophesies.

9 Books in the sixth bale: Thomas Aquinas *Summa theologica*, Part I; Hugh of St Cher, Postils on John; Petrus Lombardus *Sententiarum libri IV*; Thomas Aquinas, Commentary on Petrus Lombardus *Sententiae*, Book IV; Augustine *Epistulae*; Boethius *Philosophiae consolatio*; Thomas Aquinas, Commentary on Aristotle's *Physica*; Thomas Aquinas, Commentary on Aristotle's *Metaphysica*; Part II of Thomas Aquinas *Summa theologica*; Thomas Aquinas *Summa contra gentiles*; a listing of works ?; a collection of the works of Anselm of Canterbury; glossed versions of the books of Isaiah, Jeremiah and Kings; quires of the works of Bartholomew of Brescia, an unidentified James, and Berengarius Fredolis.

10 Books in the seventh bale: Henricus de Segusio, Cardinal Bishop of Ostia *Summa de titulis decretalium*; *Liber sextus decretalium*; *Constitutiones Clementinae*; glossed Book of Solomon; Thomas Aquinas, Commentary on Peter Lombard's *Sententiae*, Books II and III; a Mariale; glossed psalter and the books of the Minor Prophets; Gregory *Registrum*; Bernard of Clairvaux *De consideratione*; Eusebius *Historia ecclesiastica*; Martin of Troppau *Cronica pontificum et imperatorum*; Thomas Aquinas *Quaestiones de malo* and presumably *Quaestiones de potentia dei*; exceptions to the works of Gregory; Anselm of Canterbury *Liber de similitudinibus*; exposition on Esther and Judith.

11 MS: 'Comperta' bracketed against whole section on both f. 3r and f. 3v.

12 Cash sum bracketed against both this and the next entry.

13 MS: 'frotalibus'.

14 MS obscure. Perhaps for 'honore'.

15 MS obscure: WAM 9226 has 'domini Rogeri Side'.

16 Willelmus de Monte Lauduno (Mont Lauzun), perhaps his *Lectura super Clementinas*, unpublished (given the legal interests of Southam: for legal books loaned to Southam by Westminster Abbey, see *English Benedictine libraries: the shorter catalogues*, pp. 611–13).

17 See also **21/10**, Exeter's listing of the goods he held for Mag. Thomas Southam.

18 From this point onwards, the text is only in WAM 9225*.

19 Perhaps the Scotti merchants of Piacenza.

20 Followed by a blank space in MS.

21 MS: 'extor\our/sit'.

22 ff. 7 and 8 are blank.

21/9 Letter from John Bokenhull to Nicholas Litlington, Abbot of Westminster, about the estate of Cardinal Langham, 6 November [1377] *WAM 9233*

One paper, folded in the past as a letter, with two groups of three pairs of slits cut through the paper for a wrapping tie, and traces of red wax on the dorse near two of these pairs.

Endorsed with the address: 'Reverendissimo in Cristo patri ac domino domino N. abbati Westmonasterii domino meo metuendissimo'; and in a second hand: 'Bokenhull' '.

[*Recto*][1]
Reverendissime pater et domine mi humili recommendacione premissa. Scire velit vestra dominacio reverenda quod xi° die Octobris applicuit Avunon' dominus meus prior vestri monasterii incolumis atque sanus. Resque et alia bona fabrice monasterii predicti per bone memorie dominum meum jam defunctum legata recepit et disposuit de eisdem ad utilitatem et commodum monasterii prefati. Unde duodecim ballas plenas dictis rebus convenit cum quodam mercatore nomine Andrea Ticii mercatore sufficienti ad portandum seu portari faciendum apud Brugis infra tres menses a xvii° die Octobris continue ini*t*urandos. Quasquidem ballas promisit liberare in Brugis dicto domino priori seu eius procuri ad hoc legitime constituto in termino prefato unde idem dominus prior constituit Johannem Drapper et Willelmum Colyn procures suos ad recipiendum dictas ballas in loco predicto et ad transportandum in Angliam divina favente gracia secure. Quibus negociis sic peractis idem dominus prior et ego pro negociis monasterii versus Romam arripiemus infra breve iter nostrum. Ceterum pater reverendissime vestre paternitati reputo fore notum quod dominus noster papa de prioratu de Durhurst in cura vacant*e* michi graciose providit prout in litteris confectis vestre paternitati transmissis plenius continetur. Verumque propter peccatem[2] adversarii mei incumbentis non sum ausus redire ad partes ita cito sicut proposui. Ideo secundum ordinacionem vestrum si adversarius meus velit michi facere litem stabo in curia ad defensionem cause mee quia habeo jus clarum ut dicunt michi omnes vel redibo ad partes quia secundum ordinacionem vestram omnia negocia mea regulabo. Scio enim quod sine adjutorio vestro non possum perficere quod incepi. Ideo pater piissime momentate filii vestri et sibi de largifluo benignitatis vestre dono graciarum digni elargiri et pro eo penes dominum regem et alios proceros regni sic mediare ut idem filius vester per clemenciam paternam et diligenciam possit effectualiter consequi quod intendit dictumque prioratum obtinere juxta litteras apostolicas pacifice et quiete. Dominacionem vestram quod michi suo subdito mandet et precipiat quelibet sibi grata conservet altissimus feliciter et longene. Scriptum Avunon' vi° die Novembris.

Humilis servitor vester et subditus
Johannes Bokenhull'

Notes
1 In the same hand as the address on the dorse.
2 Perhaps for 'peccationem'.

21/10 Goods of Cardinal Langham received by Brother Richard Exeter, 11 March 1378 *WAM 6604*

A paper, roughly square, rolled up. The dorse is blank. Part printed in *English Benedictine libraries: the shorter catalogues*, pp. 625–6. Exeter was Prior of Westminster in 1377–82 and went to Avignon to receive Langham's goods on behalf of the monastery.

Bona subscripta recepit frater Ricardus Excestr' xi die Marcii per manus J.

Drapere et manent in custodia penes eum sed excepit \ hiis / que exprimuntur in fine

In primis recepit i calicem argenti et deauratum
Item ii fiolas argenti
Item i thuribulum argenti et deauratum
Item i navem argenti pro incenso imponendo sine cocleario
Item i cuppam argenti et bene deauratam
Item i tabulam volubilis argenti et deauratam cum ymaginibus interius insertis
Item i seynt*ure* de serico viridis coloris
Item iiii novaculas de quibus timeo ne rubigo eas consumat.

Item recepit libros infrascriptos
In primis recepit librum memoriale decreti Johannis[1]
Item xviii quarterni noviter scripti de sanitate et de pace
Item unum ex quatuor[2]
Item primum secunde sancti Thome[3]
Item compilactio theologie cum aliis libris in uno volumine contentis
Item scolastica historia[4]
Item expositor super psalterium
Item postille super Eccliasticum
Item Ysidor*us* de summo bono[5]
Item i confessionale cum aliis diversis processis. Que omnia sunt et erunt parata.

Item recepit unam modicam techam coopertam nigra veste in qua sunt ossa etc.
Item recepit ii nochys ad modum viii botonum cum gemmis in toto contextis.
Item recepit i magnum sigillum argenti quondam domini nostri Cantuariensis.
Item recepit capellum domini nostri Cantuariensis cum suis pertinenciis.
Item recepit pallium sigillatum quondam domini nostri Cantuariensis.

Ista \ ultima / reposuit dictus frater R. Excestr' in thesaurio in quadam cista cum aliis bonis domini nostri cardinalis. Et erunt ibi < ad > usque adventum magistri T. de Southam.

Notes
1 MS repeats 'Johannis'. Books identified in *English Benedictine libraries: the shorter catalogues*, pp. 625–6; this volume probably Johannes Faventinus, *Summa in decretum*, unprinted.
2 *Unum ex quatuor*, printed in *PL* 68, cols. 255–358.
3 Thomas Aquinas *Summa theologica*, I^a IIe, printed in *STO*, iv–xii.
4 Petrus Comestor *Historia scholastica*, printed in *PL* 198, cols. 1053–1722.
5 Isidorus Hispalensis (Isidore of Seville) *Sententiae* (also known as *De summo bono*), *CPL* 1199.

21/11 Account of expenses of monks of Westminster at Avignon, about the goods of Cardinal Langham, and in Rome, after March 1378 *WAM 9228*

One paper, written in a hand similar to the main hand of WAM 9223*. The sheet is approximately the same size as a page of the inventory of Langham's goods, WAM 9225*. No endorsements, but traces of an applied seal in red wax in two places. Passages in square brackets have been added by a second hand.

Expense domini Johannis de Fervygho monachi Westmonasterii qui venit Avunon' x... Julii anno domini M^{o}CCC^{mo}lxxvii et ibi moratus est in comitiva magistri Thome de Southam usque ad vii diem Septembris inclusive et sic sunt viii septimane cum dimidia qualibet septimana i flor. camere ascendit ad viii flor. camere et vii gross. computato flor. ad iii s. sterlingorum.

Item pro aliis necessariis xi gross.
Item pro papiro i gross. et di.
Item liberata eidem domino Johanni diversis vicibus vi flor. camere.
Item liberata eidem domino Johanni in recessu suo ad Angliam x flor. camere.
Item pro caligis i flor.

Summa xxiii fr. ix gross. xii d.

Item pro domino Willelmo Colchestre monacho Westmonasterii qui intravit Avunon' cum clerico suo xxiiii die Julii anni predicti et ibi moratus est cum suo clerico in societate dicti Thome usque xix diem Augusti et sunt iiii septimane exceptis duobus diebus. Unde qualibet septimana pro se et < per > clerico unum flor. cum di. ascendit ad vi flor. camere et post eius recessum remansit clericus suus per duas septimanas ascendit ad i flor. camere.
Item liberata dicto domino Willelmo Colchestr' una capa tunica et capicium de nigro et scapularium et cuculla precii xxii flor. camere et v gross.
Item pro tunica et capicio pro eodem iii fr.
Item pro collobio simplici rotundo empto ab Hagyno Judeo viii flor. camere.
Item eidem pro expensis versus Romam xl flor. camere.
Item in Roma recipere debet xx flor. camere.
Item pro cambio Cxxx flor. v flor. camere
Item pro equo de Avunon' ad Massiliam xv gross.
Item Gerardo pro neccessariis i flor. camere.
Item dicto Gerardo in recessu suo versus Angliam x flor. camere.
Item Albertolo de Medio*la*no pro ca*mera* in primis iii flor.
Item alia vice eidem x flor. camere.
Item clerico dicti Albertoli i flor. camere.

Summa Cxxii fr. xiii gross.

Summa totalis Cxlvii fr. vii gross.

Item expense facte per Johannem Draper xx fr.
In primis recepit < Parisius > Parisi*i*s a mercatoribus xx fr.
Item apud Brugg' x fr.
Item Avunon' ab eisdem ii fr.
Item a magistro T. de Southam Avunnon' eundo versus Romam ix die Marcii quindecim flor. camere qui faciunt xiiii fr.
Item in Roma x flor. camere qui faciunt ix fr. iiii gross.
Item in Avunon in infirmitate sua viii fr. vi gross.
Item pro equo versus partes Anglie xvi fr.
Item pro expensis suis versus Angliam x fr.
Item pro botis i fr.
Item [in uno ventr...l..... et sotularibus] v gross.

Summa iiii^{xx}x fr.

Summa totalis omnium summarum CCxxxviii fr. vii gross. Faciunt de moneta nostra lix marcas [viii s. iii d.] sterlingorum que summa debetur magistro T. de Southam.

21/12 Receipt from the Prior and Convent of Canterbury for a vestment bequeathed by Cardinal Langham, 16 August 1379 *WAM 9221**
A narrow strip of parchment, with a turn-up, with a fragment of a round seal of the Prior and convent of Christ Church Canterbury, in red wax, an ecclesiastical building with three arches, on cords of natural (brown) silk. Folded into six. Endorsement, in a late fourteeenth- or early fifteenth-century hand: 'Acquietancia contra priorem et conventum ecclesie cathedralis Cantuariensis de vestimento eidem a cardinali legato'. CCA, Register G, f. 212v, is a copy of the receipt.

Noverint universi quod nos Johannes permissione divina prior ecclesie Cristi Cantuariensis et eiusdem loci capitulum fatemur recepisse ex legato reverendi in Cristo patris domini Simonis episcopi Penestrensis cardinalis cardinalis Cantuariensis vulgariter nuncupati ecclesie sue Cantuariensi facto unum vestmentum cum paramentis debitis a reverendo patre domino Nicholao abbate monasterii Westmonasterii et eiusdem monasterii priore unde reverendum in Cristo patrem Petrum cardinalem Papilonensem dicti domini Simonis testamenti executorem et omnes alios executores eiusdem aquietamus per presentes. Data in domo nostra capitulari Cantuariensi sub sigillo nostro communi xvii kal. Septembris anno domini millesimo trescentesimo septuagesimo nono.

21/13 Receipt from the Prior and Convent of Ely for a vestment bequeathed by Cardinal Langham, 10 February 1380 *WAM 9224*
A narrow strip of parchment, without a seal. Slightly wider at the left-hand end, but no evidence for a tongue and seal. It has been folded horizontally and vertically into eight. Endorsement, in a late fourteeenth- or early fifteenth-century hand: 'Acquietancia contra priorem Eliensem de vestimento eidem per dominum cardinalem Cantuariensem legato'.

Pateat universis per presentes quod nos Johannes prior ecclesie cathedralis Eliensis et eiusdem loci capitulum recepimus de reverendis et religiosis viris domino abbate priore et conventu monasterii Westmonasterii quoddam vestimentum nobis et ecclesie nostre per venerabilem patrem et dominum Simonem dei gracia cardinalem Penestrini legatum videlicet unam casulam de panno viridi aureo deaspino et duas capas cum duabus tunicellis eiusdem secte. De quo quidem vestimento fatemur nos esse persolutos dictosque dominum abbatem priorem et conventum monasterii Westmonasterii inde fore quietos per presentes. In cuius rei testimonium sigillum commune capituli nostri presentibus est appensum. Data apud Ely in domo nostra capitulari x^{o} die mensis Februarii anno regni regis Ricardi secundi post conquestum tercio.

21/14 Memorandum about the estate of Cardinal Langham, *c.*1380 *WAM 9229*
One long, narrow paper, with four pairs of slits cut through it, where it was folded up and sent, sealed like a letter.

[*Recto*] Reverende pater ut servetur voluntas domini mei bone memorie qui voluit omnia bona sua ubicumque fuissent inventa ad fabricam monasterii vestri applicari prout in testamento suo evidenter apparet dignemini advertere ad infrascripta.

Unde scire velitis quod dominus W. Palmer' de anno domini M^{mo}CCC^{mo}lxxiii^{o} secundum computacionem ecclesie Romane die secunda mensis Januarii in prioratu Rofensi illo videlicet die quo dominus meus < ultimo > recessit de Anglia versus Brugges et creditur quod nos fuistis tunc temporis presens recepit omnia beneficia domini mei in Anglia ad firmam pro mille CCC^{tis} lx^{a} marcis sterlingorum preter archidiaconatum Eboracensem quem dominus tunc non optinuit set ex postea et de dicta summa idem W. deberet ponere in reparacionibus domorum in beneficiis eiusdem triginta marcas omni anno et triginta marcas debuisset distribuisse inter pauperes in dictis beneficiis existentes prout in instrumento publico sigillo interusque tam domini quam Willelmi sigillato cuius copiam sub instrumento publico vobis mitto plenius continetur unde de anno domini etc. lxxv^{to} de frutibus dictorum beneficiorum qui ascendit ad mille CCC marcas de < p...lt > claro. Dominus hic nichil recepit nec aliquis nomine suo qui poterit constare per aliquas evidencias.

Item de eodem anno debentur CC^{te} marce de archidiaconatu Eboracensi.

Item de anno domini M^{mo}CCC^{mo}lxxvi^{to} quo anno et de mense Julii dominus cuius anima sit in pace mortuus est debetur nobis dicta summa videlicet mille quingente marce et ultra \ unde / lx marce quas forsan dictus W. non distribuit pro illo anno quas quidem summas debetis recupare ab eodem W. qui erat obligatus domino et nullus alius firmarius. Et licet firmarii quibus < ..... > ipse tradidit ipsa beneficia ad firmam non solverint. Dictus W. tenetur quia dominus non tradidit alicui beneficia ad firmam nisi sibi. Et si ipse W. pro labore suo aliqua velit deducere non audietur quia dominus modicum ante mortem suam dedit sibi CC marcas sterlingorum de quibus C deberet retinere pro labore suo et alias centum debuisset distribuere inter consanguineos domini. De quibus centum solidos tradidit fratri Waltero dicti domini germano. Quidam autem fecerit de residuo non audivi.

Item de ecclesia de Someresham si solverit xx^{ti} li. magistro Ade de Eston' cui dicta ecclesia comendatur pro reparacionibus ut scribitis non debet audiri nec sibi allocari quia sine mandato vestro solvit et habuit pecunias paratas de summa integra ut predictum est pro reparacionibus faciendas.

Item si domini cardinales qui habent eius beneficia de presenti adpetant racione reparacionum dictus W. habet respondere juxta summam quam recepit quantum ad defectus contingentes in tempore dicti domini mei.

Item si dictus W. velit se excusare quia solvit huiusmodi peccunias Johanni Credi aut sociis suis non debet audiri quia dicta societas michi dixit quod de redditibus beneficiorum domini de anno lxxv^{to} non receperunt denarios sed < d > quod dictus W. habuit in mandatis a domino ad deponendum pecuniam beneficiorum illius anni in custodia nostra preter CC li. recipere debuissetis pro fabrica monasterii.

Item quia dicitur michi quod aliqui petunt pecunias eis debitis de tempore domini mei bonum est inquirere qui sunt et quid et quantum et qua de causa petunt. Dicitur enim quod dominus Ricardus Rave*ni*sher' dicit dominum meum bone memorie fore sibi obligatum in C^{m} li. sterlingorum.

Item dominus Ricardus Chesterfyld petit nescio quantum.

Item dominus W. Palmere petit ut audio magnam summam.

[*Dorse*] Item \ mitto / vobis unam indenturam factam inter dominum et Lumbardos de certa summa pecunie videlicet xx^{ti} milibus florenorum. Si dominus receperit vel non nescio quia non habeo aliquas evidencias.

21/15 Fragment of a quittance, probably from the official of the Archbishop of Canterbury, to [?]Thomas Southam, of all actions resulting from the execution of the will of Simon Langham, May 1385. *WAM 63960*

21/16 Acquittance of Henry Yevele and Stephen Love, masons (*cementarii*), of London for £20 received from the Abbot and Convent of Westminster, for making the tomb of Simon Langham, 6 November 1394. *WAM 6318*

22 William Lenn, Bishop of Worcester

22/1 Will of William Lenn, Bishop of Worcester, made while he was Bishop of Chichester, 29 December 1363 *LPL, Register of William Whittlesey, ff. 128v–129r*

In nomine sancte et individue Trinitatis patris et filii et spiritus sancti amen ego Willelmus miseracione divina Cicestrensis episcopus licet indignus sanus mente iminentem omni carni necessitatem mortis precognans volens diei mortis incertitudinem prevenire testamentum meum sive hanc meam ultimam voluntatem condo in hunc modum. In primis lego animam meam deo corpusque meum ad sepelliendum ubi me contigerit ab hac luce migrare prout amicis meis tempore mortis michi assistentibus visum fuerit. Vellem tamen et rogo si fieri possit quod corpus meum sive ossa deferantur postea ad ecclesiam Cicestrensem et sepelliantur coram altare beate Marie Magdalene ante ostium eiusdem capelle sicut transitur ad capellam beate Marie virginis. Item lego ad feretrum beati Ricardi in ecclesia Cicestrensi x marcas sterlingorum. Nolo tamen quod liberentur capitulo set quod executores mei inde faciant fieri aliquam ymachinem vel ornaturam argenteam deauratam ad tantum valorem in dicto feretro. Item lego ad fabricam dicte ecclesie x li. sterlingorum expendendas circa dictam fabricam per visum executorum meorum. Item lego et volo restitui ecclesie predicte capitulo libros de capella mea et ornamenta alia ac mitram et baculum et alia que ab ipsis recepi et si aliqua deficiant quod solvatur eis vera estimacio sic quod emantur inde dicto capitulo res consimiles et non tradatur eis in pecunia numerata. Item volo quod debita mea omnia solvantur precipua videlicet Waltero de Berneye civi London' C li. sterlingorum magistro Thome de Bocton' canonico Eboracensi xxxvii li. vi s. viii d. sterlingorum et aliis alia debita si qua sunt que singula singulariter eis lego. Item volo quod ante ostium dicte capelle ubi elegi michi sepulturam ponatur unus lapis marmoreus planus [*f. 129r*] insculptus de ymagine cuiusdam pontificis et litteris de nomine meo ad majorem mei memoriam et ut fideles ibidem transeuntes pro anima mea facilius excitentur orare. Et volo quod quamcito fieri commode poterit post mortem meam executores mei faciant poni et fieri in dicta capella in loco ad hoc apto et magis oportuno ymagines bene operatas et bene depictas domini resurgentis et beate Marie Magdalene genuflexo apparentis ad modum et similitudinem sicut sculpebantur in meo parvo sigillo et quod faciant depingi de novo de bona pictura et durativa capellam predictam de historia beate Marie Magdalene dexteram sive australem eius partem et sinistram partem in qua scilicet capud beati Ricardi reponitur de historia beati Ricardi. Item volo quod duo sacerdotes celebrent in dicta capella per unum annum integrum post mortem meam et cuilibet eorundem dentur C s. et volo quod celebrent pro anima mea et anima magistri Ricardi de Wymondeswold' et animabus patris et matris mee et omnium fidelium defunctorum et quod singulis diebus dominicis celebrent de resurreccione et diebus lune de beata Maria Magdalene ceteris vero diebus prout devocio sua eis dederit. Item lego Roberto Wyk' qui servivit michi a puericia et modicum sibi dedi xl li. Item lego Elene sorori mee xx li. pro sustentacione sua. Item lego Margarete sorori mee x li. Item lego servientibus meis Rogero Shire et predicto Roberto Wyk' Thome Cridye domicellis Simoni de Massyngham et Ricardo de Rugham nepotibus meis Edwardo Barbour et Willelmo Phelip' presbiteris ac Johanni Chenny et Rogero de Chalghton' cuilibet eorum C s. et preter hoc Rogero Shire et Roberto Wyk' predictis cuilibet eorum C multones. Item lego xliii s. iiii d. sterlingorum ad distribendum inter fratres minores in pios usus pro anima mea et anima fratris Roberti de Sta*u*nton' quondam fratris minorum. Item lego xx s. ad distribuendum inter pauperes realiter commorantes in hospitali beate Marie Magdalene et beati Jacobi prope Cicestr' et beate Marie Cicestr' ac leprosos de Loddesdon' pro anima mea et anima bone memorie domini Johannis de Langeton' quondam Cicestrensis episcopi. Item volo quod successori meo pro ruinis et defectibus ac reparacionibus ubicumque ad me pertinentibus solvantur CCC marcas sterlingorum si illis contentari voluerit et me et executores meos super hiis plene quietare et liberare infra annum a tempore mortis et in illum eventum illas sibi lego habita consideracione quod modico tempore fui episcopus et quod modicum recepi ab executoribus predecessoris me*i* et de illis que ab eis recepi fui deceptus fere ad medietatem estimacionis et nichilominus valde multa expendi circa reparaciones secundum tempus ita breve et multa plura fecissem si potuissem circa hoc vacasse propter impedimenta perversorum circa hoc et alia michi prestita. Et rogo attente successorem meum quod circa premissa ad ista attendant quod si premissa summa contentari noluerit aut per se vel per alium impedimentum prestiterit quominus executores mei libere de bonis meis disponere poterint secundum voluntatem meam seu huiusmodi ruinas vel defectus taxari fecerit vel procuraverit vel bona mea seu aliquam partem eorundem sequestrari propter hoc fecerit vel procuraverit adimo sibi exnunc dictum legatum CCC marcarum et volo quod taxentur arbitrio boni viri super quo dictum successorem meum ac illum vel illos qui hec taxabit vel taxabunt seu taxari facient vel faciet aut taxari procurabit vel procurabunt onero prout michi voluerint coram summo judice respondere quod premissa debite considerent et justiciam michi faciant in hac parte et spero quod in eventum illum non taxabuntur ad tantam summam sed hoc legatum nichilominus feci propter quietem sucessoris mei et executorum meorum si dictus successor ill*is* contentari voluerit modo et forma premissis. Residuum vero bonorum meorum quod superfuerit post premissa omnia soluta et completa volo dividi in iiii^or^ partes quarum unam volo expendi circa faciendum summum altare novum in ecclesia Cicestrensi usque ad summam xx li. si tantum fuerit in illa porcione et si quid plus fuerit expendatur in fabrica ecclesie. De reliquis tribus porcionibus volo quod habeat unam porcionem Elena soror mea predicta et liberi sui pro sustentacione sua. Aliam porcionem suam habeat Margareta soror mea et liberi sui et terciam porcionem volo expendi in pios usus pro anima mea et matris mee ac patris mei et animabus omnium fidelium defunctorum. Huius autem testamenti mei executores facio Thomam de Lexham rectorem ecclesie beate Marie de Feltewell' Norwicensis diocesis Willelmum de Thufford' Thomam le Hunte Rogerum Schire ac Robertum Wyk'. Item lego prefato magistro Thome de Lexham Hostiensem meum in lectura[1] ut faciat orari pro anima mea. Supplico humiliter caritatis intuitu omnibus Cristi fidelibus ut si in aliquo sim eis debitor vel erga aliquem minus bene me habui vel deliqui hoc velint michi pro dei misericordia relaxare et specialiter familiares meos et servientes exoro ut mei velint habere memoriam et cum deus in futurum eis dededit uberiorem fortunam de meis velint necessitatibus et indigenciis cogitare valeant omnes fideles et specialiter Cicestrensis ecclesia et devoti filii mei civitatis et diocesis Cicestrensis in domino Jhesu Cristo cum benediccione mea paterna licet indigna cuius misericordie et ipsorum oracionibus et suffragiis me commendo. Istud testamentum meum feci coram me recitari et volo esse meam ultimam voluntatem die xxix mensis Decembris anno domini millesimo CCC^mo^lxiii presentibus Ada Fe*u*rothir notario publico Willelmo Stonh*a*rde Johanne Rokewode Johanne Chilterne Thoma Pope et aliis multis testibus ad hoc vocatis et rogatis.

Notes

1 Henricus de Segusio, Cardinal Bishop of Ostia *Lectura super decretales*, printed Strassburg, 1512.

22/2 Probate, at Lambeth, 26 November 1373. *LPL, Register of William Whittlesey, f. 129r.*

22/3 Commission to the Prior of Worcester to commit the administration of the goods of the Bishop of Worcester to executors named in the will and to other suitable persons, Lambeth, 26 November 1373. *LPL, Register of William Whittlesey, f. 129v.*

22/4 Letter to Walter, Prior of Worcester, instructing the executors named in the will or other suitable persons to administer the deceased's goods. The executors named in the will are Mag. Thomas Lexham, Mag. William Thirford, archdeacon of Gloucester, and Mag. Robert Wyk', along with Adam Feurother named in a private letter to the Archbishop of Canterbury, 3 April 1374. *LPL, Register of William Whittlesey, f. 66r.*

22/5 Final acquittance of the executors of William Lenn, Canterbury, 9 December 1374. *CCA, Register G, f. 178v and f. 206v.*

23 Llywelyn ap Madoc ab Ellis, Bishop of St Asaph

23/1 Will, 10 November 1369, with confirmations 4 October 1372, 17 January 1374, and confirmation with additions, 12 October 1375

LPL, Register of Simon Sudbury, ff. 88v–89r

In dei nomine amen ego Lewelinus filius Madoc episcopus Assavensis sanus mente et corpore prout ad presens percipere possit aut sentire \ timens / tamen incertitudinem finis vite mee propter pestilenciam que violenter < regat > \ regnat / hiis diebus senciens insuper quod dum corpus sanitate viget mens interior semet ipsa coll*a*ta pleniori utitur racione testamentum meum condo ordino facio in hunc modum. In primis confisus merit*is* et precibus sanctissimi Assaphi episcopi et confessoris patronique mei lego animam meam deo omnipotenti et beatissime Marie virgini matri eiusdem et omnibus sanctis corpusque meum sepelliendum [*f. 89r*] in coro ecclesie cathedralis Assavensis juxta magnum altare ubi evangelium ad magnam missam legi consuetum est. Deinde volo et precipio per executores meos satisfieri creditoribus meis fideliter et competenter pro eorum labore et servicio. Item lego omnia vasa argentea que emi de Henrico de Salbur' ad fabricam ecclesie cathedralis Assavensis ita quod vendantur per teshaurium ecclesie predicte juxta visum et ordinacionem canonicorum Assavensium et meorum executorum et precium eorum fiat fideliter et absque dolo et fraude ad fabricam cathedralis antedicte. Siquis illa vasa alio modo alienavit quam supra dictitur sentenciam excommunicationis incurrat ipso facto quam sentenciam placeat domino meo archiepiscopo pro anima mea et utilitate ecclesie cathedralis Assavensis sueque suffragine confirmare. Item lego oves meas ac quicquid de meis ovium generis sit sororibus meis inter eas equaliter dividendas. Item lego Gruff*uth* ap Ieuan Grach' nepoti meo librum decretalium[1] et spectaculum judiciale[2] unum ciphum de massar*u* et unum ciphum de argento et vi coc*l*iaria et ii ollas de ere. Item lego Lewellino ap Ieuan nepoti meo equum quem consuevit equitare unum ciphum de masser' i ollam. Item lego Mad*oc* ap Gra*n*w Leyt unum[3] equum i ciphum de masser' et i ollam. Item lego Mad*oc* ap Ior*werth* Goch' i ollam i ciphum de masser'. Item lego Gruff*uth* ap Lewellyn ap Kynwr*i*t iiii coc*l*iaria deaurata i ollam i ciphum de masser' et i ciphum de argento. Item lego domino Edmundo ap Gruff*uth* capellano meo i ciphum de masser' et i ciphum parvum de argento.[4] Item lego utencilia domus mee ultra superius legata inter nepotes meos filios sororum mearum equaliter dividenda excepto quod de plumbo fiat i vas circa corpus meum in sepeltura. Item \ lego / pro anima mea \ xx s. / fratribus predicatoribus de Rudlan[5] et xx s. fratribus minoribus de Lanwaes[6] et Carmilit*is* de Dynbych'[7] xx s. vicariis de coro ecclesie Assavensis xl s. Item lego ad fabricam et reparacionem pont*is* de Kynwyt[8] xx s. Factis et solutis funeralibus meis et solutis debitis universis me concernentibus lego residuum omnium bonorum \ meorum / pro missis celebrandis et ad alios pios usus juxta ordinacionem executorum meorum et ad hoc testamentum meum exequendum infrascriptos facio et ordino executores videlicet Gruff*uth* ap Ieuan canonicum Assavensem dominum Edy*n*y*v*et vicarium de Grisfort[9] Madoc de Gronw Loyt nepotem meum. Scripta manu mea propria in manerio de Alltym'[10] die sabbati proximo ante festum sancti Martini episcopi et confessoris anno domini millesimo CCC^{mo} sexagesimo nono.

Istud testamentum meum volo permanere prout superius jacet nisi contingerat ne aliud ordinari per codicillos vel alia via quacumque. Data apud Alltym' anno domini millesimo CCC[mo]lxxii die lune proximo post festum sancti Michaelis archangeli.

Totum scriptum manu mea propria istud testamentum meum volo quod stet in suo robore prout superius continetur. Data apud Alltym' die martis proximo post sancti Hillarii anno domini millesimo CCC[mo] septuagesimo tercio.

Alia copia testamenti dicti episcopi Assavensis
In dei nomine amen ego Lewelinus episcopus Assavensis sanus mente licet non corpore volo pro hac mea[11] ultima voluntate quod infrascriptum testamentum meum in hoc rotulo pergameni contentum manu mea propria scriptum ac sigillo meo privato signatum valeat et stet prout melius et plenius continetur in eodem et omnia legata contenta in eodem valeant cum effectu una cum infrascriptis legatis et data in die veneris proximo post festum sancti Dionis*ii* anno domini millesimo CCC[mo]lxxv[to]. Item lego Ith*el* ap D*avi*d' ap Mad*oc* i bovem. Item lego[12] cuilibet de servientibus meis infrascriptis i bovem videlicet Jac coco Mad*oc* ap Gruff*uth* Iorw*erth* panetar*io* Tud*ur* Gogh' E*ignion* ap Bled*dyn*. Item lego Madoco ap Gronw Loyt nepoti meo liberacionem de omnibus et singulis debitis in quibus michi extiterat obligatus. Item lego D*avi*d' ap Gad'[13] xx s. Item Mad*oc* Mo*e*l i portiforium meum parvum. Item lego Gruff*uth* ap Ieuan nepoti meo Hostiensem meum in summa[14] et rosar*io*[15] ac specular*ium*[16] meos. Item Angh*ara*t sorori mee blada existencia apud Yvaerdref.[17] Item lego Mad*oc* ap Ior*werth* nepoti meo omnia blada mea existencia apud Landegla.[18] Item volo quod Ie*u*af' Effeiriat[19] habeat portiforium meum quod habet penes se ad vitam suam et post mortem ipsius executores mei vel eorum unus dent illum portiforium presbitero oranti pro anima mea. Item lego Madoc famulo palfridi i bovem. Et ad istud testamentum meum ac hanc ultimam voluntatem meam fideliter ut premittitur exequendum ordino facio et constituo hos executores videlicet Gruff*uth* ap Ieuan canonicum Assavensem Madoc ap Gronw Loyt Mad*oc* Moel et Ede*n*' ap Gruff*uth* rectores ecclesiarum de Lanwair in Kodewein[20] et Wydefrod.[21] In cuius rei testimonium sigillum meum privatum hoc testamento meo aponi feci. Hiis testibus magistro Gruff*uth* ap Ieuan canonico Assavensi Madoc' ap Gronw Mad*oc* ap Ior*werth* et Mad*oc* Moel. Data apud manerium de Alltym' die veneris proximo post festum sancti Dionisii \ anno domini M[o]CCC[o]lxxv[o] predicto. / Et ego El*is* natus D*avi*d' Englefeld' clericus Assavensis diocesis publicus auctoritate apostolica notarius premissis omnibus et singulis dum sic agerentur et fierent una cum prenominatis testibus presens interfui eaque sic fieri vidi et audivi signoque meorum nomine consuetis signavi rogatus in fidem et testimonium premissorum sub die veneris supradicto pontificatus sanctissimi in Cristo patris et domini nostri domini Gregorii divina providencia pape xi[mi] anno quinto indictione xiii[a].

Notes

1 Probably Gregory IX, *Decretales*, printed in *Corpus iuris canonici* ed. E. Friedberg (2nd edition, 2 vols., Leipzig, 1922) ii, cols. 1–928.

2 Probably Willelmus Durandus, *Speculum judiciale*, printed Frankfurt, 1602.

3 MS: 'uni''.

4 MS: 'agento'.

5 Rhuddlan, Flintshire.

6 Llanfaes, Anglesey.

7 Denbigh.
8 Cynwyd, Merionethshire.
9 Gresford, Denbighshire.
10 Alt Meliden, also known as Meliden, Flintshire.
11 MS: 'mera'.
12 MS repeats 'item lego'.
13 Perhaps erroneously for Mad*oc*.
14 Henricus de Segusio, Cardinal Bishop of Ostia *Summa super titulis decretalium*, printed Rome, 1473.
15 Guido de Baysio *Rosarium seu apparatus ad decretum*, printed Strassburg, 1473.
16 The copy above, note 2, probably of Willelmus Durandus *Speculum judiciale*.
17 Y Faerdref, 'the maer's settlement': a common place-name, in this instance with no evidence to localise it.
18 Llandegla, Denbighshire.
19 i.e. 'offeiriad', the priest.
20 Llanfair-yng-Nghedewain, i.e. Llanfair in Cedewain: Newtown, Montgomeryshire.
21 Whitford, Flintshire.

23/2 Grant of probate by Mag. Nicholas de Chaddesden, Dean of Arches, to Dom. Gruffuth ap Ieuan [Grath], canon of St Asaph, and Madoc ap Gronw Loyt, executors named in the testament, Dom. Madoc Moel declining to act in this capacity, London, 7 December 1375. *LPL, Register of Simon Sudbury, ff. 89r–89v.*

23/3 Commission to Mag. Ithel ap Roppert', archdeacon of St Asaph, Mag. Lewis Treffawr and Mag. Hugh Kyffin, canons of St Asaph, to hear the accounts of the executors of Bishop Llywelyn. Given at Lambeth, 24 May [1376]. *LPL, Register of Simon Sudbury, f. 20r.*

23/4 Acquittance of the executors, 17 November 1376. *LPL, Register of Simon Sudbury, f. 92v.*

24 Roger Martival, Bishop of Salisbury

Agreement and composition between the executors of Roger Martival, Bishop of Salibsury, and the keeper of the choristers, the vicars of the church of Salisbury, and the lieutenant of the Dean, and the Chapter of Salisbury, 21 September 1344 *Muniments of the Dean and Chapter of Salisbury, Press IV, Box W/1344 (wills)*

Both parts of the indenture of agreement, each a single membrane, lettered A and B, are sealed on a tag at the foot, with a fragment of green wax remaining with indenture A. Both texts have been damaged by damp, A more seriously than B. The text below is based on A, with passages transcribed in square brackets taken from B unless otherwise indicated. Indenture A is endorsed in a mid to late fourteenth-century hand: 'Testamentum domini Rogeri de Mortivall' de C s. legatis choristis ecclesie Sarum et vicariis xl li. in perpetuum'. Indenture B is endorsed: 1. In a mid fourteenth-century hand: 'Tangens custodem chorustarum et comunitatem vicariorum pro disposicione D li.' 2. In a mid fourteenth-century hand: 'Pro capitulo contra Worth''. 3. In a mid to late fourteenth-century hand: 'Littera testimonialis Roberti de Martivall' episcopi Sarum de voluntate sua quomodo affectavit augere statum vicariorum et chorustarum unde oneravit executores suos qui ipsi ordinarent etc. unde post litem motam inter vicarios et chorustas ex una et dictos executores ex altera \ parte / ita concordatum est de concessu omnium quorum interest que ipsi executores solverent quingentas libras monete ad usum vicariorum et chorustarum quod et fecerunt ad purchassandum inde aliquod certum de quo choruste perciperent in perpetuum annuatim C s. et vicarii predicti perciperent xl li. annuatim ita quod singuli vicarii ex illis denariis singulis diebus \ haberent / in perpetuum obulos ultra id quod vicarii solebant percipere in ecclesia Sarum etc.'

In[1] dei nomine amen hec indentura testatur quod cum recolende memorie dominus Rogerus de Martivall' quondam Sarum episcopus in suo testamento legitime ordinasset et vellet quod si post comparacionem [et mortificacionem] terrarum sive reddituum aut possessionum secundum formam testamenti sui huiusmodi pro capella sua de No*u*esle aliquod residuum superit ita notabile quod inde possit emi aliquod perpetuum in adjutorium sustentacionis puerorum chorustarum ecclesie Sarum quod [taliter emeretur et si] solutis debitis suis et legatis provisum esset dicte capelle secundum formam testamenti predicti et dictis chorustis aliqua talis summa de bonis suis residua fuerit [unde sic] provideri posset vicariis ecclesie Sarum quod singuli eorum habere possent [inde] singulos obolos ultra ea que tunc de eadem ecclesia perceperunt quod sic provideretur eisdem ac canonicus Sarum custos predictorum chorustarum a venerabilibus viris capitulo Sarum [deputatus] et vicarii predicti legata predicta sibi in dicto testamento relicta peterent auctoritate et consensu tenentis locum domini decani et capituli supradicti sibi ab eiusdem testamenti executoribus ministrari.[2] Iidem executores pretendebant quod cum celeritate qua predictus canonicus custos chorustarum et dicti vicarii predicti petebant testatoris disposicionem huius legatorum juxta formam testamenti eiusdem adimplere non poterant nec tenebantur de jure fuissetque super hiis legatis inter dictos custodem chorustarum et vicarios ac executores predictos suborta questionis materia[3] demum inter ipsos custodem chorustarum et vicarios ac executores predictos auctoritate consilio et consensu expresso tenentis locum domini decani ecclesie Sarum et eiusdem capituli prehabitis in hac parte ac de canonico[4] custode dictorum chorustarum ac omnium et singulorum vicariorum ecclesie Sarum et executorum predictorum ac aliorum quorum interest voluntate et consensu unamini concurrentibus eciam [omnibus] et singulis que in hac parte requirebantur de jure pro multis vitandis periculis que verisimiliter accidere poterant in premissis aliisque certis \ ex / causis veris et legitimis de quibus dictis tenenti locum decani et capitulo legitime constitit atque constat concordatum est et compositum inter partes predictas super dictis legatis pro bono et utilitate ecclesie ac chorustarum [et] vicariorum Sarum sponte et libere in hunc modum. Videlicet quod executores testamenti predicti solvent dictis canonico custodi chorustarum et vicariis ecclesie Sarum pro legatis suis predictis quingentas libras sterlingorum ad usum predictorum puerorum chorustarum et vicariorum eiusdem ecclesie Sarum et non in usus alios convertendas. Item videlicet quod pueri choruste predicti centum solidos imperpetuum in adjutorium sustentacionis eorum et vicarii predicti quadraginta libras habeant annuatim de aliquo perpetuo de dictis quingentis libris per custodem et dictos vicarios providendas. Ita quod ipsi vicarii singuli singulis diebus singulos habeant obolos imperpetuum ultra id quod percipere solebant in ecclesia

Sarum predicta prout in testamento continetur predicto. Quas quidem quingentas libras executores predicti solverunt integre canonico custodi chorustarum et vicariis supradictis in dictorum tenentis locum decani et capituli et notarii auctoritate apostolico pupplici presencia de consensu expresso et auctoritate dicti tenentis locum decani et capituli Sarum predicti. Promiserunt eciam predictus canonicus custos chorustarum et vicarii memorati et singuli eorumdem et coram tenente locum decani et capitulo ac executoribus supradictis juramentum ad sancta dei eva*u*ngelia prestiterunt quod predictas quingentas libras in usus dictorum chorustarum et ipsorum vicariorum et non in usus alios quatenus in eis est fideliter et quamcito comodo poterunt de dictis quingentis libris et non ultra nisi velint convertent ut premittitur et prout in testamento disponitur antedicto et quod eandem peccuniam vel aliquam eius partem canonicis vicariis vel aliis quibuscumque personis nullatenus mutuabunt [nec] alienabunt ad tempus vel perpetuo aliquo genere seu titulo alienacionis seu translacionis quocumque nisi dumtaxat in usus predictos. Volentes et concedentes expresse quod quilibet de cetero in Sarum ecclesie vicarium admittendus in sui [admissione] prestet coram dicto capitulo simile juramentum quodque dictos executores vel eorum aliquem eorumve heredes vel executores circa dicta legata eorumve occasione vel ea tangencia quovismodo seu propter aliqua que in testamento continentur predicto directo vel [per] obliquum per se vel per alios nunquam imperpetuum infestabunt vel molestabunt nec procurabunt quantum in eis est vel permittent aliqualiter infestari vel eciam molestari. Unde nos tenens locum decani et capitulum \ Sarum / ac custos chorustarum et vicarii omnes et singuli supradicti considerantes et legitime pro certo scientes quod huiusmodi concordia et composicio pro bono et utilitate dicte ecclesie ac chorustarum et vicariorum omnium et singulorum eiusdem necnon auctoritate [et] consensu [nostro] tenentis locum decani et capituli dictorum canonici custodis ac vicariorum dicte ecclesie et executorum predictorum expresso consensu legitime processerunt bonamque fidem equitatem et veritatem agnoscere cupientes fatemur in dictorum executorum predictique [pupplici notarii] presencia et ex causis predictis solucionem dictarum quingentarum librarum sterlingorum predictis custodi chorustarum et vicariis integre factam esse et pro eisdem legatis fore nobis in omnibus plenarie satisfactum. Ipsos igitur dicti testamenti executores et eorum quemlibet [ipsorumque heredes] et executores et executorum executores ab omni jure et ab omnibus et omnimodis accionibus querelis et demandis nobis tenenti locum decani et capitulo ac ecclesie supradictis ac nobis chorustarum custodi[5] ac chorustis et vicariis omnibus et singulis supradictis [pro dictis legatis] vel eorum occasione seu ea tangencia contra dicti testamenti executores seu eorum aliquem quomodolibet competentibus et [competituris] quatenus nos tenentem locum decani et capitulum ac ecclesiam supradictam concernunt et eciam quatenus ad nos custodem chorustarum et chorustas et nos [omnes et] singulos vicarios supradictos [nostrum] ve aliquem attinent auctoritate et consensu expresso tenentis locum decani et capituli predictorum pro nobis et successoribus nostris in hiis scriptis ex certa sciencia totaliter liberamus acquietamus et eosdem imperpetuum in hac parte reddimus et sponte fatemur presencium tenore quietos. Nosque custos chorustarum et vicarii supradicti omnes et singuli nos et successores nostros ad omnium et singulorum premissorum observacionem fidelem prout superius conscribuntur auctoritate et consensu expresso dictorum tenentis locum decani et capituli quatenus nos concernunt tenore presencium obligamus. In quorum omnium et singulorum testimonium atque fidem quia sigilla nostra executorum videlicet ac canonici custodis chorustarum et vicariorum ecclesie Sarum predicte pluribus sunt ignota sigillum commune venerabilium virorum dominorum capituli ecclesie Sarum[6] predicte personaliter apponi procuravimus huic scripto per modum indenture confecto. Et nos tenens locum et capitulum Sarum predicti ad predictorum canonici custodis chorustarum et vicariorum ac executorum predictorum personalem instanciam et rogatum sigillum nostrum ecclesie predicte commune eidem scripto indentato apposuimus in premissorum omnium et singulorum testimonium et memoriam perpetuam sic gestorum predictoque notario pupplico mandavimus et injunximus quod hoc scriptum indentatum pro majori securitate muniat pupplico suo signo consueto cum fuerit requisito. Data in domo nostro capitulari Sarum die vicesima prima mensis Septembris anno domini millesimo CCC° quadragesimo quarto.

Et[7] ego Johannes de Hemingby clericus Lincolniensis diocesis publicus auctoritate apostolica notarius auctoritate[8] et consensu dictorum venerabilium virorum tenentis locum decani et capituli ut premittitur superius prestitis ac dictis concorde et composicioni super dictis legatis dictarumque quingentarum librarum pro eisdem legatis [muneracioni] et solucioni ut predicitur ac premissioni et juramentorum dictorum custodis chorustarum et vicariorum prestacionibus in modo et forma predictis dictoque tenentis locum decani et capituli ac predictorum custodis chorustarum et vicariorum omnium et singulorum ab omni jure et omnibus accionibus querelis et demandis eis competentibus et competituris pro legatis predictis ac confessionibus et obligacionibus suprascriptis ut predicitur predictique sigilli communis capituli ecclesie Sarum predicte huic scripto indentato apposicionem ac premissis omnibus et singulis que et prout supra scribicionem[9] una cum testibus inferius nominatis sub anno ab incarnacione domini nostri Jhesu Cristi [secundum computaticionem ecclesie Anglicane][10] millesimo trecentesimo quadragesimo quarto indiccione xii^a^ pontificatus sanctissimi in Cristo patris et domini domini Clementis divina providencia papa vi^ti^ anno tercio mensis Septembris die vicesima prima in domo capitulari ecclesie Sarum predicte presens fui [eaque] sic fieri vidi et audivi ac ad mandatum et minacionem dominorum tenentis locum decani ecclesie cathedralis Sarum et eiusdem capituli predictorum necnon per canonicum custodem chorustarum et vicarios supradictos ac per executores predictos rogatus me subscripsi signumque meum publicum et consuetum quo utor utrique parti huius scripti indentati apposui et hoc scriptum eodem signo munivi in fidem et testimonium premissorum. Presentibus predictis locum tenente decani et capitulo Sarum predictis ac custode chorustarum ac vicariis omnibus et singulis et executoribus memoratis. Presentibus eciam discretis viris dominis Roberto de Whytlegh' presbitero [Roberto de Olney][11] Roberto de Worthe Edmundo filio Johannis de Wynterborn' magistro Henrico de Lutegarshale auctoritate apostolica notario publico et aliis in magna multitudine testibus ad premissa vocatis specialiter et rogatis.

Notes

1 The letters 'ABCDEFGHIKLMNOPQRS' are written across the head of the two indentures.

2 MS B: 'eiusdem executoribus testamenti ministrari'.

3 MS B: 'materia questionis'.

4 MS: 'canonici'.

5 MS B: 'custodi chorustarum'.

6 MS B: 'Sarum ecclesie'.
7 Preceded by a notarial sign. The notary's attestation is in a second hand.
8 MS: 'auctoritati'.
9 MS B: 'scribuntur'.
10 Passage in square brackets in MS A only.
11 Passsage in square brackets in MS A only.

25 Simon Mepham, Archbishop of Canterbury

25/1 List of ornaments delivered by Dom. Hugh de St Margaret, sacrist of Christ Church, Canterbury, to Dom. Thomas de Woghope, keeper of the chapel of Simon Mepham, Archbishop of Canterbury, 8 September 1328 *CCA, Register Q, ff. 130r–130v*

Ornamenta ecclesiastica liberata ad capellam domini S. archiepiscopi

Ornamenta ecclesiastica subscripta in duabus cistis rubeis amalatis liberata fuerunt ad capellam venerabilis patris domini Simonis dei gracia Cantuariensis archiepiscopi tocius Anglie primatis die nativitatis beate Marie anno domini M°CCC^mo^xxviii° per indenturam factam inter dominum Hugonem de sancta Margareta tunc sacristam ecclesie Cristi Cantuar' et dominum Thomam de Woghope custodem capelle dicti patris videlicet

Crux portatilis argentea

Item mitra domini Johannis archiepiscopi

Item baculus eiusdem argenteus et operatus

Item cirothece domini R. de Wynchelese archiepiscopi cum perulis et gemmis in platis quadratis et magnis tassellis rotundis

Item anulus pontificalis magnus cum saphiro oblongo et quatuor parvi pramis cum quatuor margaritis

Item tres acus aurei ad palleum quilibet cum uno rubino baleys et ii smaragdinis et ii saphiris

Item ii sandalia cum galochis de rubeo samitto brudat*is* armis regis Anglie

Item calix i cum patena argentea et deaurata intus et extra cum nodo in medio cum perulis et gemmis operat*o* ponderis xlii s.

Item ii urcioli argentei unde i deauratus et alius amalatus ponderis xxii s.

Item ii candelabra argentea cum tribus pedibus argenteis domini R. archiepiscopi predicti

Item ii thurribuli argentei et deaurati ponderis lxxiii s. iiii d.

Item vas ad thus cum cocleario argenteo ponderis xxii s.

Item vas argenteum ad aquam benedictam ponderis lxxiii s. iiii d.

Item aspersorium argenteum ponderis xiii s. iiii d.

Item pixis eburnea ad oblat*iones*

Item crismatorium argenteum domini Walteri archiepiscopi

Pro domino archiepiscopo[1]

Item capa chori i

Casula i

Tunica et dalmatica

Item tunica et dalmatica pro diacono et subdiacono de rubeo samitto brudate cum arboribus aureis et cum aurifrigio de perulis et avibus operato

[*f. 130v*] Item ii cape de rubeo samitto cum ii tassell*is* auri pro ii clericis capelle
Item alba i cum amictu et cingulo brudat*is* cum coronacione beate Marie ex parte una et matre et filio ex parte altera pro domino archiepiscopo
Item stola et manipulus cum scutis consutis et brudatis
Item corporalia brudata cum crucifixo et coronacione beate Marie
Item ii albe cum amictibus pro diacono et subdiacono de serico consut*is*
Item stola i et duo manipuli pro diacono et subdiacono brudati
Item palla altaris cum frontell*o* de scutis brudat*o*
Item palla i sine frontell*o*
Item manutergium i ad manus
Item pannus i ad sacrarium
Item campana i ad summarium capelle
Item equs i summarius cum tapeto et barehid' et alio harnasio pertinenti precii x li.
Item magnus liber qui dicitur pontificale domini Johannis archiepiscopi
Item biblia domini R. archiepiscopi supradicti

Notes
1 On the right of the text, rather than in the margin, bracketed against the next three entries.

25/2 Probate granted by Richard, Prior of Christ Church, Canterbury, in the great chapel in the monastery, to Mag. Laurence Fastolf and Dom. Thomas de Woghope, executors named in the will, the other executors so named declining the task, 7 November 1334. *CCA, Register G, f. 5v of the libellus inserted between ff. 24 and 25.* A further copy of the grant of probate is in *CCA, Register Q, f. 190v*, where it is dated 7 kal. November, 26 October 1334.

25/3 Acquittance by Robert, Prior of Christ Church, Canterbury, of Mag. Laurence Fastolf, as executor of the will of Archbishop Simon, 8 October 1348. *CCA, Register G, ff. 99v–100r.*

26 Richard Mitford, Bishop of Salisbury

26/1 Will, 29 April 1407 *LPL, Register of Thomas Arundel, vol. I, ff. 237v–238v*
In nomine sancte et individue Trinitatis patris et filii et spiritus sancti humane nature prothoplausti rubigine contaminata condicio mortalitatis flebilem ob sui demeritum subegit senteneiam cuius licet certissime nemo vivens preter creatorem prescivit horam huic est quod ego Ricardus[1] Medeford ecclesie Sarum minister licet indignus premissa sedula cordis intencione revolvens et vocacionem meam exemplo patrum meorum humiliter exspectans sana mentis mee existens memoria die penultima mensis Aprilis anno domini millesimo quadringentesimo septimo in manerio meo de Poterne condo testamentum meum in hunc modum. In primis comendo et lego animam meam omnipotenti deo qui cum suo precioso corpore redemit ac sancte Marie virgini et sancto Ricardo patronis meis et omnibus sanctis corpusque meum ad sepeliendum in ecclesia Sarum antedicta ubi jam pro me ordinatum existit. Item lego summo altari dicte ecclesie duo turribulia argentea et in parte deaurata cum cathenis argenteis ad usum ecclesie

et altaris antedictorum. Item lego eidem ecclesie ad usum eiusdem imperpetuum baculum meum pastoralem ad cuius facturam recepi de implimento baculum antiqum pastoralem de ligno inferius compositum valoris argenti eiusdem baculi antiqui quinque marcas. Item lego eidem ecclesie et capelle beate Marie ibidem vestimentum meum de albo bradekyn videlicet tria fruntalia pro altari dicte capelle duo tuallas de panno lineo tria ridella de albo tartarin cum cordulis unum pannum pro lectrino de secta fruntelliorum quatuor capas de eadem secta et quintam albam capam de panno deaurato unam casulam duas tunicas tres albas tres amictas cum parurio de secta quatuor caparum huiusmodi duas stolas tres manipulos unum casum pro corporali cum panno lineo benedicto in eodem tres zonas pro vestimentis predictis de filo albo. Item lego cuilibet canonico Sarum ecclesie notorie existenti in exequiis meis die sepulture mee et in vigilia ad placebo et dirige quinque solidos. Item lego cuilibet vicario dicte ecclesie consimili modo interessenti xx d. Item lego cuilibet alii capellano cantarias in dicta ecclesia habenti et simili modo interessenti xx d. Item lego cuilibet choriste altariste et aliis dicte ecclesie ministris superius non nominatis modo predicto interessentibus x d. Item volo quod expense mee funerales in die sepulture mee faciende fiant secundum discrecionem executorum meorum subscriptorum. Item lego et ordino ad distribuendum inter pauperes magis indigentes die sepulture mee predicte xx marcas ut quilibet pauper illuc veniens duos habeat denarios. Item lego xvi li. xiii s. iiii d. centum capellanis bone conversacionis diocesis Sarum curatis et non curatis juxta disposicionem executorum meorum subscriptorum infra mensem meam mortem proximam sequentem solvendos ut quamdiu eis placuerit orent pro anima mea parentumque meorum ac omnium [*f. 238r*] fidelium defunctorum cuilibet videlicet eorum iii s. iiii d. Item lego magistro Waltero Medeford fratri meo unum missale optimum uno excepto et unum calicem cum quo deservitur in oratorio meo cum duobus cruettis quadratis de argento. Item lego predicto magistro Waltero totum apparatum pro oratorio meo deputatum cum una nola argentea pro oratorio huiusmodi deputata. Item lego eidem magistro Waltero unum ciphum argenteum deauratum cum uno wrech' in cipho et cooperculo de vynes. Item lego eidem unum parvum salarium rotundum cum coooperculo de argento deaurato. Item lego eidem magistro Waltero unum par pelvium de argento et in parte deauratum quas habui de dono predicti magistri Walteri ad usum capelle mee. Item lego eidem magistro Waltero unam pelvem de argento ponderis iii li. xix s. ii d. cum lavacro eiusdem de argento ponderis xxxv s. v d. Item lego Alicie sorori mee uxori Henrici Hunte xxvi li. xiii s. iiii d. Item lego predicte Alicie meam robam meliorem de scarlet videlicet unum mantellum furratum cum menevero cum surcot*e* et capicio de eadem secta furrat*is* cum menevero. Item lego Roberto Hunte filio sororis mee predicte totam armaturam meam ad corpus meum armandum pertinentem qualitercumque. Item lego Alianore Margarete et Alicie filiabus sororis mee predicte cuilibet earum xiii li. vi s. viii d. Item lego predicte Alianore unam robam de panno blodio videlicet unum mantel cum capicio furrato de menevero cum uno surcote eiusdem secte furrato cum bis*e*. Item lego predicte Margarete unam robam de panno viridi videlicet unum mantel cum capicio furrat*is* cum menevero cum uno surcote eiusdem secte furrato cum bis*e*. Item lego predicte Alicie filie sororis mee unam robam de scarleta videlicet unam clocam et capicium furrata cum menevero et surcote eiusdem secte furrato cum bis*e*. Item lego Johanne cognate mee uxori Hugonis Bisle x li. Item lego Matilde cognate mee uxori Ricardi Osbern' x li. Item lego Johanne uxori Ricardi Lovell' cognate mee x li. Item lego Elizabethe uxori Johannis Hydeney cognate mee x li. Item lego Dionisie uxori Johannis Perys cognate mee x li. Item lego eisdem quinque sororibus et cognatis meis omnia vasa mea stannea inter eas equaliter dividenda. Item lego quinque cognatis meis supranominatis quinque lectos parvos cum suis apparitibus de melioribus exceptis quinque lectis optimis cum suis apparatibus quibuscumque. Item tamen quod predicte pecunie prefatis quinque sororibus et cognatis meis per me legate singulis earum liberentur vel earum maritis et quod mariti predicti quilibet eorum executoribus meis ante liberacionem dicte pecunie firmiter obligentur quod in eventum quo morietur quivis eorundem uxore sua superstite de dimittendo uxori sue predicte tunc viventi predictis decem libras quas ex legato meo recepit sine diminucione quacumque. Item lego supradicte Johanne cognate mee uxori Hugonis Bisle unum chimer de scarlet cum capicio de eadem secta ambo furrata cum menevero. Item lego supradicte Matilde cognate mee uxori Ricardi Osbern' unum chimer de violet cum capicio de eadem secta ambo furrata cum menevero. Item lego Elizabethe cognate mee uxori Johannis Hideney unum surcote de viridi melle[2] furratum cum bis*e* et capicium eiusdem secte furratum cum menevero. Item lego Johanne cognate mee uxori Ricardi Lovell' unum surcote de moustierdevilliers furratum cum bis*e* et capicium eiusdem secte furratum cum menevero. Item lego Dionisie uxori Johannis Piers cognate mee unum surcote de vi*o*let*o*[3] melle furratum cum bys*e* et capicium eiusdem secte furratum cum menevero. Item lego Alianore uxori Johannis Medeford' cognati mei unum surcote de murre furratum cum bis*e* et capicium eiusdem secte furratum cum menevero. Item lego altari capelle ubi corpus meum erit tumulatum in ecclesia Sarum vestimentum meum rubium quod nuper habui de domino Georgio Louthorp' ad deserviendum misse obitus mei quamdiu duraverit. Item lego matri magistri Walteri Medeford x marcas. Item lego Johanni Medeford' et uxori sue x marcas. Item lego Elie Hakeborne x li. Item lego Johanni Medeford' de Genge et Thome fratri suo utrique eorum lxvi s. viii d. Item lego filie dicti Johannis nuper uxori Willelmi de Cambre x marcas. Item lego Alicie filie dicte Johannis ad ipsius maritagium lxvi s. viii d. Item lego priorisse de Bromhale xiii s. iiii d. Item lego cuilibet alii moniali ibidem vi s. viii d. Item lego magistro Henrico Chicheley unam cupam deauratam cum cooperculo sculptam cum sex foliis et cum i trayle de foliis. Item lego domino Thome Wysbech unam cupam[4] deauratam cum cooperculo operat*o* cum uno wrech de liliis et una rosa super pomellum cooperculi. Item lego magistro Johanni Chandeler' unam cupam cum cooperculo deaurato sculptam[5] cum serpentibus. Item lego Johanni Gaweyn unam cupam argenteam cum cooperculo eiusdem. Item lego Johanni Wylmyndon' unam cupam de argento cum cooperculo. Item lego cuilibet executori meo inferius nominato C s. ita tamen iidem subeunt onus executorium [*f. 238v*] testamenti mei predicti. Item lego domino Johanni Wythir subdecano Sarum x li. Item do et lego domino Andree Swynford' x marcas. Item lego cuilibet alteri capellano capelle mee famuliari meo tempore mortis mee existenti C s. Item lego Willelmo Tippe clerico vi marcas. Item lego Johanni Edwynde clerico vi marcas. Item Johanni Tydemershe lego C s. Item lego Willelmo Shepton C s. Item lego Nicholao Caperon' clerico C s. Item lego Roberto camerario meo quinque marcas. Item lego Johanni Russell' quinque marcas. Item lego Rogero Cook quinque marcas. Item lego cuilibet generoso tam clerico quam laico cui per prius legatum in specie relictum non est meo famuliari existenti in servicio meo tempore decessus mei lxvi s. viii d. Item lego cuilibet valetto tam clerico quam laico cui perantea legatum in specie non relinquitur infra hospicium meum tempore exitus mei famuliari xl s. Item lego cuilibet garcioni tam clerico quam laico existenti[6] in servicio meo famuliari tempore mortis mee xx s. Item lego priorisse de Rouspar xiii s. iiii d. Item lego Johanne Glasham moniali eiusdem domus xx s. Item lego cuilibet moniali eiusdem domus de Rouspar[7] vi s. viii d. dicta Johanna Glasham dumtaxat excepta. Item lego priorisse et conventui de Kyngton' Michaelis ad dividendum equaliter inter easdem xl s. Item lego cuilibet domui fratrum mendicancium infra diocesem Sarum existencium ad celebrandum et orandum pro anima mea xx s. Item lego cuilibet domui fratrum mendicancium in Oxon' ad celebrandum et orandum pro anima mea xx s. Item lego domine de Cury unam cupam cum cooperculo deaurato quam habui de dono domini Johannis Frank. Item lego eidem domine unum ewer cum tribus foraminibus. Item lego Roberto Hunte filio sororis mee predicte xiii li. vi s. viii d. Item lego reverendissimo in Cristo patri ac domino domino Thome dei gratia Cantuariensi archiepiscopo meum pontificale optimum supplicans humiliter paternitati sue quatinus exhibere dignetur bonam dominacionem suam executoribus meis in execucione testamenti mei facienda. Et ad istud testamentum meum bene et fideliter exequendum ordino facio et constituto executores meos magistrum Walterum Medeford' fratrem meum dominum Georgium Louthorp magistrum Rogerum Harewell' dominum Thomam Wysbech' canonicos Sarum Laurencium Drewe et Johannem Wylmyndon'. Et honorabilem virum magistrum Henricum Chichele dicte ecclesie Sarum cancellarium ac Johannem Gaweyn armigerum dictorum executorum supervisores in execucione omnium premissorum facienda. Residuum vero omnium bonorum meorum tam vivorum quam mortuorum superius non legatorum do et lego predictis magistro Waltero fratri meo et Rogero Harewell' una cum legatis eisdem superius relictis ut ipsi Walterus et Rogerus deum pre oculis habentes cum consilio et supervisione dicti Johannis Wylmyndon' inter executores superius nominatos disponant et ordinent pro salute anime mee et pro animabus parentum et benefactorum meorum ut voluerint respondere coram summo judice. In cuius rei testimonium huic testamento meo una cum notarii mei infrascripti signo et subscripcione eiusdem sigillum meum apposui. Data apud Poterne predict*o* die et anno domini supradictis presentibus discretis viris dominis Johanne Wyther' subdecano ecclesie cathedralis Sarum Andrea Swynford' rectore ecclesie parochialis de Mauston' et Thoma Thirlewall' clerico ac aliis testibus ad premissa vocatis specialiter et rogatis.

Et ego Johannes Holand' clericus Exoniensis diocesis publicus auctoritate apostolica notarius premissis testamenti faccionem ordinacionem constitucionem donacionem et disposicionem ac omnibus aliis et singulis dum sic ut premittitur per venerabilem in Cristo patrem et dominum dominum Ricardum dei gratia Sarum episcopum sic testantem sub anno mense die et loco prescriptis una cum prenominatis testibus presens interfui eaque sic fieri vidi et audivi ac de mandato eiusdem venerabilis patris occupatus per alium scribi feci et in hanc publicam formam redigi signumque meum hic apposui consuetum in fidem et testimonium omnium premissorum.

Notes

1 MS: 'Ricadus'.

2 Possibly for 'medle'.
3 MS: 'vilet'.
4 MS omits 'cupam'.
5 MS: 'scultam'.
6 MS: 'existentis'.
7 MS: 'Roupar'.

26/2 Grant of probate to Mag. Walter Mitford, Lambeth, 11 May 1407. *LPL, Register of Thomas Arundel, vol. I, ff. 238v–239r.*

26/3 Commission to Mag. John Chaundeler, Dean of Salisbury, and Mag. Adam Mottron, canon of Salisbury, for committing the administration of the goods of Bishop Mitford to his executors named in his will, proved before the Archbishop; the names of the executors to be certified to the Archbishop by letters patent; 10 May 1407. *LPL, Register of Thomas Arundel, vol. I, f. 239r.*

26/4 Acquittance of Mag. Walter Mitford and Mag. Roger Harwell, executors, by the Archbishop of Canterbury, Lambeth, 27 June 1407. *LPL, Register of Thomas Arundel, vol. I, f. 239v.*

26/5 Indenture of receipt to Mag. Walter Mitford and Mag. Roger Harwell, executors, for goods, ornaments and jewels bequeathed to Salisbury Cathedral, the items described in exactly the same words as in the will, in the presence of the Dean, Dom. Thomas Wysbych and Mag. William Spaldewyk', canons of Salisbury, 31 July 1407. *Salisbury Cathedral Library, Salisbury DCM.* Printed in HMC, *Report on various collections*, i, pp. 350–1, omitting the opening clause and the witness clause.

27 Guy Mone, Bishop of St David's

Will, 17 August 1407 *LPL, Register of Thomas Arundel, vol. I, ff. 246v–247r*
In nomine sancte et individue Trinitatis patris et filii et spiritus sancti ego Guido dei gracia Menevensis episcopus bone et sane mentis ac corporis laudes deo considerans quod breves dies hominis sunt quod nil hora mortis incersius testamentum meum ex deliberacione michi desuper tradita decimo septimo die mensis Augusti anno domini millesimo CCCC^{mo} septimo in manerio meo de Charleton' Roffensis diocesis condo in hunc modum. In primis omnipotenti deo creatori meo et beatissime virgini matri sue ac omnibus sanctis eius animam meam et corpus meum sepeliendum in ecclesia conventuali de Ledys Cantuariensis diocesis videlicet in cancello dicte ecclesie conventuali in parte boriali juxta magnum altare. Item volo et constituo quod in exequiis meis quinque cerei ponderis cuiuslibet cerei quinque lib. ad ardendum in eisdem exequiis meis in die sepulture mee. Item volo et ordino quod unus pannus de nigro russeto ponatur super corpus meum cum cruce de panno lineo et quod idem pannus meis exequiis completis pauperibus distribuatur. Item volo quod xx^{ti} quatuor vestiantur de russeto panno die exequearum mearum et quod iidem pauperes teneant circa corpus meum xx^{ti} quatuor torticios de bona assisa tempore exequearum mearum quibus exequiis completis ad usum illius ecclesie de Ledis predicte iidem torticii

remaneant. Item volo quod quilibet pauper veniens ad exequeas meas habeat et recipeat de bonis meis unum denarium monete Anglicane in die sepulture mee ad orandum pro anima mea. Item volo et ordino quod executores mei cum omni festinacione possibili post decessum meum x milia missarum pro anima mea faciant celebrari et ad hoc eosdem exortor in nomine domini nostri Jhesu Cristi sicut inde in extremi judicii examine voluerint respondere. Item volo lx trigentalia beati Gregorii pro anima mea celeriter celebrentur. Item lego dicte ecclesie conventuali de Ledis si corpus meum ibi sepelliri contigerit ad orandum pro anima mea xl li. sterlingorum ita quod illi xl li. expendantur in reparacione et emendacione ipsius ecclesie juxta dispocicionem executorum meorum. Item lego ecclesie collegiate de Maydenston' magnum portiforium et magnum missale que nuper per Wennocum Chamburleyn clericum meum scribi feci ita quod iidem libri ibidem remaneant pro perpetuo. Item volo et ordino quod executores mei tres capellanos bone et honeste conversacionis sumptibus meis[1] ad celebrandum super illud altare prope quod sepultus ero septem annis continuis inmediate decessum meum sequentibus et volo quod predicti executores mei si eis videbitur expedire capellanos huiusmodi amoveant et in loco eorum deputent alios et subregent secundum disposicionem desuper eis datam tociens quociens eis videbitur expediens et honestum. Item lego cuilibet capellano interessenti exequiis meis et missam ibidem celebranti [*f. 247r*] duos solidos missam vero non celebranti duodecim denariis. Item lego reverendissimo in Cristo patri et domino domino Thome dei gracia Cantuariensi archiepiscopo unum ciphum aurum precium xl li. et eciam xl li. in pecunia numerata. Item lego operi sancte et venerabilis ecclesie Cantuariensis xl marcas. Item lego Henrico Pomfret civi et cellar*ari*o London' C marcas quas dictus Henricus et Simon Do*st*er michi debent per eorum scriptum obligatorium. Ad istud testamentum et meam ultimam voluntatem perimplenda Drugonem Barentyne Willelmum Walderne et Henricum Pomfreyt cives London' Thomam Rede domicellum de partibus Wallie magistrum Robertum Raulyn canonicum meum in ecclesia cathedrali Menevensi ac Willelmum Maydenston' camerarium meum ordino facio et constituo meos executores ac eis residuum omnium bonorum non legatorum do et lego ut ipsi huiusmodi residuum bonorum meorum michi in pios usus pro salute anime mee animarumque amicorum meorum et omnium fidelium defunctorum disponant meliori modo quo poterint et sciverint prout coram summo judice in die extremi judicii voluerint inde respondere.

Notes

1 MS: 'meiis'.

28 Michael Northburgh, Bishop of London

28/1 Will, 23 May 1361, and grant of probate, 15 September 1361

Guildhall Library, London, MS 25271/47 (formerly MSS of Dean and Chapter of St Paul's, A., Box 67, no. 47)

One membrane, with a further membrane containing the instrument of probate annexed: the tongue for the seal of this last has been put through a slit in the first membrane, and sealed on the further side. Seals: 1. Main will sealed on a tongue now with only a fragment of a seal in red wax surviving. 2. Vesica-shaped, in green wax, now a fragment, with a bishop in pontificals, attached to the probate and threaded through the will. Endorsements: 1. Contemporary note of probate in the Husting Court of London, 13 December 1361: 'Istud testamentum fuit probatum proclamatum et irrotulatum in hustengo London' de communibus placitis tento die lune in festo sancte Lucie anno regni regis Edwardi tercii post conquestum tricesimo quinto. Lucas.' The probate entry on the court roll is summarised in *CCH*, ii, pp. 61–2. 2. In late fourteenth-century hands: 'Testamentum Michaelis nuper episcopi London''; 'Sol''; 'R. Wodel''; 'xliio'.

The will is discussed by R.M. Haines, 'Michael Northburgh', *ODNB*, xli, pp. 130–2.

In nomine et fide summe sanctissime Trinitatis ac dulcis Jhesu pro me crucifixi dulcissimeque et benignissime genitricis sue Marie beatissime delectricis dei Magdalene apostolorum Petri et Pauli et Andree et virginum beatarum Katerine Margarete et Fredeswyde ac omnium sanctorum ego Michael minister et servus indignus ecclesie Londoniensis sanus mente ac die decimo kal. Junii anno domini millesimo CCC^{mo} sexagesimo primo aio testandum ordino et facio testamentum meum in hunc modum. In primis comendo miseram peccatricem animam meam passioni mere gracie et miserie salvatoris meritisque et precibus dicte sue genitricis et ceteribus sanctorum corpusculumque ministri peccati humandum ut ingressu occidentali porte majoris dicte ecclesie Londoniensis videlicet extra portam ac pro lapide tegenti[1] corpus sculpturoque transeuntes movere poterit adorandum lego viginti li. Item pro expensis funeralibus volo vestiri panno nigro vel albo aut gresio die sepulture viginti pauperes quorum quilibet teneat in manu circa funus in ecclesia unam torcheam sex lib. cere vel parvum ultra et cum octo cergiis seu cereis circa feretrum transient exequias[2] primo die. De aliis diebus disponant executores mediocriter prout viderint expedire. Volo autem et precipio quatenus plus possum sepulturam meam fieri dum facies absque putredine monstrari poterit cum insigneis ut convenit presulatus. Item lego centum presbiteris pro me inmediate post mortem continuatis diebus celebrantibus religiosis et aliis per executores meos cominus eligendis quotiens celebraverint sex denarios vel augeatur numerus presbiterorum missarum et pecunie eorundem arbitrio executorum. Item lego pro maritagio pauperum puellarum que tales esse se jurent et vicinie fama publica comprobentur in diocese et civitate London' centum li. videlicet pro centum vel quinquaginta puellis arbitrio executorum. Item lego totidem simplicibus non mendicantibus set domum et familiam tenentibus maxime nativis episcopatus Londoniensis totidem li. ita videlicet quod sint opinione puplica bone fame victum de terrula aut labore vel artificio perquirentes. Item lego pro sustentacione duodecim scolarium in jure civili et canonico Oxon' pro quadriennio centum li. et magistro eorum cum eis continue commoranti qui erit presbiter et scolaris et cotidie si poterit pro vivis et mortuis quibus teneor ex sanguine aut beneficio aut meo delicto celebrabit viginti li. Item lego ecclesie conventuali sancte Trinitatis London' videlicet eius fabrice decem li. Item monasterio de Lesnes decem li. ut in utroque monasterio habeam missas. Item pauperibus monialibus de Chesthunte quot sunt moniales tot marce ut dicat quelibet pro me primo anno vicesies psalterium beate Marie virginis et Davidi et presbiter eorum in missa qualibet nominatim pro me oret. Item lego eis unum vestimentum cum pleno aparatu de panno serico et pertinenciis auriatis quod habui nuper de monialibus de Iclinton'. Item lego abbatiis de Westm' et Berkyng' hospitalibus sancti Johannis et beate Marie monasteriis \ monialium / de Wykes et Stratford' cuilibet eorum quadraginta solidos ut in monasteriis virorum celebrentur pro me quo cicius poterint viginti misse et pro hiis quibus teneor ut prefertur. In monasteriis vero mulierum totidem dicantur psalteria Davidi. Item prioratibus de Berden' et the Le cuilibet viginti solidos \ ut / pro me totidem missas dicant. Item lego camere London' decem li. Item ad vias lutosas in Essex' decem li. Item lego Michaeli Fre libros juris civilis quos habet si in studeo perserveret et scolis.[3] Et Cynn*um*[4] meum et opus meum magnum quod voco concordiam juris et canonum. Item lectum meum rubeum laneum et unam integram armaturam missale sine nota bibliam parvam tres discos argenti cum tot salceriis unum byker vocatum Katerina quatuor cocliaria duas mappas et tot manutergia. Item pejorem amiciam meam et capam clericalem et aulam integram quam sibi comodam. Item lego Thome fratri suo si ordine non mendicantium ingredi voluerit decem li. quarum due solvantur pro paramento et residue ipso professo. Item lego cuilibet scutiferorum meorum tempore mortis mecum existenti cuilibet valecto preter Simonem in hospicio meo existenti secundum arbitrium executorum meorum. Simoni vero cum nubere voluerit centum solidos et unam robam de meis minoris valoris. Sin autem nubere voluerit xl s. et robam. Pagis autem et garcionibus prout meruerint executorum concienciis oneratis. Omnibusque meis remitto quicquid per inobedienciam aut negligenciam in me deliquerunt ut orent pro me. Si autem scient vel maliciose male egerint id studient reformare. Hec autem lego eis si nichil insolitum petant pro feodo et de receptis per eos bene et competenter respondeant. Item lego Ricardo de Ambraslee unum ciphum argenti et unum mazerum et viginti solidos et aliquem de lectis \ meis / post tres meliores cum duobus linthiaminibus et alba culcitra si nichil exegat pro feodo. Item lego Johanni de Cantebrugg' piscenario London' si execucionem testamenti mei velit assumere duos discos argenti et duo salsaria et usum tenementorum que perquesivi de eo in parochiis sanctorum Petri et Benedicti ad terminum vite sue. Item lego magistro Johanni filio suo rosarium meum et velit in missis suis et precibus me recomendat habere quem sibi placuerit et unum ciphum argenti et si coexecutor patris sui esse pro me voluerit majorem bibliam meam et aliam legendam sanctorum. Item Rose Hay aliquam capam furratam et aliqua vasa coquine et viginti solidos in quibus michi tenetur. Item lego in North*e*burgh' cuilibet filiolo seu filiole matris mee xi d. Et lx s. distribuendos ibi ut sint precipui Hugo filius Willelmi Basilia et Agnes Bate. Item lego Agneti Hakeney unum anulum et xx s. de debito quo michi tenetur. Item lego domino successori meo si racionabiliter fuerit in exaccionem pro reparacionibus communibus quod solo executorum arbitrio committo et quantum in me est estimo mille marce quia in brevi tempore meo multa feci et reparavi et plurima perquesivi mitram meam meliorem et anulum pontificalem ut facere velit de me in suis missis memoriam et hec relinquat successoribus suis eis cum a capitulo pecierint perpetuo tradenda. Item cuilibet vicario sancti Pauli xl d. Cuilibet choriste xii d. Parvis canonicis inter se lx s. et cuilibet alii minori ministro ecclesie xii d. Item lego anchorisce sancti Egidii leprosorum xl d. et duobus anacoritis sancti Laurencii de judaismo x s. et leprosis de Hakeneye v s. et cuilibet alteri anchorisse London' in civitate vel suburbio infra limites diocesis iii s. Item cuilibet ordini fratrum London' et Carmelitarum de Maldon' unam marcam. Item lego x ulnas boni panni linei domine Marie Dairel et unam marcam. Item lego Johanni North*e*burgh' de Greyby scutifero iiii li. in quibus michi tenetur et ad maritagium filie sue xl s. Item domino Johanni Greyby C s. Item lego duo milia li. hic ad fundandum construendum et complendum quamcitius executores mei hoc facere poterunt quandam domum ordinis Cartusiensis juxta ritum et modum eiusdem ordinis in loco Neuchirchehawe vulgariter nuncupato ubi est ecclesia annunciacionis beate Marie virginis quem locum et patronatum eiusdem perquesivi de domino Waltero de Ma*u*ny milite. Item lego eidem domui cum completa et perfecta fuerit duas pelves argenti meliores quas habeo administrandas in magno altari eiusdem domus et vas meum argenti aymelatum in quo poni soli corpus Cristi et meliorem stopam argenti quam habeo pro aqua benedicta cum aspersorio eiusdem et cum campanella argenti et \ ad / meliorem complecionem dicti operis et dotacionem eiusdem ampliorem lego omnes terminos meos quos habeo in quibuscumque locis usque ad quadriennum post tempus mortis mei. Et nichilominus omnes redditus meos et tenementa quos et que London' habeo et reversiones tenementorum que Johannes de Cantebrugg' tenet de me ad terminum vite sue in civitate London' et omnes alias reversiones quas habeo in eadem civitate lego eidem domui imperpetuum possidend*um* redditibus infrascriptis dumtaxat exceptis. Item lego eidem domui omnes libros meos divini servicii per me non legatos. Item duo meliora integra vestimenta que post mortem meam reperientur. Quod si domus predicta juxta voluntatem meam huiusmodi fieri non poterit tunc prefati redditus tenementa cum reversionibus predictos lego executoribus meis infrascriptis ad vendendum et disponendum de eisdem pro salute anime mee prout eis videbitur melius expedire et voluerint in die judicii respondere. Item eiusdem loci patronatum et omne jus quod in dicto loco habeo cum pertinenciis suis quantum ad me attenet vel poterit attenere lego successoribus meis episcopis London' humiliter regnans eos ob honorem Jhesu Cristi et beatissime Marie virginis et sancti Pauli contratenus ordinancionem dicte domus faciendam et fabricacionem ac compleccionem eiusdem operis cum diligencia supervidant et intendant eisdem. *De magna cista* Item lego ad faciendum unam cistam que stabit in thesauro sancti Pauli mille marcas in eadem includendas de quibus possit quilibet \ pauper / et plebeus sub bono et excedente pignore mutuo recepere x li. decanus et canonici majores xx li. vel xl marcas sub huiusmodi pignore episcopus xl vel vix l et alii nobiles vel burgenses civitatis London' xx li. usque ad annum et preferantur ceteris ministri ecclesie. Post annum autem fiat preconizacio et subhastacio seu licitacio ad crucem in sermone quod infra xiiii dies luat quilibet pignus suum sub pena vendicionis. Et si non veniat fiat vendicio absque dolo quo plus poterit reservando excessu debiti domino pignoris vel eius executoribus vel si nullus habeat quod sciatur pro anima sua in usu aumenti ciste quem puro reputo cedat in episcopo decano et custode operis veteris fabrice usus apparat majus pius. Volo enim quod decanus qui fuerit habeat unam clavem vel eo nolente senior residenciarius canonicus aliam et terciam dominus custos qui jurabunt si placeat fideliter implere ipsius ciste ordinacionem et habeant pro labore et meritum et potestatem recipiendi pro se vel pro uno amico per eos eligendo C s. ultra summas prenominatas vel si opus est disponant executores pro meliori securitate ciste cum bono consilio et jurent mutuantes quod nunquam ordinacioni facte aut faciende contraibunt per prohibiciones inhibiciones preces minas litteras aut aliter qualitercumque sub pena amissionis pignoris vel alicui nocumentum inde procurabunt et qui fraudem in hiis fecerit aut dolo versatus fuerit aut cistam voluntarie minuerit aut dampnificaverit malediccionem dei et beate matris sue sancti Pauli et omnium sanctorum incurrat. Nosque in ipsum quantum possumus trina monicione premiss*orum* execucionem domino committemus in hiis scriptis excommunicacionis sentenciam fulminamus. Item lego redditus omnes quos noviter feci[5] circa pallacium meum sic dividendos quod episcopus qui pro tempore fuerit habeat illos omnes qui sunt ex parte orientali porte posterioris palacii salva domo supra portam quam lego quantum in me est pro perpetuo custodibus operis veteris dum in ea voluerint permanere et larem fovere. Ita quod solvant annuatim ut moris est ministris ecclesie in festo Magdalene unam marcam pro facienda processione. Redditus vero ex parte occidentali sic lego dividendo ut medietas vicineorum porte cedat uni presbitero in ecclesia perpetuo pro me parentibus et ceteris quibus teneo perpetuo celebraturo per episcopum qui fuerit preficiendo. Alia vero medietas cedat in usus perpetuos monasterii cui duo milia li. legavimus sicut supra si eandem domum adimpleri contigerit alioquin eandem medietatem lego executoribus meis ut ipsi de ea disponant et ordinent in alios pios usus prout saluti anime mee viderint convenire. Et volumus quod quandocumque aliquis episcopus huic legato contravenerit per quod hoc legatum effectum non habuerit quod civitas London' habeat ad mundacionem fossarum omnes redditus supradictos per viam legati in quantum eis inde legare poterimus. Non videtur enim nobis quod debeat aliquis episcopus tanto beneficio justo judicio contrarire et quod omnes consenciant humiliter supplicamus. Huius testamenti mei constituo executores venerabiles viros magistrum Michaelem Fre Johannem de Cantebrugg' et magistrum Johannem filium suum in quos plenissime confido et Thomam Frowyk' et rogo dictos executores meos hortor et moneo sub obtestacione divini judicii quatenus voluntatem meam predictam in omnibus fideliter exequantur. Et si voluntas mea juxta ordinacionem meam predictam in toto vel in parte quod absit adimpleri non poterit tunc volo quod executores mei de hiis in quibus voluntas mea sit adimpliri non poterit ordinent prout pro salute anime mee viderint facienda. Et volo et consencio quod ipsi emere possint de bonis meis vere et fideliter estimatis sicut aliis vendere possint et valuit super quo ipsorum conciencias onero. Et quod de residuo bonorum si quod fuerit juxta eorum conciencias pro anima mea disponant in usus quos noverint magis pios. Si quis aut executorum meorum decesserit quod absit volo quod non ad executores mortui set potestas tota plene redeat ad superstites qui sibi assumant alium quem voluerint loco sui competens ei salarium statuentes. In cuius rei testimonium sigillum meum presentibus est appositum et appensum.

Notes

1 MS: 'tegente'.

2 MS: 'exequie'. A classical expression, 'exsequias ire', to go to the funeral: *LS*, p. 701, *sub* exsequiae.

3 His books are noted briefly in Cavanaugh, 'Books', pp. 617–18.

4 One of the works of Cinus of Pistoia, perhaps his *Lectura in codicem*, printed Strassburg, *c.*1475, or his commentary on Justinian's *Digestum vetus*, printed Lyons, 1527.

5 Preceded in the left margin by a note in a late fourteenth- or early fifteenth-century hand: 'Nota: memoranda pro custode veteris operis pro sacerdote sustinendo'.

28/2 Attached grant of probate to Mag. Michael Fre, Mag. John de Cantebreg' and Thomas Frowyk, executors named in the will, 15 September 1361, by William Whittlesey, official of the court of Canterbury, London, on letters from the Archbishop of Canterbury, dated at Otford, 13 September, 1361.

28/3 Commission to Mag. William Whittlesey (*de Witlesey*), official of the court of Canterbury, for proving the will of Michael, Bishop of London, 13 September 1361. *LPL, Register of Simon Islip, f. 181v.*

29 Thomas Percy, Bishop of Norwich

29/1 Will, 25 May 1368 *LPL, Register of William Whittlesey, ff. 105v–106r*
In dei nomine amen nos Thomas permissione divina Norwycensis episcopus xxv die Maii anno domini M^o^CCC^mo^lxviii^o^ in plena sanitate mentis in oratorio nostro apud Southelmham facimus et constituimus testamentum nostrum in hunc modum. In primis animam nostram deo commendamus qui eam redemit sanguine suo et corpus nostrum ad sepeliendum in ecclesia nostra cathedrali[1] Norwycensi ante chorum ecclesie supradicte. Item legamus ecclesie nostre cathedrali supradicte vestimentum nostrum principale cum pertinenciis suis. Item legamus eidem ecclesie unum cros nostrum et unum librum pontificalem quem habuimus ex dono ab executoribus Willelmi quondam predecessoris nostri immediati. Item legamus domine Margarete de Ferers sorori nostre unam cuppam deauratam cum uno aquario eiusdem secte quam comes de Suff' dedit \ nobis. / Item legamus domine Matilde de Nevyll' sorori nostre unam cuppam deauratam cum aquario eiusdem quam dominus comes Arundell' dedit nobis. Item legamus domino Henrico de Percy nepoti nostro unum anulum cum uno ruby meliorem quem habemus. Item legamus domino Thome de Percy nepoti nostro unum godet deauratum quem dominus Edwardus de sancto Johanne dedit nobis. Item legamus magistro Willelmo de Blyth' archidiacono Norff' calicem nostrem meliorem cum fial*a* eiusdem secte et unum ciphum deauratum cum armis nostris in coopertorio eiusdem ciphi sculptum ad modum calicis et unum par de paternoster*es* de auro cum firmaculo eisdem annexo et ii pelves de argento cum armis nostris in fundo et unum ciphum de argento planum quem habuimus ab executoribus reverende domine matris nostre. Item legamus domino Willelmo de Swynflet archidiacono Norwyc' unum ciphum deauratum cum armis domini Bardolf' cum coopertorio. Item legamus eidem duo cocliaria auri et unam aulam tinctam super panno lineo factam linure. Item legamus eidem unum vestimentum quod emimus de eodem. Item legamus domino Ricardo A*n*la*n*by i ciphum deauratum cum armis nostris et coopertorio eiusdem et unum par de paternoster*es* de laumbre cum firmaculo eisdem annexo. Item legamus Willelmo de Aton' nepoti nostro unam cuppam deauratam cum uno aquario eiusdem secte deaurato quam domina de Wynkfeld' dedit nobis. Item legamus capelle beate Marie in campis Norwyc' x li.

Item legamus priorisse et monialibus de Flexton' x li. Item legamus omnes libros nostros qui continentur in una indentura magistro Willelmo de Blyth' archidiacono Norff' ad terminum vite sue et volumus quod post decessum suum dicti libri vendantur et fiant pro anima nostra et sua vel quod donentur aliquibus locis indigentibus ad celebrandum pro animabus nostris. Item legamus capellam nostram cotidianam de viridi cum calice et paxbred*e* et fioles et vestiment*is* ad eandem pertinentibus capelle nostre in palacio ibidem perpetuis temporibus permansuram. Item legamus domino Stephano de Cressyngham vestimentum nostrum dominicale et unam crucem de auro cum pede deaurato cum sancta cruce in medio crucis. Item legamus magistro Johanni de Wynston' unam tabulam de Lumbardia depictam et unum missale quod emimus ab eodem. Item legamus domino Willelmo de Malbus unum maser' cum uno 'T' in fundo et x marcas. Item domino Johanni de Catton' unum aliud maser et x marcas. Item legamus Thome de Watton' x li. et i alium maser. Item legamus domino de Lekyngfeld' C s. Item legamus domino Johanni Roldeston' receptori nostro unum ciphum vocatum Lyon'. Item legamus cuilibet de parvis clericis de capella xl s. Item legamus Johanni Ly*n*ons xl s. Item legamus magistro Willelmo de Kexby C s. Item legamus Thome de Lekyngfeld' pauperi scolari commaranti apud Cantebrugg' lx s. Item legamus Ricardo de Thorton' xl s. Item legamus Roberto de Yver lx s. Item Roberto Caly lx s. Item legamus Willelmo Fe*m*er x marcas. Item legamus Willelmo Bea*u*ner camerario nostro lectum nostrum meliorem brouderatum cum omnibus tapitis pertinentibus eidem et robam nostram de scarleto cum furruris et omnibus pertinentibus ad eandem et lx s. Item legamus Alicie uxori dicti Willelmi lx s. Item legamus Willelmo de Ho*t*ham lx s. Item legamus Thome Barbour iiii li. Item legamus Ricardo de Naserton' coco nostro x marcas. Item legamus Johanni de Estrik' iiii li. Item legamus Johanni de Geryng' vi li. Item legamus Thome de Catton' lx s. Item legamus Ade Wodword' xx s. Item legamus Patricio pistori iiii li. Item legamus filio suo vi s. et viii d. Item legamus Henrico brasiatori lx s. Item legamus Rogero Rand' C s. Item legamus Mar*ie* uxori dicti Rogeri Rand C s. Item legamus Johanni Quinton faulkonario xl s. et omnes faulcones nostros et tercilet gentil et laneres. Item legamus Henrico Kutet xl s. Item legamus Johanni No*u*ble C s. Item legamus Johanni Fouler C s. Item legamus Rogero de aula xx s. Item legamus Roberto de Maldon' xl s. Item legamus Willelmo Kutet xl s. Item legamus Johanni Waryn lx s. et omnes cellas nostras. Item legamus Henrico Hunte iiii li. Item legamus Willelmo Feutrer xl s. Item legamus Thome Thornegg' lx s. Item legamus Waltero de garderoba lx s. Item legamus Johanni Dalton' xl s. Item legamus lotrici xiii s. iiii d. Item legamus Roberto Gylyot lx s. Item legamus Johanni Carter xx s. Item legamus Willelmo Chariotter xl s. Item legamus Johanni Soule de coquina xx s. [*f. 106r*] Item legamus Johanni o þe male falconario xx s. Item legamus Willelmo de boteria xl s. Item legamus Willelmo squiller xx s. Item legamus Willelmo de coquina xiii s. iiii d. Item legamus Willelmo de pistrina[2] xiii s. iiii d. Item legamus Nicholao Geryng' xl s. Item legamus Willelmo Ho*n*e garcioni de charett*e* vi s. viii d. Item legamus garcioni carect*e* de coquina vi s. viii d. Item Petro garcioni venatoris xx s. Item legamus Johanni de Lokyngton' garcioni de camera C s. Item Johanni Go*u*sill' garcioni de camera lx s. Item legamus Henrico Fouler xx s. Item legamus Johanni de Helerton coco xx s. Item legamus Henrico paget lotricis vi s. viii d. Item legamus Johanni paget fouler x s. Item legamus paget porter vi s. viii d. Item legamus paget palfreys vi s. viii d. Item Roberto paget faulkonarii vi s. viii d. Item legamus paget de pultria vi s. viii d. Item legamus ad distribuendum pauperibus die sepulture nostre lx li. Item legamus pro luminaribus circa corpus nostrum x li. Item legamus clericis dicentibus psalteria circa corpus nostrum lx s. Item legamus magistro Willelmo Ferour lx s. Item legamus Ricardo de Castro Bernardi parcario nostro apud Northelmham lx s. Item legamus Ricardo Ha*n*nell' parcario nostro de Southelmham xx s. Item legamus Johanni parcario de Hoxm' xx s. Item legamus Willelmo de Goldesburgh' xx s. Item legamus cuilibet de pauperibus nostris quos pascimus cotidie xiii s. iiii d. Item legamus Johanni Coto*u*n C s. Et quicquid residuum fuerit de bonis nostris sive de fructibus non legatis nec assignatis volumus et ordinamus quod per visum et disposicionem executorum nostrorum distribuantur pauperibus et sacerdotibus pro anima nostra celebraturis et pro debitis nostris solvendis si que fuerint ad que solvenda teneamur. Ad istud testamentum nostrum exequendum constituimus executores nostros dominum Henricum de Percy dominum de Alnwyk' magistrum Willelmum de Blyth' archidiaconum Norff' dominum Willelmum de Swynflet archidiaconum Norwic' dominum Ricardum de A*n*la*n*dby vicarium de Mildnale et dominum Willelmum Malbus rectorem de Whetacre.

Notes

1 MS: 'c\at/h''.

2 MS: 'pistria'.

29/2 Grant of probate to Dom. William de Swynflet, archdeacon of Norwich, one of the executors named in the will, Saltwood, 16 August 1369. *LPL, Register of William Whittlesey, f. 106r.*

29/3 Commission to the Prior of Norwich Cathedral Priory and Mag. Richard Wodelond', rector of the church of Lambeth, Norwich and Winchester dioceses, to commit the administration of the goods in addition to Dom. Henry de Percy, lord of Alnwick, Mag. William de Blyth', archdeacon of Norfolk, Dom. Richard de A*n*la*n*dby, vicar of Mildenhall, and William Malbus, rector of Wheatacre, executors named in the will. A full inventory of the deceased's goods and account of their administration are to be rendered by the feast of the Purification [2 February]. Probably 16 August 1369. *LPL, Register of William Whittlesey, f. 106r.*

29/4 Acquittance of the executors, Lambeth, 21 October 1370. *LPL, Register of William Whittlesey, f. 106r.*

30 Walter Reynolds, Archbishop of Canterbury

30/1 Indenture listing ecclesiastical ornaments delivered to Robert Ambroys, clerk of Archbishop Reynolds, by Brother Richard de Sharstede, sacrist of Christ Church, Canterbury, 30 September 1315. The ornaments are (a) 'mitra preciosa et baculus pastoralis cedrinus' bequeathed by John Pecham to the church of Canterbury for the use of his successors (b) 'vestimentum integrum de rubeo samito desuper cum ramunculis arborum auro brudatis videlicet capa chori casula tunica et dalmatica pro domino archiepiscopo et tunica et dalmatica pro diacono et subdiacono', bequeathed by Robert Winchelsey to the church of Canterbury for the use of his successors (in the codicil to his will, *Winchelsey register*, ii, p. 1343). *LPL, Register of Walter Reynolds, f. 282v.*

30/2 Receipt from the Archbishop to H., Prior of Christ Church Cathedral Priory, Canterbury, for the precious mitre ('mitram illam preciosam') bequeathed by John Pecham to the church of Canterbury. Croydon, 17 January 1320. *LPL, Register of Walter Reynolds, f. 285r.*

30/3 Will, 11 November 1327. *CCA, Chartae Antiquae A14.* Transcribed and discussed in J.R. Wright, 'The testament or last will of Archbishop Walter Reynolds of Canterbury 1327' *Mediaeval Studies* 47 (1985) pp. 445–73. It is endorsed with a note of probate before the Prior and Chapter of Canterbury on 28 November 1327. Also printed are the receipts of the Crown's keepers of temporalities, which show the receipt of jewels, etc., in three almost identical indentures: TNA SC 6/1128/7–8, and E 372/173/44. The will was also transcribed in *Sede vacante wills*, pp. 67–72; and calendared in HMC, *Appendix to Fifth Report*, p. 460.

30/4 Letters of Henry de Eastry, Prior of Christ Church, Canterbury, absolving and releasing Dom. Thomas de Stowe as an executor of the will of Walter Reynolds, the will having been proved before the Prior, *sede vacante*, in chapter, Canterbury, 27 November 1327. *CCA, Register Q, f. 121r.*

30/5 Receipts to the executors, 30 November 1327 *CCA, Chartae Antiquae A41A*

Two small, rectangular membranes, sewn together at the foot with white thread. Mem. 1: Dorse blank. No trace of seal. Mem. 2: Endorsed 'De bonis domini W. archiepiscopi liberatis domino Hugoni sacriste'; and 'A infra'.

[*Mem. 1r*] Universis presentes litteras inspecturis Henricus prior ecclesie Cristi Cant' et eiusdem loci capitulum salutem et pacem. Noverit universitas vestra quod nos tempore confeccionis presencium recepimus et habuimus a discretis viris magistris Johanne de Bruytone Johanne de Reddeswelle Roberto de Reddeswell' Ad*e* de Penynton' dominis Radul*pho* de Wynlesore Johanne de camera Ricardo de Kynton' et aliis domini Walteri dei gracia Cantuariensis archiepiscopi tocius Anglie primatis defuncti familiaribus et sibi dum vixerat assistentibus unum anulum magnum pontificalem cum lapide saphirino magno ornatum in circumferencia cum admiraldis quem idem pater inter vivos feretro beati martiris Thome assignavit et inter anulos suos alios alias dicto feretro collatos in cono dicti feretri orientali ex parte australi voluit collocari. De quo quidem anulo nobis plenarie fore satisfactum et universaliter omnes vicem dicti defuncti qualitercumque gerentes liberamus per presentes eciam si in testamento dicti defuncti de eodem anulo mencio subsequenter habeatur. Item recepimus ab eisdem magistris et aliis de consilio dicti defuncti ex causa depositi unum vestimentum rubium broudatum cum octo garniamentis broudatis de auro de passione sancti Thome quod nobis dicitur esse legatum in testamento dicti patris cum duobus pannis eiusdem secte sic broudatis pro altari cooperiendo subtus et supra et duobus ridillis auro cubatis eiusdem secte. Item unum crismatorium argentuum. Item duo portephor*ia*. Item tres acus de auro pro palleo < quod dictus pater de nostra ecclesia apud se habuit dum vixit ex causa comodati. Item recepimus ab eisdem > \ Item / duas cruces argenteas portatiles \ quas[1] dictus pater[2] de nostra ecclesia apud se habuit dum vixit / ex causa comodati. Item recepimus ab eisdem unum baculum pastoralem. Item unum librum pontificalem et duas cerotecas auro munitas et albis margaritis que futuro proximo archiepiscopo Cantuariensi legata dicunt et ut ea sibi restituamus in eventu. Ad quod quidem faciendum nos expresse obligamus tam dictis magistris quam eciam in persona magistri Johannis de Wymbourn' notarii publici hoc stipulanti archiepiscopo Cantuariensi proximo futuro cum super hoc ex parte alicuius eorum ydonee fuerimus interpellati. In cuius rei testimonium sigillum nostrum commune presentibus fecimus apponi. Data in domo nostra capitulari die festi sancti Andree anno domini millesimo CCC^{mo} vicesimo septimo.

Istam[3] acquietanciam petebant executores testamenti domini W. archiepiscopi in testamento suo nominati.

[*Mem. 2r*] Universis pateat per presentes quod nos Henricus permissione divina prior ecclesie Cristi Cantuar' et eiusdem loci capitulum tempore confeccionis presencium recepimus et habuimus a discretis viris magistris Johanne de Bruyton' Johanne de Reddeswell' Roberto de Reddeswell' Ade de Penyton' dominis Radul*ph*o de Wyndesor' Johanne de camera Ricardo de Kyngton' et aliis domini Walteri dei gracia Cantuariensis archiepiscopi tocius Anglie primatis defuncti familiaribus et sibi dum vixerat assistentibus ex causa depositi unum baculum pastoralem. Item i librum qui dicitur pontificale et duas cirothecas auro munitas et albis margaritis que futuro archiepiscopo Cantuariensi legata dicuntur et ut ea sibi restituamus in eventum. Ad quod quidem faciendum nos expresse obligamus tam dictis magistris quam eciam in personam magistri Johannis de Wymbourne notarii publici hoc stipulanti archiepiscopo Cantuariensi proximo futuro cum super hoc ex parte alicuius eorum congrue fuerimus interpellati. Item recepimus ab eisdem i anulum magnum pontificalem cum lapide saphirino magno oblongo ornatum in circumferencia sex amiraldis et sex rubinis quem idem pater inter vivos feretro beati martiris Thome assignavit et inter anulos suos alios alias dicto feretro collatos in cono dicti feretri orientalis ex parte australi voluit collocari < in > \ de / quo quidem anulo nobis plenarie fore satisfactum et universaliter omnes vicem dicti defuncti qualitercumque gerentes liberamus per presentes eciam si in testamento dicti defuncti de eodem anulo mencio subsequenter habeatur. Item recepimus ab eisdem magistris et aliis de consilio dicti defuncti ex causa depositi unum vestimentum rubeum brudatum cum octo garniamentis brudatis de auro de passione sancti Thome quod nobis dicitur esse legatum in testamento dicti patris cum duobus pannis eiusdem secte scilicet brudatis pro altari cooperiendo subtus et supra et ii ridellis auro cubatis eiusdem secte restituendis illis quibus de jure fuerint restitiuendum. Item recepimus ab eisdem i crismatorium argenteum. Item ii portiforia. Item iii acus de auro pro pallio. Item ii cruces argent*i* portatiles que dictus pater de \ nobis et / nostra ecclesia apud se habuit dum vixit ex causa comodati. In cuius rei testimonium has litteras nostras fieri fecimus sibi patentes. Data in capitulo ii kal. Decembris anno domini M^{o}CCC^{mo}xxvii^{o}.

Istam acquietanciam habent executores et omnia suprascripta restituerunt excepto libro qui dicitur pontificale qui penes eos remansit.

Notes
1 Inserted passage in second hand.
2 MS repeats 'pater'.
3 This sentence in a further hand.

31 Thomas de Ringstead, Bishop of Bangor

31/1 Will, 3 December 1365 *LPL, Register of Simon Islip, ff. 245v–246r*
Testamentum fratris Thome episcopi Bangorensis factum Salopie tercio die Decembris anno domini millesimo CCClxv. In primis lego animam meam deo creatori meo et corpus meum ad sepeliendum in domo fratrum predicatorum London'. Lego eciam illi loco aulam meam totam ad serviendum circa altare et non alibi cum omnibus blantalibus xx li. Item lego fabrice ecclesie Bangor C li. ita tamen quod si successor episcopus Anglicus fuerit alioquin relinquo illud judicio executorum meorum. Si contendat vel litigat pro aliqua reparacione ecclesie domorum vel maneriorum nichil habeat de isto legato quia ego non plus habui ab executoribus predecessoris mei post expensa facta per quinquennium in curia de arcubus. Item lego xl li. ad providendum de vestimentis vel calicibus ecclesiis magis indigentibus de diocese Bangorensi quod melius explorari poterit per fideles viros omni favore excluso sic cum nulla pecunia dividatur nec det illis ecclesiis sed provideatur per executores vel de vestimentis vel de aliis necessariis et distribuantur ille xl li. in rebus et non pecunia et que plus indigerint plus habea*nt*[1] sic cum \ quod / indigencia ista attendatur pene paupertatem parochi*alem* et non aliter. Item lego C li. pro v scolaribus mittendis Oxon' vel Cantebregg' aptissimis qui possunt inveniri de diocese Bangorensi absque personarum accepcione et habeat quilibet eorum iiii^{or} marcas quamdiu ista pecunia duraverit quolibet anno. Nolo[2] tum quod pecunia ista aliquo modo ingrediatur manus parentum predictorum scolarum sed executores ordinent de aliquo fideli religioso vel alio in ipsa universitate qui per singulas ebdomadas eis communes suas ministret et posset prospicere de profectu et quamcito invenerit aliquem eorum non proficientem amoveatur et alius loco sui subrogetur semper tum de dicta diocese. Et ponantur isti prima ad studium juris civilis vel canonici et eligantur tales qui sunt pauperes et non alii super animas executorum. Ponatur annuatim in manibus huius distributoris quantum sufficet in anno pro tot scolaribus et non plus. Et distributor nullo modo sit Wallicus. Item fratribus heremitarum sancti Augustini de Huntyngdon' pro anima matris mee ibidem sepulte et patris mei et Rogeri avunculi mei x li. Item amice mee Aubr*eie* lego x li. que moratur apud H*er*tleborgh' et solvantur sibi celeriter. Item lego conventui fratrum predicatorum Cicestr' pro anima domini Rogeri de Ryngestede ibidem sepulti x li. ut eciam orent pro anima mea. Item conventui Cantebregg' fratrum predicatorum lego meum missale pro animabus parentum meorum et domini Rogeri avunculi mei. Item brevarium meum magnum conventui eidem Cantebregg' et ponatur in cathena perpetua in choro in medio inter priorem et magistrum regentem quod si contingat librum illum propter quamcumque causam amoveri nisi infra tres

dies reponatur volumus quod conventus predicatorum London' extunc proprietatem et titulum habeat in eodem. Item lego fratri Thome episcopo Lamburgensi xl marcas. Item lego xx^ti li. ad faciendum unam cistam infra conventum Cantebregg' de quo studentes possunt[3] pro sufficienti pignore et non aliter quilibet recipere x s. quando indiguerint de qua magister regens et magister studentium claves portent et fidelem compotum et racionem reddant omni anno per tres dies ante festum translacionis sancti Thome ac pecuniam integre ibidem dimittant. Alioquin si defecerint volo quamdiu superjunxerit unus executor quod ipse possit et teneatur dictas xx^ti li. ad usum conventus fratrum predicatorum London' transferri post mortem eorundem executorum. Rogamus provincialem qui pro tempore fuerit quod dictam peccuniam ad conventum London' pro anima nostra transferat quamcito invenerit quod peccunia predicta non fuerit integra in festo predicto translacionis sancti Thome et in ipsa cista simul congregata post quem diem *n*oluimus quod apperiatur cista usque ad [*f. 246r*] festum omnium sanctorum set clausa maneat sigillo prioris signata et claves sigillate sigillo magistri regentis remaneant in custodia prioris toto tempore vacacionis. Item lego fratri Waltero Newport' ordinis predicatorum xl s. Item lego fratri Johanni Somburn' ordinis sancti Augustini London' xl s. Item lego fratri Gilberto Pekham magistro ordinis fratrum minorum xl s. Item lego fratri Johanni Cherleton' heremite Cestr' xl s. Item lego domino Nicholao vicario de Chymeleye viii marcas. Item volo quod anima Thome Daunvers participet specialiter de omnibus elemosinis nostris. Item respiciantur fratres Willelmus de Deylm*er*ssh' Henricus Flor' Johannes Thorneton' Northampton' quilibet eorum ad minus xl s. Item respiciantur omnes servitores mei juxta laborem. Item provideatur semper quod executores habeant expensas illi qui laborant. Item lego fratri Davido de Sternyngton' lx s. Item lego domino episcopo Ossorensi Johanni Thatenhale omnes anulos meos parvos. Item lego mantellum meum melius quod habeo cum capucio sorori Johanne Simonis ordinis predicatorum de Derteford vel quod habeat valorem viii marcas. Item lego fratribus Pencors et Ricardo Wyn magistris sacre theologie ac Willelmo Huse sacre theologie professori cuilibet eorum lx s. pro anima mea et matris mee Emme et Rogeri Ryngsted' ac fratris Willelmi Ryngestede fratris mei si vivant isti fratres. Alioquin habeant conventus eorum pro eadem causa et addatur istis magister Stephanus Co*u*lyngg'. Item fratribus Roberto Wynch' et Thome Langeford cuilibet eorum lx s. pro animabus predictorum ac eciam specialiter Thome Eliensis episcopi. Item ordinetur unus frater in conventu Cicestr' ad celebrandum per annum pro animabus Rogeri de Ryngestede domini Thome Eliensis episcopi specialiter pro anima Thome de Cestria quondam clerici mei et habeat conventus illo anno C s. Et rogamus conventum illum quod admittant illas animas ad omnia < illa > \ sua / suffragia. Item lego fratri Bernardo Herman ordinis predicatorum v marcas et fratri suo eiusdem ordinis ii marcas et ad orandum pro me. Item volo quod inter illos quinque qui debent mitti ad scolas sit Lewelinus ap Howel clericus unus quamdiu duraverint premissa. Item lego Willelmo Danv*er*s pro anima mea x marcas. Item Johanni Hancock' lx s. Item parvo Willelmo de camera lx s.[4] Item sororibus nostris apud Derteford' x li. Item domine Margarie Fokerham sanctimoniali de Romeseye xl s. Item domine Margarie Artur sanctimoniali Ambusbury xl s. Item monialibus de Chesthunte iiii li. Item David ap Bleth*in* v marcas. Item \ volo / quod post obitum meum xx marce liberantur Lore et Matilde sororibus quas dominus Thomas Lamburgensis episcopus bene novit ad distribuendum inter pauperes. Volo tum quod dicte Lora et Matilda habeant ex elemosino xl s. deductos de[5] xx marcis penes ipsas. Item lego socio meo fratri Thome de Ivylcestr' brevarium meum parvum cum lecto meo in quo morior xx[ti] li. Item lego fratri Johanni Beauchamp sacre theologie professori missale meum parvum pro anima mea et Rogeri de Ryngestede. Item lego ecclesie Bangorensi baculum meum pastoralem quem fieri feci de novo. Item lego conventui predicatorum Sarum x marcas. Item lego magistro Radulpho Ryngestede fratri meo magnum ciphum argenteum quem portant tres leones cum ii cuppis deauratis et eorum cooperculis. Item lego conventui predicatorum[6] London' mitram meam novam cum anulo meo pontificali rubeo et ii phiolas novas i bassinum argenteum commune de meis vestimentum novum de velweto totum cum capa et turribulum novum cum i navi pro incenso et i clocleario pro eadem et fiat sumptibus meis unus baculus pastoralis precium xx marcarum ad minus ita quod quando aliquis dominorum episcoporum voluerit honorare locum illum in festivitatibus vel in ordinibus inveniat omnia parata ut oret semper conventus pro animabus parentum meorum et specialiter pro anima domini Rogeri Ryngested' avunculi mei et fratris Willelmi de Ryngestede fratris mei. Et rogamus eciam priorem et conventum qui pro tempore fuerint ibidem London' ut recipiant fratrem Thomam de Ivilcestria socium meum amore mei ad moram perpetuam in predicto conventu. Cetera omnia videlicet vasa argentea cum omnibus que ad capellam pertinent vendantur et distribuantur pro anima mea et animabus patris et matris mee Rogeri de Ryngstede avunculi mei et Thome Eliensis episcopi. Et si qua residua fuerint post funeraria legata debita et expensas executorum distribuantur conventibus fratrum predicatorum Guldeford Cicestr' Chelmesford Cant' Arrundell' Wynton' Turrwe ordinis predicatorum et precipue et ante omnia ubi sunt persone sanctiores. Item lego conventui Cicestr' ordinis predicatorum vestimentum rubeum secundum melius quod habeo cum aurifrisu in memoriam domini Rogeri de Ryngestede et Thome episcopi Eliensis. Item i coopertorium eidem conventui de sindone rubeo ad ponendum super tumbam avunculi mei in diebus anniversarorum suorum. Item lego magistro Edmundo Hengham si effectuose prosequatur causam meam ad honorem dei et ecclesie C marcas. Et si non prosequatur causam et transferat se ad aliud beneficium nichil habeat. Item lego fratri meo Radulpho coopertorium meum cum flour de lys. Executores autem meos ad perficiendum omnia et singula premissa facio et constituto reverendum patrem fratrem Thomam episcopum Lamburgensem et magistrum Radulphum de Ryngestede fratrem meum fratrem Johannem Beauchamp' ordinis predicatorum fratrem Nicholum de Mo*n*yngton' eiusdem ordinis quibus addatur dominus Thomas de Thorp' rector ecclesie de Tydde. Et nolo quod aliquis istorum solus habeat potestatem acquietanciam facere sed duo ad minus. In quorum omnium testimonium sigillum meum presentibus est affixum. Hiis testibus Willelmo de Wolmeston' publico auctoritate apostolica notario fratre Thoma de Ivelcestria ordinis predicatorum Johanne Havekot Henrico Boteler' et aliis.

Notes

1 MS: 'habeat'.

2 MS: 'volo'.

3 MS repeats 'possunt'.

4 At this point the MS has the passage 'Item domine Margerie Artur sanctimoniali Ambusbury xl s. Item monialibus de Cheshunte secundum discrecionem fratris Thome', deleted by subscript

dots as far as 'Cheshunte'. The section appears in the text below without the clause about brother Thomas.

5 MS omits 'de'.

6 MS: 'predicto'.

31/2 Probate granted by Nicholas de Chaddesdenn, the Archbishop's commissary, to Dom. Thomas [de Illeye], Bishop of Lviv (*Lambergensis*), Mag. Ralph de Ryngestede, Brother Nicholas de Mo*n*yngton' and Dom. Thomas de Thorp, rector of the church of Tydd, executors named in the will, with power to include Brother John de Beauchamp also named as executor in the will if he should be received in the due form. London, 9 February 1366. *LPL, Register of Simon Islip, f. 246r.*

31/3 Acquittance by Robert, Prior of Canterbury, of the executors, 3 September 1366. *CCA, Register G, f. 132r.*

32 Inventory and valuation of the goods of John de Sandale, Bishop of Winchester, 2 November 1319, delivered to the Exchequer 24 April 1322 *BL Add. MS 57334*

John de Sandale had a long career as a royal administrator and on his death the Crown was concerned to secure sufficient goods to ensure the payment of any debts outstanding on his accounts. In contrast to most other documents in this volume, this document was not prepared either by the bishop or his executors. The inventory and valuation were compiled on the King's instructions to account for the property taken into royal hands, noting to whose custody they had been committed. The document identified goods that would normally belong to the executors, for example, the acreage of land sown and the crop concerned, as well as stock – which might ultimately belong to the next bishop. Other items, such as hay and forage, which belonged to the Crown during a vacancy, were also identified. At the same time, the inventory gave an overview of the resources, including household goods, that belonged to the incumbent of the richest see in England.

An Exchequer fashion roll of seven rotulets, the last rotulet consisting of two membranes. The roll was derived from a number of separate documents, and this document itself was worked through on several occasions, as follows:

1. The first five rotulets, the front of the sixth and part of the dorse of the seventh, contain appraisals of the manorial goods of the Bishop. These were written by the principal hand of the text, from a document or documents which had already been audited, as the principal hand wrote 'probatur' after each of the manorial totals as the text was written up. That this part of the document was a fair copy can be seen by some of the changes subsequently made to the text, for example, for Overton, where the copyist misread 'vi' as 'xi', and in the account for Rimpton, where nine boviculi valued at 27*s.* could be added in subsequently without an impact on the total. This hand also numbered each rotulet at the foot.
2. A second hand then worked through these sections of the roll, checking the totals and making some changes, before also marking each of them 'probatur'.

3. A number of other clerks worked through the roll on separate occasions: one marked almost every manorial section with an 'S' (perhaps for 'solutum') in the margin – sometimes preceding the name of the manor in the margin, sometimes appearing after it, but in this edition placed after the manorial name in each case. A further clerk or clerks added marginal notes largely about the responsibility of the keepers of the bishopric during the vacancy for sums for hay, forage and litter, usually for less than the amount entered in the account, probably implying that some at least had been used before the keepers could take charge of it or that this was their share of it. Another clerk worked through the text, possibly as part of the auditing process, noting where tallies supported some of the statements: a marginal 'ta'' or 'tal'' appears in these cases.
4. Each of the first six rotulets was examined and a total for the rotulet was given at the foot of the dorse (or the recto in the case of rotulet six), along with a note 'examinatur'. 'Examinatur', in another hand, also appears in the margin against manorial entries on rotulets four, five and six.
5. The inventory of household goods on rotulets six and seven was written up in slightly different fashion. Marginal totals were given probably by the main hand of this text, although it is just possible they were written by a second hand. Many were struck out and another hand wrote totals centred in the text, along with 'probatur'. The final sequence of totals on the dorse of rotulet seven is harder to confirm, amid deletions. A final note added to the roll records its delivery to the remembrancer of the Exchequer on 24 April 1322.

In this edition, the entries made at the second audit, in 2. above, are given between pairs of single square brackets, as is the work noted in 5. of the hand totalling the sections. The work of the other clerks described above has not been individually identified in the text, to avoid encumbering it with evidence of process; but the work of these hands has been distinguished by placing it between pairs of double square brackets.

[*Rot. 1r*] Imbreviacio et appreciacio bonorum et catallorum que fuerunt domini Johannis de Sandale nuper Wynton' episcopi die veneris in festo commemoracionis animarum anno regni regis Edwardi filii regis Edwardi xiii° quo die idem episcopus obiit facte coram Adam de Lymbergh' et Ricardo de Pottesgrave ad hoc assignatis per breve domini regis et ad eadem bona in manu domini regis seisanda

Whetleie. S'. In manerio de Whetleie fuerunt die predicto in grangia per estimacionem xii juratorum xxiiii qr. siliginis precii qr. v s. Summa vi li. Et viii qr. de ordeo precii qr. iii s. vi d. Summa xxviii s. Item l qr. avene precii qr. xviii d. Summa lxxv s. Item ii qr. de pisis et vescis precii in toto iiii s. viii d. Item est ibi fenum ad valenciam xxx s. Item ii carectate straminis precii xvi d. Item iii affri precii cuiuslibet xii s. Summa xxxvi s. Item xii boves precii cuiuslibet viii s. Summa iiii li. xvi s. Et ii vacce precii xiii s. iiii d. in toto. Et ix strek' precii cuiuslibet v s. Summa xlv s. Item i carecta vetus et debilis precii iii s. Item i pelvis cum lavatorio precii di. marce. Item ii olle eree precii di. marce. Item ii parve olee eree precii iiii s. Item ii patelle eree precii xviii d. *Ta'* Item xiii pecia meremii precii in toto viii s. Item iii mense precii in toto xii s. Item x acre seminate cum siligine precii acre iii s. iiii d. Summa xxiii s. iiii d.

Summa xxvi li. iiii s. vi d. Probatur [Probatur]

Brampton'. *S'*. Item habuit apud Brampton' die predicto xviii qr. siliginis precii qr. v s. Summa iiii li. x s. Et vi qr. ordei precii qr. iii s. vi d. Summa xxi s. Et liiii qr. avene precii qr. xviii d. Summa iiii li. xii d. Item xxii carectatas feni precii xliiii s. Item viii carectatas litere precii carectate viii d. Summa v s. iiii d. Item v acras seminatas cum siligine precii acre iii s. iiii d. Summa xvi s. viii d. *Ta'* Item iii affros precii xx s. Item viii boves precii cuiuslibet viii s. Summa lxiiii s. Item viii vaccas precii cuiuslibet vi s. viii d. Summa liii s. iiii d. Item v boviculos et vi juvencas precii cuiuslibet v s. Summa lv s.

Summa xxii li. x s. iiii d. Probatur [Probatur]

Omnia bona predicta committuntur Thome de Arkeseie capellano et Hugoni le Botiller custodienda ad opus domini regis preter animalia que remanent penes Robertum de Sandale.

Esshere. *S'*. Idem defunctus habuit ibidem per estimacionem juratorum ii qr. frumenti precii viii s. Et x qr. avene precii qr. xiiii d. Summa xi s. viii d. Item xxi pecias meremii precii xvi s. in toto. Item l lag. viridis succe precii lag. iiii d. Summa xvi s. viii d. Et i pressuram cum iiii cuvis pro vinis faciendis precii xx s. Item xviii garbas frumenti et xxx garbas avene in grangia apud Northwode pertinentes ad dictum manerium precii xii d. in toto.

Summa lxxiii s. iiii d. Probatur [Probatur]

Bona illa committuntur Gilberto le Forester Ricardo Derling' Johanni Sel*v*en et Hugoni Wytehor' per indenturam custodienda ad opus domini regis.

Ta' Item fuerunt ibidem die predicto i taurus xii vacce et ii boves qui per Johannem de Burton' ballivum de precepto executorum defuncti elongantur precii capitis vi s. viii d. Summa C s.

Summa C s. Probatur [Probatur]

Becheswortb. *S'*. Idem defunctus tenuit manerium predictum nomine custodie racione minoris etatis Rogeri Husee qui erit etatis xvi annorum in festo purificacionis beate Marie proximo futuro. Et sunt ibi in grangia per estimacionem juratorum viii qr. frumenti precii qr. v s. Summa xl s. Et xxiiii qr. ordei precii qr. iii s. iiii d. Summa iiii li. Et xxxiiii qr. avene precii qr. ii s. Summa lxviii s. Et i qr. de vescis precii iii s. iiii d. Et ii affri precii xiii s. iiii d. in toto. Et v boves precii cuiuslibet viii s. Summa xl s. Item i sus precii ii s. Et ii hoggetti porci precii ii s. Et iiii^{or} porcelli precii ii s. Et fenum appreciatum ad iii s. Et i dolium cisare precii vi s. viii d. Et litera precii ii s. Item xiii acre seminate frumento precii acre iiii s. Summa lii s. Et i currus precii ii s. Et ii pecie maheremii precii vi d. Et est ibi maheremium de quadam boveria prostrata post tempus quo habuit custodiam ibidem quod non appreciatur pro eo quod executores dicti defuncti tenentur reedificare domum illam ibidem.

Summa xv li. xvi s. x d. Probatur [Probatur] [[Probatur]]

Bona predicta committuntur Willelmo Husee et Johanni de Burton' per indenturam custodienda ad opus domini regis.

Ta' Johannes de Burton' ballivus vendidit ibidem xii porcos post mortem episcopi et iiii^{xx}ii hogastros precii capitis ii s. Summa iiii li. ii s. De quibus hoggastris et vi porcis de xii porcis predictis nondum est discussum si debeat onerari penes dominum regem nec neque asserit illas esse catallum suum proprium set debet respondere de vi porcis precii capitis ii s. Summa xii s.

Summa iiii li. xiiii s. Probatur [Probatur]

Farnham. S'. Custodes de feno et foragio lxxiiii s. Idem defunctus habuit ibidem die predicto per estimacionem xii qr. frumenti precii qr. vi s. Summa lxxii s. Et viii qr. de ordeo jemali precii qr. v s. Summa xl s. Et viii qr. ordei precii iii s. iiii d. Summa xxvi s. viii d. Et xviii qr. avene precii qr. ii s. iiii d. Summa xlii s. Et ii qr. brasei ordeici precii qr. iii s. iiii d. Summa vi s. viii d. Et iiii qr. brasei avene precii qr. ii s. iiii d. Summa ix s. iiii d. Item xvi acras seminatas frumento precii acre v s. Summa iiii li. Item fenum appreciatum ad C s. Et literam precii iiii s. Et iii bus. pisarum precii xv d. Et ii equos carectarios precii xx s. in toto. Item iiii affros precii cuiuslibet viii s. Summa xxxii s. Et ii coria ii boum precii ii s. Item i carectam ferratam precii iiii s. Et xlvii bidentes precii cuiuslibet xviii d. Summa lxx s. vi d. Et ii cignos precii viii s. Item est ibi maheremium ordinatum pro quadam aula construenda apud Esshere tempore Henrici episcopi predecessoris predicti Johannis quod ad l s. appreciatur. Item vii baliste precii vii s. Dicunt eciam quod Johannes de Heiden' thesaurius dicti episcopi et Nicholus le Spicer de London' asportare fecerunt usque ad domum Augustini de Burnham denarios usque ad summatum unius equi ut apparebat et a domo sua denarios illos usque London' cariare fecerunt pro humacione etc. Dicunt eciam quod Thomas de Folquardby habuit ibi magnam summam denariorum que fuerunt ipsius episcopi. Nesciunt tamen ubi eos detulit. Item sunt ibi iii cuve et i barellus pro piscibus cariandis precii xvi d.

Summa xxviii li. xvi s. ix d. Probatur [Probatur]

Ta' Item fueruent ibi die predicto ii recia pro piscibus capiendis precii iiii li. Et venduntur ibidem xxxi multones precii cuiuslibet xviii d. Summa xlvi s. vi d. Et i olla et i patella debiles eree precii v s. in toto que elongantur per Thomam de Sandale quondam constabularium castri predicti et inde respondere debet.

Summa vi li. xi s. vi d. [Probatur]

Bona predicta committuntur Johanni de Waghle Johanni de Radesole Roberto Heved et Johanni Cok' per indenturam custodienda ad opus domini regis.

i Examinatur

[*Rot. 1d*] *Benteley. S'. Custodes de feno xxxi s. viii d.* Fuerunt ibi die predicto per estimacionem ix affri precii cuiuslibet x s. Summa iiii li. x s. Et x boves precii cuiuslibet x s. Summa C s. Et estimantur ibi de frumento in grangia lxii qr. precii qr. v s. Summa xv li. x s. Item ii qr. drageti precii vi s. Item viii qr. avene precii qr. xx d. Summa xiii s. iiii d. Et iiii^{xx}xii acre seminate frumento precii acre iiii s. Summa xviii li. viii s. Et iiii acre de ordeo yemali precii acre ii s. vi d. Summa x s. Item in granario de frumento i bus. di. frumenti precii xi d. qua. Et fenum appreciatum ad xxvi s. viii d. Et litera precii v s.

Summa xlvi li. ix s. xi d. qua. Probatur [Probatur]

Bona committuntur Willelmo St*int* et Johanni le Charecter per indenturam custodienda ad opus domini regis.

Le Welde. S'. Custodes debent respondere de x s. de feno et foragio ibidem. Fuerunt ibidem die predicto vi affri precii cuiuslibet vi s. viii d. Summa xl s. Et xvi boves precii cuiuslibet x s. Summa viii li. Item i vacca precii iiii s. Item lx multones precii cuiuslibet ii s. Summa vi li. Et C oves matrices precii cuiuslibet xviii d. Summa vii li. x s. Lv hoggastri precii cuiuslibet xii d. Summa lv s. Item i bidens et iii oves matrices de aventicio precii cuiuslibet xviii d. Summa vi s. Item per estimacionem de frumento xlviii qr. precii qr. v s. Summa xii li. Item xvi qr. ordei precii qr. iii s. iiii d. Summa liii s. iiii d. Item de ordeo jiemali v qr. precii qr. iii s. Summa xv s. Et lvi qr. avene precii qr. ii s. Summa Cxii s. Item in granario vi bus. frumenti precii iii s. ix d. Et i qr. ii bus. avene precii ii s. vi d. Item xliiii acre seminate frumento precii acre v s. Summa xi li. Item fenum appreciatum ad viii s. Item litera precii ii s. Et xii capones precii cuiuslibet ii d. Summa ii s. Item i gallus et vi galline precii cuiuslibet i d. Summa vii d. Et iii auce precii cuiuslibet iii d. Summa ix d. Et i pullus precii xviii d. Et iiii vituli precii cuiuslibet xvi d. Summa v s. iiii d.

Summa lx li. xxi d. Probatur [Probatur]

Bona predicta committuntur Thome Calli et Philippo Godhyve custodienda ad opus domini regis.

Ta'[1] Fuerunt ibi die predicto v vacce que venduntur per J. de Heyden' precii cuiuslibet di. marce. Summa xxxiii s. iiii d. Et lix bidentes precii cuiuslibet ii s. Summa Cxviii s. per eundem J. de Heydene. Et xxvii oves matrices precii capitis xviii d. Summa xl s. vi d. eidem J. de Heydene. Et iii hurtardi precii capitis xviii d. Summa iiii s. vi d. eidem J. de Heydene.

Summa ix li. xvi s. iiii d. Probatur [Probatur]

Sutton'. S'. Ibidem per estimacionem xliiii qr. frumenti precii qr. vi s. Summa xiii li. iiii s. Et xxxii qr. ordei precii qr. iii s. Summa iiii li. xvi s. Et iiii qr. ordei precii qr. ii s. viii d. Summa x s. viii d. Et xl qr. avene precii qr. ii s. Summa iiii li. Et iii qr. pisarum precii qr. ii s. Summa vi s. Et iii affri carectarii precii capitis viii s. Summa xxiiii s. Et i affrus precii iiii s. Et xxiiii boves precii capitis x s. Summa xii li. Et vii vacce precii cuiuslibet di. marce. Summa xlvi s. viii d. Et i taurus precii x s. Et iiii boviculi precii capitis iiii s. Summa xvi s. Et iii boviculi i anni precii capitis iii s. Summa ix s. Item iiii vituli precii capitis xii d. Summa iiii s. Item i aper precii ii s. Et i sus precii ii s. Et l multones precii capitis xviii d. Summa lxxv s. Et CC oves matrices precii capitis xvi d. Summa xx marce. Et iiii hurtardi precii capitis xviii d. Summa vi s. Et vi^{xx}xiiii hoggastri precii capitis x d. Summa Cxi s. viii d. Et seminantur ibi xlviii acre de frumento precii acre v s. Summa xii li.

Summa lxxv li. xiii s. viii d. Probatur [Probatur]

Bona predicta committuntur Thome Yacelyn Thome atte Putte et Ricardo Acreman custodienda ad opus domini regis.

Ta' Johannes de Heydene recepit ibidem xl s. de vi vaccis venditis ibidem precii vacce di. marce. Et xlviii s. de xvi porcis venditis precii capitis iii s. Et xxxiii s. iiii d. de xx porciculis venditis precii capitis xx d. Et vii li. x s. de C multonibus venditis precii capitis xviii d. Et vi li. xiii s. iiii d. de C ovibus matricibus venditis precii capitis xvi d.

Summa < xxii li. xii s. vii d. > Probatur [\ xx li. iiii s. viii d. / Probatur]

Alreford'.[2] *S'.* Ibidem per estimacionem liiii qr. frumenti precii qr. v s. vi d. Summa xiiii li. xvii s. Et lx qr. ordei precii qr. iii s. Summa ix li. Et lxii qr. avene precii qr. ii s. Summa vi li. iiii s. Et iii qr. de pisis et vescis precii qr. ii s. Summa vi s. Et xliiii acre seminate frumento precii acre iiii s. vi d. Summa ix li. xviii s. Et ii equi carectarii precii xxiiii s. in toto. Et i affrus precii viii s. Et xx boves precii capitis x s. Summa x li. Item i vacca precii vi s. Item ii juvence precii x s. Et ii boviculi et vii juvence etatis i anni precii cuiuslibet iii s. Summa xxvii s. Et vi vituli precii capitis x d. Summa v s. Et lxvi multones precii cuiuslibet ii s. Summa vi li. xii s.

Et CClxxv oves matrices precii capitis xviii d. Summa xix li. xvii s. vi d. Et Clxxix hoggastri precii cuiuslibet x d. Summa vii li. ix s. ii d.

Summa iiii^{xx}viii li. iii s. viii d. Probatur [Probatur]

Ta' Ibidem Johannes de Heydene ix vaccas et i juvencam precii capitis vi s. Summa lx s. Et i taurum precii viii s. Et CC multones precii cuiuslibet ii s. Summa xx li. Item C oves matrices precii cuiuslibet xviii d. Summa vii li. x s. Item i affrum precii viii s. Et Willelmus de Heywode prepositus vendidit i bovem pro x s. et ii tauros pro xx s. et i boviculum pro vi s. Et iii s. receptis de ii quercubus venditis ibidem prostratis per escaetorem.

Summa xxxiii li. v s. Probatur [Probatur]

Bona predicta committuntur Willelmo le Bacheler Johanni atte Ware Rogero Hardy et Willelmo de Heywode preposito custodienda ad opus domini regis.

Byworth'. S'. Custodes debent respondere ibidem de feno et foragio precii xiii s. Per estimacionem ibidem xxv qr. et di. frumenti precii qr. vi s. Summa vii li. xiii s. Et xxi acre seminate frumento precii acre ii s. iiii d. Summa xlix s. Et x qr. ordei precii qr. iiii s. Summa xl s. Et xxxv qr. avene precii qr. ii s. viii d. Summa iiii li. xiii s. iiii d. Et ii qr. de pisis et vescis precii iiii s. in toto. Et fenum appreciatum ad x s. Et foragium precii vi s. Et iii affri precii ix s. in toto. Et xii boves precii capitis v s. Summa lx s. Et Cl multones precii capitis xv d. Summa ix li. vii s. vi d.

Summa xxx li. xi s. x d. Probatur [Probatur]

Et bona predicta committuntur Johanni Gocelyn et Nicholao Gunnote per indenturam custodienda ad opus domini regis.

Sevenhampton'. S'. Custodes debent respondere de lxv s. de feno et foragio. Per estimacionem ibidem iiii^{xx}xi qr. di. di. bus. frumenti precii qr. v s. iiii d. Summa xxiiii li. viii s. iiii d. Et xlviii qr. ordei precii qr. iii s. iiii d. Summa viii li. Item bericorne iii qr. precii qr. ii s. viii d. Summa viii s. Et C qr. avene precii qr. ii s. Summa x li. Item iiii qr. pisarum precii qr. ii s. iiii d. Summa ix s. iiii d. Et vi qr. de vescis precii qr. ii s. Summa xii s. in toto. Et xxxviii boves precii capitis v s. Summa ix li. x s. Item ix vacce precii capitis iiii s. Summa xxxvi s. Et ii tauri precii i v s. et alterius iii s. Summa viii s. Et vi vituli superannales precii capitis xviii d. Summa ix s. Et iiii boviculi precii capitis iii s. Summa xii s. Et ii juvence precii capitis xviii d. Summa ix s. Et iiii boviculi precii capitis iii s. Summa xii s. Et ii juvence precii in toto vi s. Et vi vituli precii capitis vi d. Summa iii s. Et iii equi carectarii precii in toto xxx s. Et iii affri precii xxx s. in toto. Et Clxxv multones precii capitis xx d. Summa xiiii li. xi s. viii d. Et ix hurtardi precii capitis xx d. Summa xv s. Et CCxv oves matrices precii capitis xvi d. Summa xiiii li. vi s. viii d. Et Cxl hoggastri precii capitis xii d. Summa vii li. Et i carecta ligata cum ferro precii vi s. viii d. Et iiii caruce cum ferramento et apparatu precii x s. Et ii hercie precii iiii d. in toto. Et fenum appreciatum ad xx s. Et litera precii l s. Et i ancer et iii auce precii xvi d. in toto. Et i olla enea precii ii s. Et i tina precii iii d. Et fimus precii xvi d. *Incrementum xii d.* Et li acre seminate frumento precii acre ii s. iiii d. Summa Cxix s.[3] Et viii acre seminate de sprigg' precii acre xv d. Summa x s.

Summa vii li.< xiiii > [\ xv s./] xi d. Probatur [Probatur]

Et bona predicta committuntur Ricardo Basset Willelmo S*u*ard Johanni Emme et Ade le Charetter per indenturam custodienda ad opus domini regis.

[Summa ...iiii^{xx}v li. ...x s. qua. Probatur][4]

[*Rot. 2r*] *Wolvessey. S'. Custodes debent respondere de xliii s. ii d. de feno.* Ibidem per estimacionem lx qr. frumenti precii qr. vi s. Summa xviii li. Et xxxiiii qr. ordei precii qr. iiii s. Summa vi li. xvi s. Et xvi qr. avene precii qr. iii s. iiii d. Summa iiii marce. Item fenum appreciatum ad iiii li. Item v affri precii cuiuslibet xiii s. iiii d. Summa v marce. Et i carecta ligata ferro precii x s. Item i carecta ad fimum precii iii s. iiii d. Et xxxii acre seminate frumento precii acre v s. Summa viii li. Item i qr. iii bus. pisarum precii qr. iii s. Summa iiii s. i d. ob. Item i dolium cisare ibidem precii vi s. viii d.

Summa xliiii li. i d. ob. Probatur [Probatur]

Ta'[5] Bona predicta committuntur Thome Durant Henrico de Medstede et Johanni de Biketon' per indenturam custodienda ad opus domini regis.

Johannes de Heidene ibidem ii equos carectarios precii lx s. quos idem Johannes abduxit oneratos cum argento et jocalibus. Nescitur tamen ubi nec ad cuius usum. Escaetor ibidem unam carectatam feni precii ii s. et iii qr. avene precii qr. iii s. iiii d. Summa x s.

Summa lxxii s. Probatur.

Twyford'. S'. Custodes ibidem debent respondere de xxxvi s. viii d. Ibidem de estimacion*e* lxx qr. frumenti precii qr. vi s. Summa xxi li. Et lxx qr. ordei precii qr. iiii s. Summa xiiii li. Et iiii^{xx} qr. avene precii qr. ii s. viii d. Summa x li. xiii s. iiii d. Item v qr. de vescis precii qr. iii s. vi d. Summa xvii s. vi d. Item fenum appreciatum ad xxx s. Item litera ad valenciam vi s. viii d. Et iiii equi carectarii precii cuiuslibet xiii s. iiii d. Summa iiii marce. Et ix affri precii cuiuslibet x s. Summa iiii li. x s. Et xli boves precii capitis xiii s. iiii d. Summa xli marce. Item iii coria iii boum precii cuiuslibet ii s. vi d. Summa vii s. vi d. Et ii sues precii cuiuslibet iii s. vi d. Summa vii s. Et xv porcelli de tribus quarteriis anni precii cuiuslibet xx d. Summa xxv s. Et viii porciculi precii cuiuslibet ix d. Summa vi s. Et CCCii multones precii cuiuslibet ii s. Summa xxx li. iiii s. Et CCCxlii oves matrices precii cuiuslibet xviii d. Summa xxv li. xiii s. Et Clix hoggastri precii cuiuslibet xii d. Summa vii li. xix s. Et v pelles hoggastrorum precii cuiuslibet iii d. Summa xv d. Et Cxx acre seminate frumento precii acre iiii s. vi d. Summa xxvii li. Et ii carecte ligate ferro debil*es* precii xiii s. iiii d. in toto.

Summa Clxxvi li. xiii s. vi d. Probatur [Probatur]

Merewell'. S'. Custodes de feno et foragio ibidem xi s. viii d. Ibidem per estimacionem xxxiiii qr. frumenti precii qr. vi s. Summa x li. iiii s. Et xl qr. ordei precii qr. iiii s. Summa viii li. Et iiii^{xx} qr. avene precii qr. ii s. viii d. Summa x li. xiii s. iiii d. Et iii qr. pisarum precii qr. iii s. Summa ix s. Item fenum appreciatum ad liii s. iiii d. Item litera appreciata ad v s. Item de equicio in parco de Merewell' xviii jumenta cum xvii pullanis precii cuiuslibet cum pullano xxiiii s. Summa xx li. viii s. Et i jumentum sine pullano precii xviii s. Item quoddam aliud jumentum debile precii vi s. viii d. Et xvi hurtardi precii cuiuslibet ii s. Summa xxxii s.

Summa lv li. ix s. iiii d. Probatur [Probatur]

Ta'[6] Johannes de Heydene ibidem xx li. viii s. de CC ovibus matricibus et iiii hurtardis venditis Henrico de Lyme precii capitis ii s. Et x li. receptis de CC hoggastris venditis eidem Henrico precii cuiuslibet xii d. Et iiii li. xi s. vi d. receptis de lxi ovibus matricibus venditis precii capitis xviii d.

Johannes Sterie quondam prepositus de l s. receptis de l hoggastris venditis precii capitis xii d. Et xvii s. iii d. receptis de ii qr. vii bus. frumenti sic venditis.

Summa xxxviii li. vi s. ix d. Probatur

Stokes. S'. Custodes de feno et foragio xxiiii s. Ibidem per estimacionem lii qr. frumenti precii qr. vi s. Summa xv li. xii s. Et xxvi qr. ordei precii qr. iii s. Summa < lxxvi s.> [\ lxxviii s. /] Et lx qr. avene precii qr. ii s. viii d. Summa viii li. Et vi qr. fabarum precii qr. iiii s. Summa xxiiii s. Item i qr. pisarum precii iiii s. Et iii qr. de vescis precii qr. ii s. viii d. Summa viii s. Et fenum appreciatum ad viii marcas. Et litera precii iiii s. Et iii jumenta affraria precii cuiuslibet i marce. Summa xl s. Et viii boves precii cuiuslibet x s. Summa iiii li. Et iii coria boum precii cuiuslibet ii s. Summa vi s. Et ii boviculi etatis ii annorum precii x s. Et iii boviculi etatis i anni precii cuiuslibet iii s. iiii d. Summa x s. Et vi vituli precii capitis xii d. Summa vi s. Item i carecta ligata ferro precii viii s. Et xl acre seminate frumento precii acre iiii s. vi d. Summa ix li. Item xv capones precii capitis ii d. Summa ii s. vi d. Et i gallus et viii galline precii capitis i d. Summa ix d. Item ii anceres et iiii auce precii capitis iii d. Summa xviii d. Et lardarium precii in toto xxvi s. viii d.

Summa liii li.< vi s. > [\ viii s. /] i d. Probatur. [Probatur]

Johannes Eilleward prepositus debet respondere de xxi s. receptis de iii qr. di. frumenti venditis ibidem.

Merdon'. S'. Custodes ibidem xxvi s. viii d. de feno et de xxvi s. viii d. de litera ibidem. Ibidem per estimacionem Clxx qr. frumenti precii qr. vi s. Summa li li. Et xl qr. ordei precii viii li. videlicet qr. iiii s. Item Cx qr. avene precii qr. ii s. viii d. Summa xiiii li. xiii s. iiii d. Et iiii qr. pisarum precii qr. iiii s. Summa xvi s. Et ii qr. de vescis precii qr. ii s. vi d. Summa v s. Item fenum appreciatum ad xl s. Item xi affri precii capitis viii s. Summa iiii li. viii s. Item iiii equi carectarii precii capitis xii s. Summa xlviii s. Item liiii boves precii capitis i marce. Summa xxxvi li. Et i taurus precii x s. Et xiii vacce precii capitis viii s. Summa Ciiii s. Et v boviculi etatis ii annorum precii capitis v s. Summa xxv s. Et vi boviculi precii capitis iiii s. vi d. Summa xxvii s. Et viii vituli precii capitis xviii d. Summa xii s. Item i aper precii iii s. iiii d. ii sues precii v s. Et x porci etatis di. anni precii cuiuslibet xx d. Summa xvi s. viii d. Item xxvii porcelli precii capitis xvi d. Summa xxxvi s. Item Cxx oves matrices precii capitis xviii d. Summa ix li. Item Ciiii^{xx}iiii hoggastri precii capitis xii d. Summa ix li. iiii s. Item ii pelles ii hoggastrorum precii iii d. Item Cxxv acre seminate frumento precii acre iiii s. vi d. Summa xxviii li. ii s. vi d. Item iii carecte ligate ferro precii xx s. in toto. Item ix pecie maheremii precii cuiuslibet pecie ii s. Summa xviii s. Item litera precii xxvi s. viii d.

Summa Ciiii^{xx}i li. ix d. Probatur [Probatur]

Ta' Johannes de Heydene ibidem xxvi s. viii d. de iiii boviculis iii annorum venditis. Et lii s. de xiii porcis venditis. Et xxvi li. xiiii s. de CClxvii multonibus venditis videlicet quilibet pro ii s. Et xii li. xv s. receptis de Clxx ovibus matricibus venditis quelibet pro xviii d.

Summa xliii li. vii s. viii d. Probatur

ii Examinatur

[*Rot. 2d.*] *Craule. S'. Custodes de litera iii s.* Ibidem per estimacionem xlviii qr. frumenti precii qr. vi s. Summa xiiii li. viii s. Et iiii^{xx} qr. ordei precii qr. iiii s. Summa xvi li. Et iiii^{xx} qr. avene precii qr. ii s. viii d. Summa x li. xiii s. iiii d. Et ii qr. pisarum precii viii s. in toto et di. qr. de vescis precii xv d. Et in granario xii bus. frumenti precii ix s. Item iii equi carectarii precii capitis x s. Summa xxx s. Et vi affri precii capitis viii s. Summa xlviii s. Item i carecta ligata ferro precii vi s. viii d. Item xxii boves precii capitis x s. Summa xi li. Et xiiii vacce precii capitis vi s. viii d. Summa iiii li. xiii s. iiii d. Item vi boviculi etatis iii annorum precii capitis v s. Summa xxx s. Item vi boviculi etatis ii annorum unde iii masculi precii capitis iii s. iiii d. Summa xx s. Item vii vituli precii capitis xiiii d. Summa viii s. ii d. Item lxx multones precii capitis ii s. Summa vii li. Et CCi oves matrices precii capitis xviii d. Summa xv li. xviii d. Et xviii hurtardi precii capitis ii s. Summa xxxvi s. Et CCiiii^{xx}xiiii hoggastri precii cuiuslibet xii d. Summa xiiii li. xiiii s. Et xlvi acre seminate frumento precii acre iiii s. Summa ix li. iiii s. Et litera ad valenciam iii s. Et iii pelles iii multonum precii x d.

Summa Cxii li. xv s. i d. Probatur [Probatur]

Ta' Ibidem Johannes de Heidene recepit xxv li. de qua\dam/ summa denariorum recepta de CCCC multonibus venditis. Et Johannes de Kirkeby \ prepositus / habet residuum denariorum illorum videlicet xv li. quia vend*itis* quilibet pro ii s. Et idem prepositus respondere debet de denariis receptis de CCiiii^{xx}xviii ovibus matricibus venditis quelibet pro xviii d. unde summa xxii li. vii s. Et de iiii s. receptis de ii hurtardis venditis. Et de xxiii s. iiii d. receptis de iii qr. di. frumenti venditis precii qr. di. marce.

Summa lxiii li. xiiii s. iiii d. Probatur

Alta Clere. S'. Custodes debent respondere de xxxii s. de feno et foragio. Ibidem per estimacionem xx qr. frumenti precii qr. v s. Summa C s. Et xvi qr. ordei precii qr. iii s. iiii d. Summa liii s. iiii d. Et viii qr. de drageto jemali precii qr. ii s. vi d. Summa xx s. Et xxvi qr. avene precii qr. ii s. Summa lii s. Et iii qr. de alio drageto precii qr. ii s. Summa vi s. Et fenum ad valenciam xl s. Et litera precii ii s. Item ii equi carectarii precii xxvi s. viii d. Et vii boves precii cuiuslibet x s. Summa lxx s. v vacce precii cuiuslibet vi s. Summa xxx s. Et iii boviculi annales precii capitis iii s. iiii d. Summa x s. Et xx vituli precii capitis xvi d. Summa xxvi s. viii d. Et xii coria vaccarum precii cuiuslibet xiiii d. Summa xiiii s. Et iii coria boum precii cuiuslibet xviii d. Summa iiii s. vi d. Et iiii coria boviculorum precii cuiuslibet viii d. Summa ii s. viii d. Item i taurus precii xii s. Et v pullani trium annorum precii capitis xxx s. Summa vii li. x s. Et iiii^{or} pullani ii annorum precii capitis xxiiii s. Summa iiii li. xvi s. Et vii pullani i anni precii capitis xx s. Summa vii li. Item Clxiii multones precii capitis ii s. Summa xvi li. vi s. Item i carecta ferrata debilis precii vi s. viii d. Et seminantur ibidem ii qr. di. frumenti super x acr*as* et valet acra v s. Summa l s. Item in granario ii qr. di. frumenti precii qr. v s. Summa xii s. vi d.

Summa lxii li. xi s. Probatur [Probatur]

Ta' Johannes de Heidene ibidem ii pullanos iii annorum precii cuiuslibet iiii marcarum unde summa Cvi s. viii d. Et x li. xviii s. de Cix multonibus venditis precii capitis ii s. qui denarii liberantur eidem J. de Heidene. Et venduntur iiii vacce pro xxvi s. viii d. precii capitis di. marce. Et ii vacce pro viii s. in toto quia dubitabatur de morina eorundem. Et ii vacce venduntur pro vi s. propter eandem causam ut dicebatur et i vacca pro ii s. Et denarii predicti videlicet xlii s. viii d. sunt in manibus Johannis Gatting' prepositi. Et idem prepositus debet respondere de x s. receptis de maheremio vendito per escaetorem.

Summa xviii li. xvii s. iiii d. Probatur [Probatur]

Burgh' Clere. S'. Custodes debent respondere de < xvi > \ xxi / s. de feno et foragio. Ibi per estimacionem etc. Cx qr. frumenti precii qr. iiii s. viii d. Summa xxv li. xiii s. iiii d. Et xxiiii qr. ordei precii qr. iii s. Summa lxxii s. Et vi qr. drageti precii qr. ii s. viii d. Summa < xviii s. > [\ xvi s. /] Et xvi qr. mixtilionis precii qr. iii s. Summa xlviii s. Et iiii^{xx} qr. avene precii qr. ii s. Summa viii li. Et iiii^{or} qr. pisarum precii qr. ii s. Summa viii s. Et ii qr. minutarum pisarum precii qr. xx d. Summa iii s. iiii d. Et fenum ad valenciam xvi s. Et litera precii v s. Et iii equi carectarii precii capitis vi s. viii d. Summa xx s. Et xl boves precii capitis xiii s. iiii d. Summa xxvi li. xiii s. iiii d. Item CCCCxxxvi oves matrices precii cuiuslibet xvi d. Summa xxxix li. xvi d. Item ii coria ii boum precii iii s. Et iiii^{xx}xii acre seminate frumento precii acre iiii s. Summa xviii li. viii s. Item i carecta ligata ferro precii di. marce. Item seminantur de ordeo jemali mixto cum frumento iiii qr. super viii acr*as* et valet acra iii s. iiii d. Summa xxvi s. viii d.

Summa Cxix li. < ii s. > viii d.[7] Probatur [Probatur]

North' Waltham. S'. Estimantur ibi xii qr. frumenti precii qr. vi s. Summa lxxii s. Et xii qr. ordei precii qr. iii s. iiii d. Summa xl s. Et vii qr. drageti precii qr. xviii d. Summa x s. vi d. Item l qr. avene precii qr. ii s. iiii d. Summa Cxvi s. viii d. Et in granario i qr. frumenti precii vi s. et di. qr. drageti precii ix d. Et xii affri precii capitis vi s. viii d. Summa iiii li. Et Cxii multones precii capitis xx d. Summa ix li. vi s. viii d. Et xlviii acre seminate de drageto precii acre ii s. Summa iiii li. xvi s. Et \x/xxix acre seminate de frumento precii acre ii s. vi d. Summa iiii li. xvii s. vi d.

Summa xxxv li. vi s. i d. Probatur [Probatur]

Memorandum Et venduntur ibi post diem predictum iiii^{xx}xi multones precii capitis xx d. Summa vii li. xi s. viii d. per preceptum J. de Heydene qui recepit denarios predictos.

Summa vii li. xi s. viii d.

Nutangre. S'. Estimantur ibi de frumento l qr. precii qr. v s. Summa xii li. x s. Item x qr. ordei precii qr. iii s. Summa xxx s. Et vi qr. de bere precii qr. iii s. Summa xviii s. Et liiii qr. avene precii qr. ii s. Summa Cviii s. Et i qr. pisarum precii ii s. iiii d. Et i qr. de vescis precii ii s. Item ii equi carectarii precii ix s. Summa xviii s. Et i carecta ligata ferro debil*is* precii iiii s. Item i bos precii viii s. Et corium i bovis precii ii s. Item v affri precii capitis vii s. Summa xxxv s. Clxxii multones precii capitis ii s. Summa xvii li. iiii s. Et Cl hoggastri precii capitis xi d. Summa vi li. xvii s. vi d. Et sunt ibi seminate de frumento xi qr. vii bus. frumenti super xliiii acr*as* precii acre iiii s. Summa viii li. xvi s. Item x acre et di. seminate de drageto yemali precii acre iii s. Summa xxxi s. vi d.

Summa lviii li. vi s. iiii d. Probatur [Probatur]

Venduntur ibi post mortem episcopi C multones quilibet pro ii s. Summa x li. et liberantur J. de Heydene denarii predicti. Et xl multones per ballivum quilibet pro xx d. Summa lxvi s. viii d. et denarii sunt in man*ibus* prepositi.

Summa xiii li. vi s. viii d. Probatur [Probatur]

[[Summa totalis ex utraque parte M^{l}iiii^{xx}vii li. vii s. iiii d. ob.]][8]

[*Rot. 3r*] *Overton'. S'. Custodes vi s. de feno et foragio. Examinatur.* Estimantur ibi de frumento in grangia xxxv qr. precii qr. v s. iiii d. Summa ix li. vi s. viii d.[9] Et xxxiiii qr. ordei precii qr. iii s. iiii d. Summa Cxiii s. iiii d. Et viii qr. drageti precii qr. ii s. Summa xvi s. Et xxx qr. avene precii qr. ii s. iiii d. Summa lxx s. Et iii qr. pisarum precii qr. iii s. Summa ix s. Et fenum appreciatum ad iiii s. Et litera precii ii s. Et Cl multones precii capitis ii s. Summa xv li. Et CCxxxviii oves matrices precii capitis xx d. Summa xix li. xvi s. viii d. Et Clix hoggastri precii capitis xiii d. Summa viii li. xii s. iii d. Item x affri precii capitis ix s. Summa iiii li. x s. Et ii boves precii xvi s. Item i carecta ligata ferro precii iiii s. Item i ancer et iii auce precii cuiuslibet iii d. Summa xii d. Et seminantur de frumento xix qr. videlicet super lxi acr*as* videlicet super acr*am* ii bus. di. precii acre iiii s. Summa xii li. iiii s.

Summa iiii^{xx}i li. iiii s. xi d. Probatur [Probatur]

Examinatur. Et venduntur per preceptum J. de Heydene CCxiiii multones precii capitis ii s. Summa xxi li. viii s. Et xxx multones quilibet pro xx d. Summa l s. Et CCxii oves matrices quelibet pro xx d. Summa xvii li. xiii s. iiii d. Et xxxii oves venduntur quelibet pro xvi d. Summa xlii s. viii d. Et ii equi carectarii pro xxvi s. viii d. unde Willelmus Aykheved debet respondere de precio unius equi et Nicholus de Wodemancote ballivus de precio alterius equi. Et x coria boum venduntur precii cuiuslibet ii s. Summa xx s. quos denarios J. Heyden recepit. Et venduntur coria ii vaccarum mortuarum pro iii s. Et corium i boviculi pro xv d. qui in morina comp*utum* post mortem dicti episcopi. Et debentur per Thomam prepositum de Waltham x s. viii d. de viii vitulis sibi venditis post mortem dicti episcopi quilibet pro xvi d. Et in manibus prepositi sunt xxx s. recepti de v qr. frumenti venditis precii qr. vi s. Et v s. recepti de i qr. di. curalli venditis. Et lxv s. recepti de lx hoggastris venditis precii capitis xiii d. Et xii d. recepti de pellibus ii ovium matricum in morina.

Summa li li. xvi s. vii d. Probatur [Probatur]

Wydhey. S'. Custodes debent respondere de iii s. de feno et foragio. Ibi estimantur xxxiiii qr. frumenti precii qr. v s. iiii d. Summa ix li. xvi d. Et xvii qr. ordei precii qr. iii s. iiii d. Summa lvi s. viii d. Et ii qr. et di. drageti precii qr. ii s. iiii d. Summa v s. x d. Et iiii qr. de alio genere drageti precii qr. ii s. viii d. Summa x s. viii d. Et xix qr. avene precii qr. ii s. Summa xxxviii s. Et ii equi carectarii precii xxiiii s. in toto. Et i carecta ferrata debilis precii iii s. iiii d. Et xvi boves precii cuiuslibet x s. Summa viii li. Et CCiiii^{xx}xvi multones precii capitis ii s. Summa xxix li. xii s. Et i qr. di. pisarum precii iii s. Et i qr. de vescis precii ii s. Item pellis unius multonis mortui post mortem episcopi precii v s. Et fenum precii ii s. Et litera precii xii d. Et seminantur ibidem xxiiii acre de frumento precii acre iiii s. Summa iiii li. xvi s. Item xxii acre drageti precii acre iii s. Summa lxvi s.

Summa lxii li. ii s. iii d. Probatur [Probatur]

*Esshem*an*sworth'. S'. Custodes debent respondere de x s. de feno et foragio.* Estimantur ibi xxxii qr. frumenti precii qr. iiii s. Summa vi li. viii s. Et xii qr. ordei precii qr. iii s. iiii d. Summa xl s. Et xxxiiii qr. avene precii qr. ii s. Summa lxviii s. Et v qr. de ordeo jemali precii qr. ii s. Summa x s. Item i qr. ordei et fabarum precii xx d. Et i qr. de vescis precii ii s. Et est ibidem fenum precii x s. Et i qr. pisarum precii ii s. Item v affri precii cuiuslibet v s. Summa xxv s. Et xvii boves precii cuiuslibet x s. Summa viii li. x s. Et CC multones precii cuiuslibet ii s. Summa xx li. Et Cxxv oves matrices precii capitis xx d. Summa x li. viii s. iiii d. Et v pelles ovium precii cuiuslibet iii d. Summa xv d. Item vii hogastri precii capitis xii d. Summa vii s. Et ii pelles hoggastrorum precii iii d. Item i carecta debilis precii xii d. Et litera precii xii d. Et seminantur ibi xxi acre de vi qr. di. frumenti precii acre v s. Summa Cv s.

Summa lix li. vi d. Probatur [Probatur]

Dounton'. S'. Custodes vii li. xvi s. de feno. Estimantur ibidem iiii^{xx} qr. frumenti precii qr. v s. Summa xx li. Et Clx qr. ordei precii qr. iii s. iiii d. Summa xxvi li. xiii s. iiii d. Et lxx qr. avene precii qr. ii s. iiii d. Summa viii li. iii s. iiii d. Et v qr. pisarum precii qr. iii s. iiii d. Summa xvi s. viii d. Et v qr. de vescis precii qr. ii s. viii d. Summa < xv s. x d. > [\ xiii s. iiii d. /] Item fenum appreciatum ad x li. Et vi equi carectarii precii cuiuslibet x s. Summa lx s. Et xvi affri precii cuiuslibet viii s. Summa vi li. viii s. Et xlvi boves precii cuiuslibet x s. Summa xxiii li. Item i taurus precii xii s. Et xx vacce precii cuiuslibet viii s. Summa viii li. Et v boviculi etatis ii annorum precii cuiuslibet v s. Summa xxv s. Item ix boviculi etatis unius anni precii cuiuslibet iiii s. Summa xxxvi s. Et iii vituli precii cuiuslibet xviii d. Summa iiii s. vi d. Et CCCClv multones precii cuiuslibet xxi d. Summa xxxix li. xvi s. iii d. Item xiiii hurtardi precii cuiuslibet xviii d. Summa xxi s. Item CCCxxix oves matrices precii cuiuslibet xvi d. Summa xxi li. xviii s. viii d.[10] Item CClx hoggastri precii cuiuslibet [xi d.][11] Summa xi li. xviii s. iiii d. Et iiii^{xx} capri precii cuiuslibet xii d. Summa iiii^{or} li. Et ii apri precii in toto vi s. Et iiii sues precii cuiuslibet iii s. Summa xii s. Et ix porciculi precii cuiuslibet xv d. Summa xi s. iii d. Et xlii porcelli precii cuiuslibet vi d. Summa xxi s. Item vi cigni videlicet iii paria de eyrers precii in toto xxx s. Item viii cigni etatis i anni precii cuiuslibet iiii s. Summa xxxii s. Item viii pulli de hoc anno precii cuiuslibet iii s. Summa xxiiii s. Item ii pavones precii in toto ii s. Et vi pavones precii cuiuslibet viii d. Summa iiii s. Item iii pullani femelli quarum i trium annorum de equicio precii lxvi s. viii d. et alia de eodem equicio ii annorum precii liii s. iiii d. et tercia i anni de eodem equicio precii xxx s. Item ii pull*an*i de hoc anno affrorum precii in toto iiii s. Item ii carecte ligate ferro precii xiii s. iiii d. Et i corium i jumenti precii xviii d. Et i ancer et iii auce precii in toto xii d. Et Cxxxvi acre seminate frumento precii acre iiii s. vi d. Summa xxx li. xii s.

Summa CCxxxv li. < xiii s. > [\ x s. vi d. /] Probatur [Probatur]

Ta' Et venduntur ibidem iii pullani affrorum etatis unius anni precii cuiuslibet viii s. Summa xxiiii s. Et ii pullani de hoc anno precii in toto iiii s. Et corium i bovis precii ii s. Et ii boviculi etatis ii annorum pro x s. in toto. Et CCxl multones precii cuiuslibet xxi d. Summa xxi li. Et lx multones pro C s. videlicet quilibet pro xx d. Et CCC oves matrices pro xx li. quelibet pro xvi d. Et xii porci venduntur pro xxiiii s. videlicet quilibet pro ii s. Et iiii porc*i* venduntur pro v s. iiii d. quilibet pro xvi d. Item venduntur ibidem v qr. frumenti qr. pro v s. Summa xxv s. Et xii qr. vii bus. ordei precii qr. iiii s. Summa li s. vi d. Et iiii qr. vii bus. avene precii qr. ii s. iiii d. Summa xi s. iii d. ob. Et vi bus. de frumento molendini precii iii s. ix d. Et vi bus. brasei molendini precii ii s. vi d.

Summa liiii li. iii s. iiii d. ob. [Probatur]

iii Examinatur

[*Rot. 3d*] *Bisshopton'. S'. Custodes xlix s. iiii d. de feno et foragio.* Per estimacionem ibidem l qr. frumenti precii qr. v s. vi d. Summa xiii li. xv s. Et C qr. ordei precii qr. iii s. iiii d. Summa xvi li. xiii s. iiii d. Et lxx qr. avene precii qr. ii s. iiii d. Summa viii li. iii s. iiii d. Et v qr. pisarum precii qr. iii s. Summa xv s. Et CCi multones precii cuiuslibet ii s. Summa xx li. ii s. Et CCxviii oves matrices precii cuiuslibet xviii d. Summa xvi li. vii s. Et Clx hogastri precii cuiuslibet xi d.

Summa vii li. vi s. viii d. Et i jumentum precii x s. Et i carecta ligata ferro precii viii s. Et xviii boves precii cuiuslibet xi s. Summa ix li. xviii s. Item i taurus precii xii s. Et xiii vacce precii cuiuslibet vi s. Summa lxxviii s. Et v boviculi annales precii cuiuslibet iii s. iiii d. Summa xvi s. viii d. Et ii vituli precii cuiuslibet ii s. vi d. Summa v s. Et i ancer et iiii^{or} auce precii xv d. Et fenum appreciatum ad lxvi s. viii d. Et litera precii xvi d. Et lxxii acre seminate frumento precii acre v s. Summa xviii li. Item i pelvis cum lavatorio precii ii s.

Summa Cxxi li. xv d. Probatur [Probatur]

Ta' xi li. Venduntur ibidem Cx multones precii cuiuslibet ii s. Summa xi li. et denarii liberantur J. de Heydene. Et C oves matrices venduntur precii cuiuslibet xviii d. Summa vii li. x s. Et i pullanus affri precii x s. similiter venditur. Et x qr. ordei precii qr. iii s. iiii d. venduntur. Summa xxxiii s. iiii d. Et denarii predicti sunt in manu Roberti Burdayne prepositi.

Summa xx li. xiii s. iiii d. Probatur [Probatur]

Funtel. S'. Custodes x s. de feno. Estimantur ibidem iiii^{xx} qr. frumenti precii qr. v s. iiii d. Summa xxi li. vi s. viii d. Et iiii^{xx}x qr. ordei precii qr. iii s. iiii d. Summa xv li. Et iiii^{xx} qr. avene precii qr. ii s. iiii d. Summa ix li. vi s. viii d. Et fenum appreciatum ad x s. Et ii equi carectarii precii xx s. Et xvi boves precii cuiuslibet xiiii s. iiii d. Summa x li. xiii s. iiii d. Et Cliii multones precii cuiuslibet ii s. Summa xv li. vi s. Et i carecta precii v s. Et seminantur lxiiii acre de frumento precii acre v s. Summa xvi li. Et remanent in granario ii qr. ii bus. frumenti precii ut supra. Summa xii s. Et ii bus. mixtilionis precii x d. Item i aper et i sus precii ii s. in toto.

Summa iiii^{xx}x li. ii s. vi d. Probatur [Probatur]

Ta' viii li. Venduntur ibidem xix porci pro xxxiiii s. Et C multones pro x li. Et ii pulli affrorum unus etatis ii annorum pro viii s. et alius huius anni pro ii s. vi d. Et Walterus Schone prepositus debet respondere de omnibus denariis predictis preter viii li. quas Johannes de Heidene recepit.

Summa xii li. iiii s. vi d. Probatur [Probatur]

Cnoel. S'. Custodes ibidem de feno et litera vii li. xxi d. ob. Item ibi per estimacionem lxx qr. frumenti precii qr. iiii s. vi d. Summa xv li. xv s. Et C qr. ordei precii qr. iii s. iiii d. Summa xvi li. xiii s. iiii d. Et xxii qr. avene precii qr. ii s. Summa xliiii s. Et fenum appreciatum ad vi li. xiii s. iiii d. Et litera ad valorem x s. Et iiii^{or} equi carectarii precii cuiuslibet xvi s. Summa lxiiii s. Item ii jumenta affrorum precii cuiuslibet viii s. Summa xvi s. Item i bos precii v s. Et xx vacce precii cuiuslibet vi s. viii d. Summa vi li. xiii s. iiii d. Et xii boviculi annales precii cuiuslibet iii s. Summa xxxvi s. Et iiii^{or} vituli precii cuiuslibet xviii d. Summa vi s. Et CCC iiii^{xx}xvii multones precii cuiuslibet ii s. Summa xxxix li. xiiii s. Et xxv hurtardi precii cuiuslibet xviii d. Summa xxxvii s. vi d. Et DCxlvi oves matrices precii cuiuslibet xviii d. Summa xlviii li. ix s. Et CCCxxii hogastri precii cuiuslibet x d. Summa xiii li. viii s. iiii d. Et i aper precii iii s. Et ii sues precii v s. in toto. Et vi porci precii xii s. in toto. Et xxix hogetti \ porcorum / precii cuiuslibet xvi d. Summa xxxviii s. viii d. Et ix porcelli precii cuiuslibet vi d. Summa iiii s. vi d. Et iiii qr. frumenti precii qr. v s. Summa xx s. Et i qr. curalli precii iii s. iiii d. Et iiii qr. ordei precii qr. iii s. iiii d. Summa xiii s. iiii d. Et i biga precii x s. Et iiii^{or} carecte precii ii marcarum in toto. Et vi^{xx} acre frumenti precii acre v s. Summa xxx li. Item i ancer et iiii^{or} auce precii xv d. in toto. Et xiii pelles multonum et iiii pelles ovium precii cuiuslibet iiii d. Summa v s. viii d.

Summa Ciiii^{xx}xv li. viii s. iii d. Probatur [Probatur]

Et venduntur ibidem vi coria boum pro xv s. in toto. Et ii coria vaccarum venduntur i pro ii s. et aliud pro xviii d. Et CCCx multones venduntur videlicet CCx multones pro xxi li. quilibet pro ii s. et C multones venduntur pro viii li. vi s. viii d. precii cuiuslibet xx d. Et CCl oves matrices precii cuiuslibet xviii d. Summa xviii li. xv s. Et denarii predicti remanent penes Johannem atte Ligh' prepositum.

Upton' Cnoel. S'. Fenum et litera ibidem xv s. de quibus debent respondere custodes. Per estimacionem ibidem de frumento xii qr. precii qr. v s. iiii d. Summa lxiiii s. Item xxvi qr. ordei precii qr. iii s. Summa lxxviii s. Item de ordeo jemali iii qr. precii qr. ii s. iiii d. Summa vii s. Item de avena xxiiii qr. precii qr. ii s. viii d. Summa lxiiii s. Item ii jumenta affrorum precii x s. in toto. Et i pullus masculus etatis i anni precii ii s. Item xv boves precii cuiuslibet x s. Summa vii li. x s. Et Cxxiii multones precii cuiuslibet ii s. Summa xii li. vi s. Item fenum appreciatum ad x s. Et litera precii v s. Et i carecta debilis precii iii s. Item i qr. de vescis precii qr. xviii d. Et di. qr. pisarum precii xvi d. Item xxvi acre et di. seminate frumento precii iiii s. Summa Cvi s. Et xii acre de ordeo jemali precii acre ii s. vi d. Summa xxx s.

Summa xxxviii li. xvii s. x d. Probatur [Probatur]

Et venduntur ibidem iiii multones precii cuiuslibet ii s. Summa viii s. Et vii qr. vii bus. frumenti precii qr. v s. iiii d. Summa xlii s. Et i qr. di. de curallo precii in toto vi s. Et i qr. v bus. de drageto jemal*i* precii in toto iiii s. i d. Et Robertus atte Hull' prepositus debet respondere de denariis predictis.

Summa < lxx s. i d. ob. > [\ lx s. i d. /] Probatur [Probatur]

Taunton' cum membris. S'. Custodes ibidem de feno et foragio vii li. xiiii s. Ibidem per estimacionem CCxxv qr. frumenti precii qr. vi s. viii d. Summa lxxv li. Item DCC qr. avene precii qr. ii s. Summa lxx li. Item fenum appreciatum ad x li. *Hull'* Item apud Hill' xxxii boves precii cuiuslibet x s. Summa xvi li. Item ii bige precii xiii s. iiii d. Et iiii^{xx}xv acre seminate frumento apud Hull' precii acre v s. Summa xxiii li. xv s. *Holewey* Item apud Holewey xxiii boves precii cuiuslibet x s. Summa xi li. x s. Et ii bige precii xiii s. iiii d. Item fenum[12] appreciatum ad lx s. Item in eodem manerio C acre seminate frumento precii acre v s. Summa xxv li. *Stapelgrave* Item apud Stapelgrave xxi boves precii bovis x s. Summa xi li. Et ii bige precii xiii s. iiii d. Et fenum appreciatum ad xxx s. Et liii acre seminate frumento precii acre v s. Summa xiii li. v s. Item litera ad valenciam iiii s. Et apud Taunton' xl qr. pisarum precii qr. iii s. Summa vi li. Item i pelvis cum lavatorio ii olle enee cum i patella precii x s. in toto.

Summa CClxviii li. xiiii s. Probatur [Probatur]

[[Summa totalis ex utraque parte M^{l}CCCxliii li. ob. Probatur]][13]

[*Rot. 4r*] *Neylesborne. S'. Custodes ibidem de feno et foragio li s. viii d.* Estimantur ibidem lx qr. frumenti precii qr. vi s. viii d. Summa xx li. Et lx qr. avene precii qr. ii s. Summa vi li. Et i qr. mixtilionis precii v s. Et fenum appreciatum ad lxvi s. viii d. Et litera precii v s. Et xxiiii boves precii bovis xiii s. iiii d. Summa xvi li. Et ii bige precii xiii s. iiii d. Et ii pelles ii bidentum precii iiii d. Et lvii acre seminate frumento precii acre v s. Summa xiiii li. v s. Et xix acre seminate de siligine precii acre iii s. Summa lvii s.

Summa lxiii li. xii s. iiii d. Probatur [Probatur]

Tal' Venduntur ibidem iiii boves precii xxvi s. viii d. Et vi^{xx}xv multones precii multonis x d. Summa Cxii s. vi d. Et i ovis matrix precii x d. Et ii pelles ii bidentum precii iiii d. Et v qr. avene precii qr. xxii d. Summa ix s. ii d.

Summa vii li. ix s. vi d. Probatur

Pondeford'.[14] *S'. Custodes ibidem de feno et foragio lviii s. iiii d.* Per estimacionem ibidem xl qr. frumenti precii qr. viii s. Summa xvi li. Et iiii^{xx} qr. avene precii qr. ii s. Summa viii li. Et xxxii boves precii bovis xvi s. Summa xxv li. xii s. Et lxi porc*i* precii porc*i* xv d. Summa lxxvi s. iii d. Et x vituli precii capitis xviii d. Summa xv s. Item i ancer et iii auce precii cuiuslibet iiii d. Summa xvi d. Et xxiiii^{or} capones precii in toto iiii s. Et i gallus et v galline precii cuiuslibet i d. ob. Summa ix d. Item iii plaustra precii xv s. in toto. Et fenum appreciatum in toto ad lxvi s. viii d. Et litera appreciata ad v s. Et Cxx acre seminate frumento precii acre v s. vi d. Summa xxxiii li.

Summa iiii^{xx}xi li. xvi s. Probatur [Probatur]

Ta' x li. iii s. vi d. Et venduntur ibidem xxiii vacce precii capitis vii s. vi d. Summa viii li. xii s. vi d. Et ii coria ii boviculorum que coria venduntur pro iii s.[15] Et vi boviculi venduntur precii capitis iii s. Summa xviii s. Et i taurus venditur pro x s. < *Memorandum* > Et fuerunt die predicto xi annales precii cuiuslibet iii s. [\ et venduntur. /] Summa xxxiii s. Et xxxix porci venduntur precii cuiuslibet ii s. Summa lxxviii s. Et vii qr. avene precii qr. ii s. Summa xiiii s.

Summa xvi li. viii s. vi d. Probatur [Probatur]

Rympton'. S'. Custodes debent respondere de lxvi s. viii d. de feno et litera. Estimantur ibidem xxxiiii qr. frumenti precii qr. v s. viii d. Summa ix li. xii s. viii d. Et liii qr. avene precii qr. ii s. viii d. Summa vii li. xvi d. Et xx qr. fabarum precii qr. iii s. iiii d. Summa lxvi s. viii d. Et fenum appreciatum ad lx s. Et ii jumenta affrorum precii xx s. in toto. Et xxxii boves precii capitis x s. Summa xvi li. Et iiii bige precii xx s. in toto. Et i carecta precii vi s. viii d. Et i ancer et iiii^{or} auce precii cuiuslibet iii d. Summa xv d. Et i gallus et v galline precii cuiuslibet i d. ob. Summa ix d. Item litera precii vi s. viii d. Et Cix acre seminate de frumento precii acre iiii s. Summa xxi li. xvi s. Item ii olle enee i patella enea i pelvis cum lavatorio precii viii s. in toto.

Summa lxiiii li. Probatur [Probatur]

Ta' Venduntur ibidem xv qr. frumenti precii qr. vi s. Summa iiii li. x s. Et viii qr. frumenti venduntur precii qr. v s. iiii d. Summa xlii s. viii d. Et xii qr. avene pro xxii s. precii qr. ii s. viii d. Et xii qr. fabarum venduntur pro xl s. precii qr. xl d. Et xxi s. viii d. receptis de viii qr. i bus. fabarum venditis precii qr. ii s. viii d. Et iii boves pro xxvii s. iiii d. venduntur in toto. Et i taurus venditur pro x s. Et xvi vacce venduntur precii vacce vii s. Summa Cxii s. Et ix boviculi etatis trium annorum precii capitis iii s. Summa xxvii s. \ Et ix boviculi etatis ii annorum precii capitis iii s. Summa xxvii s. /[16] Et x vituli precii capitis xiiii d. Summa xi s. viii d. Item i aper precii iii s. Item ii sues cum porcell*is* precii in toto vi s. viii d. Et xvi hogastri precii capitis xiii d. Summa xvii s. iiii d. Et iiii porc*i* precii vi s. viii d. in toto. Et i porcus precii iii s. Et i carecta precii vi s. viii d. Et i jumentum cum pullano precii xiii s. iiii d.

Summa xxiiii li. xviii s. Probatur

Biterne. S'. Custodes episcopatus debent respondere de xxx s. vi d. de feno et foragio. Per estimacionem ibidem ii qr. frumenti precii in toto viii s. Et xii qr. drageti precii qr. iii s. Summa xxxvi s. Et xiiii qr. avene precii qr. ii s. Summa xxviii s. Et i qr. pisarum et vescarum precii ii s. Item fenum appreciatum ad lx s. Et foragium precii vi d. Et xii acre seminate frumento precii acre ii s. Summa xxiiii s. Et in granario i qr. ii bus. frumenti precii v s. in toto. Item ii equi carectarii precii xiii s. iiii d. in toto. Et ii affri precii x s. in toto. Item viii boves precii cuiuslibet vi s. viii d. Summa liii s. iiii d. Et v vacce precii capitis iiii s. Summa xx s. Et vi bovetti precii capitis ii s. Summa xii s. Et v vituli precii in toto v s. Et xxx multones precii capitis x d. Summa xxv s. Et iiii^{xx}ix oves matrices precii capitis ix d. Summa < lxvii s. vi d. > [\ lxvi s. ix d. /] Item i carecta ferrata cum hernasio precii vi s. viii d. Et i caruca cum ferro et hercia precii ii s. Et maheremium precii xviii d. Et ii cuve precii xii d. Et i olla enea precii xviii d. i patella cupra precii iiii d. Et i corium cuiusdam vacce precii xii d.

Summa < xxvi li. xv s. viii d. > [\ xix li. ii s. xi d. /] Probatur [Probatur] Bona predicta committuntur Johanni A*ce* Galfrido Edmund' Johanni de Westesid' et Petro Hederede per indenturam custodienda ad opus domini regis.

Waltham. S'. Custodes ibidem xvi s. viii d. de feno et foragio. Per estimacionem ibidem lxx qr. iii bus. frumenti precii qr. iiii s. Summa xiiii li. xviii d. Et xxii qr. di. ordei precii qr. ii s. viii d. Summa lx s. Et iiii^{xx} qr. avene precii qr. ii s. Summa viii li. Et ii qr. pisarum et vescarum precii iiii s. in toto. Et iiii equi carectarii precii in toto xxv s. Et xliii boves precii capitis vi s. viii d. Summa xiiii li. vi s. viii d. Et corium cuiusdam bovis precii xviii d. Et i taurus precii vi s. viii d. Et xvii vacce precii capitis v s. Summa iiii li. v s. Et ii bovetti et ii juvenca precii capitis iii s. Summa xii s. Et iii boviculi et iii juvenca precii capitis xiii d. Summa vi s. vi d. Et Cliiii multones precii cuiuslibet xvi d. Summa x li. v s. iiii d. Et viii hurtardi precii capitis xvi d. Summa x s. viii d. Et CCl oves matrices precii capitis x d. Summa x li. viii s. iiii d. Et C hoggastri precii capitis v d. Summa xli s. viii d. Item i aper precii ii s. Et ii sues et vi porci precii capitis ii s. Summa xvi s. Item viii porcelli precii capitis x d. Summa vi s. viii d. Et vii porcelli juniores precii cuiuslibet vi d. Summa iii s. vi d. Item ii cigni veteres precii v s. Et ii cigni juniores precii iii s. iiii d. Et i ancer et iiii^{or} auce precii cuiuslibet iii d. Summa xv d. Item i gallus et v galline precii ix d. in toto. Et fenum appreciatum ad x s. Et foragium appreciatum ad vi s. viii d. Et i carecta ferrata cum hernasio precii vii s. et iiii^{or} caruce cum apparatu precii v s. viii d. in toto. Et i olla enea precii xii d. Et vetus maheremium precii xii d. Et i batella precii vi s. viii d. Item i cista precii vi d. Et iii magne cuve precii vi s. viii d. in toto. Et ii parve cuve precii in toto ix d. Et iii kuvelini precii in toto vi d. Et iii cuve pro lardario precii ix d. Et viii^{xx}viii acre seminate precii acre ii s. Summa xvi li. xvi s. Item i pressura pro cisera facienda precii ii s.

Bona predicta committuntur Ade de Yelle preposito huius manerii Ricardo Reynald' Petro Herberd et Johanni Bues \ per indenturam /[17] custodienda ad opus domini regis.

Summa iiii^{xx}x li. xviii s. vi d. Probatur [Probatur]

iiii Examinatur

[*Rot. 4d*] *Drokeford'.*[18] *S'. Custodes ibidem iii s. x d. de feno et foragio* Per estimacionem ibidem xvi qr. vi bus. frumenti precii qr. iiii s. iiii d. Summa lxxii s. vii d. Item xx qr. ordei precii qr. ii s. viii d. Summa liii s. iiii d. Et xxx qr. avene precii qr. ii s. Summa lx s. Et ii qr. pisarum et vescarum precii iiii s. in toto. Et fenum appreciatum ad v s. Et foragium precii vi d. Et ii equi carectarii precii xviii s. in toto. Et iii affri precii xv s. in toto. Et xviii boves precii in toto vi li. Et i taurus precii vi s. viii d. Et xii vacce precii capitis v s. Summa lx s. Et v boviculi precii capitis iii s. Summa xv s. Et iii boviculi precii vi s. in toto. Item v vituli annales precii capitis x d. Summa iiii s. ii d. Item CCxx multones precii capitis xiiii d. Summa xii li. xvi s. viii d. Et vi hurtardi precii capitis xiiii d. Summa vii s. Et CCiiii^{xx} oves matrices precii capitis x d. Summa xii li. ix s. ii d. Et Cxxiiii hoggastri precii capitis vi d. Summa lxii s. Item i aper precii ii s. et ii sues vi porci precii capitis ii s. Summa xvi s. Item xvi porc*i* minores precii cuiuslibet xii d. Summa xvi s. Item viii porcelli precii cuiuslibet iiii d. Summa ii s. viii d. Item i ancer et iiii^{or} auce precii auce iii d. Summa xv d. Item i gallus v galline et v pulli precii xi d. in toto. Item i carecta ferrata cum hernesio precii iiii s. vi d. Item i carecta pro fimis precii xii d. Et ii cupe pro femis imponendis precii iiii d. Item ii carecte non ferrate precii xii d. Item iii caruce cum apparatu precii iii s. in toto. Item pelvis cum lavatorio precii xii d. Item i olla enea precii xii d. Item patella enea precii xii d. Item fimus precii v d. Item ii cuve precii viii d. Item ii scale precii ii d. Et xl acre seminate frumento precii acre ii s. Summa iiii li.

Summa lvii li. viii s. [Probatur]

Bona inventa apud Drokeford[19] committuntur Henrico le Wrey preposito Willelmo atte Brok' Johanni le Longe et Henrico De*n*el per indenturam custodienda ad opus domini regis.

Hameldon'. S'. Custodes episcopatus debent respondere de x s. de feno ibidem. Per estimacionem ibidem C qr. frumenti precii qr. iiii s. Summa xx li. Et viii qr. de sprig' precii qr. ii s. Summa xvi s. Et Cvi qr. ordei precii qr. ii s. viii d. Summa xiiii li. ii s. viii d. Et Cxl qr. avene precii qr. ii s. Summa xiiii li. Et i qr. fabarum precii iii s. Et iiii qr. pisarum precii qr. ii s. iiii d. Summa ix s. iiii d. Et ii qr. de vescis precii iiii s. in toto. Et xxxiii acre seminate frumento precii acre ii s. vi d. Summa iiii li. ii s. vi d. Item fenum appreciatum ad x s. Et foragium ad iii s. Et ii equi carectarii precii xx s. Et ix affri precii cuiuslibet vi s. viii d. Summa lx s. Et vi boves precii capitis vi s. viii d. Summa xl s. Et i taurus et vi vacce precii capitis v s. Summa xxxv s. Et vi boviculi precii capitis iiii s. Summa xxiiii s. Item viii boviculi precii capitis iii s. Summa xxiiii s. Et vii hurtardi precii capitis xvi d. Summa ix s. iiii d. Et CClix multones precii capitis xv d. Summa xvi li. iii s. ix d. Et CClix oves matrices precii capitis xii d. Summa xii li. xix s. Et Cxii hogastri precii capitis viii d. Summa lxxiiii s. viii d.[20] Et i aper precii iii s. Et iiii sues precii viii s. in toto. Item xxviii porci precii capitis ii s. vi d. Summa lxx s. Item xiii porc*i* precii capitis xviii d. Summa xix s. vi d. Item xxvi porcelli precii cuiuslibet x d. Summa xxi s. viii d. Item iii carecte ferrate precii i x s. et alterius iiii s. et tercius iii s. Summa xvii s. Item i rota ferrata precii xii d. Item ii caruce cum ferramento et apparatu precii iiii s. Item i ancer et iiii^{or} auce precii xv d. in toto. Item i gallus et v galline precii ix d. in toto. Item ii olle enee precii ii s. viii d. Item i vitulus precii x d. Item ii patelle enee precii xviii d. Item i pelvis cum lavatorio precii xviii d. Item ii scale precii vi d. Et maheremium precii xii d. Et fimus precii iii s. iiii d.

Et bona predicta committuntur Willelmo in the Dene Willelmo de Cheddon' et Willelmo Coker per indenturam custodienda ad opus domini regis.

Summa Cv li. < xvii s. ix d > [\ xiiii s. ix d. /] Probatur [Probatur]

Est Moenes. S'. Custodes xlvii s.[21] *de feno et foragio.* Per estimacionem ibidem CC qr. frumenti precii qr. iiii s. Summa xl li. Et xl qr. ordei precii qr. iii s. Summa vi li. Et vi qr. fabarum precii qr. iii s. Summa xviii s. Et CCC qr. avene precii qr. ii s. Summa xxx li. Et liiii boves precii capitis vi s. viii d. Summa xviii li. Et xv vacce precii capitis v s. Summa lxxv s. Et xviii boviculi precii capitis iii s. iiii d. Summa lx s. Et ix boviculi precii capitis xviii d. Summa xiii s. vi d. Et i vitulus precii xii d. Item iiii equi carectarii precii capitis xv s. Summa lx s. Et xxvi affri precii capitis vi s. viii d. Summa viii li. xiii s. iiii d. Et ii carecte ferrate cum hernasio precii xvi s. in toto. Et ix caruce cum ferramento et apparatu precii cuiuslibet xviii d. Summa xiii s. vi d. Et DCCCiiii multones precii capitis xvi d. Summa liii li. < xvi s. > [\ xii s. /] Et ix hurtardi precii capitis xviii d. Summa xiii s. vi d. Et DCC oves matrices precii capitis xiii d. Summa xxxvii li. xviii s. iiii d. Et CCCC hogastri precii capitis x d. Summa xvi li. xiii s. iiii d. Et iii apri precii capitis iii s. Summa ix s. Et v sues precii sue iii s. Summa xv s. Et xxxii porci precii capitis iii s. Summa iiii li. xvi s. Et xxxi minores precii capitis xviii d. Summa xlvi s. vi d. Et xx porcelli precii cuiuslibet iii d. Summa v s. Et v cigni unde ii veteres precii vi s. viii d. Et iii minores precii vi s. Summa xii s. viii d. Et i ancer xxiii auce precii cuiuslibet iii d. Summa vi s. Et xxiii capones precii cuiuslibet ii d. Summa iii s. x d. Et i gallus et v galline precii ix d. in toto. Et ii dolia plena cisare precii in toto xvi s. Et i pelvis cum lavatorio precii in toto ii s. Et iii olle enee precii ii s. Et i patella enea precii ii d. Item i cacabus precii xvi d. Item fenum appreciatum ad xxxii s. Et foragium precii xv s. Et CCxl acre seminate frumento precii acre ii s. Summa xxiiii li. Et ii tauri precii vi s. viii d. in toto. Et i alius taurus precii v s. Et maheremium borde et poukwayn precii vi s. viii d. Et fimus precii iii s. iii d.

Summa CClxii li. < xvi s. > [\ xii s. /] v d. Probatur [Probatur]

Bona predicta committuntur Thome de Burle Johanni de Tygehale Martino atte Brugge Willelmo atte Strode Thome de Compe Roberto Hugh' Odino de Combe Willelmo Randulf' et Rogero atte Sele per indenturam custodienda ad opus domini regis.

[[Summa ex utraque parte DCCCiiii li. xi d.]]

[*Rot. 5r*] *Farham. Custodes xxvi s. viii d. de feno.* Per estimacionem ibidem xlix qr. et di. frumenti precii qr. iiii s. Summa ix li. xviii s. Et xxxiii qr. ordei precii qr. iii s. Summa iiii li. xix s. Et xl qr. avene precii qr. ii s. Summa iiii li. Et vii qr. pisarum precii qr. ii s. Summa xiiii s. Et viii qr. de vescis precii qr. ii s. Summa xvi s. Et fenum appreciatum ad xxvi s. viii d. Et ii equi carectarii precii xiii s. iiii d. in toto. Et iiii affri precii xx s. in toto. Et Cliiii multones precii capitis xiiii d. Summa viii li. xix s. viii d. Et i aper precii ii s. Et ii sues precii in toto iiii s. Et xviii porc*i* precii capitis xiiii d. Summa xxi s. Et x porcelli precii capitis viii d. Summa vi s. viii d. Et ii pavones femelli cum ii pullis precii cuiuslibet iiii d. Summa xvi d. Et i ancer et iiii^{or} auce precii cuiuslibet iii d. Summa xv d. Et ii carecte ferrate cum hernesio precii i vi s. viii d. et alterius ii s. Summa viii s. viii d. Et ii caruce cum ferramento et apparatu precii in toto iii s. iiii d. Et i olla enea precii xx d. Item i dolium vacuum pro elemosina episcopi colligenda precii iiii d. Et ix jumenta de quibus ii steriles precii cuiuslibet xiii s. iiii d. Summa vi li. Et vii pullani unde vi masculi et i femellus precii capitis vi s. viii d. Summa xlvi s. viii d. Item fimus precii xiiii d. Item xlviii acre seminate frumento precii acre ii s. Summa iiii li.

xvi s. Et xviii boves precii capitis vi s. viii d. Summa vi li. Et i taurus precii vi s. viii d. Et v vacce precii capitis v s. Summa xxv s.

Summa lv li. xii s. < iiii d. > Probatur \ [v d. Probatur] /

Bona predicta committuntur Willemo atte Lane Ende Willelmo de Yullme Henrico atte Hoke et Henrico le Fevre per indenturam salvo custodienda ad opus domini regis.

Et memorandum quod v s. recepti de iii vitulis venditis sunt in manu Willelmi prepositi eiusdem manerii.

Summa v s.

Brokhampton'. S'. Custodes v s. de feno. Per estimacionem ibidem xxi qr. frumenti precii qr. iiii s. Summa iiii li. iiii s. Et v qr. ordei precii qr. ii s. viii d. Summa xiii s. iiii d. Et viii qr. avene precii qr. ii s. Summa xvi s. Et ii qr. fabarum precii vi s. in toto. Et iii qr. pisarum precii vi s. in toto. Et iiii qr. de vescis precii vi s. viii d. in toto. Et i qr. mixtilonis precii iii s. Et iiii boves precii xxvi s. viii d. in toto. Et iii coria boum precii v s. in toto. Et ii affri precii xiii s. iiii d. in toto. Item i mulus precii ii s. Et ii asini precii iiii s. in toto. Et i pullus asini precii ii s. Item i carecta ferrata precii vi s. viii d. Et i caruca cum ferramento et apparatu precii xviii d. Et i corda canabi pro carect*a* ligand*a* precii ii d. Et i patella enea precii xii d. Item i urciolus precii vi d. Item i pelvis cum lavatorio precii xii d. Item fenum appreciatum ad v s. Item ii dolia vetera vacua precii vi d. Item iiii^{or} cuve precii in toto xvi d. Item iiii ciste unde i precii xii d. et precium aliarum trium ix d. Item fimus precii viii d. Item i petra ad molendum in molendino aquatico precii xxvi s. viii d. Item xiiii acre seminate frumento precii acre iiii s. Summa lvi s.

Summa xiii li. x s. ix d. Probatur [Probatur]

Et bona predicta committuntur Ricardo acte Halle Willelmo Robiste Ricardo Conqueraunt et Willelmo Trakkem*ere* per indenturam custodienda ad opus domini regis.

Waltham sancti Laurencii. S'. Examinatur. Custodes xv s. de feno et foragio. Per estimacionem ibidem vii qr. et di. frumenti precii qr. iiii s. vi d. Summa xxxiii s. ix d. Et xvii qr. v bus. mixtilonis precii qr. iii s. iiii d. Summa lviii s. ix d. Et viii qr. vi bus. ordei precii qr. iii s. Summa xxvi s. iii d. Et xii qr. drageti precii qr. ii s. Summa xxiiii s. Et xxxi qr. avene precii qr. xx d. Summa li s. viii d. Et ii qr. et di. pisarum precii qr. iii s. Summa vii s. vi d. Et vii affri precii capitis xii s. Summa iiii li. iiii s. Et xvii vacce precii capitis vi s. viii d. Summa Cxiii s. iiii d. Item i vitulus precii viii d. Et iii hurtardi precii capitis xvi d. Summa iiii s. Et iiii^{xx} oves matrices precii capitis xvi d. Summa Cvi s. viii d. Et lxxvii agni precii capitis viii d. Summa li s. iiii d. Et viii casei precii cuiuslibet iii d. Summa ii s. Et i patella enea precii ii s. vi d. Et iii boketta precii in toto iii d. Et i caruca precii ii s. Item v borde de fago precii iii d. Et i ventatorium precii viii d. Item i bussellum ligatum cum ferro precii iiii d. Et ii crebri et i ridelus precii iii d. Item fenum appreciatum ad xi s. Et foragium precii x s. Item xxii acre seminate frumento cum mixtilone precii acre ii s. Summa xliiii s. Et xxx s. argenti in manu prepositi.

Summa xxxiii li. v s. ii d. Probatur [Probatur]

Pyllingbere. S'. Examinatur. Custodes vii s. de feno et foragio. Per estimacionem ibidem xii qr. frumenti precii qr. iiii s. Summa xlviii s. Et x qr. de mixtilone precii qr. iii s. iiii d. Summa xxxiii s. iiii d. Et viii qr. drageti precii qr. ii s. Summa xvi s.

Et xxx qr. avene precii qr. xx d. Summa l s. Et i equus carectarius et i jumentum precii viii s. in toto. Et ii affri precii v s. iiii d. in toto. Et ix boves precii capitis viii s. Summa lxxii s. Et xi vacce precii capitis viii s. Summa iiii li. viii s. Et xi vacce pejores precii capitis vi s. viii d. Summa lxxiii s. iiii d. Et iii boviculi precii capitis vi s. viii d. Summa xx s. Et v boviculi et v juvence precii capitis v s. Summa l s. Et ix vituli superannales precii capitis ii s. vi d. Summa xxii s. vi d.[22] Et x vituli annales precii capitis xii d. Summa x s. Et xxx multones precii capitis xv d. Summa xxxvii s. vi d. Et xxxviii oves matrices precii capitis xii d. Summa xxxviii s. Et xxxix hoggastri precii capitis vii d. Summa xxvi s.[23] Et i qr. frumenti in grangia precii iiii s. Item i qr. vii bus. mixtilonis precii qr. iii s. iiii d. Summa vi s. iii d. Item i ventalium precii iiii d. Item i mensura que vocatur bussel precii iiii d. Item i saccus precii ii d. Item ii crebri et i ridellus precii ii d. Et xix casei precii cuiuslibet ii d. Summa iii s. ii d. Item i cuvara precii ii d. Item i patella enea precii vi d. Item i tripes precii iii d. Item ii boketta precii ii d. Item i formula pro case*is* inficiend*is* precii iii d. Item fenum appreciatum ad vi s. Item foragium precii v s. Item i caruca cum ferramento et alio apparatu precii iii s. Item i carecta cum apparatu precii xii d. Item maheremium novum apto carpentatum et preparatum ad quandam bercariam inde faciendam precii xxxiii s. iiii d. Et vi s. vi d. sunt in manibus prepositi de bosco vendito et ii s. iii d. recepti de pannagio. < [[Postea executores dicti defuncti onerant se]] >
[Memorandum de xix acris de mangcorn' precii acre ii s. iii d.] [[Et onerantur inde < in una summa per s..... recept' in .... >]] [[in indentura]][24]

Summa xxxiii li.˙ < v s. > [\ x s. /] x d. [Probatur]

Et bona predicta committuntur Alexandro atte Brugge Johanni de gardino Willelmo Joldwine Ade de Thurmere et Henrico atte Felde per indenturam custodienda ad opus domini regis.

Culham. S'. Examinatur. Memorandum custodes de feno et foragio xiii s. Per estimacionem ibidem vi qr. et di. frumenti precii qr. iiii s. Summa xxvi s. Et xiii qr. mixtilonis precii qr. iii s. iiii d. Summa xliii s. iiii d. Et viii qr. ordei precii qr. iii s. Summa xxiiii s. Et iii qr. drageti precii qr. ii s. Summa vi s. Et xi qr. avene precii qr. xx d. Summa xviii s. iiii d. Et vi affri precii capitis vi s. Summa xxxvi s. Et i taurus precii vi s. viii d. Et xv vacce precii capitis vi s. Summa iiii li. x s. Et iiii boviculi precii capitis ii s. Summa viii s. Et v boviculi precii capitis xviii d. Summa vi s. vi d. Et vi vituli precii capitis vi d. Summa iii s. Et i ancer et iiii^or^ auce precii in toto xv d. Et xi capones precii cuiuslibet i d. ob. Summa xvi d. ob. Item ii galli et ix galline precii xi d. in toto. Et fenum precii xx s. Et foragium precii vi s. i patella enea precii xviii d. Et lxi acre seminate cum mixtilone precii acre ii s. Summa vi li. ii s.

Summa xxi li. xxii d. ob. Probatur [Probatur]

Et bona predicta committuntur per indenturam Willelmo Cuverich' et Roberto Croyly per indenturam custodienda ad opus domini regis.

v Examinatur

[*Rot. 5d*] *Wergrave. S'. Examinatur. Custodes x s. de feno ..... iii s. de foragio.* Item ibidem per estimacionem xviii qr. ii bus. frumenti precii qr. iiii s. Summa lxxiii s. Et xxvii qr. v bus. mancorn' precii qr. ii s. iii d. Summa lxii s. i d. ob. qua. Et xxi qr. de ordeo precii qr. iii s. Summa lxiii s. Et iiii qr. drageti precii viii s. in toto. Et xxxi qr. avene precii qr. xx d. Summa li s. viii d. Et xiiii boves precii capitis vi s. Summa iiii li. iiii s. Et i taurus precii ii s. Et xxi vacce precii capitis vi s. Summa vi li. vi s. Et ii boviculi precii viii s. in toto. Et v juvence precii capitis iiii s. ix d. ob. Summa xxiii s. ix d. ob. Et iiii boviculi precii capitis xviii d. Summa vi s. Et x vituli precii cuiuslibet ii d. Summa xx d. Item ii equi carectarii precii in toto xx s. Item hernasium ad eosdem precii xii d. Item i carecta ligata ferro precii x s. Item i carecta pro femis precii x d. Item iiii jumenta affrorum precii in toto xxvi s. viii d. videlicet cuiuslibet vi s. viii d. Et[25] ii caruce cum ferramento et toto apparatu precii iiii s. Item i pullanus masculus precii iiii s. Et iii hurtardi precii cuiuslibet xviii d. Summa iiii s. vi d. Item iiii multones precii capitis xx d. Summa vi s. viii d. Et C oves matrices precii capitis xv d. Summa vi li. v s. Item lix hoggastri precii capitis ix d. Summa xliiii s. iii d. Item ii apri precii i iii s. et alterius ii s. Summa v s. Item ii sues precii v s. in toto. Et xi porci precii cuiuslibet ii s. Summa xxii s. Item xviii porcelli precii capitis ix d. Summa xiii s. vi d. Item i ancer et iii auce precii xvi d. in toto. Et i gallus et v galline precii ix d. in toto. Item hercia precii iiii d. Item i corda precii iiii d. Et fenum appreciatum ad xxx s. Et foragium precii xii s. Item i olla enea precii x d. ii patelle enee precii xvi d. Et i pelvis cum lavatorio precii xii d. Et i tripes precii iii d. Et iii mense cum trestellis precii xii d. Et ii dolia plena cisare precii xiii s. iiii d. Item ii cuve precii vi d. Item i tina precii ii d. Item i bussellum ligatum cum ferro precii vi d. i saccus precii iiii d. ii crebri precii ii d. ii ridels precii ii d. Item i ventorium precii viii d. Item i formula cum ped*ibus* ad supersedendum[26] precii iii d. iii formule ad supersedendum precii iii d. Et i mola pomerie cum pressura precii iiii s. i archa precii vi d. Item iiii pavones unde ii galli et ii femelli precii iiii s. in toto. Item liiii acre seminate de sprigg' precii acre ii s. Summa Cviii s.

Summa xlix li. iii s. viii d. qua. Probatur [Probatur]

Et bona predicta committuntur Johanni atte Lake Johanni atte Forde Roberto atte Bere et Willelmo de Werdle per indenturam custodienda ad opus domini regis.

Westwicomb'. S'. Examinatur. Custodes lvi s. iiii d. de feno et foragio. Per estimacionem ibidem lxx qr. frumenti precii qr. iiii s. Summa xiiii li. Et iiii qr. de sprigg' precii qr. iii s. Summa xii s. Item viii qr. drageti et viii qr. ordei precii qr. ii s. vi d. Summa xl s. Et l qr. avene precii qr. ii s. Summa C s. Item vii boviculi precii capitis iiii s. Summa xxviii s. Et xx vacce precii capitis x s. Summa x li. Et xi boviculi precii capitis iii s. Summa xxxiii s. Item xii vituli precii capitis ii s. Summa xxiiii s. Item ii hurtardi precii in toto iii s. iiii d. Et lx multones precii capitis xviii d. Summa iiii li. x s. Item xvi oves matrices precii capitis xvi d. Summa xxi s. iiii d. Et xxii hogastri precii capitis xiiii d. Summa xxv s. viii d. Et xvi agni precii capitis x d. Summa xiii s. iiii d. Item ii apri precii in toto vi s. Et ii sues precii v s. in toto. Item xxii porci precii capitis ii s. Summa xliiii s. Et xxiii porcelli precii capitis vi d. Summa xi s. vi d. Et i ancer et iiii^or auce precii in toto xx d. Et i gallus et iiii^or galline precii in toto vii d. ob. Et ii equi carectarii precii in toto xxvi s. viii d. Et xii affri precii cuiuslibet x s. Summa vi li. Item i carecta ferrata cum hernasio precii xiii s. iiii d. Item i carecta pro fimis precii vi d. Item ii caruce cum apparatu precii iiii s. Et iiii hercie precii viii d. in toto. Item ii corde ad carect*as* ligand*as* precii viii d. Item fenum precii liiii s. iiii d. Et foragium precii ii s. Et i olla enea precii ii s. Et i patella enea precii xii d. Item i tripes precii ii d. Item ii dolia plena cisare precii xvi s. Et xl acre seminate cum sprigg' precii acre ii s. Summa iiii li.

Et vetus maheremium precii ii s. Item MDC latthes precii centene vi d. Summa viii s. Item viiiM tegularum precii ii s.

[[Excedit]] Summa lxiii li. xii s. ix d. ob. [Probatur]

Et bona predicta committuntur per indenturam Ricardo atte Vuning' Johanni Leȝewe juniori Willelmo atte Hurne et Johanni Nicol custodienda ad opus domini regis.

Ivyngho. S'. Examinatur. Custodes debent respondere de lx s. de feno et foragio. Per estimacionem ibidem CCviii qr. vii bus. frumenti precii qr. iiii s. Summa xli li. xv s. vi d. Et xviii qr. de sprigg' precii qr. iii s. Summa liiii s. Et xviii qr. ordei precii qr. iii s. iiii d. Summa lx s. Et v qr. fabarum precii qr. ii s. viii d. Summa xiii s. iiii d. Et Clx qr. avene precii qr. ii s. ii d. Summa xvii li. vi s. viii d. Et fenum precii C s. Et foragium precii xl s. Et maheremium precii v s. Item i molendinum pro pomis molandis precii vi s. viii d. Et ii ventatoria lignea precii ii s. in toto. Item i carecta precii ii s. Item ii currus ferrati pro fimis cariandis precii x s. Item ii equi carectarii precii xl s. in toto. Item v caruce cum ferramento et apparatu precii xv s. in toto. Et xl boves precii capitis vi s. viii d. Summa xiii li. vi s. viii d. Item i juvenca precii x d. Item iiii^{or} vituli precii capitis iiii d. Summa xvi d. Item xxx multones precii capitis xx d. Summa l s. Item Cx oves matrices precii capitis xx d. Summa ix li. iii s. iiii d. Et lvi agni precii capitis xv d. Summa lxx s. Item i aper ii sues et xxiiii^{or} porci precii cuiuslibet iii s. Summa iiii li. xii d. Item xxi porc*i* precii capitis xvi d. ob. Summa xxviii s. x d. ob. Item i cignus precii iii s. iiii d. Item i ancer iiii^{or} auce precii cuiuslibet iii d. Summa xv d. Item i pelvis cum lavatorio precii ii s. Item ii olle enee precii vi s. in toto. Item i patella enea precii xvi d. Item ii scale precii vi d. Item fimus precii xii d. Item i busellum ligatum cum ferro precii vi d. iii crebri precii iii d. Item ii corde de canabo pro carect*is* ligand*is* precii vi d. Item ii hercie precii iii d. Item iiii bus. mixtilonis de lucro molendini precii xvi d. Item i saccus precii ii d. vi forme precii xvi d. Item ii ciste veteres precii vi d. Item i corbellus portabilis precii ii d. Item i carecta pro fimis cariandis precii x d. Item ii mense cum trestellis precii x d. Item li acre seminate frumento precii cuiuslibet iiii s. Summa x li. iiii s. Item xv acre i roda seminate cum sprigg' precii acre iii s. Summa xlv s. ix d.

Summa Cxxiiii li. iiii s. ob. Probatur [Probatur]

Bona predicta committuntur Rogero Vag' Jacobo Weremod Henrico le Bedel et Thome le Reve per indenturam custodienda ad opus domini regis.

Morton'. S'. Examinatur. Custodes debent respondere de vi s. viii d. de feno et foragio. Per estimacionem ibidem xx qr. frumenti precii qr. iii s. iiii d. Summa lxvi s. viii d. Et xx qr. drageti precii qr. ii s. iiii d. Summa xlvi s. viii d. Et xii qr. pisarum et fabarum precii qr. xvi d. Summa xvi s. Item \ ii / carecte sine ferro cum hernasio precii iii s. in toto. Et iiii equi carectarii precii i xvi s. et aliorum trium xviii s. in toto. Et iii caruce cum ferramento et apparatu precii xxviii d. in toto. Item xxvii boves precii cuiuslibet vi s. viii d. Summa ix li. Et xii vacce precii cuiuslibet v s. Summa lx s. Et ii boviculi precii vi s. viii d. in toto. Item vi vituli precii capitis xiiii d. Summa vii s. Et i ancer et viii auce precii cuiuslibet iii d. Summa ii s. iii d. Item i gallus et v galline precii in toto vi d. Item i olla enea sine pedibus precii xii d. Item i patella enea precii xii d. Et i ventatorium precii xii d. Item ii sacci precii iii d. Item i vanga ferrata precii i d. Item i tribula precii i d. Item ii crebri et i ridel precii iii d. Item CC tegule precii xii d. Item CCCC lath*es* precii ii s.

in toto. Et fenum precii xxvi s. viii d. Et foragium precii x s. Item ii hercie precii vi d. Item i mensa cum trestellis precii vi d. Item alie mense et forme precii iii d. Item i dolium vacuum precii vi d. Item iii corde pro carect*is* ligand*is* precii vi d. Item xiiii acre seminate cum frumento precii acre iii s. Summa xlii s.

Summa xxv li. xii s. viii d. [Probatur] [[Probatur]]

Bona predicta committuntur Galfrido Peris Willelmo atte Colvrehous Henrico atte Nasshe et Willelmo preposito per indenturam custodienda ad opus domini regis.

[[Summa totalis ex utraque parte CCCCxx li. xix s. ii d. ob. qua.]][27]

[*Rot. 6r*] *Witteneye. S'. Custodes ibidem lx s. de feno.* Ibi per estimacionem lxviii qr. vi bus. frumenti precii qr. iiii s. Summa xiii li. xv s. Et lxxvi qr. ordei precii qr. iii s. Summa xi li. viii s. Et xvi qr. drageti precii qr. ii s. vi d. Summa xl s. Et lx qr. avene precii qr. ii s. Summa vi li. Et de pisis xii qr. iii bus. precii qr. ii s. vi d. Summa xxx s. xi d. qua. Et fenum precii viii li. Et braseum de exitu molendini ii qr. precii vi s. in toto. Item de tolcorne vi bus. precii ii s. iii d. Et iii equi carectarii precii cuiuslibet xiii s. iiii d. Summa xl s. Item ii carecte ferrate debiles precii cuiuslibet iiii s. Summa viii s. Et vii boves et i vacca precii capitis v s. Summa xl s. Et iii vituli annales precii capitis xii d. Summa iii s. Et iiii^{or} jumenta precii cuiuslibet xiii s. iiii d. Summa liii s. iiii d. Et iii pullani etatis ii annorum unde precii i xiii s. iiii d. et aliorum duorum xiii s. iiii d. Et ii pulli femelli superannales precii cuiuslibet v s. Summa x s. Item ii pulli annales precii cuiuslibet xx d. Summa iii s. iiii d. Et Ciiii^{xx}xiiii multones precii capitis ii s. Summa xix li. viii s.[28] Et Ciiii^{xx}xiiii oves matrices precii capitis ii s. Summa xix li. viii s. Item vi[29] hurtardi precii capitis ii s. Summa xii s. Et xlv hogastri precii capitis xii d. Summa xlv s. Et xxx porci precii cuiuslibet iii s. precii in toto iiii li. x s. Et i aper precii iii s. iiii d. Et ii sues cum viii porcellis precii v s. Et xxx porc*i* campestres precii capitis xx d. Summa l s. Et i ancer et iii auce precii cuiuslibet iii d. Summa xii d. Item ii olle i urciolus i patella pelvis cum lavatorio precii v s. Item i dolium ad imponendum elemosinam precii iiii d. Item iiii^{or} scale precii xvi d. Item lx crates pro ovili construendo precii xx d. Item fimus precii xx d. Item de terra seminata cum frumento lxxiiii acre precii acre ii s. Summa vii li. viii s. Et xiii s. iiii d. in manibus prepositi de viii multonibus venditis precii capitis xx d. Et de lvi multonibus et ovibus matricibus per ipsum venditis precii cuiuslibet xxi d. ob. Summa C s. iiii d. Et xii d. de uno apro debili et infirmo vendito. Et v s. de corio unius tauri vendito. Et xxiii boves precii in toto vi li. x s. vi d. Et xxx s. de coriis xiii boum mortuis diverso precio. Et xxvii s. de vi boviculis venditis. Et vii s. de v boviculis venditis. Et ii d. de coriis ii vitulorum. Et xxxii s. de viii vaccis venditis diverso precio. Item vii coria vii vaccarum mortuarum de morina precii vi s. ix d. in toto qui denarii sunt in manibus Ricardi Wytherod prepositi. Item est ibi securis precii iii d. Et i crowe precii xii d. Et x mense cum trestellis et x forme precii xiii s. iiii d. Item iii howes precii ix d.

Summa Cxxvii li. xv s. iii d. qua. Probatur [Probatur]

Bona predicta committuntur Roberto White Ricardo de Wytherod et Simoni Wykyng' per indenturam custodienda ad opus domini regis.

Harewell'. S'. Custodes debent respondere ibidem de xliiii s. de feno et foragio. Ibi per estimacionem xlvi qr. et ii bus. frumenti precii qr. iiii s. Summa ix li. v s. Et lx qr.

ordei precii qr. iii s. iiii d. Summa viii li. vi s. viii d. Et xii qr. drageti precii qr. ii s. viii d. Summa xxxii s. Item i qr. fabarum precii < qr. > ii s. Et v qr. pisarum et vescarum precii qr. ii s. viii d. Summa xiii s. iiii d. Item fenum precii lx s. Et foragium precii iiii s. Et xvi boves precii capitis x s. Summa viii li. Et ii equi carectarii precii x s. Item i carecta debilis precii iii s. iiii d. Et ii currus precii vi s. Et i carecta pro fimis precii xii d. Et iiii^{xx}v oves matrices precii capitis xiiii d. Summa iiii li. xix s. ii d. Et ii caruce cum ferramento et hernasio precii iiii s. Et i olla enea precii iii s. iiii d. i patella enea precii iiii d. Item i pelvis cum lavatorio precii xviii d. Item maheremium et borde pro i molendino aquatico construendo precii C s. Item xiii acre et di. seminate frumento precii acre ii s. Summa xxvii s. Item solughbemes[30] precii ix d.

Summa xliiii li. v d. Probatur [Probatur]

Ta' Et venduntur ibidem \ i bos / pro xiii s. iiii d. et i sus cum ix porcellis precii vi s. Item xv porc*i* pro xv s. Item viii porc*i* pro ix s. ii d. Et fenum precii x s. Et ii carectate focalis pro xii d. Et xiii multones et oves matrices pro xv s. ii d. Que denarii sunt in manibus Rogeri Trendel prepositi.

Summa lxix s. viii d. Probatur [Probatur]

Et bona predicta committuntur Rogero Trendel Waltero Fot Willelmo Bartelat et Johanni le Baroun per indenturam custodienda ad opus domini regis.

Abberbury. S'. Custodes debent respondere ibidem de feno precii xxxiii s. iiii d. Ibidem per estimacionem xxxii qr. vii bus. frumenti precii qr. iiii s. Summa vi li. xi s. vi d. Item iiii^{xx}xi qr. et di. siliginis precii qr. iii s. Summa xiii li. xiii s. vi d. Et Cxxx qr. drageti precii qr. ii s. iiii d. Summa xv li. iii s. iiii d. Et xliiii qr. v bus. avene precii qr. ii s. Summa iiii li. ix s. iii d. Et ii qr. pisarum precii iiii s. in toto. Et fenum appreciatum ad liii s. iiii d. Et iii equi carectarii precii ii equorum xlviii s. in toto et precii tercii vi s. viii d. Item i niger pullus qui venit de Harewell' precii xxii s. Item i pullus discoloratus precii x s. Et xxiii boves precii capitis vi s. viii d. Summa vii li. xiii s. iiii d. Et ii tauri precii xiii s. iiii d. in toto. Et xi vacce precii capitis v s. Summa lv s. Et iiii boviculi precii capitis iii s. iiii d. Summa xiii s. iiii d. Et ix boviculi precii capitis ii s. vi d. Summa xxii s. vi d. Et i vitulus precii xii d. i sus precii ii s. ii porci precii v s. in toto. Et vi porc*i* precii capitis xvi d. Summa viii s. Et vii porcelli precii in toto ii s. iiii d. Et i hurtardus precii xvi d. Et Ciiii^{xx}xv multones et oves matrice precii capitis xvi d. Summa xiii li. Item ix pavones unde v galli et iiii^{or} gallini precii capitis vi d. Summa iiii s. vi d. Item i ancer et iiii auce precii in toto xv d. Item i carecta ferrata cum hernasio precii vi s. Item i carecta pro fimis cum[31] rotis debilibus precii ii s. Item ii olle i patella i urciolus i pelvi*s*[32] cum lavatorio et tripode precii vi s. viii d. Item i cuva i kuvelyn et i alveus precii vi d. Item ii paria liminum nova ad carect*as* precii viii d. In iii scale precii xviii d. Item xl crates ovili precii ii s. Et ii mense cum trestellis et ii formule precii in toto xii d. Item fimus precii xii d. Item iiii^{or} acre seminate frumento precii acre ii s. ii d. Summa viii s. viii d. Item Cxvi acre seminate siligine precii acre ii s. Summa xi li. xii s. Item stallus pro bidentibus precii vi d.

Summa iiii^{xx}vii li. viii s. vi d. Probatur [Probatur]

Ta' Et vend*i*tur stipula per prepositum precii vi s. viii d. Et foragium precium xix d. Item corium i vacce pro ii s. Item iiii porci venduntur pro x s. Et xlvi multones et oves matrices precii iiii li. xii s. Et xl crates ovili precii iii s. Et ix d. ob. de ix caseis. Et iii d. de iii lag. lactis venditis.

Summa Cxvi s. iii d. ob. Probatur [Probatur]

Et bona predicta committuntur Willelmo Whiting' Johanni Askil Thome Bereward et Ricardo Beche Winde[33] per indenturam custodienda ad opus domini regis.

Brightewell'. S'. Custodes episcopatus ibidem debent respondere de xl s. de feno. Ibidem per estimacionem xxx qr. frumenti precii qr. iiii s. Summa vi li. Item x qr. siliginis precii qr. iii s. Summa xxx s. Item iiii^xx^x qr. ordei precii qr. iii s. Summa xiii li. x s. Item xx qr. drageti precii qr. ii s. Summa xl s. Item iiii qr. pisarum precii viii s. in toto. Et i qr. et di. mixtilonis precii iii s. in toto. Et fenum precii lx s. Et iii equi carectarii precii xxx s. in toto. Et vi affri precii capitis iiii s. Summa xxiiii s. Et i jumentum precii vi s. viii d. Et xxxiiii boves precii capitis vi s. viii d. Summa xi li. vi s. viii d. Item i taurus precii ii s. vi d. Et xiii vacce precii capitis iiii s. Summa lii s. Et viii boviculi precii cuiuslibet xii d. Summa viii s. Et i sus precii ii s. Et xvii porcelli precii cuiuslibet viii d. Summa xi s. iiii d. Item i ancer et iiii^or^ auce precii xv d. in toto. Et xi capones precii xxii d. in toto. Et i gallus et v galline precii ix d. in toto. Et xlviii acre seminate frumento precii acre ii s. Summa iiii li. xvi s. Et xlv acre seminate cum siligine precii acre xviii d. Summa lxvii s. vi d. Item i carecta ferrata cum hernasio precii v s. Item i carecta pro fimis precii xviii d. Et fimus precii xii d. Item i civera precii iii d. Item ii olle enee precii iii s. Et ii urcioli precii xii d. Et ii patelle precii ii s. Item i pelvis cum lavatorio precii vi d.

Summa liii li. xv s. ix d. Probatur [Probatur]

Et venduntur ibi viii vacce precii capitis iiii s. vi d. Summa xxxvi s. Et viii boviculi precii capitis iii s. Summa xxiiii s. Et iii porc*i* precii cuiuslibet xxii d. Summa v s. vi d. Item i pullanus precii xviii d. Et i affrus precii vi s. viii d.

Summa lxxiii s. viii d. Probatur [Probatur]

Et bona predicta committuntur Roberto le Cart*er*e preposito et Ricardo West per indenturam custodienda ad opus domini regis.

[[Summa istius partis CCCxxv li. xix s. vi d. ob. qua. Probatur]]

vi Examinatur

[*Rot. 6d*] *Sandale* Bona que fuerunt domini Johannis de Sandale nuper Wyntoniensis episcopi apud Sandale
In primis i dolium de venacione non plenum precii[34]
Item i pipa de vernache non plena precii C s.
Item xii haubergeons precii in toto xl s.
Item ii jaumbers de maille precii viii d.
Item vi paunces de maille precii xii d.
Item i gasingale precii x d.
Item ii trappe de maille precii x s.
Item i pisane precii vi d.
Item v aketons albi precii in toto xx s.
Item v bacinett*es* de ferro precii v s.
Item ii cirotece de plat*a* debiles precii iiii d.
Item i par*e* de quisseus de ferro precii xii d.
Item i par*e* de quisseus de linge teill*e* precii vi d.
Item ii paria de jaumbers de ferro precii xviii d.
Item ii paria de polenis de ferro precii viii d.

Item i blason' precii viii d.
Item vii selle pro runcyns cum ii frenis precii xvi s.
Item iii capelle de verins precii in toto vi d.
Item de lardario iiii carcosia boum precii in toto xx s.
Item xxx casse multonum precii in toto xx s.
Item i missale in quadam cista precii x li.
Item i portiforium precii x s.
Item i doublet' precii x s.
Item una carta de libertatibus episcopatus Wyntoniensis cum aliis diversis memorandis
Item i cista continens i bibliam precii x marcarum
Item i biblia precii l s.
Item i par decretorum precii v marcarum[35]
Item i par decretalium precii v marcarum[36]
Item i portiforium precii lxxiii s. iiii d.
Item i gradale precii xx s.
Item aliud gradale precii di. marce
Item iiii libri de romaunces precii xx s.
Item ii albe de secta usitate quarum parure sunt de armis regum Anglie et Francie cum i stola et cum ii fanons et ii amicz absque paruris[37] precii xx s.
Item i tunicle dalmaticle de eadem secta precii xl s.
Item i alba de velvet' stragulata cum stola fanon et amiz precii x s.[38]
Item i frontale ultra altare et aliud super altare stragulat*a* precii xx s.
Item ii cape de choro de raffata precii ii marcarum
Item alia capa de choro de samito rubeo cum linatura de sindone precii viii s.
Item i superpellicium precium vi d.
Summa lxiii li. xvii s. viii d. [Probatur] [[Probatur]]

Item i saccus de garderoba domini precii iii s.
In eodem i roba de camelett' linata de sindone viridi cum mantello et cloche precii xl s.
Item i roba de marberyn linata sindone viridi precii ii marcarum
Item i supertunica de tirteyn et i collobium de nigro panno precii di. marce
Item iiii paria linee tele precii vi s.
Item ii paria lintheaminorum precii x s.
Item i culcitra apta pro lecti coopertorio cooperta de indea et i culcitra de eadem secta cum iii curtinis et i spervera de samyt' indea precii x marcarum
Item i canevaz de carde cum ii peciis usitatis et debilibus precii ii s. vi d.
Item i coopertorium ad modum culcitre de sindone viridi precii xxx s.
Item iiii tapeta nova de viridi Paris' precii xxvi s. viii d.
Item iiii tapeta de indea usitate precii xx s.
Item i bal' de dates continens CCxvi \ lib. / precii centene xvi s. Summa xxxiiii s. vi d.
Memorandum Item ii barelli uterque quasi mensura iiii^{xx} lag. pleni de sucre pulvere albo et aliis speceriis precii[39]
Item l lib. cinomomi precii lib. ix d. Summa xxxvii s. vi d.
Item i flasket precii in toto xvi d.
Item vi bolion' amigdolarum continentes $M^{l}i$ quart. xiiii lib. precii cuiuslibet centene xviii s. Summa < ix li. ii s. ii d. > \ ix li. vi s. ix d. /

Item i pecia cere continens Ci quart. xxvii lib.
Item i pecia cere continens Ci quart. xxiiii lib.
Item[40] i pecia cere continens C di. iiii lib.
Item i pecia cere continens Ci quart. xxi lib.
Summa de istis Diiii quart. xx lib. precii centene lx s. Summa valet xvii li. xv s. viii d. ob. preter iiii li. xii s. que remanent in manu R. de Sandale.

Item i pecia cere continens Ci quart. xiiii lib.
Item i pecia cere continens Ci quart. xxi lib.
Continent CCiii quart. vii lib. precii ut supra. Summa viii li. viii s. ix d.

Summa [liiii li. ix s. iiii d. ob. Probatur]

Item i fardellum trussatum et frectatum in quo continentur de croco xxxvi lib. precii lib. iii s. iii d. Summa vi li.
Item lxviii lib. di. de geng*e*vre precii lib. ii s. Summa vi li. xvii s.
Item xl lib. de galinga precii lib. xi d. Summa xxxvi s. viii d.
Item xxx lib. de galiophiro precii lib. iii s. viii d. Summa C s. < x d. > [\ x s. /]
Item xxx lib. de maces precii lib. iii s. vi d. Summa Cv s.
Item xii lib. de quibibes precii lib. iiii s. viii d. Summa lvi s.
Item xxx lib. de poivre precii lib. x d. Summa xxv s.
Item xii lib. cimini precii lib. i d. Summa xii d.
Item vi lib. de saundr*es* precii lib. xii d. Summa vi s.
Item xxx lib. de racemis Corincialibus precii lib. iiii d. Summa x s.
Item vi flaskett*es* precii ix s.
Item lxxii ulne naperie precii ulne x d.[41]
Item xxx ulne manutergii precii ulne iiii d. Summa istorum lxx s.
Item C di. canabi pro naperia precii lx s.
Item xxxii ulne manutergii precii in toto xii s.
Item C di. ulne canabi grossi precii in toto li s.
Item xxxviii ulne naperie precii in toto xxi s. vii d.
Item iiii^{xx}iiii ulne linee tele precii in toto xliii s.[42]
Item xxvii ulne linee tele precii in toto xv s. ix d.
Item iii ulne canabi pro lect*is* faciend*is* precii xviii d.
Item ii pecie naperie de Dynaunt' continentes iiii^{xx}xv ulnas precii in toto lv s.
Item x manutergia in i pecia precii viii s. ix d.
Item i pecia de sauvenapes continens in toto xxxv ulnas precii in toto x s. ii d. ob.
Item i pecia de manutergio precii in toto v s. iii d.
Item i pecia de manutergio precii in toto vi s. viii d.
Item xxx ulne linee tele precii in toto xx s.
Summa < xlix li. vi s. ii d. Probatur > [xlix li. xv s. iiii d. ob.]

Summa istius partis rotuli Clxviii li. ii s. v d. [Probatur]

[*Rot. 7r, mem. 1*] Inventarium bonorum Johannis de Sandale nuper Wyntoniensis episcopi apud Suthwerk' inventorum

Capella In primis i casula almatica dealmatica de variis coloribus de Tars' precii xxvi s. viii d.

Item i capa chori de velvecto stragulato et skaccato cum casula dealmatica et tunica de eadem secta precii iiii li.
Item i casula iii cape chore tunica et dealmatica cum ii frontellis de viridi precii viii li.
Item ii tunice de viridi de taffata precii xx s.
Item ii casule cum corporal*ibus* precii xxvi s. viii d.
Item i capa chori broudata de imaginibus precii x li.
Item i alba cum paruris broudat*is* cum imaginibus et stola et fanon*a* de eadem secta precii lxvi s. viii d.
Item i alba cum paruris broudat*is* de historia passionis Cristi cum stola fanon*a* et amicta de eadem secta precii xl s.
Item i alba cum paruris broudat*is* de imaginibus apostolorum cum amicta et stola de eadem secta precii xxvi s. viii d.
Item i casula iiii tunice iii cape iii albe iii amicte ii stole et iii fanone de nigro panno de taffata precii Cvi s. viii d.
Item xiiii pecie cuiusdam libri qui vocatur pontificale precii vi s. viii d.
Item i superaltare precii ii s.
Item i parva tabula pro altari depicta precii vi s. viii d.
Item i tabula argenti amelata ordinata pro pace danda in capella precii xv s.
Item i frontale ante altare de panno de camocha viridi broudatum cum imagine sancte Trinitatis cum ii angelis insensantibus cum i superfrontali i panno ad lectrinum de consimili panno et consimili broudato cum imagine beate Marie virginis et aliis imaginibus precii x li.
Item i alba debilis cum paruris panni de Turkys cum amict*a* stola et fanon*a* et iii tuellis dedicatis et i auriculari pro altari precii x s.
Item i missale precii xxvi s. viii d.
Item i gradale precii xx s.
Item i casula iii cape chori i tunica i dealmatica ii frontallia de albo panno de Turky precii xii li. Et liberantur priori beate Marie de Suthwerk' pro ornamento corporis defuncti die sepulture eiusdem.
Item ii candelabra ponderis lx s. et valent lx s.
Item ii pelves \ argenti / ordinantes pro altari ponderis xlv s. et valent xlv s.
Item ii fioli argenti pro altari ponderis xx s. et valent xxvi s. viii d.
Item i crux argenti et deaurata cum pede amelat*o* et ingravat*o* ponderis xxxi s. viii d. precii xlv s.
Item i navis argenti pro incenso cum cocleario argenti ponderis xxv s. et valet xxvi s. viii d.
Item i calix cum patena argenti deaurat*i* ponderis xxvi s. viii d. precii xl s.
Item i turribulus argenti deauratus cum cathenis argenti non deauratis ponderis l s. et valet[43] lxx s.
Item i vas argenti cum ysopo argenti ordinat*a* pro aqua benedicta in capella ponderis lxvii s. vi d. precii iiii li. x d.
Item i campanella argenti ordinata pro capella ponderis v s. precii vii s.
Item i pixis eburnea ligata argento precii iii s. iiii d.
Item i campana enea pro capella precii iiii s.
Item i orfreys broudata de diversis capitibus precii C s.
Item in quodam coffino x pecie de orfreis cum pipis de auro et in parte amellate de armis reg*um* Anglie quas defunctus habuit de domino rege
Item iii pecie de orfreis et di. de filo auri quas similiter rex dedit eidem

Item i crux depicta in i casula et i alia crux antiqua de ebore precii in toto vi s. viii d.
Item ii casule v cape chori de baudekyns usitat*e* precii cuiuslibet v s. Summa xxxv s.[44]
Item ii panni ad aurum precii xl s.
\ Item iii manutergia i frontale de ca*nu*bo cum broudatis precii v s. /[45]
iiii^{xx}i li. x s. vi d.
[Summa iiii^{xx}i li. xv s. vi d. Probatur]

Aula Item v tapeta de armis diversis et papejaies precii xv s. Et iii tapeta debilia et lacerata precii vi s. Et i dosserium de diversis armis precii xiii s. iiii d. Et ii dosseria de indea pou*n*drata de \ iii / foliis[46] rubiis cum bordura de armis regum Anglie et x pecie pro costis aule et camere de eadem secta precii xxx li.
Item i tapetum precii x s.
< *xxxii li. iiii s. iii d.* >
[Summa xxxii li. iiii s. iiii d. Probatur]

Camera Item ii culcitre veteres et usitate precii xiii s. iiii d.
Item ii culcitre de card*e* inde*o* nove precii xx s.
Item i contrepoint de sindone rubio coopert*um* precii viii s.
Item ii sarges rubi*i* de quibus i remanet in ecclesia de Suthwerk' super tumbam precii x s.
Item i carpetum pro capella precii vi s. viii d.
Item i coopertorium de burnecto furratum de griseo precii xl s.
Item i canevaz de card*e* inde*o* in quo trussantur omnia predicta precii xviii d.
Item i contrepoint' coopert*um* de sindon*e* inde*o* precii xiii s. iiii d.
Item i blank*et* precii x s.
Item iiii tapeta de indeo precii xvi s.
Item ii contrepointz coopert*a* de albo sindon*e* precii viii s.
Item ii curtyns de card*e* inde*o* cum sperver de eadem secta precii xiii s. iiii d.
Item i canevaz de indeo precii ii s. vi d.
Item i roba de russecto brustekyn cum furrura de griseo de v garniamentis et ii capuciis preter mantellum qui furratur de agnis de Lindes' precii vi li. xiii s. iiii d.
Item i roba de sanguineo de vi garniamentis furratis de vario preter mantellum qui furratur de grosso vario precii vi li. xiii s. iiii d.
Item i roba de ta*une* en greyn de vi garniamentis de i furrura de vario ii de griseo et mantellum de agnis de Lindeseie et clok' non furrat*us* precii iiii li. xiii s. iiii d.
Item ii supertunice i cloca et ii capucia de russecto brustekyn furrata de griseo cum mantello furrato de agnis de Lindeseie precii lxvi s. iiii d.
Item i roba cum v garniamentis et ii capucia de melle linata de sindon*e* viridi precii xl s.
Item i corset de panno ta*u*nato de camoca furrat*o* de vario precii xx s.
Item ii cloches non furrati novi de pers precii xxvi s. viii d.
Item i cloch' de pers furratus de biss' cum capuci*o* furrat*o* de eadem secta precii xvi s.
Item i supertunica cum capuci*o* de camelino de Triple linata cum panno de taphata inde*a* cum mantello de secta precii xx s.
Item ii paria cirotecarum de panno unde i par \ furratus / de vario et alius de biss' precii ii s.

Item v sacci ad pannos et ii bahud' precii cuiuslibet xl d. Summa xxiii s. iiii d.
Item ii cloches debiles de nigro panno precii viii s.
[*Rot. 7r, mem. 2*] Item iii albe tunice de blanket' unde i furrata de agnis precii vi s. viii d.
Item iiii ulne de albo panno novo precii ulne ii s. vi d. Summa x s.
Item xii coffr*es* iiii paniers precii cuiuslibet xx d. Summa xxvi s. viii d.
< *xxxix li. viii s. iiii d.*>

[Summa xxxix li. viii s. iiii d. Probatur]

Jocalia remanencia in custodia executorum impignorata et vendita
In[47] primis i anulus auri cum rubecto bono precii C li.
Item i anulus auri cum rubecto precii xx marcarum
Item iii anuli auri cum balesiis precii cuiuslibet xl s. Summa vi li.
Item i anulus auri cum emeraldis precii v marcarum
Item vi anuli auri cum safiris precii cuiuslibet xx s. Summa vi li.
Item i anulus auri ingravatus ad modum sigilli precii xx s.
Item i pixis amelat*a* cum armis reg*um* Anglie in qua est bonus rubectus \ precii / xxvi s. viii d.
Item i anulus auri cum rubecto et ameraldi*s* precii iii s. iiii d.
Item i ciphus de mazre cum cooperculo argenti precii C s.
Item i navis argenti ponderis vii marcarum precii viii marcarum
Item vi pelves argenti ponderis xxi lib. x s. Summa xxi li. x s.
Item xl disce argenti et xxxviii salsarii argenti ponderis lvi lib. xx d. Summa lvi li. xx d.
< *CCxix li. xx d.* >

[Summa CCxix li. xx d. Probatur]

Item[48] xx ciphi plati ponderis xii lib. ii s. vi d.
Item iiii chargeours ponderis ix lib. xiii s. iiii d.
Item iii olle argenti ponderis xi lib. vi s.
Item ii disce pro speciebus et i parva argenti ponderis Ci s. viii d.

Summa ponderis predictorum jocalium xxxix lib. xvii s. vi d.

Item i ciphus albus cum pede et cooperculo argenti precii xxix s.
Item i ciphus albus cum pede et cooperculo precii xxvii s. vi d.
Item i ciphus albus cum pede et cooperculo precii xxx s. viii d.
Item i ciphus albus cum pede et cooperculo precii xxxii s.
Item i olla et i aquarium argenti precii v marcarum iii s. iiii d.
Item i calix precii iiii^{or} marcarum
Item ii phioli argenti precii xxx s.
Item ii missalia et i portiforium Cvi s. viii d.
< *liii li. x s.*>

[Summa < liii li. x s. Probatur >]
[Summa lviii li. xvi s. viii d.] [[Probatur]]

Equi domini J. quondam Wyntoniensis episcopi venditi per executores
Grisell'[49] de Goldinton' venditus[50] magistro G. de Middelton' pro xx marcis
Bayard' de Wynteney carectarius venditus Ricardo de Reynham pro xiii s. iiii d.
Item ferand' Brewer et bayard' de Smethfeld' carectar*ii* venditi H. de Copsted' pro xxvi s. viii d.

Morellus de Clere carectarius venditus J. de Merkingfeld' pro xxvi s. viii d.
Baiard Dikheved et lyard de longa carecta venditi magistro G. de Middelton' pro iiii li.
Bulsi[51] venditus domino T. de Folquardby pro iiii li.
Morellus somerus de butelleria venditus J. de London' pro xl s.
Grisell' de Founteyns venditus magistro R. de Norton pro viii marcis
Grisell' pullanus venditus magistro W. de Staunford' pro iiii marcis
Baiard' de Ebor' venditus archidiacono Wynton' pro vi marcis
Baiard' de aula venditus W. le Blount' pro xl s.
Lyard de sancto Albano venditus Henrico de Staldewell' pro iiii marcis
< *xliii li. vi s. viii d.* >

[Summa xliii li. vi s. viii d. Probatur]

Jocalia[52] In primis i anulus cum safiro magno orientali precii liii s. iiii d.
In i anulus auri cum safiro precii xxvi s. viii d.
Et i anulus auri cum rubecto precii xiii s. iiii d.
Et i anulus auri cum camuto precii vi s. viii d.
Et i anulus auri cum safir*o* precii iii s. iiii d.
Et i anulus auri cum i pelicot' precii iii s. iiii d.
Et i anulus auri cum pelicot' magno precii xii s.
Et i anulus auri cum safir*o* precii vi s. viii d.
Et i anulus auri cum pelicot' precii iii s. iiii d.
Et i anulus auri cum safiro quadrato precii xxvi s. viii d.
Et i anulus auri cum quodam gernet precii iiii s.
Et i anulus auri cum i ameralda precii xx s.
Et i anulus auri cum safir*o* precii v s.
Et i anulus auri cum safir*o* precii x s.
Et i anulus auri cum safir*o* precii xxvi s. viii d.
Et i anulus auri cum safir*o* precii x s.
Et xix anuli cum rubect*is* et ameraldi*s* precii cuiuslibet <u>xii d.</u> Summa xix s.
Et i anulus auri cum safir*o* precii x s.
Item i anulus pontificalis cum magno safiro circumamicto cum xii ameraldis parvis precii Cvi s. viii d.
Item i nuchea que vocatur mors' ad capam chori cum i camahuto albo magno precii xxvi s. viii d.
Item v safiri mediocres sine auro in toto iiii li.
Item i anulus magnus de cristallo cum safiro bono ut creditur virtuoso circumamicto rubectis et emerald*is* parvis inclusis in quadam pixide de cupro precii xxvi s. viii d.
Precium istius anuli pro rege non ...dit[53] *in summa totalis istius rotuli* Item i anulus auri cum baliso quadrato pro rege precii x li.
Item i firmaculum auri cum iii rubectis et iii meraldis precii xl s.
Item i firmaculum precii xiii s. iiii d.
Non appreciatur Item i zona que fuit Roberti de Wynchelse quondam archiepiscopi Cantuariensis tenetur pro reliquio
Item i loculus de serico precii iiii s.
Item i scrinenium in quo jocalia predicta ponuntur precii iii s.
Item i ciphus de jaspide cum pede argenti et deaurato precii lx s.
Item i liber qui vocatur Sidrak' precii v s.[54]

Item i parvus picherus de vitr*eo* albo hernisiato cum argento precii vi s. viii d.
Item i liber predicacionis precii ii s.
Item i alius liber de sermonibus diversorum predicatorum precii xii d.
Item i ciphus de nuce nigra cum pede et cooperculo argenti et deauratis precii xl s.
Item i nux minor cum argento deaurat*o* et cum cooperculo non deaurato precii xxx s.
Item i firmaculum auri precii vi s. viii d.
Item i jocale cum lingua serpentis ad modum frondis deauratum ponderis xxix s. precii xl s.
Item i ciphus argenti cum pede et cooperculo planus pro rege ponderis lv s. x d.
Item xi burse de serico broudate precii cuiuslibet iiii s. xliiii s.
Item iii zone de serico precii cuiuslibet xv d. Summa iii s. ix d.
Item ii coclearia argenti pro speciebus ponderis iii s. viii d. Et valent iii s. viii d.
Item i ciphus de mazre cum cooperculo argenti plano precii xxvi s. viii d.
Item i par cultellorum magnorum cum mans' de jasper precii x s.
Item alius par cultellorum magnorum cum mans' de ebore precii v s.
Item ii ciphi de mazre veteres precii x s. in toto.
Item i par cultellorum magnorum cum mans' de cristallo precii xiii s. iiii d.
Item alius par cultellorum cum mans' de cristallo prec' vi s. .....
Item i par cultellorum cum mans' de jaspide precii vi s. viii d.
Item i ciphus de mazre cum pede argenti turci et deaurati amellatus in fundo precii xvi s.

[Summa xliiii li. xvii s. vi d. Probatur] [[Probatur]]

[< Summa totalis istius partis Dxiiii li. iii s. xi d. Probatur >]
[[Summa totalis istius partis Dxix li. x s. vii d.]]

[*Rot. 7d., mem. 1*] *Garderoba* Item iiii^{xx}iii ulne de canabo precii in toto xx s. ix d.
Item i pecia naperie continens xiiii ulnas precii in toto vii s.
Item i pecia mapparum continens v mappas et quelibet mappa vii ulnas precii ulne vi d. Summa xviii s. vi d.
Item i pecia de manutergio que continet iii manutergia quodlibet de vii ulnis precii ulne ii d. ob. Summa iii s. vi d.
Item i pecia continens iiii manutergia unde ii continent utraque vii ulnas et alia ii continent iii ulnas precii ii d. ob. Summa v s. iii d.
Item iiii ulne linee tele precii ulne vi d. Summa ii s.
Item i cathedra trussabilis de ferro precii ii s.
Item ii chapelle precii iii s.
Item i casula pro eisdem chapellis precii ii s.
Item ii bulge veteres precii vi d.
Et v ulne et di. de burnecto precii ulne iii s. Summa xvi s. vi d.
Item vi coffr*es* et ii paniers precii cuiuslibet xx d. Summa xiii s. iiii d.
< *lxxv s. x d. Probatur* >

[Summa iiii li. xiii s. iii d. Probatur]

Item[55] iiii fraels de ficubus precii[56]
Item i ball' de rys continens CCCC precii[57]
Item i bale de dates gemellatis non integra precii[58]

Item i morterium ereum cum pestello precii vi s. viii d.
Et i morterium lapideum precii vi s. viii d.
< *xiii s. iiii d.* >
[Summa xiii s. iiii d. Probatur]

Libri Item i biblia cooperta cum corio rubeo precii lxvi s. viii d.
Et quartus liber quarte partis pantheologi cooperta de albo corio precii i marce[59]
Item Hostiensis in ii voluminibus in corio viridi precii iiii li.[60]
Item prefacio sancti Bernardi abbatis cum corio nigro precii i marce[61]
Item exposicio quorundam ewangelii secundum Marcum de corio nigro precii x s.
Item quedam vetustissima decret*a*[62] in corio rubeo precii iii s. iiii d.
Item Pritianus gramatic*a* cum corio bullito precii xviii d.[63]
Item quedam summa de viciis compilata per fratrem Willelmum in corio rubeo precii vi s. viii d.[64]
Item exposicio quorundam ewangelii secundum Matheum de corio rubeo precii v s.
Item i biblia in romanis[65] in albo corio precii i marce.
Item i liber de romanc*is* precii x s.
Item quoddam vetus gradale precii ii s.
Item i liber qui vocatur Innocent' precii xx s.[66]
Item i phalterium precii x s.
Item quedam statuta r*egni* precii ii s.
Item i liber de cantu organico precii ii s.
Item i liber qui vocatur tresor precii xx s.[67]
Item quoddam aliud phalterium precii xiii s. iiii d.
[Summa xiiii li. xii s. vi d. Probatur]
Et i liber qui dicitur pontificale magnus liberatur priori Wynton' quia fuit eiusdem prioris.
Item i zona quo defunctus utebatur dum vixit cum ii alvers. Et i bursa de serico non appreciantur.

Equi remanentes
Item magnus palefridus pro rege
Item magnus palefridus baiard' precii x li.
Item morellus somerus butellarie precii xx s.
Item baiard de capella precii liii s. iiii d.
Item vayron carectarius precii xxvi s. viii d.
Item liard' carectarius precii xiii s. iiii d.
Item liard' carectarius precii xx s.
Baiard' de Gernemue precii x s.
Item feraunt de Ledes precii xx s.
Item feraunt pro coffr*es* pro butellaria precii liii s. iiii d.
Item liard Carnan nullius precii ultra xviii d.
Item morellus carectarius precii xiii s. iiii d.
Item ii carecte et i longa carecta hernasiate precii xxxvii s.
< *xxiii li. viii s. vi d.* >
[Summa xxiii li. viii s. vi d.]

Coquina Ibi i magna olla ponderis iiii^{xx}x lib. precii lib. i d. ob. precii in toto xi s. iii d.
Et \ i / alia olla ponderis xl lib. precii v s.
Et ii olle ponderis lx lib. precii vii s. vi d.
Et i olla magna ponderis lx lib. precii xii s. vi d.
Et i olla ponderis xx lib. precii lib. ii d. ob. precii iiii s. ii d.
Item ii urcioli et i calestourium ponderis xxx lib. precii vi s. xi d.
Item i patella cuprea pene nova preci xiii s. iiii d.
Item alia patella minor precii vi s. viii d.
Item alia patella precii vi s. viii d.
Item alia patella precii vi s. viii d.
Item ii patella in parte fracte et debiles precii iii s.
Item ii patelle ferri et fricatorium precii iiii s.
Item ii craticule ferri precii ii s. vi d.
Item micatorium precii xii d. Item i ferrum ordinatum ad supportandum ollas et patellas in coquina precii ii s. vi d.
Item iiii haste ferri cum iii tribulis precii iii s.
Item i parva hasta precii ii d.
Non respondentur Item v olle enee ponderis Cxxx lib. precii lib. ii d. ob. Item ii calestouria enea conjuncta in pondere cum predictis v ollis ponderis x lib. precii in toto cum predictis ollis preter ferrum eiusdem appositum. Summa xxix s. ii d.
< *vi li. v s. iiii d.* >

[Summa vi li. v s. iiii d. Probatur]

Item i anulus auri cum i emeralda precii xx s. Item i anulus auri cum peridot' precii ii s. vi d. Item i zona de filo argenti harnisiata argento deaurato ponderis xliii s. iiii d. Et valent xliii s. iiii d. Item ii cornua de ebore i majus cum zona de viridi serico et hernisiatum argento precii lx s. Item aliud minus similiter hernisiatum precii xl s.
< *viii li. v s. x d.* >

[Summa viii li. v s. x d. Probatur]

Et memorandum quod ista bona in ultimo panello superius scripta tam restituuntur de omnibus bonis de quibus compertum fuit per inquisitionem coram dominis W. de Norwico et J. de Foxle apud Suthwerk captam que elongabantur per familiares dicti defuncti.

Ta' Item in balliviis de Farnham Sutton' Alta Clere Twyford' Dounton' et Taunton' cum membris et apud Wolvessey < et Becheworth > sunt iiii^{xx}ix caruce cum herciis et actilliis precii cuiuslibet ii s. Summa viii li. xviii s.
Et in eisdem balliviis fima appreciata in toto ad xlii s. iiii d.
< *xi li. iiii d.* >

[Summa xi li. iiii d. Probatur]

Item sunt ibidem x qr. drageti precii qr. ii s. Summa xx s. Et iii pecie maheremii precii xii d. Item triturantur ibidem post diem predictum v qr. drageti precii qr. ii s. Summa x s. Et elongantur per Henricum de Scaldewell'. \ Summa xxxi s. / Et elongatur i equus per quemdam Nicholum clericum escaetoris precii iiii marcarum.

< *iiii li. iiii s. iiii d.* >

[Summa iiii li. iiii s. iiii d. Probatur]

Et memorandum quod omnia bona apud Suthwerk' inventa remanent in manibus executorum sub sigill*is* predictorum Ade Ricardi et Radul*ph*i de Rudham salvo custodienda ad opus domini regis.

[Summa totalis precii bonorum ex ista parte rotuli lxxiii li. iiii s. vi d. Probatur]

Quia inferius < Summa totalis precii bonorum tam ex altera parte rotuli quam ex ista usque huc videlicet bonorum inventorum in manerio de Suthwerk' Diiii^{xx}vi li. iii s. v d. In ista summa continentur partem que inseruntur in alia parte rotuli huic rotuli consut*is* \ et ..... / hoc rotulo superiori ex utraque parte tunc

Summa totalis precii bonorum inventorum apud Suthewerk' Diiii^{xx}vii li. viii s. v d. [Probatur] >

[*Rot. 7d., mem. 2*] *Jeveneye. S'. Prepositus debet respondere de x s. de feno.* Item in manerio de Yeveneie idem episcopus habuit bona et catalla videlicet xxx qr. frumenti precii qr. iiii s. Summa vi li. Et vi qr. fabarum precii qr. iii s. Summa xviii s. Et xxx qr. ordei precii qr. iii s. Summa iiii li. x s. Et xxvi qr. avene precii qr. ii s. Summa lii s. Et xvii qr. pisarum et vescarum precii qr. ii s. Summa xxxiiii s. Item fenum[68] precii xvi s. Et foragium precii ii s. vi d. Et ii equos caretarios precii xvi s. in toto. Et vi affros precii capitis v s. Summa xxx s. Et iiii boves precii capitis v s. Summa xx s. Et vi vaccas precii vacce iiii s. Summa xxiiii s. Et ii boviculos precii iii s. in toto. Et ii sues cum ix porcellos precii v s. x d. in toto. Item ii capones precii iiii d. in toto. Et i carectam ligatam ferro cum hernasio precii vi s. Et i carectam pro fimis precii ii s. Et i carucam cum hernasio precii xviii d. Et xviii acras seminatas cum frumento precii acre iii s. Summa liiii s.

Summa xxiiii li. xv s. ii d. [Probatur]

Bona predicta committuntur Willelmo Pleinam*our* Thome le Fullere Thome Pleinam*our* et Johanni Bynorth' per indenturam custodienda ad opus domini regis.

Merdele. S'. Item habuit in manerio de Merdele xxvi qr. frumenti precii qr. iiii s. Summa Ciiii s. Et iiii qr. mixtilonis precii qr. iii s. Summa xii s. Et xx qr. drageti precii qr. ii s. vi d. Summa l s. Et xl qr. avene precii qr. ii s. Summa iiii li. Et xxiii acras seminatas cum frumento precii acre ii s. Summa xlvi s. Item iiii acras seminatas cum mixtilone precii acre xviii d. Summa vi s. Et ii equos carectarios precii xx s. Et vi affros precii capitis v s. Summa xxx s. Et i carectam ferratam cum hernasio precii vi s. viii d. Et i carucam cum apparatu precii ii s. Et ii mensas cum trestellis formul*is* et tabul*is* precii xvi d. Item i alveum precii xii d. Et i cuveram precii iii d. Et fenum precii vi d.

Summa xvii li. xix s. ix d. [Probatur]

Bona predica committuntur Radulpho Elienore Roberto atte Sightre Ade atte Oke et Waltero West juniori.

[Summa predictorum ii maneriorum xlii li. xiiii s. xi d.]

Postea termino sancti Hillarii eodem anno xiii^{o} apud Ebor' predicto Johanne de Heidene plenius examinato per predictum Adam de Lymberg' de denariis quos idem episcopus habuit apud Wolveseie et alibi die obitus sui cognovit quod idem episcopus habuit eodem die in denariis CC marcas de quibus ipse ut executor ipsius episcopi fecit administracionem etc.

Summa CC marcas

< Summa totalis ex parte ista huius rotuli superiori rotulo consuti Clxxvi li. xix d. [Probatur] >

Summa totalis omnium bonorum predictorum preter bona non appreciata < vM^{l}CCCCiiii^{xx}xix li xv ... ix d. >

Summa[69] totalis de precio bonorum jocalium equorum et aliorum inventorum apud Suthwerk et apud Sandale DCClv li. x s. x d. Probatur

Summa totalis aliorum bonorum et catallorum inventorum in maneriis predictis \ preter Suthwerk' et Sandale / MMMMDCCxlii li. xviii s. viii d. ob. qua.

Summa totalis dictarum duarum summarum totalium vM^{l}CCCCiiii^{xx}xviii li. ix s. vi d. ob. qua. Probatur

Hunc[70] rotulum liberavit hic Adam de Lymbergh' rememorditorio de scaccario domini regis xxiiii die Aprilis anno regni regis Edwardi filii regis Edwardi quinto-decimo.

Inventarium de bonis et catallis que fuerunt Johannis de Sandale nuper episcopi Wyntoniensis defuncti per Adam de Lymbergh et Ricardum de Pottesgrave ad hoc assignatos per breve regis

Notes

1 Bracketed against the whole paragraph.
2 MS has a double 'f', i.e. a capital, mid-word, rather than the 'sf' of the modern form, Alresford.
3 MS: 'Cxix s.' over erasure.
4 In a further hand, in the bottom left corner of the roll.
5 Bracketed against both the following entries.
6 Bracketed against both the following entries.
7 MS: deletion made in the hand that wrote the second 'probatur'.
8 The total should be £1158 9*s.* 4½*d.*, including £190 17*s.* 5*d.* in the 'tallies' sections.
9 MS should total £9 11*s.* 8*d.*
10 MS: 'xxi li. xviii s. viii d.' written over erasure.
11 MS: 'xi d.' written over erasure.
12 MS blotted.
13 The total is £1320 0*s.* 0½*d.*, including the 'tallies' sections.
14 MS has a double 'f' for a capital mid-word.
15 MS: 'que coria venduntur pro iii s.' over erasure.
16 MS: insertion in a different hand to the text and the work of the auditors, without affecting the total.
17 MS: insertion in a further hand.
18 MS has a double 'f' for a capital form mid-word.
19 MS has a double 'f' for a capital form mid-word.
20 MS: 'xiiii s. viii d.' over erasure, in a further hand.
21 MS omits 's.' in 'xlvii s.'
22 MS: total written over erasure, by main hand of text.
23 The total should be 26*s.* 9*d.*

24 MS: 'in indentura' added by a further hand.
25 MS repeats 'Et'.
26 MS: 'superedend''.
27 The total, taking account of the corrections, is £419 19*s.* 2¾*d.*
28 MS: 'i' of 'xix' written over erasure.
29 MS: 'vi' written over erasure.
30 MS: 'so' written over erasure.
31 MS: 'pro'.
32 MS: 'pelvi', written off edge of membrane.
33 MS: blank space precedes 'Winde'.
34 No value given.
35 Gratian *Decretum*, printed in *Corpus iuris canonici* ed. E. Friedberg (2nd edition, 2 vols., Leipzig, 1922) i.
36 Gregory IX *Decretales*, printed in *Corpus iuris canonici*, ii, cols. 1–928.
37 MS: 'parures'.
38 This entry is bracketed to the one following in an ink different from that of the main text.
39 No value given.
40 MS: preceded in margin by *n' r'* ; possibly for 'nota', 'respicere'.
41 This entry is bracketed with the one following for the valuation.
42 MS: the first 'i' in 'xliii s.' is an insertion in main hand.
43 MS: 'ponderis ..... valet' over erasure, in main hand.
44 This entry written over an erasure.
45 MS: possibly inserted after the total below was written.
46 i.e. trefoils.
47 Preceded by a later marginal note, '*o.o*', possibly late fourteenth- or fifteenth-century; the notes in 48, 49 and 52 were probably made at a similar date.
48 Preceded by a later marginal note, '*d*'.
49 Preceded by a later marginal note, '*a*'.
50 MS: 'vend'' extended as a past participle throughout this section.
51 MS: possibly 'Bulsis'.
52 MS: later note in margin, '*f.*' Parts of this section are laid out two entries to the line.
53 MS obscure; the sense is that this item was not included in the total on the roll.
54 The French original of Sidrak and Bokkus: see *Sidrak and Bokkus: a parallel-text edition from Bodleian Library, MS Laud Misc. 559 and British Library, MS Lansdowne 793* ed. T. Burton (2 vols., Early English Text Society, original series, 311–12; 1998–9).
55 This section is written intermittently in two columns.
56 No value given.
57 Unit of weight omitted: lib. ? No value given.
58 No value given.
59 Part four of Alexander of Hales *Summa theologica* ed. B. Klumper *et al.* (6 vols., Quaracchi, 1924–79, and in progress).
60 Henricus de Segusio, Cardinal Bishop of Ostia, probably *Summa super titulis decretalium*, printed Rome, 1473.
61 Works of Bernard of Clairvaux.
62 Perhaps a further copy of Gratian's *Decretum*, as note 35.
63 Priscianus Caesariensis *Institutiones grammaticae*, Books I–XVI; *CPL* 1546.
64 Willelmus Peraldus *Summa de vitiis et virtutibus*, printed Basel, 1469.
65 A bible in French.
66 Perhaps Innocent IV *Apparatus in quinque libros decretalium*, printed Strassburg, 1477.
67 Possibly *Thesaurus novus. Sermones de tempore et de sanctis*, attributed by some to Petrus de Palude (*c.*1275–1342), printed Strassburg, 1483.
68 MS repeats 'Item fenum'.
69 The next three entries are all in the same, additional hand, following on from the striking out of the total in the line immediately before. In the first of these entries, the concluding 'Probatur' is probably in another hand.
70 This entry is in a further hand.

33 John Sheppey, Bishop of Rochester

33/1 Will, 21 September 1360 *LPL, Register of Simon Islip, ff. 169v–170r*
In nomine sancte ac individue Trinitatis patris et filii et spiritus sancti ego frater Johannes de Scapeya eiusdem Trinitatis miseracione ecclesie cathedralis Roffensis licet indignus episcopus die vicesimo primo mensis Septembris anno domini nostri Jhesu Cristi millesimo CCC^{mo}lx^{o} compos mentis et sane memorie ac habens omnium sensuum meorum umacitatem et usum solo gressu pedum meorum excepto condo testamentum meum per hunc modum. In primis lego animam meam dulcissimo creatori supplicans sibi quatinus eam collocare dignetur inter animas nunc beatas et si in presenti sit impedimentum aliquod quare non debeat ibi poni quod dignetur illud michi revelare ut possim de illo per suam graciam purgare ante finem vite mee. Item lego corpus meum ad sepeliendum in ecclesia cathedrali Roffensi ubi executores mei infra nominandi ordinaverint cum consensu prioris. Item lego pro expensis funeralibus meis videlicet pro distribucione facienda inter pauperes et aliis necessariis a die mortis mee usque ad crastinum sepulture C marcas. Et nolo[1] quod habeam circa corpus meum plures quam xxiiii^{or} cereos. Nolo eciam et de hoc onero consciencias executorum meorum quod ad sepulturam meam vocent vel invitent aliquem militem seu hominem de patria aut dominam set volo quod invitent abbatem de Boxle cum priore de Ledes ut ipsi cum priore Roffensi ponant in terra vel sarcaphago miserum corpus meum. Item volo quod statim spiritu exalato executores mei London' Derteford' Roff' Newynton' et Sydyngbourne palam faciant proclamari ut si cui sim debitor veniat ad certum diem et locum per executores assignandos recepturus quod sibi debetur habito super debito plano et legitimo documento et quod hoc fiat onero consciencias executorum meorum ante omnia legata vel leganda solvenda. Item lego domino meo Cantuariensi archiepiscopo qui erit pro tempore mortis mee et quibusdam ministris suis sub condicionibus infrascriptis et non aliter l marcas videlicet soli domino. Item cancellario v marcas auditori causarum xl s. registrario suo ii marcas et apparitori i marcam sub condicionibus istis ut subsequitur quod quamcito executores mei venerint ad dictum dominum Cantuariensem ad testamentum probandum et postea cum inventario fideli et compoto de administracione et facto illorum dumtamen ad alterius instanciam non fiat contradiccio maliciosa. Prefatus dominus Cantuariensis libere stet predictorum executorum juramento et eis incontinenti det acquietanciam sufficientem quatenus ad suum officium pertinent necnon quod ipse et ministri sui predicti sint amici prefatis executoribus meis si successor meus vel alius in curia dicti domini archiepiscopi velit eos impetere minus juste alioquin volo quod predicta legata prefatis domino et suis ministris nullam habeant juris vel roboris firmitatem. Item lego priori et capitulo meis Roffensibus in recompensacionem defectuum meorum negligenciarum expensarum per me factarum preter vel contra eorum voluntates et consensus vel detencionem bonorum eorum penes me non restitutorum si que vel que fuerint C marcas includendas in cista communi sub tribus clavibus famosis et applicandas ad reparaciones faciendas infra monasterium super quo prioris gestorum clavium predictarum necnon omnium monachorum de secunda et tercia leccione qui erunt pro tempore consciencias onero. Item lego priori et capitulo supradictis vestimentum meum album videlicet casulam tunicam et dalmaticam pro episcopo si affuerit tunicam et dalmaticam pro diacono et subdiacono et iiii^{or} capas cum albis stol*is* et phanon*is* ridell*is* et

frontell*o* de eadem secta. Item lego eiusdem priori et capitulo mitram meam novam de opere Johannis de Coloigne salvo quod successor meus immediatus habebit sub certis condicionibus infra scribendis et non aliter usum dicte mitre ad terminum vite sue dumtaxat prout in hoc testamento mee ultime voluntatis inferius describetur. Item lego eisdem priori et capitulo l virgas panni linei et l virgas panni de canabo ad faciendum inde linthiamina pro hospitibus venientibus ad dictum monasterium. Item lego cuilibet monacho professo et sacerdoti dimidiam marcam et professo non sacerdoti v s. Item lego officio cellerarie C lib. piperis. Item lego priori Roffensi unum triper de iii peciis quondam prioris hospitalis in uno hanaperio. Item lego priori et capitulo predictis unum biker cum cooperculo morandum semper in refectorio in mei memoriam quod michi dedit Johannes de Middelton' victuallarius Cales' et volo quod inde potet presidens in refectorio obitus mei die et alias quando ei placuerit. Item lego fratri Willelmo de Hadloo si superstes fuerit tempore mortis mee unam robam meam quam voluerit eligere. Item eidem xii virgas panni linei et xii virgas panni de canabo. Item lego fratri Willelmo de Strode x virgas panni nigri de bruneto pro una capa et tunica et omnes furvellos meos et v s. pro cariagio eorundem. Item fratri Johanni Morell' sex ulnas panni de bruneto pro una capa scolastica et xx s. pro aliis suis neccessariis. Item lego successori meo immediato unum vestimentum novum de indico pulverizato cum scalopis cum toto apparatu videlicet casul*a* stol*a* phanon*a* cap*a* alb*a* tunic*a* dalmatic*a* frontell*o* et coopertura anologii. Item lego eidem sub eisdem condicionibus aulam cum papilionibus quam emi a Nicholao Mary*v*y et unam aliam quam emi ab eodem pro xxv li. et valet multo plus et est de opere de aras et existit in custodia abbatisse de Mallyng'. Item lego eidem sub eisdem condicionibus pro tribus tabulis aule sue majoris duas mappas et pro majori mensa ii surnappas cum tuallis competentibus et ad lavandum ante prandium vi tuallas. Item lego eidem unam magnam pelvem cum lotorio suo de latonia. Item lego eidem sub eisdem condicionibus iii pelves de argento cum ii lotoriis in quarum pelvium fundo sunt arma de Hadloo et xxiiii scutellas argenteas cum x et viii salsaria ii salaria argentea et xxiiii coclearia. Item lego sub eisdem condicionibus pro coquina sua unum robynet ereum duos pottos majores duas patellas meliores de coquina [*f. 170r*] et ii postenettis cum omnibus gromis meis ferreis. Item lego eidem sub eisdem condicionibus C marcas in pecunia vel in valore et aliis rebus in toto vel in parte juxta avisamentum executorum meorum cum una calice meliori preter calicem de capella episcopi ab antiquo cum ii phiolis argenteis quibus utebar communiter in capella majori una cum ii pelvibus trussabilibus cum ii phiolis quondam magistrorum Roberti de Chikwell' et Johannis Barnet quos pelves et phiolas volo quod dimittat ecclesie Roffensi ad usum perpetuum pontificum futurorum. Et hec omnia legata successori meo immediato lego sibi sub condicionibus istis videlicet quod not impetat nec prosequatur contra executores meos pro reparacione aliqua facienda per eos vel per me et eciam quod quamcito requisitus fuerit per executores meos heredes vel executores eorundem ad faciendum eis acquietanciam sufficientem de omnibus de quibus possunt per eum impeti de consuetudine vel de jure et nisi ista fecerit volo quod omnia et singula sibi legata sunt invalida et nullius roboris sint vel virtutis. Dumtamen executores mei sibi offerant legata predicta intencionis tamen mee existit quod implementum ab antiquo consuetum futuro episcopo persolvatur. Item lego Johanni de Kenyngton' vi discos argenteos domino Roberto de Lodesdon' xx s. Ade clerico xl s. Willelmo Cheyne C s. et i ciphum argenteum plateum. Johanni de Fynchynfeld C s. et unum ciphum argenteum plateum. Nicholao de Fav*er*sham C s. et unum ciphum argenteum plateum. Ade Tewdre xx s. Ricardo atte Welde xl s. Stephano de Bereham xx s. Nicholao de The*u*ford xl s. Johanni Sewale de South*e*flete ii marcas. Johanni Doure panitario meo vi marcas et unum ciphum argenteum plateum. Johanni Barbour camerario meo x marcas et unum ciphum argenteum plateum. Johanni Moys valletto camerario lx s. Et pro eo quod camerarii dominorum de quadam curialitate et permissione clamant haberi post mortem dominorum zonam et quicquid appendet cultellos bursam et quicquid continetur in ea exceptis sigill*is* et aliis secretis scripturis domini lectum et totum apparatum et sepius contigit quod in fraudem tales camerarii ordinarunt de preciosioribus pannis episcopi lectum suum ideo declaro quod camerarius habeat unum canevas' ii materas duo linthiamina duo plumaria unum la*un*gelum unam quiltam bonam de nulla alia secta i cov*er*let cum i testre duobus tapetis et iii ridellis et non plus. Et volo quod de hoc contentetur et erunt cov*er*lyt et testre et tapete cum papilionibus. Item volo quod per executores meos ordinetur unus lectus de pannis extravagantibus et inter se non convenientibus et illum lectum lego Johanni Moys predicto. Item lego Johanni Barbour et Johanni Moys predictis omnia vasa et instrumenta mea ad conficiendum species dividenda inter se. Item lego Roberto Ferrour xl s. Tribus garcionibus in coquina cuilibet illorum di. marcam. Item lego Elwyne i marcam. Item parvo Rogero xl s. Item lego Alicie sorori mee xx marcas et omnes furruras meas omnimodas nondum applicatas ad opus. Item lego Petro filio predicte Alicie totum staurum vivum et mortuum cum omnibus aliis rebus existentibus in et super terris et terras meis et meas apud la Hoke nisi ante mortem de predictis aliter ordinetur et tunc volo quod predictus Petrus habeat C marcas. Item cum per finem levatam habeam statum in manerio de M*er*ston' cum omnibus pertinenciis suis in comitatu Kanc' per xv annos et ultra ad terminum vite mee per unum annum integrum lego prefato Petro totum catallum meum vivum et mortuum et quod michi debebitur de eisdem manerio et pertinenciis per illos quindecim annos. Item lego Willelmo Cheyne Johanni de Fynchyngfeld' et Petro consanguineo meo omnimodas armaturas meas dividendas per equales porciones in valore. Item lego Nicholao Mary*v*y unum anulum cum uno rubino de bales quondam Alicie Neele qui quidem anulus cum rubino suo amoto de sua capsula aurea in quadam capsula lignea in qua est magnus numerus lapidum smaragdorum qui valent ad minus in omni foro C marcas de dono domini regis. Item lego domino Rogero de Chest*re*feld unam cuppam cum cooperculo deaurat*am*. Item domino Ricardo de Chestrefeld unam cuppam cum cooperculo deaurat*am*. Item lego Waltero Whitehors scutifero domini mei regis unum ciphum argenteum cum cooperculo et uno aquario argenteo. Item lego cuilibet executorum meorum hic nominandorum xx li. xii scutellas argenteas xii salsaria et duos chargeours dumtamen accipiant onus ministrandi et de facto ministrent alioquin ille qui non ministrat nichil inde habeat. Item lego domino Willelmo dei gracia Wintoniensi episcopo et Anglie cancellario unum anulum cum diademante cum scriptura quadam in amicicia non propter valorem rei in se set propter meam memoriam amici sui nimium supplicans sibi tanquam persone de qua plus confido quatinus inter alias solicitudines suas velit in justicia sua supervidere facta executorum meorum cum indignerint et eos protegere contra malignantes et eos ut predicitur defendere et tueri tanquam providens supervisor. Huius autem testamenti mee ultime voluntatis executores ordino et constituo ex certa sciencia magistrum Thomam de

Bradwell rectorem ecclesie de Shorham et capelle de Otteford officium meum dominum Robertum de Pleseley rectorem ecclesie de Suth*e*flete et dominum Stephanum Randulph' rectorem ecclesie de Couden'. Et residuum omnium bonorum meorum tam manibus meis quam in manibus aliorum quorumcumque existencium committo prefatis executoribus meis ut ipsi ordinent et disponant pro anima mea prout melius viderunt expedire. Et si habundet residuum respiciant pauperes parochianos meos et tenentes meos. Volo et concedo quod si aliqua bona vel res de bonis meis sint venalia quod executores mei habeant prerogativam emendi eadem solvendo tantum quantum alii dare vellent pro eisdem. Data et acta apud la Place juxta Lamheth' die et anno supradictis. Et ego Johannes episcopus predictus cum manu mea tremula in testimonium omnium premissorum sigillo beatissimi patroni mei consignavi.

Notes

1 MS: 'volo'; the negative sense is also picked up by 'nolo eciam' at the start of the next sentence.

33/2 Acquittance of Mag. ..... Bradewelle, Dom. Robert de Pleseley and Dom. Stephen Randulph', the executors, Charing, 5 July 1363. *LPL, Register of Simon Islip, f. 195r.*

34 William Spridlington, Bishop of St Asaph

34/1 Will, 30 June 1381, with notarial confirmation, 6 September 1381 *LPL, Register of William Courtenay, ff. 196v–197v*

In dei nomine amen anno ab incarnacione domini millesimo CCC^{mo}lxxxi die ultima mensis Junii in manerio de Althmehedyn[1] in Wallia ego Willelmus episcopus Assavensis sanus mente et corpore sciens me tamen viam universe carnis transire ac volens de bonis meis a deo michi collatis meam propriam disponere voluntatem testamentum meum condo facio et ordino in hunc modum. In primis lego animam meam deo omnipotenti creatori redemptori et salvatori meo et corpus meum ad sepeliendum in choro ecclesie cathedralis Assavensis ad capud austral*e* magni altaris sub basso lapide concordanti cum pavimento. Et ordino et lego fabrice eiusdem ecclesie quadraginta solidos sterlingorum et meum librum vocatum catholicon'[2] in eadem ecclesia ad infor*ma*cionem et instruccionem ministrorum deo serviencium in eadem perpetuis temporibus remansurum et summo altari eiusdem ecclesie meum calicem majorem deauratum per totum et annellatum extra in parte. Item lego xl s. ad distribuendum equaliter inter perpetuos vicarios et alios capellanos eiusdem ecclesie et unam marcam ad distribuendum equaliter inter parvos vicarios choristas et sacristam eiusdem ecclesie. Item lego ad expensas funerales et ad distribuendum die sepulture mee xl li. Item lego fabrice [*f. 197r*] ecclesie sancti Albani de Sprydelyngton' xx s. et ad divina ministranda in eadem ecclesia sancti Albani unum vestimentum in parte usitatum videlicet i casulam i albam i amictam cum corporali stola fanon*a* et zona. Item lego vicario eiusdem ecclesie xiii s. iiii d. et unum garnamentum de vestibus meis precium x s. vel in denariis x s. ultra dictam marcam sibi legatam. Item fabrice ecclesie sancti Hillarii de Spridelyngton' xiii s. iiii d. et i vestimentum in parte usitatum videlicet i casulam i albam i amictam cum corporali stola fanon*a* et zona. Item lego rectori eiusdem ecclesie sancti Hillarii xiii s. iiii d. Item lego fabrice ecclesie de Weldon' xiii s. iiii d. et summo altari eiusdem ecclesie unum calicem videlicet minorem calicem de meis tribus calicibus[3] et i vestimentum in parte usitatum videlicet i casulam i albam et i amictam cum corporali stola fanon*a* et zona ad morandum in eadem ecclesia in augmentacionem cultus divini que vestimenta dictis tribus ecclesiis legata volo quod habeant de vestimentis[4] meis que habeo ad presens nisi dedero alicui earundem ecclesiarum aliquod vestimentum ante mortem meam post confeccionem presentis testamenti. Item lego domino Ricardo fratri meo meum majus missale meum majorem ciphum mazer' et meum nott cum pede que erant domine Thome Besevill' unum librum vocatum oculus sacerdotis[5] unum lectum de worstede blew operatum in brouder*atum* dictum videlicet lectum continentem i cov*er*lett i tester' utrumque operatum ut supra i cilatouram largam cum tribus ridellis de carde bleu cum uno materac' syngle quod erat dicti domini Thome cum ii linthiaminibus i canevace unam duodenam vasorum stanne videlicet xii platella xii potag*er*s et xii sausers et ii chargeours in parte usitat*a* i mappam mensalem de opere Parisiensis longitudinis vii ulnarum ad minus cum uno manutergio eiusdem operis et longitudinis et unum manutergium curtum eiusdem operis et i sanap' de tela linea dicte longitudinis ii cofres trussabiles que fuerunt dicti domini Thome ii pelves de lathon' cum ii lavatoriis et i amys de grys et i superpellicium. Item lego Willelmo filio Roberti fratris mei unum lectum non broudatum videlicet i cov*er*lett i testr' i par linthiaminum i blanket vel i materac' i canvace x li. in auxilium sustentacionis sue ad scolas i par decretalium[6] i par de Clementin*is*[7] et aliquas vesturas ad valorem xl s. vel xl s. ultra dictis x li. et i peciam argenti ponderis xx^ti^ s. ad minus et sex coclearia argenti. Item Thome filio nepoti*s* mei i peciam argenti cum ymagine sancti Johannis Baptiste cum cooperculo eiusdem sex coclearia argenti et i mazer' ligatum cum argento et i lectum videlicet i cov*er*let i tester' ii linthiamina i materac' vel i blanket et i canevace i hab*er*jon i jakke album et i bacynett vel i palett juxta ordinacionem executorum meorum et C s. sterlingorum in auxilium filiorum et filiarum suorum. Item lego domino Ricardo de Stokes i mazer' ligatum de argento deaurato quod fuit Johannis de Stokes fratris sui et i byker argenti ad modum calicis cum cooperculo eiusdem cum pomello annellato et cum signo 'W.S.' coronato infra cooperculum et i quintfoil in summitate pomelli et ii cofres trussabiles que fuerunt Roberti de Spridelyngton'. Item lego domino Rogero de Wymondham i mazer' argento ligatum quod fuit Beatricis Besevill' ii pecia argenti de una secta cum annell*o* in fundo utraque cum i homine et domicella et i duodenam vasorum stanni garniti ut supra cum duabus ollis utraque de uno potello de stanno et ii cofres trussabiles que fuerunt domini Thome Roblot. Item lego Ricardo de Cristulton' ii pecias argenti vel xl s. sterlingorum. Item lego Johanni Brigge seniori servienti meo C s. et utensilia domus videlicet de vasis stanni enei et lignei ad valenciam xx[ti] s. ad minus et unum lectum integrum pro statu suo condecenti. Et Johanni Brigg' filio suo xl s.[8] sterlingorum et i lectum videlicet unum cov*er*lett i tester' ii linthiamina i blankett et i canvenace. Item lego Johanni Braytoft coco meo x marcas sterlingorum et de pannis sive de utensilibus domorum ad valenciam xl s. ad minus juxta ordinacionem executorum meorum. Item lego camerario meo qui tempore mortis fuerit unum lectum viridum videlicet i cov*er*lett i tester' cum dimidia celura iii ridellos ii linthiamina i blanket unum canevace et xl s. sterlingorum. Item domino Johanni de Lichefeld' i peciam argenti valoris xx[ti] s. ad minus et i librum vocatum

Barth*olomeum* de proprietatibus rerum.[9] Item lego domino Hugoni de Wolaton' unam vel duas pecias argenti ponderis xl s. ad minus et sex coclearia argenti et meum parvum portiforium meum librum vocatum rationale divinorum officiorum[10] et meum ordinale. Item lego Waltero de Stokes de Spridelyngton' si superstes fuerit quatuor li. sterlingorum et Willelmo de Fernebergh' garcioni coquine mee quinque marcas Ricardo West de Spridelyngton' i marcam et cuilibet garcioni sive ancille de servientibus meis apud Ly*v*eden' x s. argenti. Et si aliquis eorundem serviencium steterit in servicio meo ultra unum annum ante mortem meam unam marcam. Et si aliquis steterit in servicio meo ultra ii annos ante mortem meam xx^ti^ s. Et remitto Ade de Cokerham de Rothelan'[11] totum debitum in quo michi tenetur de tempore quo fuit receptor meus de exitibus decanatus Assavensis. Item lego fratribus predicatoribus Oxon' lx s. Item lego Magot*e* Bole de Ly*v*eden' i peciam argenti ponderis unius marce argenti ad minus et unum garnamentum cum capucio de vestibus meis valoris [*f. 197v*] unius marce ad minus suffic*ienter* furratum cum pelluris et cuilibet servienti meo apud Althmelyden' et Llanlwey[12] qui steterit in servicio meo ultra unum annum ante mortem meam di. marcam. Item lego Johanni filio Ricardi le Cooke de Weldon' xl s. argenti. Item lego Alicie de comitatu Lincoln' nuper servienti mee tam apud Spridelyngton' quam apud Ly*v*eden' xx^ti^ s. argenti. Item lego domino Willelmo de Messyngham unam peciam argenti ponderis xx^ti^ s. ad minus et domino Johanni de Wymondham i peciam argenti ponderis xx^ti^ s. ad minus. Item lego Johanni Godard camerario meo xx^ti^ s. sterlingorum. Roberto mareschall*o* C s. et unum lectum integrum pro statu suo condecenti juxta ordinacionem executorum meorum. Roberto Hardy xl s. Janyn pistori meo xx^ti^ s. Thome de Lampton garcioni camere mee xx^ti^ s. Et cuilibet alteri garcioni camere coquine stabuli aut alterius officii i marcam. Et magistro Johanni coco meo ad presens xx^ti^ s. et Johanni clerico capelle mee xx^ti^ s. Item lego cuilibet executori recipienti in forma juris administracionem presentis testamenti mei et facienti execucionem eiusdem C s. sterlingorum ultra expensas racionabiles quas fecerint in execucione eiusdem testamenti et ultra legata eis superius ordinata. Et volo et ordino quod maneria de Chirchefeld' et Ly*v*eden' et omnia alia terra et tenementa ibidem in quibus domini Ricardus de Stokes Ricardus de Spridelyngton' et Rogerus de Wymondham et alii sunt feoffati vendantur post mortem meam si ante non fuerint vendita et denarii inde provenientes liberantur executoribus meis pro debitis meis solvendis et pro execucione testamenti facienda. Volo eciam et ordino quod residuum omnium bonorum meorum ultra debita mea soluta et legata mea predicta et expensas funerales et alias expensas que racionabiliter oportet et debeant fieri dividantur in duas partes equales et una pars sive medietas tocius residui ordinetur et solvatur capellanis pro anima mea parentum amicorum et omnium benefactorum meorum divina celebrantibus et hoc quamcicius poterit post mortem meam in locis competentibus tam apud Spridelyngton' quam alibi juxta ordinacionem executorum meorum. Et alia medietas dictorum bonorum meorum distribuatur et solvatur servientibus meis et pauperibus debilibus viduis et aliis tenentibus meis qui sunt in paupertate prostrati et in aliis elemosinis et primo et principaliter pauperibus tenentibus meis et aliis de parochia de Weldon' Spridelyng' Llanellwy Althm' et Ly*v*eden' et alibi juxta bonam ordinacionem et discrecionem executorum meorum et hoc sub periculo animarum suarum et ita cicius quam bene poterit fieri absque dilacione aliquali. Et volo eciam quod omnia alia testamenta mea ante confeccionem presentis testamenti mei facta nullum habeant vigorem sed sunt revocata et adnullata et ea per presentes revoco et adnullo et ad hanc meam integram et ultimam voluntatem in forma predicta exequendam et execucionem presentis testamenti mei et administracionem bonorum meorum faciendam dominos Ricardum de Stokes Ricardum de Spridelyngton' Rogerum de Wymondham Hugonem de Wolaton' et Johannem Brigg' seniorem executores meos ordino facio et constituo per presentes sigillo meo signato in testimonium premissorum. Et ad majorem securitatem et noticiam omnium fidelium in futurum signum et subscripcionem Ricardi de Cristulton' notarii publici infrascriptum presentibus apponi procuravi. Data et acta die loco et anno domini supradictis. Presentibus tunc ibidem discretis viris domino Johanne de Wymondham rectore ecclesie de Machynlleyth' Assavensis diocesis et Roberto Wyvill' de comitatu Leycestr' testibus in premissis.

Subscripcio notarii Et ego Ricardus Matheu de Cristulton' clericus Lichfeldensis diocesis publicus apostolica et imperiali auctoritate notarius predicti testamenti et omnium contentorum in eodem interpositorum et lecture facte et habite coram prefato reverendo patre domino Willelmo episcopo sic ut premittitur testante ipsius nomine et de ipsius speciali mandato prefatum testamentum et omnia in eodem superius denotata suum merum factum et suam ultimam voluntatem esse pro tunc expresse et ex certa sciencia sua ut asseruit recognoscenti in camera principali eiusdem testantis infra hospicium habitacionis sue infra parochia de Alhmundi[13] Salop' Lichfeldensis diocesis situata die sexta mensis Septembris anno domini suprascripto indiccione quarta pontificatus sanctissimi in Cristo patris et domini nostri domini Urbani divina providencia pape vi^{ti} anno quarto una cum prenominatis testibus et pluribus aliis presens interfui eaque sic ut premittitur fieri vidi et audivi ac de requisicione et mandato dicti venerabilis patris Willelmi episcopi testantis signum meum consuetum una cum sigilli sui appensione presentibus per alium scriptum me subscribendo apposui in fidem et testimonium \ omnium / premissorum.

Notes

1 Alt Meliden, now Meliden, Flintshire.

2 John of Genoa (Johannes Januensis) (compiler) *Catholicon*, printed Mainz, ?1460.

3 MS: 'calicis'.

4 MS: 'vestimentibus'.

5 Willelmus de Pagula *Oculus sacerdotis*, unpublished.

6 Gregory IX *Decretales*, printed in *Corpus iuris canonici* ed. E. Friedberg (2nd edition, 2 vols., Leipzig, 1922) ii, cols. 1–928.

7 The *Liber septimus decretalium*, known as the *Constitutiones Clementinae*, printed in *Corpus iuris canonici*, ii, cols. 1129–1200.

8 MS repeats 'xl s.'

9 Bartholomeus Anglicus *De proprietatibus rerum*, printed Frankfurt, 1601.

10 Willelmus Durandus the elder *Rationale divinorum officiorum*, printed Mainz, 1459.

11 Rhuddlan, Flintshire.

12 St Asaph, Flintshire.

13 St Alkmund, Shrewsbury.

34/2 Grant of probate, committed to the executors named in the will, reserving the power of committing it also to Dom. Richard de Stokes and Dom. John Brugg. In the chapel at Croydon, 1 May 1382. *LPL, Register of William Courtenay, f. 197v.*

34/3 Acquittance of the executors, Dom. Richard de Spridlyngton', Dom. Roger de Wymondham, and Dom. Hugh de Wolaton. Otford, 5 June 1386. *LPL, Register of William Courtenay, f. 198r.*

35 John Stratford, Archbishop of Canterbury

35/1 Will, 1347 *CCA, Chartae Antiquae W219.* See the catalogue of probate documentation for references.

35/2 Declaration of the refusal of Mag. Richard Wachaun (Vaughan), archdeacon of Surrey, to take on the executorship of Archbishop Stratford's will, to which he has been named along with Robert, Bishop of Chichester, John de Lecch', John de Pulteney, knight, Dom. John de Eccleshall, clerk, and Dom. Richard de Twynerton, clerk, 10 September 1348. *CCA, Chartae Antiquae W222.*

35/3 Grant of probate and insinuation (publication) of the will by Robert, Prior of Canterbury, and the monks assigned by the chapter there, to Dom. Robert, Bishop of Chichester, Ralph, Bishop of London, Mag. John de Lecch' and Mag. Richard Vaughan, archdeacon of Surrey, and to John de Pulteneye, knight, Dom. John de Egleshale, and Richard de Twynerton, clerk, executors named in the will, 13 October 1348. *CCA, Register G, ff. 96v–97r; and Register Q, f. 203v.*

35/4 Letters of Robert, Prior of Canterbury, to Ralph, Bishop of London, exonerating him from the administration of the will of John Stratford, 29 October 1348. *CCA, Register G, f. 97r; also Register Q, ff. 215v–216v.*

35/5 The claim of Ralph, Bishop of London, to be exonerated from the administration of John Stratford's will; Mag. Henry Cocham, proctor of the Bishop of Chichester, and Walter de Merston, proctor of the Bishop of London. Given the first law day after SS. Simon and Jude (29 October), 1348; case based on infirmity and other reasons. The proctors exhibit their letters, both dated 25 October 1348. Commission granted by the Prior of Canterbury and the chapter of Christ Church, transferring execution to the Bishop of Chichester, 29 October 1348. *CCA, Register G, ff. 97v–98v; also Register Q, ff. 215v–216v.*

35/6 Account of the executors of John Stratford, Archbishop of Canterbury, 1349 *CCA, Chartae Antiquae A37*
Summarised in HMC *Appendix to Fifth Report*, p. 444; and by R.M. Haines, *Archbishop John Stratford*, pp. 509–13. A roll of one membrane. The recto is laid out in three columns. There are no medieval endorsements.

Inventarium omnium bonorum bone memorie domini Johannis de Stratford quondam archiepiscopus Cantuariensis factum per executores eiusdem episcopi anno domini millesimo CCC^{mo} quadragesimo nono

Thesaurus In primis inveniuntur in thesauro CCCiii li. xv s.
Debita defuncti Item debentur defuncto CCCCii li. xiii s. iiii d.
Capella et libri eiusdem Item inveniuntur in capella libri vestimenta et alia diversa ad valenciam M^{l}C li. iii s. viii d.
Libri Item inveniuntur libri diverse facultatis ad valenciam CC li. vi s.
Vasa argentea Item inveniuntur vasa argentea ad valenciam DCiiii^{xx}iiii li. xxi d.
Jocalia Item inveniuntur jocalia ad valenciam CCCCvi li. x s.
Garderoba et armatura Item inveniuntur robe lecti panni et armatura ad valenciam CC li. xiiii s.
Aula Item inveniuntur diversa dorsoria et bancaria ad valenciam xxvi li. xiii s. iiii d.
Panetria boteleria Item inveniuntur mappe tuelle et alia vasa ad valenciam xx li. xvi s. viii d.
Coquina Item inveniuntur vasa enea et alia diversa ad valenciam xx li. xx d.
Lardarium Item inveniuntur carcosia boum et baconum ad valenciam xiii li. vi s. viii d.
Stabulum Item inveniuntur ibidem palefridi et alii equi cum carect*is* ad valenciam Ciiii^{xx}i li. iii s. iiii d.
Blada in granariis Item inveniuntur ibidem \ blada / diversi generis ad valenciam Cxii li. x s.
Blada in grangiis Item inveniuntur ibidem diversi generis ad valenciam M^{l}CCCxxxiii li. vi s. viii d.
Staurum vivum Item inveniuntur in omnibus maneriis diversa animalia ad valenciam M^{l}CCiii li. xii s. iii d. preter implementa
Lana Item inveniuntur tam de lana grossa quam agn*ina* ad valenciam CCC li.

Summa tocius recepte[1] viM^{l}Dix li. xiiii s. iiii d.

Expense post obitum domini cum expensis funerariorum DCCiiii^{xx}ii li. iiii s. ii d. qua.
Debita soluta Solvuntur diversis creditoribus M^{l}C li. xiii s. ix d.
Legata et alia ordinata tempore vite domini M^{l}CCCiiii^{xx} li. vi s.
Elemosine solute Solvuntur prioribus de North*e*gate et Herbaldo*u*ne xxx li.
Vadia soluta Solvuntur diversis servientibus pro vadiis aretro existentibus x li.
Feoda soluta Solvuntur diversis senescallis et aliis pro feodis[2] aretro existentibus Ciiii^{xx}iiii li. iii s. iiii d.
Rewarda ballivorum et serviencium In donis diversis servientibus pro magno labore C li. xii s.
Expensa forinseca In diversis expensis forinsecis factis post obitum domini DCCCxxxvii li. xiiii s. i d.
Soluta capellanis celebrantibus pro anima predicti domini Solvuntur quinquaginta capellanis celebrantibus pro anima defuncti Clxvi li. xiii s. iiii d.
Liberata domino regi de bladiis in grangiis Liberantur domino regi in bladis sibi venditis \ pro / quibus denariis non solvuntur M^{l}CCCxxxiii li. vi s. viii d.

Summa tocius expense[3] vM^{l}ixCxxv li. xiii s. iiii d. qua.

Notes

1 MS: 'tocius recepte' in a second ink over an erasure.

2 MS: 'feodo'.
3 MS: 'tocius expense' in a second ink over an erasure.

35/7 Acquittance by Robert, Prior of Christ Church, Canterbury, of Robert, Bishop of Chichester, having heard his account of the administration of the will of John Stratford, of all goods in the diocese and province of Canterbury, 13 July 1349. *CCA, Register G, f. 115v; also Register Q, ff. 215v–216v.*

36 Ralph Stratford, Bishop of London

Summary of the account of the executors, *c*.1356 *LPL, Register of Simon Islip, f. 126r*

Summarium compoti executorum episcopi Londoniensis

Memorandum quod summa inventarii extendit se ad MDCCCxxvi li. xii s. xi d.

Summa omnium expensarum liberacionum et solucionum compoto computatum est MDxxxii li. xv s. xi d. qua. Et sic remanet in pede dicti compoti in manibus executorum CCiiii^{xx}xiii li. xvi s. xi d. ob. qua. De quibus dicti executores postea domino episcopo Londoniensi solverunt in persolucione MCC marcarum et liii li. iiii^{xx}ix li. xiii s. iiii d. in monetis et unum annale pontificale precium x marcarum et i dorsarium de Lumbardia precium xl s. et assignaverunt eidem domino episcopo iiii^{xx}v li. xiii s. ob. de debitis diversorum creditorum. Item solverunt Thome Scharnebrok' xx marcas. Item executoribus magistri Halam Hothum et executoribus domini Nicholai Hosebonde lxxvi li. xiii s. iiii d.

Summa CClxxiii li. xix s. viii d. ob.

Et adhuc remanent xix li. xvii s. iii d. qua.

Inde in manibus Willelmi Wokyngdon' et socii sui iiii li. ii s. viii d. Item in manibus Willelmi Asselot xxvii s. xi d. ob. Item remanet i crux precium xxx s. Item i gladius precium xxx s. Summa viii li. x s. vii d. ob. Et sic remanent xi li. vi s. vii d. ob. qua. qui consistunt in precio rerum appreciatarum in inventario que sunt in manibus executorum. Necscitur pro quanto vendere poterunt.

Item executores habebunt pro maritagio J. Band lx li. de quibus satisfaciendum est pro expensis dicti J. et domine comitisse Northampton' et familiaribus domini episcopi defuncti qui disposuit eos remunerari juxta discrecionem executorum de residuo si quod esset.

37 Robert Stratford, Bishop of Chichester

37/1 Will, 9 April 1362 *LPL, Register of Simon Islip, f. 185r*
In dei nomine amen per presens publicum instrumentum cunctis appareat evidenter quod anno ab incarnacione domini millesimo CCC^{mo}lxii^{do} indiccione quintodecimo pontificatus sanctissimi in Cristo patris et domini nostri domini Innocencii divina providencia pape sexti anno decimo mense Aprilis die nono constitutus personaliter in mei notarii publicii infrascripti ac testimonio subscriptorum presencia venerabilis in Cristo pater et dominus dominus Robertus dei gracia Cicestrensis episcopus in camera manerii sui de Aldyngbourne Cicestrensis diocesis compos mentis ut michi videbatur licet corporis inbecillis jacens in lecto egritudinis suum condidit fecit et ordinavit testamentum ultimam suam continens voluntatem in hunc modum. In primis idem venerabilis pater personas infrascriptas ad suam ultimam voluntatem exequendam suos nominavit et fecit ordinavit executores videlicet discretos viros magistros Henricum Cockham cancellarium Johannem de Wendlingburgh' thesaurarium et me Robertum de Wendlingburgh' canonicum ecclesie Cicestrensis dominum Willelmum Horewyk rectorem ecclesie de Bury senescallum hospicii dicti patris Ricardum Clere marescallum eiusdem et Ricardum Cha*u*nz de Apuldham[1] Cicestrensis diocesis. Ordinavit eciam et voluit quod primo et precipue sua debita solveruntur creditoribus suis per executores predictos. Et quod iidem executores de bonis ipsius patris respicerent et remunerarent familiares eiusdem patris prout eisdem executoribus videretur fore faciendum quodque iidem executores caperent de bonis dicti patris per eosdem administrandos bene et sufficienter pro labore suo in hac parte circa administracionem bonorum eiusdem patris faciendam impendendo. Et quod premissis factis de residuo bonorum patris memorati disponerent prout utilitati et saluti anime sue videretur eis expedire. Acta sunt hec que supradixi sub anno indiccione pontificatu mense die et loco supradictis presentibus \ discretis / viris domino Roberto de Hampton' rectore ecclesie de Nytimbr' Cicestrensis diocesis Roberto de Clow camerario dicti patris et Johanne de Herem*u*ndesworth' valetto camere eiusdem patris testibus ad premissa vocatis specialiter et rogatis.

Et ego Robertus Hyne de Wendlingburgh' clericus Lincolniensis diocesis publicus apostolica auctoritate notarius supradicti testamenti sive ultime voluntatis et executorum predictorum ordinacioni testimonioque supradictorum vocacioni et rogacioni ceterisque omnibus et singulis prout superius per me scribuntur dum sic ut premittitur per venerabilem patrem supradictum sub anno indiccione pontificatu die et loco ac mense predictis agerentur et fierent una cum testibus supradictis presens interfui eaque sit ut predixi fieri vidi et audivi propriaque manu scripsi et in hanc publicam formam redigi meoque signo consueto signavi rogatus.

Notes
1 The MS shows no sign of abbreviation, even though one might expect a form similar to 'Apul*der*ham' for the modern Appledram.

37/2 Probate granted to Mag. Henry Cookham, chancellor of Chichester Cathedral, Robert de Wendlynghburgh', canon of Chichester Cathedral, and

William Horewyk', rector of Bury, executors named in the will, 26 April 1362. *LPL, Register of Simon Islip, f. 185r.*

37/3 Acquittance of the executors, Mag. Henry Cokham, chancellor of Chichester Cathedral, Mag. Robert Wendlyngburgh', canon of Chichester Cathedral, and Dom. William de H*orew*yk. The executors have shown an inventory of the goods of the deceased, valued at £2,653 16*s*., from which they have accounted for debts, legacies paid, and other expenses of £2,344 14*s*. 4*d*., leaving £309 1*s*. 8*d*. in their hands, as shown in the foot of the account, with which the executors, following the will of the deceased, wish to found a perpetual chantry in Chichester Cathedral for the soul of the deceased and all the faithful departed. The executors are discharged from any further account. Charing, 25 June 1365. *LPL, Register of Simon Islip, f. 207v.*

38 Richard Swinfield, Bishop of Hereford

Receipts and quittances given to the executors, 1317–47

38/1 26 April 1317 *HCA 1024*

One membrane, a narrow strip, with two tongues running from the bottom left, each with a fragment of a seal. 1. Oval, a fragment in green wax, now 18 mm × 16 mm, a bishop in pontificals, a crozier held in his left hand, with a figure kneeling to his right; fragments of lettering, now illegible. 2. Oval, a fragment in green wax, the seal of the deanery of Hereford *ad causas*, a forward-facing, tonsured head. Contemporary endorsement: 'Acquietancia R. de Oxinden' de v marcis receptis in partem solucionis x marcarum sibi legatarum'.

Universis pateat per presentes quod ego Ricardus de Oxindenn' recepi et habui a domino Johanne de Kemes' thesaurario Herefordensi executore et suis coexecutoribus testamenti venerande memorie domini Ricardi de Swynefeud quondam Herefordensis episcopi quinque marcas legalium sterlingorum in partem solucionis decem marcarum quas idem venerabilis pater michi in suo testamento legavit. In cuius rei testimonium has meas acquietancie litteras dictas quinque marcas videlicet medietatem pecunie michi legate ut premittitur continentes feci patentes et quia sigillum meum pluribus est ignotum sigillum decanatus Herefordensis ad causas apponi presentibus procuravi. Data Hereford' xxvi^{a} die mensis Aprilis anno domini millesimo CCC^{mo} septimodecimo.

38/2 28 April 1317 *HCA 1001*

One membrane, with fragments of two seals in green wax, both on tongues running from the bottom left. Seals: 1. A shield of arms, a lion rampant facing left. 2. The seal of the deanery of Hereford *ad causas*, a forward-facing tonsured head, ... ATVS ..... Contemporary endorsement: 'Aquietancia Thome de Rethyng' de xl s. pro expensis suis in servicio domini factis cum renunciacione sua super exacione sua imposterum facienda'.

Universis pateat per presentes quod ego Thomas de Rethyng' recepi et habui a domino Johanne de Kemes' thesaurario Herefordensi executore et suis coexecutoribus testamenti sancte memorie domini Ricardi de Swinefeud quondam Herefordensis episcopi quadraginta solidos legalium sterlingorum pro servicio meo in negociis eiusdem domini episcopi coram justic*iis* domini nostri regis itinerantibus apud Cant' et pro expensis meis in suis negociis in Cancia quam quidem pecuniam me recepisse et dictos executores inde quietos esse fateor per presentes renuncians per has meas litteras omnibus exacionibus querelis et demandis quas contra executores predictos coram quibuscumque movere potero in futuro salvis michi et uxori mee legatis nobis in testamento domini episcopi supradicti. In cuius rei testimonium sigillum meum presentibus est appensum et quia sigillum meum pluribus est ignotum sigillum decanatus Herefordensis ad causas apponi presentibus procuravi. Data Hereford' die jovis promixo post festum sancti Marci evangeliste anno domini M^{mo}CCC^{mo} septimodecimo.

38/3 28 April 1317 *HCA 1015*
One membrane, a narrow strip, with a fragment remaining of a tongue running from the left, with no trace of a seal. Contemporary endorsement: 'Aquitancia priorisse et conventus de Acornebur' de v marcis eis legatis'.

Universis Cristi fidelibus pateat per presentes quod nos Katerina priorissa de Acornebury et eiusdem loci conventus recepimus et habuimus a discretis viris domini Johanne de Kemeseye thesaurario Herefordensi et a ceteris coexsecutoribus suis testamenti bone memorie domini Ricardi dei gracia nuper Herefordensis episcopi quinque marcas sterlingorum quos nobis intuitu caritatis in suo testamento reliquit. In cuius rei testimonium sigillum nostrum commune presentibus est appensum. Data in capitulo nostro de Acornebury die beati Vitalis martiris anno domini millesimo trecentisimo septimodecimo.

38/4 30 April 1317 *HCA 1009*
One membrane, with a stub from a tongue at the bottom left. The endorsement has been partly cut away. Contemporary endorsement: 'Acquietancia W. de Duur' et R. de Boklond' de script..... tangentibus terras de Wymelyngewe..... et Estenorr' receptis de executoribus domini Ricardi quondam Herefordensis episcopi'.

Tenore presencium pateat universis quod nos Walterus de Duur' et Ricardus de Boklonde recepimus et habuimus ab executoribus venerande memorie domini Ricardi de Swinefeud quondam Herefordensis episcopi omnes litteras cartas munumenta et scripta alia quecumque tangencia terras et tenementa nostra in Wymelyngewelde et Estenor' renunciantes in hiis omni exacioni quam ea occasione contra executores predictos facere poterimus in futurum. In cuius rei testimonium sigilla nostra huic acquietancie sunt appensa. Data Hereford' die sabbati proxima post festum sancti Marci evaungeliste anno domini millesimo CCC^{mo} septimodecimo.

38/5 30 April 1317 *HCA 1025*
One membrane, a narrow strip, with the remains of a stub from a tongue at the bottom left. Contemporary endorsement: 'Aquietancia Walteri de Du*u*r' de munimentis et cartis de Bromȝord Hoddesbach''.

Tenore presencium litterarum pateat universis quod ego Walterus de Du*ur*' recepi et habui ab executoribus bone memorie domini Ricardi de Swynefeud quondam Herefordensis episcopi omnes litteras cartas munumenta et scripta alia quecumque tangencia omnes terras et tenementa mea in Bromyard forinceca et extrinceca que fuerunt in custodia domini episcopi memorati renuncians per presentes omni exacioni quam ea occasione facere potero in futurum. In cuius rei testimonium sigillum meum presentibus est appensum. Data Hereford' die sabbati proxima post festum sancti Marci evaungeliste anno domini millesimo trecentesimo septimodecimo.

38/6 30 April 1317 *HCA 1043*
One membrane, a narrow strip, with two stubs at the bottom left, possibly with the remains of a third for a wrapping tie. Contemporary endorsement: 'Aquitancia Rogeri de Gatesden' de equo ei legato liberato eidem'.

Universis pateat per presentes quod ego Rogerus de Gatesden' recepi et habui ab executoribus bone memorie domini Ricardi de Swynefeud quondam Herefordensis episcopi unum equm bayum cum curvo dorso qui vocatur bayard de Dor' precii centum solidorum de quali precio idem pater michi in suo testamento unum equm legavit. In cuius rei testimonium sigillum meum presentibus est appensum et quia sigillum meum pluribus est ignotum sigillum officii domini archidiaconi Herefordensis apponi presentibus procuravi. Data Her' die sabbati proximo post festum sancti Marci evaungeliste anno domini $M^{mo}CCC^{mo}$ septimodecimo.

38/7 30 April 1317 *HCA 1045*
One membrane, a narrow strip, with a seal on a tongue running from the bottom left, and a stub from a second tongue also at the bottom left. Seal: oval, 22 mm × 16 mm, in green wax; a shield, a chevron between three animals or ?martlets; legend: [SIGILL'] RICARDI DE BOKELOND (the first word is no longer present, but was when the Morgans prepared their catalogue of the seals, summarised in F.C. Morgan and P.E. Morgan *A concise list of seals belonging to the Dean and Chapter of Hereford Cathedral* (Hereford, 1966)). Contemporary endorsement: 'Aquitancia Ricardi de Boklond' de v marcis in partem x marcarum ei legatarum'.

Universis pateat per presentes quod ego Ricardus de Boklond' recepi et habui a domino Johanne de Kemes' thesaurario Herefordensi executore et suis coexecutoribus testamenti venerande memorie domini Ricardi de Swynefeud nuper Herefordensis episcopi quinque marcas sterlingorum in partem solucionis decem marcarum quas ipse dominus episcopus michi in suo testamento legavit. In cuius rei testimonium sigillum meum presentibus est appensum et quia sigillum meum pluribus est ignotum sigillum decanatus Herefordensis ad causas apponi presentibus procuravi. Data apud Hereford' ultima die mensis Aprilis anno domini millesimo CCC^{mo} septimodecimo.

38/8 30 April 1317 *HCA 1046*
One membrane, a narrow strip with stubs from two tongues at the bottom left.

Contemporary endorsement: 'Aquitancia priorisse de Cornebur' de i cuppa quod fuit patris sui ei restituta'.

Universis pateat per presentes quod ego Katerina de Geynvyle priorissa de Acornebur' recepi et habui a domino Johanne de Kemes' thesaurario Herefordensi executore et suis coexecutoribus testamenti venerande memorie domini Ricardi de Swynefeud nuper Herefordensis episcopi unum ciphum argenteum quem ipse michi assignavit dum vixit et quem bone memorie frater Galfridus de Geynvyle pater meus de Hibernia sibi misit. In cuius rei testimonium sigillum meum privatum una cum sigillo domus nostre communi presentibus est appensum. Data apud Acornebur' predictam die sabbati proximo post festum sancti Marci evaungeliste anno domini M^{mo}CCC^{mo} septimodecimo.

38/9 2 May 1317 *HCA 1048*
One membrane, a narrow strip, with a stub from a tongue at the bottom left. Damaged by water: missing letters supplied below in square brackets. Contemporary endorsement: 'Aquitancia Johanne de Glouc' de di. marca et i coopertorio'.

Universis pateat per presentes quod ego Johanna de Glouc' relicta Willelmi Vynt quondam civis Hereford' recepi et habui a domino Johanne de Kemes' thesaurario Herefordensi executore et suis coexecutoribus testamenti venerande memorie domini Ricardi de Swynefeud nuper Herefordensis episcopi dimidiam marcam et unum coopertorium de russeto pellibus cuniculorum furratum in suo testamento michi legata. In cuius rei testimonium sigillum meum presentibus est appensum et quia s[igillum] meum pluribus est ignotum sigillum decanatus Herefordensis ad causas presentibus apponi procuravi. Data apud Hereford die l[une] in crastino apostolorum Philippi et Jacobi anno domini M^{mo}CCC^{mo} septimodecimo.

38/10 3 May 1317 *HCA 1037*
One membrane, a narrow strip, now with no trace of a tongue. Contemporary endorsement: 'Acquietancia domini T. de marisco presbiteri de i supertunica cum i capucio bene forrato'.

Tenore presencium pateat universis quod ego Thomas de marisco de Bos' recepi et habui a domino Johanne de Kemes' thesaurario Herefordensi executore et suis coexecutoribus testamenti sancte memorie domini Ricardi de Swynefeud quondam Herefordensis episcopi unam supertunicam clausam coloris rubii forratum de biso cum uno capucio forrato de minuto vario quam quidem supertunicam cum dicto capucio idem pater michi in suo testamento legavit. In cuius rei testimonium sigillum meum presentibus est appensum. Data apud Bosebur' die martis in festo invencionis sancte crucis anno domini M^{mo}CCC^{mo}xvii^{o}.

38/11 [3 May 1317] *HCA 2724*
One membrane, a narrow strip, missing the left edge. The hand is similar to other receipts for 1317 and the feast of the Invention of Holy Cross fell on a Tuesday in this year. No contemporary endorsements.

..... quod ego Johanna Eseger de Ledebur' recepi et habui a domino Johanne de

Kemes' thesaurario Herefordensi executore et suis coexecutoribus ..... de Swinefeud quondam Herefordensis episcopi unam robam coloris azur*e* de seisona estivali liniatam de viridi sindone videlicet .....unicam apertam capam et mantellum cum duobus capuciis et secundis manicis quam quidem robam de predictis garniamentis idem ..... In cuius rei testimonium sigillum meum presentibus est appensum. Data Ledebur' die martis in festo invencionis sancte crucis .....

38/12 5 May 1317 *HCA 1005*

One membrane, with two tongues running from the bottom left with seals, and a third, a wrapping tie. Seals: 1. Oval, 14 mm × 12 mm, in green wax, a bird or possibly a hawking scene. 2. Round, 16 mm in diameter, in green wax, three (?)sheaves. The legends on both seals are illegible. Contemporary endorsement: 'Acquientancia Elianore Racy de i roba recepta ab executoribus testamenti domini Ricardi quondam Herefordensis episcopi'.

Universis pateat per presentes quod ego Elianora uxor Rogeri Racy recepi et habui a domino Johanne de Kem' thesaurario Herefordensi executore et suis coexecutoribus testamenti sancte memorie domini Ricardi de Swynefeud quondam Herefordensis episcopi unam robam cum quinque garniamentis et capuciis ab eandem coloris de flore vesce liniatam de nigra sindone quam robam idem pater michi in suo testamento legavit. In cuius rei testimonium sigillum meum una cum sigillo Rogeri mariti mei predicti presentibus est appensum. Data apud Bos' die jovis proximo post festum invencionis sancte crucis anno domni M^{mo}CCC^{mo}xvii^{o}.

38/13 5 May 1317 *HCA 1011*

One membrane, a narrow strip, with no trace of a tongue or seal. Contemporary endorsement: 'Aquitancia A. de Ailyneton' de vi marcis in partem sui legati'.

Universis pateat per presentes quod ego Adam de Ailyneton' rector ecclesie de Willardesl' recepi et habui a domino Johanne de Kemes' thesaurario Herefordensi executore et suis coexecutoribus testamenti recolende memorie domini Ricardi de Swynefeud nuper Herefordensis episcopi sex marcas sterlingorum in partem solucionis decem marcarum quas ipse dominus episcopus michi in suo testamento legavit. In cuius rei testimonium sigillum meum litteris presentibus manu mea scriptis appendi. Data apud Hereford' die jovis proximo post festum invencionis sancte crucis anno domini M^{o}CCC^{mo} septimo decimo.

38/14 9 May 1317 *HCA 1028*

One membrane, a narrow strip, with a seal on a tongue running from the bottom left. Seal: vesica-shaped, 26 mm × 18 mm, in green wax, a face in profile looking to the right, with on the left side, a flat dish with a foot, holding the head of St John the Baptist. Legend: ..... CAND : IOHIS : IN..... Contemporary endorsement: 'Aquitancia domini J. de Kem' de i cuppa coclearis et quissinis'.

Universis pateat per presentes quod nos Johannes de Kemeseye thesaurarius Herefordensis recepimus et habuimus die lune proximo post festum sancti Johannis ante portam Latinam ab executoribus venerande memorie domini Ricardi de Swynefeud nuper Herefordensis episcopi unam cuppam argent*i* deauratam et bossatam cum floribus liliorum cum pede et cooperculo platto precii quadraginta solid*orum*. Item recepimus ab eisdem sex coclearia argent*i* precii sex solidorum. Item recepimus ab eisdem decem bancaria videlicet omnia bancaria que fuerunt eiusdem domini episcopi. Item recepimus ab eisdem tres quissinos de scarleto cum vineis consutis et scutis precii viginti solidorum. Que omnia idem dominus episcopus una cum aliis nobis in suo testamento legavit. In cuius rei testimonium sigillum nostrum presentibus est appensum. Data apud Hereford' die lune predicta anno domini millesimo CCC^{mo} septimodecimo.

38/15 9 May 1317 *HCA 1031*

One membrane, a narrow strip, probably with the remains of a tongue at the bottom left. Contemporary endorsement: 'Aquietancia Johannis de Tyb*er*ton' de lecto et legato domini'.

Universis pateat per presentes quod ego Johannes de Tib*er*ton' quondam subcubicularius venerande memorie domini Ricardi de Swynefeud nuper Herefordensis episcopi recepi et habui ab executoribus ipsius lectum eiusdem domini episcopi cum toto apparatu precii quatuor librarum duorum solidorum et sex denariorum. Item recepi ab eisdem quatuor marcas quas ipse michi legavit. Item recepi ab ipsis decem solidos pro stipendio meo annali prout continetur in testamento predicto. In cuius rei testimonium sigillum meum presentibus est appensum et quia sigillum meum pluribus est ignotum sigillum decanatus Herefordensis ad causas apponi presentibus procuravi. Data apud Hereford' die lune proximo post festum sancti Johannis ante portam Latinam anno domini M^{o}CCC^{mo} septimodecimo.

38/16 10 May 1317 *HCA 1030*

One membrane, a narrow strip, with two tongues, each with a seal, running from the bottom left. Seals: 1. Oval, 20 mm × 15 mm, in green wax, the Virgin with a child on her lap; legend S' ..... 2. Oval, in green wax, a foward-facing, tonsured head, the seal of the deanery of Hereford *ad causas*. Contemporary endorsement: 'Aquitancia domini Ade de Aylyneton' de x marcis iiii cocleariis sibi legatis'.

Universis pateat per presentes quod ego Adam de Ailyneton' quondam clericus familiaris venerande memorie domini Ricardi nuper Herefordensis episcopi recepi et habui a domino Johanne de Kemes' thesaurario Herefordensi executore et suis coexecutoribus testamenti domini episcopi supradicti decem marcas sterlingorum et quatuor coclearia argent*i* michi in testamento predicto legata. In cuius rei testimonium sigillum meum presentibus est appensum et quia sigillum meum pluribus est ignotum sigillum decanatus Herefordensis ad causas apponi presentibus procuravi. Data apud Hereford' die martis proximo post festum sancti Johannis ante portam Latinam anno domini millesimo trecentisimo septimodecimo.

38/17 12 May 1317 *HCA 1019*

One membrane, a narrow strip with two seals on tongues running from the bottom left. Seals: 1. Oval, in green wax, 21 mm × 17 mm, an engraved (?)gem of the Virgin seated with a child, the sun to her left, possibly the moon to her right; no legend. 2. A fragment of a vesica-shaped seal in green wax, a bishop in pontificals looking to the left, with a crozier in his hand. Contemporary endorsement: 'Aquietancia domini Johannis de Wyteneye de i missali'.

Universis pateat per presentes quod ego Johannes de Whiteneye vicarius in ecclesia Herefordensi successor domini Walteri de Banastre capellani quondam in ecclesia predicta divina celebrantis pro anima domini Willelmi le Rous recepi et habui ab executoribus venerande memorie domini Ricardi de Swynefeud nuper Herefordensis episcopi unum preciosum missale de usu Herefordensi in cuius fine scribuntur meditaciones beati Ancelmi[1] quod ipse dominus episcopus ab eodem domino Waltero dudum ex accommodato recepit. In cuius rei testimonium sigillum meum presentibus est appensum et quia sigillum meum pluribus est ignotum sigillum officialitatis Herefordensis apponi presentibus procuravi. Data apud Hereford' in festo ascensionis dominice anno eiusdem M^mo^CCC^mo^ septimodecimo.

Notes

1 Anselm of Canterbury *Meditationes*, published in *S. Anselmi Cantuariensis archiepiscopi omnia opera* ed. F.S. Schmitt (6 vols., Edinburgh, 1946–61) iii, pp. 76–91; for references to manuscript collections, Sharpe, *Latin writers*, p. 60. Noted in B.G. Charles and E.D. Emanuel, 'Notes on old libraries and books', *National Library of Wales Journal* 6 (1950) pp. 353–72, at p. 354, and Cavanaugh, 'Books', p. 839.

38/18 14 May 1317 *HCA 1004*

One membrane, with a stub from a tongue running from the bottom left. Contemporary endorsement: 'Acquietancia Egidii le Ferour de xl s. sibi legatis receptis ab executoribus domini Ricardi quondam Herefordensis episcopi'.

Tenore presencium pateat universis quod ego Egidius le Ferour recepi et habui a domino Johanne de Kemes' thesaurario Herefordensi executore et suis coexecutoribus testamenti bone memorie domini Ricardi de Swynefeud quondam Herefordensis episcopi quadraginta solidos legalium sterlingorum quos idem pater michi in suo testamento legavit. In cuius rei testimonium sigillum meum presentibus est appensum et quia sigillum meum pluribus est ignotum sigillum decanatus Herefordensis ad causas apponi presentibus procuravi. Data Her' die sabbati proximo post festum ascensionis domini M^mo^CCC^mo^xvii^o^.

38/19 14 May 1317 *HCA 1021*

One membrane, a narrow strip, with a stub from a tongue running from the bottom left. Contemporary endorsement: 'Acquietancia domini R. de Kynges*n*od' de xx s. ei legatis'.

Tenore presencium pateat universis quod ego Ricardus de Kynges*n*ode rector ecclesie de Colewell' Herefordensis diocesis recepi et habui a domino Johanne de Kemes' thesaurario in ecclesia Herefordensi executore et suis coexecutoribus testamenti sancte memorie domini Ricardi de Swynefeud quondam Herefordensis episcopi viginti solidos sterlingorum quos idem pater michi in suo testamento legavit. In cuius rei testimonium sigillum meum presentibus est appensum et quia sigillum meum pluribus est ignotum sigillum decanatus Herefordensis ad causas apponi presentibus procuravi. Data Herefordie die sabbati proxima post festum ascensionis domini anno domini M^mo^CCC^mo^xvii^o^.

38/20 14 May 1317 *HCA 1040*

One membrane, a narrow strip, with two tongues running from the bottom left, both with seals. Seals: 1. Vesica-shaped, 30 mm × 20 mm, in green wax, the seal of the deanery of Hereford *ad causas*; legend: .....NATVS ..... 2. ?Oval, now 20 mm × 9 mm, in green wax, a standing ?episcopal figure, most of the right-hand side broken off; lettering illegible. Contemporary endorsement: 'Acquietancia R. subpistoris de xx s. receptis ab executoribus domini'.

Tenore presencium pateat universis quod ego Ricardus dictus le Mareschal recepi et habui a domino Johanne de Kemes' thesaurario Herefordensi executore et suis coexecutoribus testamenti sancte memorie domini Ricardi de Swynefeud quondam Herefordensis episcopi viginti solidos sterlingorum quos idem pater michi in suo testamento legavit. In cuius rei testimonium sigillum meum presentibus est appensum et quia sigillum meum pluribus est ignotum sigillum decanatus Herefordensis ad causas apponi presentibus procuravi. Data Herefordie die sabbati proximo post festum ascensionis domini anno domini M^{mo}CCC^{mo}xvii^{o}.

38/21 14 May 1317 *HCA 1041*

One membrane, a narrow stip, with a stub from a tongue at the bottom left. The top edge of the document has the bottom of letters from the last line of another document. Contemporary endorsement: 'Acquietancia Johannis de Barwe'.

Pateat universis per presentes quod ego Johannes de Barewe recepi viginti solidos argenti a venerabilibus viris dominis Johanne de Kemeseye Johanne de la Felde et magistro Roberto de Icclesham canonicis Herefordensibus ac domino Rogero de Breynton' executoribus testamenti bone memorie domini mei domini Ricardi de Swynefeld'[1] nuper episcopi Herefordensis quos viginti solidos idem episcopus dominus meus in testamento suo legavit. De quibus quidem viginti solidis fateor me plenarie solutum et predictos[2] executores fore quietos per presentes imperpetuum. In cuius rei testimonium sigillum meum presentibus est appensum. Data Hereford' die sabati proximo ante festum sancti Ethelberti regis et martiris anno domini millesimo trecentesimo septimo decimo.

Notes

1 MS has a double 'f' mid-word for a capital.

2 MS: 'predictis'.

38/22 16 May 1317 *HCA 1020*

One membrane, a narrow strip with part of a tongue running from the left at the foot, with no trace of a seal. Contemporary endorsement: 'Aquietancia Ricardi de Torneiston' de xx s. legatis'.

Universis pateat per presentes quod ego Ricardus de Torneston recepi et habui ab executoribus testamenti sancte memorie domini Ricardi de Swynefeud quondam Herefordensis episcopi viginti solidos legalium sterlingorum quos idem venerabilis pater michi in suo testamento legavit. In cuius rei testimonium sigillum meum presentibus est appensum et quia sigillum meum pluribus est ignotum sigillum decanatus Herefordensis ad causas apponi presentibus procuravi. Data Her' die lune proximo post festum ascensionis domini anno domini millesimo trecentesimo septimodecimo.

38/23 16 May 1317 *HCA 1042*
One membrane, a narrow strip, with two stubs from tongues or wrapping tie at the bottom left. Contemporary endorsement: 'Aquietancia fratrum beati Augustini de Lodelowe'.

Pateat universis per presentes quod nos prior et fratres ordinis sancti Augustini de Lodelowe habuimus et recepimus die confeccionis presencium per manus executorum Ricardi dei gracia quondam episcopi Herefordie viginti solidos sterlingorum de qua solucione nos prior et fratres fatemur predictos executores esse quietos. In cuius rei testimonium presentibus literis acquietancie sigillum officii prioris apposuimus. Data apud Lodelowe die lune proxima ante festum Pentecost*es* anno domini M^mo^CCC^mo^ septimodecimo.

38/24 17 May 1317 *HCA 2062*
One membrane, a narrow strip, with two seals, each on a tongue running from the bottom left, along with the torn stub from a wrapping tie running from the same place. Seals: 1. Oval, 24 mm × 17 mm, in green wax, a fragment of the seal of the deanery of Hereford *ad causas*. 2. Oval, 23 mm × 18 mm, in green wax, the seal of William de Wike, two figures, on the left, identified in the catalogue entry as St Michael with a shield and spear piercing a dragon; and on the right, a mitred figure. There are three architectural arches at the top. Legend: S' WILLI DE ..... Contemporary endorsement: 'Aquietancia Johannis de Schel*v*ing' de C s. sibi legatis'.

Universis pateat per presentes quod ego Johannes de Schel*v*ing' recepi et habui ab executoribus testamenti sancte memorie domini Ricardi de Swynefeud quondam Herefordensis episcopi centum solidos legalium sterlingorum quos idem venerabilis pater michi in suo testamento legavit. In cuius rei testimonium sigillum meum presentibus est appensum et quia sigillum meum pluribus est ignotum sigillum decanatus Herefordensis ad causas apponi presentibus procuravi. Data Her' die martis proximo post festum ascensionis domini anno domini M^o^CCC^mo^ septimodecimo.

38/25 17 May 1317 *HCA 1016*
One membrane, a narrow strip, now with no remains of a tongue. Contemporary endorsement: 'Acquitancia Henrici de Wyk' de xx s. sibi legatis'.

Tenore presencium pateat universis quod ego Henricus de Wyk' recepi et habui ab executoribus testamenti sancte memorie domini Ricardi de Swynefeud quondam Herefordensis episcopi viginti solidos legalium sterlingorum quos idem venerabilis pater michi in suo testamento legavit. In cuius rei testimonium sigillum meum presentibus est appensum. Data Her' die martis proxima post festum ascensionis domini anno domini millesimo trecentisimo septimodecimo.

38/26 17 May 1317 *HCA 1006*
One membrane, with a seal on a tongue running from the bottom left and a wrapping tie. Seal: oval, 22 mm × 17 mm, in green wax, the seal of William de Wike, as **38/24**. S' WILLI DE WIKE ..... Contemporary endorsement: 'Acquietancia J. et S. fratrum de Wyk' de xl s.'

Universis pateat per presentes quod nos Johannes ac Stephanus de Wyk' recepimus et habuimus ab executoribus testamenti sancte memorie domini Ricardi de Swynefeud quondam Herefordensis episcopi quadraginta solidos legalium sterlingorum quos idem pater nobis in suo testamento legavit. In cuius rei testimonium sigillum magistri Willelmi de Wyk' fratris nostri apponi presentibus procuravimus. Data Her' die martis proximo post festum ascensionis domini anno domini millesimo trecentisimo septimo.

38/27 18 May 1317 *HCA 1003*
One membrane, now with no trace of a tongue or seal. Contemporary endorsement: 'Aquitancia Ricardi Wynchecou' de xx s.'

Universis pateat per presentes quod ego Ricardus de Wynchecoumbe recepi et habui ab executoribus testamenti sancte memorie domini Ricardi de Swynefeud quondam Herefordensis episcopi viginti solidos sterlingorum quod idem pater michi in suo testamento legavit. In cuius rei testimonium sigillum meum presentibus est appensum et quia sigillum meum pluribus est ignotum sigillum decanatus Herefordensis ad causas apponi presentibus procuravi. Data Her' die mercurii proximo post festum ascensionis domini anno domini M^{o}CCC^{mo} septimodecimo.

38/28 18 May 1317 *HCA 1008*
One membrane, with no trace of a tongue or seal. Contemporary endorsement: 'Aquitancia domini Nicholai de Ak' de vi s. legatis garcionibus suis'.

Tenore presencium pateat universis quod ego Nicholus de Aka porcionarius in ecclesia de Ledebur' Herefordensis diocesis recepi et habui ab executoribus testamenti sancte memorie domini Ricardi de Swynefeud quondam Herefordensis episcopi ad opus Willelmi et Radul*ph*i garcionum meorum sex solidos sterlingorum eis legatis in testamento domini episcopi supradicti. In cuius rei testimonium sigillum meum presentibus est appensum. Data Hereford' die mercurii proximo post festum ascensionis domini anno eiusdem M^{mo}CCC^{mo}xvii^{o}.

38/29 18 May 1317 *HCA 1010*
One membrane, with remains of a tongue at the bottom left, but most now missing, including the seal. Contemporary endorsement: 'Acquietancia Willelmi Persevale de xx s. legatis'.

Universis pateat per presentes quod ego Willelmus Perceval recepi et habui ab executoribus testamenti sancte memorie domini Ricardi de Swynefeud quondam Herefordensis episcopi viginti solidos sterlingorum quos idem pater michi in suo testamento legavit. In cuius rei testimonium sigilllum meum presentibus est appensum et quia sigillum meum pluribus est ignotum sigillum decanatus Herefordensis ad causas apponi presentibus procuravi. Data apud Her' die mercurii proximo post festum ascensionis domini anno domini millesimo trecentisimo septimodecimo.

38/30 18 May 1317 *HCA 1026*
One membrane, a narrow strip with a stub from a tongue (possibly with a stub

from a second tongue or a wrapping tie) at the bottom left. Contemporary endorsement: 'Aquitancia magistri Ricardi de Nonyton' de libris sibi legatis'.

Universis pateat per presentes quod ego Ricardus de Nonyton' canonicus Herefordensis recepi et habui ab executoribus venerande memorie domini Ricardi de Swynefeud nuper Herefordensis episcopi unum veterem librum summarum et eva*u*ngelia glosata secundum Marcum et Lucam in uno volumine[1] quos idem venerabilis pater michi in suo testamento legavit. In cuius rei testimonium sigillum meum presentibus est appensum. Data Her' die mercurii proximo post festum ascensionis domini anno domini M°CCC° septimodecimo.

Notes

1 Noted in B.G. Charles and E.D. Emanuel, 'Notes on old libraries and books', *National Library of Wales Journal* 6 (1950) pp. 353–72, at p. 354, and Cavanaugh, 'Books', p. 839.

38/31 18 May 1317 *HCA 1044*

One membrane, a narrow strip, with a seal on a tongue running from the bottom left and a stub from a wrapping tie. Seal: oval, 24 mm × 18 mm, in green wax. Two heads, separated by a crossed key and sword over a pointed arch; in the arch, the top half of a figure in an attitude of prayer, facing left. The head on the left is tonsured, facing right; the head on the right faces left. There is a small cross to the left of the crossed key and sword. Lettering illegible. Contemporary endorsement: 'Aquitancia \ Willelmi de / molendino de xx s. ei legatis'.

Tenore presencium pateat universis quod ego Willelmus de molendino de Bosebur' recepi et habui ab executoribus testamenti bone memorie domini Ricardi de Swynefeud quondam Herefordensis episcopi per manus domini Nicholai de Ak' porcionarii in ecclesia de Ledebur' viginti solidos sterlingorum michi legatos in testamento predicto. In cuius rei testimonium sigillum dicti domini Nicholai presentibus est appensum. Data Her' die mercuii proximo post festum ascensionis domini anno eiusdem M^mo^CCC^mo^xvii°.

38/32 19 May 1317 *HCA 1023*

One membrane, a narrow strip, with a stub at the bottom left from a tongue. Contemporary endorsement: 'Aquietancia magistri R' de Ham' de pecunia sibi soluta pro suis garcionibus ex legato'.

Universis pateat per presentes quod ego Ricardus de Hamonasch' canonicus Herefordensis recepi et habui ab executoribus venerande memorie domini Ricardi de Swynefeud nuper Herefordensis episcopi duodecim solidos sterlingorum ad opus quatuor garcionum meorum quos ipse eisdem in suo testamento legavit. In cuius rei testimonium sigillum meum presentibus est appensum. Data apud Hereford' die jovis in octavis ascensionis domini anno eiusdem M°CCC°xvii°.

38/33 21 May 1317 *HCA 1013*

One membrane, a narrow strip, now with no trace of a tongue. Contemporary endorsement: 'Acquietancia Rogeri le Barbor de ..... s. sibi legatis'.[1]

Universis pateat per presentes quod ego Rogerus le Barbour recepi et habui a domino Johanne de Kemes' thesaurario Herefordensi executore et suis coexecutoribus testamenti sancte memorie domini Ricardi de Swynefeud quondam Herefordensis episcopi xx s. legalium sterlingorum quos idem venerabilis pater michi in suo testamento legavit. In cuius rei testimonium sigillum meum presentibus est appensum et quia sigillum meum pluribus est ignotum sigillum decanatus Herefordensis ad causas apponi presentibus procuravi. Data Her' die sabbati proximo post festum ascensionis domini anno domni M°CCC°xvii°.

Notes
1 MS: 'legatum'.

38/34 22 May 1317 *HCA 1012*
One membrane, a narrow strip, with two tongues running from the bottom left, each with a seal. Seals: 1. Round, in brown wax, 20 mm × 20 mm, with the initials MC, possibly IHC, below an arch, lettering illegible. 2. Oval, in green wax, 28 mm × 22 mm, a forward-facing, tonsured head (as **38/1**). Contemporary endorsement: 'Acquietancia Johannis de Stildon' de di. marca'.

Universis pateat per presentes quod ego Johannes de Stildon' recepi et habui ab executoribus testamenti sancte memorie domini Ricardi de Swynefeud quondam Herefordensis episcopi dimidiam marcam legalium sterlingorum quam idem venerabilis pater michi in suo testamento legavit. In cuius rei testimonium sigillum meum presentibus est appensum et quia sigillum meum pluribus est ignotum sigillum decanatus Herefordensis ad causas apponi presentibus procuravi. Data Her' die dominica proxima post festum ascensionis domini anno domini M°CCC°xvii°.

38/35 12 July 1317 *HCA 1002*
One membrane, with, on a tongue running from the bottom left, an oval seal in red wax, 21 mm × 13 mm: two figures, a standing ?bishop on the left, possibly holding two aspergilla; figure on right kneeling. Lettering illegible. Contemporary endorsement: 'Acquietancia Ade de Hervynton' de i anulo aureo sibi legato'.

Pateat universis quod ego Adam de Herwynton' recepi et habui ab executoribus testamenti pie memorie domini Ricardi de Swynefeud nuper Herefordensis episcopi unum anulum aureum cum saphiro cum quo idem pater fuit in episcopum consecratus et quem michi in suo testamento legavit. In cuius rei testimonium sigillum meum huic acquietancie est appensum. Data London' die martis proximo post festum translacioni beati Benedicti abbatis anno domini millesimo CCC^{mo}xvii°.

38/36 13 July 1317 *HCA 1007*
One membrane, with a seal on a tongue running from the left and a short section of second tongue. Seal: oval, 37 mm × 25 mm, in green wax, a poor impression, with two seated figures and an illegible legend. Contemporary endorsement: 'Acquietancia Ade de Cranbrok et Gonnoner*e* uxoris sue de xx marcis'.

Pateat universis quod nos Adam de Cranebrok et Gunnora de Boynton' uxor mea recepimus et habuimus ab executoribus testamenti pie memorie domini Ricardi de Swynefeud nuper Herefordensis episcopi viginti marcas sterlingorum michi Gunnore predicte in testamento eiusdem patris legatas quam quidem pecuniam nos recepisse et dictos executores inde inperpetuum fore quietos per presentes fatemur. In cuius rei testimonium sigilla nostra presentibus sunt appensa et quia sigilla nostra pluribus sunt ignota sigillum venerabilis viri domini prepositi ecclesie de Wyngeham Cantuariensis diocesis apponi presentibus procuravimus. Data London' et apud Wyngeham die mercurii proxima post festum translacionis beati Thome martiris anno domini M^{mo}CCC^{mo}xvii^{o}.

38/37 13 July 1317 *HCA 1017*
One membrane, a narrow strip, now with no remains of a tongue. In this document and in **38/38–42**, **44–7**, the feast is the translation of St Benedict the Abbot (11 July), rather than the saint's day (21 March). Contemporary endorsement: 'Acquietancia fratrum et sororum hospitalis de Northegath' Cant' de xl s.'

Pateat universis quod nos fratres et sorores hospitalis de Northgate Cant' recepimus et habuimus ab executoribus testamenti pie memorie domini Ricardi de Swynefeud nuper Herefordensis episcopi quadraginta solidos sterlingorum nobis in testamento dicti patris legatos. In cuius rei testimonium sigilla prioris et priorisse domus predicte presentibus sunt appensa. Data Cantuar' die mercurii proxima post festum sancti \ Benedicti / abbatis anno domini M^{mo}CCC^{mo}xvii^{o}.

38/38 13 July 1317 *HCA 1029*
One membrane, a narrow strip with a stub from a tongue at the bottom left. Contemporary endorsement: 'Acquietancia priorisse et sororum hospitalis sancti Jacobi Cant' de xl s.' There is a gap between 'Jacobi' and 'Cant'', suggesting that the endorsement was written while the receipt was held closed by a wrapping tie.

Pateat universis quod nos priorissa et sorores hospitalis sancti Jacobi extra civitatem Cant' recepimus et habuimus ab executoribus testamenti bone memorie domini Ricardi de Swynefeud nuper Herefordensis episcopi quadraginta solidos sterlingorum nobis in testamento suo legatos. De qua quidem pecunia dictos executores quietos esse fatemur per presentes. In cuius rei testimonium sigillum domini decani Cant' procuravimus hiis appendi. Data Cantuar' die mercurii proximo post festum sancti Benedicti abbatis anno domini M^{mo}CCC^{mo}xvii^{o}.

38/39 13 July 1317 *HCA 1032*
One membrane, a narrow strip; no tongue, but part torn away at the bottom left as if there had been one. Letters in square brackets are supplied: the membrane is torn away at this point. Contemporary endorsement: 'Acquietancia fratrum [predi]catorum Cant' xl s.'

Pateat universis quod nos prior et conventus fratrum de ordine predicatorum Cant' recepimus ab executoribus testamenti pie memorie domini Ricardi de Swynefeud nuper Herefordensis episcopi quadraginta solidos sterlingorum nobis in testamento suo legatos. In cuius rei testimonium ego prior predictus sigillum meum huic acquietancie apposui. Data Cant' d[ie mer]curii proximo post festum sancti Benedicti abbatis anno domini $\mathrm{M^{mo}CCC^{mo}xvii^{o}}$.

38/40 13 July 1317 *HCA 1038*
One membrane, a narrow strip, with a stub from a tongue at the bottom left. Contemporary endorsement: 'Acquietancia vicarii et parochianorum de Boctone de xxvi s. viii d.'

Pateat universis quod ego Thomas vicarius ecclesie de Bocton' Cantuariensis diocesis recepi et habui ab executoribus testamenti bone memorie domini Ricardi de Swinefeud nuper Herefordensis episcopi duas marcas sterlingorum distribuendas inter pauperes parochianos ecclesie de Bocton' predicte quas quidem duas marcas idem pater pauperibus parochianis predictis in suo testamento legavit. In cuius rei testimonium sigillum discreti viri commissarii venerabilis viri domini rectoris ecclesie de Bocton' una cum sigillo meo presentibus est appensum. Data Cant' die mercurii proximo post festum sancti Benedicti abbatis anno domini $\mathrm{M^{mo}CCC^{mo}xvii^{o}}$.

38/41 14 July 1317 *HCA 1014*
One membrane, a thin strip, now with no trace of a tongue. Contemporary endorsement: 'Acquietancia Michaelis de Berham de uno anulo sibi legato'.

Pateat universis quod ego Michael de Bereham canonicus in ecclesia Herefordensi recepi ab executoribus testamenti bone memorie domini Ricardi de Swynefeud nuper Herefordensis episcopi unum anulum aureum preciosum[1] quem dominus Robertus de Borgat' quondam abbas Radyng' contulit dicto patri et quem idem pater michi in suo testamento legavit. In cuius rei testimonium sigillum meum presentibus est appensum. Data Cant' die jovis proximo post festum sancti Benedicti abbatis anno domini $\mathrm{M^{mo}CCC^{mo}xvii^{o}}$.

Notes
1 MS: 'preciosum' written over an erasure and followed by a long line filler.

38/42 14 July 1317 *HCA 1022*
One membrane, a narrow strip, with a seal on a tongue running from the bottom left, with a stub from a second tongue. Seal: vesica-shaped, in green wax, 25 mm × 19 mm; a church or ecclesiastical building of two storeys, with a pointed roof; S' DECA..... CANTUARIE Contemporary endorsement: 'Acquietancia Johannis Osebarn' Wymarc uxoris sue de xx s.'

Pateat universis quod nos Johannes Osebarn et Wymark uxor mea recepimus ab executoribus testamenti pie memorie domini Ricardi de Swynefeud nuper Herefordensis episcopi viginti solidos sterlingorum michi Wymark predicte in testamento dicti patris legatos de qua pecunia dictos executores quietos esse inperpetuum per presentes fatemur. In cuius rei testimonium sigilla nostra presentibus sunt appensa et quia sigilla nostra pluribus sunt ignota sigillum domini decani \ Cant' / ad nostrum rogatum presentibus est appensum. Data Cant' die jovis proximo post festum sancti Benedicti abbatis anno domini $\mathrm{M^{mo}CCC^{mo}xvii^{o}}$.

38/43 14 July 1317 *HCA 1036*
One membrane, a narrow strip, with a seal on a tongue running from the bottom left and a second tongue or wrapping tie. Seal: a fragment, vesica-shaped in red wax, possibly a figure in pontificals; lettering illegible. Contemporary endorsement: 'Acquietancia fratrum minorum Cant' de xl s.'

Pateat universis presentem seriem inspecturis quod pridie id. Julii anno domini M^{o}C^{o}C^{o}C^{o}xvii^{o} satisfactum est creditoribus fratrum minorum Cantuar' in xl solidis sterlingorum pro anima bone memorie domini Ricardi quondam episcopi Herefordensis nuper defuncti per manus magistri Ricardi Hamenherse executoris dicti domini. In cuius rei testimonium sigillum officii gardiani dicti loci presentibus est appensum.

38/44 14 July 1317 *HCA 1039*
One membrane, a narrow strip, with a seal on a tongue running from the bottom left, along with a stub remaining from the wrapping tie. Seal: a fragment of an oval or vesica-shaped seal in green wax, 20 mm × 17 mm, a building of two storeys in the centre (as **38/42**); legend: ..... DECAN..... Contemporary endorsement: 'Acquietancia magistri et presbitorum Cant' de xx s. sibi legatis'.

Pateat universis per presentes quod nos magister and presbiteri hospitalis presbiterorum Cant' recepimus et habuimus ab executoribus bone memorie domini Ricardi de Swynefeud nuper Herefordensis episcopi viginti solidos sterlingorum nobis in testamento dicti patris legatos de qua quidem pecunia predictos executores fatemur esse quietos per presentes. In cuius rei testimonium sigillum decanatus Cantuariensis presentibus apponi procuravimus. Data Cant' die jovis proximo post festum sancti Benedicti abbatis anno domini M^{o}CCC^{mo}xvii^{o}.

38/45 14 July 1317 *HCA 1047*
One membrane, a narrow strip, now with no trace of a tongue. Contemporary endorsement: 'Acquietancia Symonis de Scel*v*yng' de x marcis'.

Pateat universis quod ego Simon de Schel*v*yng' recepi et habui ab executoribus testamenti bone memorie domini Ricardi de Swynefeud nuper Herefordensis episcopi decem marcas sterlingorum quas idem pater michi in suo testamento legavit de quibus decem marcis predictos executores inperpetuum fore quietos fateor per presentes. In cuius rei testimonium sigillum meum presentibus est appensum et quia sigillum meum pluribus est ignotum sigillum domini decani Cantuariensis apponi presentibus procuravi. Data Cant' die jovis proximo post festum sancti Benedicti abbatis anno domini M^{mo}CCC^{mo}xvii^{o}.

38/46 15 July 1317 *HCA 1027*
One membrane, a narrow strip, originally with two tongues running from the bottom left, of which the upper one is now only a stub. Fragment of a vesica-shaped seal, now 33 mm × 20 mm, in green wax; probably a standing figure in pontificals; no legend remaining. Contemporary endorsement: 'Acquietancias de Colehull' de C s.'

Pateat universis quod ego Thomas de Coleshulle recepi et habui ab \ executoribus / testamenti pie memorie domini Ricardi de Swynefeud nuper Herefordensis episcopi centum solidos sterlingorum michi in suo testamento legatos de qua quidem pecunia dictos executores quietos esse fateor per presentes. In cuius rei testimonium sigillum meum presentibus est appensum et quia sigillum meum pluribus est ignotum sigillum venerabilis viri domini prepositi ecclesie de Wyngeham apponi presentibus procuravi. Data apud Wyngeham die veneris proximo post festum sancti Benedicti abbatis anno domini M^mo^CCC^mo^xvii^o^.

38/47 16 July 1317 *HCA 1033*
One membrane, a narrow strip, with no tongue but a torn area of parchment, bottom left, where one would have been. Contemporary endorsement: 'Acquietancia T. de Retlyng' de xx s.'

Pateat universis me Thomam de Retlyng' recepisse et habuisse ab executoribus testamenti bone memorie domini Ricardi de Swynefeud nuper Herefordensis episcopi viginti solidos sterlingorum pro una roba michi debita de seisona estivali post mortem eiusdem domini episcopi. In cuius rei testimonium sigillum meum presentibus est appensum. Data Cant' die sabbati proximo post festum sancti Benedicti abbatis anno domini M^mo^CCC^mo^xvii^o^.

38/48 17 July 1317 *HCA 1018*
One membrane, a narrow strip, now with no trace of a tongue. Contemporary endorsement: 'Acquietancia Margerie de Brok de x marcis sibi legatis'.

Tenore presencium pateat universis quod ego Thomas de la Felde procurator legitimus Margerie de Brok' filie Isabelle de la Dane quondam sororis bone memorie domini Ricardi de Swynefeud nuper Herefordensis episcopi defuncti recepi et habui ab executoribus testamenti eiusdem domini Ricardi decem marcas sterlingorum quos quidem[1] dominus Ricardus eidem Margerie domine mee in suo testamento legavit quam quidem peccuniam me integre recepisse et dictos executores a dicta peccunia quietos esse fateor per presentes. In cuius rei testimonium sigillum decanatus Cantuariensis presentibus apponi procuravi. Data Cant' xvi kal. Augusti anno domini M^o^ CCC^o^ xvii^o^.

Notes
1 MS obscure.

38/49 2 August 1317 *HCA 1035*
One membrane, a narrow strip with a fragment of a seal on a tongue running from the bottom left. Seal: vesica-shaped, now 30 mm × 24 mm, in green wax; two standing ecclesiastical figures, each in a pointed arch; legend unclear. Contemporary endorsement: 'Acquietancia magistri Willelmi de Svanton''.

Pateat universis quod ego Willelmus de S*u*anton' rector ecclesie de Cherring' recepi et habui ab executoribus felicis memorie domini Ricardi de Swynefeud nuper Herefordensis episcopi unum anulum aureum cum saphiro et cum quadam emerauda in eodem quem dictus pater michi in suo testamento legavit. De quo anulo cum dictis lapidibus preciosis dictos executores quietos clamo per presentes. In cuius rei testimonium sigillum jurisdiccionis ecclesie mee de Cherryng' huic acquietancie apposui. Data London' secundo die mensis Augusti anno domini M°CCC°xvii°.

38/50 9 September 1317 *HCA 2677*
One membrane, a narrow strip, with a stub at the bottom left from a tongue. No contemporary endorsements.

Pateat universis per presentes quod nos decanus et capitulum Herefordenses collectores procuracionis dominorum Gaucelini et Luce de Flisc' cardinalium a curia Romana in Anglia transmissorum recepimus per manus domini Nicholai de Ya*n*ewrth' capellani ac in hac parte receptoris nostri ab executoribus bone memorie domini Ricardi nuper Herefordensis episcopi undecim libras sexdecim solidos et quatuor denarios racione procuracionis supradicte eisdem cardinalibus de bonis \ ipsius episcopi / spiritualibus temporalibus et mobilibus in decanatu et archidiaconatu Herefordensi existentibus debite pro primo anno more eorum in Anglia videlicet de qualibet marca quatuor denarios. In cuius rei testimonium sigillum ipsius domini Nicholai presentibus est appensum. Data Heref' die veneris in crastino festi nativitatis beate Marie anno domini M°CCC° septimodecimo.

38/51 15 [no month] 1317 *HCA 1034*
One membrane, a narrow strip, with a stub at the bottom left for a tongue. Damaged by water. Contemporary endorsement: 'Littere acquietancie dominorum decani et capituli London' de C s. .....cutoribus ..... Herefordensis episcopi ....tuor ..... eisdem'.

Tenore presencium pateat universis nos decanum et capitulum ecclesie sancti Pauli London' habuisse et recepisse ab ..... bone memorie Ricardi de Swinefeud quondam episcopi Herefordensis centum solidos sterlingorum quos idem R..... ..... de qua quidem pecunia dictos executores fore quietos in perpetuum concedimus per ....gocia presentibus est appensum. Data in capitulo nostro London' xv die ....decimo.

38/52 31 July 1320 *HCA 1372*
Letters of William Reynolds, Archbishop of Canterbury, to Adam Orleton, Bishop of Hereford, instructing him to hear the account of the executors of Bishop Swinfield. Given at Lambeth. One membrane.

38/53 6 February 1327 *HCA 1068*
One membrane, a narrow strip, with a fragment of a vesica-shaped seal in green wax on a tongue, running from the left, and a wrapping tie. Damaged by water. Printed in *Charters and records of Hereford Cathedral* ed. W.W. Capes (Cantilupe Society, 3; 1908) pp. 220–1, where it is incorrectly dated 1337. Contemporary endorsement: 'Acquietancia capituli de legatis episcopi Ricardi'.

Universis fidelibus pateat per presentes quod nos S. decanus ecclesie cathedralis Herefordensis et eiusdem loci capitulum facta calculacione sive compoto cum dominis Johanne de la Feld et Rogero de Breynton' nostris confratribus et concanonicis executoribus testamenti bone memorie domini Ricardi dei gracia dudum nostri episcopi Herefordensis comperimus ipsos ecclesie nostre satisfecisse de particulis infrascriptis nobis et ecclesie nostre predicte legatis usque ad quadraginta libras decem et novem solidos et octo denarios quos nobis persolverunt super compoto videlicet de viginti marcis sterlingorum argenti pro fenestris vitreis in domo capitulari noviter construenda facienda. Item de quingenta marcis ad construccionem eiusdem dom... ...pitularis. Item de centum marcis ad emendum redditum pro sustentacione duorum capellanorum celebraturorum perpetue divina in ipsa ecclesia pro anima dicti patris. Item de centum marcis ad emendum redditum pro melioracione distribucionis faciende annuatim die obitus dicti patris. Item de centum marcis pro construcione feretri sancti Thome predecessoris dicti patris. Item de centum marcis ad emendum redditum annuum ad distribuendum vicariis et clericis qui interim celebracioni misse beate Marie virginis cotidie in ecclesia predicta celebrande. Ipsos de particulis prout in ipsius patris testamento plenius et seriosius continetur quietos esse fatemur et penitus liberatos. In cuius rei testimonium sigillum nostrum commune presentibus duximus apponendum. Data in domo nostra capitulari Herefordensi sexto die mensis Februarii anno domini millesimo CCC^{mo} vicesimo sexto.

38/54 5 March 1328 *HCA 1051*

Letters of Adam Orleton, Bishop of Hereford. He has received a mandate from Walter, Archbishop of Canterbury, dated at Lambeth, 31 Jul [2 kal. August] 1320 to hear and determine the account of the executors of Bishop Swinfield. He has therefore called before him Dom. John de la Felde and Dom. Roger de Breintone, canons of Hereford, the surviving executors, who have rendered to him the account of their administration, and whom he now acquits of their charge. London, 5 March 1328. One membrane.

38/55 15 April 1340 *HCA 1069*

One membrane, a notarial instrument. Contemporary endorsement: 'Aquietancia H. de Estenore'.

In dei nomine amen. Per presens publicum instrumentum cunctus appareat evidenter quod anno ab incarnacione domini millesimo trecentesimo quadragesimo indiccione octava pontificatus sanctissime in Cristo patris domini Benedicti divina providencia pape xii anno sexto die quintadecima mensis Aprilis Henricus de Estenore pauper ut asseruit consanguineus bone memorie domini Ricardi de Swynefeud' dudum Herefordensis episcopi defuncti in castro venerabilis in Cristo patris domini Ade dei gracia Wyntoniensis episcopi apud Farnham Wyntoniensi diocese in mei notarii publici et testimonium subscriptorum presencia personaliter constitutus fatebatur se recepisse a venerabili viro domino Rogero de Breynton' testamenti dicti patris defuncti executore ibidem tunc presente unam summam peccunie racione et nomine legati residui bonorum dicti patris defuncti in ipsius testamento eidem Henrico ut dixit relicti et de eadem peccunie summa racione et nomine dicti legati residuum bonorum predictorum sibi fuisse et esse integre satisfactum et plenarie persolutum ac omni juri accioni et liti sibi contra prefatum dominum Rogerum executorem supradictum qualitercumque competentibus vel competituris racione dicti legati pure sponte et absolute renunciavit et ea dicto executori remisit expresse. Acta sunt hec presentibus[1] venerabilibus et discretis viris magistris Johanne de Orleton canonico Herefordensi et Johanne de Usk' officiali Wyntoniensi testibus ad premissa vocatis specialiter et rogatis.

[*Notarial sign*] Et ego Johannes de Beautre clericus Wygorniensis diocesis publicus apostolica auctoritate notarius supradictis confessioni renunciacioni et remissioni prefati Henrici anno domini indiccione pontificatu mense die et loco suprascriptis una cum predictis testibus presens fui easque sic fieri vidi et audivi scripsi et in hanc publicam formam redegi meoque signo consueto signavi rogatus in testimonio premissorum. Rasuram vero verborum remisit expresse. Acta sunt hec presentibus superius in hoc instrumento contentes feci et approbi ego notarius predictus.

Notes
1 MS: the first four words of this sentence are written over an erasure.

38/56 1342 × 1352 *HCA 1925*
Notarial instrument, now partly cut away, temp. Pope Clement VI. One membrane.

.... Racy of Bosebury, a blood relation of Bishop Swinfield in the third degree, acknowledging that he or she has been paid in full by Dom. Roger de Breynton, canon of Hereford, the portion bequeathed in the Bishop's will. In the presence of John de Rysebury, clerk (and at least one other individual, whose name is now cut away), and attested by Thomas de Bokenhulle, clerk of the diocese of Hereford, notary public by papal authority.

38/57 5 April 1342 *HCA 1070*
Notarial instrument testifying to the renunciation by Juliana Schort of Eastnor, diocese of Hereford, a poor (*pauper*) relation of Bishop Swinfield in the second degree of consanguinity, in the house of Dom. Roger de Breynton', canon of Hereford and executor of Swinfield, of all claim resulting from the clause in the Bishop's will concerning poor blood relations of the Bishop. In the presence of Dom. Simon de Radenore and Dom. Richard de Aust', clerks, and attested by Philip de la More, clerk of the diocese of Exeter, notary public by papal authority. One membrane.

38/58 9 April 1342 *HCA 3163*
Notarial instrument testifying that Roger Racy of Bosbury and Richard de Aust, proctors of Eleanor the wife of the said Roger and of Richard, Roger, Juliana and Alice their children, blood relations of Bishop Swinfield, appeared in Hereford Cathedral, and stated that Dom. Roger de Breynton', canon of Hereford and executor of Swinfield, had satisfied them of all claims resulting from a legacy in the Bishop's will. In the presence of John de Ministreworth' and John de Stanford' and attested by Philip de la More, clerk of the diocese of Exeter, notary public by papal authority. One membrane.

38/59 14 April 1342 *HCA 1071*
Notarial instrument testifying to the renunciation by Thomas de Nonynton', of the diocese of Canterbury, a poor (*pauper*) relation of Bishop Swinfield within the

fourth degree of consanguinity, in the cathedral church of Hereford, of all claim against Dom. Roger de Breynton', canon of Hereford and executor of Swinfield, recognising him to have paid in full any legacy due under the Bishop's will, with a quitclaim to Roger, his heirs and executors. In the presence of Dom. Roger de Hompton and Robert de Wokenhull', clerks, and attested by Philip de la More, clerk of the diocese of Exeter, notary public by papal authority. One membrane.

38/60 8 January 1347 *HCA 1072*
Notarial instrument testifying to the renunciation by Juliana daughter of Roger Racy, a blood relation of Bishop Swinfield, in the house (*mansio*) at Hereford of Dom. Roger de Breynton', canon of Hereford and executor of Swinfield, recognising him to have paid in full her share from the residue of the goods of the Bishop bequeathed in his will, 40*s*. having been paid to her in cash at that point by the hands of William Bourdon'. Juliana acknowledges the full and final payment of the share and agrees not to sue against the executors for it in future. In the presence of Dom. John de Lugardyn and Dom. William de la Mersche, priests, and attested by William Bourdon', clerk of the diocese of Canterbury, notary public by papal authority. One membrane.

39 Tideman, Bishop of Worcester

39/1 Commission for levying sums in order to pay the debts of the Bishop, who has died intestate, 5 December [1402] *LPL, Register of Thomas Arundel, vol. I, f. 196v*
The item immediately preceding the commission is dated 21 November 1402.

[*f. 196v*] *Commissio ad levandum et exigendum quascumque pecuniarum summas episcopi Wigorniensis decedentis ab intestato et ad solvendum creditoribus recepta ab eis acquietanciis* Thomas permissione divina etc. dilecto in Cristo filio magistro Ricardo Wynchecombe archidiacono Gloucestr' salutem etc. Cum bone memorie quondam venerabilis frater noster dominus Tyddemannus ultimus Wigorniensis episcopus nuper ab intestato decedens mortis sue tempore in tantum fuit ere alieno gravatus quia omnia bona que dimisit creditoribus suis vix in x^{mo} denario ex provida defalcacione prehibita satisfacere sufficiunt de implemento ecclesie Wigorniensis et reparacionibus que percepit fieri sicut deberet ex debito justicie venerabili fratri nostro domino Ricardo dei gracia episcopo ipsius inmediato successori cum instancia id petenti restitucio moderata unde inspecto et examinato inventario et vero valore ac exilitate bonorum huiusmodi ac omnia debita tam Wigorniensi ecclesie quam creditoribus memoratis ut equitas racionis et honestatis observetur ubique non unus totum sed unusquisque prout bona suppetunt modicum quid accepiat. Ad levandum recipiendum et exigendum vice et auctoritate nostris quascumque pecuniarum summas debitas et pervenientes de vendicione bonorum huiusmodi et de eisdem pecuniis sic receptis tam predicto episcopo et ecclesie sue Wigorniensi de denariis quos sibi ex equa defalcacione ordinavimus quam ceteris personis et creditoribus memoratis et in cedula hiis annexa descriptis juxta moderacionis formam eciam in eadem cedula specifice designatis receptis primitus ab eodem episcopo et ceteris creditoribus memoratis anticopis et sufficientibus acquietanciis in hac parte vobis conmittimus[1] vices nostras et plenam tenore presencium potestatem. Data in manerio nostro de Lamh' quinto die mensis Decembris anno domini et translacionis supradictis.

Defalcacio debitorum episcopi Wigorniensis
In primis Ricardo episcopo Wigorniensi pro reparacionibus CCC marce
Johanni Shirwynd lxiii s. iiii d.
Item Johanni Trygge xx s.
Item Johanni Blakeden xxvi s. viii d.
Item rectori sancte Katerine de Colman x li.
Item Rogero Walden' xiii li. vi s. viii d.
Item Nicholao Mo*u*nketon xx li.
Item Johanni Wodelok xiii li. vi s. viii d.
Item Henrico Cambregg vi li. xiii s. iiii d.
Item Johanni Luk xxvi s. viii d.
Item Johanni Romald x s.
Item Waltero Saymour x li.
Item Johanni Lodelowe x s.
Item Rogero Barbour xiii s. iiii d.
Item Johanni Weston vi li. xiii s. iiii d.
Item Willelmo Cro*u*ell' xiii li. vi s. viii d.
Item magistro Ricardo Wych vi li. xiii s. iiii d.
Item Johanni Bathe xii li.
Item pro stipendio famulorum x li.
Item sacriste Wigorniensis ecclesie viii li.

Notes
1 MS: 'co', followed by 6 minims and 'ttimus'.

39/2 Commission of the Archbishop addressed to the Deans of Worcester and Gloucester, John Swepedewe and Thomas Pany, clerks, and William Wenmue and John Walter, *literatis*. Reliable information has been received that very many people in the province of Canterbury are withholding 'nonnulla bona vasa argentea et vestimenta et alia jocalia' formerly belonging to the Bishop of Worcester, either by virtue of pledges, or out of concealment, to the peril of the soul of the Bishop and his creditors. The addressees are to warn those holding the goods that they be delivered to Mag. R. Wichecombe, archdeacon of Gloucester, within a given term, assigning to those who were owed 'aliqua liquida summa' by the deceased either satisfaction or sufficient security. All contradicting this are to be cited. n.d. December 1402. *LPL, Register of Thomas Arundel, vol. I, f. 197v*

39/3 Letters of the Archbishop: whereas Bishop Tideman of Worcester died intestate, and whereas his successor, Richard, has petitioned for sums towards repairs of the properties of the bishopric, and upon enquiry the dilapidations have been found to amount to £2,396, greatly exceeding the deceased's goods, the Archbishop orders 300 marks to be paid from the goods towards the dilapidations for Richard, Bishop of Worcester, reserving the balance of the estate for the payment, with moderate default, of Bishop Tideman's creditors to whom it is known at the time of his death he was bound in sums greater than his possessions. In turn, Richard and his executors are not to be held liable for a sum greater than 300 marks in respect of the dilapidations. Given at Mortlake, n.d. *c.*December 1402. *LPL, Register of Thomas Arundel, vol. I, f. 198r.*

40 Alexander Tottington, Bishop of Norwich

40/1 Will and codicil, 20 April 1412 *LPL, Register of Thomas Arundel, vol. II, ff. 165r–166v*

In dei nomine amen nos Alexander permissione divina Norwicensis episcopus vicesimo die Aprilis anno domini millesimo CCCC^{mo} duodecimo in plena sanitate mentis et corporis infra manerium nostrum de Thorp juxta Norwicum existentes condimus facimus et constituimus nostrum testamentum in hunc modum. In primis commendamus animam meam deo omnipotenti qui eam redemit suo sanguine precioso et corpus nostrum sepeliendum in ecclesia nostra cathedrali Norwici in capella beate Marie eiusdem juxta fontem sub quadam petra marmoria prius ibidem ea de causa per nos posita dum in officio prioris ibidem administravimus. Item lego ad distribuendum inter pauperes die sepulture nostre denariatim xx li. Item in die nostre septennarie cuilibet pauperi illuc venienti ob. et in die tricennarie ob. Item legamus et assignamus pro sumptibus nostrorum funeralium racione nostre sepulture faciende quantum nostris executoribus infrascriptis pro meliori videatur expedire et similiter tantum pro sacerdotibus inveniendis pro anima nostra celebraturis quantum eisdem executoribus nostris pro nostro meliori videatur expedire. Item legamus et concedimus priori et conventui ecclesie nostre cathedralis predicte ad orandum et celebrandum pro anima nostra certam summam peccunie per executores nostros annuatim eisdem liberandam de proventibus manerii nostri de Brundale proveniendam sub certis modo et forma in quodam codicillo nostro plenius specificatis. Item legamus ad distribuendum inter pauperes tenentes nostros apud Hoxne xx s. et ad reparacionem ecclesie parochialis eiusdem xx s. Apud Southelmham inter pauperes tenentes nostros xx s. et ad reparacionem cuiuslibet ecclesie parochialis eiusdem vi s. viii d. Apud Eccles inter pauperes nostros tenentes xiii s. iiii d. et ad reparacionem ecclesie eiusdem vi s. viii d. Apud Thornage inter pauperes tenentes nostros xiii s. iiii d. et ad reparacionem eiusdem ecclesie xx s. Apud Thornham inter pauperes tenentes nostros xx s. Item ad reparacionem eiusdem ecclesie xx s. Apud Lamtham inter pauperes tenentes nostros xx s. Item ad reparacionem eiusdem ecclesie vi s. viii d. Apud Merston' inter pauperes tenentes nostros xiii s. iiii d. et ad reparacionem ecclesie eiusdem vi s. viii d. Apud Blofeld' inter pauperes tenentes nostros xiii s. iiii d. et ad reparacionem ecclesie eiusdem vi s. viii d. Apud Boyton' inter pauperes tenentes nostros xiii s. iiii d. et ad reparacionem ecclesie eiusdem vi s. viii d. Apud Northelmham inter pauperes tenentes nostros xx s. et ad reparacionem ecclesie eiusdem xx s. Apud Thorp inter pauperes tenentes nostros xiii s. iiii d. et ad reparacionem ecclesie eiusdem vi s. viii d. Apud Geywode inter pauperes tenentes nostros xx s. et ad reparacionem ecclesie eiusdem vi s. viii d. Apud Batesford inter pauperes [*f. 165v*] tenentes nostros x s. et ad reparacionem ecclesie eiusdem vi s. viii d. Apud Wykes Episcopi inter pauperes tenentes nostros vi s. viii d. Apud Terlyng inter pauperes tenentes nostros et parochianos ibidem xx s. et ad reparacionem ecclesie eiusdem xiii s. iiii d. Aput Totyngton' inter pauperes parochianos ibidem xx s. et ad reparacionem ecclesie eiusdem xx s. Item legamus priorisse et conventui de Campesse xl s. Item priorisse et conventui de Bungey xx s. priorisse et conventui de Flixton xx s. abbatisse et conventui de Brusiȝerd' xx s. priorisse et conventui de Redelyngfeld' xx s. priorisse et conventui de Carhowe xx s. priorisse et conventui de Thefford'[1] xx s. abbatisse et conventui de Marham xx s. priorisse et conventui de Schouldham xx s. priorisse et conventui de Blacbergh' xx s. ac priorisse et conventui de Crabhous xx s. ut ipse moniales orent pro anima nostra et animabus omnium amicorum nostrorum quibus tenemur et omnium fidelium defunctorum. Residuum vero omnium bonorum nostrorum non legatorum legamus et donamus nostris executoribus infrascriptis ad perficiendum nostram ultimam voluntatem et solvendum omnia debita nostra et ulterius ad disponendum inde pro anima nostra prout eis et anime nostre saluti melius videatur expedire et prout voluerint coram deo respondere. Et si bona nostra non sufficiant ad perficiendum omnia legata nostra tunc volumus et concedimus quod de omnibus et singulis legatis nostris parcellatim fiat defalcacio juxta discrecionem et voluntatem omnium executorum nostrorum administracionem nostrorum bonorum in forma juris recipiencium. Huius autem testamenti sui cuiuscumque alterius ultime nostre voluntatis debite perficiendum nostros facimus ordinamus et constituimus executores videlicet magistros Thomam Dallyng Willelmum Bernham et Johannem Thornham clericos ac Edmundum Oldehalle armigerum et Willelmum Paston. Presentibus discretis viris magistris Hugone Bridham et Johanne Excestre notariis publicis Johanne Disse Johanne Barton' rectore ecclesie parochialis de Dounham ac Roberto Edyman rectore de Brisele Willelmo Alman Ricardo Gegg et Thoma Bockyng et aliis testibus ad premissis vocatis specialiter et rogatis. In cuius rei testimonium presenti testamento nostro clauso sigillum nostrum fecimus apponi. Data die loco et anno domini supradictis. Et nostre consecracionis anno quinto.

Hec est ultima voluntas nostri Alexandri permissione divina Norwicensis episcopi infra manerium nostrum de Thorp' juxta Norwicum per nos facta et de mandato nostro scripta vicesimo die mensis Aprilis anno domini millesimo CCCC^{mo} duodecimo preter aliam nostram voluntatem in quodam testamento nostro sub data presencium confectam specificatam quod quidam testamentum et contenta in eodem non intendimus per presentes revocare set pocius nostram voluntatem executoribus nostris infrascriptis per presentes lucidius declarare et notificare. In primis volumus et ordinamus quod prior et capitulum ecclesie Norwicensis eorumque successores habeant et teneant post mortem nostram in suos proprios usus imperpetuum manerium nostrum de Brundale cum suis juribus et pertinenciis universis cuius verus valor annuus se extendit hiis diebus ad decem libras monete Anglie sub ista condicione si ipsi voluerint suis propriis sumptibus et expensis huiusmodi manerium nostrum sibi ipsis videlicet ad officium celerarii[2] eorundem appropriare et ex licencia regia illud notificare quamcito poterint post mortem nostrum atque presentem nostram ordinancionem seu ultimam voluntatem de et super cantaria unius capellani perpetui inter eosdem celebraturi de novo eregendo sub modo et forma infrascriptis debite adimpleverint cum effectu videlicet quod incontinenti post mortem nostram habeamus inter capitulares nostros et confratres cantariam unius capellani perpetui videlicet unius monachi professi in capella sancte Marie virginis nostre cathedralis ecclesie antedicte in qua nostram elegimus sepulturam quolibet die ad sextam horam matutinalem eiusdem diei imperpetuum de cetero celebraturi [*f. 166r*] pro anima nostra ac animabus bone memorie domini Henrici dudum Norwicensis episcopi Johannisque patris nostri et Agnetis matris nostre parentum parochianorum et omnium fidelium defunctorum. Qui quidem capellanus predictus cotidie post dictam missam sic per ipsum celebratam dicat ad tumulum nostrum 'De profundis' cum oracionibus sequentibus videlicet 'Deus qui inter apostolicos sacerdotes famulos tuos Herbertum et Alexandrum' etc. 'Inclina' etc. pro fidelibus defunctis et quod semel in septimana unam missam celebret de requiem pro anima nostra et animabus predictis. Item quod quilibet monachus de conventu[3] Norwici cum septimana pro ordine in forma prescripta huiusmodi missam celebret si voluerit et in fine eiusdem septimane in qua sic ut premittitur celebraverit recipiet pro labore suo per manus dicti celerarii seu alterius cuiuscumque huiusmodi officium occupantis de proventibus dicti manerii nostri vel officii dicti celerarii duos solidos bone et legalis monete Anglie ad quam celebracionem in forma prescripta ac dicte pecunie solucionem ut premittitur bene et fideliter faciendas et observandas volumus dictum officium celerarii firmiter obligari. Item volumus et ordinamus quod dicti prior et capitulum Norwicenses annuatim nostrum anniversarium predicta ecclesia nostra cathedrali imperpetuum teneant ut moris est prout faciunt pro aliis episcopis Norwicensibus. Et quod tunc quilibet monachus in eadem ecclesia nostra ad placebo dirige et missam eiusdem anniversarii nostri ibidem personaliter presens existens recipiet per manus dicti celerarii vel cuiuscumque alterius officium dicti celerarii occupant pro tempore xii d. Item volumus et ordinamus quod totum commodum residuum de dicto manerio nostro de Brundale annuatim proveniens per celerarium predictum pro[4] tempore existentem recipiatur ac per eundem in usum et commodum officii sui predicti expendatur et comittatur. Item damus concedimus et legamus dicte ecclesie nostre cathedrali nostram capellam in die sepulture nostre corpus nostrum ad eandem ecclesiam nostram deferendam antecedentem videlicet unam mitram baculum pastoralem unum vestimentum integrum de panno[5] operato cum[6] unum calicem unum par fiolarum argenti unum deosculatorium cum tintinabulo et pixide pro pane de argento unum par candelabrorum et unum thurribulum de argento cum equo et apparatu huiusmodi capellam deferenti ac unum equm in curru nostro tunc forsitan nostrum corpus deferenti anterius deambulantem sic ut predicta ecclesia nostra cathedralis per nos qui in eadem a nostre juventutis flore usque in finem utinam ad laudem et honorem dei cursum vite nostre confirmavimus suo jure et consuetudine laudabili hactenus observatis libere congaudeat et deberet et possessionem pacifice et quiete. Item legamus et assignamus ecclesie nostre predicte nostrum missale novum de usu monachorum per nos compositum cum tribus vestimentis pro capellano nostro predicto cum uno calice cum duobus corporalibus et uno pare fiolarum argenti ad altare ubi dictus noster capellanus ut premittitur celebrabit imperpetuum remansura. Item legamus ecclesie nostre predicte duo portiforia nova que eciam fecimus scribi et componi de usu monachorum quorum majus portiforium in camera prioris dicte ecclesie nostre pro tempore existentis ad usum suum imperpetuum remanebit ac minus portiforium penes fratrem Ricardum Middelton' ad terminum vite sue remanebit eciam si extra dictum monasterium[7] Norwicense morietur ita quod post eius mortem ad predictum monasterium revertatur. Item legamus et assignamus dicte ecclesie nostre cathedrali unum novum portiforium et pulcrum non notitatum secundum usum Sarum per nos compositum et honeste reponetur juxta discrecionem executorum nostrum in eadem ecclesia nostra cathedrali ut peregrini et alii presbiteri huiusmodi ecclesiam causa devocionis visitantes super eodem libro suas horas canonicas congrue poterint dicere ut causam provide habeant ad orandum pro anima nostra in futurum. Item damus et legamus ad summum altare dicte ecclesie nostre cathedralis unam pulcram capam argenteam et deauratam ibidem ad nostri memoriam impertuum remansuram. Et ad refectorium[8] eiusdem ecclesie unam peciam argenteam et deauratam cum cooperculo eiusdem secte de cedre honeste apparatam cum argento et de iburneo sic circumscriptam 'Siphus Alexandri' servetur ab hostio meandri ac officio hostiarii eiusdem ecclesie nostre duo lecta integra secundum disposicionem executorum meorum. Item volumus et ordinamus quod si contingat aliquo casu interveniente dictos priorem et capitulum nostrum predict*os* seu canonicum Norwicensem [*f. 166v*] seu quemquam legatoriorum nostrorum aut aliquem eorum aut quemvis aliquem alium nomine suo vel alieno nostros executores in nostro testamento constitutos videlicet magistros Thomam Dallyng et Willelmum Bernham clericos Johannem Thornham Edmundum Oldehalle et Willelmum Paston vel aliquem eorundem execucione vel administracione nostre ultime voluntatis vel occasione licite administracionis bonorum nostrorum quovis modo impedire molestare implicare perturbare vexare vel inquietare quod absit pretextu cuius impedimenti vexacionis inquietacionis seu perturbacionis huiusmodi bona nostra ideo fuerint et sint diminuta que non sufficiant ad solvendum debita nostra et ad perficiendum legata nostra quominus nostra presens ultima voluntas et alibi in nostro testamento plenius specificata suum debitum poterit sortiri effectum quod tunc nostra presens voluntas seu alia ordinacio et omnia alia legata hic et in dicto testamento nostro plenius specificata in quantum concernunt dictos priorem et capitulum cannonicum aut nostros legarios antedictos aut alios quoscumque in casu predicto contingentes pro nullo habeantur ac suo robore careant et effectu. Et in casu predicto volumus et ex certa sciencia ordinamus quod licitum sit executoribus nostris predictis quantum voluerint de dictis legatis nostris juxta eorum discrecionem parcellatim defalcare et penes se retinere et si necesse fuerit huiusmodi legata in parte vel in toto tollere dictumque manerium de Brundele sicut alia bona nostra non legata vendere ac de eisdem omnibus et singulis libere disponere ad honorem dei et anime nostre salutem pro sue libito voluntatis prout eis melius videbitur expedire predictis nostris legatis et donacionibus omnino non obstantibus. Item volumus et ordinamus quod si aliquo dictorum executorum nostrorum aliqua de bonis nostris vendenda pro justo et competenti precio voluerit emere tantum solvendum pro eisdem consociis suis executoribus quamcumque alia persona discreta et indifferens voluerit solvere pro eisdem bonis tunc idem executor noster licite posset huiusmodi empcionem facere quem volumus in hac parte aliis auferri quacumque constitucione in contrarium edicione non obstanti. Item legamus cuilibet notario de nostro consilio xx s. Item cuilibet armigero nostro xx s. Item cuilibet valetto nostro xiii s. iiii d. Et cuilibet garcioni nostro vi s. viii d. Item legamus cuilibet executorum nostrum administracionem bonorum nostrorum in forma juris recipienti pro suo labore x marcas. In cuius rei testimonium presenti codicillo nostro clauso nostram ultimam voluntatem in se continenti sigillum nostrum fecimus apponi. Data die loco et anno domini supradictis. Et nostre consecracionis anno quinto.

Notes
1 MS: the double 'ff' probably intended as a capital.
2 MS: 'celelar''.
3 MS: 'conventui'.
4 MS: 'per'.
5 Followed in MS by a blank space.
6 Followed in MS by a blank space.
7 MS obscure, possibly conflating two words: 'dcmonen'.
8 MS: 'refectorum'.

40/2 Grant of probate for the testament and codicil to Mag. William Berham and William Paston, 4 May 1413. *LPL, Register of Thomas Arundel, vol. II, f. 166v.*

40/3 Commission to William Milton, archdeacon of Buckingham, delegating to him the power of admitting to the administration another of the executors named in the will, certifying the same to the Archbishop of Canterbury, 4 May 1413. *LPL, Register of Thomas Arundel, vol. II, f. 166v.*

41 John Trefnant, Bishop of Hereford

41/1 Will, 1 March 1404; notarial copy, 21 March 1404 *LPL, Register of Thomas Arundel, vol. I, f. 207r*

Although the will is dated 1 March 1403, i.e. new style 1404, the date of the notarial copy, 21 March 1404, must be 1404 new style, rather than 1405, as the document was written in the presence of the Bishop – who died between 26 March and 23 April 1404.

In dei nomine amen per presens publicum instrumentum cunctis appareat evidenter quod anno ab incarnacione domini secundum cursum et computacionem ecclesie Anglicane millesimo CCCC^{mo} quarto indiccione xiime pontificatus sanctissimi in Cristo patris et domini nostri domini Bonifacii divina providencia pape noni anno xv^{to} xxi^{mo} die mensis Marcii in manerio reverendi in Cristo patris ac domini domini Johannis dei gracia Herfordensis episcopi de Prestebury Wygorniensi diocese in quadam alta camera ibidem in mei notarii publici et testium subscriptorum presencia in lecto egritudinis personaliter constitutus dictus reverendus pater videns sibi mortis periculum iminere sanus mente licet debilis corpore testamentum suum sive ultimam voluntatem condidit et ordinavit in hunc modum et sub forma que sequitur verborum. In dei nomine amen ego Johannes permissione divina Herfordensis episcopus sanus mente licet aliquantulum eger corpore de inevitabili fine precogitans qui fuit et est omnibus et singulis mortalibus ordinatus condo testamentum meum in hunc modum. In primis lego animam meam deo omnipotenti redemptori meo beate Marie et omnibus sanctis corpusque meum sepeliendum in capella australi ecclesie Herfordensis que dicitur sancte Anne et volo quod circa funus meum juxta arbitrum executorum meorum huius testamenti fiat. Item volo quod iidem executores mei persolvant omnia debita mea et ad hoc pure et simpliciter ac sine fraude do et concedo eis omnia et singula bona mea mobilia et immobilia in quibuscumque rebus existencia ut ordinent et disponant prout secundum deum et sinceram conscienciam eis ac omnibus bonis hominibus sincere et bone consciencie videbitur faciendum ad que omnia et singula peragenda constituto et ordino infrascriptos executores meos videlicet dominum Johannem dei gracia episcopum Assavensem dominum Ricardum Kyngeston' decanum de Wyndesore magistrum Raginaldum Wolston' dominos Johannem Proute[1] Hugonem Harper et Thomam Busshebury canonicos ecclesie Herfordensis et Ricardum de la Bere Thomam Wallewayn' ac Willelmum Wallewayn fratrem suum et Johannem Crosset rectorem ecclesie de Hertilbury Wygorniensi diocese. In cuius rei testimonium sigillum meum rotundum huic presenti testamento meo apponi feci. Data in manerio meo de Prestbury primo die mensis Marcii anno domini millesimo CCCC^mo^ tercio. Acta sunt hec prout suprascribuntur et recitantur sub anno domini indictione pontificatus mense die et loco predictis presentibus tunc ibidem discretis viris magistro Rogero Andrew publico auctoritate apostolica notario Johanne Hampton Willelmo Barre et Edmundo Webbeley presbiteris Johanne ap Oweyn' Willelmo Charlton' Johanne Goth Waltero Aylston' clericis Herfordensibus testibus ad premissa vocatis specialiter et rogatis. Et ego Johannes de Went clericus Landavensis diocesis publicus auctoritate apostolica notarius premissis omnibus et singulis dum sic ut premittitur agerentur et fierent sub anno domini indictione mense die et loco predictis una cum prenominatis testibus presens interfui eaque omnia et singula sic fieri vidi et audivi scripsi publicavi et in hanc publicam formam redigi signoque et nomine meis consuetis signavi rogatus et requisitus in fidem et testimonium premissorum.

Notes

1 MS obscure; probably John Prat, who held the prebend of Gorwell and Overbury (J. Le Neve *Fasti ecclesiae Anglicanae 1300–1541. II Hereford diocese* ed. J.M. Horn (London, 1962) p. 25).

41/2 Grant of probate to Mag. Reginald Wolston, canon of Hereford, Dom. John Gresset, rector of the parish church of Hartlebury, executors named in the will, Lambeth, 23 April 1404. *LPL, Register of Thomas Arundel, vol. I, f. 207r.*

41/3 Commission to Mag. Roger Hore, canon of Hereford, for committing the administration of the estate to other executors named in the will, Lambeth, 24 April 1404. *LPL, Register of Thomas Arundel, vol. I, f. 207r.*

41/4 Inventory, *c*.1404 *HCA 2126*

A roll of one membrane, indented at the head; written in a single hand, with additions in a further hand, and a total at the end in a third. The head of the roll has faded badly, and there is some water damage. The sections preceding the book list are laid out in two columns, with the first two sections in the first column. Endorsements: 1. At the head, in an early to mid fifteenth-century hand, 'Inventarium Johannis Trevenant episcopi Herefordensis'. 2. At the foot, in an early to mid fifteenth-century hand, 'Inventarium de libris etc. J. episcopi Herefordensis. Et vasis argenteis.' The section listing books was published first in *Charters and records of Hereford Cathedral* ed. W.W. Capes (Hereford, 1908) pp. 259–62; in more detail by B.G. Charles and H.D. Emanuel, 'Notes on old libraries and books' *National Library of Wales Journal* 6 (1950) pp. 353–72, at pp. 355–60; and is noted in Cavanaugh, 'Books', pp. 874–8.

Memorandum quod reverendus in Cristo pater dominus Johannes Trefnant episcopus Herefordensis emit infrascripta de executoribus domini Johannis Cl*ouve* militis videlicet

In primis vii hanap argent dendor*e* de poys lviii s. precii C s.
Item ii salers cover*t* poys lx s.
Item ii pot*es* dargent de poys de vii liv. vi s.
Item i bacyn dargent de poys Cvi s.
Item i alt*re* bacyn dargent de poys de Cxvi s.
Item ii ewers dargent de poys de iiii liv. viii s. viii d.
Item ii charj*ou*rs dargent de poys de vii liv. v s.
Item v esquils dargent de poys de viii liv.
Item vii esquils dargent de poys de ix liv. viii d.
Item vi esquils dargent de poys viii liv. xii s.
Item i pot*e* dargent *d*endore*e*[1] de poys viii liv. xv s. precii xii li.
Item i ewrer argent et end*ore* de poys xlvi s. viii d. precii iiii li.
Item iii candelabra dargent et endore precii xiiii li.
Un ..... rev..... ..... xl *s*.[2]

Summa lxxxxviii li. xiiii s. iiii d.[3]

Item empta sunt vasa infrascripta a magistro Thoma de Busshebury
In primis ii pelves ii lavatoria xii scutelle xii sauseria et ii olle de argento precii xlvi li. viii s. iiii d.
Item i calix de argento precii C s.
Item i cyphus argenti deauratus cum coopertorio deaurato cum longo pede precii xl s.
Item i calix d*e*auratus precii iii li.
Item i tabuleta de auro puro cum salutacione beate virginis cum ymaginibus sancti Georgii et sancte Katerine ex una parte et ymaginibus sancti Cristofori et sancte Margarete ex alia parte cum diversis lapidibus preciosis et uni omnibus precii xxiii li.
Memorandum sunt de dono comitis Arrundell'[4] Item i magnus cyphus argenti cum uno aquario deaurato precii C s.
Item i cyphus cum longo pede et coopertorio deaurato et ii parvis ciphis de nuce cum coopertoriis deauratis precii C s.

Summa lxxxix li. viii s. iiii d.

Item memorandum quod[5] empta sunt infrascripta vasa argenti de Thoma P..... aurifabro ac cive London'
In primis vii scutelle vi sausers ii charjurs de argento precii xxxvi li. ..... s.
Item xii gacie de argento cum ii coopertoriis argenti precii xx li. iii s. iiii d.
Item xii coclearia argenti unde i coclearium perd...[6] precii xxxv s. ii d.
Item viii coclearia argenti precii xxvi s. viii d.
Item ii salers cum ii coopertoriis argenti precii iiii li.
Item i parvum salerium argenti precii viii s.
Item ii pelves argenti precii xii li. xii s. viii d.
Item i halywat*er*stok' cum i ysopo de argento precii C s.
Item i campanella de argento precii *l* s.[7]
Item osculatorium de argento precii xxx s.

Item ii fiale de argento precii xl s.
Item i olla argenti precii iii li. viii s.
Item i cyphus cum coopertorio de argento deaurato precii xl s. Non reperitur.[8]
Item i turribulum de argento deaurato precii iii li. xi s. iiii d.
Item i cyphus de testa gryffonis cum coopertorio deaurato emptus per W. *C*oykyn de Johanne Sa*u*ndres precii iii li.
Item i cyphus cum coopertorio deaurato habitus a magistro Roberto Prys valoris xxviii s.
Item ii coclearia deaurata cum i bifur*cito*[9] valoris vii s.
Item i tabuleta aurea valoris vi marcarum.
Item i cyphus cum coopertorio deauratus habitus a domino Johanne Gode-m*o*ston' valoris iii li.

Summa Cii li. xi s. ii d.

Summa totalis vasorum argenti CClxxxix li. xiii s. x d.

Sequitur inventarium de libris domini J. Trefnant episcopi Herefordensis
In primis i misale melius incipiens in secundo folio post kalendarium 'reverencia et timor' '[10] valoris xxiiii li.
Item aliud missale incipiens in secundo folio post kalendarium 'usque ad festum' in rubro valoris viii marcarum.
Item aliud missale de usu Herefordie in duabus partibus videlicet in collatario incipienti in secundo folio 'tifica in membris' valoris xxv s. et epistolario incipienti in secundo folio 'peccata sua' valoris xxv s. l s.
Item i gradale de usu Sarum incipiens in secundo folio 'in principio' valoris vi marcarum.
Item i manuale incipiens in secundo folio post kalendarium 'tate spiritus' valoris xl s.
Item i aliud gradale de usu Sarum[11] incipiens in secundo folio 'sequentibus' valoris iiii marcarum.
Item i pontificale incipiens in secundo folio 'exorciste spiritus' valoris xl s.
Item i parvum portiforium quod incipit in secundo folio 'd' Go.....'[12] valoris v marcarum.
Item i psalterium de grossa littera incipiens in secundo folio psalterii 'monte sancto' valoris viii s.
Item aliud psalterium novum nondum liminatum[13] incipiens in secundo folio 'a*ut*' quis' valoris xv s.
Item lectura Ricardi de Saluzeto super forciato veteri[14] incipiens in secundo folio 'ecclesie ut ...' valoris v marcarum.
Item Au*gustin*us super prima parte psalterii[15] et Hugo de sacramentis[16] in eodem volumine incipiens in secundo folio 'explicit psalmus' valoris iiii marcarum.
Item textus forciati veteris[17] incipiens in secundo folio 'tulit' valoris vi s. viii d.
Item alius textus forciati veteris incipiens in secundo folio 'senator' etc. valoris x s.
Item unum volumen in quo continentur ordo judiciarius[18] et casus super codice et institu*cionibus*[19] cum questionibus Bar*tholomei* Brixensis[20] incipiens in secundo folio 'enim contra se' valoris xl s.
Item Bartholomeus de proprietate rerum[21] incipiens in secundo folio 'sive localis' valoris vi marcarum.
Item textus novem collationum[22] incipiens in secundo folio 'complentes' valoris xx s.

Item Augustinus de civitate dei[23] incipiens in secundo folio 'quas solet coruptorum' valoris iii marcarum.
Item cronica Martiniana[24] incipiens in secundo folio 'corum in alt...' x s.
Item summa Azonis super codice et aliis[25] cum lectura Jacobi de Belviso super libro feudorum[26] incipiens in secundo folio 'cum cleric*is*' valoris xl s.
Item pars lecture Cyni super forciato veteri[27] incipiens in 2° folio 'ipsam voluntatem' valoris x s.
Item i formularium magnum cum diversis formis litterarum incipiens in secundo folio 'ministraciones secularium' valoris xx s.
Item casus decretales cum lectura Petri Sampsonis[28] incipiens in secundo folio 'considerans' valoris iii marcarum.
Item secunda pars speculi historialis[29] incipiens in secundo folio 'occupaverant' valoris v marcarum.
Item Cynus super codice[30] incipiens in secundo folio 'do l i'[31] valoris vii marcarum.
Item secunda secunde[32] incipiens in secundo folio 'nos visuros' valoris xl s.
Item summa confessorum incipiens in secundo folio 'et libellis' valoris iii li.
Item summa Azonis super codice[33] et casus super forciato novo ac eciam casus Viviani super inforciato[34] incipiens in secundo folio 'et ita forciatum § hiis enim pact*is*' valoris xl s.
Item Mandagodus[35] super formulis eleccionum cum una cotacione biblie et pluribus extravagantibus incipiens in secundo folio 'bilitas patitur' valoris xx s.
Item i codex[36] antiquus incipiens in secundo folio 'excellentissimus' valoris x s.
Item i lectura super collacionibus cum glosa Bartholi super novem collacionibus[37] incipiens in secundo folio 'statim haberet effectum' valoris xl s.
Item lectura Andree de Ysservia super x collacionibus[38] incipiens in secundo folio 'observari primitus' valoris lx s.
Item racionale divinorum officiorum[39] incipiens in secundo folio 'sic et spiritualis' valoris lx s.[40]
Item Willelmus de Cunio super forciato veteri et codice[41] incipiens in 2° folio 'glo quia illud' valoris xl s.
Item libellus domini Johannis de La*n*disco super titulo institucionum de accionibus et aliis diversis[42] incipiens in secundo folio 'num nisi destruat' valoris xiii s. iiii d.
Item prima pars lecture Henrici Boyc super decr*etalibus*[43] incipiens in secundo folio 'gnitatibus' etc. valoris x marcarum.
Item exposicio super speculo judiciali[44] per ordinem alphabeti incipiens in secundo folio post tabulam 'cum inopta' valoris xx s.
Item textus sentenciarum[45] incipiens in secundo folio 'tatem usum' valoris xx s.
Item declaracio super Valerio Maximo edita a fratre Dionisio de Burgo sancti sepulcri[46] incipiens in secundo folio 'narrato que' etc. valoris xl s.
Item liber de exemplis sacre scripture incipiens in secundo folio 'ad peticionem' valoris xx s.
Item lectura Bar*tholi* composita super decr*eto*[47] incipiens in secundo folio 'commissione' valoris xx s.
Item lectura domini Baldi de Perusio super codice[48] incipiens in secundo folio 'et forciatum de usufructu' valoris xxx s.
Item Valerius Maximus super momoralibus[49] Romanorum[50] incipiens in secundo folio post tabulum 'bus diis' valoris xx s.
Item i liber de papiro minoris forme coopertus pelle rubea continens diversas

questiones et tractatum de censura ecclesiastica cum aliis diversis incipiens in 2° folio 'nostro sci*licet*' valoris xl s.
Item opusculum domini Viviani super inforciato[51] incipiens in 2° folio 'pensionem de cenaculo' valoris vi s. viii d.
Item secunda pars domini H. Boyc super decr*etalibus*[52] incipiens in secundo folio 'et G... hic' valoris vii li.
Item libellus de regimine civitatis[53] incipiens in secundo folio 'dicitur vero' valoris vi s. viii d.
Item historia scolastica[54] incipiens in secundo folio 'eciam hic' valoris xl s.
Item lectura Bartholi super parte inforciati[55] incipiens in secundo folio 'universitas corporum' valoris xl s.
Item lectura super xii libro forciati veteris cum aliis incipiens in secundo folio 'et ii° .....'[56] valoris xx s.
Item historia tripartita[57] incipiens in secundo folio 'sompno repugnans' valoris xx s.
Item summa Britonis super diccionibus biblie[58] incipiens in secundo folio 'actitus ta' cum[59] exposicionibus prologorum biblie[60] valoris xxx s.
Item i volumen in quo continentur decretales incipiens in secundo folio 'per veram poterit' etc. et vi^us^ liber incipiens in secundo folio 'magistratum regimini' etc. cum extravagantibus bene glosatis per cardinalem[61] valoris vi marcarum.
Item liber vi incipiens in secundo folio 'rum subdictorum' etc. glosatus per Johannem cardinalem cum aliis ii glosatoribus scilicet Johanne Andree et archidiaconi[62] valoris vi marcarum.
Item novella super vi[63] incipiens in secundo folio 'ad partem contrariam' valoris x marcarum.
Item Innocencius[64] incipiens in secundo folio 'et tunc sufficit' etc. valoris vi marcarum.
Item i biblia incipiens in secundo folio '*in* extremis finibus mundi' etc. valoris x marcarum.
Item i par decretorum[65] incipiens in secundo folio 'di facultas' valoris x marcarum.
Item novella in secunda parte decr*etalium*[66] incipiens in secundo folio 'crear' solet' valoris x marcarum.
Item rosarium[67] incipiens in secundo folio 'et die quod est opus nunc' valoris x marcarum.
Item Clementine incipiens in secundo folio 'textus vobis sub ullam' etc. cum tribus glosatoribus suis videlicet Ȝesell' Johanne et Guillelmo de Monte Haudino[68] valoris v marcarum.
Item lectura domini Pauli super Clementinis[69] incipiens in secundo folio 'sualitas nam' etc. valoris xx s.
Item i liber de papiro de decisionibus rote et aliis dubiis decisionibus et allegacionibus eiusdem domini episcopi in publicis relacionibus[70] et alia diversa qui incipit in secundo folio 'in c' querela' etc. valoris l s.
Item forciatum vetus[71] incipiens in secundo folio in titulo 'de insti' et de jure instituerunt certas' etc. ii marcarum.
Item inforciatum incipiens in secundo folio '*cule* predictum' etc. valoris xl s.
Item forciatum novum incipiens in secundo folio 'meminisse oportet' etc. valoris xl s.
Item parvum volumen incipiens in secundo folio 'libri instituticionum quedam sibi constituerunt' etc. valoris iii li.

Item liber codex incipiens in secundo folio 'judicio tui culminis' etc. valoris xx s.
Item Hostiensis in summa[72] incipiens in secundo folio 'de excess' prela' valoris x marcarum.
Item prima pars Johannis in novella super decr*etalibus*[73] incipiens in secundo folio 'rari auctorem' etc. valoris xvi marcarum.
Item prima pars lecture Hostiensis super decreto[74] incipiens in secundo folio 'dixit declarat' ' etc. valoris vii marcarum.
Item lectura Hostiensis in secunda parte decr*eti* incipiens in secundo folio 'xxiii q' i' militar' ' etc. valoris vii marcarum.
Item questiones Oldradi cum aliis diversis[75] in uno volumine quod incipit in secundo folio post tabulam 'apparet quod post' etc. valoris vi marcarum.
Item lectura Jacobi de Bruticariis super codice[76] incipiens in secundo folio 'sibi impositum' etc. valoris iii li.
Item lectura Bartholi super inforciato[77] incipiens in secundo folio 'ut in § fuerat' etc. valoris vi marcarum.
Item lectura Bartholi super forciato veteri[78] incipiens in secundo folio 'tenet hanc partem' etc. valoris vi marcarum.
Item lectura eiusdem Bartholi super forciato novo[79] incipiens in secundo folio 'edi privat' l i' valoris x marcarum.
Item unum volumen de papiro continens plura opuscula doctorum in primis i lecturam super collacionibus incipiens in secundo folio 'a' sed cum testator' valoris vii marcarum.
Item i volumen continens diversa videlicet lecturam Lapi super vi libro et Clementinis[80] et extravagantibus glosat*is* per Zessel'[81] cum aliis diversis incipiens in 2° folio '*nimie*tatis'[82] valoris xl s.
Item speculum judiciale[83] incipiens in secundo folio 'forme eciam instrumentorum' etc. valoris vi marcarum.
Item Hugusius super decreto[84] in secundo folio 'ga consuetudo' etc. valoris vi marcarum.
Item tabula terminorum juris per litteras alphabeti incipiens in secundo folio post tabulam 'adversati*ve* autem etc.' valoris xl s.
Item unum grossum volumen de papiro minoris forme coopertum cum albo corrio de diversis lecturis repeticionibus et questionibus quod incipit in secundo folio 'J i Johannes graciosum' etc. valoris iii li.
Item unum volumen de papiro ligatum in pelle rubeo continens scripta diversorum super eleccione Urbani vi et scismate sedando incipiens in secundo folio[85] valoris xx s.
Item liber Quintiliani in declamacionibus[86] incipiens in secundo folio 'scriptus' valoris vi s. viii d.
Item summa que dicitur gramadica profundi[87] cum summa et notulis magistri Cessar'[88] incipiens in secundo folio 'tinorum sunt' valoris v s.
Item Albertanus super doctrina filii sui[89] incipiens in secundo folio 'eciam apostolus' valoris vi s. viii d.
Item i catholicon[90] incipiens in secundo folio[91] valoris xii marcarum.
Item legenda aurea[92] incipiens in secundo folio[93] valoris iii li.

Summa CClxxi li. v s. viii d.[94]

Item una mitra levis alba noviter empta pro vi marcarum.
Item unum par vestimentorum de albo panno videlicet iii albe cum iii amictis ii

tunicellis ii capis una casula stola manipul*o* et cinctoriis neccessariis etc. valoris xl li.
Item[95] unum pontificale novum quod incipit in secundo folio[96] valoris xx marcarum xl marcarum.
Item unum collacarium quod incipit in secundo folio[97] valoris x marcarum.

Notes

1 The start of this word is unclear.
2 This entry, which is very faded, added in a second hand or ink.
3 MS: 'iiii s. iiii d.' in another ink, possibly over an erasure.
4 The marginal note probably refers to both the succeeding entries.
5 MS: 'memorandum quod' faded and obscure.
6 MS obscure.
7 MS obscure.
8 MS: 'Non reperitur' in another hand.
9 MS obscure, presumably a fork.
10 Single quotation marks have been used to indicate the passages quoted from the second folio. Some are followed by 'etc.', and this word has been placed outside the quotation marks, although in some instances it is just possible it was part of the text.
11 MS damaged by water: 'usu Sarum' most probable reading, under ultraviolet light.
12 MS obscure: the 'd'' may be an ampersand.
13 MS: 'l' followed by three minims, with a suspension. Possibly 'liniatum'.
14 Commentary on the first part of Justinian's *Digest*, ascribed to Ricardus de Saluzeto (?Saluzzo, in north Italy).
15 Augustine of Hippo *Enarrationes in Psalmos*, *CPL* 283; ed. E. Dekkers and J. Fraipont (*CCSL*, 38–40; 1956).
16 Hugh of St Victor *De sacramentis Christianae fidei*, edited in *PL* 176, cols. 173–618.
17 The first part of the *Digest*: Justinian *Digestum* I–XXIV, 2 ed. T. Mommsen and P. Krüger, in *Corpus iuris civilis* ed. P. Krüger, T. Mommsen, R. Schöll and W. Kroll (3 vols., Berlin, 1872–7) i. See W.P. Müller, 'The recovery of Justinian's *Digest* in the Middle Ages' *Bulletin of Medieval Canon Law* 20 (1990) pp. 1–29, for the make up of this work in the Middle Ages.
18 See A. Van Hove *Prolegomena ad codicem iuris canonici* (2nd edition, Mechlin, Rome, 1945) p. 452. Probably the *Ordo iudiciarius* of Tancred of Bologna, printed in *Pillii, Tancredi, Gratiae Libri de iudiciorum ordine* ed. F. Bergmann (Göttingen, 1842; reprint Aalen, 1965) pp. 89–314.
19 Unidentified cases on Justinian's *Code* and *Institutes*. For the development of Justinian's works, J.A. Brundage *The medieval origins of the legal profession: canonists, civilians, and courts* (Chicago, 2008) p. 58.
20 Bartholomeus Brixiensis (Bartholomew of Brescia) *Quaestiones dominicales et veneriales*, printed Rouen, 1511.
21 Bartholomeus Anglicus *De proprietatibus rerum*, printed Frankfurt, 1601.
22 The abbreviated Latin version of the *Novellae* of Justinian was known as the *Authenticum* and was commonly arranged in nine *collationes*; printed: *Authenticum in novem collationes digesti* ed. P. Krüger (Berlin, 1877). See also note 37 below.
23 Augustine of Hippo *De civitate dei*, *CPL* 313; ed. B. Dombart and A. Kalb (*CCSL*, 47–8; 1955).
24 Martinus Polonus (Martin of Troppau) *Chronicon pontificum et imperatorum* ed. L. Weiland (MGH, Scriptores, 22; 1872) pp. 377–482.
25 Azo *Summa super codice et institutis*, printed Speyer, 1482.
26 Jacobus de Belviso *Lectura summam autenticorum et usus feudorum elucidans*, printed Lyons, 1511.
27 Cinus of Pistoia, Commentary on Justinian's *Digestum vetus*, printed Lyons, 1527.
28 Petrus Sampson, *Lectura decretalium*, unpublished.
29 Probably Vincent of Beauvais *Speculum historiale*, printed Douai, 1624.
30 Cinus of Pistoia *Lectura in codicem*, printed Strassburg, *c.*1475.
31 MS: 'do l j'.
32 Part of Thomas Aquinas, *Summa theologica*, II^{a} IIe: *STO*, iv–xii.
33 Azo *Summa super codice et institutis*, as note 25; other works possibly unpublished.
34 Vivianus Tuscus *Casus longi* on Justinian's *Codex*, *Digestum vetus* and *Inforciatum*, printed Freiburg, *c.*1494.
35 Willelmus de Mandagoto *De electionibus*, printed Paris, 1506.

36 Justinian *Codex*, printed in *Corpus iuris civilis* ed. T. Mommsen, P. Krüger, R. Schöll and W. Kroll (3 vols., Berlin, 1872–7) ii.

37 Works of Bartolus de Saxoferrato (Bartolus of Sassoferrato), commentaries on the nine *collationes* of the *Authenticum* (note 22 above); his *Lectura super iuris civilis*, with his commentaries on the whole of Justinian's *Codex* and the *Digest*, was published at Lyons, 1481/2. For other works of Bartolus on the *Corpus iuris civilis*, see below, notes 55, 77–9.

38 Andreas (de Rampinis) de Isernia, perhaps his *Peregrina lectura*, printed Lyons, 1533–4.

39 Willelmus Durandus the elder *Rationale divinorum officiorum*, printed Mainz, 1459.

40 A second hand has written 'vacat' around this entry, with the letters 'va' before it and 'cat' after.

41 Guillelmus de Cuneo *Lectura digesti veteris* (unpublished except for the *prohemium*, B. Brandi *Notizie intorno a Guillelmus de Cunio. Le sue opere e il suo insegnamento a Tolosa* (Rome, 1892) pp. 104–13); *Lectura codicis*, printed Lyons, 1513.

42 Not traced: a work of John de Landisco/Laudisco on Justinian's *Institutes*.

43 Henry Bohic *Distinctiones in v libros decretalium*, printed Lyons, 1498: the first part; the second part is below, see note 52.

44 Either Willelmus Durandus the elder *Speculum judiciale*, printed Strassburg, 1473; or commentary on it.

45 Petrus Lombardus *Sententiarum Libri VI*, edited in *PL* 192, cols. 521–962, and by I. Brady (3 vols., *Spicilegium Bonaventurianum*, 4–5; Grottaferrata, 1971–81).

46 The unpublished gloss of Dionigi da Borgo San Sepolcro on Valerius Maximus *Facta ac dicta memorabilia*: see below, note 50.

47 A work of Bartolus de Saxoferrato, perhaps a commentary on Gratian's *Decretum*, but possibly on collections of more recent *Decretales*. His complete works were published in 5 vols. at Basle in 1588–9: *Opera quae nunc extant omnia* ...

48 Baldus de Ubaldis *Lectura super I–IX codicis*, printed Venice, 1480–1; *Lectura super X–XII codicis*, printed Milan, 1492.

49 For 'memorabilibus'.

50 Valerius Maximus *Facta ac dicta memorabilia*, printed Strassburg, before 1470.

51 A work by Vivianus Tuscus on the *Inforciatum*: see note 34 above.

52 The second part of Henry Bohic's work, note 43 above.

53 Given the other works in this library by Bartolus de Saxoferrato, this may be his *De regimine civitatis*: printed in D. Quaglioni *Politica e diritto nel trecento Italiano* (Florence, 1983).

54 Petrus Comestor *Historia scholastica*, edited in *PL* 198, cols. 1053–722; ed. A. Sylwan (*CCCM*, 191; 2005), Genesis only.

55 Bartolus de Saxoferrato, commentary on part of the *Inforciatum*: see above, note 37.

56 MS possibly 'et quod .....'

57 Cassiodorus (and Epiphanius) *Historia tripartita*, *CPL* 899; *Historica ecclesiastica tripartita* ed. W. Jacob and R. Hanslik (Corpus scriptorum ecclesiasticorum Latinorum, 71; Vienna, 1952).

58 William Brito *Expositiones vocabulorum Bibliae* ed. L.W. and D.A. Daly (Padua, 1975).

59 MS repeats 'cum'.

60 William Brito *Expositio in prologos Bibliae*, unpublished.

61 A volume of decretals, with continuations, the *Liber sextus*, with decretals from Gregory IX to Boniface VIII (*Corpus iuris canonici* ed. E. Friedberg (2nd edition, 2 vols., Leipzig, 1922) ii, cols. 933–1124), and the *Extravagantes*, probably those of Boniface VIII, both of which were glossed by Cardinal Jean le Moine (the *Glossa aurea* on the *Liber sextus*, printed Venice, 1585; the glosses to the *Extravagantes* partly incorporated in the *Glossa ordinaria* to the *Extravagantes communes*).

62 Another copy of the *Liber sextus*, with the glosses of Cardinal Jean le Moine, Johannes Andreae (gloss printed, Mainz, 1465) and Guido de Baysio, 'archidiaconus' (printed Milan, 1490).

63 Johannes Andreae, *Novellae in sextum*, printed Rome, 1476.

64 Given the other works on canon law in Trefnant's library, this is probably Innocent IV *Apparatus in quinque libros decretalium*, printed Strassburg, 1477.

65 Gratian *Decretum*, printed in *Corpus iuris canonici*, i.

66 Johannes Andreae *Novellae in decretales*, printed Venice, 1489.

67 Guido de Baysio *Rosarium seu apparatus ad decretum*, printed Strassburg, 1492.

68 The *Liber septimus*, or *Constitutiones Clementine*, containing the continuation of the decretals to Clement V (1314), edited in *Corpus iuris canonici*, ii, cols. 933–1124; with the glosses of Jesselin de Cassagnes, unpublished; Johannes Andreae, printed Mainz, 1460; and William of Mont Lauzun, unpublished.

69 Paulus de Liazariis *Lectura super Clementinas*, unpublished.

70 Decisions of the papal rota: for the circulation of these, Brundage, *Medieval origins of the legal profession*, pp. 579–80; possibly with some of Trefnant's own cases.

71 This and the next four entries contain the key texts for medieval civil law: Justinian's *Digest* in its three medieval sections, the *Old Digest*, the *New Digest* and the *Inforciatum*, along with Justinian's *Institutes*, and the *Code*. See above, note 17, for references. The *Parvum volumen*: a standard collection of Roman law, Justinian *Codex*, X–XII.

72 Henricus de Segusio, Cardinal Bishop of Ostia *Summa super titulis decretalium*, printed Rome, 1473.

73 A further copy of Johannes Andreae *Novellae in decretales*: see note 66.

74 Henricus de Segusio, Cardinal Bishop of Ostia *Lectura super decretales*, printed Strassburg, 1512. The manuscript, as is the case here, is often found in two volumes.

75 Oldradus de Ponte *Consilia et quaestiones*: many of the *consilia* circulated in manuscript; printed in varying numbers, e.g. Rome, 1472; Rome, 1478. For discussion, K. Pennington, <http://faculty.cua.edu/pennington/12981-z.htm>, accessed 4 April 2010.

76 Jacobus Buttrigarius *Lectura super codice*, unpublished.

77 Bartolus de Saxoferrato *Lectura super infortiatum*, printed Perugia, 1474/5. See note 37 above for related works, and notes 78–9.

78 Bartolus de Saxoferrato *Lectura super digestum vetus*, printed in two parts, part 1, Naples, 1471/2; part 2, Perugia, 1471/2.

79 Bartolus de Saxoferrato *Lectura super digestum novum*, printed in two parts, part 1, Venice, 1471; part 2, Venice, 1473.

80 Lapus Tactus, Abbot of San Miniato *Lectura super sexto*, printed Rome, 1589; *Lectura super Clementinas*, unpublished; *Lectura super extravagantibus*, not recorded.

81 The gloss of Jesselin de Cassagnes on John XXII's *Extravagantes*, printed in early editions of the *Corpus iurus canonici* (Paris, 1500, etc.).

82 This word may start with 8 minims.

83 Willelmus Durandus the elder *Speculum judiciale*; see note 44 above for this work and commentary.

84 Huguccio, Bishop of Ferrara (d. 1210) *Summa super decreta*, unpublished; i.e. probably not Hugutio of Pisa: the distinction is made in Professor Sharpe's listing, citing W.P. Müller *Huguccio: the life, works and thought of a twelfth-century jurist* (Washington DC, 1994) pp. 35–66.

85 The MS omits words here: it has a caret at this point to indicate an insertion, but no words have been added.

86 Pseudo-Quintilian *Declamationes xix maiores* ed. L. Håkanson (Stuttgart, 1982).

87 A work of Jacobus de Aesculo (Giacomo di Ascoli), for whom see T. Yokoyama, 'Zwei Questionen des Jacobus de Aesculo über das Esse Obiectivum' in *Wahrheit und Verkündigung. Michael Schmaus zum 70. Geburtstag* ed. L. Scheffczyk, W. Dettloff and R. Heinzmann (2 vols., Munich, 1967) i, pp. 31–74, at pp. 31–6.

88 A work of Magister Caesar, for whom see *Une grammaire latine inédite du XIII siècle* ed. C. Fierville (Paris, 1886).

89 Perhaps a work of Albertanus of Brescia.

90 John of Genoa (Johannes Januensis) (compiler) *Catholicon*, printed Mainz, ?1460.

91 Followed by a blank space in the MS.

92 Jacobus de Voragine *Legenda aurea* ed. T. Graesse (3rd edition, Breslau, 1890).

93 Followed by a blank space in the MS.

94 The total is in a third hand.

95 This entry and the next are additions in a further hand.

96 Followed by a blank space in the MS.

97 Followed by a blank space in the MS.

41/5 Acquittance of Mag. Reginald Wolston', canon of Hereford, and John Cresset, rector of the church of Hartlebury, and their co-executors of the will of Bishop Trefnant, London, 4 April 1406. *LPL, Register of Thomas Arundel, vol. I, f. 207r.*

42 Thomas Trillek, Bishop of Rochester

42/1 Will, 11 December 1372 *LPL, Register of William Whittlesey, ff. 126v–127r*

In nomine domini nostri Jhesu Cristi gloriose viriginis Marie matris eius cunctorumque civium supernorum instante misera mortis hora nemini percentis corporis dissolucionem senciens iminere ego Thomas Trillek' miseracione divina Roffensis ecclesie minister indignus sanus mente licet debilis corpore confiteor altissimo peccata mea clementem ipsius misericordiam humiliter postulans pro commissis ac obitum meum cupiens provisione testamentaria prevenire testamentum sive ultimam voluntatem meam xi die mensis Decembris anno domini millesimo CCC^mo^lxxii^do^ condo et ordino in hunc modum. In primis animam meam peccatricem quanto devocius possum lego et commendo Jhesu Cristo redemptori ac salvatori meo beatissime et gloriosissime virgini matri sue nutissimoque apostolo sancto Andree patrono meo necnon omnibus sanctis dei et corpus meum ad sepelliendum in ecclesia cathedrali Roffensi. Item lego pro expensis meis funerariorum et distribucione pauperum id quod executoribus meis infrascriptis justum et equum visum fuerit. Item lego tribus capellanis per unum vel uni capellano per tres annos pro anima mea parentum amicorum meorum et omnium fidelium defunctorum celebraturis pro ipsorum stipendio viginti li. Item lego priori ecclesie cathedrali Roffensi decem li. cuilibet monacho presbitero celebranti [*f. 127r*] ibidem sex solidos et octo denarios cuilibet monacho eiusdem loci in ordine sacerdotali minime constituto tres solidos quatuor denarios. Item lego Isabelle uxori Ricardi Rous xl s. Item lego Agneti que fuit uxor Ed*wardi* FitzJon xl s. Item lego Margarete Lo*v*el xl s. Item lego magistro Roberto de Bourn' x li. Item lego Rogero Digge x marcas. Item lego domino Willelmo Durrant x marcas. Item lego domino Ed*wardo* de Malmeshull x marcas. Item lego Jacobo de Pecham quinque marcas. Item lego Philippo La*n*waram x marcas. Item lego domino Willelmo Hagham centum solidos. Item lego magistro hospitalis[1] de Strode x li. Item lego Willelmo Kirkeby triginta tres solidos et quatuor denarios. Item lego Johanni Baker de Cobham xx s. Item lego Philippo Cha*um*b*er*leyn xl s. Item lego Johanni Ne*ne* xx s. Item lego Johanni Treiuly[2] x s. Item lego Bartholomeo Baker vi s. et viii d. Item lego Johanni Ode*n*ay x s. Item lego Johanni La*n*waran x s. Item lego Thome Rous vi s. et viii d. Item lego Thome Smyth' vi s. viii d. Residuum vero bonorum meorum non legatorum lego executoribus meis infrascriptis ut ipsi ordinent et disponant de bonis huiusmodi pro anima mea sicut eis melius et salubrius juxta eorum arbitrium videbitur expedire. Huius autem testamenti sive ultimi voluntatis mei facio ordino executores meos magistrum Robertum de Bourne rectorem ecclesie de Suthflet et dominum Willelmum Durrant rectorem ecclesie sancti Michaelis ad ripam regine London'. In quorum omnium testimonium premissorum sigillum meum feci presentibus apponi.

Notes

1 MS: 'hospitali'.
2 MS: the 'i' is an insertion.

42/2 Grant of probate to Dom. William Durra*un*t, rector of St Michael Queenhithe, London, and Mag. Robert de Bourne, executors named in the will. Charing, 3 January 1373. *LPL, Register of William Whittlesey, f. 127r.*

42/3 Acquittance of Dom. William Durraunt, executor, Canterbury, 31 August 1374. *CCA, Register G, f. 177r.*

43 Roger Walden, Bishop of London

43/1 Will, 31 December 1405 *LPL, Register of Thomas Arundel, vol. I, ff. 227r–228r*

In nomine sanctissime Trinitatis patris et filii et spiritus sancti amen ego Rogerus Walden ex benigna dei clemencia permittente Londoniensis episcopus muneritus et indignus sciens et senciens quod humane vite series dum in huius mundi pelago fluctuoso naufraga fuerit tota crebro quatitur turbine procellarum et in exilio cui pro pa*tria*[1] digne committitur luctui semper exponitur et labori nec est finis sue miserie quousque sperans exul a patria miserum carnis relinquat hospicium et naturalem sibi locum repetat ubi sperat frui patria post exilium post luctum leticia requie post laborem et quia illuc tendentibus est necesse domui sue prius bene exponere secundum quod morituro precepit dominus Ezechie[2] idcirco dum michi a domino sana racionis et memorie datur incolumitas meum de bonis meis in forma que sequitur condo ordino et facio testamentum. In primis lego et commendo animam meam domino Jhesu Cristo meo et tocius humani generis redemptori ipsius ineffabilem exorans clemenciam quatinus eam post laboris miseriam in celesti requie cum celestibus faciat civibus habitare. Item lego corpus meum cum ex hac luce migraverit tradendum ecclesiastice sepulture aut in ecclesia cathedralis sancti Pauli Londoniensis aut in quadam nova capella quam de novo feci fieri in ecclesia conventuali canonicorum sancti Bartholomei juxta Smethfelde ad electionem et ordinacionem reverendissimi in Cristo patris et domini mei Thome dei gracia Cantuariensis archiepiscopi qui me de sub pedibus hominum jacentem et pulvere ad Londoniensis ecclesie apicem sublimavit. De bonis autem meis que michi contulit clemencia salvatoris sic dispono volo ordino et lego videlicet quod ultra et preter expensas ad honorem et laudem dei [*f. 227v*] racione funeris mei servi sui faciendas quas committo disposicioni ordinacioni et discrecioni executorum meorum omnia debita mea quecumque quibuscumque personis ex quacumque causa vel occasione sint debita secundum bonorum meorum sufficienciam integre persolvantur absque difficultate seu contradictione quamcicius hoc comode fieri poterit. Et deinde legata subscripta legatariis quibuscumque plene et integre persolvantur. Item lego dicto domino meo Cantuariensi unum librum in quo continentur pastoralia beati Gregorii[3] cum aliis. Item lego ecclesie Cristi Cantuariensi unam capam ad chorum de rubio panno auri aurifrigiato cum margaritis in cuius aurifrigiis ymagines archiepiscoporum Cantuariensium et in retro pendulo scutali eiusdem martirum sancti Thome continentur. Item lego ecclesie mee cathedrali sancti Pauli Londoniensi meum optimum frontale pro summo altare. Item lego priori et conventui ecclesie conventualis sancti Bartholomei juxta Smethfelde illa duo vestimenta mea que dicti prior et conventus possident in presenti. Item volo et ordino quod executores mei juxta eorum omnium discrectionem de bonis meis predictis gardonent et remunerent servientes meos quibus nunc teneor pro retroactis serviciis et ante mortem meam tenebor pro futuris tunc temporis non gardonatis aut remuneratis. Item de bonis meis inmobilibus sic dispono ordino et volo primo videlicet quod immediate post mortem meam Johannes Walden frater meus et alii cum ipso in manerio de Totenham tunc temporis feoffati duos de executoribus meis subscriptis post ipsum Johannem fratrem meum in presenti testamento nominatis feoffent in eodem manerio cum pertinenciis suis habendum et tenendum eis in feodo simplici sub tali condicione quod ipsi duo sic feoffati immediate postea de eodem manerio de Totenham cum pertinenciis suis refeoffabunt eundem Johannem fratrem meum et Idoniam uxorem suam tenendum eisdem Johanni fratri meo et Idonie et heredibus masculis de corpore ipsius Johannis fratris mei procreandis. Et si contingat ipsum Johannem sine herede masculo de corpore suo procreato obire extunc volo quod illud manerium cum pertinenciis suis post mortem dicte Idonie per dictos feoffatos vendatur precio quo poterit cariori et quod pecunia inde percepta per omnes executores meos tunc superstites onus administracionis huius testamenti mei habentes in operibus pietatis et caritatis uno cum residuo bonorum meorum modo infrascript*o* expendatur. Item volo et ordino quod immediate post mortem meam Ricardus Scot et alii cum eo in manerio de[4] Dedham cum pertinenciis suis in comitatu Essex' una cum advocacionibus ecclesiarum de Revenhale et Bulmer' feoffati feoffent dictum Johannem fratrem meum et dictam Ydoniam uxorem suam in manerio de Dedham predicto et in advocacionibus ecclesiarum predictarum feoffent eundem Johannem fratrem meum tenendum manerium de Dedham predictum cum suis pertinenciis eisdem Johanni et Idonie heredibus et assignatis ipsius Johannis imperpetuum et dictas advocaciones ecclesiarum predictarum eidem Johanni fratri meo heredibus et assignatis suis imperpetuum sub condicione tali quod idem Johannes eisdem feoffatis in manibus solvat pro eisdem manerio de[5] Dedham et advocacionibus ecclesiarum predictarum mille libras argenti vel securitatem sufficientem faciat eisdem feoffatis pro predictis mille libris eis solvendis infra annum dictum feoffamentum proximum sequentem. Et si idem Johannes dictas mille libras sic solvere recusaverit volo quod tunc immediate post mortem meum omnes dicti feoffati in dicto manerio de Dedham et advocacionibus ecclesiarum predictarum cum eorum pertinenciis eadem manerium et advocaciones cum eorum pertinenciis vendant precio carissimo que poterunt et quod pecunia tunc pro eisdem percepta una cum pecunia de manerio de Totenham[6] eciam cum residuo bonorum meorum sub forma infrascripta expendatur. Item volo \ et / ordino quod immediate post mortem meam omnes illi qui tunc in manerio sive tenemento de Bonhunte sive Elmedon' in comitatu Essex' fuerint feoffati feoffent in eodem manerio sive tenemento de Elmedon' predictum Johannem fratrem meum una cum reversione manerii sive tenementi de Bonhunte predicta post decessum supradicti Ricardi Scot tenendum eidem Johanni fratri meo et heredibus masculis de corpore suo procreandis. Et si contingat eundem Johannem sine herede masculo de corpore suo procreato obire quod tunc iidem feoffati dictum manerium sive tenementum de Elmedon cum suis pertinenciis una cum reversione manerii sive tenementi de Bonhunte predicta post mortem dicti Ricardi Scot dent et inde feoffent priorem et conventum ecclesie sancti Bartholomei predictum licencia domini regis et aliorum dominorum quorum interest obtenta sumptibus eorundem prioris et conventus habendum et tenendum eisdem priori et conventui sub tali condicione quod iidem prior et conventus perpetuo inveniant tres canonicos divina celebrantes pro anima mea et animabus quibus teneor in capella quam de novo fieri feci in ecclesia conventuali sancti Bartholomei predicta ex parte boriali eiusdem cum securitate sufficienti facienda pro eisdem tribus canonicis sic ibidem inveniendis prout iidem prior et conventus et iidem feoffati poterint concordare. Et si iidem prior et conventus eadem maneria sive tenementa cum eorum pertinenciis sic habere sub condicionibus predictis recusaverint volo quod tunc [*f. 228r*] eadem maneria sive tenementa cum eorum pertinenciis per ipsos tunc inde feoffatos vendantur et quod pecunia inde recepta una cum aliis pecuniis et residuo predictis per dictos executores meos in forma inferius descripta fideliter expendatur. Residuum vero omnium bonorum meorum superius non legatorum simul cum pecuniis de vendicione maneriorum tenementorum et advocacionum ecclesiarum mearum subscriptarum recipiendis do et lego ordinacioni ac disposicioni executorum meorum subscriptorum ut ipsi de bonis et pecuniis predictis ordinent et fideliter disponant pro salute et remedio anime mee et animarum Ricardi regis Anglie secundi Anne regine consortis sue Johannis Waltham nuper episcopi Sarum animarumque parentum et benefactorum meorum ac omnium fidelium defunctorum in operibus caritatis prout eorum conscienciis decreverint plus deo placere. Huius autem testamenti mei ordino facio et constituto executores Johannem Walden' fratrem meum Ricardum Clyderow Johannem Shordiche juniorem armigeros magistrum Willelmum Bulcote magistrum Henricum Hamerton Johannem Bernard Thomam Wysebech' et Ricardum Scot clericos. Et volo et ordino quod in omni actu huius testamenti execucionem concernente dictus Johannes Walden' frater meus et Ricardus Scot presencialiter intersint vel execucioni huiusmodi dent consensum et precipue dictus Johannes frater meus cuius consensum in omni actu huiusmodi requiri volo eciam et haberi. Data apud Hadham die ultima mensis Decembris anno ab incarnacione domini secundum cursum et computacionem ecclesie Anglicane millesimo CCCC^{mo} quinto presentibus discretis viris magistro Willelmo Bryght in decretis bacallario domino Johanne Teyngton' presbitero et Johanne Mychell' armigero. Item ordino et constituto supervisores huius testamenti reverendum in Cristo patrem dominum Ricardum Clyfforde episcopum Wygorniensem et dominum Ricardum Kyngeston' canonicum ecclesie Londoniensis humiliter supplicans eisdem ut ipsi pro deo dignent habere respectum tenerum ad premissa. Item volo et ordino quod quilibet executorum meorum libere et licite possit emere de bonis meis vendendis quicquid sibi placuerit et in empcione huius ceteris preferatur dumtamen precium rei vendende juxta omnium eorum consciencias sit taxatum quacumque constitucione in contrarium edita non obstante.

Notes

1 MS obscure: 'pa', probably followed by a 't', just possibly an 'o', with a suspension.
2 Perhaps a reference to Ezekiel 3: 18.
3 Gregory the Great, *De cura pastorali*, *CPL* 1712.
4 MS omits 'de'.
5 MS omits 'de'.
6 MS: 'dotenham'.

43/2 Grant of probate to Richard Clyderow and John Schordich the younger, esquires, Mag. William Bulcote, Mag. Henry Hamerton', John Bernard and Richard Scot, clerks, reserving to the Archbishop the power of committing the administration to Thomas Wysbeche named as a co-executor in the will, 20 January 1406. *LPL, Register of Thomas Arundel, vol. I, f. 228r.*

43/3 Acquittance by Thomas Arundel, Archbishop of Canterbury, of the executors, John Walden', Richard Cliderow, John Shordich the younger, esquires, Mag. William Bulcote, Mag. Henry Hamerton, Mag. John Bernard, Mag. Richard Scot and Mag. Thomas Wysbech, London, 17 May 1406. *LPL, Register of Thomas Arundel, vol. I, f. 230v.*

43/4 Articles of Richard Scot, relating to the execution of the will, after 1406 *BL Stowe Charter 624*
One membrane

[*Recto*] These bethe the articlis þat schewen how the will of my lord Sir Roger Walden sumtyme Bisshop of London' aft*ir* the wryting in his testament are brokyn and nouȝt < fuff > fulfillyd

First my lord Sir Rog*er* Walden seyth in his testament Quod ultra et preter expensas ad honorem et laudem dei racione funeris mei servi sui faciendas quas committo disposicioni ordinacioni et discrecioni executorum meorum omnia debita mea quecumque quibuscumque personis ex quacumque causa vel occasione sint debita secundum bonorum meorum sufficienciam integre persolvantur absque difficultate seu contradictione quamcicius comode fieri poterit. And how this is p*er*f*our*myd I drede me in my conscience for ther as was owyng a M^{l} marc'. We made an ende *with* þe executo*ur*s of him þat hit was due to for xl li. and toke acquita*u*nce etc.

Dedham Item volo et ordino quod immediate post mortem meam Ricardus Scott et alii cum ipso in manerio meo de Dedham cum suis pertinenciis in comitatu Midd'[1] una cum advocacionibus ecclesiarum de Revenale et Burmer' feoffati feoffent Johannem fratrem meum et Idoneam uxorem suam heredes et assignatos suos sub tali condicione quod idem Johannes eisdem feoffatis in manibus solvat M^{l} li. argenti vel securitatem sufficientem faciat eisdem feoffatis pro predictis M^{l} li. eis solvendis infra annum dictum feoffamentum proximum sequentem. But nevirtheles þowh it be write a M^{l} li. in his testament it was accordid þat he schulde paie but vC li. þe which is unpayd unto this day so þat my seyd lordis will is brokyn etc.

Totenham Item volo quod inmediate post mortem meam Johannes Walden frater meus et alii cum ipso in manerio de Totenham tunc temporis feoffati duos de executoribus meis subscriptis post ipsum Johannem fratrem meum in presenti testamento nominatis feoffent in eodem manerio cum pertinenciis suis habendum et tenendum eis in feodo simplici sub tali condicione quod ipsi duo sic feoffati inmediate postea de eodem manerio de Totenham cum pertinenciis suis refeoffabunt eundem Johannem fratrem meum et Idoneam uxorem suam tenendum eisdem Johanni fratri meo et Idonie et heredibus masculis de corpore ipsius Johannis fratris mei procreandis. Et si contingat ipsum Johannem sine herede masculo de corpore suo procreato obire extunc volo quod illud manerium cum pertinenciis suis post mortem dicte Idonie per dictos feoffatos vendatur precio quo poterit cariori et quod pecunia inde percepta per omnes executores meos tunc superstites onus administracionis huius testamenti mei habentes in operibus caritatis et pietatis una cum residuo bonorum meorum modo infrascripto expendatur. The whiche is not fulfyllyd for aft*ir* that Totenham was soold ther was lent unto \ a / *cer*teyn *per*sone CC li. of that monye of the which I Sir Richard Scot \ resceyvid / a C li. the which I the seyd Richard dispendid it in dettis payng and in almesdede ȝevyng as my seyd lordes will was and am redy to schewe how. And when I the seyd Richard axid of þe same *per*son the tothir C li. he seyd that he was diffendid by Rob*ert* Warner' þat he schuld paie me noon. And a nothir C li. þe same Rob*ert* Warner holdith still in his owne hande to what entent I wote nevir and so my seyd lord is will is not fulfillid.

Elmedon' Bonhunt Item volo quod maneria sive tenementa de Elmedon' et Bonhunt cum eorum pertinenciis per ipsos tunc inde feoffatos vendantur et quod pecunia inde percepta una cum aliis pecuniis et residuo predicto per dictos executores meos in forma inferius discripta fideliter expendatur. The whiche is not fulfillyd for John Walden ȝaff Edelmedon' to ii^{o} of his *ser*v*a*u*n*t*is* and Bonhunt to Idoigne his wif t*er*me of hir life. And I Sir Richard Scott wote well þat this was nevir my lordis will nor I assentyd nevir ther*e*to.

*ii plas*is *in Seint Barth'*[2] Also S*ir* Rog*er* Walden p*ur*chasid ii plasis w*ith*in the cloos of þe priory of Seint Bartilemewz in Smythfeld to him and to John his brothir for t*er*me of lx yer*is* and aft*ir* the dissees of the seyd John to þe executo*ur*s and assignees of Rog*er* Walden. And aft*ir* John Walden died Ideyn' his wif occupied hit and payd noo peny and sche hadde also ther in othir neccessariis and my lord hadde nevir p*ro*ffit ther*e*of.

Item volo in omni actu huius testamenti execucionem concernente dictus Johannes Walden' frater meus et Ricardus Scott presencialiter intersint vel execucioni huiusmodi dent consensum et precipue dictus Johannes frater meus cuius consensum in omni actu huiusmodi requiri volo eciam et haberi etc. To þe which act*is* I was nevir p*re*sent nor prevy ther*e*to.

Also the seyd John Walden foryaf to Piers Crull' an obligac*io*n of vii^{xx} li. the which*e* was due to my seyd lord S*ir* Roger without assent of alle the executo*ur*s.

Also þ*er* is payd of my seyd lord S*ir* Roger Waldens good*is* for dette and beqwest of John Walden as þe p*er*cell beren witnesse iiii^{xx}xiiii li. ii s. x d.

[*Dorse*] Also S*ir* John Bernard oon of the executo*ur*s made acquita*u*nce to the Priour of Seint Bartilimewes of an obligac*io*n of xl li.

Fait aremembr*er* q*e* ordeigne est p*ar* lemys[3] de lez execut*ours* de Rog*er* Walden de lez detrez q*e* serro*u*nt paiez p*ar* Richard Clyderow as div*er*sez p*er*sonez cest assav*oir*

Enp*ri*mez a luy mesmez del ordeigna*u*nce dez ditz execut*ours* C li.
Item a s*ieur* Joh*a*n Bernard de le dette a luy due outr*e* le pris*e* de le perll' a luy assignez lxvii li. viii s. iiii d.
Item a s*ieur* Ric*hard* Scot xxviii li. vi s. viii d.
Item a s*ieur* Joh*a*n Newport x li.
Item a s*ieur* Joh*a*n < Ra*u*l > Ra*u*kdich' cano*u*n x li.

Item a Henri Pountfrett viii li.
Item a Laurence Wotton' xl li.
Item a la femme de Molkyng xx li.
Item a Johan Pope pelter pur Selby xx li.
Item a Johan Horton' hakeneyman iiii li. vi s.
Item rest due a dite Richard Clederow de lez xx li. a luy devisez par mounsieur Roger Walden viii li. xiiii s. iii d.
Item a Walter Burgeys vi li. xiii s. iiii d.

Summa totalis CCCxxiii li. xiii s. vii d. dount le dit Richard Clyderow ad en mayns Cxl li. iiii s. xi d. Item in i obligacion de mester Nicholl Danyell Ciiii[xx]vi li. xiii s. iiii d. Et sic remanent in lez mayns du dit Richard Clyderow clerement outre lez parcelles avauntditz lxiiii s. viii d.

Notes

1 *Recte* Essex.
2 This clause is not in the will.
3 Perhaps for 'lavys'.

44 John Waltham, Bishop of Salisbury

44/1 Will, 2 September 1395 *TNA PROB 11/1 (5 Rous), ff. 32r–33r*

In nomine sanctissime et individue Trinitatis patris et filii et spiritus sancti gloriosissime dei genitricis virginis Marie specialis patrone mee ac utriusque Johannis Baptiste scilicet et evaungeliste et tocius celestis curie amen. Lacrimosa semper imutabilis imbecillitatis humane condicio in hac valle miserie statum firmum et permanencem non agnoscit sed inperpetuo motu consistens occulto quodam et inconsiderato cursu dierum ad finem naturaliter preordinatum continue labitur inrevercens et qui visibilem pretendunt essenciam invisibiliter[1] tendunt ad non esse testante propheta quia homo vanitati similis factus quasi flos egrediens cito conteritur et velut umbra pertransiivit dies eius quod ego Johannes piisima dei permissione Saresburiensis episcopus licet indignus ad recentem memoriam reducens et intra mee mentis archana jugi meditacione revolvens ac attendens quod crescentibus \ donis /[2] augentur raciones donorum dum tempus adhuc superest et michi sanus animi et mentis integritudo assistens de bonis divina clemencia et bonitate michi collatis ad ipsius laudem et dispensacionis mee memoriam racionem reddendam disponere et ordinare ac mee mortis indubie horam incertam testamentaria faccione prevenire decrevi in hunc modum. In primis siquidem in sinceritate et privitate fidei catholice existens omnipotenti deo et domino nostro Jhesu Cristo animam meam quam precioso cruore redemit lego et eam sibi intenciori devocione qua possum cum omnimodis desideriis commendo et corpus meum sepeliendum in ecclesia mea Saresburiensi in loco ubi per discrecionem supervisorum et executorum testamenti mei ac decani et capituli ecclesie mee predicte congruius et convenciencius fieri poterit et de sepultura exequiis et funeralibus meis volo et ordino quod supervisores et executores predicti faciant et disponant prout eis ad honorem dei melius videbitur expedire. Item volo et ordino quod hospicium meum simul et integre continuetur et continueatur saltim de illis qui voluerint remanere per unam mensem post sepulturam meam vel quousque servientes mei congrue et racionabiliter remunerentur. Item lego ecclesie mee predicte melius et preciosius vestimentum meum ut ipsi de ecclesia predicta pro anima mea et salubri statu domini Willelmi Lescrop' dum viverit et pro anima sua cum ab hac luce migraverit cum cuius bonis datum vestimentum in magna parte provisum fuit omnipotenti deo et beate Marie semper virgini specialiter evocare teneantur et obligentur. Item lego eidem ecclesie mee ad orandum pro anima mea vestimentum meum de panno aureo et de blodio cum fronterio cum capis et toto apparatu eidem vestimento pertinentibus et duo integra vestimenta mea alba melius par candelabrorum pro capella et melius par turribulorum meorum ac eciam meum melius missale. Item volo et ordino quod maneria mea de Steventon' in comitatu Berk' et Westbury in comitatu Wiltes' cum pertinenciis simul cum advocacione ecclesie dicti manerii de Steventon' in quibus dominus Rogerus Walton' clericus mecum seisatus existit domino nostro regi super execucionem voluntatis mee in hoc exequi voluit indilate donentur et concedantur ad effectum et sub condicione quod ipse eadem maneria cum pertinenciis et advocacionem statim et immediate det et concedat priori et conventui ecclesie sive prioratus sancti Johannis Baptiste de Sandelford ordinis Augustini mee Sarum diocesis et ecclesiam predictam salva porcione vicarie eiusdem ecclesie prout jam vocatur habendum et tenendum sibi et successoribus suis ad inveniendum decem canonicos regulares ordinis predicti ultra numerum canicorum ibidem prius ordinatorum divina celebraturos simul cum priore et canonicis ibidem prius stabilitis ad honorem et laudem dei et beate Marie semper virginis sancti Johannis Baptiste et sancti Johannis Eva*u*ngeliste omniumque sanctorum dei pro salubri statu domini nostris regis predicti dum viverit et pro anima sua cum ab hac luce migraverit et pro anima mea ac animabus parentum amicorum et benefactorum nostrorum imperpetuum. Item volo et ordino quod advocacio et jus patronatus prioratus predicti in quibus dominus Johannes Chitt*er*ne et alii mecum feoffati existunt remaneant Johanni de Waltham nepoti meo et heredibus suis imperpetuum. Item volo quod manerium et soca ac terre tenementa et redditus mea in Waltham post mortem Johanne sororis mee que ea habeat ad terminum vite sue ac manerium meum de Borstall' cum pertinenciis in comitatu Kancie et manerium meum de Pl*esel*ey cum pertinenciis in comitatu Derbeie remaneant predicto Johanni nepoti meo et heredibus suis imperpetuum. Item lego eidem Johanni custodiam omnium terrarum et tenementorum que sunt de hereditate Johanne filie et heredis Roberti Grey de Rotherfeld' in manu et custodia mea existencium habendum usque ad legitimam etatem predicte Johanne ac maritagium eiusdem Johanne. Item \ lego / dicto domino nostro regi omnes pecias de berillo et cristallo quas habeo non garnisatas et omnes perulas non positas in operibus meliorem anulum meum et meliorem ciphum meum aureum prout intitulatur in inventario meo. [*f. 32v*] Item lego eidem domino meo regi mille marcas quod ipse faciat et disponat pro anima sua et anima mea prout sibi placuerit et melius videbitur expedire. Item lego certis dominis amicis et servientibus mea certa res et bona prout intitulantur in quodam inventario meo sub sigillo meo signato et huic testamento meo conjuncto vel ligato. Item lego dominis archiepiscopo Cantuariensi et archiepiscopo Eboracensi utrique videlicet eorum novem pannos aureos preciosos de una secta ut quilibet eorum unum vestimentum inde faciat et postquam usum inde ad suam voluntatem habuerit illud relinquat et dimittat ecclesie sue proprie ad exorandum pro se et me imperpetuum. Item lego dicto domino archiepiscopo Cantuariensi omnes orfreias paruras et pecias quas habeo operatos de perulis et nondum positas in vestimentis et unum bonum anulum cum uno saphiro. Item lego dicto domino archiepiscopo Eboracensi unum alium bonum anulum cum uno saphiro. Item lego fabrice ecclesie mee predicte centum marcas et cuilibet canonico residenciario eiusdem xl s. cuilibet vicario eiusdem ecclesie viginti et sex solidos et octo denarios et cuilibet choriste tresdecim solidos et quatuor denarios necnon decem marcas inter ceteros ministros ipsius ecclesie distribuendos. Item lego cuilibet domui religiose possessionate mee diocesis centum solidos. Item lego ecclesie beate Marie Lincoln' ad exorandum pro anima mea vestimentum meum viride de panno damasco. Item lego abbati et conventui Westmonasterii centum solidos abbati et conventui de Thornton' centum solidos abbati et conventui de Welhowe centum solidos abbati et conventui de Parco Lude centum solidos abbati et conventui de Selby centum solidos. Item lego priorisse de Stikeswold' viginti marcas et eidem priorisse ac conventui eiusdem domus centum solidos. Item lego priorisse et conventui de No*n*necotom centum solidos ac priorisse et conventui de Grymesby centum solidos. Item lego singulis fratribus quatuor ordinum mendicancium in civitate London' et universitatibus Oxon' Cantebr' et in villa de Grymesby ac in domibus ordinum predictorum infra dioces*i*m meam in conventibus commorantibus sex solidos et octo denarios ad exorandum specialiter pro anima mea. Item lego Johanne sorori mee quinquaginta marcas et unum ciphum argenteum deauratum ac omnes lectos utensilia et mobilia mea apud Waltham existencia et unam robam meam integram furratam. Item lego Cecilie sorori mee viginti libras et unam pelvem ac unum aquarium argentea ac eciam unam aliam robam meam integram furratam. Item lego Johanni Moigne marito suo decem libras et unum ciphum argenteum deauratum et unum equm valoris viginti marcarum. Item lego cuilibet capellano capelle mee quinque marcas. Item lego cuilibet alii clerico excedenti etatem viginti annorum quadraginta solidos et cuilibet choriste dicte capelle mee viginti solidos. Item lego Willelmo Candelesby viginti marcas. Item lego matri sue et filiabus suis quadraginta libras. Item lego ecclesie de Waltham vestimentum meum rubeum cum toto apparatu orfreciat*o* cum panno albo aureo et viginti marcas distribuendas inter pauperes homines dicte ville. Item lego cuidam paupercule mulieri amice mee vocate Katerine viginti marcas. Item lego quingentas marcas distribuendas inter pauperes homines diocesis mee juxta discrecionem executorum meorum ad exorandum pro animabus meis et dominorum Johannis Bacon et Nicholai Spaigne et omnium fidelium defunctorum. Item lego centum marcas distribuendas juxta discrecionem executorum meorum inter pauperes de consanguinitate et parentela mea. Item volo quod mille psalteria et milies placebo et dirige cum commendacione per indigentes quamcito fieri poterit dicantur pro anima mea et animabus omnium aliorum pro quibus orare teneor et remunerentur competenter ea dicentes juxta discrecionem executorum meorum. Item lego rectori ecclesie parochialis sancte Brigide London' rectori sancti Andree in Holborn London' et rectori sancti Dunstani in la West videlicet cuilibet eorum quadraginta solidos. Item volo quod providantur quamcito comode fieri poterit centum vestimenta competencia de panno cerico de quibus detur cuilibet ecclesie parochiali quam tempore meo occupavi sive fuerit simpliciter parochialis vel annexa archidiaconatui prebende capelle vel hospitali per me occupatis simul cum quadraginta solidis pauperibus parochianis singularum huiusmodi ecclesiarum erogandis et residua vestimenta dentur aliis ecclesiis indigentibus juxta discrecionem executorum meorum. Item lego pauperibus fratribus et sororibus hospitalis de Shirbourne Dunolmensis diocesis centum solidos. Item lego Ricardo Moriell' Nicholo Carreu Johanni Gowayn Willelmo Stourton' Janico Dorcass' Johanni Walden' Andree Neweport Ricardo Clyderowe Willelmo Willecotes Thome Bonham Laurencio Dru Johanni Worth Ricardo Lambard' Johanni Mosdale et familiaribus scutiferis hospicalis mei videlicet cuilibet eorum decem marcas. Item lego Johanni Scalby [*f. 33r*] Thome Belesby et Johanni Humble*corn*' familiaribus scutiferis meis videlicet cuilibet eorum unum equm valoris decem librarum. Item lego Johanni Gilbert camerario meo viginti libras Johanni Aston garderobario meo decem marcas et cuilibet alii valecto hospicalis mei quinque marcas. Item lego cuilibet garcioni camere mee quadraginta solidos et cuilibet alii garcioni hospicalis mei viginti et sex solidos et octo denarios et cuilibet pagetto hospicalis mei tresdecim solidos et quatuor denarios. Item lego Johanni Candelesby Willelmo Dyones et Henrico Harburgh' videlicet cuilibet eorum viginti libras. Et volo quod omnes alii servientes mei in isto testamento vel inventario non nominati remunerentur recionabiliter per executores meos juxta illorum discrecionem. Item lego cuilibet executorum meorum admittenti onus presentis testamenti mei viginti libras. Item lego Johanni Sapurton decem libras et Elene uxori sue viginti libras ac unam robam meam integram. Item remitto et condono domino Baldwino Berford decem libras quas michi debet per scriptum suum obligatorium. Item lego Johanne Langdale moniali de Wilton' viginti marcas. Item lego Cecilie sorori mee predicte custodiam et maritagium Thome filii sui et terrarum et tenementorum eiusdem in auxilium eiusdem sororis mee et liberorum suorum. Item volo et desidero quod si ossa corporis patris mei fideliter reperiri poterint tunc ipsa ossa capiantur et reponantur juxta ossa matris mee et ordinetur unus lapis de marmore in memoriam eorundem. Alioquin ordinetur lapis in memoriam matris mee inscriptus juxta discrecionem executorum meorum. Item lego et volo quod quadraginta libre statim post mortem meam solvantur abbati et conventui de Lesnes ad usum et utilitatem domus sue quas quidem quadraginta libras habeo in custodia mea ad usum predictum de elemosina domini regis. Item volo quod ordinetur et stabiliatur de bonis meis juxta discrecionem executorum meorum in ecclesia mea predicta unus obitus sive anniversarium pro anima mea singulis annis imperpetuum celebrandum. Item lego volo et ordino quod residuum rerum jocalium et bonorum meorum vendantur et denarii inde provenientes satisfacto inde prius de debitis meis et omnibus quibus dampnum vel offensam aliqualiter intuli vel feci distribuantur juxta discrecionem supervisorum et executorum mei testamenti in missarum celebracionibus elemosinarum largicionibus ac aliis oracionibus ac operibus pietatis. Huius autem testamenti mei et ultime voluntatis mee executores nomino facio deputo et constituto dilectos michi in Cristo dominum Willelmum Lescrop militem dominum Rogerum Walden' magistrum Radul*ph*um Selby magistrum Willelmum Waltham magistrum Ricardum Holm dominum Georgium Louthorp' dominum Thomam Haxey magistrum Ricardum Pittes canonicos ecclesie mee Willelmum Holym Willelmum Dyones capellanos et Johannem Gowayn domicellum quos omnes et singulos onero et exoro ut hoc testamentum meum et hanc meam ultimam voluntatem debite exequantur et quantum in eis est adimpleant et faciant adimpleri sicut coram deo voluerint respondere. Supervisores autem huius testamenti mei ac ultime mee voluntatis creo ordino et facio reverendos in

Cristo patres dominos archiepiscopos Cantuariensem et Eboracensem quos humiliter deprecor et requiro quatinus hoc presens testamentum meum et meam ultimam voluntatem debite et solicite quatenus opus fuerit supervideant ipsaque execucioni debite faciant demandari. In quorum omnium et singulorum testimonium acque fidem presentem paginam sive presens testamentum ultimam voluntatem meam continens sigilli mei magni appensione feci fideliter communiri. Data in manerio de Sonnyng' Sarum diocesis secundo die mensis Septembris anno domini millesimo CCC^{mo} nonogesimo quinto indiccione tercia pontificatus sanctissimi in Cristo patris et domini domini Bonefacii divina providencia pape noni anno sexto et sub anno regni dicti domini nostri regis decimonono.

Notes
1 MS: 'in' inserted at start of word.
2 Inserted in margin in a seventeenth-century hand.

44/2 Probate of the will, with the inventory annexed as a codicil, before the Archbishop of Canterbury, granted to William Lescrop, knight, Roger Walden', Richard Holm, George Louthorp' and Richard Pittes, canons of Salisbury, and Dom. William Holym and Dom. William Dyones, chaplains, named as executors in the will, in the oratory at Lambeth, 26 September 1395. *TNA PROB 11/1 (5 Rous), ff. 33r–33v.*

44/3 Acquittance for legacies to the Archbishop of Canterbury, 4 October 1395. *TNA PROB 11/1 (5 Rous), f. 33v.*
Noverint universi per presentes nos Willelmum permissione divina Cantuariensem archiepiscopum tocius Anglie primatem et apostolice sedis legatum recepisse et habuisse a venerabilibus viris dominis Rogero Walden' thesaurario Anglie Willelmo Lescrope domini nostri regis camerario magistro Willelmo Waltham canonico Sarum et sociis suis executoribus testamenti bone memorie domini Johannis nuper episcopi Sarum bona subscripta in testamento ipsius episcopi nobis legata videlicet duas pelves argenteas deauratas habentes in fundo arma dicti episcopi. Item unum ciphum altum de berillo cum coopertorio operat*o* et ornat*o* cum auro. Item unum anulum aureum cum uno saphiro. Item unum alium anulum aureum cum saphiro quo dictus episcopus utebatur in missa et pro vestimentis faciendis ad divini cultus augmentum novem pannos aureos cum champo rubio unius secte. Item duas orfreias pro una capa de champo viridi operatas cum perlis continentes duodecim tabernacula cum ymaginibus. Item duas orfreias pro una casula de eodem opere continentes undecim tabernacula cum ymaginibus. Item unum frontorium strictum cum champo viridi operatum de perlis. Item unum capucionem pro dorso unius cape de eodem opere. Item quatuor paruras pro almiciis de eodem opere. Item quatuor orfreias strictas currentes et longas de champo viridi. Item quatuor alias breves de eodem opere in una pecia. Item sex paruras pro tribus albis de champo rubeo operatas cum perlis cum uno pellicano in quolibet. Item sex paruras[1] de eodem opere. Item tres paruras pro almiciis de champo rubeo operatas de perlis cum diversis ymaginibus. Condicio autem huius legati pro vestimentis ut premittur fiendis est hoc ut nos Willelmus archiepiscopus antedictus de vestimentis aureis supradictis faciamus fieri vestimentum vel vestimenta pro cultu divina juxta vim et effectum testamenti predicti quorum usum habeamus nos per totam vitam nostram et

postquam nos contigit ab hac luce subtrahi remaneant dicta vestimenta ecclesie nostre Cantuariensi imperpetuum ad orandum pro anima nostra et anima ipsius Johannis episcopi quamquidem condicionem nos permittimus fideliter adimplere et prefatos executores de predictis bonis per nos receptis quietamus et imperpetuum liberamus per presentes. In cuius rei testimonium sigillum nostrum fecimus hiis apponi. Data in manerio de Cherleton' quarto die mensis Octobris anno domini millesimo CCC^{mo} nonogesimo quinto ac regni regis Ricardi secundi decimo nono. Et nostre translacionis anno xv^{mo}.

Notes

1 MS: 'paruas'.

WORD LIST AND GLOSSARY

This word list has four purposes. Firstly, it identifies and defines all words in the edited texts that are not in *LS*, *RMLWL*, *DMLBS*, *AND*, *OED* and *KMED*. In addition, it includes words that are in *RMLWL*, *DLMBS*, *AND* and *OED* where the usage is different, where the example in this edition is within 30 years of the earliest recorded use, or where orthography may make it difficult to trace the word. Secondly, it is intended to help in cases of ambiguity, where words have similar orthography but different meanings. It is, thirdly, integral to the editorial process: it sets out the assumptions and practices in extending contracted and abbreviated forms of words; it indicates where expansions have been made silently, or where suspensions have been dropped; and it records the choices that have been made in terms of case, gender and number where the manuscripts supply little or no evidence. The fourth purpose is to make plain the conventions adopted in expanding some grammatical constructions, particularly where there is a divergence from classical Latin or ambiguity.

actill' (**32**): equipment. Extended to *pl.* forms in *-ia*, *-iorum*, *n.*
actinentibus (**2/1**): appurtenances, other things belonging.
affr' (**32**): draught-horse. Extended to forms in *-us*, *-i*, *m.* Extended to the *adj.* form, *affrarius*, *-a*, *-um*, in the expression *jumentum affrarium*, a mare draught-horse.
aier': *see* **eyrers**.
aketon (**32**): acton, a padded jerkin worn under mail (*AND*). Treated as *m.*
allocacione (**18/2**): hiring.
almat' (**32**): dalmatic (ecclesiastical vestment). Extended to *almatica*, *-e*, *f.*
altar': altar. Extended in **2/1**, **21/8** and **40/1** to forms in *-e*, *-is*, *n.*
annal' (**36**): ring. Extended to forms from *annale*, *-is*, *n.*, an unusual form, possibly used inadvertently matching the following word, *pontificale*.
anniversar': annual feast, anniversary. In **44/1**, extended to forms in *-ium*, *-ii*, *n.*
anolog' (**33/1**): reading desk, lectern (*RMLWL*). Extended to forms from *-ium*, *-ii*, *n.*
antiphonar' (**2/1**, **6/2**, **12/2**): an antiphoner, book of antiphons. Extended on **2/1** and **12/2** to forms in *-ium*, *-ii*, *n.*; and on **6/2** to forms from *-e*, *-is*, *n.*
antiqum (**6/2**): old. Extended to forms from *antiqus*, *-a*, *-um*, not *-uus*.
aqua' (**2/2**), **aquar'** (**32**): ewer. Extended to forms from *aquarium*, *-ii*, *n.*
arg' argent': silver, *sb.* and *adj.* As *sb.*, extended to forms from *argentum*, *-i*, *n.*; as *adj.*, to forms from *argenteus*, *-a*, *-um*. Treated as a *sb.* on **6/2**, **12/1**, **21/10**, **32**; as an *adj.* on **25/1**, **31/1**, **33/1** and **35/6**; and as a *sb.* or *adj.*, following the MS, on **12/2**, **18/1**, **18/2** and **28/1**.
arrerag' (**18/2**): arrears. Extended to forms from *arreragia*, *-orum*, *n. pl.*
aspersor' (**25/1**): a sprinkler for holy water. Extended to forms in *-ium*, *-ii*, *n.*
aurei (**6/2**): of gold. Treated as a *sb.* by the MS.

auriat' (**28/1**): of gold, golden. Treated as a *sb.* by the MS; extended to forms in *-us, -i, m.*

aven': oats. On **18/2**, extended to *pl.* forms, *-e, -arum, f.* (no evidence on MS whether it was intended to be *sing.* or *pl.*); and on **32**, extended in *sing.* forms, *-a, -e, f.*, following MS.

bahud' (**32**): a container or wrapper of animal hide used for transporting valuable textiles, a barehide (*AND* bahu; *OED* barehide 1450). Not extended.

baiard' (**32**): bay, colour of horse, and sometimes its name. Not extended.

bal' (**32**): bale, possibly in the sense of packages or of specific quantities when used of fruit, spices or rice (*OED* bale *sb.*[3]; *AND* bal[3]). Not extended.

bales', **balis'** (**32**): a balas ruby (*DLMBS* balasius; *AND* balais; *OED* balas). Extended to forms in *-us, -i, m.*

banc' (**18/2**): royal court at Westminster. Extended to forms in *-us, -i, m.*

bancar' (**35/6**, **38/14**), **bankar'** (**12/2**), **banker'** (**11/1**), **banquer'** (**6/2**): a banker, a seat. Extended on **35/6** and **38/14** to forms from *-ium, -ii, n.*; and on **6/2**, **11/1** and **12/2** to forms from *-um, -i, n.*

barell' (**32**): barrel. Extended to forms in *-us, -i, m.*

bass' (**31/1**): basin. Extended to forms from *bassinum, -i, n.*

batell' (**32**): boat. Extended to forms in *-a, -e, f.*

batellag' (**18/2**): transport (by boat), boat hire. Extended to forms in *-ium, -i, n.*, in *sing.*

baudkino, **baudekini** (**2/1**); **baudekyns** (**32**): a rich textile, an Italian, figured silk, loosely from *Baldacco*, an Italian form of Baghdad (*RMLWL*; *OED* baudekin *c.*1300; Monnas, *Merchants*, p. 301).

bere, **bericorne** (**32**): barley (*OED* bear *sb.*[2]), perhaps a coarser form than the *ordeum* which appears as well in both instances, the accounts for Nuthanger and Sevenhampton.

bidens (**32**): sheep. Extended to forms from *bidens, bidentis, f.*, with *bidentum* as *gen. pl.* (not extended on MS).

bis' (**38/10**): byss, a cloth, probably a fine linen, uncoloured (*OED* byss *sb.*1, *c.*1324). Extended to forms from *-um, -i, n.*

bis' (**26/1**), **biss'** (**32**): squirrel skin (*AND* bis[1]; E.M. Veale *The English fur trade in the later Middle Ages* (2nd edition, London Record Society, 38; 2003) pp. 216, 228). Extended to *bise* on **26/1**; not extended on **32**.

blaneo, **blani**, **blandio** (**21/8**): describing or qualifying types of textile, in two examples cheaper woven silks (satin and taffeta: Monnas, *Merchants*, p. 297); in a third case 'two cloths with the arms of England'. Possibly associated with *KMED* blaunner, blaundener, blander, a material of black and white colour (principally used to describe a fur, like ermine). *See also* blantalibus, below.

blanket' (**32**): blanket; an undyed (that is, uncoloured, or natural white) woollen material, used for clothing (*AND* blanchet; *OED* blanket *sb.*, 1, *c.*1300). Not extended.

blantalibus (**31/1**): *abl. pl.* Meaning unclear: fabric furnishings of the hall, or parts belonging to it.

blason' (**32**): shield (*AND* blason).

blod' (**6/2**, **9/1**): blue. Extended on both as *adj.* to forms in *-ius, -ia, -ium*; and on **9/1**, as *sb.* to forms in *-ium, -ii, n.*

bokacyne (**6/2**): a cotton textile (*OED* bocasin 1485; Monnas, *Merchants*, p. 301).

bokett' (**32**): bucket. Extended to forms in *-um, -i, n.*
bolion' (**32**): probably a bale, perhaps a measured amount (of almonds). *AND* has *bolioun* in the sense of bullion, and *bolion*, a knob or ball, which may be cognate, in the sense of referring to a solid mass of material; see also the discussion in *OED*, bullion[1] and bullion[2], a quantity that has been boiled together. Not extended.
bord' (**18/2**, **32**): board. Extended to forms in *-a, -e, f.*
boteler' (**35/6**), buteller' (**32**): buttery. Extended to forms in *-ia, -ie, f.*
boton' (**21/10**): button, stud. Extended as if from *boto, botonis*, no gender expressed.
bover' (**32**): cowshed. Extended to forms in *-ia, -ie, f.*
bovett' (**32**): young cattle, typically in their third or fourth year, sometimes steers and bullocks, as opposed to heifers; sometimes unclear. Extended to forms in *-us, -i, m.*
bovicul'(**32**): calf at least a year old. Extended to forms in *-us, -i, m.* Sometimes encompasses female calves, e.g. Crawley: 'Item vi boviculi etatis ii annorum unde iii masculi', and sometimes excludes them, e.g. Waltham 'Et iii boviculi et iii juvenca precii capitis xiii d.' Compare *MRC*, p. 778.
bras' (**6/2**, **32**): malt. Extended to forms in *-eum, -ei, n.*
brustekyn (**32**), **bradekyn** (**26/1**): a type of cloth or describing a type of cloth – *russetto brustekyn*; an embroidered fabric (*KMED* brussekyn, *n.*, 1349, from *brusdé, p.pl.* of *broder*, to embroider). Not in *OED* or *AND*.
bulg' (**32**): bag, or saddle-bag. Extended to forms in *-a, -e, f.*
burnect' (**32**): burnet, a fine, dark cloth (*OED* burnet *sb.*[1], 2. 1284, a wool-dyed cloth of superior quality; *AND* brunet).
buss' (**32**): a measure for a bushel. Extended to forms from *bussellum, -i, n.*
buteller': *see* **boteler'**.

calcituar' (**18/2**): footwear. Extended to forms in *-a, -e, f.*
calestour' (**32**): a heater, or brazier; here a container made of brass. Extended to forms in *-ium, -ii, n.*
camelett' (**32**): camlet, a costly, Eastern fabric, probably woven in mohair or silk (*OED* camlet, *c.*1400; *AND* camelot, chamelet; Monnas, *Merchants*, p. 301).
camelino de Triple (**32**): a rich fabric, reputed to have been bought through Tripoli (the port for Aleppo). Presumably similar to camlet: *AND* camelin; *OED* cameline *sb.*[1], *c.*1400, argues that this is camel hair, but whatever contemporaries believed, it was probably mohair or silk.
camocha (**32**): a fine silk textile (*RMLWL* camaca; Monnas, *Merchants*, p. 301, lampas silk).
camut' (**32**): cameo. Extended to forms in *-us, -i, m.*
canab' (**18/2**, **32**): hemp, or a coarse textile made from hemp, canvas. Extended to forms in *-us, -i, m.*
canevaz (**32**): *see* **carde**.
capelle, **chapell'** (**32**): hats (military) (*AND* chapel[1]). Latin forms extended to *-a, -e, f.*
capic' (**26/1**), **capuc'** (**31/1**, **32**), **capucionem** (**44/3**): a hood, headdress. Extended on **26/1**, **31/1** and **32** to forms in *-ium, -ii, n.*; the form in **44/3** is *m.*
capitular' (**2/1**): a capitulary, or chapter book. Extended to forms in *-ium, -ii, n.*

capr' (**32**): goat. Extended to forms from *caper*, *capri*, *m.* (*m.* as a collective, but many of the goats at Downton must have been female).
carcos' (**32**, **35/6**): carcass. Extended to forms in *-ium*, *-i*, *n.*
carde (**32**): a textile fabric, probably of linen at this date (*OED* carde; *AND* carde[1]). The expression 'canevaz de carde' possibly means a piece of fabric employed in a manner typical of canvas, to wrap something, or as hangings.
carect' (**18/2**), **carectar'** (**32**): of a cart, *adj.*, as in *equi carectarii*, cart-horses. Extended to forms from *carectarius*, *-a*, *-um*.
carectat' (**32**): cart-load. Extended to forms in *-a*, *-e*, *f.*
carn' (**18/2**): flesh. Extended from forms of *caro*, *carnis*, *f.*, in *pl.*, following MS.
carpet' (**32**), **carpit'** (**18/2**): carpet. Extended on **32** to forms in *-um*, *-i*, *n.*; and on **18/2** to forms in *-a*, *-e*, *f.*, following MS.
cas' (**26/1**): case. Extended to forms in *-um*, *-i*, *n.*
cass' (**32**): carcass. Extended to forms in *-a*, *-e*, *f.*
celur' (**6/2**, **12/2**, **34/1**): celure, a textile canopy (*OED* celure). Extended on **12/2** and **34/1** to forms in *-a*, *-e*, *f.*; not extended on **6/2**.
cendat': *see* **sandoco**.
cent' (**32**): a hundred. Extended to forms from *centena*, *-e*, *f.*
cergiis (**28/1**): cierge, a wax candle or taper (*OED* cierge *sb.*), distinguished from 'cereis' and 'torcheam', both also of wax.
chimer' (**9/1**, **26/1**): a chimer, a loose, upper robe, especially one worn by a bishop (*OED* 1375). Extended on **9/1** to forms in *-us*, *-i*, *m.*, where it is accompanied by a masculine form of an *adj.*; on **26/1**, where there is a suspension, extended to forms in *-a*, *-e*, *f.*, otherwise treated as English and not extended.
ciph' (**32**): cup. Extended to forms in *-us*, *-i*, *m.*, following MS.
cisar' (**32**): cider. Extended to forms in *-a*, *-e*, *f.*
classic' (**18/2**): peal of bells. Extended to forms in *-a*, *-e*, *f.*
clausur' (**19/1**): close, cloister, enclosed area. Extended to forms in *-a*, *-e*, *f.*
cloches (**32**): cloaks (*AND* cloke), but different to a *mantellum*. Treated as *m.* with Latin adjectives on rot. 7r.
coclear' (**2/1**, **12/2**, **21/10**, **25/1**, **29/1**, **32**, **33/1**, **38/14**), **cocliar'** (**28/1**), **cloclear'** (**31/1**): spoon. Extended to forms from *-ium*, *-ii*, *n.*
coffr' (**32**), **cofr'** (**34/1**): coffer, especially a strong box, chest (*AND* coffre; *OED* coffer *sb.*, *c.*1300). Extended in italics on **32**; on **34/1**, treated as an English word, extended to *cofres*; *cofr' trussabil'*, coffers to hold trussed bundles.
collectar' (**2/1**), **collatar'** (**41/4**): a book of collects. Extended to forms in *-ium*, *-ii*, *n.*
colleg' (**19/1**): collegiate. Extended to forms in *-us*, *-a*, *-um*.
color' (**2/1**): colour. Extended to forms from *color*, *-is*, *m.*, using the genitive to express colour, for example, 'vestimentum integrum purpurei coloris'.
comp' (**18/2**): to account, or, as *sb.*, an account (document) or the process of audit. Extended as *vb.* to forms from the present tense of *computare*, and as *sb.*, to forms from *compotus*, *-i*, *m.*
concord' (**18/2**): concordance. Extended to forms from *concordancia*, *-e*, *f.*
contrepoint (**32**): a bed cover, later a counterpane (*OED* counterpoint *sb.*[2], 1423; *AND* conterpoint).
coopert' (**9/1**): cover. Extended to forms from *coopertorium*, *-i*, *n.*, following one example on MS.
corbell' (**32**): basket. Extended to forms in *-us*, *-i*, *m.*

cot' (**18/2**): coat, cloak. Extended to forms in *-a, -e, f.*
crates (**32**): hurdles.
crismator' (**25/1**): chrism cloth, or chrismatory. Extended to forms in *-ium, -ii, n.*
Crist': Christ. All forms in *χρ* extended to *Cristus, -i, m.*, rather than *Christus*, following P. Chaplais, 'The spelling of Christ's name in medieval Anglo-Latin: "Christus" or "Cristus" ?' *Journal of the Society of Archivists* 8 (1986–7) pp. 261–80. There is no evidence that 'Ch' forms were intended in any of the MSS.
crowe (**32**): probably a crow-bar (*OED* crow *sb*[1], 5, *c.*1400); at 12*d.*, this is an expensive item.
cupp' (**18/2**): cup. Extended to forms in *-a, -e, f.*
curall' (**32**): small corn of wheat, unless another corn specified. Extended to forms in *-um, -i, n.*
curr' (**32**): coach, or a form of cart or wagon. Extended to forms in *-us, -us, m.*
cuvar' (**32**): perhaps a vat or tub, similar to *cuva*; *OED* cowl *sb.*[2] may be cognate. Extended to forms from *cuvara, -e, f.*
cuvell' (**18/2**): wedge. Extened to forms in *-a, -e, f.*

dalmat', **dealmatic'** (**32**), **dalmaticul'** (**6/2**): dalmatic (ecclesiastical vestment). Extended to forms in *-a, -e, f.*, in **6/2** in *pl.*
deaspino (**21/8**): diapered.
die (**23/1**, **38**): day. Treated as *m.* where no evidence for gender.
dioc' (**31/1**): diocese. Extended to *diocese* in *abl.*, rather than *diocesi*; there is no evidence for either form.
disc' (**32**): dish. Extended to forms in *-a, -e, f.*: *adj.* describing dishes appear in *f.*
discolor' (**32**): 'discoloured', possibly 'pale', *adj.* Extended to *discoloratus, -a, -um.*
dorsar' (**36**), **dorsor'** (**35/6**), **doser'** (**6/2**), **dosser'** (**32**): a dossal, or back cloth. Extended to forms in *-ium, -ii, n.*
draget' (**32**): dredge, mixed corn of barley and oats. Extended to forms in *-um, -i, n.*

earundem, **eorundem**: of them. Abbreviated forms extended to this rather than *earumdem, eorumdem*, except **39/1**, where the MS writes in full the form *eorumdem.*
eburn' (**2/1**): of ebony, black wood. Extended to forms in *-eus, -ea, -eum.*
emerald', **amerald'**, **merald'** (**32**): emerald. Extended to forms in *-a, -e, f.*; not extended on MS.
epistolar' (**2/1**), **ep'lar'** (**41/4**): book of the epistles. Extended to forms from *epistolarium, -ii, n.*
equ' (**38/6**): horse. Extended to forms from *equs, -i, m.*, following one example written out in full.
ereum (**33/1**): brazen, of brass or similar mix of metals. *Adj.*, treated similarly to *eneus, -a, -um.*
evangelizar' (**6/2**): the gospels. Extended to forms in *-ium, -ii, n.*
event' (**21/7**): event, occasion. Extended to forms in *-us, -us, m.*
expens' (**31/1**): expenses, costs. Extended to *pl.* forms in *-e, -arum, f.*
eyrers (**32**), **aier'** (**6/2**): nesting or breeding pair, in the expression 'paria de eyrers', swans at Downton (**32**); and 'de cignis aier*iis*', at Stortford (**6/2**). *OED*

aerie, *sb.*, a nest, restricts this to birds of prey or birds building nests in high places, but neither would apply to swans. *AND* eire[2] extends this to dragons; and eirer[1], nestling, *adj.* to pigeons and herons; but as a *vb.*, eirer[2] is confined to birds of prey.

f' (**41/4**): Justinian's *Digest.* Extended to forms from *forciatum, -i, n.*
fab' (**32**): beans. Extended in *pl.*, following MS, to forms in *-e, -arum, f.*
fagett' (**18/2**): faggot, firewood. Extended to forms in *-us, -i, m.*
fanon' (**13**, **32**, **34/1**), **phanon'** (**33/1**): fanon, an embroidered band, originally like a napkin, attached to the left hand of the celebrant and other clergy at mass; a maniple (*OED* fanon 1418). Extended to forms in *-a, -e, f.*
fardell' (**32**): fardel, bundle. Extended to forms in *-um, -i, n.*
feret' (**28/1**), **feretr'** (**18/2**): bier. Extended to forms from *feretrus, -i, m.*
ferr' (**6/2**): iron. Extended to forms as *sb.*, from *ferrum, -i, n.*, rather than as an *adj.*, *ferreus*, on the analogy of *argentum.*
ferr' (**18/2**): horseshoe, ironwork, *sb.* Extended to forms from *ferrum, -i, n.*
ferr' (**32**): ironwork for ploughs, *sb.* Extended to forms from *ferramentum, -i, n.*, in *sing.* only.
ferr' (**32**): with iron equipment, or iron in part, *adj.* Extended to forms from *ferratus, -a, -um*, especially *carecta ferrata*, a cart with wheels with iron tyres.
ferraunt (**32**): a grey horse, sometimes a horse's name (*AND* ferant[1]).
fial' (**29/1**), **fiol'** (**21/10**), **phiol'** (**33/1**): phial. Extended to forms in *-a, -e, f.*
fibul' (**21/8**): bole, or knob. Extended to forms in *-a, -e, f.*
flasket (**32**): flasket, a small wooden cask (*AND*; *OED* considers it a basket, but does not cite an example earlier than 1460).
flat' (**9/1**): plain, unornamented. Not extended.
floscul' (**2/1**): little flower. Extended to forms in *-us, -i, m.*
for' (**35/6**): forensic, external, out of the normal course. Extended as *adj.* from *forinsecus, -a, -um.*
formul' (**32**): form, in the sense of both a mould and a seat. Extended in *-a, -e, f.*, following one example (meaning a seat) written out in the Ivinghoe account.
fricator' (**32**): frying pan (*RMLWL* frixatorium). Extended to forms in *-ium, -ii, n.*
frount' (**6/2**): a front, a hanging for the front of an altar (*OED* front, *sb.*, 9b, 1533). Not extended.
frontell' (**33/1**), **frountell'** (**6/2**), **fruntell'** (**26/1**): an altar frontal, a smaller hanging than the front (*OED* frontal, *sb.*, 2a, 1381). Not extended on **6/2**; extended on **33/1** to forms from *-um, -i, n.*; and on **26/1** to forms from *-ium, -ii, n.*, following one example on MS of *fruntalia, acc. pl.*
fumus (**18/2**): funeral (for *funus*). It may mean 'the body at the funeral' in 'Item solutis pro feretro ligneo de novo facto ad fumus portandam vi s. x d.' Treated as forms of *fumus, -us, f.*
funer' (**28/1**), **funeral'** (**26/1**): funeral, *adj.* Extended to forms from *funeralis, -e.*
funerar' (**18/1**, **35/6**, **42/1**): funeral, *sb.* Extended to forms from *funeraria, -orum, n. pl.*
furrur' (**33/1**): fur. Extended to forms in *-a, -e, f.*
furvellos (**33/1**): small, dark coloured, pieces of cloth, a diminutive form of a *sb.*, derived from *furvus, -a, -um* (*LS*).

gacie (**41/4**): bowls, jars, troughs (*RMLWL* gata).
galioph' (**32**): cloves. Extended to *galiophirum*, *-i*, *n*.
galoches (**6/2**): galoshes, a wooden shoe or sandal fastened to the foot with thongs or leather (*OED* galosh 1377).
gasingale (**32**): a piece of armour (*AND* gasyngale).
gemell' (**32**): referring to dates (*bot.*), literally 'forked branch', or 'arranged in pairs', perhaps 'on the vine', or with the fruit remaining on short sticks. Extended as if from *gemellatus*, *-a*, *-um*.
godet (**29/1**), **godett'** (**12/2**): a drinking cup (*OED* godet 1383). Extended on **12/2** to forms in *-us*, *-i*, *m.*, gender taken from following *adj.*; not extended on **29/1**.
graduar' (**6/2**): a gradual. Extended to forms in *-ium*, *-ii*, *n*.
granar' (**32**): granary. Extended to forms in *-ium*, *-ii*, *n*.
grang' (**32**): barn. Extended to forms in *-ia*, *-ie*, *f.*
gremialia (**21/8**): aprons.
grisell' (**32**): grey horse, sometimes a horse's name. Not extended.
gromis (**33/1**): kitchen equipment, here of iron, probably a hook or crook (*OED* crome, cromb *sb.*).
gwanag', **ganag'** (**20**): land under cultivation. Extended to forms in *-ium*, *-ii*, *n*.

herc' (**32**): harrow, *sb*. Extended to forms in *-ia*, *-ie*, *f.*
heremit' (**31/1**): a hermit. Extended to forms in *-a*, *-e*, *m*.
hernas', **hernes'** (**32**): harness, equipment. Extended to forms in *sing.* only, in *-ium*, *-ii*, *n*.
hernis' (**32**): set with, fitted with; or fitted with equipment. Extended to forms from *hernisiatus*, *-a*, *-um*.
her*o*u*n*cell' (**18/2**): small or young herons (*OED* heronsew). Extended to forms in *-us*, *-i*, *m*.
hog', **hogg'**, **hogastr'**, **hoggastr'** (**32**): sheep in its second year. Extended as second declension, from *hog(g)aster*, *-i*, *m.*, following the Downton account, which has *hoggastr'*, whereas the others mainly use *hogg'*.
hog', **hogg'** (**32**): pig in its second year. Extended to forms from *hog(g)ettus*, *-i*, *m*.
howes (**32**): possibly saddle-cloths (*OED* house sb^2).
hurtard' (**6/2**, **32**): ram. Extended to forms in *-us*, *-i*, *m*.

implementum (**18/2**, **33/1**, **35/6**, **39/1**): the quota of stock and equipment on the lands of the bishopric to be passed to the succeeding bishop.
incens' (**21/10**): incense. Extended to forms from *-um*, *-i*, *n*.
ind', **indea** (**32**): blue. Extended as *sb.* to forms in *-a*, *-e*, *f.*, and as *adj.* to forms in *-eus*, *-ea*, *-eum*.

jemali, **jiemali**, **yemali** (**32**): winter, *adj.* Where the word appears with an abbreviation, extended to forms in *-is*, *-e*.
jument' (**32**): mare. Extended to forms from *jumentum*, *-i*, *n.*, following MS.
juvenc' (**32**): heifer. Extended to forms in *-a*, *-e*, *f.*
juvent' (**18/2**): 'assistance', or 'help' (*RMLWL* juvamen). Extended as if from *juventum*, *-i*, *n*.

kuvelini, **kuvelyn** (**32**): small tub(s) or vat(s); diminutive of *cuva*.

lactric' (**20**): animals in milk (*DLMBS* lactrix 1230). Extended to forms from *lactrix, lactricis, f.*

lan' (**18/2**): wool. Extended to forms in *-a, -e, f.*, in *sing.*

larder' (**20**): for store, the larder. Extended to forms in *-ium, -ii, n.*

laton' (**33/1**), **lathon'** (**34/1**): latten (metal). Extended on **33/1** to forms in *-ia, -ie, f.*; not extended on **34/1**.

laungel' (**33/1**): a woollen blanket. Extended to forms in *-um, -i, n.*

lavator' (**32**): ewer. Extended to forms in *-ium, -ii, n.*

legatt' (**18/2**): legacy. Extended to forms in *-um, -i, n.*

liard', **lyard'** (**32**): dapple-grey, colour of horse and sometimes its name (*AND* liart). Not extended.

liberat' (**4/1**): livery, clothing. Extended to forms from *liberatura, -e, f.*

lign' (**18/2**, **32**): wooden, *adj.* Extended to forms in *-eus, -ea, -eum.*

limin' (**32**): cart-shafts. Extended as if from *limo, liminis, m.*

linge teill' (**32**): linen cloth (*AND* linge[1]).

locul' (**32**): a small lock, a twist, in this case of silk (*OED* lock *sb.*[1], 2, 1300; *DMLBS* loculus: examples refer to containers rather than this sense). Extended to forms in *-us, -i, m.*

lotor' (**33/1**): a laver, ewer. Extended to forms in *-ium, -ii, n.*

Magd' (**22/1**): Magdalen. Extended to *Magdalene* as an invariable form.

man' (**32**): hands. MS uses both *sing.* and *pl.* in the expression 'in the hands of'; where it is not written out on the MS, it has been extended in *pl.* in italic.

mancorn', **mangcorn'** (**32**): a mixed corn, a maslin, usually wheat and rye (*OED* mongcorn). Not extended.

mans' (**32**): handles (*AND* manche[1], manz; Latin forms not noted in *DMLBS*). Not extended.

mantell' (**32**): cloak. Extended to forms in *-um, -i, n.*

manuterg' (**32**): towel (linen). Extended to forms in *-ium, -ii, n.*

marberyn (**32**): 'like marble' (*AND* marbrin), but here probably referring to the patterning of a fabric.

martilog' (**2/1**): calendar of saints or benefactors; book of obits. Extended to forms in *-ium, -ii, n.*

maser' (**12/2**, **29/1**), **massar'** (**23/1**), **mazer'** (**34/1**): mazer, a wooden drinking cup. Not extended, except in one case on **23/1** where it is possibly treated in the MS as a 4th declension noun, 'de massaru'. Most occurrences on **29/1** have no suspension. On **34/1**, it is treated as *n.*

materac' (**34/1**): mattress. Not extended.

meandri (**40/1**): a menial, literally 'lesser man' (*RMLWL*, *DMLBS* meandri *sb.*, *pl.* form; here it is a *gen. sing.*, but probably a *coll. sing.*)

melle (**32**): medley, mixed cloth, of wool (*AND* medler[2]; *OED* medley *sb.* 3, 1438).

menever' (**26/1**): miniver, dressed squirrel skins. Extended to forms in *-um, -i, n.*

mercur' (**38**): Wednesday. Extended to *mercurii* in the expression *die mercurii.*

micator' (**32**): a grater. Extended to forms in *-ium, -ii, n.*

mixtil, **myxtil'** (**6/2**); **mixtilion'**, **mixtilon'** (**32**): maslin, a mixed corn of wheat and winter barley on **6/2**, and probably of wheat and rye on **32**. Extended to forms from *mixtil(i)o, -onis*, on **32**; no evidence for gender on **32**. On **6/2**, extended to forms from *myxtilio, -onis, f.*

moce: *see* **mors'**.

molandis, **molendis** (**32**): for the milling of, *gerundive*. The main hand in **32** writes this in varying forms, with *a* and *e*.

mors' (**32**), **moce** (**6/2**): morse, the clasp or buckle fastening a cope (*DLMBS* morsus *sb*. 4. (both 2nd and 4th declension); *OED* morse *sb*. 1, 1404). Not extended. Not in *AND*.

mortar' (**18/2**): mortar, for pounding food. Extended to forms in *-ium*, *-i*, *n*.

motelyn' (**6/2**): parchment from sheep, contrasted to *velym*. Not extended.

moustierdevilliers (**26/1**): a mixed, grey cloth; made from wool or linen (*OED* musterdevillers).

muneritus (**43/1**): endowed with grace (*RMLWL* munus).

Nich'us: Nicholas, man's name. Extended to forms from *Nicholus*, *-i*, *m*., unless there is evidence for a stem in forms other than the *nom*. in *-a*.

nouchis (**21/8**): ouches. Treated as *n*.

orfreys (**32**): orphreys. Treated as *f*.

ovili (**32**): sheepfold. The *abl*. form is *ovili*, e.g. on the Witney account.

pag' (**12/2**): a page (a child servant). Extended to forms from *pagettus*, *-i*, *m*.

pailett*es* (**6/2**): pallet, small bed (*OED* pallet *sb* 2., 1374).

palefrey (**18/2**): palfrey. Treated as *n*. in MS.

paniers (**32**): large baskets (*AND* paner; *OED* pannier *sb*.[1], 1, *c*.1300).

pann' (**18/2**): cloth. Extended to forms in *-us*, *-i*, *m*.

pannag' (**32**): pannage. Extended to forms in *-ium*, *-ii*, *n*.

parament' (**28/1**): apparel. Extended to forms in *-um*, *-i*, *n*.

Paris' (**32**): a textile fabric, used for tapets; probably silk woven in Paris (Monnas, *Merchants*, p. 4 n. 38, citing wardrobe accounts of Edward II). Not extended; not traced in *DMLBS*, *OED* and *AND*, but see *KMED* Paris *sb*[1] b.

patell' (**32**): bowl. Extended to forms in *-a*, *-e*, *f*.

paternoster' (**29/1**): rosary. Treated as indeclinable; probably an English form.

pec' (**18/2**): a piece of silver plate. Extended to forms in *-ia*, *-ie*, *f*.

pecten (**2/1**): comb. Extended to forms from *pecten*, *-inis*, *m*.

pelicot' (**32**): a precious stone, a chrysolite (*AND* pelitote; *OED* peridot, *sb*. a.; U.T. Holmes, 'Medieval gem stones' *Speculum* 9 (1934) pp. 195–204, at p. 199). Not extended.

pelv' (**18/2**): basin. Extended to forms from *pelvis*, *-is*, *f*.

pelvinar' (**2/1**): cushion or pillow, a variant of *pulvinarium*. Extended to forms in *-ium*, *-ii*, *n*.

perit' (**4/1**): completed. For *peract'*, i.e. from *perago* rather than *pereo*.

pers (**32**): a dark coloured, fine cloth, typically a dark blue, and sometimes referring to a material of that colour and quality (*DMLBS* persicus 4b., *sb*., 1200; *OED* perse, *a*. and *sb*.[2] 1366; *AND* pers, earliest citation as a blue cloth is in *Chichele register*).

peryll' (**21/8**): pearls. Never extended on MS; extended editorially in italics.

pestell' (**18/2**, **32**): pestle. Extended to forms in *-um*, *-i*, *n*.

phalterium (**32**): the psalter.

phanon': *see* **fanon**.

phiol': *see* **fial'**.

pis' (**18/2**, **32**): peas. Extended in *pl.* to forms in *-e*, *-arum*, *f.*, following one example on **32.**

pitanc' (**18/2**): pittance, a special, supplementary dish of food. Extended to forms in *-ia*, *-ie*, *f.*; treated as *sing.*

plat' (**32**, **33/1**): plate, *adj.*, of bullion, usually silver, made from sheets of metal. The sense of 'plating', to cover with a precious metal, as in gilding, is recorded in *DLMBS* platare b., from 1386, with a reference to the second metal (plates of gold on silver); but the examples in **32** and **33/1** do not refer to a second metal (for the technique, M. Campbell, 'Gold, silver and precious stones' in *English medieval industries: craftsmen, techniques, products* ed. J. Blair and N. Ramsay (London, 1991) pp. 107–66, at pp. 131–2). Extended on **32** to forms in *-us*, *-a*, *-um*; and on **33/1** to forms in *-eus*, *-ea*, *-eum.*

platell' (**21/8**, **34/1**): small plates. Extended on **21/8** to forms in *-a*, *-e*, *f.*; and on **34/1** to forms in *-um*, *-i*, *n.*

plumar' (**33/1**): a pillow, or featherbed. Extended to forms in *-ium*, *-ii*, *n.*

pond' (**32**), **ponder'** (**18/2**, **25/1**, **32**): weight. Extended as a *sb.* to forms from *pondus*, *-eris*, *n.*; in expressions like 'vasa ponderis iii lib.', to *gen. sing.*

porc' (**32**): pig. Extended to forms in *-us*, *-i*, *m.*; where the value of the animal is below 2*s.*, extended in italic, as the word intended may have been *porcellus* or *porciculus.*

porcicul' (**32**): small piglet. Extended to forms in *-us*, *-i*, *m.* In the Twyford account, the *porcelli* are described as 9 months old and worth 20*d.* each; the *porciculi* are younger, and worth 9*d.* each; however, in the Downton account the *porcelli* are worth 6*d.* each, and the *porciculi*, 15*d.*

portag' (**18/2**): carriage, transport. Extended to forms in *-um*, *-i*, *n.*

postenett' (**33/1**): posnet, a handled pan. Extended to forms in *-a*, *-e*, *f.*

poukwayn (**32**): a wagon for carrying 'pooks', hay or unthreshed corn (*DMLBS*, poukewaynum, 'poke-wain', ? haycart; 1327; one example of 1276 in L.F. Salzman *Building in England down to 1540: a documentary history* (revised edition, Oxford, 1966) p. 352; *OED* pook *sb.* and *vb.* 1587).

pramis (**25/1**): gemstones, prase, a leek-green quartz or plasma (*AND* prasme; *OED* prase; *RMLWL* prama). As written in MS.

prebend' (**18/2**): fodder. Extended to forms in *-a*, *-e*, *f.*

prec': value, price. Extended throughout to forms in *-ium*, *-ii*, *n.* In valuations, e.g. *prec' gallin'*, extended to *precium* in all instances except on **18/2**, **25/1**, **32** and **38/15**, where a *gen. sing.* form is used.

processionar' (**6/2**): a processional, service book. Extended to forms in *-ium*, *-ii*, *n.*

pull' (**32**): a foal, a chick (also used for cygnets in the Downton account, and pea-chicks at Fareham). For both, extended to forms from *pullus*, *-i*, *m.* The form *pullanus* is only used where the MS employs it directly.

pullan' (**32**): a foal. Extended to forms in *-us*, *-i*, *m.* The Downton account has *pullan' femell'.*

quisseus (**32**): cuisses, armour for protecting the upper part of the thigh (*OED* cuisse; *AND* cuissier).

quissin' (**38/14**): cushion. Extended to forms in *-us*, *-i*, *m.*

quorundam (**32**): of which. Abbreviated forms extended to this rather than *quorumdam.*

Rad' (**2/1**): Ralph. Extended to forms from *Radulphus*, *-i*.
raffata (**32**): a fabric, possibly the same as taffeta (a shiny silk).
rebinat' (**6/2**): land left fallow, after three ploughings (*RMLWL*).
redill': *see* **ridill'**.
reperpand': (**18/2**) for forms of *preparare*, to prepare.
ridel', **ridell'** (**32**): riddle, sieve. Extended to forms in *-us*, *-i*, *m*., where Latin is intended; some examples have no suspension, and the unextended form *ridel* (and variants) has been kept.
ridill' (**34/1**), **redill'** (**19/1**): curtain. Extended to forms in *-us*, *-i*, *m*.
robynet (**33/1**): a cauldron. Not in *OED*, but presumably a smaller cauldron than a robin: C.M. Woolgar *The great household in late medieval England* (1999), p. 140, for a reference to Thomas of Lancaster acquiring two brown robins and four copper bowls for £20 (n. 17, citing TNA DL 28/1/13, mem. 3d).
rub' (**6/2**, **12/1**, **31/1**, **32**, **38/10**, **43/1**): red, or 'with a ruby' (**31/1**). Extended as *sb*. on **38/10** to forms in *-ium*, *-ii*, *n*. Treated as *adj*. and extended to forms in *-eus*, *-ea*, *-eum* throughout **6/2** and **31/1**; and to forms in *-ius*, *-ia*, *-ium* on **12/1** and **43/1**. **32** uses forms in both *-ius* and *-eus*: extended to forms in *-eus*, *-ea*, *-eum*. where abbreviated to *rub'*.

sabatinorum (**6/2**): a slipper or form of shoe, possibly an overshoe, one example here made of damask (*KMED* sabatin *sb*. a, 1448; *OED* sabatine 1460). Fifteenth-century examples usually occur in lists with sandals; in **6/2**, galoshes are also listed.
sacc' (**32**): sack. Extended to forms in *-us*, *-i*, *m*.
saf' (**32**): sapphire. Extended to forms from *safirus*, *-i*, *m*. (examples of *safiro*, *abl*., on MS).
sallar' (**12/2**): a salt. Extended to forms in *-ium*, *-ii*, *n*.
sals' (**32**), **salsar'** (**12/2**, **18/2**, **28/1**, **33/1**), **salcer'** (**28/1**): saucer. On **32**, extended to forms from *salsarius*, *-i*, *m*.; on the others, extended to forms in *-ium*, *-ii*, *n*.
samite (**2/1**), **samyt'** (**32**): samite, a fine silk (*AND* samit; *OED*, 13--; Monnas, *Merchants*, pp. 297–8, 302).
sanap' (**34/1**), **surnapp'** (**33/1**): a cloth to protect a tablecloth, to lie over it (*RMLWL* sanappa, supermappa; *AND* sauvenappe). There are two senses here, protecting and over-lying, although the consequences in terms of what the cloth did are probably the same. Extended on **33/1** to forms in *-a*, *-e*, *f*.; not extended on **34/1**.
sandal' (**6/2**), **sidaliorum** (**28/1**): sandals. In **6/2**, appears in two forms, *sandalia*, *-ium*, and *sandalina*, *-orum*, both *n. pl*.; in **21/8** perhaps *sindaliorum* was intended.
sandoco, **sandaco**, **cendat'** (**2/1**): a textile, of green and red. Extended to forms in *-us*, *-i*, *m*. Note, however, *LS* sandix: vermilion; and *RMLWL*, sandix: madder, woad, or weld. May be cendal, a silk: Monnas, *Merchants*, p. 302.
sarges (**32**): serge, a textile fabric, possibly of silk (*AND* sarge; *OED* serge 1386).
saundr*es* (**32**): red sanders, colouring used in cooking.
scalop' (**33/1**): scallop shells. Extended in *pl*. in *abl*. to *-is*.
scons' (**2/1**), **skonces** (**6/2**): sconce, screened light (*RMLWL*). Extended on **2/1** to forms in *-a*, *-e*, *f*.; not extended on **6/2**.

scrinen' (**32**): a chest or wallet for precious items or muniments (*RMLWL*). Extended to forms in *-ium*, *-ii*, *n*.
scutali (**43/1**): a shield? Treated as if from *scutale*, *-is* (form not in *LS* or *RMLWL*).
scutell' (**33/1**): dish or bowl. Extended to forms in *-a*, *-e*, *f.*
sell' (**18/2**): saddle. Extended to forms in *-a*, *-e*, *f.*
septennar' (**40/1**): seventh day, although the form looks as if it means 'seventh anniversary'. Treated as *sb.*, and extended to forms in *-ia*, *-ie*, *f.*
servicum, **servicium** (**18/2**): service. MS uses forms in both *-um*, *-i*, and *-ium* and *-ii*, *n*.
sidaliorum: *see* **sandal'**.
sindon, **sindone** (**32**): sindon, a fine linen (*OED*).
skaccato (**32**): checked, *adj.*
solughbemes (**32**): ploughbeams (*OED* sullow *sb*, 2.).
sommar' (**18/2**): sumpter horse, a pack-horse. Extended to forms in *-ium*, *-ii*, *n*.
specer' (**32**): spicery. Extended in *pl.* to forms in *-e*, *-arum*, *f.*
sprigg' (**32**): rye (not in *OED*, but see *RMLWL*, sprigetum; *MRC*, p. 797, sprygg'). Not extended.
stall' (**32**): sheepcote. Extended to forms in *-us*, *-i*, *m*.
steignat' (**6/2**): stained or painted. Extended to forms in *-us*, *-a*, *-um*.
stipul' (**32**): stubble. Extended to forms in *-a*, *-e*, *f.*
stirk' (**20**), **strek'** (**32**): young cattle, both bullocks and heifers. Extended to forms in *-us*, *-i*, *m.*, following MS.
stol' (**33/1**): stole, ecclesiastical vestment. Extended to forms in *-a*, *-e*, *f.*
stott' (**6/2**, **18/2**): steer. Extended to forms in *-us*, *-i*, *m*.
stragulatus (**32**): striped, or panelled, of cloth.
suffragine (**23/1**): suffragan bishop. An unusual form, *dat.* of *suffragina*, *-e*, *f.*
super: on, about, prep. **2/1**: used on the first roll with both *acc.* and *abl.*; extensions of following *sb.* made in *acc.* unless evidence to the contrary. **32**: no evidence for case of following *sb.*: extended in italics. **41/4**: following *sb.* extended in *abl.* after the use of MS.
superannal' (**32**): over the age of one, *adj.* Extended to forms in *-is*, *-e*.
superpellic' (**32**): surplice. Extended to forms in *-ium*, *-ii*, *n*.
surnapp': *see* **sanap'**.

taffat', **taphat'** (**32**): taffeta, a plain, tabby weave, silk (Monnas, *Merchants*, pp. 297, 302). Extended to forms in *-a*, *-e*, *f.*
tap' (**32**), **tapet'** (**6/2**, **32**, **33/1**): tapet, an ornamented cloth, a hanging. On **6/2** and **33/1**, extended to forms in *-a*, *-e*, *f.*; on **32**, extended to forms from *tapetum*, *-i*, *n*.
Tars' (**32**), **Tarsen'**, **panno Tarsen'** (**2/1**): silks, possibly originally from, or thought to be from, Tarsus in Asia Minor (*RMLWL*; Monnas, *Merchants*, p. 302). Not extended.
tartaryn (**6/2**): a plain silk (Monnas, *Merchants*, p. 302).
ta*une* (**32**): tawny, a brownish colour (*AND* tauné; *OED* tawny *sb*. 2, 1426.)
tegul' (**32**): tile. Extended to forms in *-a*, *-e*, *f.*
tester' (**34/1**): the tester of a bed. Not extended.
thimiaterio (**2/1**, **2/2**): censer (*RMLWL* thymaterium). Extended to forms in *-us*, *-i*, *m.*, to agree with *adj.* following.
thuribul' (**21/10**): thurible. Extended to form from *-us*, *-i*, *m*.

tirteyn (**32**): a rich silk cloth from the East (*Dictionnaire de l'ancienne langue française et de tous ses dialectes du IXe au XVe siècle* ed. F. Godefroy (10 vols., Paris, Abbeville, 1880–1902) from 1295; possibly the same as tartarin, *OED* tartarin *sb*[1], 2, and *AND* tartarin, citing *Chichele register*).
tolcorne (**32**): tolcorn, multure, the miller's share of corn as a consideration for grinding it.
tortic' (**9/1**, **18/2**): torch, a large candle, of wax in **18/2** (*OED* tortis, 1, 1375). Extended to forms in *-us*, *-i*, *m.*
trestell' (**32**): trestle. Extended to forms in *-um*, *-i*, *n.*
tribul' (**32**): tool or shovel. Extended to forms in *-a*, *-e*, *f.*
tricennar' (**40/1**): thirtieth day, or month's mind. Treated as *sb.*; extended to forms in *-ia*, *-ie*, *f.*
triper (**33/1**): ?an ecclesiastical book, a troper.
tuall' (**26/1**, **33/1**), **tuell'** (**32**, **35/6**): towel. Extended to forms in *-a*, *-e*, *f.*
tulee (**2/1**): sandaco tulee, a twilled cloth (*OED* twilly, *adj.* and *sb.*).
turc' (**32**): 'wrought', twisted, of silver (*AND* tort, tortre[1]; *RMLWL* torculatus). Extended to forms in *-us*, *-a*, *-um*.
Turkys (**32**): an oriental, fine cloth.

urc'olus (**32**): cruet, ewer for holy water. Extended to *urciolus* where abbreviated.

valenc' (**32**, **34/1**): value. Extended to forms in *-ia*, *-ie*, *f.*, in *sing.* On **32**, used for the value of hay and litter; may imply a different process to appraisal, 'fenum appreciatum ad', perhaps not done by the jury, as the use of the two phrases is mutually exclusive.
varyon' (**32**): skewbald, of a horse, coloured white and bay, sometimes also a name (*AND* vairon).
vas' (**11/1**, **31/1**): vessels. Extended to forms from *vasum*, *-i*, *n.*
velvett' (**12/2**): velvet, cloth. Not extended.
ventator', **ventor'** (**32**): winnowing fan. Extended to forms in *-ium*, *-ii*, *n.*
verins (**32**): of iron (*AND* ferrin).
vernache (**32**): an Italian wine (*OED* vernage).
vesc' (**32**, **38**): vetch. On **32**, extended in *pl.*, to forms in *-e*, *-arum*, following examples in *abl. pl.*, *vescis*. On **38**, there is no evidence for the extension: extended in *sing.* to forms in *-a*, *-e*, *f.*
victual' (**33/1**): victualler. Extended to forms from *victuallarius*, *-i*, *m.*
violacio (**21/8**): used to describe a cloth of gold.
virid' (**6/2**, **26/1**): green. Extended to forms from *viridis*, *-e*, *adj.*
vitr' (**2/1**): of glass, *adj.* Extended to forms in *-eus, -ea, -eum.*

wrech' (**26/1**): wreath. Not extended.

ydria (**21/8**): holy water stoup (*RMLWL* hydriola).

INDEX OF PERSONS AND PLACES

Personal names and place-names have been stardardised and brought together in a single entry, where the principal forms are listed. Bishops are listed with the see held at death (or final see in England and Wales), with work elsewhere identified in that entry. Peers have been numbered following the *Complete peerage of England, Scotland, Ireland, Great Britain, and the United Kingdom* ... ed. G.E. Cokayne, revised Vicary Gibbs *et al.* (13 vols., 1910–59). In Welsh names, modern orthographic practice has been used and forenames have been modernised. Welsh patronymics have been ordered by the last patronymic, rather than by first name, to facilitate reference in cases where a surname is employed (e.g. Edmund ab Eignion Lloyd has been placed under Lloyd). Other individuals have been identified as far as possible. The names of a bishop's executors have not been cross-referenced under each bishop, as they appear in the Catalogue of Probate Documentation. Places in England and Wales are identified by their pre-1974 county.

INDEX OF SUBJECTS

INDEX OF BOOKS

ANONYMOUS WORKS